CLASSICAL PHILOSOPHY

Collected Papers

Series Editor

TERENCE IRWIN
Professor of Philosophy
Cornell University

A GARLAND SERIES

Series Contents

VOLUME
5

ARISTOTLE'S ETHICS

Edited with introductions by
TERENCE IRWIN
Sage School of Philosophy
Cornell University

GARLAND PUBLISHING, INC.
New York & London
1995

Library of Congress Cataloging-in-Publication Data

Classical philosophy : collected papers / series editor, Terence Irwin.
p. cm.
Includes bibliographical references.
Contents: v. 1. Philosophy before Socrates — v. 2. Socrates and his contemporaries — v. 3. Plato's ethics — v. 4. Plato's metaphysics and epistemology — v. 5. Aristotle's ethics — v. 6. Aristotle: substance, form and matter — v. 7. Aristotle: metaphysics, epistemology, natural philosophy — v. 8. Hellenistic philosophy.
ISBN 0-8153-1829-4 (v. 1 : alk. paper). — ISBN 0-8153-1830-8 (v. 2 : alk. paper). — ISBN 0-8153-1832-4 (v. 3 : alk. paper). — ISBN 0-8153-1833-2 (v. 4 : alk. paper). — ISBN 0-8153-1834-0 (v. 5 : alk. paper). — ISBN 0-8153-1835-9 (v. 6 : alk. paper). — ISBN 0-8153-1836-7 (v. 7 : alk. paper). — ISBN 0-8153-1837-5 (v. 8 : alk. paper)
1. Philosophy, Ancient. I. Irwin, Terence.
B171.C53 1995
180—dc20 95-5168
CIP

Printed on acid-free, 250-year-life paper
Manufactured in the United States of America

Contents

Series Introduction

The aim of this series is to collect some previously published work on Greek philosophy in a form in which it will be accessible to students and teachers. The pieces reprinted here were originally published in English and were almost all published in journals, though some appeared in collections of essays and a few as chapters of books. (I will refer to them, irrespective of their origin, as "papers" or "essays.")

The most difficult task for the compiler of such a collection is to decide what to exclude, since one has to choose from a large number of good essays published over the past 150 years. In this area of Anglophone scholarship, academic journals (as opposed to periodicals such as *Westminster Review* or *Athenaeum* aiming at a wider audience) began in the second half of the nineteenth century. The *Journal of Philology* (originally the *Journal of Classical and Sacred Philology*) was first published at Cambridge in 1854. *Mind* (originally a journal of both philosophy and psychology) began in Edinburgh in 1876. In the late nineteenth century these were followed by the *Classical Quarterly*. In the United States the first specialized journals began in the late nineteenth century, attached to universities; the *American Journal of Philology*, for instance, was founded at Johns Hopkins University and the *Philosophical Review* at Cornell University. In these journals, and the many other Classical and philosophical periodicals that have been founded in the twentieth century, essays on Greek philosophy have appeared regularly. The earliest essay chosen (by Henry Sidgwick) comes from the *Journal of Philology* in 1872. Also included are essays from the early 1990s and—though this was not part of my plan—essays from most of the decades in between.

The first journal devoted to ancient philosophy was *Phronesis* (not confined to English), which began in 1955. More recently *Oxford Studies in Ancient Philosophy*, *Apeiron*, *Ancient Philosophy* (all in English), *Revue de Philosophie Ancienne*, *Elenchos*, and *Methexis* have appeared. Some of the best recent work appeared in these specialized journals, and their growth indicates the increasing interest in Greek philosophy. It would be regrettable, however, if essays in this area were confined to the specialized journals.

Fortunately, important essays continue to appear in journals such as the *Classical Quarterly* and the *Philosophical Review*, which aim to reach a more general classical or philosophical audience.

The different journals publishing work in Greek philosophy tend, not surprisingly, to attract somewhat different essays and readers of this collection will notice different styles and approaches. Linguistic, literary, historical, and philosophical skills (and, no doubt, others) are all necessary for the full understanding, appreciation, and enjoyment of Greek philosophical texts, and it would be foolish to take the difference between "Classical" and "philosophical" essays too seriously. Included is an excerpt from the work of George Grote, whose contributions to the study of both Greek history (in his *History of Greece*) and Greek philosophy (in his books on Plato and on Aristotle) were of the highest importance. In Grote's time, of course, scholars in either of these areas did not need to read as much as now; moreover, the scholar had the benefit of a private income, and therefore did not hold a teaching position in a university. In practice most writers on ancient philosophy, having limited means, limited leisure, and limited knowledge, write primarily as Classicists or as philosophers.

Classical studies and philosophy have evidently not been static over the past 150 years; and the study of Greek philosophy has been deeply influenced by developments in its "parent" disciplines. A few examples will illustrate the point:

1. Nineteenth-century Classical scholars (here partly influenced by Biblical criticism) show a great deal of confidence in their ability to divide texts into "earlier" and "later" versions or sections and to recognize the work of "editors," or "redactors" or "interpolators." The sort of treatment given to the *Book of Genesis* and to the *Iliad* was also thought suitable for Plato's *Republic* and for Aristotle's *Ethics* and *Metaphysics*.

2. In the early twentieth century Classical studies were strongly affected by the latest trends in anthropology. These trends entered the study of Greek philosophy, and especially of the Presocratics, through the work of F.M. Cornford.

3. In the twentieth century Anglophone philosophy passed through the rise and fall of trends associated with logical positivism and its successors. These trends affected not only philosophers' views of which parts of Plato or Aristotle are deemed nearly true or hopelessly false but also their views of what, if anything, in the history of philosophy is worth studying.

4. Anglophone scholarship as well as Anglophone philosophy has been affected, to varying degrees, by the developments in

philosophy connected with Heidegger, Gadamer, Derrida, and their disciples. Greek philosophers play a central role as heroes or villains or both in these philosophers' views of philosophy and its history; and these views in turn have affected the questions raised about the Greek texts themselves.

These different trends in Classics and philosophy have caused the "Classical" and the "philosophical" aspects of the study of Greek philosophy to converge or diverge at different times. An extreme example of divergence is illustrated by Cambridge from (roughly speaking) 1900 to 1970. G.E. Moore, C.D. Broad, and Ludwig Wittgenstein were central figures in the development of Cambridge philosophy; but their conception of philosophy did not include any central place for the study of ancient philosophy. F.M. Cornford and W.K.C. Guthrie were the leading figures in the study of Greek philosophy in Cambridge; their conception of the right approach to ancient philosophy did not include any serious engagement with philosophy in general. Oxford between 1918 and 1945 presents a different picture; here the philosophers who took Plato and Aristotle seriously (for instance, H.H. Joachim, W.D. Ross, and H.W.B. Joseph) were regarded by some of their colleagues as intellectual dinosaurs.

No doubt these historical pictures are rather crude and exaggerated, but they may suggest the sort of thing that can happen when the relation between the study of Greek philosophy and its parent disciplines becomes unbalanced. It seems safe to say—without naive optimism—that the present situation is less unbalanced than it was in either of these extreme pictures. It would be wrong to suggest that the study of Greek philosophy has an assured and stable place in either parent discipline; since these disciplines are themselves developing, *nothing* has an assured place in them. It seems reasonable to claim, however, that a fairly wide range of Classicists and philosophers recognize a legitimate place within their disciplines for the study of Greek philosophy and that, conversely, most serious students of Greek philosophy recognize their obligation to learn from both Classics and philosophy.

The essays in this series were not chosen to illustrate anything in particular about the history of scholarship or about the different methods used in approaching Greek philosophy. I believe, however, that the essays in these volumes display the different skills and approaches of the philologist, the historian, and the philosopher. Some volumes are more heavily weighted in one direction than in the other; Volumes 1 and 2, for instance, contain more contributions that discuss historical and literary questions, while some of the essays on Aristotle are more evidently philosophical. One of the incidental but nontrivial benefits of studying Greek philosophy is the opportunity that it gives us to understand the approaches of these different disciplines and to see how they influence each other.

The general aim in selecting essays is quite vague: to collect some of the best work (so far as it is available within the limits mentioned above) on some important questions in Greek philosophy. I have, however, kept in mind (though probably not constantly or consistently) some slightly more precise criteria:

1. The essays naturally vary in the degree of difficulty and in the comprehension level that they presuppose in readers. I hope, however, that most of them are accessible to readers who are not already specialists in Greek philosophy, but rather students seeking aid in writing a paper, more advanced students beginning research, or specialists in other disciplines who want some idea of what has been going on in this area.

2. On the whole I tried to pick essays that raise issues of philosophical interest, whether or not the authors approach the issues from a primarily philosophical point of view. In doing this I was influenced by the twentieth-century tendency to bring the study of Greek philosophy closer to philosophy. This is not the only tendency (as I mentioned above), but it is prominent enough to affect the general character of essays published in journals.

3. The essays are not all recent. I sought some older essays—those that often are difficult to find, especially for students without ready access to old or well supplied libraries. Moreover, they often deserve to be read again and not simply to be cited in bibliographies and footnotes.

4. I collected some essays that examine different sides of a question to give readers some sense of the debate and dialogue that are characteristic of the best work in this area. In some cases I picked out one contributor to a debate and left it to readers to follow up the references that will acquaint them with the other sides of the issue.

5. In allotting space to different topics, I was guided by the quantity of good work available in journals in English. The allocation of space, therefore, does not reflect my own view about the relative importance of different topics in Greek philosophy; it reflects my view about the quantity and quality of the work done in different areas. Readers should bear this point in mind when they see, for instance, that this collection is heavily weighted toward Plato and Aristotle and that one whole volume (Volume 6) is devoted to questions related to Aristotle's doctrine of substance. If I had been thinking simply of the relative importance of different

topics, or seeking to point out directions for future research, I might have tried a different distribution of space.

6. Some readers may reasonably regret the fact that Greek philosophy after Aristotle is squeezed into one volume and that this volume does not go beyond the Hellenistic schools. Once again this decision reflects my view about the quantity and quality of material available for this collection. Some of the best work on Hellenistic philosophy, for instance, has appeared in collections of essays.

7. I made some effort to avoid reprinting essays that are easily accessible elsewhere. This criterion explains the absence of some deservedly well-known essays by, for instance, Gregory Vlastos, Harold Cherniss, and G.E.L. Owen; their work is available in the volumes of their collected essays. I have also tried to avoid extensive duplication of other useful and readily available collections, including those by Alexander Mourelatos and by D.J. Furley and R.E. Allen on the Presocratics, by R.E. Allen and by Gregory Vlastos on Plato, and by Jonathan Barnes, Malcolm Schofield, and Richard Sorabji on Aristotle. I have not been rigid in avoiding overlap, however; I have included some essays whose importance seemed to make them indispensable for a volume in this series, even if they were already reprinted elsewhere.

I am confident that by applying these criteria I have collected a body of important essays that, hopefully, will be useful to a fairly wide range of readers. I must disabuse readers, however, of any tendency to believe that these volumes collect the crème de la crème of work in Greek philosophy or that I suppose everything included here is superior to everything not included. The very fact that the collection is drawn entirely from work in English means that it cannot represent the full range of important work on Greek philosophy; some of the best work has been published in other languages—especially French, German, and Italian. The fact that the collection is confined almost entirely to journals also means that it misses some important work. Some of the most important contributions in several areas—especially in recent years—are in books rather than essays. Moreover, some important work—once again, especially in recent years—appears in collections of essays that have been published as books. These collections include the twelve volumes of Symposia Aristotelica published since 1957, and the five volumes of Symposia Hellenistica published since 1980. Other omissions from the present collection can be explained by the fact that some journals charge permission fees beyond the means of the publisher of this series.

In fairness to the authors of these essays readers should realize that the essays are reprinted in the form in which they appear in the journal or book from which they are taken. This means that they do not necessarily represent the current views of the authors. In many cases I picked essays that began or contributed to a discussion or controversy; in some of these cases authors may well have decided, in the light of later discussion, to modify some of their initial views. Readers should regard these essays as participants in a conversation. I hope that once readers listen to these earlier participants they also will want to continue the conversation.

INTRODUCTION

Aristotle's ethical theory is probably the most intensively studied aspect of his philosophy in the English-speaking world since at least 1807, when the University of Oxford first required candidates for a degree to pass a public examination *in literis humanior-ibus*. Moral philosophy was a large component of this examination and Aristotle and Butler were the main sources studied. From the mid-nineteenth century onward commentaries on the Greek text, translations, and articles—both philological and philosophical—have appeared in considerable numbers; more recently books devoted to the *Ethics* itself, or dealing with the *Ethics* in the course of a treatment of issues in moral philosophy, have become more and more frequent. This means that the secondary literature in English on the *Ethics* is far larger than anything that can be found in any other modern language; the compiler of an anthology could usefully fill three or four volumes of the size of this one.[1]

I did not try to convey the variety or scope of this large body of secondary literature. Instead I confined myself to some essays that illustrate some of the topics in the *Ethics* that have been prominent in recent discussion.

This volume begins with two papers reminding us that Aristotle's ethical works do not consist simply of the *Nicomachean Ethics*. Three ethical treatises belong to the Aristotelian Corpus, but the *Eudemian Ethics* and *Magna Moralia* tend to suffer neglect; there is, for instance, no modern English commentary on the whole Eudemia*n Ethics*, or on any part of the *Magna Moralia*.[2] In the case of the *Magna Moralia* this neglect has probably been encouraged by the belief that the work is spurious. John Cooper's essay defends both the authenticity (suitably qualified) and the philosophical value of the *Magna Moralia*, arguing that it preserves the substance of an early course of Aristotle's, and that its discussion of particular issues throws some light on their treatment in the other *Ethics* and on Aristotle's relations to Plato. Cooper's conclusions about the authenticity of the *Magna Moralia* have been controverted.[3] Regardless of his accuracy, Cooper's point-by-point comparison is the only satisfactory way to decide about the philosophical connections between the different treatises.

In the twentieth century (in contrast to the nineteenth) the authenticity of the Eudemian Ethics has been generally accepted, but readers still differ about 1) whether it is earlier or later than the *Nicomachean Ethics*, 2) whether the two works differ on significant points of doctrine, or merely in details of exposition, and 3) whether one or the other work is better on this or that issue. Rather large claims were made for the superiority of the Eudemian *Ethics* and these foster the view that it is the latest and most mature statement of Aristotle's position.[4] D.J. Allan's essay does not discuss the first or the third of these issues. He confines himself to the second issue and studies the way in which the *Eudemian Ethics* presents its arguments and conclusions. His essay, like Cooper's, is useful not only because of the specific topics it discusses, but also because it provides an example of the kind of thing that needs to be done to form a clearer view of the character of each ethical treatise. Some readers are perhaps too eager to draw conclusions about the *Eudemian Ethics* or *Magna Moralia* as a whole on the strength of insufficiently careful study of its doctrine and argument; Cooper and Allan show what kinds of questions need to be raised.

Allan's essay leads naturally into the two essays in Part 2, which deal with the methods of argument and inquiry that Aristotle uses in his Ethics. Since some of his methods of argument are practiced in other works too these two essays may also serve as an introduction to the study of Aristotle's methods in general.[5] Jonathon Barnes studies the methods, presuppositions, and aims of Aristotle's arguments, and compares ethics with other areas of study. Timothy Roche's essay takes up a particular question about Aristotle's methods, discussing the relation between Aristotle's ethical arguments and the conclusions that he reaches in other areas of his philosophy.[6] Roche's arguments are especially helpful when compared with the treatment of metaphysical and psychological topics by W.F.R. Hardie and Jennifer Whiting (in Part 3) and by Cooper and David Charles (in Part 4).

All of Aristotle's ethical works begin with a discussion of the human good, which is identified with *eudaimonia*. Translators normally use the term "happiness" for *"eudaimonia,"* but some suggest that this is misleading, recommending "flourishing" as a better rendering because it avoids the associations with feelings of pleasure and satisfaction that—it is assumed—make "happiness" inappropriate. Richard Kraut's and J.C. Dybikowski's essays discuss this issue of the relation between eudaimonia and happiness;

in doing so they throw some light on the nature of happiness and on the nature of *eudaimonia*. Troels Engberg-Pederson's essay allows us to compare the conclusions of Kraut's and Dybikowski's arguments with the use that Aristotle makes of an appeal to *eudaimonia* in a specific passage of the *Ethics*, where he considers what is involved in acting "for the sake of *eudaimonia*."

Once we understand what Aristotle means by "*eudaimonia*," we can consider what states or activities he actually identifies with being *eudaimôn*. Two sorts of answers to this question are offered:

1. Some argue, by appeal to Book X of the *Nicomachean Ethics*, that Aristotle identifies happiness with intellectual contemplation.

2. Others argue, mainly by appeal to the rest of the *Nicomachean Ethics* (and sometimes to the other ethical works), that Aristotle identifies happiness with virtuous activity, including the expression of the moral virtues as well as contemplation.

Reasons for holding one or the other of these views are surveyed in Hardie's essay. David Keyt examines the passages in Book X that seem to support the first view, but concludes that the passages, in fact, do not support the first view.[7]

Whiting and Cooper's essays are relevant to a choice between the two views of the nature of happiness. Whiting's paper discusses Aristotle's much-criticized claim that happiness is identified with the fulfillment of the human function. This is often taken to support the view that the human good consists exclusively in intellectual activity. Cooper discusses the place of external goods (i.e., those that are not within the agent's control) in happiness. Aristotle rejects the Socratic view (accepted by the Cynics and Stoics) that virtue is sufficient for happiness but he also insists that happiness is relatively stable in the face of ill fortune. Careful examination is needed to determine whether he has a stable position between these extremes.[8]

Since Aristotle defines happiness as an activity of the soul in accordance with complete virtue in a complete life a full understanding of his views on happiness requires an understanding of his conception of virtue. Parts 4 and 5 discuss questions that are relevant to the understanding of virtue. Part 4 deals with general questions about virtue (primarily virtue of character, in contrast to virtue of intellect) and Part 5 deals with some of the specific virtues.

Cooper's essay connects Aristotle's moral psychology with the Platonic division of the soul (which is discussed especially in Volume 3, Part 3). Stephen Leighton examines the special role that

Aristotle assigns to the emotions in moral virtue. These two essays form a basis for evaluating the assumptions made by Rosalind Hursthouse in her discussion of Aristotle's claim that virtue is a mean between two extremes. This claim is closely related to Aristotle's views about rational and non-rational motivation. It also is presumed to involve acceptance of a certain conception of virtue as moderation or compromise. Hursthouse's paper considers these two aspects of the doctrine of the mean and criticizes some attempts to connect them closely.

Aristotle requires the virtuous person to decide on (*prohaireisthai*) the virtuous action for its own sake. Charles and Kraut discuss different questions raised by this requirement. Some questions arise from the fact that virtuous people may decide on an action for several different reasons (e.g., using up surplus wood, erecting a fence, performing a difficult and time-consuming task, helping one's neighbor, acting justly, etc.). How many of these are relevant to the virtuous person's choice and in what way are they relevant? By answering these questions perhaps we can understand Aristotle's assertion that virtuous people decide on virtuous actions "for the sake of the fine," and we can see the relation between choosing for the sake of the fine, choosing for their own sake, and choosing for the sake of happiness.[9] (Here we return to some of the questions raised by Engberg-Pederson's essay, and by Christopher Kirwan and Nicholas White in Part 2 of Volume 3.)

The virtues discussed in Part 5 illustrate different areas of conduct that Aristotle tries to explain through his account of virtue. Temperance is primarily concerned with control of one's non-rational appetites. Magnanimity is concerned with honor, but more generally with the virtuous person's attitude to external goods, and so it is relevant to the issues discussed in Cooper's paper in Part 3. It is concerned with both one's attitude to oneself and one's attitude to others, and so it raises questions that are further discussed in Aristotle's treatment of friendship and justice.

Two papers anticipate some of the essays on Hellenistic Ethics in Volume 8. A.A. Long presents some reasons for supposing that the questions raised by Aristotle influence Stoic ethics. While it is easy to contrast Aristotelian with Stoic ethics it is often illuminating to consider how far the Stoics may fairly be understood as giving answers to Aristotelian questions, and why we might suppose that Stoic or Aristotelian answers are preferable. If we raise these questions, we may conclude that the Stoic and the Aristotelian positions are not as far apart as they may appear to be in some ancient sources and in some modern accounts. Julia Annas's essay pursues this last question further by considering the later Peripatetic presentations of Aristotle's ethics. These later presentations draw considerably on Stoic and other post-Aristotelian doctrines to an extent that we may find surprising. Annas argues, however, that we ought to take seriously the claims of these later sources to present the essentials of Aristotelian ethics.

Notes

1. Two useful collections of papers are J. Barnes, M. Schofield, and R. Sorabji, eds., *Articles on Aristotle*, 4 vols. (London, 1975–9), of which vol. 2 is on ethics and politics; A.O. Rorty, ed., *Essays on Aristotle's Ethics* (Berkeley, 1980).
2. A translation with commentary of Books I, II, and VIII is M.J. Woods, *Aristotle: Eudemian Ethics*, 2nd ed. (Oxford, 1992). The only modern commentary on the *Magna Moralia* is F. Dirlmeier, *Aristoteles: Magna Moralia* (Berlin, 1964).
3. See C.J. Rowe, "A reply to John Cooper on the *Magna Moralia*," *American Journal of Philology* 96 (1975), 160–72; A.J.P. Kenny, *The Aristotelian Ethics* (Oxford, 1978).
4. See especially Kenny, *The Aristotelian Ethics*.
5. See also G.E.L. Owen, "*Tithenai ta phainomena*" in M. Nussbaum, ed., *Logic, Science, and Dialectic* (London, 1986).
6. An example of the sort of view that Roche is opposing is T.H. Irwin, *Aristotle's First Principles* (Oxford, 1988).
7. For some other contributions see J.M. Cooper, *Reason and Human Good in Aristotle* (Cambridge, Mass., 1975); J. Whiting, "Human Nature and Intellectualism in Aristotle," *Archiv für Geschichte der Philosophie* 68 (1986), 70–95; Cooper, "Contemplation and Happiness: A Reconsideration," *Synthèse* 72 (1987), 187–216; R. Kraut, *Aristotle on the Human Good* (Princeton, 1989); G. Lawrence, "Aristotle and the Ideal Life," *Philosophical Review* 102 (1993), 1–34.
8. See also T.H. Irwin, "Permanent Happiness," *Oxford Studies in Ancient Philosophy* 3 (1985), 89–124; M.C. Nussbaum, *The Fragility of Goodness* (Cambridge, 1986); S. White, *Sovereign Virtue* (Stanford, 1992).
9. See also T.H. Irwin, "Aristotle's Concept of Morality," in *Proceedings of the Boston Area Colloquium in Ancient Philosophy* 1 (1985), 115–43.
10. A recent collection of papers is D. Keyt and F. Miller, eds., *A Companion to Aristotle's Politics* (Oxford, 1991).

THE *MAGNA MORALIA* AND ARISTOTLE'S MORAL PHILOSOPHY.

It has been nearly fifteen years since Franz Dirlmeier published his defense of the authenticity of the *Magna Moralia.*[1] Reviews of the work were not numerous.[2] Nor can it be said that published discussions of Dirlmeier's views have provided the critical evaluation of his arguments and conclusions that the importance of the subject certainly demands.[3] For, obviously, if Dirlmeier is right, and the *Magna Moralia,* at any rate in content, is the work of Aristotle himself, composed earlier than either of the other two extant expositions of his moral philoso-

[1] *Aristoteles*: *Magna Moralia,* übersetzt und kommentiert von Franz Dirlmeier (Berlin, 1958).

[2] I know of only one full serious review, that by Düring in *Gnomon* 33 (1961), 547-57. Only three other reviews seem to have appeared (Gigon in *Deutsche Literatur-Zeitung* 83 (1961), 14-19, C. Fabro in *Paideia* 16 (1961), 206, and P. Pédech in *Erasmus* (1961), 358-59, none of which is very searching. (Pédech, drawing no distinction between Dirlmeier's views in his commentary and the argument of his 1939 article, attributes to him belief in a second-century date for the *Magna Moralia*!) In addition D. J. Allan devotes part of his review of Dirlmeier's commentary on the *Eudemian Ethics* (*Gnomon* 38 [1966], 138-49: see pp. 142-43) to a rebuttal of some of Dirlmeier's claims for the *Magna Moralia.* Gigon and Allan do not, while Düring does, accept Dirlmeier's thesis of the substantial authenticity of the work. See also Düring's *Aristoteles* (Heidelberg, 1966), 438-44.

[3] Treatments of Dirlmeier's views on the *Magna Moralia* occur in Gigon, "Die Sokratesdoxographie bei Aristoteles," *Mus. Helv.* 16 (1959), 174-212 (esp. 192 ff.), Philip Merlan, *Studies in Epicurus and Aristotle,* (Wiesbaden, 1960), 83-93, and Karl Bärthlein, "'Ὀρθὸς λόγος in den *Magna Moralia,*" *Archiv f. Geschichte d. Philos.* 45 (1963), 213-58. Pier Luigi Donini, in his dissertation, *L'Etica dei Magna Moralia* (Torino, 1965) deals often and in detail with Dirlmeier's interpretations of particular points; he accepts somewhat mechanically the traditional view of the work's authenticity, but regards it (pp. 222-25) more as an independent work by an aristotelizing Hellenistic writer than as in any sense a commentary on or condensation of the two Aristotelian *Ethics.* This is certainly an improvement over the older versions of the traditional view, but seems, as will be clear from what I say below, pp. 338 ff., an inadequate theory for many passages of the *Mag. Mor.*

phy, we have in this work an extremely valuable tool for tracing out Aristotle's philosophical development, as also for the interpretation and evaluation of his moral philosophy itself.

The importance of the *Magna Moralia* in this latter connection deserves emphasis, since it tends to go unmarked by most non-philosophical scholars, Dirlmeier included. First, on some issues the simpler treatment found in the *Magna Moralia* presents more adequately a basic insight which the other, more elaborate treatments tend to obscure;[4] these insights can be claimed for Aristotle, if the treatise is genuine, and used to bring into clearer focus the theories of the other ethical writings. Secondly, in several instances the *Magna Moralia* includes discussions of important and difficult points never explicitly faced in the other treatises: the most noteworthy instance of this is the discussion of the question what to do in case the rules of two virtues dictate conflicting actions in a particular situation (*Mag. Mor.* 2.3.1199 b 36–1200 a 11).[5] Thirdly, where the *Magna Moralia* differs in doctrine from either of the other treatises the exact determination of the differences, if they can be presumed to be due to Aristotle himself, always throws interesting new light on the theories and arguments of the other version. Thus the *Magna Moralia* (1.33.1193 b 24-30) explains justice as a mean between getting more and getting less than one's share. If

[4] Thus *Mag. Mor.* 1.16 comes closer to recognizing the importance of intention in determining responsibility than the elaborated, but negative, treatment in *Eth. Nic.* 3.1. Likewise the account of the "final good" in *Mag. Mor.* 1.2 is a necessary supplement to *Eth. Nic.*'s much less straightforward and distinct treatment. Again *Mag. Mor.* 2.7. 1204 b 4-1205 a 6 gives a much clearer version of Aristotle's rebuttal of Speusippus' doctrine that pleasure is a γένεσις than *Eth. Eud.* 6.12 (= *Eth. Nic.* 7.12) 1152 b 33 ff. does. (Though the difficulty of the latter version is not caused by overelaboration.) The exposition of the theory of the three types of friendship in *Mag. Mor.* 1208 b 36-1209 a 36 has important implications for the origin of the theory (cf. esp. 1208 b 10 ff.) which help to bring the theories of *Eth. Eud.* and *Eth. Nic.* into better focus.

[5] The other four problems discussed in *Mag. Mor.* 2.3.1199 a 14 ff. are of varying interest. But they and the opening chapters of the treatise (1.1-3), which discuss various ways a thing can be good and to which nothing quite corresponds in the other treatises, should not be overlooked by any student of Aristotle's moral philosophy.

the treatise is genuine then its account of justice both serves to explain the occasional half–survival of the same view in *Eudemian Ethics* 4 (= *Nicomachean* 5) and to point up the nature and degree of Aristotle's later achievement in getting beyond such a restricted understanding of justice (on this see further below, section 2). Again, the fact that the *Magna Moralia* consistently, clearly and repeatedly (1184 a 29-38, b 33-39 with 1204 a 26-29, 1185 a 25-26, 36-39, 1208 b 3-6) maintains a unified conception of εὐδαιμονία as consisting, without discrimination, of the exercise of both the moral and the intellectual virtues, cannot but throw important new light on the related theories of the *Nicomachean* and *Eudemian Ethics*.[6]

In all these ways then, as well perhaps as others,[7] the *Magna Moralia* is a very important document for scholars and philosophers interested in understanding Aristotle's moral philosophy—*if* it is, in fact, Aristotle's work. In this paper I will try to

[6] I think something similar should be said about the *Mag. Mor.'s* well–known emphasis on ὁρμαὶ φυσικαί and φυσικὴ ἀρετή as necessary presupposition for the acquisition of moral virtue (1198 a 8-9). I believe careful reflection will show that the *Eth. Nic.*'s theory of virtue is incompatible with this thesis. The notion of φυσικὴ ἀρετή appears in the *Eth. Nic.* only in books 6 & 7, which are also *Eudemian* books, and even there (1144 b 1 ff.) Aristotle does not make it, or ὁρμαὶ φυσικαί, a *necessary presupposition* of (complete) moral virtue.

[7] Dirlmeier (commentary on *Eth. Eud.*, pp. 366-67, 492-93, 497-98) revives the view of Spengel (*Über die unter dem Namen des A. erhaltenen ethischen Schriften*, 499-503) and von Arnim (*Sitzungsberichte d. Wien. Akad.* 202 (2), p. 96, and *Rhein. Museum*, 76 (1927), 114-15, that the present concluding chapters of the *Eth. Eud.*, 8.1-3) in fact have been misplaced in our MSS. from the end of book 6, and that therefore *Eth. Eud.*, like *Mag. Mor.*, concluded with the treatment of friendship. His and their chief argument is that the corresponding chapters of *Mag. Mor.* (2.7.1206 a 36-10) do precede the treatment of friendship. Dirlmeier's motive for wanting to make this adjustment is apparently to underscore the truth that *Eth. Eud.* 8.3 is not to be interpreted as the counterpiece to *Eth. Nic.* 10. 6-8, with its intellectualist revision of the definition of εὐδαιμονία. This motive I applaud; though the truth in question is not made doubtful by reading these chapters where they stand. But so far as I can see they cannot have preceded book 7, since at 8.3.1249 a 17-18 Aristotle refers back to the argument of book 7.2. 1235 b 30 ff.—an argument, indeed, found nowhere else in the Corpus. Dirlmeier's invention (op. cit. p. 497-98) of a passage for *Eth. Eud.* 6 in which the same thing was said is gratuitous at best.

show, mostly by considering the philosophical content of the work, that the *Magna Moralia* can only be plausibly interpreted as, in substance at any rate, the work of Aristotle, representing an earlier stage in the development of his moral philosophy than either the *Eudemian* or the *Nicomachean Ethics.* In this I agree with Dirlmeier. But as I am not persuaded by his treatment of the more narrowly philological grounds on which scholars have tended to reject the treatise, I first indicate what I take to be the main inadequacies of Dirlmeier's views on the date and method of composition of the work. But though Dirlmeier does not, in my judgment, adequately meet the philological grounds of objection to the treatise, these objections can be very largely disarmed, and I will suggest a way in which this can be done. My hope is that once it is seen clearly that the state of our text does not require, or even strongly suggest, the inference that someone other than Aristotle is the author of the *Magna Moralia,* the arguments from its content which I advance in section 2 will then be admitted to weigh the balance strongly in favor of its Aristotelian origin.

I

A large part of Dirlmeier's commentary (which, with its introduction, runs to three hundred and eighty-odd pages) is devoted to rebutting the charges that have been made against the *Magna Moralia*'s authenticity. The grounds of objection have chiefly fallen into four groups. (1) Matters of language and style in which the *Magna Moralia* seems to diverge sharply from the admittedly genuine works; (2) a few personal and other references allegedly pointing toward a post-Aristotelian date; (3) supposed Stoic influences in terminology and doctrine; (4) a general impression, very strong in a few relatively isolated passages, that the author of the *Magna Moralia* wrote with the *Eudemian* and *Nicomachean Ethics* open before him, excerpting, condensing and abbreviating so as to produce a kind of handbook of Aristotelian moral theory.[8] Dirlmeier, following von

[8] I omit mention of Jaeger's claim ("Ein Theophrastzitat in der *Gr. Ethik,*" *Hermes* 64, (1929), 274-78) that the *Mag. Mor.* cites Theophrastus at 1198 b 9-20. This claim was always suppositious, and Dirlmeier disposes of it effectively (pp. 354-56).

Arnim, shows, I think, that the passages which have been thought to betray Stoic influence do not do so.[9] What he says on the other heads, however, is open to serious objection in several ways.

To begin with, the view he adopts about the *Magna Moralia*'s peculiarities of language and style is strained and dubious in itself and hardly consistent with his treatment of some of the personal references.[10] Dirlmeier recognizes, as he must, that the *Magna Moralia* was not written down in its present form by Aristotle. His strategy, however, is to reduce the influence of Aristotle's "editor"[11] to the minimum, viz., to "externals" of language.[12] Stylistic peculiarities he hopes to account for in another way. The treatise has always struck readers as pedantic and schoolmasterly, consisting as it does of discussions for the most part simply strung together, without much attempt at large-scale composition, and with frequent personal and quasi-dramatic touches, such as references to the author in the first person singular, use of second person singular where Aristotle more normally uses impersonal τις, introduction of objections by personifying the counterargument or by a subjectless "he says," and such practices as beginning an explanation or defense of a thesis by διὰ τί; ("And why so? Because . . ."). These, and other such, peculiarities Dirlmeier seeks to explain partly by the idea that the *Magna Moralia* is an early work, composed by the young logician Aristotle in the style of the *Topics*,[13] and

[9] See, for example, pp. 439; 202-5, 257-58, 349-50; 268-69; 291 (not that everything he says is correct, or that more might not be said). Dirlmeier is also right (pp. 118-19, 423) to reject Tennemann's objections to the *Mag. Mor.*'s "moralistic" conception of god at 1207 a 6-17.

[10] Düring has also noticed this incongruence (*Gnomon* 33, pp. 552, 557).

[11] So Dirlmeier, without adequate discussion, characterizes the interloper. See below, pp. 7 ff.

[12] It should be acknowledged that Praechter (*Die Philosophie des Altertums*, ed. 12, p. 370 n. 1) and Theiler (*Hermes* 69[1934], 353-79) anticipated Dirlmeier in arguing for the independent Aristotelian origin of the content of the *Mag. Mor.*, while allowing the actual writing to have been done by someone else.

[13] This he thinks accounts for the serial ordering of arguments and some of the dryness of exposition. I find his arguments from the supposed affinity of *Mag. Mor.* to *Topics* (itself much overstated) extremely dubious: see below p. 336.

partly by the unfalsifiable but rather disparate hypothesis that the *Magna Moralia,* unlike the other treatises, preserves Aristotle's actual classroom style.

By emphasizing its affinities to the *Topics* (and other early logical works) Dirlmeier commits himself to a date for the work perhaps as early as the early 350's and certainly not later than about 350.[14] But this is hardly compatible with the reference (1197 b 22) to Mentor, the man who betrayed Aristotle's friend Hermeias to the Persian king; this, as Dirlmeier recognizes in passing (see his comment ad loc.) could not have been written before about 342 at the earliest. And similarly the passage (1205 a 23) referring to Neleus, son of the exemplary Coriscus, can hardly have been written before about 340 and perhaps dates from considerably later.[15] Dirlmeier also runs into difficulties over the reference (2.15.1212 b 23 ff.) to, and implied defense of, the doctrine of god as self–thinker. For since he accepts a late date for *Metaphysics* Λ he must, most implausibly, imagine the reference not to be to Aristotle's own argument in Λ but to an otherwise entirely unknown Academic pre–cursor.[16] The *Metaphysics* reference will cause no difficulty if, as I am inclined to believe in any case, (the main body of) Λ is an early work.[17] But the other two passages pose considerable obstacles to Dirlmeier's defense of the *Magna Moralia*: at the very least, if the treatise was composed before about 350 then some special explanation must be provided for the occurrence of the references to Mentor and Neleus. But Dirlmeier seems not to have even noticed the discrepancy.

Thus Dirlmeier's treatment of the stylistic peculiarities of the treatise is both unconvincing in itself and at variance with his way of handling the references to Mentor and Neleus. He

[14] For this dating of the *Topics* see Düring, *Aristotle's Protrepticus* (Göteborg, 1961), p. 287.

[15] On Mentor and Neleus see Düring, *Gnomon* 33, p. 552, as well as Dirlmeier ad loc. (Dirlmeier accepts Wilamowitz's correction of the manuscripts at 1205 a 23: see Wilamowitz, "Neleus von Skepsis," *Hermes* 62 [1927], 371.)

[16] Cf. Merlan, loc. cit. and Düring op. cit. pp. 550-51.

[17] In fact if *Mag. Mor.* is authentic and an early work, the appearance of the reference to *Metaph.* Λ becomes a very strong additional argument in favor of an early date for Λ.

is no more convincing in what he says about the linguistic oddities of the work. As noted above, Dirlmeier maintains that the "editor" who prepared Aristotle's manuscript for publication limited himself to providing some of the "externals" of language in which to clothe Aristotle's thoughts (p. 147). At one place, indeed, Dirlmeier goes to the extreme of claiming that the "editor" betrays his presence *only* in his preference for ὑπέρ with genitive where Aristotle would write περί (p. 185)! In fact, however, on Dirlmeier's own account elsewhere, un-Aristotelian language is much more prevalent than that in the treatise. Thus the use of τὸ ὅλον as adverb (meaning "in general," "on the whole") is, at least given its frequency in this work, certainly un-Aristotelian (cf. Dirlmeier's comment, p. 156). There is also the remarkable fact, noted by Dirlmeier on p. 158, that Ionic forms of οἶδα are not merely frequent in the *Magna Moralia,* but the only ones used at all. And other less striking usages might be cited as well.

When the number and pervasiveness of these linguistic peculiarities is taken properly into account, I think Dirlmeier's hypothesis of an "editor" who published Aristotle's own lecture notes with a few light alterations of language is untenable. The very mention of an *editor* who not only touches and patches here and there, but regularly supplies some of the *prepositions* and *adverbs* is really quite suspect. No other work of Aristotle, all of which, one supposes, were at least lightly edited, shows any such features. How *did* it happen that the supposed original Aristotelian manuscript of the *Magna Moralia,* and it alone, underwent such treatment? Dirlmeier attempts no answer and no plausible one suggests itself.

The very least that one must infer from these facts about the language in which the treatise is written is that if it contains Aristotle's own notes put out by someone else, this man was no mere editor. He must have worked from an original text which was very incomplete, since he found it necessary to write at many places ὑπέρ where Aristotle, if he had written up the same materials, would have written περί, and his own idiom shows also, as I have noted, in other ways throughout the work. But if the materials were incomplete enough to require the "editor" to compose many of the actual sentences in his own words, there must have been plenty of opportunity, and perhaps in some cases actual need, for him to fill out the argument here and there, both by adding examples and in other ways. Once you admit, as Dirlmeier reluctantly does, and as one must, that the work was actually written out in someone else's words than Aristotle's, you must expect to find *some* substantive intrusions in the text, so that Dirlmeier's insistence on the total authenticity of the work's contents would in any case have to be tempered. (So the simplest hypothesis, I should think, by which Dirlmeier could reconcile his early date for the *Magna Moralia* with references in the text to Neleus and Mentor would be to suppose that these were added later by the "editor".)[18] If, then, our text originated in a manuscript of Aristotle's own, we must reckon with the strong probability that this manuscript was very incomplete and has been considerably filled out by whoever prepared it for publication.

It is of course possible for all we are likely ever to know, that this is how our text came into being. But there is a simpler and more natural way, on the hypothesis of the substantial authenticity of the *Magna Moralia*'s contents, of accounting for all the genuinely un–Aristotelian aspects of style and language found in the treatise, without indulging in conjectures about an Aristotelian manuscript whose condition might have seemed to call for just the sort of expansion we seem to find in the *Magna Moralia*. This is by the supposition that the *Magna Moralia* is a student's published notes of a course of Aristotle's, not based on any Aristotelian manuscript but on what he actually heard Aristotle say. Editing, if any, would be of his own old notes, not Aristotle's. In setting down his notes originally he would naturally have written partly in his own idiom and style; in preparing them for publication, or for his own later use in lectures, he could easily have added the examples of Neleus and Mentor, and perhaps filled out the notes in other ways. In this way all the linguistic facts could be plausibly ac-

[18] This is a better guess than Düring's supposition (op. cit. p. 557) that Theophrastus (or someone) added them on the occasion of his reading Aristotle's notes to a beginning ethics class in the Lyceum. Does Düring then suppose also that Theophrastus (or whoever) was identical with Dirlmeier's "editor?"

counted for and such facts as the appearance of the references to Mentor and Neleus easily accommodated. I need not claim that this hypothesis *does* correctly explain the genesis of our *Magna Moralia*; it is enough to point out that, in advance of a study of the treatise's contents, this possibility stands completely open, and is in itself no less believable than the generally current hypothesis of a post–Aristotelian author who worked primarily from Aristotelian sources known to us independently of his version.

II

But is the substance of the treatise Aristotle's own work, rather than a pastiche of the other *Ethics*? Dirlmeier here does what one must do, namely read right through the work testing each section to see how it compares with the corresponding passages, if any, in the other treatises. I think there is no doubt that he proves the insufficiency of the standard view, that the *Magna Moralia* has its origin in a condensation and distillation of the *Eudemian Ethics* or of the *Eudemian* and *Nicomachean* both. There are in fact only two fairly brief passages where in organization and argument the *Magna Moralia* "follows" the *Nicomachean* in preference to the *Eudemian*.[19] Elsewhere the affinities are all to the *Eudemian*. But I agree with Dirlmeier that no one who reads the *Magna Moralia* carefully and sensitively, noticing and understanding the points of divergence in form, organization, and argument, can believe that it derives directly from the *written text* of either or both of the other *Ethics*. Dirlmeier is not, however, always careful enough to distinguish this kind of independence, which he amply establishes, from that kind of independence he wishes to prove: that of a work composed without knowledge of the others, and by the same author. For, even if the *Magna Moralia* is thus textual-

[19] 1.5.1185 b 13-9. 1187 a 4 (corresponding roughly to *Eth. Nic.* 2), and 2.13-14 (1212 a 28-b 23) (on the sense in which the good man loves himself, corresponding to *Eth. Nic.* 9.8). How comes it that *Mag. Mor.*, the earliest ethics, deals with these matters in a way which in the end (*Eth. Nic.*) Aristotle finds on the whole satisfactory, while yet during the interim (*Eth. Eud.*) he sees fit to alter his treatment quite considerably? Dirlmeier doesn't even face the question squarely. See below, p. 347 f.

ly independent, it might still have been composed as a handbook of Aristotelian moral philosophy by someone other than Aristotle: the author might have learned his philosophy from reading (or hearing) the *Eudemian Ethics,* and then composed his handbook without consulting the texts as he went along. Dirlmeier repeatedly emphasizes that Aristotle himself wrote the *Nicomachean Ethics* without working directly from the text of the *Eudemian*: why should not a second party have done the same in the *Magna Moralia?*

To prove its Aristotelian authorship Dirlmeier relies principally on matters of form and language. In the first place, there is the alleged affinity, already mentioned, to the *Topics* and other logical works: he calls the *Magna Moralia* "Ethica logice demonstrata" (p. 175), and says it is composed *more topico* (p. 205), "with the logical interest" predominating. It seems to me highly questionable whether anything much can be made of these claims. The *Topics* consists for the most part of somewhat disjoint analyses of modes of argument, because its interest is predominantly in the *form* of valid and invalid arguments of a very wide range of types. The interest is in the study of the arguments themselves, and not so much in any large–scale *theory* of arguments; hence, the disjointedness, serial order, etc. In the *Magna Moralia* the predominant interest is in any case in the *content* of the arguments, such interest in form as there is being simply that of the self–respecting philosopher concerned for the validity of his reasoning.[20] So the disjointedness here certainly does not have the same causes. Nor does Dirlmeier cite any reason to expect a man in turning from work on a handbook on dialectical argumentation to lecturing, or composing a book on ethics, to treat this new and different subject matter in a somewhat similar handbook style. Hence such

[20] It is, in any case, rather the *Eth. Eud.* than the *Mag. Mor.* which betrays in its mode of exposition Aristotle the young logician: the emphasis on ὑποθέσεις and deduction which marks that work (cf. D. J. Allan "Quasi–mathematical method in the *Eudemian Ethics,*" in *Aristote et les problèmes de méthode,* ed. S. Mansion, Louvain, 1961) is surely to be interpreted as the application of the *Posterior Analytics'* Theory of scientific reasoning to the subject matter of ethics—as the *De Caelo* is its application to cosmology.

affinities as there may be to the *Topics* provide no strong argument in favor of Aristotelian authorship.

On the other hand, Dirlmeier also emphasizes many matters of linguistic usage, and small matters of style, of which some link the *Magna Moralia* to the logical works, some to Plato and the Academy. These observations, spread through his commentary, are varyingly impressive; [21] but my own sense is that cumulatively they are not sufficient to settle the question of authorship. The author, if not Aristotle, might himself have spent time at the Academy, perhaps while Aristotle was a member, thus picking up mannerisms, distinctions, etc., linking him to the Academy in general and to the Aristotle of the *Organon* in particular.

Thus, while one must attach some weight to considerations of language and style, further arguments are clearly needed. Such arguments can only be founded on the philosophical content of the work. Dirlmeier does on occasion take note of philosophical divergences which can plausibly be explained on the theory that the *Magna Moralia* presents less mature Aristotelian doctrine,[22] but he seems to shy away from such judgments (perhaps on the ground that they are too "subjective"). Certainly judgments of this kind are frequently inconclusive; but often, also, they are not. I think there are many passages of the *Magna Moralia* of which "immaturity" of doctrine is an extremely plausible explanation [23]—and a much more plausible one than the alter-

[21] Among the most interesting are the formulary resemblances between doctrines in *Mag. Mor.* (and *Eth. Eud.*) and the Academic *Definitiones*: cf. pp. 104, 215, etc.; noteworthy, too, is the *Mag. Mor.*'s listing (1185 b 5-6) of *ἀγχίνοια, εὐμάθεια* and *μνήμη* as intellectual virtues: as Dirlmeier rightly observes (p. 207) these are repeatedly referred to as virtues by Plato, but are not listed in *Eth. Eud.* 5 (= *Eth. Nic.* 6), while again they turn up in the *Definitiones*.

[22] Most notably with respect to the shifting uncertainty of the *Mag. Mor.* as to whether the intellectual virtues, to which however, it never refuses to grant the title of "virtue," are grounds of praise: pp. 208-9, 345-46, 352-53.

[23] I list just a few of the most important of these: 1184 a 8-14 (definition of *τέλειον*, which, as the context [a 3-38] shows, covers what in *Eth. Nic.* is divided between *τέλειον* and *αὔταρκες*); 1188 b 18-24 (what are called in *Eth. Nic.* 3.1 *μικταὶ πράξεις*—the conception though not the name is prominent also in *Eth. Eud.*, cf. 1225 a 1-33—are, with-

native, that someone whose knowledge of Aristotle's teachings was drawn from the *Eudemian* and/or *Nicomachean Ethics,* wittingly or unwittingly, made alterations of the kind we find in *Magna Moralia.* Indeed, in two cases I think it can be practically demonstrated that this explanation is correct. When one adds the fact that the author himself claims to be Aristotle, by referring to the *Analytics'* doctrine of the syllogism as his own (1201 b 25), I think the matter is settled.

The two passages I think are decisive are 1.1.1182 b 6-1183 b 8, the critique of an abstract or universal Good, and 1.33, on justice.

All three of the ethical treatises insist that ethics, as a practical and not a merely theoretical inquiry, ought to concern itself only with concrete questions about the good of human beings, and not at all with whatever more universal or abstract goods there may be. In the *Nicomachean Ethics* (1.6) the sole object of attack and rejection is the Platonic Form of the Good, against which Aristotle argues both that there isn't any such thing and that if there were ethics should take no account of it. In the *Eudemian Ethics* (1.8) the chief focus of the discussion is again on the Platonic theory, and these same two points are again made (1217 b 16-23, 25-1218 a 32, as against 1217 b 23-25, 1218 a 33-38), but there is in addition a brief section (1218 a 38-b 6) dealing separately with the claims for attention of something called τὸ κοινὸν ἀγαθόν, "the common good." We are evidently (cf. 1218 a 8-15, *Mag. Mor.* 1182 b 12-14) to understand this as what all good things are supposed to have in common, regarded now *not* as something separated apart from those good things (as a Platonic Form would be) but had or possessed in common by each of them equally: in short, good regarded as a proper universal instead of as a Form. In the *Magna Moralia,* interest in the "common good" (introduced as τὸ κοινὸν ἐν ἅπασιν ὑπάρχον ἀγαθόν, 1182 b 11-12) expands to such an extent

out comment, treated as ἀκούσια); 1193 b 10-18 ("legal justice" is not πρὸς ἕτερον, which contradicts *Eth. Eud.* 4 [*Eth. Nic.* 5] 1129 b 25-27; but the later version has, by deeper reflection, discovered a different and important way in which "legal justice" *is* πρὸς ἕτερον); 1208 b 36-1209 a 36 (the theory of the three εἴδη of friendship is developed in the course of treating an ἀπορία and not simply announced as in *Eth. Nic.*, 1155 b 18-19, and in effect, in *Eth. Eud.*, 1236 a 16).

that it dominates the discussion (1182 b 10-1183 a 24), while the Platonic theory is relegated to a relatively brief final section (1183 a 24-b 8) ; and though the main arguments are significantly different from those in the *Eudemian* and *Nicomachean Ethics,* it is only against the common good, and not against the Form, that the author makes any of the points made in the other treatises (cf. 1183 a 7-23 with *Eth. Eud.* 1217 b 35-41, *Eth. Nic.* 1096 a 29-34).

This altered main interest of the *Magna Moralia* is certainly not easily explained as the work of a post–Aristotelian. For, among other reasons, Aristotle's mature theory makes the claim that "good" is said in all the categories grounds for treating it as a word not of one but of many senses. On this view there cannot *be* anything which all good things as such have in common, so that the idea of a *κοινὸν ἀγαθόν* must be regarded as empty. On this the *Eudemian* (1217 b 25-35) and the *Nicomachean Ethics* (1096 a 23-29) agree.[24] This is why the *Nicomachean* does not even mention a *κοινὸν ἀγαθόν*, other than the Platonic Form, and why the *Eudemian* treats it only in passing and as subsidiary to the Form. Why then does a supposed post–Aristotelian writer take such a strong and independent interest in the unhypostatized *κοινὸν ἀγαθόν*? One might, of course, invent a controversy among Aristotle's successors on this point for the *Magna Moralia* to be engaged in, but for this there is no warrant. In fact close study of the texts shows that special interest in a non–Platonic *κοινὸν ἀγαθόν* marks a stage of Aristotle's *own* thinking, a stage *earlier* than that of the *Eudemian Ethics.* It follows that the *Magna Moralia,* which betrays this interest, reports Aristotle's argumentation at that earlier time.

It is well known that in his essay *On Ideas* Aristotle rebutted the Platonists' argument "from the sciences" (*Metaph.* A 9, 990 b 12) by pointing out that even if this argument proves there

[24] Even if *ἀγαθόν* is treated as a *πρὸς ἓν λεγόμενον* (cf. G. E. L. Owen "Logic and metaphysics in some earlier works of Aristotle," *Aristotle and Plato in the Mid-Fourth Century*, ed. Düring–Owen, Göteborg, 1959, pp. 163-90, esp. p. 180) it remains true that the word has many senses, with no common definition covering all its instances. So that the later reservations of the *Eth. Nic.* (1096 b 26-31) do not affect this point.

are things besides particulars, it does not prove there are Forms: for "there are besides particulars the things they have in common (τὰ κοινά), which *we* maintain are the objects of the sciences." [25] This theory of κοινά, as an alternative to Platonic hypostatization, appears also in the logical works; [26] and it is plainly about κοινά in this Aristotelian sense that the *Magna Moralia* is speaking when it says: ἕτερον γὰρ τῆς ἰδέας τοῦτο δόξειεν ἂν εἶναι. ἡ μὲν ἰδέα χωριστὸν καὶ αὐτὸ καθ' αὑτό, τὸ δὲ κοινὸν ἐν ἅπασιν ὑπάρχει (1182 b 12-14). So the suggestion that political science must in the first instance get to know τὸ κοινὸν ἀγαθόν amounts to the claim both that there is a κοινόν in this Aristotelian sense in the case of "good," and that political science must study it.

In the *Nicomachean* and *Eudemian Ethics* the corresponding suggestion about the Form is disposed of in two stages: as noted above, Aristotle argues first that there is no such object of study, and secondly that even if there were it would not help the political scientist, or any other specialist, to know about it.[27] The *Magna Moralia,* however, argues only that political scientists must not concern themselves with the κοινὸν ἀγαθόν (nor with the Platonic Form), without denying the existence of any κοινὸν ἀγαθόν, whether "separated" or not. In fact, the *Magna Moralia* has no qualms about actually stating the common definition of "good" (1182 b 20-21); whereas the argument of the two *Ethics* clearly implies that there is no such definition. *Magna Moralia* is content to deny to political science any need to be concerned with it, while yet affirming its existence. The principal argument of the *Eudemian* and *Nicomachean Ethics*

[25] Alexander of Aphrodisias, in *Metaph.* 79.17-19, citing the Περὶ Ἰδεῶν (cf. 79.5): ἔστι γὰρ παρὰ τὰ καθ' ἕκαστα τὰ κοινά, ὧν φαμεν καὶ τὰς ἐπιστήμας εἶναι.

[26] E.g., *Topics* 178 b 36 ff., as a solution to the Third Man; cf. *Metaph.* B. 6 1003 a 8-12, Z. 13.1039 a 1-3.

[27] *Eth. Eud.* states this program explicitly (1217 b 19-25), and *Eth. Nic.* plainly follows it implicitly (1096 a 17-b 31 on existence, b 31-1097 a 14 on usefulness). At 1218 a 37-b 1 *Eth. Eud.* apparently means to affirm the corresponding two points about a nonseparated κοινόν (so also D. J. Allan interprets: "Aristotle's Criticism of Platonic Doctrine concerning Goodness and the Good," *Proc. of the Arist. Soc.* 64 [1963-64], 227): in any case it certainly follows from what is argued at 1217 b 22-35 (cf. ὥσπερ οὖν οὐδὲ τὸ ὂν ἕν τι ἐστι περὶ τὰ εἰρημένα, οὕτως οὐδὲ τὸ ἀγαθόν, b 33-34) that there is no κοινὸν ἀγαθόν.

against its existence, that because "good" is said in all the categories it must have so many different senses, is not even adumbrated anywhere in the *Magna Moralia.* It is true that the claim is made (1183 a 9-10) that "good" is said in all the categories, but this thesis is put to a quite different use. The argument here (1183 a 7-23)[28] is that even in a single category, like that of time, what is good is not the subject of a single science; rather the doctor knows when is a good time for an operation, and the pilot when is a good time to sail, and so on. If then in *each* category one finds not one but many sciences dealing with good, so much the less will one expect to find a single science dealing with what is good in all the categories at once. This is a straightforward argument *a fortiori,* and does not depend on or involve the theory that good is a πολλαχῶς λεγόμενον.

The argument of this section of the *Magna Moralia* therefore has the following features. (1) It concentrates specially on the proposition that political science should have in view in its reasonings the realization of the "common" good, an unhypostatized *universale in rebus.* (2) It does not deny, but affirms, the existence of such a "common" good. (3) It is familiar with the doctrine of categories, and holds that there are items in all of them which are good, but does not argue on this basis that "good" is ambiguous and that there is no goodness common to all good things. It would seem that we have here the record of a stage of Aristotle's thinking about "good" which antedates both that preserved in the *Eudemian* and that of the *Nicomachean Ethics.* At this time he himself accepted the ex-

[28] It corresponds to *Eth. Eud.* 1217 b 35-1218 a 1 (*not* to b 25-35) and *Eth. Nic.* 1096 a 29-34 (*not* to a 23-29). Dirlmeier's failure to see that two separate arguments are given in *Eth. Eud.* and *Eth. Nic.* leads him wildly off in his analysis of *Mag. Mor.* 1183 a 7-23: see pp. 176-77. The same failure, in the case of *Eth. Eud.*, has led Allan (op. cit. pp. 284-86, cf. esp. his way of running together the two arguments in his summary on p. 285) to misunderstand the clear meaning of 1217 b 33-35, which states as the conclusion of a completed, *independent* argument that there is no unified science of goodness because there is nothing common to all good things as such. (On this Owen is right, "Logic and Metaphysics in some Earlier Works of Aristotle," Owen–Düring op. cit. pp. 165-66).

istence of a κοινὸν ἀγαθόν alongside the other κοινά whose existence he proposed as an alternative to Forms. This is why he deals more fully with the suggestion that politics must study this than with the corresponding suggestion about the Platonic Form. The former was for him a live question, while the latter was not. Later, when he came to think that because there are good things in all the categories good must be a πολλαχῶς λεγόμενον, so that there is no such κοινόν, the question ceased to be a live one. He then naturally recast his treatment of the "abstract good" so as to make it a historical, anti-Platonic discussion such as we find in the *Eudemian* and *Nicomachean Ethics.* Certainly no follower of Aristotle's, whether wittingly or unwittingly, can have produced our text out of the more orthodox arguments of the other works.

These considerations show conclusively, I think, that at least the part of the first book just analyzed goes back to some Aristotelian text or discussion earlier than either *Eudemian* or *Nicomachean Ethics.* Examination of the *Magna Moralia*'s treatment of justice will show that this is no isolated case. This can be done relatively briefly, since two of the points that need to be taken account of have been mentioned already.[29]

Magna Moralia 1.33, like the *Eudemian–Nicomachean* account of justice, begins with a distinction between two senses of τὸ δίκαιον. First, there is the sense of the word in which, because the law of the city enjoins the performance of virtuous acts of all kinds, and anything enjoined by the law can be called δίκαιον, "just" acts would include acts of virtue of whatever kind, brave, temperate, pious and the rest. (Commentators of the *Nicomachean Ethics* call this "justice" in the universal sense.) Secondly, and more narrowly, there is a sense of the word in which only fair dealing counts as just action, and it is naturally with justice in the second sense of the word that both discussions are primarily concerned. The *Magna Moralia,* however, draws the distinction in an importantly different way from the *Eudemian–Nicomachean* account. The *Magna Moralia,* noting that fairness and unfairness consist in attitudes one has to other people and their good, contrasts the narrower with the broader sense of justice as respectively relational and non–

[29] Above, p. 328 and note 23.

relational: the temperate man, who will of course also be just in the broad sense, need stand in no particular relation to others in doing (at least some of) his temperate actions (1193 b 12-17). But the *Eudemian–Nicomachean* account makes it a principal part of its theory that in both senses justice is a relational notion:[30] insofar as a temperate man can be regarded also as just (in the universal sense) he must think of his actions as conforming to the law and therefore as contributions to the general good which it is the aim of the law to promote. The contradiction here is quite explicit. Universal justice ἀρετὴ μέν ἐστι τελεία, ἀλλ' οὐχ ἁπλῶς ἀλλὰ πρὸς ἕτερον (*Eth. Nic.*=*Eth. Eud.* 1129 b 26-7); ἀλλὰ τὸ δίκαιον τὸ πρὸς ἕτερον ἄλλο τοῦ εἰρημένου κατὰ νόμον δικαίου ἐστίν (*Mag. Mor.* 1193 b 15-16). It is surely incredible that anyone writing a compendium of Aristotelian ethics who knew the other treatment should thus boldly contradict his main source.[31]

But on the assumption of authenticity it is not difficult to account for this divergence. It is plain that the *Magna Moralia* takes a much too simple view of the relation of universal, or legal, justice to the particular virtues enjoined by it—and that the *Eudemian–Nicomachean* account shows deeper insight and more sophistication. The author of the *Magna Moralia* simply equates acts of (universal) justice with acts of temperance, courage and so on, as the case may be, and hence, naturally enough, infers that acts of (universal) justice have no necessary relation to other persons. But this is wrong, and in the other discussion Aristotle takes some pains (1129 b 25-1130 a 8) to ex-

[30] It is this fact that, Aristotle implies (1130 b 1-2), makes the double usage of the word at once intelligible and difficult to see through (1129 a 26-28).

[31] The contradiction consists in the affirmation and denial that τὸ κατὰ νόμον δίκαιον is πρὸς ἕτερον, something that consists in a relation to others. It is plain that πρὸς ἕτερον bears this same sense in both statements. The fact that καθ' ἑαυτόν ("by himself," "solitary," *Mag. Mor.* 1193 b 13, 15) contrasts with πρὸς ἕτερον differently than καθ' αὑτόν ("in himself," "for his own advantage," *Eth. Nic.* 1129 b 33), ἁπλῶς (1129 b 26) or πρὸς αὑτόν (1130 a, 6, 7) do (P. Trude, *Der Begriff der Gerechtigkeit in der aristotelischen Rechts- und Staatsphilosophie*, Berlin, 1955, pp. 59-62, cited with approval by Dirlmeier, p. 313), does not imply that πρὸς ἕτερον has a different sense there. Provided the sense is the same the contradiction remains.

plain why: as already noted, an act of (say) temperance is only also an act of (universal) justice if done *as* owed to someone else (perhaps the community as a whole, or the ruler, or some fellow citizen, Aristotle suggests [1129 b 14-19, 1130 a 5]). Aristotle seems to have in mind two different ways in which a virtuous act might be regarded as a contribution to someone else's good. First, some acts of courage are undertaken in defense of the life and property, not of the agent himself, but of others, and a corresponding point might be made for temperance, good temper and other virtues.[32] Now on this ground one could only argue that a person displays justice in the universal sense when exercising some virtue to the material benefit of some other person besides himself—by bravery in battle, or leaving someone else's wife unseduced, and so on. But one could not maintain that *private* acts of bravery (defending merely oneself) or temperance (not overeating), etc., showed (universal) justice. Secondly, however, Aristotle seems also to have in mind a way in which *all* virtuous acts, whether publicly or merely privately beneficial in the way just noted, can be thought of as πρὸς ἕτερον. For in a well-organized city, according to Aristotle, the laws aim to advance the happiness of all the citizens in common (1129 b 14-19), so that, since happiness consists partly in morally virtuous action, the law "bids us to live according to each of the virtues and forbids us each of the vices" (1130 b 23-24). Hence one may regard one's virtuous disposition and its exercise, whether private or public, as a contribution to the well-being of the city just in themselves: it is in the exercise of one's own virtue, whatever the circumstances, that one makes one's fundamental contribution to the communal good.

Now in making this second point Aristotle marks an essential advance on the theory of the *Magna Moralia.* For even the *Magna Moralia*'s solitary temperate man can, from this point of view, also be acting for social ends and so be acting πρὸς ἕτερον: he need only regard his own temperance as just in itself part of the communal good. It would thus seem that the *Eudemian–Nicomachean* account shows the fruit of deeper reflection, which enabled Aristotle to correct the earlier, over-hasty classification

[32] This seems to be the point Aristotle relies on at 1129 b 31-1130 a 8: see esp. b 33-35.

of justice in the broader sense as not consisting in a relation to others. Certainly the facts can very easily be accommodated in this way, while, as noted above, they can hardly be squared at all with the hypothesis of a post-Aristotelian author familiar with the orthodox doctrine.

This theory of the origin of the *Magna Moralia*'s discussion of justice is also suggested by other facts. Thus the *Magna Moralia* gives an account of "particular" justice, justice in the sense of fair dealing, which from the point of view of the *Nicomachean Ethics*, is both restricted in scope and very poorly articulated. The restricted scope comes out already in the definition of the just man as the man who wants to have what is equal—neither getting more by acting unjustly nor getting less by being unjustly treated (1193 b 25-30), than his share.[83] Obviously in this conception justice and injustice only show themselves in situations where a man is actually competing with others for some good thing: the just man limits his competitiveness and desire for gain in ways in which the unjust man does not. Justice, in effect, is fairness in making or accepting distributions between oneself and others (1193 b 20-23); the more general case of parent or arbitrator or judge distributing goods where he is not party to the distribution is not taken account of in the definition at all.[84] In fact, justice on this definition seems perfectly to exemplify the *Magna Moralia*'s general thesis about the moral virtues (1186 a 33, b 33-34, 1190 b 7, etc.), that they are μεσότητες τῶν παθῶν. Justice turns out to be essentially the proper control of one's competitive instinct for gain: the just man has neither too much, nor too little, but the right amount of this πάθος. Now not only does this view make justice the exact counterpart of the other moral virtues (without the disruptions caused in the theory of the mean by Aristotle's recognition in the *Eudemian* and *Nicomachean Ethics*

[83] Compare *Eth. Eud.* 2.3.1221 a 4: κέρδος—ζημία—δίκαιον and the theory of *two* opposed vicious types (the κερδαλέος and the ζημιώδης) adumbrated at a 23-24. The limitation evident here was corrected by the time the detailed treatment of book 4 was composed. Contrast *Eth. Nic.* 2.7.1108 b 7-8.

[84] Hence the situation of the judge or arbitrator, which rightly occupies the center of the discussion in *Eth. Eud.* (*Eth. Nic.*), is only alluded to briefly in *Mag. Mor.*, in a kind of appendix (1196 a 34-b 3).

of the anomalous character of justice [cf. 1133 b 32 ff.]), but it is also a very natural first sketch for a Greek and a student of Plato's *Republic* to have produced. The general equation of πλεονεξία (graspingness) with ἀδικία would certainly predispose any Greek to the sort of account the *Magna Moralia* gives, and this predisposition would certainly be reinforced for Aristotle, if he is the author of that account, by the way in which Thrasymachus in the *Republic* builds on this usage in his theory of what injustice is.

Here again, the *Eudemian–Nicomachean* treatment shows the fruits of further reflection. In their theory the circumstances of justice are generalized to include indifferently the assignment of the right amount of goods (and evils), no matter who the persons may be to whom the assignment is made (cf. 1134 a 1-6). And because the case where a man is assigning goods to himself is a special case, Aristotle rightly tends to avoid it, discussing instead the actions of judges and arbitrators.[35] On this improved conception it is not essential to justice that a just act involve the renunciation of possible, but unjust, gain on one's own part. And, on the other side, the motives to injustice could, in principle, be quite varied: not merely excessive desire for gain, but also simple hatred and willful arbitrariness, can now be accommodated. The essential thing is whether or not the right assignment of goods has been made—and the motives leading someone to fail to make it are now a subsidiary question. The *Nicomachean Ethics,* by defining the virtues as means in passion *and action* (1106 b 16-17),[36] perhaps intends to make room for virtues like justice, which, so understood, is a virtue of action only, with no peculiar range of emotion under its control. In any case the official *Nicomachean* account of justice as a mean (1133 b 29 ff.) mentions only actions and not passions. (It is interesting to notice, however, that even in this later treatment the appeal of the *Magna Moralia*'s more primitive

[35] This is the true source of what some commentators have found to be objectionably legalistic in Aristotle's account. The judge looms so large primarily because he represents the general case, where the facts can be observed free from the confusions introduced by considering the special case concentrated on by Plato and the earlier Aristotle.

[36] The *Eth. Eud.* is less explicit than *Eth. Nic.* in including actions as well as passions, but cf. e.g., 2.3.1220 b 21-35, esp. πράξει (b 25).

scheme is not completely overcome. In one passage (1136 b 34-1137 a 4) Aristotle assimilates the judge who knowingly hands down an unjust decision to Thrasymachus' grasping man, who is motivated by excessive desire for gain: according to Aristotle, even if he does not profit materially from the transaction, the judge at least gets an excess of *some* good—gratitude, perhaps, or revenge! Here Aristotle plainly writes under the influence of the old, restricted conception of justice; on his own current theory he ought to feel no need at all to treat the judge as a πλεονέκτης, and it is certainly to be regretted that he did not take the opportunity here once and for all to break the old tie between ἀδικία and πλεονεξία.)

The upshot is that although Aristotle takes the essential first step in *Eudemian Ethics* 4 (=*Nicomachean* 5) toward getting beyond the oversimple conception of justice as consisting essentially in the limitation of one's competitive instinct for gain, he never freed himself entirely of this idea. He recognizes the essential irrelevance of the identities of the parties to a distribution, but does not, apparently, have a clear grasp of the consequences. Both the success and the failure support the thesis that the *Magna Moralia*'s theory of justice is the work of a less mature Aristotle.

I think that my examination of the philosophical content of the *Magna Moralia's* theory of justice shows beyond reasonable doubt that that theory was constructed by Aristotle himself at some time before the composition of the *Eudemian Ethics.*[37] I have shown the same for the *Magna Moralia*'s critique of a universal Good. Many other passages could be added, but I think these are decisive.

The only significant doubts about this conclusion, so far as I can see, are prompted by the two passages where, as I said above,[38] the *Magna Moralia* "follows" the *Nicomachean Ethics* in fairly clear preference to the *Eudemian*—to which, however, on my account, it is chronologically closer. Why Aristotle should have revised, in the *Eudemian Ethics,* the treatment accorded

[37] The same conclusion could be reached, I think, from a consideration of the *Magna Moralia*'s failure to distinguish distributive, corrective and "reciprocal" justice and their spheres.

[38] P. 335 and note 19.

to these matters in the *Magna Moralia,* only to revert to it in the *Nicomachean,* is certainly not easy to say. On the other hand, one must not expect to explain *everything*: Aristotle can have had motives for doing what seems unfathomable to us. I do not think the facts are entirely inconsistent with the supposition of the priority of the *Magna Moralia*'s version of these two passages;[39] but in any case, the anomaly, difficult as it is to explain, must not be allowed to outweigh the arguments for authenticity presented above.

I have defended both the substantial authenticity of the *Magna Moralia* and its importance as a source for the study of Aristotle's moral philosophy. But I have also emphasized the undoubted, though not precisely determinable, influence of an intermediary on the transmitted record of what Aristotle said. One is not infrequently tempted to find this influence at work in the exposition of the detail of Aristotle's arguments.[40] This is

[39] On the question of *Mag. Mor.* 1.5.1185 b 14-1187 a 4 see D. J. Allan, "*Magna Moralia* and *Nicomachean Ethics,*" JHS 77, pt. 1 (1957), 7-11; Dirlmeier, *Magna Moralia* pp. 145-46; Allan, *Gnomon* 38, pp. 142-43; Dirlmeier, commentary on *Eth. Eud.*, ed. 2, 143. As for Allan's claim that the author of *Mag. Mor.* here cites the (*Nicomachean*) *Ethics* by name (1185 b 15), and thereby shows himself not to be Aristotle: (1) Dirlmeier shows that the reading ἐκ τῶν ἠθικῶν would not *normally* mean, and so probably does not mean, "from the *Ethics.*" (I do not think he succeeds in showing that it *could* not mean that.) (2) Dirlmeier's (and in effect Stock's) own favored translation, "from the phenomena (*Erscheinungen*) of moral character," "from the (observed) facts about character," which is in itself possible enough, does not fit the context: if these facts of character can be *observed* then they are not ἀφανῆ and there is no need to consider what is observed to happen in matters of bodily health as a visible indication of what happens in the formation of character. (3) I therefore agree with Spengel and others (most recently Düring, *Gnomon* 33, p. 551) that we should emend to ἐκ τῶν αἰσθητῶν ("from observable facts"): I take Stobaeus' ἐκ τῶν αἰσθήσεων (II.7, Wachs. p. 137, 25) to be very strong grounds for this alteration, given the well-known fact that his text is plainly based at this point ultimately on the *Magna Moralia.* If this is correct the question of priority must be decided on internal grounds alone, if at all.

[40] Likely cases which can be briefly indicated include 1187 a 35-b 4 (compare *Eth. Eud.* 1222 b 20-1223 a 8), 1188 b 25-26 (which seems to betray a formal structure for the argument of chapters 12-16 like that of *Eth. Eud.* 2.7-9, but without any other sign that this is so);

indeed to be expected. But I do not find any evidence that the writer has, either deliberately or through oversight or incapacity, altered any important element of Aristotle's teaching in the lectures being reported. The proof of this is the degree to which convincing and good philosophical sense can be made of at least the main drift of all the *Magna Moralia*'s discussions, together with the fact that the sense which emerges requires to be explained not as derivative from, but as the ancestor of, the mature Aristotelian doctrine. This means that the *Magna Moralia* can only be used with care in giving an account of the genesis and content of Aristotle's moral theory; but it can and must be used.

JOHN M. COOPER.

UNIVERSITY OF PITTSBURGH.

also certain arguments which hardly make sense as they stand can be presumed to be faulty reports, e. g., 1205 a 7-15.

D. J. ALLAN
GLASGOW

Quasi-mathematical method in the *Eudemian Ethics*

This paper will be so largely concerned with the use of hypotheses that it seems quite appropriate to begin by indicating some foundations of my discussion which there is not space to defend at length.

There is a general consensus of opinion, with which I agree, that the Eudemian version of the *Ethics* is not by Eudemus, but by Aristotle; while, thanks to researches begun nearly a century ago by Rassow, Jackson and Cook Wilson, and continued by Mansion, Festugière and others, the mystery of the books common to the Eudemian and Nicomachean treatises has been to a great extent cleared up. Scholars have not, I submit with all due respect, been equally successful in explaining what is the chronological, or other, relation between the two treatises. The view has, of course, recently prevailed that it is chronological, and that the Eudemian version is the earlier. Thomas Case maintained that the *Eud. Eth.* is an incomplete and weaker draft of the Nicomachean system; while Jaeger assigned it to the period of Aristotle's residence at Assos. This conclusion is assumed by Dirlmeier and, yet more recently, by Gauthier. But it has not gone unchallenged; Schächer decided, on the basis of a study of passages dealing with friendship, that the *Nic. Eth.* is the earlier version, while Verbeke has pointed to features of the first and tenth books of the Nicomachean treatise which seem to mark it as relatively close to Platonism. Personally, I have in the end found it hardly possible to apply throughout the view that the *Eud. Eth.* is nearer to Platonism, and have thus come to think that the primary need is still for phenomenological description of the Eudemian system, aimed at discovering what really are the significant differences between the versions. This study of the method formulated and employed in the *Eud. Eth.* has been undertaken with such an object in view [1].

The method which an author adopts in an inquiry is largely determined by his conception of its purpose, and we may begin by asking whether our two versions set before themselves the same general aim. It is well known that the *Nic. Eth.* begins by speaking of the *politikos* and addresses itself throughout to him, *i.e.* to the statesman, not the political theorist. The beginning of the treatise drives home the point that *politikê* is the most august of all the practical arts. At the end, the need for

[1] The references are to: A. MANSION, *Autour des Éthiques attribuées à Aristote,* Rev. Néoscol. de Phil., 33 (1931); A. J. FESTUGIÈRE, *Aristote: le Plaisir,* (1936); E. J. SCHÄCHER, *Studien zu den Ethiken...,* (1940); G. VERBEKE, *L'idéal de la perfection humaine chez Aristote et l'évolution de sa noétique,* in Fontes Ambrosiani XXV (1951).

The question 'to which of our two versions do the disputed books belong ?' cannot fairly be posed, inasmuch as our mss. tell us that the passage is common to both versions, not that it belongs to one or the other; still less should it be confidently answered. Many scholars however do in fact answer it: an example is to be found in Prof. Theiler's recent German translation of *De Anima,* where we are told that the three books are Nicomachean with the exception of the passage on pleasure in VII, which is Eudemian. But modern analysis of the text — in which a leading part may be claimed for English scholars — has made it clear that both V and VII contain material which belongs to both versions: though of course we can hardly attempt to make a distribution where the first editors apparently abandoned the attempt to do so. It was placed beyond dispute by Jackson in 1878 that the account of degrees of ἀδικία in V ch. 8 goes closely together with the *Eudemian* treatment of voluntary action. The earlier Eudemian books have prospective references, wanting in *Nic. Eth.,* to the discussion of ἀκρασία and ἡδονή in the common book VII. This has been shown by Festugière among others. It has further been shown by Rassow and Cook Wilson that book VII contains doublets, of which in a few instances one passage betrays itself by its vocabulary as Eudemian. This result is, with minor reservations, accepted by Gauthier. Munro, Fritzsche, Jackson and Grant all wrongly claimed the books *in toto* for the *Eud. Eth.*

well-conceived legislation is emphasized; a treatise on politics is projected, and its principal subjects enumerated.

Very different are the beginning and end of the Eudemian treatise. Here the author announces it as his purpose to show that moral value, goodness and pleasure are all combined in 'happiness', if this last is properly defined. He says that his aim is at present practical, and consists in finding an answer to the double question: ἐν τίνι τὸ εὖ ζῆν καὶ πῶς κτητόν. He proceeds to speak in the following terms of the need experienced by every man to form a clear conception of the good life:

> «Every man who is able to live at his own discretion will wish to dwell upon these matters and to set before himself, like a target by reference to which he will undertake all his actions, his view of the good life — honour, or reputation, or wealth, or education; to have neglected to introduce system into one's life is a sign of considerable folly. Now the first question which he will wish to decide at leisure, yet without undue delay, for himself is this: wherein does the good life consist, and what, under the conditions of human existence, are its pre-requisites ?» (*Eud. Eth.* I 2, 1214 b 6-14).

Each man, then, must answer *for himself* the old riddles addressed by Meno to Socrates, whether *aretê* arises by learning, by discipline, by good fortune or in some other way. The Eudemian treatise, though its inquiry seems to be occasionally termed *politikê,* is not meant for the statesman, but is designed to assist the individual in such deliberation. This fact was perceived long ago by Sir A. Grant. It is of course recognised *more Aristotelico* that man is a social being; an examination of justice and friendship will be no less necessary here than in giving advice to the statesman, and its practical result is not likely to be dissimilar. For, as is said in the common book VI 9, 1142 a 9, «yet perhaps one cannot (consider, or provide for) one's own good without being a householder and citizen». The same book makes *politikê* a genus of which statesmanship, household management and personal prudence are the species. Still, the *Eud. Eth.* is *not* the first half of a comprehensive «philosophy of human affairs», as the *Nic. Eth.* claims to be

(X 10, 1181 b 14). It culminates neither in exaltation of the contemplative life, nor in a promise of research into the forms of government, but in fulfilment of the promise made in the opening paragraph: The man of 'complete virtue', ***kalokagathia,*** is characterized by his choosing for their intrinsic goodness that highest class of goods which are 'the valuable'. His life is happiness; and it has been demonstrated that the truly good coincides with the truly pleasant — it is the subjectively good and pleasant which may diverge. Therefore his life combines value, pleasure and goodness. (Jaeger's contention that the *Eud. Eth.* is linked to an *Urpolitik* is in my opinion no longer defensible).

The Eudemian treatise is, then, self-contained. As though in compensation it rests more heavily than the Nicomachean does upon the *Metaphysics.* To single out a notable point, whereas that version — omitting VII 15, 1154 b 26 as being really part of the Eudemian discussion of pleasure — speaks of the gods only in terms of prevailing opinion, the Eudemian repeatedly builds upon the Aristotelian theology of the *Metaphysics* and assumes knowledge of this on the reader's part.

Formal Statement of method

In setting up his target, a man is naturally most influenced by opinions widely held. We may exclude fantastic opinions, and we should start from such apparent problems as are 'proper to' the investigation (ἀπορίαι ... οἰκεῖαι, I 3, 1215 a 3). It must be decided first of all whether happiness is «a disposition of the soul, as some of the σοφοὶ καὶ πρεσβύτεροι have said; or, though this is indeed a requisite, it is more requisite to perform *actions* of a certain type». (I 4, 1215 a 22-25). Most people would agree that it is a form of life and activity. But wise men and the multitude are by no means in agreement about the scope of this activity, and it has long been observed that men pursue one of three ends, — knowledge, honour and pleasure. Excluding for the time being the life of pleasure, we may take as our starting-point an investigation of *phronesis* and *aretê.* Are they, as Socrates maintained, the same ?

At this point the writer lays down some general rules of method, which are briefly recalled again in book II (I 6, 1216 b 26-1217 a 17; II 1, 1220 a 15-22). This explicit treatment of method is not very sensational. Readers of the treatise will have at the outset some true, but vague and unarticulated ideas about the subject with which it deals (apparently both definitions and propositions). The ethical philosopher will conduct a series of exchanges of a vague expression for a more precise one, and by the same process will reveal 'the why' in addition to knowledge of the fact. Finally, the validity of his analysis will be confirmed from experience, *i.e.* from prevailing opinion and unsophisticated moral judgment. We are advised (1217 a 10) to consider separately the fact demonstrated and the reasons alleged for it, (i) because such proof sometimes wanders off into pretentious irrelevance, so that men with experience and practical competence are taken in by those who have neither, and (ii) because a true fact may be made to emerge from false reasoning.

Now this fails to prepare the reader for the most singular feature of the method which the author actually uses, and the subsequent exemplification of these maxims appears to me of much greater interest and novelty than the maxims themselves. Right down to the point at which his definition of moral excellence is secured, fairly far on in the treatise, he is translating into practice his methodical preface; but there emerges a fact to which he does not explicitly call attention, namely that he sets before him a mathematical pattern of deduction. (Let me add to avoid misunderstanding that, as far as I can see, one might think it advantageous to adopt such a pattern without holding that the precision of mathematics can be reproduced in the ethical sphere). My plan in the remainder of this paper is to follow in detail, and with reference to the structure rather than the substance of the argument, the process by which the definitions of happiness and moral excellence are reached in books I and II of the *Eud. Eth.*

The absolute good

General consent is first claimed for the proposition that happiness is the greatest and most intensely good of human goods (I 7, 1217 a 21). The word 'human' is eliminated in favour of 'achievable by man' (τῶν ἀνθρώπῳ πρακτῶν ἄριστον, a 30-40). Next the expression 'best' or 'intensely good' or as one may paraphrase it, *summum bonum*, is analysed:

«Broadly speaking, there are three opinions on this subject. They (*sc.* Plato and others) say that the *summum bonum* is to be equated with the absolute good (αὐτὸ τὸ ἀγαθόν); and that the absolute good is that, in which are combined the attributes of being first among goods, and immanent cause of goodness in other things (ᾧ ὑπάρχει τό τε πρώτῳ εἶναι τῶν ἀγαθῶν, καὶ τὸ αἰτίῳ τῇ παρουσίᾳ τοῖς ἄλλοις τοῦ ἀγαθὰ εἶναι). These two attributes, our friends say, are combined in the Idea of the good» (8, 1217 b 2-6).

Others find the absolute good in an immanent general concept of goodness (κοινὸν ἀγαθόν). Our author brings objections against both views — to the former, on the ground that the assumption of Ideas is open to criticism thoroughly familiar to his audience, and to the latter, on the ground that goodness is a πολλαχῶς λεγόμενον and that goods do not share in a common concept, as species of a genus do. These two parties, then, have mishandled the notion, useful in itself, of 'the absolute good'. It remains to go over to a third view — that the attributes of an absolute good are to be seen combined in the *ultimate good achievable by man.* Such an argument imposes upon the author a proof that any purpose (οὗ ἕνεκα) is the cause of activities which precede it in time, and are undertaken in order to give it reality. He does give this proof, and makes a distinction between cause of goodness and cause of existence. The illustration of going for a walk for the sake of health is used: the walk, as an efficient cause, brings health into existence. But the end, health, causally infuses goodness into the means used.

No quotation is perhaps necessary to show that in the *Nic. Eth.* Aristotle does not proceed in the same way. He there treats as equivalent the assertion of a Platonic Idea and the use of the expression 'absolute...'. The search for the absolute good is consequently a wild goose chase. The author of the *Eud. Eth.* joins with enthusiasm in the search, and is in full agreement about the description of the bird that is being hunted. It would seem to me that the key to this difference in the style of criticism is, not that the Eudemian version shows closer sympathy with Platonism — its manner of introducing the discussion, placed side by side with the Nicomachean equivalent, can only seem cool and abrupt — but that the passage is integral to the discourse on method which immediately precedes it. The Platonist is to be disabused of his errors by reasoning from premisses which he admits, and which are true, but not in the way in which he supposes.

Definition of Happiness

The inquiry of the first book has shown us that happiness means 'chief good attainable by man'. At the outset of book II the author formulates some hypotheses, which he says are derived either from popular reasoning or from induction; from these he proceeds to infer that a life of good activity of soul is the chief good attainable by man. Since things identical with the same thing are identical with one another, he is also then in a position to say that happiness is a life of good activity of soul; and with this he has secured his 'more precise' definition of happiness. Notable points here are the formal statement of the hypotheses which will be required (II 1, 1218 b 31-1219 a 18), the frequent use of ὑποκείσθω, and the Euclidean way in which reference is made to the assumptions or to the initial vague definition. I summarize the passage:

Hypothesis I a. Goods are of two kinds, external goods and those of the soul. b. The latter are more desirable than the former. (Based on exoteric reasoning).

2 a. Excellence has a meaning where, and only where, its subject has a function or use.

b. By excellence is meant: disposition ideally adapted to the performance of a function.

This is based upon a survey of instances, which at the same time proves that the *soul* has a function, and will also have an excellence as defined in 2 b.

3 a. Let the better function be that which belongs to the better disposition; b. Let it be granted that, as dispositions stand in relation to one another, so do their functions or uses.

4. Let *end* be equivalent to function, and let its definition be: highest or ultimate good, for whose sake all else is done.

Now evidently there is more goodness in the achieved function than in the disposition which brings it into play. For the function is the end, *i.e.* that for which all else, including the disposition, exists (Hypothesis 4). And (special case of this) whereas a function is sometimes the same as the exercise of the disposition, sometimes a product additional to this — in the former case exercise is a higher good than disposition.

Further, whenever a thing admits of excellence, as explained in 2 a, that thing and its excellence have the same function and are differentiated by manner of performance: good shoemaking does not produce something more than a shoe, but makes shoes well; and so in similar cases.

That soul has a function has already been agreed; let it now be assumed (Hyp. 5) that this function is to *instil life*. And by this let waking life be meant; sleep is to be viewed as a kind of non-functioning. Hence (by the proposition last secured) the function of human soul-excellence is good human life: and by the preceding proposition such life (*sc.* rather than mere disposition of excellence) is the chief good attainable by man [2]. But in book I it was seen on the basis of prevailing views that happiness means the chief good attainable by man. Therefore

[2] Aristotle, if he is the author, is here assuming a psychology at variance with his own: (a) in his system, life is not co-extensive with waking life, and sleep is not ἀργία ψυχῆς, for the vegetative soul is then still operating; (b) in *De Anima* I 4, 408 b 13 we read: «it is perhaps better to say, not that the soul has pity or learns or thinks, but that the man does so with the soul». Here the *Nic. Eth.* which speaks of a function of man is in closer accord with the *De Anima*:

Nic. Eth., I 6, 1098 a 7 ἔργον ἀνθρώπου = ψυχῆς ἐνέργεια κατὰ λόγον ἢ μὴ ἄνευ λόγου.

Eud. Eth., II 1, 1219 a 24 ψυχῆς ἔργον = τὸ ζῆν ποιεῖν.

happiness and good human life, or functioning of human soul-excellence, are equivalent. Taking up another point made in tial to happiness. Thus in conclusion happiness of man means book I, we must add that completeness (τὸ τέλειον) is essen-exercise of complete excellence in a complete human life. This account of the genus and definition of happiness must be checked from experience (II 1, 1219 a 40 ff.). It does, in fact, square with «beliefs which we all hold».

Definition of Excellence

Among the hypotheses used in advancing to a «clear» definition of happiness was a provisional, and quite general, definition of ἀρετή, namely: βελτίστη διάθεσις ἢ δύναμις ἑκάστων ὅσων ἐστί τις χρῆσις ἢ ἔργον (Hyp. 2 b in the above enumeration). The next task is to make this more precise, and to secure a definition specially suited to the moral form of excellence. The distinction between two main types of excellence, the moral and the intellectual, and the accompanying subdivision of the human soul, has not yet been required in the Eudemian argument: it is now very briefly stated (II 1, 1220 a 5-12. This corresponds to *Nic. Eth.*, I 13, 1102 b 13-1103 a 10).

Having reminded us once more of the need to advance from the true-but-vague to the true-and-clear, the author proceeds as follows (I summarize the first part, and quote in translation II 3, 1220 b 21-37). Two propositions are plain from a survey of instances, and may become hypotheses:

6. A best disposition is brought into being *by* a best procedure; and in every sphere it is *from* best dispositions that best actions follow (ὑποκείσθω δὴ πρῶτον ἡ βελτίστη διάθεσις ὑπὸ τῶν βελτίστων γίγνεσθαι κ.τ.λ., II 1, 1220 a 23).

7. It is by the same movements or actions performed in a different manner that all dispositions are both formed and destroyed, *e.g.* health is secured by proper nourishment, excercise and climate, but lost by the same things improperly applied (ἔτι πᾶσαν διάθεσιν κ.τ.λ., 1220 a 26).

Applying the new hypotheses, any excellence of soul — the

time to speak specifically of moral excellence has not yet come — (a) is produced by the best treatment, and (b) issues in the performance of the best activity, of soul; (c) is both gained and lost by the same circumstances operating upon soul in a different manner. Further, it is among these circumstances that excellence of soul, when established, is operative.

Concerning moral excellence two questions arise for consideration: what is the 'best' treatment, whereby it is produced ? and, what are the circumstances among which it operates ? The answer to the first question is 'a mean between extremes, fixed by our perception'; to the second 'pleasures and pains' [3].

To arrive at this result, the writer first considers habit. The same point is made as in *Nic. Eth.*, II 1, 1103 a 17, that the name ἦθος (character) indicates a prolongation of ἔθος (habit). Upon what subject does training through habit operate ? Evidently upon one which, though it is not endowed with imperative (ἐπιτακτικός) reason, can respond to rational command. Now in the human soul is found an element which answers to this description. It is by reference to this element and, to be more definite, to its δυνάμεις or to its ἕξεις, that a man is said to be ποιός τις (his powers and dispositions are significant of his character or ἦθος) [4].

How, then, is good character distinguished from bad ?

«These distinctions being made, we can proceed to the point that where a continuous and divisible subject is given, there may be excess, deficiency and a mean; and these may be judged (i) by comparison with each other, or (ii) by human perception: for instance in

[3] It seems to me that II 1, 1220 a 34 σημεῖον δ'ὅτι περὶ ἡδέα —— 2, 1220 a 39 δῆλον must be either an interpolation, or a note inserted in its wrong place. It would be inappropriate to mention a *sign* of a fact not yet proved.

[4] The mss. at II 2, 1220 b 11 have: Μετὰ ταῦτα ἡ διαίρεσις ἐν τοῖς ἀπηλλαγμένοις τῶν παθημάτων καὶ τῶν δυναμέων καὶ τῶν ἕξεων.

διειλεγμένοις Rassow, ἐπηλλαγμένοις Bernays, διηλλαγμένοις Spengel, ἑπομένοις vel ἐχομένοις Bender.

The emendations are futile, and, without being able to discuss the interpretation here, I suggest one of these translations: (1) 'in the cancelled version' — for this use of ἀπαλλάττομαι passive compare Plato, *Rep.* VIII 559 b and IX 571 b — or (2) 'in the separate section' (as one might say in the arts of the gymnastic trainer, doctor, builder, helmsman, and in every conceivable action, with science and art, or without science and art. For movement is a continuum, and action is a movement.

«The mean judged by human perception is always the best action. For this corresponds to the requirements of science and reason. This is also everywhere productive of the best disposition. And theory as well as induction will show the truth of this: for contraries annihilate each other, and extremes are contrary both to one another and to the mean, (for the mean assumes either character in comparison with an extreme, *e.g.* the equal is greater than the less, but is less than the greater).

«Of necessity, then, excellence of character is concerned with a kind of intermediates, and is itself a kind of mean state: we have therefore to ask, *what* kind of state ? and *what* kind of intermediates ? Let us take the following as an example and separately study each item on our list» (II 3, 1220 b 21-37).

Fourteen triads of moderate and extreme states are now set out in a table and described. The purpose of this appears to be, not exactly to justify the doctrine of the mean, but to prepare the way for the answer which will now be given to the question concerning the *special sphere* of moral virtue and vice.

Completion of definition of moral excellence

The intellectual virtues belong to the rational element in the human soul: their function is truth, concerning either a state of affairs, or a process of becoming. The latter is an allusion to the intellectual virtue of *technê,* and the wording of *Eth. Eud.* II 4, 1221 b 30 is closely similar to that of the common book VI 2, 1139 a 30 and 4, 1140 a 11).

The excellences of character belong to the appetitive element, and it can now be inferred that it is by pursuit or avoidance of *pleasures and pains* that the characters of men are discriminated and judged as good or bad. For (i) if the classification of mental phenomena already used is exhaustive, this must follow, since δυνάμεις, ἕξεις and παθήματα all have relation to pleasure and pain: and we have agreed that it is δυνάμεις and ἕξεις that are significant of character, (ii) it was shown in general terms above that the sphere of exercise is identical with the circumstances which produce the better, or worse, thing: now unquestionably it is right and wrong pursuit and avoidance of *pleasures* which makes men morally better and worse; and punishment, which is intended to be remedial of character, operates through *pain*.

Thus (II, 5, 1222 b 5-12) it follows necessarily that moral excellence, in all its several forms, is itself a mean state, and is related to intermediates, either in pleasure and pain themselves, or in their causes. But the sharpness of the opposition between mean and extremes varies in the different cases.

Moral excellence, then, is related to intermediates, and vice to extremes, of pleasure and pain: but how related ? Instead of saying 'by deliberate choice', and thus giving a definition which would correspond to *Nic. Eth.* II 6, 1106 b 36, ἕξις προαιρετική, ἐν μεσότητι οὖσα τῇ πρὸς ἡμᾶς, κ.τ.λ., the writer lays down yet another set of hypotheses, and commences his investigation of voluntary and involuntary action and of choice. At last in II 10, 1227 b 5-11 he is in a position to propound this defining formula of moral excellence:

> «a disposition to make deliberate choice of a mean, relative to our perception, in those pleasures and pains, susceptibility to which is deemed significant of character. Fondness *e.g.* for sweet or bitter tastes is *not* treated as an index of character».

In the *Nic. Eth.,* Aristotle employs by anticipation his concepts of φρόνησις and προαίρεσις when defining moral exellence. The Eudemian passage which I have attempted to analyse is formally more correct, in so far as the full analysis of προαίρεσις has been made to precede the final formulation of the definition of ἠθικὴ ἀρετή. The anticipatory reference to the 'right rule', *i.e.* to φρόνησις, is found in both versions.

Prominence of pleasure and pain in the Eudemian version

There is a difference between the versions in this argument leading to the definition of virtue, of which the effect can be traced right through the companion treatises. The assertion that virtue and vice consist in, and arise through, a right or wrong use of pleasures and pains, in the Nicomachean version *precedes* and is external to the inquiry into the τί ἐστι of moral virtue. It has only the status of a practical rule suggested to the disciplinarian. In the Eudemian argument this assertion plays its part *during* the inquiry into the τί ἐστι, and is incorporated in the actual definition of moral virtue. Place the two definitions side by side, and this is at once obvious.

Let me be precise here: the *fact* that moral virtue and vice are 'concerned with pleasures and pains' is stated with all possible emphasis in *Nic. Eth.*, where we read that «pleasure leads men to do what is wrong, and pain causes them to refrain from doing what is right» (II 2, 1104 b 8-11). My claim is that, at the point where this is said, the attempt to define moral excellence, which will include the discovery of its sphere, has not yet begun. Only at 4, 1105 b 19 does Aristotle say: μετὰ δὲ ταῦτα τί ἐστιν ἡ ἀρετὴ σκεπτέον. What we hear in *Nic. Eth.* II 5 (VI) — in the passage in which moral excellence is defined — and often later, is that it operates among emotions and actions (πάθη καὶ πράξεις); and we are shown no way of reducing these without remainder to pleasures and pains.

A first consequence of this is seen in the sketches of the particular virtues. In *Nic. Eth.* the virtue of πραότης is περὶ ὀργάς; in *Eud. Eth.*, it is said to be a mean disposition towards the *painful emotion* of anger. In *Nic. Eth.*, bravery and the two associated deficiencies are said to be concerned with τὰ φοβερά: but in *Eud. Eth.* τὸ φοβερόν is discovered by analysis to be τὸ ποιητικὸν λύπης φθαρτικῆς. In *Nic. Eth.* liberality is related to the πράξεις of taking or earning on one side, and bestowing gifts or spending on the other. In *Eud. Eth.*, this virtue is a right disposition towards the joy of receiving and the pain of giving away; and so forth.

It will be remembered that book VII and *Nic. Eth.*, book X

diverge in the manner in which they link pleasure and activity. Pleasure, according to VII 13, 1153 a 14, is ἐνέργεια τῆς κατὰ φύσιν ἕξεως ἀνεμπόδιστος. Objects which call forth such activity are the φύσει ἡδέα. They will include colours, sounds and other *sensibilia,* and also the objects of intellectual activity. In contrast to them stand the κατὰ συμβεβηκὸς ἡδέα, pleasures or rather objects productive of pleasure which are enjoyed not in the normal state, but incidentally while it is being restored after interruption. They are not really a distinct class, for the pleasure, so it is claimed, is due to the functioning of powers left unaffected by the disturbance. Under this description fall the bodily pleasures which entail previous painful want, and their objects are not φύσει ἡδέα. These will be regarded by the wise man as *not evil* rather than as goods. In respect of them he pursues ἀλυπία, freedom from desire, not continuance of pleasure. There are, however, pure pleasures, (the κατὰ φύσιν ἡδέα) which the φρόνιμος does desire, and these admit of no excess. The argument that pleasure is the chief good because it is the universal desideratum cannot be lightly rejected. When pleasure is condemned by moralists, it is because the 'incidental' pleasures are mistakenly regarded as typical.

In contrast to the doctrine of this passage, which obviously belongs to the Eudemian version, Aristotle declares in *Nic. Eth.,* X 5, 1175 b 33 that it is a *mistake* to identify pleasure and activity, and elaborates the view that pleasure is an ornament supervening upon already perfect activity. (See now the commentary of Père R. A. Gauthier, Tome II, pp. 778-81. Gauthier maintains — following Festugière — that it is an error of perspective to suppose that the distinction between activity and pleasure is for Aristotle, «the pivot of the entire anti-hedonist argument». The weight rests rather on the point that there is a qualitative difference among pleasures).

Now apparently it is the identification of pleasure and activity — the doctrine of book VII — that is normal in Aristotle's non-ethical writings [5]. Thus our companion treatises have two

[5] As I am inclined to suppose with CASE (article *Aristotle* in Encyclopaedia Britannica, 1911) and J. LÉONARD, *Le Bonheur chez Aristote,* in spite of the doubts of R. A. GAUTHIER, *op.cit.,* Vol. 3, pp. 796-797.

designations of the sphere of virtue and vice, and two analyses of pleasure. And it seems obvious enough that the one which *equates* pleasure with unimpeded activity and so allows it a substantial existence is designed to go together with the analysis which says that the sphere of action of the virtues and vices is pleasure and pain. On the other hand, the analysis which makes pleasure adjectival is in place in the treatise which — though continuing to teach as a mere practical rule that virtue is περὶ ἡδονὰς καὶ λύπας — uses for preference an alternative designation, namely πάθη καὶ πράξεις. Limitations of space forbid a fuller development of this point.

Thus, to conclude, the Eudemian version, carrying out its avowed principle of steady advance from the vague to the clear, arrives in order at a series of connected definitions:

II 1, 1218 b 37	Ἀρετή = βελτίστη διάθεσις ἢ ἕξις ἢ δύναμις ἑκάστων, ὅσων ἐστί τις χρῆσις ἢ ἔργον = Hypothesis 2.
1219 a 39	Εὐδαιμονία = ζωῆς τελείας ἐνέργεια κατ' ἀρετὴν τελείαν.
II 6, 1222 b 21	(κύριος). τῶν ἀρχῶν ὅσαι τοιαῦται, ὅθεν πρῶτον αἱ κινήσεις, κύριαι λέγονται.
1223 a 4	(ἐφ' αὑτῷ) — — ὅσων πράξεων ὁ ἄνθρωπός ἐστιν ἀρχὴ καὶ κύριος, φανερὸν ὅτι ἐνδέχεται καὶ γίνεσθαι καὶ μή, καὶ ὅτι ἐφ' αὑτῷ ταῦτ' ἐστι γίνεσθαι καὶ μή.
II 10, 1226 b 16-21	Προαίρεσις = ὄρεξις τῶν ἐφ' αὑτῷ βουλευτική — — λέγω δὲ βουλευτικήν, ἧς ἀρχὴ καὶ αἰτία βούλευσίς ἐστι, καὶ ὀρέγεται διὰ τὸ βουλεύσασθαι.
1227 b 5-10	Ἠθικὴ ἀρετή = ἕξις προαιρετικὴ μεσότητος τῆς πρὸς ἡμᾶς ἐν ἡδέσι καὶ λυπηροῖς, καθ' ὅσα ποιός τις λέγεται τὸ ἦθος ἢ χαίρων ἢ λυπούμενος.

What should be inferred from all this as regards the relation between the versions? One of two things: either Aristotle employed at first a deductive method, which he subsequently relaxed in favour of one which might reflect the natural, progressive, self-correcting movement of thought, with some sacrifice of formal strictness: he also abandoned, so far as theory was concerned, the view that pleasure and pain are the sphere of operation of virtue and vice, presumably in order to be able to range more widely in his description of good and bad states: and 'disengaged' — to borrow a word from T. Case — the pleasures of perceiving and thinking from the activities of perceiving and thinking themselves.

Or conversely the Eudemian version presupposes the Nicomachean, and is an attempt to present the same or a similar system in a stricter form: the Euclidean method, the simpler analysis of pleasure, the new definition of the sphere of moral excellence and the more copious use of the *Metaphysics* would all then tend to this purpose. Only when a total picture has been derived from several comparative studies such as this, can we fairly profess to make a choice between these explanations. If an impression must be stated, I would give it as my view that the systematizer is the later Aristotle. But there are other modes than the chronological of explaining the existence of two versions, and it need not be supposed that there was development unless the substantial differences as opposed to those of presentation are wide enough to suggest this. There is a parallel to show that a writer may have occasion for both a natural and progressive, and a deductive exposition: Descartes published his *Meditations* in 1641, and his *Principles of Philosophy* in 1644[6].

[6] It was objected at the time of the discussion of this paper at Louvain that the form of these arguments is simply syllogistic, and that there is no need to ascribe to the author a predilection for the mathematical style. But (i) the establishment of an equation between A and C by identifying each in turn with B is surely a Euclidean trick? (ii) the grouping of the requisite assumptions at the beginning (of which the frequent use of the words ὑπόθεσις, ὑπόκειμαι is an external sign) appears to me a feature of scientific treatises rather than of syllogistic debate, and (iii) my argument could have been reinforced by at least one good instance of the use of *reductio ad absurdum*: it is argued in II 7, 1223 b 3 foll. that if 'desired' = voluntary, the same acts are both voluntary and involuntary, which is impossible.

ARISTOTLE AND THE METHODS OF ETHICS

Jonathan BARNES

I

Aristotle's discussion of *ἀκρασία* in *Nicomachean Ethics* H 1 is prefaced by a brief reflexion on method :

> *δεῖ δ' ὥσπερ ἐπὶ τῶν ἄλλων τιθέντας τὰ φαινόμενα καὶ πρῶτον διαπορήσαντας, οὕτω δεικνύναι μάλιστα μὲν πάντα τὰ ἔνδοξα περὶ ταῦτα τὰ πάθη, εἰ δὲ μή, τὰ πλεῖστα καὶ κυριώτατα · ἐὰν γὰρ λύηταί τε τὰ δυσχερῆ καὶ καταλείπηται τὰ ἔνδοξα, δεδειγμένον ἂν εἴη ἱκανῶς* (1145b2-7).

The passage is neither difficult nor controversial ; but it warrants a short commentary.

The method Aristotle sketches has three components, marked by three verbs : first, *τιθέναι* ; secondly, *διαπορεῖν* ; thirdly, *δεικνύναι* ; setting down, puzzling through, proving.

The first component consists in the setting down of *τὰ φαινόμενα* ; and thethird in the proving of *τὰ ἔνδοξα*. '*Τὰ φαινόμενα*' and '*τὰ ἔνδοξα*' are not synonymous expressions ; but elsewhere they are used to designate the same class of items, and here too they doubtless have the same reference. A little later on, at 1145b20, Aristotle uses '*τὰ λεγόμενα*' to denote the same items ; and he also employs '*τὰ δοκοῦντα*'. Since *τὰ δοκοῦντα* and *τὰ ἔνδοξα* are certainly things believed, *τὰ φαινόμενα* will be beliefs or opinions of some sort ; so that '*τὰ φαινόμενα*' is likely to mean neither 'the things that are evidently the case' nor 'the things which are seen by observation to be the case' (neither 'the evident facts' nor 'the observed facts'), but rather 'the things that seem to be the case'.

And indeed, the method which Aristotle outlines would make little sense on the supposition that *τὰ φαινόμενα* were established facts (1).

Thus the first component in Aristotle's method is a matter of laying out opinions on the subject in question ; and he advises us to begin the investigation of *ἀκρασία* by setting down a doxography on that curious phenomenon.

The second component of the method is a puzzling through, *διαπορεῖν*. The term refers here, as it often does in Aristotle's writings, to a preliminary (*πρῶτον*) rehearsal or run-through of the puzzles (*ἀπορίαι*) or difficulties (*τὰ δυσχερῆ*) which the *data* of the investigation raise : having set down *τὰ ἔνδοξα*, we proceed to survey the problems they present (2).

What will those problems be ? Aristotle hopes that, after the resolution of the difficulties, all the *ἔνδοξα* may remain (*μάλιστα μὲν πάντα* ...) ; but he recognizes that such a happy result will not always be achieved, in which case we must preserve *τὰ πλεῖστα καὶ κυριώτατα*.

(1) That '*τὰ φαινόμενα*' does not mean 'the observed facts' is set beyond doubt by G. E. L. Owen, '*Τιθέναι τὰ Φαινόμενα*', in *Aristote et les Problèmes de Méthode*, ed. S. Mansion (Louvain, 1961), reprinted in *Articles on Aristotle*, ed. J. Barnes, M. Schofield, R. Sorabji, vol. I (London, 1975) : see pp. 114-5. (The point was clearly made long ago : see Sir Alexander Grant, *The Ethics of Aristotle* (London, 1885), vol. II, pp. 144-5). Owen, pp. 113-8, distinguishes two senses of '*τὰ φαινόμενα*', which he thinks Aristotle 'tends to assimilate' ; the senses are, roughly, 'the observed facts' and 'the opinions'. I think a subtler analysis is required, based on a pair of distinctions. (i) Like 'seem' in English, '*φαίνεσθαι*' in Greek may be either (a) phenomenological ('He looks pink') or (b) judgmental ('He seems guilty'). Note that this is not a distinction between what *φαίνεται* in perception and what *φαίνεται* in some other mode ; for, evidently, judgmental seeming may apply in perceptual situations ; and Aristotle at least will extend phenomenological seeming beyond the confines of perception *sensu stricto* (see e.g. *EN* Z 9, 1142a25-30 ; 11, 1143a35-b14). (ii) Unlike 'seem' in English, '*φαίνεσθαι*' in Greek may be either (a') non-veridical ('He seems to be alive (but maybe he isn't)'), or (b') veridical ('He is evidently guilty'). This distinction coincides, by and large, with the syntactical distinction between *φαίνεσθαι* + infinitive and *φαίνεσθαι* + participle. (Note that in the phrase '*ἐναργῶς φαίνεσθαι*', '*φαίνεσθαι*' is not necessarily used in sense (b') : see *EN* H 2, 1145b28, where '*ἐναργῶς*' modifies '*φαινομένοις*', not (as is usually supposed) '*ἀμφισβητεῖ*' (cf. *Protr*. fr. 9 Ross = B 97 Düring ; Plato, *Philebus* 20 C 1).) The sense of '*τὰ φαινόμενα*' with which we are concerned is got by combining (i)(b) with (ii)(a') : Aristotle surely saw that ; and although he nowhere *makes* the distinction I have just drawn, we need not suppose that he was *confused*.

(2) Sometimes '*διαπορεῖν*' means no more than '*ἀπορεῖν*' ('be puzzled', 'wonder (why)') ; but usually it means '*διέρχεσθαι τὰς ἀπορίας*', 'rehearse the puzzles', and then it is often qualified by '*πρῶτον*' : see Bonitz, *Index* 187b1-34.

Presumably, then, the initial ἔνδοξα may conflict among themselves ; and if they do conflict, we must select a consistent subset of them. That subset must be 'maximal' (τὰ πλεῖστα), i.e. it must be the largest consistent subset of the initial set of ἔνδοξα, subject to the proviso that it must include 'the most important' (κυριώτατα) members of that original set. (Aristotle does not say what 'importance' consists in : perhaps τὰ κυριώτατα ἔνδοξα are those which are most widely held, or those which have been embraced after sustained reflexion, or those whose content is most abstract or most general (3).)

One type of problem raised by τὰ ἔνδοξα will be straightforward inconsistency ; and one aspect of the process of διαπορεῖν will be the discovery of such inconsistency. But even if we are left in the end with πάντα τὰ ἔνδοξα, that result will have been attained by διαπορεῖν : what problem, other than inconsistency, can τὰ ἔνδοξα present ? Evidently, ἔνδοξα may be obscurely or inadequately expressed : they may be vague, ambiguous, apparently contradictory – in short, they may suffer from all the vices which infect human beliefs. It is only plausible to imagine that the process of puzzling will require us to take note of those vicious imprecisions.

At the beginning of the account of φιλία in the *Eudemian Ethics*, Aristotle sets out various δόξαι on the subject (H 1, 1235a4-b12), noting explicitly that ταῦτα ... πάντα δοκεῖ μὲν ὑπεναντία ἀλλήλοις εἶναι (1235b2-3). He continues :

> ληπτέος δὴ τρόπος ὅστις ἡμῖν ἅμα τά τε δοκοῦντα περὶ τούτων μάλιστα ἀποδώσει καὶ τὰς ἀπορίας λύσει καὶ τὰς ἐναντιώσεις · τοῦτο δ' ἔσται ἐὰν εὐλόγως φαίνηται τὰ ἐναντία δοκοῦντα · μάλιστα γὰρ ὁμολογούμενος ὁ τοιοῦτος ἔσται λόγος τοῖς φαινομένοις · συμβαίνει δὲ μένειν τὰς ἐναντιώσεις ἐὰν ἔστι μὲν ὡς ἀληθὲς ᾖ τὸ λεγόμενον ἔστι δ' ὡς οὔ (1235b13-18) (4).

Here 'τὰ δοκοῦντα ... ἀποδώσει' answers to 'δεικνύναι τὰ πλεῖστα' in *EN* H 1 ; and 'τὰς ἀπορίας λύσει 'corresponds to 'λύηται ... τὰ δυσχερῆ'. The

(3) *APst* A 24, 86a23, suggests that generality confers importance ; but see *EE* H 1, 1235a29-31 (cf. perhaps Plato, *Theaetetus* 206B). Plato, *Sophist* 246D, says that τὸ ὁμολογηθὲν παρὰ βελτιόνων που κυριώτερον ἢ τὸ παρὰ χειρόνων. Note that one thing may be *more* ἔνδοξον than another : *Top* Θ 5, 159n7, 22.

(4) For 'τρόπος' (Sylburg) at 1235b13 the MSS have 'λοιπός' ; Casaubon's 'λόγος' is preferred by Dirlmeier and others.

ἀπορίαι are explained (καί) as ἐναντιώσεις ; and since in some cases those ἐναντιώσεις 'remain' (μένειν : cf. καταλείπηται in *EN* H 1), it is clear that they are *apparent* inconsistencies. The inconsistencies will be apparent if one at least of the conflicting ἔνδοξα is found to be ambiguous (ἔστι μὲν ὡς ... ἔστι δ' ὡς οὔ).

The process of διαπορεῖν will discover various infelicities in the ἔνδοξα initially laid down : some of the infelicities may be due to vagueness or ambiguity of expression ; others may point to genuine incompatibilities among the ἔνδοξα. The third component of Aristotle's method, 'proof', consists simply in the 'solution', or resolution, of those problems ; 'for if the difficulties are solved ... sufficient proof has been given'. Having laid down the ἔνδοξα concerning ἀκρασία, Aristotle remarks :

> αἱ μὲν οὖν ἀπορίαι τοιαῦταί τινες συμβαίνουσιν · τούτων δὲ τὰ μὲν ἀνελεῖν δεῖ τὰ δὲ καταλιπεῖν – ἡ γὰρ λύσις τῆς ἀπορίας εὕρεσίς ἐστιν (*EN* H 4, 1146b6-8).

'Of the ἔνδοξα, some must be abandoned, others preserved ; for discovering the truth about ἀκρασία is simply a matter of solving the puzzles' (5). Once the difficulties are solved – once the original ἔνδοξα are purified or emended, and the appropriate consistent subset of them is determined – the truth is to be found, exclusively and exhaustively, in the ἔνδοξα that remain.

Put schematically, Aristotle's method amounts to this : first, garner a set of ἔνδοξα on the subject in question, call it the set $\{\alpha_1, \alpha_2, ..., \alpha_n\}$. Secondly, survey the α_i's for infelicities. Thirdly, remove those infelicities : purify the α_i's to produce a new set, $\{\beta_1, \beta_2, ..., \beta_n\}$; select the 'most important' β_i's ; and construct a maximal consistent subset of the β_i's containing those 'most important' members. Let us call the final set, the end product of the puzzling and proving, $\{\gamma_1, \gamma_2, ..., \gamma_m\}$: note that $m \leqslant n$; and that each γ_i is 'adequately proved'. The investigation is at an end : assembling the α_i's sets up the problems ; puzzling and proving, which turn the α_i's into β_i's and then pick out the γ_i's, solve the problems.

(5) For the correct interpretation of this passage, see J. A. STEWART, *Notes on the Nicomachean Ethics of Aristotle* (London, 1892), vol. II, pp. 123-4.

II

In *EN* H 1 Aristotle speaks specifically of *ἀκρασία* ; but the method he sketches is meant to have a broader application ; for in the case of *ἀκρασία* we must proceed *ὥσπερ ἐπὶ τῶν ἄλλων*. There can be no doubt that *τὰ ἄλλα* include other issues in practical philosophy : does the method extend further than that ?

In the course of his discussion of *τόπος* in *Physics Δ*, Aristotle makes a methodological remark similar in tone to the passage in *EN* H 1 :

> *δεῖ δὲ πειρᾶσθαι τὴν σκέψιν οὕτω ποιεῖσθαι ὅπως τὸ τί ἐστιν ἀποδοθήσεται, ὥστε τὰ τε ἀπορούμενα λύεσθαι καὶ τὰ δοκοῦντα ὑπάρχειν τῷ τόπῳ ὑπάρχοντα ἔσται, καὶ ἔτι τὸ τῆς δυσκολίας αἴτιον καὶ τῶν περὶ αὐτὸν ἀπορημάτων ἔσται φανερόν· οὕτω γὰρ ἂν κάλλιστα δεικνύοιτο ἕκαστον* (Δ 4, 211a7-11).

There are differences between this passage and *EN* H 1. The *Physics* does not explicitly refer to the setting down of *τὰ ἔνδοξα* ; and it adds a new component : having resolved the difficulties which the *ἔνδοξα* present, we must also exhibit their cause (6). Again, the *Physics* only applies the method to enquiries into the definition or essence of some subject matter (*σκέψιν ... ὅπως τὸ τί ἐστιν ἀποδοθήσεται*). But from the present point of view, those differences are comparatively trivial : like *EN*, the *Physics* holds that when 'the puzzles are solved, and it appears that what is believed to belong to *τόπος* actually does belong to it', then 'we shall have given the best proof possible'.

The method which Aristotle outlines in *EN* H 1, and which I shall call, somewhat grandiosely, the Method of *Ἔνδοξα*, is thus not restricted to practical philosophy : Aristotle preaches it in the *Physics* as well as in the *Ethics*. And in recent years scholars have emphasized that Aristotle practises what he preaches : the Method is no theoretical aside ; it actually governs a large part of Aristotle's philosophical researches (7). Of course, the Method of *Ἔνδοξα* is not the only method

(6) Cf. *EN* H 14, 1154a22-6 : ... *οὐ μόνον δεῖ τἀληθὲς εἰπεῖν ἀλλὰ καὶ τὸ αἴτιον τοῦ ψεύδους*.

(7) See esp. OWEN, *o.c.*, n. 1 ; and, of older studies, ch. 1 of R. EUCKEN, *Die Methode der aristotelischen Forschung* (Berlin, 1872). Aristotle's respect for *τὰ ἔνδοξα* is often contrasted with Plato's brusque dismissal of *δόξα* (e.g. W. WIELAND, *Die aristotelische Physik* (Göttingen, 1962), p. 221 : 'Diese neue Dignität der Doxa erhellt den Gegensatz zwischen Platon und Aristoteles vielleicht besser als alle inhaltlichen Differenzen') ; but see e.g., *Laws* 950BC : *θεῖον δέ τι καὶ εὔστοχον ἔνεστι καὶ τοῖσιν κακοῖς, ὥστε πάμπολλοι καὶ τῶν σφόδρα κακῶν εὖ τοῖς λόγοις καὶ ταῖς δόξαις διαιροῦνται τοὺς ἀμείνους*

Aristotle advocates : even in practical philosophy, he urges us to conduct our enquiries *διὰ λόγων*, and he contrasts such conduct with the Method of *῎Ενδοξα* (*EE* A 6, 1216b26-8) ; cf. *EN* A 8, 1098b9-12). But he nowhere suggests that any other method will lead to results which conflict with, or go beyond, the results achieved by the Method of *῎Ενδοξα*.

The Method of *῎Ενδοξα* is often construed as a method of Common Sense (8) ; and *τὰ ἔνδοξα* are taken to be common beliefs. In an autobiographical fragment, Henry Sidgwick tells the following tale :

> In this state of mind I had to read Aristotle again ; and a light seemed to dawn upon me as to the meaning and drift of his procedure – especially in Books ii, iii, iv, of the *Ethics* .... What he gave us there was the Common Sense Morality of Greece, reduced to consistency by careful comparison : given not as something external to him but as what «we» – he and others – think, ascertained by reflexion. And was not this really Socratic induction, elicited by interrogation ? Might I not imitate this : do the same for our morality, here and now, in the same manner of impartial reflexion on current opinions ? (9).

Sidgwick refers to *EN* B, *Γ* and *Δ* ; but he will not have overlooked the methodological text from H 1. He explains Aristotle's ethics as a morality of Common Sense ; and he explicitly sets himself to follow in Aristotle's footsteps. Nor is Sidgwick a lone figure : his Aristotelian conception of the methods of ethics has been widely praised and widely practised, at least among philosophers writing within the Anglo-Saxon tradition. Among his more recent disciples is John Rawls, who, like Sidgwick, explicitly traces his own view of the nature of moral philosophy back to Aristotle (10).

τῶν ἀνθρώπων καὶ τοὺς χειρόνας · διὸ καλὸν προτιμᾶν τὴν εὐδοξίαν πρὸς τῶν πολλῶν. Cf. Xenophon, *Mem* IV.vi.15 : *ὁπότε δὲ αὐτός* [i.e. Socrates] *τι τῷ λόγῳ διεξίοι, διὰ τῶν μάλιστα ὁμολογουμένων ἐπορεύετο, νομίζων ταύτην τὴν ἀσφάλειαν εἶναι λόγου*. See further K. OEHLER, 'Der Consensus Omnium als Kriterium der Wahrheit in der antiken Philosophie und der Patristik', in his *Antike Philosophie und Byzantinisches Mittelalter* (Munich, 1969).

(8) See e.g. BONITZ, *Index* 203a27 ; GRANT, *o.c.* n. 1, vol. II, p. 194 ; STEWART, *o.c.* n. 5, vol. II, p. 123 ; H. H. JOACHIM, *Aristotle-the Nicomachean Ethics* (Oxford, 1955), p. 219.

(9) H. SIDGWICK, *The Methods of Ethics* (London, 1907[7]), pp. xix-xxi ; cf. STEWART, *o.c.* n. 5, vol. I, pp. 117-8 ; vol. II, pp. 120-4. On Sidgwick's own views, see J. B. SCHNEEWIND, *Sidgwick's Ethics and Victorian Moral Philosophy* (Oxford, 1977), ch. 6.

(10) J. RAWLS, *A Theory of Justice* (Oxford, 1972), p. 51 and n. 26.

Sidgwick speaks specifically of moral philosophy; but Aristotle's Method of Ἔνδοξα spreads its net more widely, and if *τὰ ἔνδοξα* constitute Common Sense, it is tempting to enrol Aristotle in the ranks of Common Sense Philosophers. Such an enrolment was made by Sir William Hamilton in his history of the Common Sense movement. Hamilton, who believed that 'the doctrine of Common Sense, notwithstanding many schismatic aberrations, is the one catholic and perennial philosophy', traced the School back to the old poet Hesiod; but its first serious *alumnus* was Aristotle. And Hamilton expresses the essence of Common Sense philosophy in highly Aristotelian terms: 'The first problem of Philosophy ... <is> to seek out, purify, and establish by intellectual analysis and criticism, the elementary feelings and beliefs in which are given the elementary truths of which all are in possession'. 'Seek out, purify, establish': *τιθέναι, διαπορεῖν, δεικνύναι* (11).

Common Sense philosophy – and, in particular, Common Sense practical philosophy – has certain characteristic features. Thus it is descriptive in its approach: *τιθέναι τὰ φαινόμενα* is an empirical task; and the *ἔνδοξα* that 'remain' will represent, as it were, a refined sociology of moral belief. Again, Common Sense morality will be parochial: according to Sidgwick, Aristotle is giving us a *Greek* morality – and, we may safely add, a morality of the fourth century B.C. Finally, the Method of Common Sense ensures moral conservation: iconoclasm, or even a modest criticism of customary *mores*, is out of place if the answers to our practical problems are all to be found among existing opinions.

To many moral philosophers, those three traits of descriptiveness, parochialism, and conservatism are, for obvious reasons, anathema; and they will have no truck with a Method of Ethics which enshrines them. Speaking of Hume's Scotch opponents, Kant observed that 'they discovered a more convenient way to be obstinate and defiant without any insight, namely by appealing to *common sense*'; and he commented that, 'seen in the light of day, this is nothing but an appeal

(11) See Note A to Hamilton's edition of Thomas Reid's *Works* (Edinburgh, 1858[5]), esp. pp. 771-3 (Hamilton was anticipated by Hugo Grotius: see his *De iure belli ac pacis*, I.xii). George Grote criticised Hamilton at length in Appendix II to his *Aristotle* (London, 1872), pp. 269-300.

to the judgment of the crowd – applause at which the philosopher blushes but the popular coxcomb struts and triumphs'. Bentham, too,is characteristically savage : a Common Sense morality is 'a cloak, and pretence, and aliment, to despotism' (12).

Those *cris de cœur* can be expressed in less passionate and more pertinent form. Aristotle's Method of *Ἔνδοξα* consists of three parts : against each part we may raise a question. First, why begin an enquiry by collecting *τὰ ἔνδοξα* or the views of Common Sense ? Other starting-points are possible, and more immediately attractive. Secondly, why suppose that the problems of philosophy, the *ἀπορίαι* which philosophers attempt to resolve, all arise from *τὰ ἔνδοξα* ? Are there not other, and more important, sources of philosophical perplexity than Common Opinions, and does not the Method lead us to ignore those sources ? Thirdly, why rest content when *τὰ ἔνδοξα* are left behind ? there are surely truths as yet undreamed of ; and the Method bars us from reaching them.

The third of those questions is the most pressing and the most disturbing (13) : Aristotle's Method of *Ἔνδοξα* seems to be pernicious and philosophically enervating ; for it assumes, depressingly, that the answers to our ethical questions are already to hand, enshrined in *τὰ ἔνδοξα* ; and it restricts our intellectual grazing to pastures the common herd has already cropped. Is that really so ? Does Aristotle's Method, like Sidgwick's, fence us in ? In order to tackle that question, we must first look more closely at *τὰ ἔνδοξα*.

(12) KANT, *Prolegomena to any Future Metaphysics*, trans. P. G. Lucas (Manchester, 1953), pp. 8-9 ; BENTHAM, *Introduction to the Principles of Morals and Legislation*, ch. II § 14.

(13) The question is not raised by those several passages in which Aristotle ascribes a *purely* methodological function to the collection of *τὰ ἔνδοξα* (e.g. *Cael* Δ 1, 308a4-7 ; *An* A 2, 403b20-4 ; *Met* B 1, 995a24-b4). Those passages do not suggest that *τὰ ἔνδοξα* *determine* the area of legitimate inquiry (thus *Cael* Δ 1 holds that, after *τιθέναι* and *διαπορεῖν, οὕτω καὶ τὸ φαινόμενον ἡμῖν εἴπωμεν περὶ αὐτῶν* ; and *Met* B 1 urges us to consider *ὅσα τε περὶ αὐτῶν ἄλλως ὑπειλήφασί τινες, κἂν εἴ τι χωρὶς τούτων τυγχάνει παρεωραμένον*) ; and Aristotle offers practical arguments in favour of starting from *τὰ ἔνδοξα* (cf. *Cael* A 10, 279b4-12). Not all philosophers share Aristotle's taste for collecting *τὰ ἔνδοξα* ; and the fruitfulness of such collections no doubt depends in part on the psychology of the collector. But that is another story.

III

Τὰ ἔνδοξα form the subject matter of 'dialectic', and the *Topics* is a treatise on the dialectical art : the *Topics* should enable us to determine exactly what *τὰ ἔνδοξα* consist in.

And the first question here is a simple one : what does the adjective '*ἔνδοξος*' mean ? There are two traditional answers, both inspired by Boethius' Latin translation, in which he regularly turns '*ἔνδοξος*' by '*probabilis*'. Some transliterate '*probabilis*' and get 'probable' ; others translate it to get 'plausible' or 'credible' : *τὰ ἔνδοξα*, then, are either objective probabilities or subjective plausibilities (14).

But neither 'probable' nor 'plausible' is either probable or plausible as a translation of '*ἔνδοξος*' : nothing in Aristotle indicates that '*ἔνδοξος*' has either of those senses in his philosophical idiolect (15) (he possesses the words '*εἰκός*' and '*πιστός*') ; nor does Greek usage or etymology offer support. Recognizing those facts, modern scholars prefer a different rendition : for '*τὰ ἔνδοξα*' they give 'received opinion', 'accepted opinion', or the like (16). *Τὰ ἔνδοξα* may be probable, and they may be plausible ; but if so, they have those properties by accident : essentially, and *ex vi termini*, they are accepted opinions.

That modern translation fits neatly into Aristotle's discussion of *τὰ ἔνδοξα* in the *Topics*, and it points to a semantic connexion between

(14) Boethius' translation of *Top* is printed in *Aristoteles Latinus* V. 1-3, ed. L. Minio-Paluello (Brussels/Paris, 1969). Boethius regularly uses '*probabilis*' for '*ἔνδοξος*' ; but he prefers '*opinabilis*' at e.g. *Γ* 6, 119a38. Among moderns, Tricot uses 'probable' in his French translation. For 'plausible' see e.g. Alexander, in *Top* 3.18 ; 5.5 ; among moderns, Kirchmann uses 'glaubhaft' in his German translation (cf. Bonitz, *Index* 250a16). – For discussion of '*ἔνδοξος*' see : L. M. Régis, *L'Opinion selon Aristote* (Paris/Ottawa, 1935), pp. 81-8 ; J. M. Le Blond, *Logique et Méthode chez Aristote* (Paris, 1939) ; E. Weil, 'The Place of Logic in Aristotle's Thought', in Barnes, Schofield, Sorabji, *o.c.*, n. 1 ; G. Colli, *Aristoteles : Organon* (n.p., 1955), p. 917 ; W. A. de Pater, *Les Topiques d'Aristote et la dialectique platonicienne*, Études Thomistes 10 (Fribourg, 1965), pp. 75-7 ; J. Brunschwig, *Aristote : Topiques I-IV* (Paris, 1967), pp. 113-4 ; A. Zadro, *Aristotele : I Topici* (Naples, n.d.), pp. 309-10 ; J. D. G. Evans, *Aristotle's Concept of Dialectic* (Cambridge, 1977), pp. 77-85.

(15) *APr* B 27, 70a3-5, appears to support the translation 'probable' (but see Evans, *o.c.* n. 14, p. 78) ; *Top Θ* 11, 161b31, and *Rhet* A 2, 1356b27, 34, seem to favour 'plausible' (but the semblance is deceptive).

(16) Thus Pickard-Cambridge (Oxford translation) and Forster (Loeb) use 'generally accepted' (but 'generally' is quite unwarranted) ; Brunschwig (Budé) uses 'idée admise' ; Colli opts for 'fondato sull'opinione'.

'ἔνδοξος' and 'δόξα' or 'opinion'. But it has two interrelated disadvantages: first, it does not offer a translation of the adjective 'ἔνδοξος', but only of the phrase 'τὰ ἔνδοξα'; and secondly, it pays no attention to the linguistic context from which the phrase 'τὰ ἔνδοξα' is drawn. Perhaps τὰ ἔνδοξα are received opinions; but if they are, that does not tell us what the phrase 'τὰ ἔνδοξα' means.

The word 'ἔνδοξος' is no Aristotelian neologism: an ordinary Greek adjective, it occurs once in Plato, and is common in Xenophon and in the orators. A typical occurrence is this, from a speech by Demosthenes:

> *καὶ γάρ τοὶ τούτων μὲν ἐκ πτωχῶν ἔνιοι ταχὺ πλούσιοι γίγνονται, καὶ ἐξ ἀνωνύμων καὶ ἀδόξων ἔνδοξοι καὶ γνώριμοι· ὑμεῖς δὲ τοὐναντίον ἐκ μὲν ἐνδόξων ἄδοξοι, ἐκ δ' εὐπόρων ἄποροι* (VIII.66 = X.68).

The word usually has a personal subject: it is applied to men, often in conjunction with 'πλούσιος', 'γνώριμος', or the like; and it is frequently applied to cities. At least once it is used with an impersonal subject: Aeschines talks of τὰ ἔνδοξα καὶ λαμπρὰ τῶν πραγμάτων (III.231) ([17]).

The meaning of 'ἔνδοξος' in all those passages is unproblematical: 'ἔνδοξος' translates as 'reputable', 'of good repute' ([18]); and it is closely connected with that use of 'δόξα' in which it means 'reputation'. As such, it is strictly comparable to numerous other adjectives in '-δοξος', where 'δόξα' is semantically effective in the sense of 'reputation' ([19]). Aristotle himself, in passages unconnected with τὰ ἔνδοξα, uses the word 'ἔνδοξος' in that ordinary Greek sense ([20]).

'"Ενδοξος' has an uncontroversial ordinary meaning. Aristotle nowhere indicates that the adjective takes on a special sense in his phrase

(17) See also e.g. Xenophon, *Mem* I.ii.65; III.v.1; *Ages* I.19; *Oec* VI.10; Plato, *Soph* 223 B 5; [*Def*] 415 C 9; Isocrates, I.37; V.14, 52, 55, 65, 82; *Aeschines*, I.183; III.178; Demosthenes, XII.19; XVIII.219; XX.73; LXI.39. The word is late and prosy (at Theognis, 195, the right reading is 'εὔδοξος'); earlier synonyms are 'εὔδοξος', 'εὐδόκιμος', 'δόκιμος'.

(18) Cf. Ammonius, *diff* 172: *ἔνδοξος καὶ ἐπίδοξος διαφέρει· ἔνδοξος μὲν γάρ ἐστιν ὁ ἐπίσημος, ἐπίδοξος δὲ ὁ προσδοκώμενος καὶ ἐλπιζόμενος.*

(19) Eleven such compounds are found in pre-Aristotelian Greek, according to C. D. Buck and W. Petersen, *A Reverse Index of Greek Nouns and Adjectives* (Chicago, 1944), pp. 739-40.

(20) E.g. *Rhet* A 9, 1368a21, 24; *EN* Δ 2, 1122b32; cf. *EN* Δ 7, 1127a21. On *Top* A 1, 100b23, see below, n. 23.

'τὰ ἔνδοξα' [21]. There is, then, no reason to suspect him of semantic innovation : 'τὰ ἔνδοξα' means 'the reputable things' ; to collect τὰ ἔνδοξα is to collect the *reputable* views. (Boethius got it right ; for his '*probabilis*' no doubt means 'to be approved of'). Aristotle may have been the first to apply the adjective 'ἔνδοξος', to views or tenets ; and in doing so, he may have been entertained by the pun on 'δόξα'. But however that may be, in its new context, 'ἔνδοξος' retains its old sense of 'reputable' [22].

If 'τὰ ἔνδοξα' means 'the reputable things', what are τὰ ἔνδοξα ? what, in other words, are the criteria for good repute ? *Τὰ ἔνδοξα* are *δοκοῦντα* or *φαινόμενα*, beliefs or opinions ; but *φαινόμενα* or *δοκοῦντα* to whom ? whose beliefs and opinions are reputable ? Aristotle answers those questions at the beginning of the *Topics* :

> *ἔνδοξα δὲ τὰ δοκοῦντα πᾶσιν ἢ τοῖς πλείστοις ἢ τοῖς σοφοῖς, καὶ τούτοις ἢ πᾶσιν ἢ τοῖς πλείστοις ἢ τοῖς μάλιστα γνωρίμοις καὶ ἐνδόξοις* [23] (A 1, 100b21-3).

That is Aristotle's *ὅρος* or definition of *τὰ ἔνδοξα* (cf. 101a11) [24]. (It does not explain what 'τὰ ἔνδοξα' means : it defines τὰ ἔνδοξα inasmuch as it determines their scope ; it lays down the criteria of reputability [25].)

(21) But there are two entries for 'ἔνδοξος' in Stephanus' *Thesaurus* ((1) = *opinabilis* ; (2) = *gloriosus*) ; and the word is assigned two meanings by Liddell and Scott.

(22) Apart from Boethius '*probabilis*', the only correct translation of 'ἔνδοξος' I have come across is Zadro's 'notevole' ; Alexander, *in Top* 19. 19 points to the right understanding of the term.

(23) 'ἐνδόξοις' here (cf. 'ἐνδοξοτάτοις' at 101a13) evidently bears its ordinary sense of 'reputable'. Evans, *o.c.* n. 14, pp. 68n28 and 79n64, construes 'ἔνδοξος' as 'view-holding' (and 'γνώριμος' as 'understanding'), deriving its application to men from its application to beliefs. That is topsy-turvy.

(24) 'ἔνδοξος' and 'εὔδοξος' are synonyms (above, n. 17) ; compare, then, Aristotle's account of *εὐδοξία* :

> *εὐδοξία δ' ἐστιν τὸ ὑπὸ πάντων σπουδαῖον ὑπολαμβάνεσθαι ἢ τοιοῦτόν τι ἔχειν οὗ πάντες ἐφίενται ἢ οἱ πολλοὶ ἢ οἱ ἀγαθοὶ ἢ οἱ φρόνιμοι* (*Rhet* A 5, 1361a25-27).

That definition exhibits formed parallels to the *ὅρος* of *τὰ ἔνδοξα* : 'εὔδοξος' does not appear elsewhere in Aristotle, and the definition (like many in *Rhet*) may be Academic ; in that case, Aristotle's account of *τὰ ἔνδοξα* may be a naughty pastiche of an Academic definition. Note, too, Plato's idiosyncratic use of 'εὐδοξία' at *Meno* 99B, which probably puns on the two senses of 'δόξα'.

(25) The *ὅρος* requires further discussion : e.g. some passages appear to make 'ἔνδοξος' a relational term ('It is *ἔνδοξον* to *x* that *p*') – *Top* A 10, 104b8-11 ; others talk of what *seems* to be *ἔνδοξον* – e.g. A 14, 105b2.

What count as *δοκοῦντα* here? what does the domain of beliefs include? Certainly, it will include any explicit beliefs – opinions which men do or would avow (to themselves, if not *in foro publico*); and which are, in a plain sense, *τὰ λεγόμενα*. But it will also include a large and important body of implicit beliefs. Those beliefs may be roughly divided into three categories.

First, propositions which are evidently entailed by, or close corollaries of, our explicit beliefs may be ascribed to us. Thus Aristotle counts as *ἔνδοξα* propositions which are *τοῖς ἐνδόξοις ὅμοια, καὶ τἀναντία τοῖς δοκοῦσιν ἐνδόξοις εἶναι κατ' ἀντίφασιν προτεινόμενα* (*Top* A 10, 104a13-14). If I avow the belief that *p* and the proposition that *q* is intimately related (in one of various specified ways) to that belief, then I believe that *q*.

Secondly, some beliefs may be ascribed to us on the basis of our actions: what we do shows that we hold pleasure to be good, or wealth more important than virtue. There is nothing unusual in the suggestion that actions speak louder than words; and Aristotle's list of *τὰ ἔνδοξα* will include opinions which men manifest by their deeds [26].

Thirdly, there are beliefs latent in language: what we say may show our beliefs in two distinct ways; for as well as expressing what we think, our sentences may reveal beliefs which they do not express. A Greek, according to Aristotle, would only say '*προαιροῦμαι* to *Φ*' if he took *Φ*ing to be a means to, or an ingredient in, some predetermined end; and that linguistic fact shows he believes that 'we only choose what conduces to an end' (*EN Γ* 2, 1111b26-30). Of course, if you ask him 'Do you deliberate about ends?', you may well get an affirmative answer – or a blank stare of incomprehension; for at a conscious level the belief may never have been formulated. But the language we use betrays our latent opinions.

Again, the various ways in which the Greek talk about change – in particular, the various syntactical structures they employ in doing so – evince a common belief that every change consists in matter taking on form in place of privation. Ordinary Greeks do not have explicit beliefs about such abstract philosophical issues; but still they believe what

(26) See, e.g., *EN* K 2, 1172b35-1173a5 (cf. H 13, 1153b31-2): the fact that everyone *desires* (*ἐφίεται*) pleasure indicates that everyone *believes* (*δοκεῖ*) pleasure to be good. See also *Γ* 5, 1113b21-6, with Aspasius, *in EN* 76.31.

Aristotle says they do – for their very language conveys such opinions (27).

Τὰ ἔνδοξα are *τὰ λεγόμενα* ; and *τὰ λεγόμενα* (the term is not univocal) include linguistic facts, facts about syntax and facts about semantics. I stress the point for two reasons. First, the class of *τὰ πᾶσι δοκοῦντα* will surely be very small, perhaps empty, if we confine *τὰ δοκοῦντα* to explicit beliefs ; but if *τὰ δοκοῦντα* encompass the presuppositions of our linguistic usage, then in any linguistically homogeneous community there will be innumerably many *πᾶσι δοκοῦντα*. Common Sense, in other words, may be a rich treasury of opinion – so long as it is a treasury of latent opinion.

Secondly, modern philosophers of Common Sense have often linked their concern with an interest in ordinary language : ordinary language is, as it were, the vehicle for Common Sense ; and linguistic analysis may give an account of Common Sense beliefs. Aristotle shared that view ; and his known penchant for the linguistic turn is to be explained by reference to his explicit interest in *τὰ ἔνδοξα* (28).

IV

It is now easy to see why the *φαινόμενα* which we lay down at the start of our investigations may require purification and selection. Since the beliefs we are concerned with may be implicit or latent, they will have to be exhumed from the behaviour or the linguistic forms in

(27) See *Phys* A 7, with the commentary by Wieland, *o.c.* n. 7, pp. 110-40.

(28) R. M. Hare ('The Argument from Received Opinion', in his *Essays on Philosophical Method* (London, 1971)) argues that 'common moral opinions have in themselves no probative force whatever in moral philosophy' ; and he suggests that 'they appear to have probative force, and have been treated as if they had it, because of a failure to observe the distinction' between common moral opinions and the common use of moral words (p. 122). Hare thinks that this distinction 'was perhaps not *clearly* made before Moore', and 'never becomes entirely clear in either Plato or Aristotle' (p. 118). I think that a generalisation of Hare's distinction was clearly stated by Aristotle :

ταῖς μὲν ὀνομασίαις τὰ πράγματα προσαγορευτέον καθάπερ οἱ πολλοί, ποῖα δὲ τῶν πραγμάτων ἐστι τοιαῦτα ἢ οὐ τοιαῦτα, οὐκέτι προσεκτέον τοῖς πολλοῖς (*Top* B 2, 110a16-19 ; cf. Z 11, 148b20-3).

I doubt if failure to observe the distinction underlies the Argument from Received Opinion ; and certainly one can observe the distinction and still hope to discover common opinions latent in common language.

which they are entombed. *Τὰ ἔνδοξα* may be difficult to formulate, or to formulate precisely. (To that extent, at least, the Method of *Ἔνδοξα* is not purely descriptive : it calls for analytical work.)

Again, *τὰ ἔνδοξα* may conflict : if most men are at odds with the wise, or with the most reputable of the wise ; or if the wise are at odds among themselves ; or if there is dispute among the most reputable of the wise – in all those cases, opposite opinions will be equally *ἔνδοξα* (29). And the final set of *ἔνδοξα*, the γ_i's, will be smaller than the original set, the α_i's. It was once *ἔνδοξον* that the earth was stationary (for most men held it to be so), and also that the earth moved (for was not Galileo a reputable sage ?). (To that extent, at least, the Method of *Ἔνδοξα* may be partly prescriptive ; for selecting the favoured *ἔνδοξα* may involve a normative decision.)

It is plain, too, that the Method of *Ἔνδοξα* cannot be used to brand Aristotle as a Common Sense philosopher. *Τὰ ἔνδοξα* include all the propositions of Common Sense, if Common Sense is the sum of the beliefs held by all, or most, men. But *τὰ ἔνδοξα* also include minority beliefs – the opinions of sages, specialists, and savants ; and those beliefs, which may be at odds with the beliefs of *hoi polloi*, will hardly count as a part of Common Sense. Aristotle undertakes to defend Common Sense ; for he will defend *τὰ ἔνδοξα*, and *τὰ ἔνδοξα* encompass Common Sense. But in exactly the same way he is a defender of Uncommon Sense, of expertise and of the *élite*.

A proposition fails to be *ἔνδοξον* only if either no one at all believes it (in the extended sense of 'believe'), or it is believed by a group of people who include no *σοφοί* and do not constitute a large majority of men. Aristotle says little about such *ἄδοξα*. At *Rhet* A 2, 1356b36, he implies that *τὰ ἔνδοξα* will not include anything that *φαίνεται ... τοῖς παραληροῦσιν* ; at *EN* A 4, 1095a28-30, he observes that :

> *ἁπάσας μὲν οὖν ἐξετάζειν τὰς δόξας ματαιότερον ἴσως ἐστιν, ἱκανὸν δὲ τὰς μάλιστα ἐπιπολαζούσας ἢ δοκούσας ἔχειν τινα λόγον.*

Two sorts of opinions are worth *ἐξετάζειν* (i.e. *διαπορεῖν*) : 'those which are especially prevalent', i.e. those *ἔνδοξα* which *πᾶσι ἢ τοῖς πλείστοις*

(29) In *Top* Aristotle never explicitly recognizes the possibility of conflict among *τὰ ἔνδοξα* (but see perhaps A 11, 104b1-5 ; I 12, 173a19-30) ; and he appears to disallow it at Θ 5, 159b4-6, A 10, 104a11-12 (cf. Alexander, *in Top* 72.22 : *τὸ ... τῷ ἐνδόξῳ ἐναντίον οὐχ οἷόν τε ἔνδοξον εἶναι*). For such conflicts in *EN* see e.g. A 4, 1095a21-3 ; H 3, 1145b27 ; and cf. *EE* H 1, 1235b2-3 (quoted above, p. 492).

δοκεῖ ; and those which 'seem to have some reason', i.e. those *ἔνδοξα* which are accepted by *οἱ σοφοί*.

The passage in *EE* corresponding to those lines from *EN* A 4 is difficult :

> *πάσας μὲν οὖν τὰς δόξας ἐπισκοπεῖν ὅσας ἔχουσί τινες περὶ αὐτῆς [*sc. *τῆς εὐδαιμονίας] περίεργον · πολλὰ γὰρ φαίνεται καὶ τοῖς παιδαρίοις καὶ τοῖς κάμνουσι καὶ παραφρονοῦσι, περὶ ὧν ἂν οὐδεὶς νοῦν ἔχων διαπορήσειεν · δέονται γὰρ οὐ λόγων ἀλλ' οἱ μὲν ἡλικίας ἐν ᾗ μεταβάλλουσιν, οἱ δὲ κολάσεως ἰατρικῆς ἢ πολιτικῆς (κόλασις γὰρ ἡ φαρμακεία τῶν πληγῶν οὐκ ἐλάττων ἐστίν) · ὁμοίως δὲ ταύταις οὐδὲ τὰς τῶν πολλῶν · εἰκῇ γὰρ λέγουσι σχεδὸν περὶ ἁπάντων καὶ μάλιστα †περὶ ἐπισκεπτέον μόνας† ἄτοπον γὰρ προσφέρειν λόγον τοῖς λόγου μηδὲν δεομένοις ἀλλὰ πάθους · ἐπεὶ δ' εἰσὶν ἀπορίαι περὶ ἑκάστην πραγματείαν οἰκεῖαι, δῆλον ὅτι καὶ περὶ βίου τοῦ κρατίστου καὶ ζωῆς τῆς ἀρίστης εἰσίν · ταύτας οὖν καλῶς ἔχει τὰς δόξας ἐξετάζειν · οἱ γὰρ τῶν ἀμφισβητούντων ἔλεγχοι τῶν ἐναντιουμένων αὐτοῖς λόγων ἀποδείξεις εἰσίν* (1214b28-1215a7) (30).

What is to be made of that ?

First, Aristotle wants to *exclude* certain *δόξαι* from consideration, i.e. to keep them out of the initial set of a_i's (31). The excluded *δόξαι* are those of mad men (*παραφρονοῦσι* : cf. *παραληροῦσι* in *Rhet*), of the sick, of children. (Aristotle means to exclude opinions *peculiar* to those groups : evidently, a child or a madman might happen to share a view held by *οἱ σοφοί*). In addition, he excludes *τὰς τῶν πολλῶν* < *δόξας* > : that is surprising, for surely the opinions of *οἱ πολλοί* are *ἔνδοξα* ? We must distinguish between *οἱ πολλοί* and *οἱ πλεῖστοι* : opinions held by most men are indeed *ἔνδοξα* ; but opinions peculiar to *οἱ πολλοί*, the vulgar herd, should be ignored (32).

(30) '*εἰκῇ*' (MSS : '*εἰ μή*') at 1215a1 is generally accepted.

(31) Aristotle's *reason* for his exclusions is odd : 'ignore the opinions of madmen and children, because argument cannot change them' ; 'do not consider the beliefs of *οἱ πολλοί*, since they need not *λόγος* but *πάθος*' (on '*πάθους*', 1215a3, see F. Dirlmeier, *Aristoteles : Eudemische Ethik* (Berlin, 1962), p. 160). But in assembling *τὰ ἔνδοξα* we are collectors, not missionaries ; our task is to amass *data*, not to change minds. And the fact that argument will not alter an infant's opinion is no reason for excluding that opinion from the a_i's.

(32) See E. Weil, *o.c.* n. 14, p. 95 (Dirlmeier, *o.c.* n. 31, p. 160, opines that *οἱ πολλοί* are 'die massenhaft auftretenden Sophisten ..., von denen er einmal sagt : *διαλέγονται περὶ πάντων*'). Respect for the views of *οἱ πολλοί* is probably shown at *EN* A 4, 1095a18 (but see A 5, 1095b16) ; and cf. A 8, 1098b27-9 :

τούτων δὲ τὰ μὲν πολλοὶ καὶ παλαιοὶ λέγουσιν, τὰ δὲ ὀλίγοι καὶ ἐνδόξοι ἄνδρες · οὐδετέρους δὲ τούτων εὔλογον διαμαρτάνειν τοῖς ὅλοις ...

Secondly, Aristotle indicates which opinions *should* be puzzled over, or put among the initial α_i's. They are *ταύτας ... τὰς δόξας*. The manuscript reading provides no antecedent for '*ταύτας*', and thus no way to identify the α_i's. Some scholars attempt to extract an implicit antecedent from the phrase '*ἀπορίαι ... οἰκεῖαι*' : 'consider only those opinions which give rise to appropriate puzzles' (33). But that reading is difficult ; and the advice to consider 'appropriate' *δόξαι* is unilluminating – we want to be told what *δόξαι* are appropriate. Other scholars insert the phrase '*τὰς τῶν σοφῶν δόξας*' into the text, after the obelized sentence (34). There we have an antecedent for '*ταύτας*' – and a radical restriction on the Method of *Ἔνδοξα* : only expert opinions are to be admitted among the initial α_i's. But it is scarcely to be believed that here, uniquely, Aristotle should set value only on wise beliefs ; and in any case, the insertion does not make good sense in the context.

On that unsatisfactory note, I end my account of *τὰ ἔνδοξα*. Aristotle's Method of *Ἔνδοξα* does not commit him to a Morality of Common Sense ; but for all that, it is materially restrictive – it rules a large body of propositions out of philosophical court.

V

Why was Aristotle attracted by the Method of *Ἔνδοξα* ? what gives *τὰ ἔνδοξα* their claim to exclusive attention ? There is, in principle, no need to look for a general justification of the Method : *τὰ ἔνδοξα* fall into different types, and are applied in different disciplines ; perhaps one argument will explain the use of *τὰ ἔνδοξα* to establish the definitional *ἀρχαί* of physics, another will support the use of *τὰ ἔνδοξα* in practical philosophy. Perhaps the opinions of the wise are valuable in a fairly trivial sense (what is a wise man if not someone whose opinions are regularly true ?), whereas beliefs enshrined in ordinary

(33) So. e.g., Solomon in the Oxford Translation.

(34) *...καὶ μάλιστα περὶ ἐπισκεπτέον μόνας* ... (1215a1-2) lacunam post *περὶ, a* ; *περὶ + ὧν D^2* ; *περὶ τούτων τὰς τῶν σοφῶν P^b* marg.

Scholars have tried two lines of emendation. (i) Spengel, followed by Susemihl, transposes '*ἐπισκεπτέον*' to follow '*τῶν πολλῶν*' (1214b34) ; and emends '*μόνας*' to '*εὐδαιμονίας*'. (ii) Others make an insertion after '*περί*', e.g. : *...περὶ < ταύτης · ἀλλὰ τὰς τῶν σοφῶν > ἐπισκεπτέον* ... (Fritsche, Dirlmeier, Gigon (with '*ἐπιεικῶν*' for '*σοφῶν*')) ; *...περὶ < ταύτης · ἀλλὰ τὰς τῶν σοφῶν ταύτης γε περὶ > ἐπισκεπτέον* ... (Dodds).

language can have their importance vindicated by theoretical linguistics.

Scattered through Aristotle's treatises and implicit in some of his arguments, there is a wide range of considerations bearing on the value of *τὰ ἔνδοξα*. And though Aristotle never meditated long on the justifiability of his Method, he says enough to enable us to meditate on his behalf. I shall now briefly sketch one line of thought out of the many which Aristotle might have pursued.

Let us begin with another methodological passage from the *Eudemian Ethics* :

> [1] *πειρατέον δὲ περὶ πάντων τούτων ζητεῖν τὴν πίστιν διὰ λόγων, μαρτυρίοις καὶ παραδείγμασι χρώμενον τοῖς φαινομένοις* ([2a] *κράτιστον μὲν γὰρ πάντας ἀνθρώπους φαίνεσθαι συνομολογοῦντας τοῖς ῥηθησομένοις*, [2b] *εἰ δὲ μή, τρόπον γέ τινα πάντας*, [2c] *ὅπερ μεταβιβαζόμενοι ποιήσουσιν* · [3] *ἔχει γὰρ ἕκαστος οἰκεῖόν τι πρὸς τὴν ἀλήθειαν*), [4] *ἐξ ὧν ἀναγκαῖον δεικνύναι πως περὶ αὐτῶν* · [5] *ἐκ γὰρ τῶν ἀληθῶς μὲν λεγομένων, οὐ σαφῶς δέ, προϊοῦσιν ἔσται καὶ τὸ σαφῶς, μεταλαμβάνουσιν ἀεὶ τὰ γνωριμώτερα τῶν εἰωθότων λέγεσθαι συγκεχυμένως* (A 6, 1216b26-36).

The text is exceedingly difficult ; and any interpretation must be tentative (35).

Sentence [1] invites us to rely on 'arguments' (*λόγοι*) in our enquiries, and to use *τὰ φαινόμενα* (i.e. *τὰ ἔνδοξα*) as 'evidences and examples'. Sentence [2] explains *why* we should bother with *τὰ φαινόμενα*, and sentence [3] somehow supports or elucidates [2]. Sentence [4] indicates *how* we are to use *τὰ φαινόμενα* ; and [5] explains [4].

The antecedent of '*ὧν*' in sentence [4] seems to be '*τοῖς φαινομένοις*' in sentence [1] ; and '*περὶ αὐτῶν*' in 4 likewise adverts to '*περὶ πάντων τούτων*' in [1]. (Sentences [2]-[3] are thus parenthetical, and are best enclosed in brackets). According to [4] we use *τὰ φαινόμενα* to effect 'a

(35) For a useful commentary, see O. GIGON, 'Das Prooimion der Eudemischen Ethik', in *Untersuchungen zur Eudemischen Ethik*, edd. P. Moraux and D. Harlfinger, Peripatoi 1 (Berlin, 1971). The parallel text in *EN* reads :

σκεπτέον δὲ περὶ αὐτῆς [sc. τῆς εὐδαιμονίας] οὐ μόνον ἐκ τοῦ συμπεράσματος καὶ ἐξ ὧν ὁ λόγος, ἀλλὰ καὶ ἐκ τῶν λεγομένων · *τῷ μὲν γὰρ ἀληθεῖ πάντα συνᾴδει τὰ ὑπάρχοντα, τῷ δὲ ψευδεῖ ταχὺ διαφωνεῖ τἀληθές* (A 8, 1098b9-12).

The second sentence is strange : Rassow is surely right to excise '*τἀληθές*' ; I suspect we should read '*τὰ ὑπάρχειν δοκοῦντα*' for '*τὰ ὑπάρχοντα*' ; and it helps to insert '*πως*' after '*συνᾴδει*'.

sort of proof' (δεικνύναι πως) ; a sort of proof, rather than a fullblooded proof, because proof here consists – as sentence [5] explains – in replacing 'true but unclear' propositions by 'clear' propositions, i.e. 'in continually putting more intelligible things in the place of those which are customarily expressed in a confused fashion' (36). Sentences [4]-[5] thus allude to the business of 'purifying' τὰ ἔνδοξα, of replacing the α_i's by the β_i's.

Sentence [2] offers a double reason for making use of τὰ φαινόμενα : [a] 'it is best that all men should evidently agree with what we are going to say' ; and [b] 'otherwise, that all men should do so in a certain fashion'. Aristotle insists on universal agreement : he supposes, in effect, that the initial set of α_i's will be consistent. (That explains why sentence [5] refers only to 'purification').

The function of [2c] is to show how all men may agree 'in a certain fashion' : they will do so μεταβιβαζομένοι. What does that mean ? The easiest construe renders it : 'if their opinions are changed'. But that reduces Aristotle's remark to triviality – if men disagree with us, they will agree with us if their opinions are altered. Better sense is given if 'μεταβιβαζομένοι' is taken to anticipate 'μεταλαμβάνουσιν' : if we purify or reformulate men's opinion, we shall see that they do, after all, agree with us (37). It is best if the α_i's cohere ; if not, then let all the β_i's cohere.

Sentence [3] remains : its sense, and its position in Aristotle's argument, are alike unclear. It could be taken to support sentence [2] as

(36) (i) 'μεταλαμβάνειν *X* ἀντὶ *Y*' is common in the *Organon* ; it means 'put *X* in place of *Y*' – and it usually refers to the replacement of one word or phrase by a more illuminating synonym. See e.g. *APr* A 39, 49b3 ; *APst* B 11, 94b21 ; *Top* B 4, 111a8 ; E 2, 130a29 ; *Z* 4, 142b3. The genitive, 'τῶν εἰωθότων' is difficult. It cannot be partitive, dependent on 'τὰ γνωριμώτερα'. Perhaps it is comparative, after 'γνωριμώτερα' ; perhaps 'μεταλαμβάνειν τὸ *X* τοῦ *Y*' is used for '... τὸ X ἀντὶ τοῦ *Y*' (? cf. *Top* Z 11, 149a33) ; or perhaps we should add 'ἀντί' before 'τῶν εἰωθότων' (Richards). (ii) For the move from what is 'true but unclear' to what is 'clear' see *EE* B 1, 1220a15-18 ; cf. A 6, 1217a19 ; Θ 3, 1249b6 ; *EN* Z 1, 1138b25-6 ; *An* B 2, 413a11 ; *Phys* A 1, 184a16 ; Plato, *Politicus* 275A ; 281D. In such contexts (and often elsewhere) 'σαφής' means not 'lucid' but rather 'illuminating' (cf. W. J. Verdenius, 'Human Reason and God in the Eudemian Ethics', in *Untersuchungen zur Eudemischen Ethik*, pp. 286-7) : when we μεταλαμβάνειν β_i ἀντὶ α_i, we replace a dull by an illuminating account of the matter.

(37) 'μεταβιβάζειν' certainly refers to conversion, or change of belief, at *Top* Θ 11, 161a33 (cf. A 2, 101a33 ; Plato, *Phaedrus* 262B) ; and the process of conversion is schematically described at e.g. *Met* Z 3, 1029b3-12 (NB 'μεταβαίνειν'). But the word does not *mean* 'convert' ; and I do not see why the move from α_i to β_i cannot be called μεταβιβάζειν.

a whole: 'Why is it best if all men agree ... ?' – 'Because ἔχει ἕκαστος ...'. Or it could be linked particularly to [2c]: 'Why will men agree μεταβιβαζομένοι ?' – 'Because ἔχει ἕκαστος ...'. I doubt if there is any way of deciding between those two interpretations; and for my present purposes a decision does not greatly matter.

It is more important to determine the sense of [3]; and in particular, to discover the import of 'οἰκεῖόν τι'. At least two interpretations have been canvassed. First: 'everyone has something of his own to contribute to the truth' (38); i.e. each of us has managed to grasp some portion of the truth, so that the sum total of our opinions will contain a few grains of truth hidden in a mass of chaff. Compare these lines from the *Metaphysics*:

> *ὅτι ἡ περὶ τῆς ἀληθείας θεωρία τῇ μὲν χαλεπὴ τῇ δὲ ῥᾳδία· σημεῖον δὲ τὸ μήτ' ἀξίως μηδένα δύνασθαι τυχεῖν αὐτῆς μήτε πάντως ἀποτυγχάνειν, ἀλλ' ἕκαστον λέγειν τι περὶ τῆς φύσεως, καὶ καθ' ἕνα μὲν ἢ μηθὲν ἢ μικρὸν ἐπιβάλλειν αὐτῇ, ἐκ πάντων δὲ συναθροιζομένων γίγνεσθαί τι μέγεθος* (α 1, 993a30-b4) (39).

'No natural philosopher has properly grasped the truth; but each has hit upon some aspect of it; and hence from a collection of their opinions we may expect to amass a quantity of truth'. Similar thoughts may be found in the *Politics*, where they provide an argument for the value of democracy: each citizen contributes something of his own to the communal feast; and as a result the banquet is varied and nutritious (40).

On that reading of sentence [3], all men are to agree with us in a very weak sense: if we grasp the whole truth, each man will agree with us in at least one particular, viz. in his own individual contribution to the truth. It is hard to understand the agreement of sentence [2] in that meagre way.

On the second interpretation, 'οἰκεῖόν τι' means 'something proper to him', 'some part of his nature'; thus: 'Everyone has a natural aptitude for grasping truth' (41). Compare the following passage from the *Rhetoric*:

(38) So, e.g., Solomon in the Oxford Translation.

(39) At 993b1, read 'πάντως' (Erasmus, Brandis, Bonitz), for the MSS 'πάντας'.

(40) See *Pol* Γ 11; cf. E. Braun, 'Die Summierungstheorie des Aristoteles', *Jhb. Öst. Arch. Inst.*, 44, 1959, 157-84.

(41) So, e.g., Dirlmeier, *o.c.*, n. 31, p. 183.

> *οἱ ἄνθρωποι πρὸς τὸ ἀληθὲς πεφύκασιν ἱκανῶς καὶ τὰ πλείω τυγχάνουσιν τῆς ἀληθείας · διὸ πρὸς τὰ ἔνδοξα στοχαστικῶς ἔχειν τοῦ ὁμοίως ἔχοντος καὶ πρὸς τὴν ἀλήθειάν ἐστιν* (A 1, 1355a15-8).

'Men have a natural inclination (*πεφύκασιν*) towards the truth ; and that is why it is worth studying *τὰ ἔνδοξα*'.

If that is Aristotle's thought in sentence [3], we must ascribe to him one of the following arguments : 'It is best if all men agree with our results ; for everyone is naturally inclined to grasp the truth, so that dissent will be a sign of falsity' ; or : 'Men will agree with us when their opinions are purified ; for everyone has a natural aptitude for the truth, which the process of purification will reveal'.

Aristotle certainly held that men have a natural longing for the truth, and a natural disposition to attain it. The celebrated exordium to the *Metaphysics* (*πάντες ἄνθρωποι τοῦ εἰδέναι ὀρέγονται φύσει* : A 1, 980a21) probably derives from the *Protrepticus*, where Aristotle says, more expansively, that *αἱρετωτέρα καὶ τοῦ ζῆν ἐστιν ἡ φρόνησις (κυριωτέρα* <*γὰρ*> *τῆς ἀληθείας)· ὥστε πάντες ἄνθρωποι τὸ φρονεῖν μάλιστα διώκουσιν* (fr. 7 Ross = B 77 Düring) (42). And in the ethical treatises, we find passages such as this :

> *φύσει σοφὸς μὲν οὐδείς, γνώμην δ' ἔχειν καὶ σύνεσιν καὶ νοῦν · σημεῖον δ' ὅτι καὶ τῆς ἡλικίας οἰόμεθα ἀκολουθεῖν καὶ ἥδε ἡ ἡλικία νοῦν ἔχει καὶ γνώμην, ὡς τῆς φύσεως αἰτίας οὔσης* (*EN* Z 11, 1143b6-9).

Human nature is so constituted that we possess a faculty for grasping truth – even if that faculty must be refined by experience.

There is a gap between the premises that men have a natural aptitude for knowledge, and the conclusion that *τὰ ἔνδοξα* constitute a deep well of truth. But for Aristotle the gap is easily bridged : if nature does nothing in vain, and if we are naturally inclined towards truth, it follows that we do, for the most part, attain the truth. For our natural aptitudes cannot remain unexercised (in that case they would be vain, or pointless) ; nor can they be exercised without usually achieving their object (in that case they would be vain, or unsuccessful). Thus we do regularly hit upon the truth.

We cannot infer that whatever a man believes, is true ; nor even that whatever all men believe, is true. For our natural aptitudes will

(42) Text as emended by D. J. Allan.

sometimes fail us ; and it is in principle possible that they should fail us at just those points on which we are all agreed. But for all that, given Aristotle's teleology, the fact that something is ἔνδοξον must count as strong *prima facie* evidence in favour of its truth.

That argument is not explicitly unrolled in any Aristotelian text ; but I suspect that it constitutes, in Aristotle's eyes, one of several arguments for the utility of *τὰ ἔνδοξα*. Moreover, it integrates the Method of *Ἔνδοξα* into the system of Aristotle's natural philosophy. But the argument will only move those who share Aristotle's teleological leanings ; and even then it offers frail support for the Method. For the most the argument shows is that ἔνδοξα tend to be true : it cannot show that truths tend to be ἔνδοξα ; and hence it cannot warrant us in limiting to *τὰ ἔνδοξα* the potential conclusions of our philosophical investigations.

V

Rightly understood, the Method of *Ἔνδοξα* does not commit Aristotle to the conservative parochialism of Common Sense. But the Method is restrictive, in that it refuses to consider certain propositions as possible bearers of truth. We may try to explain why Aristotle was prepared to submit to that restriction ; but no explanation will also serve as a justification, and the Method itself is vicious.

Yet Aristotle's practical philosophy is not, I think, seriously marred by his Method, and that for two reasons. First the restrictions imposed by the Method are minimal : there are remarkably few propositions which Aristotle cannot, in one way or another, include among the initial α_i's ; and the process of 'purification', generously construed, will allow him still greater scope in assembling the β_i's. The Method is not formally vacuous ; but it has, in the last analysis, very little content.

Secondly, Aristotle's actual philosophising was not greatly affected by his reflexion on how philosophy ought to be conducted. In the *Ethics*, he considers – and partly defends – Socrates' bizarre views on *ἀκρασία*. In the *Physics*, he takes account of the cranky theories of Parmenides and of Zeno. In the *Metaphysics*, he argues against men who reject the law of non-contradiction. All those views are interesting and significant ; and no methodological ruminations restrained Aristotle from investigating them.

Ryle once observed that 'preoccupation with questions about methods tends to distract us from prosecuting the methods themselves. We run, as a rule, worse, not better, if we think a lot about our feet'. From time to time, Aristotle thought about his feet; and he produced one or two odd theories of running. But, like any good athlete, he forgot about theorizing when it came to the race [43].

Balliol College, Oxford.

(43) On Aristotle's 'methods of ethics' I have found the following studies particularly helpful: R. Eucken, *Ueber die Methode und die Grundlagen der aristotelischen Ethik* (Berlin, 1870); Grant, *o.c.* n. 1, pp. 391-6; Stewart, *o.c.* n. 5, vol. I, pp. 26-57; J. Burnet, *The Ethics of Aristotle* (London, 1900), pp. xxxi-xlvi; D. H. G. Greenwood, *Aristotle: Nicomachean Ethics Book Six* (Cambridge, 1909), pp. 127-44; Owen, *o.c.* n. 1; D. J. Allan, 'Quasi-mathematical Method in the *Eudemian Ethics*', in *Aristote et les Problèmes de Méthode*, ed. S. Mansion (Louvain, 1961); W. F. R. Hardie, *Aristotle's Ethical Theory* (Oxford, 1968), ch. 3; J. D. Monan, *Moral Knowledge and its Methodology in Aristotle* (Oxford, 1968); Gigon, *o.c.* n. 35.

Ancient Philosophy 8

On the Alleged Metaphysical Foundation of Aristotle's *Ethics*

Timothy D. Roche

It is widely believed that Aristotle's explicit account of moral methodology fails to give an adequate represention of his practice in the *Nicomachean Ethics*. The explicit account suggests only one method of establishing first principles in ethics—the method of dialectic.[1] But contemporary scholars seem to agree that when Aristotle proceeds to construct his moral theory, he often, though not always, appeals to the principles of his metaphysics and psychology.[2] It is thought that the *Ethics* is derived, at least in part, from Aristotle's own scientific conceptions of the human soul, the teleological development of natural organisms, and the place and function of man in the hierarchy of animate beings.

In a series of important papers, Terence Irwin has developed a sophisticated defense of the view that there is a metaphysical foundation to Aristotle's *Ethics*.[3] I believe, however, that there is no such foundation, and that Aristotle practices what he seems to preach, *viz.*, that dialectic, and a purely autonomous dialectic,[4] is the only method used to establish his ultimate moral principles.[5] In what follows, I will try to exhibit some of the difficulties I see in Irwin's argument and defend—so far as the limits of this paper will allow—my alternative reading of Aristotle's method in ethics.

Irwin's claim that Aristotle uses his metaphysics to justify his moral principles—a position I shall refer to as the metaphysical foundation hypothesis—rests on three broad contentions. The first is that Aristotle's argument in the *Nicomachean Ethics* 'requires an appeal outside ethics for the justification of ethical principles' (Irwin 1981, 223). The appeal is necessary, says Irwin, because Aristotle intends to establish the truth of his ethical principles, and the only plausible way for him to fulfill this intention is by means of arguments which rely on some of his metaphysical principles. The second claim is that it is *possible* for Aristotle to rely on his metaphysics in order to support his moral theory. Irwin defends this claim primarily by exhibiting certain connections between Aristotle's concept of a final good in the *Ethics* and his theories of substance, form, and rational soul in his metaphysics and psychology. Finally, Irwin contends that there is some textual evidence for the view that Aristotle does, in fact, ground his ethics on his metaphysics. He recognizes that Aristotle's explicit account of moral methodology makes no reference to metaphysical doctrines, but he contends that an examination of the actual arguments deployed in the *Ethics* reveals that Aristotle is *implicitly* appealing to these doctrines; and once again, Irwin's discussion primarily revolves around Aristotle's theory of the human good (Irwin 1978, 260-262 and 271n29; 1980, 40-51; 1981, 207-223).

It should be noted that the first two of these contentions, taken singly, fail to provide any direct support for the metaphysical foundation hypothesis. For even if it is true that Aristotle needs to appeal to his metaphysics in order to justify his ethics, it does not follow that Aristotle thinks he needs to do this. And, even if it is possible for Aristotle to defend his theory of the good with his metaphysics, it does not follow that Aristotle does defend his theory of the good with his metaphysics. Moreover, the claims taken together also fail to support the metaphysical foundation hypothesis. Aristotle exegesis might be a great deal easier if we were to accept the principle that whatever the Stagirite had better do, and is possible for him to do, he in fact does. But no one would seriously defend this principle.

The strength of Irwin's position is found in the conjunction of all three contentions. For if Aristotle's moral methodology is clearly untenable without a metaphysical underpinning, and it is possible for Aristotle to furnish such an underpinning, and there is textual evidence suggesting that Aristotle may be using his ontology to support central arguments of the *Ethics*, then Irwin's reasoning is quite persuasive. Certainly one should look for an interpretation which avoids saddling Aristotle with a conspicuously indefensible conception of moral argument; and if Irwin is right in claiming to have found such an interpretation (and it is a plausible interpretation of Aristotle's text), then there are good reasons to think it is an accurate account of Aristotle's method in ethics.

There are stronger reasons, however, for doubting the accuracy of Irwin's interpretation. I will argue, specifically, that it does not cohere well with the textual evidence. Moreover, I will suggest that Aristotle's method in ethics is neither conspicuously indefensible nor dependent upon his own metaphysical doctrines; therefore, there is a false dilemma at the core of Irwin's argument for the metaphysical foundation hypothesis.

I

Irwin begins his defense of the metaphysical foundation hypothesis with a process-of-elimination type of argument (Irwin 1981, 201-208). He maintains that Aristotle might establish his ethical principles in one of three ways. He might take the first principles of ethics to be self-evident truths grasped by an act of intuition. Alternatively, and as Aristotle's explicit account of moral method seems to suggest, he might defend his ethical principles with a 'merely dialectical argument'. Finally, Aristotle might appeal to principles of other disciplines, in this case his metaphysical and psychological principles, in order to justify his ethical principles. Irwin correctly rejects the first option because ethics is not a demonstrative science for Aristotle, and self-evident first principles grasped by intuition seem to be a unique characteristic of such sciences. The second option is also rejected, and Irwin concludes that Aristotle chooses to employ the final method of justification, the one which includes the use of Aristotle's distinctive metaphysical views.

The argument supporting Irwin's rejection of the second option seems questionable to me. This argument begins with, and depends upon, a certain conception of Aristotle's method of dialectical reasoning. Irwin formulates the conception roughly as follows. The first step in dialectical argument is to garner a set of ἔνδοξα (*endoxa*, common beliefs) on the subject in question. We then examine the *endoxa* for inconsistencies and consider relevant problems, i.e., questions on which there are disagreements among people. Often a problem arises from an ἀπορία (puzzle), which is brought about when arguments which seem equally forceful yield contradictory conclusions. The next step in the process is to remove the inconsistencies and puzzles. This is accomplished by winnowing out the *endoxa* responsible for the inconsistencies and knocking down the arguments which produce the puzzles. There is a constraint here, however: We must reject the fewest number of *endoxa* compatible with the aim of removing infelicities. Coherence is to be achieved with a minimum sacrifice of the common views. This process of examining the accepted opinions, puzzling through them, and solving the difficulties, is also the road towards first principles. For once we have thought through all of the problems infecting our beliefs, we may come to understand why these problems arise and how they can be permanently dissolved with the establishment of the correct moral principles (Irwin 1981, 194-199).

Irwin concludes this description of Aristotelian dialectic with the remark that such a method of reasoning would 'seek principles that generate the common beliefs and remove puzzles created by the common beliefs' (Irwin 1981, 199). More specifically, a 'merely' dialectical defense of ethical principles will consist in showing that the principles in question entail a maximal, logically harmonious subset of *endoxa*, *viz.*, those *endoxa* which have survived the process of cross-examination.

But Irwin insists that this is a clearly untenable way for Aristotle to argue towards the first principles of ethics. For he points out that Aristotle wants to persuade us that most of the *endoxa* and the most important of them, reflect the truth (Irwin 1981, 200; cf. *EN* 1145b2-7, 1179a20-23, *EE* 1235b13-18). And so, one might reasonably complain: 'If the theoretical principles are really meant to vindicate the common beliefs and show that they are true, how are the principles to be defended? They will not be adequately defended if they are only shown to be the principles that yield the common beliefs. They seem to require some independent support, but dialectical arguments do not seem to offer that' (Irwin 1981, 200-201). The problem here is one of finding an acceptable coherence theory of justification, and Irwin insists that 'Coherence between ethical principles and common ethical beliefs seems to be a rather fragile justification, allowing very little defense against a radical critic or skeptic' (Irwin 1981, 222). In order for Aristotle to persuade an opponent to accept his moral principles, he needs to do more than show that these principles are compatible with the largest possible set of consistent moral *endoxa*. For the opponent who refuses to accept the moral *endoxa* is, *ipso facto*, refusing to accept the premises of this type of argument. As Irwin points out, the 'merely dialectical' method of argument aims only at achieving a 'narrow coherence' between ethical principles and ethical common beliefs; and 'narrow coherence' is just compatibility, not justification (Irwin 1981, 207-208). It seems to follow, then, that Aristotle needs to appeal outside ethics for the justification of his moral principles; and given Aristotle's views on the methods appropriate to the justification of moral principles, the necessity of such an appeal should be quite clear to him.

One might wonder, however, whether Aristotle believes it is appropriate (or even possible) to engage in moral inquiry with a radical critic or skeptic. The *Ethics* does not direct its argument at radical critics but at people who 'have been brought up in good habits', and so presumably share certain normal ethical convictions (*EN* 1095b3; cf.

EN 1094b29-1095a12 and *EE* 1214b20-1215a8). The received views are the 'starting-points' of moral argument for Aristotle, and if the radical critic refuses to accept these views as the basis of the inquiry, he simply opts out of the discourse (*EN* 1095a30-b13; cf. 1098a33-b8). Moreover, Aristotle insists that the kind of dialectic employed in an inquiry into the truth is 'not a competition' but a cooperative venture (*Top.* 159a25). A participant in such an inquiry must accept the received views as the materials of the debate (*Top.* 160a1). Consequently, if Aristotle takes the argument of the *Ethics* to be dialectical, he may not agree that he is obliged to persuade those who eschew the proper starting-points of moral inquiry. Indeed, it would not be out of character for him to suggest that the appropriate way of dealing with someone who repudiates these starting-points is through social training, violence, or medical treatment (cf. *Meta.* 1009a18; *EN* 1104b4-16, 1180a9; *EE* 1214b34-35; *Top.* 105a3-9).

In any case, it is not clear that a radical critic will find it more difficult to abandon metaphysical principles than ethical principles. According to Irwin, the following proposition expresses a basic metaphysical view supporting the argument of the *Ethics*: A natural organism is a goal-directed system whose essence is identical to its formal, functional properties (Irwin 1981, 211). But if our hypothetical skeptic feels perfectly at ease with his abandonment of the belief that the ultimate good must be complete and self-sufficient, or that an incontinent man acts against his better judgment, or that excellence, pleasure, and wisdom are goods, then why should he hesitate about denying this metaphysical principle? Irwin says that understanding a natural organism in accordance with the metaphysical principle is 'necessary for the right explanation of the organism's other features' (Irwin 1981, 211). However, it seems that an analogous response can be made in defense of certain basic moral propositions. Indeed, Aristotle *does* appear to issue such a response. Anyone, he says, who denies that the good is that at which all things aim 'will hardly have anything more credible to say' (*EN* 1173a1-2). And he insists that anyone who denies that a man can act against his better judgment 'manifestly contradicts the φαινόμενα (*phainomena*, appearances)' (*EN* 1145b27).

But I want to put these initial complaints aside for the moment. For Irwin does appear to have good reasons for thinking that the 'merely dialectical' method of argument is fundamentally, and conspicuously, flawed; and it is this belief which leads him to ransack the *Metaphysics* in search of a solid foundation for the dialectical reasoning of the *Ethics*. So let us consider the foundation which Irwin believes he has discovered.

Since the goal of a 'merely dialectical' argument is only to achieve 'narrow coherence' between moral *endoxa* and moral first principles, and since the establishment of 'narrow coherence' patently fails to justify belief in the truth of the basic principles of a moral theory, Irwin suggests an alternative interpretation of Aristotle's argument in the *Ethics*. According to this interpretation, the real goal of the method in the *Ethics* is not to establish 'narrow coherence', but 'broad coherence'.

The method of establishing 'broad coherence' consists in (1) justifying ethical principles by reference to non-ethical principles (and non-ethical *endoxa*) and then (2) justifying the initial ethical *endoxa* by appealing back to the antecedently justified ethical principles (Irwin 1981, 207-208). Irwin says that if we take this to be Aristotle's method in ethics, then we can see that the method is not 'merely dialectical'. It is not 'merely dialectical' because it does not rely on an interlocutor's uncritical acceptance of common moral beliefs. None the less, the method continues to be dialectical in so far as it relies on beliefs the interlocutor will accept (Irwin 1981, 208).

As I have noted, Irwin defends this conception of Aristotle's methodology primarily with an interpretation of the arguments about the final good in *EN* i. These arguments, he says, are 'addressed to a human agent as a broad rational agent' (Irwin 1981, 216). A 'broad rational agent' is understood as an agent who is not only able to take given desires and arrange for their satisfaction in a final (or comprehensive) good, but an agent who has the capacity to determine, to some extent, the desires he will have in the future. A broad rational agent is capable of deliberating and then deciding which potential desires he ought to develop and which desires he ought to weaken (Irwin 1981, 211-213). Now Irwin argues that this conception of a broad rational agent is supported by Aristotle's psychological theory. In particular, it is supported by Aristotle's theories of the human soul and human essence, and his method of teleological explanation. The psychological theory is supported, in turn, by Aristotle's metaphysical doctrines concerning substance, essence, form, and matter (Irwin 1981, 208-211). Thus, Aristotle's moral argument achieves broad coherence. The theory advanced in the *Ethics* is not only supported by coherence between moral principles and moral *endoxa*. Aristotle also defends his theory with his own firmly established metaphysical doctrines.

II

Irwin's conception of Aristotle's method in ethics is subtle and complex. He recognizes that the explicit account of method in the *Ethics* precludes the view that Aristotle directly infers his moral principles from his metaphysics. For the explicit account reveals that Aristotle's moral argument takes the form of a dialectical movement from moral *endoxa* to moral principles, and then a movement back from the moral principles to explain (and thus defend) the initial moral *endoxa* (*EN* 1095a30-1095b8, 1098b9-12, 1145b2-7, 1179a20-23; cf. *EE* 1216b26-35, 1235b13-18). Irwin does not appear to ignore this evidence. Instead, he seems to formulate his argument for the metaphysical foundation hypothesis in a way that accomodates it. He suggests that Aristotle's implicit interlocutor (in the dialectical move from moral *endoxa* to moral principles) is a broad rational agent; and since the concept of a broad rational agent can be defended with Aristotle's own psychological and metaphysical doctrines, Irwin is able to conclude that the argument of the *Ethics* is both metaphysically grounded and 'dialectical throughout' (Irwin 1981, 208).

But Irwin's interpretation does not accomodate all of the textual evidence. Aristotle has a distinctly negative attitude toward using metaphysical (or physical) doctrines to support ethical conclusions: Whenever his argument in the *Ethics* approaches an issue that falls within the sphere of another science, he immediately redirects the course of the discussion, often with the reminder that the issue is οὐκ οἰκεῖος (not appropriate) or ἀλλότριος (foreign) to the argument (*EN* 1096b30-31, 1155b8-9, *EE* 1217a2, 9-10; cf. *EN* 1102a23-32, 1178a22-23). Now what explanation are we to give for this attitude? Perhaps we should recall Aristotle's well-known doctrine of the autonomy of distinct branches of philosophical knowledge (sometimes called the doctrine of 'the autonomy of the sciences'). According to this doctrine, each rational discipline, or science, has its own special principles which function as explanations or 'reasons' for the *phainomena* 'appropriate' to that discipline (*Post. An.* 72a5-7, 74b24-26; *Meta.* 1064b17-23; *Gen. An.* 748a8-12; *Rhet.* 1358a3-32). Separate domains of inquiry have different questions, methods, and goals; thus, irrelevancy and confusion result from approaching issues appropriate to one domain of inquiry with arguments, explanations, or goals peculiar to another. Consequently, if Aristotle were to incorporate his metaphysical and psychological doctrines into the defense of his moral principles, as Irwin suggests, he would contradict the doctrine of the autonomy of the sciences, a doctrine he espouses throughout the Corpus.

Irwin tries to avoid this result by arguing that we should understand the doctrine of the autonomy of the sciences to apply only to demonstrative sciences (Irwin 1981, 222-223). He points out, first, that since the principles of Aristotle's demonstrative sciences must be self-evident, grasped by intuition without inferential justification, they cannot require justifications based on inferences from the principles of other disciplines. And secondly, he reminds us that Aristotle's argument in the *Ethics* 'requires an appeal outside ethics for the justification of ethical principles' (Irwin 1981, 223). But Irwin's first claim, if accepted, implies only that the demonstrative sciences must be autonomous—it implies absolutely nothing about Aristotle's moral philosophy. So the conclusion of Irwin's argument depends, crucially, on the truth of his second claim. But as I noted at the beginning of this paper, even if we grant that Aristotle's moral argument requires a metaphysical foundation, it does not follow that *Aristotle* thinks his argument requires such a foundation. Still less does it follow that Aristotle (therefore) rejects the autonomy of moral philosophy.

Aristotle never claims that the doctrine of the autonomy of the sciences is restricted to the demonstrative sciences, and his consistent practice of shelving metaphysical issues in the *Ethics* strongly suggests that he does not so restrict it. Moreover, an examination of relevant passages of the *Ethics* shows why Aristotle *should* preserve the autonomy of moral theory.

The branch of philosophy under which Aristotle places his inquiry in the *Ethics* is πολιτική. But πολιτική, according to Aristotle does not even belong in the same general area of knowledge as metaphysics: πολιτική is a *practical* science, the goal of which is to evoke certain types of conduct, while metaphysics is a *theoretical* science, the goal of which is a true and precise account of reality (*EN* 1095a5, 1103b27, *EE* 1216b11-25, *Meta*. 993b19-23, 1025b19-28). In the *Ethics*, Aristotle not only recognizes, but emphasizes, this fundamental difference between these areas of philosophy. And what he says indicates specifically why metaphysical inquiry should not be brought into the argument for moral principles. He uses an important analogy to defend his position:

> But we must also remember what we said before and not look for ἀκρίβεια (precision) in all things alike, but in each [a precision] consistent with the subject-matter, and as much as is οἰκεῖον (appropriate) to the investigation. For a carpenter and a geometer investigate the right angle differently: The carpenter [investigates] as far as it is useful for his work, but the geometer [investigates] τί ἐστιν (what-it-is) or ποῖόν τι (what-sort-of-thing) it is; for he is a spectator of the truth. Thus we must act in the same way in other matters as well, so that τὰ πάρεργα (the appendices) do not become the greater part of our work. (*EN* 1098a26-33)

Here Aristotle associates ἀκρίβεια with investigations into the nature of things, i.e., metaphysical investigations. Elsewhere he insists that we should not expect to find ἀκρίβεια in moral investigations (e.g., *EN* 1094b12-28, 1102a23-26, 1103b34-1104a11). Therefore, if investigations into the nature of things are ἀκριβής (precise), and investigations into how we should act are not ἀκριβής, Aristotle has good reason to keep these types of investigation separate.

The passage I have quoted reveals Aristotle's true conception of the relationship between moral and metaphysical inquiries. Contrary to Irwin, Aristotle does not think that the success of his moral theory is essentially dependent upon his own metaphysical doctrines. He tells us that metaphysical discussions should be regarded as τὰ πάρεργα, mere 'appendices' ('asides', or details 'subordinate') to his discussion in ethics; and whatever specific account we give of this claim, it is certainly not the sort of claim a philosopher would make if he is concerned about supplying a metaphysical foundation for his ethics.[6]

Irwin's rejection of autonomy for Aristotle's moral theory allows him to argue that Aristotle appeals to his own psychological doctrines to support his ethical principles. He supposes that the account of the human soul in the *Ethics* is derived from the theory defended in *De Anima* (Irwin 1978, 271n28). But this does not square with what Aristotle tells us. Aristotle tells us that for the argument of the *Ethics* he 'must use' an account of the soul given ἐν τοῖς ἐξωτερικοῖς λόγοις, 'in the exoteric discourses' (*EN* 1102a26-27). It is debated whether 'exoteric discourses' refers to Aristotle's own more popular writings, or the writings of other philosophers, or simply common discussions of a given topic. But whichever one of these views is correct, it is clear that Aristotle's account of the soul in the *Ethics* is *not* drawn from his own scientific treatises (the so-called 'esoteric discourses'). It is also clear that the conception of the soul in the *Ethics* is based on *endoxa*. For if 'exoteric discourses' refers to his popular writings, then Aristotle is directing his arguments to a popular audience and, hence, should be reasoning from the views of the many (cf. *Top*. 101a31-34). And if the phrase refers to the accounts of other philosophers (e.g., the Platonists), or to widespread discussions of the topic, then it is undeniable that Aristotle's reasoning is based (directly) on received views.

III

I want now to challenge the central premise of Irwin's view, *viz.*, that Aristotle needs (and recognizes the need) to appeal to his metaphysical doctrines to defend his moral principles. My contention is that Aristotle uses a purely autonomous dialectical method in ethics. Unlike Irwin's method of 'broad coherence', a purely autonomous dialectical method does not imply that Aristotle appeals (or thinks he *needs* to appeal) directly to his own metaphysical views to give adequate support to his moral theory. This is not to say, however, that an autonomous dialectical argument in ethics cannot rely on propositions, beliefs, or presuppositions which one might label 'metaphysical'. But it is to say that if Aristotle uses any such proposition or doctrine in his argument, he does so *for the reason that* it is a received opinion of a certain kind—or it constitutes a necessary, and perhaps, generally acknowledged, condition of moral inquiry—*not because* it expresses *a pre-established metaphysical truth* or *metaphysical knowledge*.[7] I call this method 'autonomous dialectic' because the principles it establishes within a particular domain of philosophical inquiry will not depend, necessarily, on doctrines already proved within other domains of inquiry. And thus, in so far as Aristotle employs this method in the *Ethics*, he will preserve the independence of moral theory.

Let us begin with the subject matter of Aristotelian dialectic—τὰ ἔνδοξα (*ta endoxa*). Irwin translates ἔνδοξα as 'common beliefs'. But there is fairly strong evidence to suggest that ἔνδοξα literally means 'reputable things' and that Aristotle does not depart from this ordinary sense of the term.[8] To collect τὰ ἔνδοξα, then, is to collect the reputable views. In response to the question of what views are to count as reputable, Aristotle answers: 'the opinions of everyone or the majority or the wise—that is, the opinions held by all, most people, or those who are especially notable and reputable' (*Top.* 100b21-23). These opinions are either explicit or implicit.[9] They are explicit when men assert them or, under suitable circumstances, would assert them, i.e., when they count clearly as τὰ λεγόμενα, things people (would) say (*EN* 1145b2-7; cf. 1145b20 and 1152b23-24). They are implicit when: (1) they are propositions implied by, or closely connected to, our explicit opinions (e.g., *Top.* 104a13-33 and 105b1-10; cf. *EN* 1095b26-31), (2) they are revealed by the actions we perform or the kinds of lives we lead (e.g., *EN* i 5; cf. 1113b21-26, 1153b25f., 1172b35-1173a5), or (3) they are manifested by semantic or syntactic features of our language (e.g., *Top.* 105a25-31, 108a18-20, 112a32-38, 118a34-39; cf. *EN* 1103a17-20, 1111b26-30. See, also, Barnes 1980, 501).

There is a further distinction between τὰ ἔνδοξα which requires emphasis. Certain *endoxa* have, *ab initio*, greater probative force than others. This distinction holds prior to the process of cross-examination: It is not merely the difference between *endoxa* which generate puzzles and those that do not. It is the difference between *endoxa* which cannot be abandoned and those which can. The sense in which I mean 'cannot be abandoned' may be revealed by reflecting, first, on Aristotle's dialectical defense of the Principle of Non-Contradiction. Aristotle attempts to persuade his interlocutor of this principle, and ultimately his notions of substance and essence, with an argument that relies only on what the interlocutor concedes (*Meta.* iv 4 and xi 5). If the interlocutor asserts something significant (or refers to some definite object) and concedes that he has done so, Aristotle thinks he can lead him to accept some version or application of the Principle of Non-Contradiction. If, on the other hand, the interlocutor refuses to make a significant assertion, then he ceases to be a participant in a discussion. In so far as he refuses to speak of anything, he is like a vegetable, and Aristotle reminds us that there is nothing to be gained by arguing with vegetables. Thus, the assertion of something significant—or reference to something definite—and, ultimately, the Principle of Non-Contradiction itself could be abandoned only at the cost of eliminating significant speech and thought. And Aristotle can fairly argue that this is a cost even the skeptic may find too severe to accept.

Irwin recognizes that this is a dialectical argument, and a persuasive dialectical argument. Moreover, he goes on to point out that Aristotle's defense of his psychological theory is also dialectical, and also quite persuasive. In fact, Irwin shows that Aristotle's argument for his psychological theory has the same form as Aristotle's defense of the Principle of Non-Contradiction. He maintains that the *endoxa* Aristotle relies on in the argument for the psychological theory can be abandoned only at the cost of eliminating teleological explanation, but this form of explanation can be shown to be necessary for the correct understanding of nature. Although these psychological *endoxa* are not quite as indispensable as certain metaphysical *endoxa*, they are, according to Irwin, evidently strong enough to compel the assent of a skeptic.

But when Irwin moves to Aristotle's moral philosophy, he breaks off this pattern of analysis. He assumes that Aristotle would not find a purely dialectical argument acceptable for ethics. But why should we assume this? Are there no useful moral *endoxa* which Aristotle would find 'especially hard to reject', as Irwin puts it? Are there no moral *endoxa* whose abandonment is as costly for moral theory as the abandonment of certain psychological *endoxa* is for the philosophy of mind? Let us grant, for the sake of argument, that any such moral *endoxa* would not be as indispensable as the psychological *endoxa*, and even less indispensable than the metaphysical *endoxa*. Even so, Aristotle may believe that there are certain moral *endoxa* which can be abandoned only at the cost of eliminating moral philosophy; and for those who wish to participate in the life of a community, the rejection of rational discourse about how men should act and organize their political systems is clearly unacceptable.

Let us now consider Aristotle's argument for the first principle of the *Ethics*—the definition of the human good. I would like to use an analysis of this argument to illustrate what I take to be the structure of Aristotle's method of moral reasoning. According to this view, Aristotle *does* believe that there are certain purely moral *endoxa* which are 'especially hard to reject', and these *endoxa* play an important part in his moral argument.

I refer to the moral *endoxa* that cannot be (easily) abandoned as 'deep *endoxa*', and those that can be abandoned as 'surface *endoxa*'. For the most part, surface *endoxa* purport to give substantive answers to ethical questions, such as 'What is the good?' There is considerable disagreement about the right answer to a question like this, so there are numerous conflicting surface *endoxa*. Some say that the good is pleasure, others that it is honor, or virtue, or intelligence, and so on (e.g., *EN* 1095a22-25, 1095b14-1096a10, 1097b2). Deep *endoxa*, on the other hand, do not purport to give substantive answers to ethical questions. They provide the framework within which such answers are to be sought, and hence function as criteria for acceptable principles and definitions. In contrast to the surface *endoxa*, there is considerable agreement about the reputable views which count as deep. Among the wise, the agreement is often explicit. But the majority may only agree implicitly, by holding, for example, explicit opinions which entail or suggest the deep *endoxa*, or by acting in a way which reveals that they unconsciously embrace the deep *endoxa* (or by acting, and judging, in conformity with the deep *endoxa*, whether or not they consciously or unconsciously embrace them).

Aristotle argues for his definition of the human good in three stages. First, he identifies several deep *endoxa* about the good. These include: (1) the good is that at which all things (or all things with intelligence) aim (*EN* 1094a2-3; cf. 1172b14-15), (2) the good is a complete end, i.e., an end which we choose always for its own sake and never for the sake of something else (1097a25-34), and (3) the good is self-sufficient, i.e., attainment of the good implies attainment of everything essential to living well (1097b6-21; cf. 1169b5-6, 1172b26-35, *EE* 1215b15-1216a10, 1244b1-11). It is beyond question that Aristotle regards these propositions as moral *endoxa*.[10] That they are deep moral *endoxa* is clear from the following considerations. First, they are criteria for an adequate definition of the good, not proposals for such a definition. Moreover, unlike most surface *endoxa*, they enjoy nearly universal assent; and Aristotle does not regard them as problematic in the way that he regards the surface *endoxa* as problematic. They are never subjected to dialectical examination, but seem, rather, to guide that examination—they function as *constraints* on the argument for the first principle. Consider, finally, Aristotle's response to those who would deny the view that the good is that at which all things aim: 'When some object that what everything aims at is not good, surely they are talking nonsense. For what seems to all, that, we say, is; and one who destroys confidence in these things, will hardly have anything more credible to say' (*EN* 1172b35-1173a2). This is exactly the sort of response we should expect Aristotle to give if he takes the view in question to be a deep moral *endoxon*. For the rejection of deep moral *endoxa* undermines the possibility of moral inquiry and debate (*just as* the rejection of certain deep metaphysical *endoxa* undermines the possibility of all speech and thought).

Along with the deep *endoxa*, Aristotle brings into view the surface *endoxa* about the good. The good is identified with honor, pleasure, intelligence, and virtue. But these views fail to satisfy the deep *endoxa* for none of the things with which they identify the good are complete, self-sufficient, or the aim of all things (*EN* 1097a4-1097b6, 1102a2-4). All believe, however, that εὐδαιμονία (*eudaimonia*, happiness) accords with the deep *endoxa*. But this fails to settle the issue. Aristotle wants a definition of the good, not its common label.

Therefore, the second stage of Aristotle's argument is to establish a definition of the good. The argument begins with the idea that one's concept of the good of a thing is always connected to the notion of the ἔργον (*ergon*, work) of that thing. The first prem ise rests squarely on a dialectical induction: 'For just as a flute-player, a sculptor, or any artist, and, in general, for all things that have an *ergon* or action, the good and the well δοκεῖ (is believed) to reside in the *ergon*, so it would seem to be for man. . .' (*EN* 1097b25-28). Aristotle goes on to claim that the ἴδιον (unique) work of man must involve the activity of reason, for a simple survey of the activities of the various animate beings reveals that reason is a peculiar characteristic of man. The next premise connects the *ergon* of a *good* thing with ἀρετή (excellence). Aristotle points out that φαμέν (we say) that an X and a good X have an *ergon* which is specifically the same (1098a8-9). He defends this view with a παράδειγμα (model) of how 'we' speak: A lyre-player and a good lyre-player have the same *ergon*, '*and so* without qualification in all cases' (the *ergon* of an X and a good X are the same) (1098a9-10). However, 'we' attribute ἀρετή to the *ergon* of a good X (1098a11-12). The *ergon* of a lyre-player is simply to play the lyre, but one adds the qualification 'to do so well' to the *ergon* of the good lyre-player. The final premise of the argument is a special application of this principle to the *ergon* of the good man. Since the *ergon* of man is an activity of the rational part of the soul, the *ergon* of the *good* man is to perform this activity well (1098a15). Aristotle's definition of the good, and the first principle of his moral philosophy, follows immediately: 'human good turns out to be activity of soul in accordance with excellence, and if there are several excellences, in accordance with the best and most complete' (1098a16-18).

The first principle of Aristotle's moral philosophy follows from the preceding argument, not from Aristotle's ultimate metaphysical principles. Irwin maintains, however, that this argument constitutes *evidence* for the metaphysical foundation hypothesis (Irwin 1978, 261; 1980, 48-49; 1981, 216n31). Undoubtedly, many scholars would be inclined to agree with him. Monan, for example, contends that by identifying the good with the activity of man's *ergon*, Aristotle makes the good 'intrinsically relative to man's distinctive nature. . . and as a result of this identification, he has made it necessary to seek in speculative psychology for the distinctive nature of man, *as a means* to discovering the genuine realization of the notion of happiness' (Monan 1968, 107).

But the question at hand is whether there is good reason to believe that *Aristotle thinks it is necessary* to support the *ergon* argument with his own metaphysical principles. The answer to this question cannot be based merely on the fact that the premises of this argument include claims about human nature. For these premises may, nevertheless, be formulations of *endoxa*, and *endoxa* of a sort that Aristotle (and his contemporaries) would readily accept as premises for dialectical debates in ethics. Now, the precursor of Aristotle's argument is clearly the Socratic elenchus (dialectical refutation) of Thrasymachus at the end of *Republic* i (352e-354b). Moreover, near the beginning of the corresponding argument in the *Eudemian Ethics*, Aristotle tells us that his reasoning follows the pattern of an ἐπαγωγή (induction) (1218b38-1219a6). We should recall that for Aristotle, induction is one of the two main forms of dialectical argument (*Top.* 105a13-14). An example of such an argument is presented for students of dialectic at *Topics* 105a14-17; and it exhibits precisely the same structure as the core of the *ergon* argument. Thus, there is evidence for the view that Aristotle is forging the *ergon* argument directly out of traditional, and perhaps deeply entrenched, Greek moral concepts and familiar patterns of moral theorizing.

Irwin may object that Aristotle *can* support the *ergon* argument with his ontology, and thus the argument is not 'merely dialectical' (cf. Irwin 1981, 211-212). But even if we grant that the *ergon* argument *can* be defended with Aristotle's metaphysics, much more needs to be done to show that Aristotle *does* so defend it. Perhaps an interesting story may be told about how the metaphysical basis of the *Ethics* lies in the shadows, but it is difficult to see why such a basis for the *Ethics would* lie in the shadows. For Irwin insists that Aristotle recognizes that he *must* supply a metaphysical foundation for his ethics. But if this were the case, we would surely expect Aristotle at least to sketch the main lines of this foundation in the *Ethics*. That he does not is certainly evidence against the metaphysical foundation hypothesis. And what he does is certainly a problem for those who defend this hypothesis: The premises of the *ergon* argument are all explicitly linked to *what we say* or *what we believe*. And the conclusion of the argument follows deductively from premises reached through inductions based upon reputable beliefs.

Having reached the definition of the good through this process, Aristotle looks to the *endoxa* once more in order to test the adequacy of his definition. The test consists in showing that the definition captures, in some fashion, much of what people say about the good and *eudaimonia*: That the good is an activity and falls among goods of the soul, not external goods; that the *eudaimôn* lives well and does well; that *eudaimonia* involves virtue, practical wisdom, theoretical wisdom, and entails pleasure and even the posesssion of some external goods (*NE* i 8). Although surface *endoxa* may have been eliminated as adequate definitions of the good, it is important to show that the correct definition is not entirely foreign to them (1098b9-12). There are at least three reasons for this. First, and most importantly, the surface *endoxa* make up most of the *phainomena* which the first principle is intended to *explain* (cf. *EE* 1216b27-34, *EN* 1145b2-7). This explanatory function of the first principle is noted by Irwin, but I do not think it is sufficiently appreciated by him. For an autonomous dialectic in ethics does appear likely to convince us of the truth of a moral principle if it can be shown that only that principle is able to account for the various apparently conflicting *endoxa*. Aristotle's ethical first principle receives justification beyond the views it explains precisely because, he argues, it alone is able to explain them.

Second, and connected to this point, Aristotle believes that it is unlikely that all, or even most substantive conceptions of the good are radically false, i.e., have no connection whatever to the true account (*EN* 1098b26-30). If they were radically false, then no true account would be possible in the first place, since we ascend to the first principles by means of an examination of the *phainomena*. What is more, it is just implausible to think that everyone is completely off the mark. In the first place, we know that it is natural for men to strive for the truth, and nature does nothing in vain (*Meta*. 980a21, *EE* 1216b31, *Rhet*.. 1355a15). But secondly, and I think crucially, Aristotle may reasonably ask how one could persuasively argue that all (or most) of our substantive moral beliefs are mistaken. For such an argument would have to achieve two apparently incompatible goals—the wholesale (or nearly wholesale) rejection of our moral conceptual scheme, and the establishment of convincing principles of morality. It seems that a persuasive moral theory needs to be developed out of a particular moral tradition—to relinquish that tradition is, at once, to relinquish the possibility of giving an effective (or perhaps, even a comprehensible) moral argument. Finally, the ultimate goal of moral philosophy is to elicit certain types of conduct from people (*EN* 1095a5, 1103b27, 1179a35; cf. *EE* 1216b11-25, *MM* 1182a1-7). So if the definition proposed explains why commonly held beliefs are false, but not farfetched, it is likely to secure the type of conviction which helps to produce such conduct.

If the foregoing account is a roughly accurate picture of a purely autonomous Aristotelian dialectic, then it does not seem subject to Irwin's objection that it is a patently indefensible method of working towards true first principles. For it escapes the ground for the objection, that the method implies that a principle is true merely when it generates a consistent set of common opinions. The method suggests, rather, that we are justified in believing a moral principle is true when (1) we examine all of the reputable formulations of such a principle, (2) we dispose of those formulations which conflict with strongly defensible criteria for the principle, (3) we argue from reputable beliefs to a principle which satisfies these criteria, (4) we show that our principle better *explains* substantive moral opinions than any other extant proposal, and (5) no counterargument is offered to upset our account. If this is an indefensible method of doing moral philosophy, it is surely not patently indefensible. Indeed, it seems that not a few contemporary moral theorists use and defend a method similar to this.[11] And if this method is not patently indefensible, and Aristotle's explicit account of method, as well as his practice, reflects it, then Irwin requires other arguments to defend the metaphysical foundation hypothesis.[12]

Memphis State University

NOTES

[1] The claim is undisputed. For a detailed analysis of a substantial part of the explicit account, see Barnes 1980. There are also helpful discussions in Burnet 1900, xxxi-xlvi, Greenwood [1909] 1973, 127-144, Owen 1961, 85-91, le Blond 1973, 42-47, Wieland 1970, 202-230, Monan 1961, 247-271, Monan 1968, 96-115, and Cooper 1975, 67-71.

[2] Hardie 1968, 38-45, Cooper 1975, 155-180, Monan 1961, 261-271, Monan 1968, 72n and 96-115, and Irwin (see n3 for references).

[3] Irwin 1978, 252-272, Irwin 1980, 35-53, and Irwin 1981, 193-223.

[4] The notion of a 'purely autonomous dialectic' will be explained later in this paper.

[5] Nearly a century ago, Burnet 1900, v, insisted that Aristotle's moral methodology is 'dialectical throughout'. Reaction to this claim has been nothing less than vicious. It has been called 'les hypothèses les plus absurdes' by Gauthier and Jolif 1959, I.1, 88. And Hardie 1968, 36, scornfully refers to it as 'Burnet's paradox'. I am inclined to think that these types of response are motivated at least as much by Burnet's (and possibly some of his critics') views on the nature of Aristotelian dialectic, as they are by the nominal claim itself. Burnet, along with others of his period, seems to have occasionally conflated dialectic with ἐριστικὸς συλλογισμός (contentious reasoning). See Burnet 1900, xvii. Cf. Irwin 1981, 195n3 and Cooper 1975, 69n97.

[6] This point should be considered along with the fact that Aristotle rarely notes any connection between a discussion in the *Ethics* and a discussion in another part of the Corpus. And when he does refer to discussions outside of the *Ethics*, he never indicates that they are *needed* to support the arguments being advanced (cf. *EN* 1096b7-8, 30-31, 1139b26-27, 31-33, 1174b2-3). Now a reference to a non-ethical treatise is a natural place to find textual evidence for Aristotle's alleged reliance on his metaphysical doctrines in the *Ethics*. But Aristotle never even suggests in such places that the discussions to which he refers are essential to the defense of his moral principles. It is difficult to believe Aristotle recognizes that he *must* appeal to his metaphysical principles in order successfully to defend his moral principles when he consistently fails to indicate this.

[7] It is possible that Aristotle argues from certain received opinions in the *Ethics* which also happen to be metaphysical views he would endorse. Indeed, one would hope that any metaphysical assumptions in the *Ethics* are consistent with Aristotle's own metaphysics. And in fact I believe this is the case. But if Aristotle relies on such opinions in his moral argument, it does not follow that he does so because he believes his *own* metaphysical doctrines must be used to support his ethics. It may be useful to illustrate this point. Irwin contends that Aristotle employs the concept of a 'broad rational agent' in his moral argument *in order to* ground his ethics on his firmly established metaphysical principles. I deny this, but not because Aristotle fails to assume that his interlocutor in the *Ethics* is a broad rational agent. I deny it because Aristotle assumes his interlocutor is such an agent for the simple reason that people generally think of themselves in this way. Aristotle's goal in the *Ethics* is to persuade his audience to accept his moral principles. Since it is implausible to think his audience does *not* already believe that people are broad rational agents, it is clear that Aristotle does not need to appeal to his own metaphysical doctrines to persuade his audience. And it is difficult to see how Irwin would reply to this argument, for he readily admits that the concept of a broad rational agent 'rests on fairly firm and undisputed' received opinions (Irwin 1981, 211-212).

[8] The evidence, which consists mainly in Greek usage and etymology, is expertly presented by Barnes 1980, 498-500. Here one may note that the inadequacy of rendering *endoxa* simply as 'common beliefs' seems to be suggested by Aristotle's procedure in the *Ethics* itself. The Socratic doctrine that there is no such thing as incontinence might be an *endoxon* for Aristotle (cf. *EN* 1145b2-7 and 1145b21-31). Furthermore, the Platonic theory of transcendent Forms is included among the opinions which Aristotle claims ἐξετάζειν (to examine: *EN* 1095a25-30). The procedure and language here reminds us of the initial process of collecting *endoxa* for dialectical scrutiny. But neither the Socratic doctrine, nor the Platonic theory, can reasonably be thought a *common* belief. Since they are advanced by 'the wise', however, they certainly count as *reputable* beliefs. Cf. *Top*. 104b18-105a2.

[9] I owe this point to Barnes 1980, 501-502.

[10] (1) 'The good is that at which all things aim' is used by Plato at *Resp*. 505e, *Phlb*. 20d and 60a, *Grg*. 499e, and *Symp*. 206a. It appears at *EN* 1172b14-15 in Aristotle's statement of one of Eudoxos' arguments for the identity of pleasure and the good. Most significantly, Aristotle includes it among τόποι (argument patterns) to be used in dialectical and rhetorical debate: *Top*. 116a19-20, *Rhet*. 1362a23, 1363a8-9, 1363b14, 1365a1. (2) The precursor of Aristotle's concept of a strictly complete end is found in Plato, *Resp*. 375a-358a (cf. *Leg*. 697b-c and *Phlb*. 20d-e, 22b, 61a, and 67a). Eudoxos uses the notion in another argument for the identity of pleasure and the good (cf. *EN* 1172b20-23). And again, Aristotle includes the view in his lists of

τόποι and premises of enthymemes: *Top*. 116a29-30, 116b22-23, 118b25-26, 116b37-39, *Rhet*. 1363b12f., 1364a1-5 (cf. 1362a21f., *Pol*. 1280b40-1281a3, *MM* 1184b7-10, *EN* 1176b30-31). (3) The self-sufficiency of the good life (or happiness) is regarded as unproblematic by Plato (cf. *Lysis* 215a-b, *Phlb*. 20d-e, 22b, 60b-e, 67a). Aristotle clearly regards it as a received opinion and thus a principle on which dialectical and rhetorical proofs can be based: Compare *EN* 1097b6-21 with 1172b26-35; also see *Top*. 117a16-18, *Rhet*. 1362b10-12, 1360b14f., 1360b19-29, 1362a21-29, 1363b12-21.

[11] For example, Rawls 1971, 46-53 and 1974, 5-22; Daniels 1979, 256-282 and 1980, 83-103.

[12] I am grateful to Michael Wedin, John Malcolm, and Alan Code for tough criticism during the earliest stage of my thoughts about Aristotle's moral methodology. The penultimate draft of this paper was very profitably discussed with Alasdair MacIntyre, Richard Kraut, and my colleagues, Terry Horgan, David Hiley, and Tom Nenon. I also thank Ronald Polansky and two anonymous referees for *Ancient Philosophy*. They provided me with helpful suggestions for improving the essay.

BIBLIOGRAPHY

Barnes, J. 1980. 'Aristotle and the Methods of Ethics' *Revue Internationale de Philosophie* **34** 490-511.

le Blond, J.M. 1973. *Logique et méthode chez Aristote*. Paris: J. Vrin.

Burnet, J. 1900. *The Ethics of Aristotle*. London: Methuen.

Cooper, J. 1975. *Reason and Human Good in Aristotle*. Cambridge, MA: Harvard University Press.

Daniels, J. 1979. 'Wide Reflective Equilibrium and Theory Acceptance in Ethics' *Journal of Philosophy* **76** 256-282.

Daniels, J. 1980. 'Reflective Equilibrium and Archimedean Points' *Canadian Journal of Philosophy* **10** 83-103.

Gauthier, R.A. and J.Y Jolif. 1958-1959. *L'éthique à Nicomaque tome I*. Paris/Louvain: Beatrice-Nauwelaerts, Publications Universitaires de Louvain.

Greenwood, L.H.G. [1909] 1973. *Aristotle, Nicomachean Ethics Book Six*. rep. New York: Arno Press.

Hardie, W.F.R. 1968. *Aristotle's Ethical Theory*. Oxford: The Clarendon Press.

Irwin, T.H. 1978. 'First Principles in Aristotle's Ethics' in P.A. French, *et. al*. edd. *Studies in Ethical Theory*. Vol. 3, *Midwest Studies in Philosophy* 252-272. Morris: University of Minnesota Press.

Irwin, T.H. 1980. 'The Metaphysical and Psychological Basis of Aristotle's Ethics' in A.O. Rorty ed. *Essays on Aristotle's Ethics* 35-53. Berkeley/Los Angeles/London: University of California Press.

Irwin, T.H. 1981. 'Aristotle's Methods of Ethics' in D.J. O'Meara ed. *Studies in Aristotle*. Vol. 9, *Studies in Philosophy and the History of Philosophy* 193-223. Washington, DC: The Catholic University of America Press.

Mansion, S. ed. 1961. *Aristote et les problèmes de méthode*. Paris/Louvain: Beatrice-Nauwelaerts, Publications Universitaires de Louvain.

Monan, J.D. 1961. 'Two Methodological Aspects of Moral Knowledge in the *Nicomachean Ethics*' 247-271 in Mansion ed. 1961.

Monan, J.D. 1968. *Moral Knowledge and its Methodology in Aristotle*. Oxford: The Clarendon Press.

Owen, G.E.L. 1961. '*Tithenai ta Phainomena*' 83-103 in Mansion ed. 1961.

Rawls, J. 1971. *A Theory of Justice*. Cambridge, MA: Harvard University Press.

Rawls, J. 1974. 'The Independence of Moral Theory' *Proceedings and Addresses of the American Philosophical Association* **48** 5-22.

Wieland, W. 1970. *Die aristotelische Physik*. 2nd ed. Göttingen: Vandenhoeck und Ruprecht.

The Philosophical Review, LXXXVIII, No. 2 (April 1979).

TWO CONCEPTIONS OF HAPPINESS

Richard Kraut

I

In this paper, I want to contrast two ways of judging whether people are leading happy lives: Aristotle's and our own. I will argue that there are some striking similarities between these two conceptions of happiness. To live happily, for both Aristotle and for us, is to have certain attitudes towards one's life, and to measure up to certain standards. Where we and Aristotle sharply disagree is over the standards to be used in evaluating lives. Roughly, he insists on an objective and stringent standard, whereas our test is more subjective and flexible. I will also argue that we have good reason to reject his conception of happiness, for his standards can be employed only by those who know things we do not. If we ever acquired such knowledge, we might make judgments about happiness that are like the ones Aristotle makes in the *Nicomachean Ethics*. We would, in other words, drop our present conception of happiness and adopt something like his.

The approach I am taking to this subject differs from the usual one. Scholars and philosophers who study the *Ethics* often claim that Aristotle has no conception of happiness at all, in our sense of the word. They notice that when his term *eudaimonia* receives the traditional translation, "happiness," a number of his points sound dubious and even silly. For example, he is made to say that everything should be sought for the sake of happiness, and that children and evil adults are never happy because they have not developed such traits as justice, courage, and self-control. Furthermore, *eudaimonia* does not name a feeling or emotion, whereas we think that happiness is, or at least involves, a certain state of mind. And so we are warned, for example, by Henry Sidgwick, that the word "happiness" that we find in translations of Artistotle does not have its contemporary meaning in English.[1] Occasionally a different translation is proposed:

[1] *The Methods of Ethics*, 7th edn. (London, 1907), pp. 92–93.

W. D. Ross suggests "well-being"[2] (despite the fact that he sticks to "happiness" in the Oxford edition of the *Ethics*); John Cooper proposes "flourishing."[3] The idea is that we should assign a meaning to *eudaimonia* that makes Aristotle disagree with us as little as possible. Since we believe that some children definitely are happy, and that some evil people might very well be, Aristotle's *eudaimonia* cannot mean "happiness" in its usual sense.

I think this approach rests on an oversimplified view both of happiness and of *eudaimonia.* Sidgwick makes the dubious claim that our term is "commonly used in Bentham's way as convertible with Pleasure."[4] Ross tells us that " 'happiness' means a state of feeling, differing from 'pleasure' only by its suggestion of permanence, depth and serenity."[5] And Cooper says that it "tends to be taken as referring exclusively to a subjective psychological state."[6] The common error here is the belief that the only thing we mean when we judge a person happy is that he is in a certain state of mind. As I will argue, we often mean something more than this: we are saying that the individual is happy because his life meets a certain standard (a subjective one). Furthermore, when Aristotle calls someone *eudaimon,* he means not only that the individual meets a certain standard (an objective one), but that he is in a certain state of mind—the very same state we say people are in when we call them happy. To think that happiness just involves a psychological condition and that *eudaimonia* does not is to get both concepts wrong.

It is an illusion, at any rate, to think that we foster a better understanding of Aristotle if we use "well-being" or "flourish-

[2] *Aristotle: A Complete Exposition of His Works and Thought,* Meridian edn. (Cleveland, 1959), p. 186. Unless otherwise noted, quotations are from the Ross translation.

[3] *Reason and Human Good in Aristotle*, (Cambridge, Massachusetts, 1975), pp. 89-90, n. 1. Cooper says that "happiness" is not a good translation since "much that Aristotle says about *eudaimonia* manifestly fails to hold true of happiness as ordinarily understood." (Ibid.) To support this point, he calls attention to Aristotle's claim at 1100*a*1-4 that a child can be called *eudaimon* only in the expectation that he will achieve *eudaimonia* as an adult.

[4] Op. cit., p. 92.

[5] Op. cit., p. 186.

[6] Op. cit., p. 89, n. 1.

ing" as translations of *eudaimonia,* rather than "happiness." If we use these words, Aristotle will be made to say that children and evil men do not attain well-being, or do not flourish. Are these claims any more plausible than the ones they are supposed to replace? If a young tree can flourish in the right conditions, why not a young person?[7] Why say that well-being is beyond the reach of children and evil people? Certainly we do things for their well-being—don't we ever succeed?

We could of course leave *eudaimonia* untranslated and let its meaning be gathered from the statements Aristotle makes about it. But that would leave unanswered a question I think we should ask: When we say that a person is leading a happy life, and Aristotle says that the same person is not *eudaimon,* do we have anything to argue about? I think we do. As I will try to show, the conception of *eudaimonia* in the *Nicomachean Ethics* is best interpreted as a challenge to the way we go about judging people to be happy. If we were convinced that what Aristotle says about *eudaimonia* is true, we would no longer believe that children or

---

[7] It would be desirable, in translating Aristotle's *eudaimonia,* to find an English expression that plays pretty much the same role in our language that *eudaimonia* played in his. On this score, "flourishing" is quite inadequate:

A. Eudaimon and its cognates were everyday words that occurred frequently not only in philosophical works, but also in Greek drama, oratory and poetry. Our term "flourishing" is less common. If a student in a philosophy course were asked, "What is human flourishing?" his first reaction would be that this is a philosopher's question that has no obvious connection with ordinary life. But when Aristotle asked in his classroom what *eudaimonia* is, his audience immediately recognized this as a common and urgent practical question. (In this respect, asking "what is happiness?" is very much like asking what *eudaimonia* is.)

B. When "flourishing" is used in common speech, it is most often attached to nonhuman subjects: ant colonies, flowers, towns, businesses, etc., are much more likely to be called flourishing than human beings. *Eudaimonia,* on the other hand, is attributed only to human and divine persons. (Notice how odd it would be to say that an animal or plant is leading a happy life. Though dogs and cats can be happy, they still do not lead happy lives; the latter expression has pretty much the same range of application as *eudaimonia.*)

C. When human beings are said to flourish, it is often meant that they flourish in a certain role or activity. For example: artists do not flourish in military dictatorships, pornographers flourish in democracies, and evil men flourish when moral standards are too lax or too strict. Roughly what is meant is that they succeed in these roles under the conditions specified. This common use of the term "flourish" is far from Aristotle's use of *eudaimonia.* When he says that an evil man cannot be *eudaimon* under any conditions, he is hardly denying that evil can flourish.

evil people can be happy. And if we began to make judgments of happiness in the way he makes judgments of *eudaimonia,* we would not be changing the meaning of "happiness."

II

Aristotle thinks that the most *eudaimon* individual is someone who has fully developed and regularly exercises the various virtues of the soul, both intellectual and moral. Such a person engages in philosophical activity (since this is the full flowering of his capacity to reason theoretically) and also in moral activities, which display his justice, generosity, temperance, etc. Though he may experience minor mishaps, he cannot have recently suffered any severe misfortunes, such as the death of close friends or dearly loved children. Aristotle thinks that a virtuous person will make the best of any situation, but that in extreme circumstances *eudaimonia* is lost. It may be regained, but only after a long period of time during which many fine things have been achieved.[8]

Consider such a person—a philosopher and a good man—at a time of life that is not marred by misfortunes. Aristotle thinks he would in these conditions be as *eudaimon* as any human being can be. I want to ask: is he a happy person? Is he in the same psychological state as any individual who is leading a happy life? When we say that someone is living happily, we imply that he has certain attitudes towards his life: he is very glad to be alive; he judges that on balance his deepest desires are being satisfied and that the circumstances of his life are turning out well. Does Aristotle's paradigm of *eudaimonia* have these same attitudes? I think so. For such a person loves the activities he regularly and successfully engages in. He thinks that exercising one's intellectual and moral capacities is the greatest good available to human beings, and he knows he possesses this

[8] This paragraph summarizes views Aristotle puts forward in several parts of the *Ethics:* I 7 1097*b*22–1098*a*20 (the function of man is to act virtuously); I 8 1099*a*31–1099*b*7 and I 9 1100*a*5–9 (the misfortunes that can spoil *eudaimonia*); I 10 1100*b*22–1101*a*13 (only major misfortunes take *eudaimonia* away, and it can be recovered); X 7–8 (the best life is philosophical). See "Aristotle on the Ideal Life" (unpublished) for my defense of the view that for Aristotle the best life combines both philosophical and ethical activities.

good.[9] Furthermore, he has all the other major goods he wants. His desire for such external goals as honor, wealth, and physical pleasure is moderate, and should be easy enough to satisfy in a normal life.[10] If, however, some great misfortune does occur—if, for example, he is totally deprived of honor—then Aristotle insists that he is no longer *eudaimon.*[11] So, the individual who is most *eudaimon* on Aristotle's theory passes our tests for happiness with flying colors. All his major goals are being achieved, to a degree that satisfies him. Knowing this, he greatly enjoys his life and has nothing serious to complain of.

Furthermore, there is a passage in which Aristotle explicitly tells us how a *eudaimon* individual will look upon his life. It occurs in the midst of an involved proof that whoever is *eudaimon* needs friends: "All men desire (life), and particularly those who are good and supremely happy (*makarious*), for to such men life is most desirable, and their existence is the most supremely

[9] As is well known, the virtuous individual does not merely act virtuously: he also chooses such acts for their own sake (II 4 1105*a*30–32), prefers them to everything else (I 10 1100*b*19–20), and realizes he is a good person (IX 9 1170*b*4–9).

[10] For the view that ethical virtue requires moderate desires for external goods, see esp. III 4 1119*a*11–20 and VII 4 1148*a*22–1148*b*4. Aristotle's doctrine that every ethical virtue lies in a mean between two extremes should be distinguished from his belief that desires for external objects should be moderate in strength, though he himself may run these two theses together. For some brief discussion, see J. Urmson, "Aristotle's Doctrine of the Mean," *American Philosophical Quarterly* 10 (July, 1973), esp. pp. 225–226.

[11] "Those who say that the victim on the rack or the man who falls into great misfortunes is happy if he is good, are, whether they mean to or not, talking nonsense" (VII 13 1153*b*19–21). Aristotle presumably does not mean that a brief experience of great physical pain, whatever its cause, is incompatible with *eudaimonia.* Otherwise, pains endured in honorable battle would also deprive someone of *eudaimonia.* No doubt, he is thinking of the rack as an instrument of punishment and therefore disgrace; the victim not only suffers pain, but also a severe loss of honor. To put the point more generally: Some external goods, like honor, are so important that they must be present, to some moderate degree, in any *eudaimon* life, and this is why severe deprivation of such goods is incompatible with *eudaimonia.* Such goods will be desired moderately by whoever understands what *eudaimonia* is, and so those who achieve *eudaimonia* will fully satisfy their desires for these major external goals. If Aristotle had held (1) that a virtuous individual can have ravenous appetites for external goods, and (2) if he had continued to hold that a *eudaimon* life need only contain a moderate amount of such goods, then (3) he would have to accept the conclusion that a *eudaimon* individual can want much more than he has.

happy (*makariōtatē*)" (1170*a*26–29). To put it somewhat differently: one who is good and highly *eudaimon* has an especially strong desire for life, and this psychological condition is based on the perception of how very desirable his life is. Now, when Aristotle says that one who is virtuous and *eudaimon* particularly desires life, he cannot mean that he will struggle to stay alive at any cost. Rather, he must mean that such individuals are more glad to be alive than others; the kind of existence they enjoy gives them a heightened love of life. As Aristotle says elsewhere (1117*b*9–13), these are the people who have the most reason to live, and therefore the thought of death—even death in battle—is especially painful to them. In their attitude towards themselves and their lives, they are the very opposite of the sort of individual who is so miserable and filled with self-hatred that he contemplates suicide (1166*b*11–28). It is undeniable, then, that the *eudaimon* individual, as Aristotle depicts him, is fully satisfied with his life. He is, in other words, a happy person.

There is another way of arriving at this same conclusion. Let us for the moment ignore Aristotle's belief that *eudaimonia* consists in virtuous activity. He has many other convictions about the *eudaimon* life besides this one, and from these alone we can infer that whoever is *eudaimon* must be happy with his life. Consider the following points, all of which Aristotle affirms or presupposes: We human beings are different from plants, in that we would never be able to attain our good with any regularity, unless we had effective desires for what we think is worthwhile. Since we are creatures with strong desires for the good, as we variously conceive it, it is natural and inevitable for us to develop a deep interest in whether or not such desires are being satisfied. An animal with first-order desires, but no strong second-order interest in whether those first-order desires are being fulfilled, would not be fully human. Put otherwise: no person would choose a life in which he remains continually unaware of whether or not he possesses the good; that would be a life befitting plants, not human beings.[12] Now, any deep desire

[12] Aristotle says in a number of places that a life of continual slumber is one no human being would choose, since it is the life of a plant. See *Eudemian Ethics* I 5 1216*a*2-6; *NE* I 5 1095*b*32-35, X 6 1176*a*34-35. The distinction between plants and animals lies in the latter's ability to perceive (*De Anima*

which develops naturally and universally is a desire which must be satisfied, if we are to attain our good. Satisfying that desire is in fact part of our good.[13] So a major human good is the second-order good which consists in the perception that our major first-order desires are being satisfied. And this second-order good is one we must have in order to be *eudaimon,* since a *eudaimon* life can have no serious deficiency (1097*b*14–15). Even if someone correctly understood his good and attained it, he still would not be *eudaimon,* if he mistakenly thought that he lacked a major part of that good. For example, suppose someone whose family is living abroad is told that they have recently been killed. Let us assume that he is deeply affected, and views his loss as a great tragedy. Even if he should discover, after a year's time, that he was misinformed, that his family has all this time been alive and well, it remains true that he lacked *eudaimonia* during that year.[14] His life may in fact have possessed every first-order good that a well-lived life requires; still, it undeniably contained a serious second-order evil. To think, over a long period of time, that dear friends or family members have recently died, is by itself a major misfortune. For it involves the perception—or, in the case imagined, the misperception—that one lacks a great

---

II 2 413*b*1-2, *NE* IX 9 1070*a*16-17); in sleep, one becomes plant-like, since perception ceases. Therefore, one of the capacities we must take advantage of, if we are to lead lives that are not plant-like, is perception. And what one presumably wants to perceive are the goods available to higher beings: the good things in one's own life, in the lives of friends and one's city, and in the fixed nature of the universe. Merely to perceive the sorts of things that other animals can detect is to escape the condition of a plant, but it is not to lead a distinctively human life (I 7 1098*a*1-3).

[13] Thus Aristotle says that pleasure is a good since all human beings desire it (X 2 1172*b*35-1173*a*4). In fact, it is so pervasive a feature of human life that all men "weave pleasure into their ideal of happiness" (VII 13 1153*b*14-15). Aristotle's own theory of *eudaimonia* also finds an important place for this good (I 8 1099*a*7-29). In general, anything that is deeply and universally desired must be part of our good.

[14] Aristotle, of course, never discusses such an example. My point is that he has beliefs which commit him to denying that the individual described is *eudaimon.* Anyone who doubts this should recall Aristotle's view that one must have practical wisdom to be *eudaimon.* Judging from his discussion of this virtue in Book VI, it is doubtful that he would ascribe it to those who have radically mistaken beliefs about their own well being. Notice especially the connection between practical wisdom and understanding (VI 10), and the importance of recognizing specific matters of fact (1141*b*15 ff., 1142*a*20 ff.).

good, and this in itself is a great evil. *Eudaimonia* involves the recognition that one's desire for the good is being fulfilled, and therefore one who attains *eudaimonia* is necessarily happy with his life. His deepest desires are being satisfied, and realizing this, he has an especially affirmative attitude towards himself and his life.[15]

Notice that in reaching this conclusion, no appeal was made to Aristotle's theory that the best life is devoted to virtuous activity. So, if the argument I have just reconstructed is correct, then all of the various and conflicting theories of the good life ought to recognize that a *eudaimon* individual, whatever else may be true of him, has a certain attitude toward his life. Even if one disagrees with Aristotle about the importance of virtue, that is no reason for denying the connection between *eudaimonia* and the perceived satisfaction of major desires. For that connection depends solely on some highly general features of human nature, and the point that a *eudaimon* life is without major defects. Therefore, any adequate theory of the best human life—whether it identifies the good with honor or pleasure or virtue—ought to characterize a *eudaimon* individual as someone who knowingly satisfies his deepest desires. Furthermore, if *eudaimonia* and desire-satisfaction are connected in the way described, then there is a fair empirical test by which competing theories of *eudaimonia* can be partially evaluated. If the individuals who are pronounced *eudaimones* by a certain theory of *eudaimonia* believe there is little reason to be alive, and are

[15] The connection between *eudaimonia* and desire-satisfaction is tacitly assumed at the beginning of *Eudemian Ethics* I 5: "While there are many different things as to which it is not easy to make a right judgment, this is especially the case with one about which everybody thinks that it is easy to judge and anybody can decide—*the question which of the things contained in being alive is preferable and which when attained would fully satisfy a man's desire*" (1215*b*15-18, tr. by H. Rackham, emphasis added). Obviously, the deceptively simple question posed here is a stand-in for the one Aristotle has been raising in the first four chapters of the *Eudemian Ethics*: "Which sort of life is most *eudaimon*?" Since Aristotle regards them as equivalent questions, he is presupposing that a life cannot be *eudaimon* unless it fully satisfies the desires of one who leads it. I take him to be talking about major desires—that is, long-standing desires which have great weight in determining how one conducts one's life. Small mishaps cannot deprive one of *eudaimonia* (*NE* I 10 1100*b*22-25), and the failure to satisfy a minor desire is a small mishap, at most.

given to thoughts of suicide, then that theory cannot be right. Contrariwise, if those who are pronounced *eudaimones* have a highly positive attitude towards their lives, and those who are alleged to be quite distant from *eudaimonia* are deeply dissatisfied with themselves, then that is some confirmation for the theory which reaches this result. A theory of *eudaimonia,* in other words, ought to harmonize, at least partly,[16] with the way people feel about their lives: that is the upshot of our argument linking *eudaimonia* and the perception that one's major desires are being fulfilled. And Aristotle can claim that his own particular theory, which connects *eudaimonia* with virtuous activity, satisfies this requirement. For, as we have seen, he thinks that the virtuous and *eudaimon* individual is especially glad to be alive, whereas the individual who most sorely lacks *eudaimonia*—the evil man, hated for his misdeeds—is given to thoughts of suicide.

Let me emphasize two points about my interpretation. First, I have not said that the word *eudaimon,* by virtue of its everyday meaning, could only have been applied to satisfied individuals. Perhaps, as K. J. Dover claims, a Greek could have applied that term, without irony or contradiction, to a person who was deeply dissatisfied with his life.[17] What I want to emphasize is that Dover's thesis about ordinary Greek usage does not conflict with my own thesis about Aristotle. The *Nicomachean Ethics* does not merely record linguistic conventions about the term *eudaimon,* and in many ways Aristotle's treatment of this subject is controversial. His idea that *eudaimonia* consists in contemplation, for example, is no part of the meaning of the word *eudaimonia,* but is instead a product of philosophical argument. Similarly, the psychological condition presupposed by Ar-

[16] I say "at least partly" because Aristotle leaves open the possibility that some lack *eudaimonia* even though they perceive that their deepest desires are satisfied. Consider, for example, a person who is not evil, but who values honor, wealth, and physical pleasure more than they are worth. Because of these defective desires, he is not a virtuous person, and he therefore lacks *eudaimonia.* Yet he might be fully satisfied with his life. Satisfaction of desire is not a sufficient condition of *eudaimonia*, but even so a theory of *eudaimonia* is dubious if it fails to correspond roughly with experience. The most important cases are at the extremes: individuals deemed *eudaimones* or *athlioi* (miserable) ought to have opposite attitudes towards their lives.

[17] *Greek Popular Morality in the Time of Plato and Aristotle* (Oxford, 1974), p. 174, and n. 5.

istotle—that *eudaimonia* requires full and conscious satisfaction of desire—is a product of his own reflections, and need not have been a linguistic convention or a matter of universal agreement. So if we ever find among Greek authors genuine cases in which a deeply dissatisfied individual is called *eudaimon,* we merely will have discovered an application of that term against which Aristotle would protest, just as he protests against those who call only the wealthy *eudaimones.*[18]

Second, I am not saying that, according to Aristotle, whoever perceives that his major desires are being satisfied is *eudaimon.* Complete fulfillment of desire is a necessary condition of *eudaimonia,* but not a sufficient one. For on Aristotle's theory, those desires must be directed at worthwhile goals, and they must be proportionate in strength to the value of those goals; otherwise, one is not *eudaimon,* however satisfied one feels. Now, it might be claimed that this is a striking difference between *eudaimonia* and happiness. If a person's desires are fully satisfied—so the claim goes—then he is happy; but, as I have just said, this condition is not sufficient, in Aristotle's eyes, for *eudaimonia.* And it might be said that this difference is enough to show that "happiness" is not a good translation of Aristotle's *eudaimonia.* In the remaining sections of this paper, I will be presenting my reply to this line of argument. For now, I would like to stress the point that, however one wants to translate Aristotle's term *eudaimonia,* one ought to have a clear understanding of the similarities and differences between that notion and our notion of a happy life. And one remarkable similarity, which scholars

[18] I doubt that Dover has found a genuine case. The lines he quotes, ibid., n. 5, are *Medea* 598-9, but the context strongly suggests that Medea is being ironic: some *eudaimon* life that would be, filled with worry and distress! If that is how she is to be understood, then her lines tell us just the opposite of what Dover reads into them. Her mental anguish is precisely what makes it outrageous to call her *eudaimon.* I am grateful to Gregory Vlastos and Elizabeth Gebhard for discussion of this point. Dover admits that *eudaimonia* "occasionally requires the translation 'happiness'." Ibid. So even if this is a poor translation in many contexts and authors (and I am not convinced it is), it may still be the most suitable translation of Aristotle. Notice that closeness of meaning is not necessarily transitive. Our expression "leading a happy life" may be close in meaning to Aristotle's term *eudaimonia*, and his use of that term may be close to the way it is used by his contemporaries and predecessors; yet some of them may mean by *eudaimon* something that is not close to our expression "leading a happy life."

have not recognized,[19] is this: A *eudaimon* individual, as Aristotle conceives him, is in the very same psychological state as a person who is living happily. Such individuals have a highly affirmative attitude towards their lives, since they perceive that their major desires are being fulfilled. In spite of the fact that "happiness" is the traditional translation of *eudaimonia,* one of the most important connections between the two concepts has curiously been ignored.[20]

III

Let us take a closer look now at how we judge whether someone is happy. The following example will help focus our ideas: Suppose a man is asked what his idea of happiness is, and he replies, "Being loved, admired, or at least respected by my friends. But I would hate to have friends who only pretend to have these attitudes towards me. If they didn't like me, I would want to know about it. Better to have no friends at all, and realize it, than to have false friends one cannot see through." Suppose that what this man hates actually comes to pass. His so-called friends orchestrate an elaborate deception, giving him every reason to believe that they love and admire him, though in fact they don't. And he is taken in by the illusion.

Is this a happy life? Is he a happy man? Some people will say

---

[19] This parallel is not mentioned by any of those who specifically discuss the relationship between *eudaimonia* and happiness: J. Austin, "*Agathon* and *Eudaimonia* in the *Ethics* of Aristotle," in J. Moravcsik (ed.), *Aristotle: A Collection of Critical Essays* (Garden City, N.Y., 1967), pp. 261-296, esp. 270-283; H. Joachim, *The Nicomachean Ethics* (Oxford, 1951), p. 28; J. Ackrill, "Aristotle on *Eudaimonia*," *Proceedings of the British Academy* 1974, pp. 3-23, esp. 12-13; S. Clark, *Aristotle's Man* (Oxford, 1975), p. 157; R. Sullivan, *Morality and the Good Life* (Memphis, 1977), p. 178; to which add the works of Sidgwick, Ross and Cooper, cited above in notes 1, 2, and 3.

[20] For an exception, see G. Watson, "Happiness and *Eudaimonia*," read at the 1977 Princeton Colloquium on Aristotle's Ethics; his argument differs from my own. Hobbes too seems to connect *eudaimonia* with happiness. He says, "That whereby (men) signify the opinion they have of a man's felicity is by the Greeks called *makarismos*, for which we have no name in our tongue." *Leviathan*, I 6, penultimate sentence. A *makarismos* is a claim that someone is *makarios* or (equivalently) *eudaimon*. So Hobbes is saying that when *A* calls *B eudaimon:* (1) *A* thinks *B*'s life is felicitous (i.e. happy), and (2) *A* is giving his opinion of (is praising or admiring) *B*'s happy life.

yes, without a moment's thought. On their view (which I will call "extreme subjectivism"), happiness is a psychological state and nothing more; it involves, among other things, the belief that one is getting the important things one wants, as well as certain pleasant affects that normally go along with this belief.[21] So the deceived man is living just as happily as he would be if he were not deceived. Just as unfounded fear is still fear, so unfounded happiness is still happiness. For consider what we would say if the deceived man became suspicious of his friends, and came upon an opportunity to discover what they really think of him. Would we say that he is finding out whether he is really happy? Wouldn't it be more natural to say that he is finding out whether his happiness has been based on an illusion?

I think extreme subjectivism is a half-truth. Our reaction to the case of the deceived man is really more complicated than this doctrine admits. We do have some tendency to say that the deceived man is happy, but at the same time we have a definite reluctance to say this. The basis for our reluctance seems to be this: When a person is asked what his idea of happiness is, he quite naturally answers by describing the kind of life he would like to lead. It would therefore be misleading for the man in the above example to reply that he will be happy whether his friends deceive him or not. That would imply that he attaches some significant value to the situation in which he is deceived. Evidently, when we ask someone, "What will make you happy? What is your idea of happiness?", we are not requesting that he specify the conditions under which he will be in a certain psychological state. It is not like asking, "What will make you angry?" Rather, it is inquiring about the standards he imposes on himself, and the goals he is seeking. And this makes us hesi-

[21] I do not intend extreme subjectivism to be naive in its view about what kind of psychological state happiness consists in. It would be naive if it held that a happy person is simply one who is, at the time, in a euphoric mood. That is far too simple and episodic an account: a happy person may be so occupied with challenging activities that he rarely experiences the sort of mood we call "feeling happy." The important thing about extreme subjectivism is that it endorses these views: when a person's conception of reality is utterly mistaken, that fact can never be the basis for denying that he is happy; even when someone deeply desires his conception of the world to be correct, his happiness does not require that desire to be satisfied; a person must be wrong if he says that his happiness depends on reality being a certain way.

tant to say that the deceived man is happy or has a happy life. Judged by his own standards of happiness, he has not attained it, though he is in the same psychological condition he would be in if he had attained it. Merely being in that psychological state is not something to which he attaches any value, and so it is odd to say that he has attained a happy life merely by being in that psychological state.[22]

I think we can improve on the way extreme subjectivism describes our use of "happiness." We are not at all reluctant to say that the deceived man *feels happy* about his life. But we are quite reluctant to say that *the life he is leading is a happy life.* And we are at sea when we have to decide whether he is *happy;* the word "happiness" seems to lean in two directions, sometimes referring to the *feeling* of happiness, sometimes to the kind of *life* that is happy. For a person to be living happily, or to have a happy life, he must attain all the important things he values, or he must come reasonably close to this standard. But one can feel happy with one's life even if one comes nowhere near this goal; one need only believe that one is meeting one's standard. The deceived man, then, has a feeling of happiness, but when he is asked what he thinks happiness is, he is not being asked for the conditions under which he will have this feeling. Rather, he is being asked for his view about what a happy life is. If he discovers that his friends were deceiving him, he should say that although his feeling of happiness was based on an illusion, it really did exist. At no time, however, was he really leading a happy life.

In what follows, I will, for the sake of convenience, use the terms "happiness" and "a happy life" interchangeably. I am not

[22] To vary the example somewhat: Suppose that, as a cruel trick, someone is voted the most popular student in his high school. In actuality, his fellow students can't stand him, but he is benighted enough to take the vote at face value. After a day of euphoria, he discovers that he has been tricked. Years later, he is asked what the happiest day of his life has been. If that day in high school was the one on which he felt most intensely happy, must he say that in fact it was the happiest day in his life? I think not. I can understand his saying that it was actually the unhappiest day of his life, however happy he felt. If the extreme subjectivist also wants to make this distinction between a happy day and a day on which someone feels happy, then he must explain why he does not distinguish a happy life from feeling happy with one's life. For further discussion, see n. 31.

denying that it is sometimes correct to call a person happy merely because he feels that way about his life. Aristotle never uses *eudaimonia* in this way, and in this respect his term differs markedly from our own. But once this point is made, an important question remains: What is the difference between being *eudaimon* and leading a happy life?

IV

On our view, a person is living happily only if he realizes that he is attaining the important things he values, or if he comes reasonably close to this high standard. Of course, this is not the only condition one must meet. One must also find that the things one values are genuinely rewarding, and not merely the best of a bad range of alternatives.[23] And perhaps further conditions are necessary as well. What I want to focus on is a certain subjectivism in our conception of happiness. On our view, a person is happy only if he meets the standards *he* imposes on his life. Even if many others consider his standards too low, and would never switch places with him, he can still have a happy life. Consider, for example, a person who is severely retarded and thus quite limited in his aims and abilities. Though we would never wish for such a fate, we still think that under favorable conditions such a person can lead a happy life. For he can achieve the things he values, given the right circumstances. It is irrelevant that more fortunate individuals have more ambitious goals and would not be satisfied if their achievements were so very limited.

Contrast this with a more objective way of determining whether people are leading happy lives. We can define "objectivism" as the view that people should not be considered happy

[23] "Attaining the important things one values" should not be construed narrowly, e.g., to mean that a happy person necessarily strives for future accomplishments, prizes, or successes. Happiness does not require "amounting to something," as that phrase is often used. One might attain the important things one values simply by being a certain sort of person, enjoying certain activities or relationships, and functioning in a certain way. Furthermore, to find an activity or goal "rewarding" is not merely to make an aseptic intellectual judgment that it is worthwhile. It is to be emotionally engaged in that activity, and to feel pleasure in its performance.

unless they are coming reasonably close to living the best life they are capable of. According to the objectivist, each person has certain capacities and talents which can be fully developed under ideal conditions. And if someone is very distant from his full development, he is not and should not be considered happy, even if he meets the standards he imposes on his life. For he could have been leading a much better life, as determined by some ideal standard. The objectivist thinks that it is not up to you to determine where your happiness lies; it is fixed by your nature, and your job is to discover it.

The objective conception of happiness is in some important ways modeled on Aristotle's conception of *eudaimonia.* He thinks that to be *eudaimon* one must completely fulfill the function of a human being, or come reasonably close to doing so. And in his opinion, most people don't know what their function is; they may not even believe that they have one. Therefore they never attain *eudaimonia,* whether they realize it or not. Now, even though the objective view of happiness is patterned after Aristotle's approach to *eudaimonia,* a modern-day objectivist need not be as narrow. The *Nicomachean Ethics* argues that there is just one life that is best for everyone—the philosophical life—but objectivists can disagree. They might believe that for each of us there is a large class of ideal lives, and that to be happy we have to come reasonably close to one of those lives. And an objectivist can also say that different types of individuals have different capacities, so that what is ideal for one person may not be ideal for another. We can think of the objectivist as a reformed Aristotelian: he wants us to make judgments of happiness in somewhat the way the *Ethics* makes judgments of *eudaimonia,* but he is free to modify Aristotle's doctrine here and there, so that his own proposal will be more reasonable.

It is important not to overestimate the differences between the subjective and objective ways of judging a person to be living happily.[24] The objectivist, like us, recognizes that a happy

[24] I will be assuming in this paper that both objectivists and subjectivists view happiness as a great good. This vague judgment, though arguable, is common in philosophy, and accurately reflects the role happiness plays in ordinary practical thought. Happiness has an important place, for example, in the ethics of philosophers as divergent as Kant and Mill. Of course, they disagree about how great a good it is; according to Mill it includes all other

person must have certain attitudes towards himself; he must be satisfied with the way his life is going, and he must find his projects fulfilling. Furthermore, we are like the objectivist in that we believe that living happily does not merely consist in having a highly positive attitude towards one's life. We agree that to lead a happy life a person must actually meet a certain standard; seeming to meet it is not enough. Finally, we resemble the objectivist in this further respect: in our assessment of how happy a person is, we take into account the extent to which he has realized his capacities. We think that if someone falls far short of developing himself, then although he may be happy, he is not as happy as he might have been. For example, even if a retarded person manages to achieve a happy life, he might have been happier had he realized to a greater degree the normal capacities of a human being. In better circumstances, he could have chosen his interests from a wider range of alternatives, and he would have found more rewarding activities for himself. Much the same can be said of normal individuals who grow up in environments that do not elicit their talents and abilities. They too might have led happier lives, though they can be successful in pursuing the things they value, and therefore be happy.[25]

---

goods, whereas Kant assigns it a smaller but still significant place in our thinking. The precise value of happiness is a difficult issue which I want to avoid. It is separate from the problem of whether objective or subjective standards are more appropriate, and so in order to focus attention on this latter issue, I have objectivists and subjectivists agree roughly that happiness is a great good. Taking this as common ground, they can more easily isolate the issues that divide them. For further comments on the worth of a happy life, see n. 38. On those who deny happiness a central role in practical thought, see B. Williams, *Morality: An Introduction to Ethics* (New York, 1972), pp. 81-88. According to Aristotle, any adequate theory of *eudaimonia* must treat that end as one that cannot rationally be renounced. The *eudaimon* life, whatever it turns out to be, must be so good that no reasonable person would choose to have something else instead. (I 7 1097*b*14-20). Many suppose that happiness, for all its importance, does not have quite the value Aristotle attributes to *eudaimonia*. But we should not infer—as J. Ackrill does—that because of this disparity "happiness" is an unsuitable translation of Aristotle's term *eudaimonia*. See p. 13 of his paper, cited in n. 19. Mill, as I have said, thinks it is a conceptual truth that happiness includes all other desirable goals. Yet those who deny this point can still mean the same thing he does by "happiness." Similarly, the fact that *eudaimonia*, as Aristotle conceives it, cannot be rationally renounced hardly shows that "happiness" is a poor translation of his term.

[25] How are we to take the claim that although someone is leading a happy

But the objectivist says that a person is not happy if he is very distant from leading the best life he is capable of. We say instead that such a person is happy, though he might have been happier. What sort of disagreement is this, and how important is it?

V

Is the difference between subjectivism and objectivism merely verbal? Does the objectivist assign a different meaning to the word "happiness?" Should we say that he is only adopting a misleading way of talking, and that he would make his point more clearly and effectively if he used a different word instead of "happiness?" We might recommend, for example, that he express himself in this way: "A person can be happy if his life meets his own standards, but *to flourish* he must realize his capacities and come reasonably close to the best life he is capable of. So one can be happy but not flourish."

I think the objectivist has good reason to reject this proposal. He is someone who sees, in a number of cases, a huge gap between the lives people are leading and the lives that would be best for them. He may want to shock them into the realization that they are doing a terrible job with their lives. In this way perhaps they will change for the better, and at any rate others will not be tempted to imitate them. Furthermore, the objectivist may succeed in changing people's minds about whether their lives have been happy. He may convince them that their

life, he could be leading a happier one? Do such statements refer to a certain psychological state which the person is currently in, and which could be more intense in different circumstances? For example, do we mean that although the individual now has a highly positive attitude towards his life, it would have been more affirmative and enthusiastic had he chosen a different life? Sometimes this is meant, but not always. I am inclined to say that our conception of happiness, though largely subjective, nonetheless contains an objective component: Certain events—the ones that severely handicap us—are misfortunes, whatever a person's standards, attitudes or feelings. And a life afflicted by bad happenstance is, to that extent, less happy than it might otherwise have been. If a blind and a sighted person have the same positive attitude towards their existence, the latter's life is nonetheless happier, since it is not marred by serious misfortune. For futher discussion, see n. 31. So subjectivism borrows from objectivism, without accepting its central idea that to live happily one must come close to one's full development.

lives have been sorely lacking in qualities whose importance they suddenly recognize. After reevaluating themselves in the light of newly acquired standards, they may thank the objectivist for making them see that they have unknowingly been leading unhappy lives.[26] Since such reevaluations do take place, it is hardly appropriate to tell the objectivist that he is misusing the word "happiness." Notice too that it is not very disturbing to be told that although one is happy one could be even happier. Quite naturally, people will reply that they are satisfied just to be happy: why should they keep striving for more and more? Why should we make radical changes in our lives, as the objectivist urges, merely to exchange a happy life for a happier one? Similarly, no one is going to be upset if he is told that he is not flourishing (most people will wonder what flourishing amounts to) or fully realizing his talents. Happiness is what people want for themselves, and the objectivist is right in his conviction that people are unlikely to change drastically for their own sake unless they believe that they are not presently leading happy lives. So if we take the word "happiness" away from the objectivist, we take away a strategic tool, which he rightly insists on using.

Furthermore, the objectivist may challenge us in the following way: "As you saw earlier, a person is not leading a happy life if he falsely believes that he is achieving his most valued goals. But can't people suffer from an illusion that is equally

[26] Suppose someone thinks back on an earlier period of his life, and decides that although he was achieving his goals and considered himself happy, those goals were actually worthless. Since he now deeply regrets having lived in that way, he may single out the days on which he became attracted to those empty ideals as the unhappiest days of his life. (See n. 22.) If this is a coherent way of describing those days, then it also makes sense for him to go further and to say that his life, during that whole period, was not happy. And if he does say this, his judgment cannot rely on a subjective conception of happiness. For he admits that (*A*) his life at that earlier time met the standards he then set, and that (*B*) he did have an affirmative attitude towards his existence. By subjective standards, he was then leading a happy life; the claim that he was then unhappy presupposes an objective conception of happiness. So when I say throughout this paper that our conception of happiness is subjective, I am oversimplifying. Subjectivism (with its objective component—see n. 25) is normally our view, but on occasion (e.g., in the example just presented), some of us make statements that presuppose an objective test of happiness. For another example, see n. 40.

bad for them, if not worse? They can have radically false beliefs about what goals they should pursue. If a person wants to lead the best life he is capable of, but is deeply mistaken about what this life consists in or how it is to be accomplished, then he is in as sorry a state as the man who is deceived into believing that he is loved by his friends. Both think they are leading a certain sort of life, but they are far from it, and so neither is living a happy life—though they may *feel* happy."

We can reply to this challenge by showing what the difficulties of objectivism are, and I will be doing that in a later section. But enough has been said to show that the objectivist is not simply adopting an arbitrary and misleading way of talking. He thinks that the way we talk about happiness deceives people into leading what is, from their own point of view, the wrong kind of life. So we would be missing his point if we were to look upon his way of judging people happy to be nothing but a misuse of the word.

Nor would it be correct to say that the objectivist is proposing a new meaning for the word "happiness." To see this, consider the following analogy: Suppose that a certain society takes tallness to be an invaluable property, though the greatest height attained is five feet. A group of scientists discovers that under optimal conditions human beings can reach a height of between five and seven feet, and they propose that steps be taken to achieve these conditions, so that young people and future generations will achieve their ideal height. To make people sense the urgent need for change, they stop calling anyone—even five-footers—tall, and they recommend that everyone else adopt this new standard. It would be a strategic mistake for them to introduce a new word to mean "attaining one's ideal height." Since "tallness" is already a familiar term for an esteemed property, they should simply deny what their society has affirmed: that a five-foot person is tall.

It would be wrong to say that these scientists are proposing a new meaning for the word "tall." To be tall is to meet or exceed a specified standard of height, and the scientists are not trying to change this definition. Rather, they are proposing a different standard. They think that tallness should no longer be a matter of exceeding the norm, but of coming close to an ideal, and there is no more a change of meaning here than in any other case in which standards for the application of a term are revised. What once passed for a good recording, for example, would no longer do so, but that hardly shows that the meaning of "good recording" has changed.[27]

The objective conception of happiness should be treated in the same way. It proposes that we drop our current subjective standard of happiness,[28] and judge each person instead by a more severe and objective test. And the objectivist can reasonably argue that when he talks about a happy life, "happy" means just what it does for the subjectivist: a happy person has a highly affirmative attitude towards his life, and comes reasonably close to attaining the important things he values; a happy life, furthermore, is one that is highly desirable from the standpoint of the person leading it. But how should we characterize that standpoint? The objectivist says that a life is desirable from your own standpoint only if it comes fairly close to your ideal life, whereas the subjectivist thinks your current goals fix the standpoint from which your life should be evaluated. This difference hardly amounts to a difference in the meaning of the term "happiness."[29]

[27] It might be suggested, contrary to what I claim in this paragraph, that a tall person is one who significantly exceeds the average height of individuals *currently alive*. If that is the correct definition, then the scientists in our imaginary society would be proposing a new meaning. But I doubt that this proposal captures the meaning of "tall person." Suppose we discover that ten billion human beings escaped from the earth in prehistoric times and have been living in a different galaxy. Their height varies from eight to ten feet. Are only some of them tall—the ones who exceed our newly computed average? Obviously, we would call *all* of them tall. And we would not be forced by the meaning of "tall" and "short" to consider all earthlings short.

[28] This is a crucial feature of objectivism, as I conceive it. It is not the mild view that on occasion we are justified in using an objective standard, and that for the most part a subjective test of happiness is legitimate. Rather, the objectivist holds that our subjective test for happiness should never be employed.

[29] It may help, at this point, to think about such expressions as: "that is a happy turn of phrase," "your plants are happy in that window," "my dog is happier when he's on the farm." These uses of the term "happy" are closely related to each other, and to the way "happy" is used when applied to human beings. A happy turn of phrase is one that is just right for the context in which it occurs: if a plant is happy in a sunny window, or a dog happy on a farm, that is because their needs and their environment are appropriately matched;

I think this bears on the question of how to translate Aristotle. For the objectivist wants us to use the expression "living happily" in very much the way the *Ethics* uses *eudaimonia.* As we have seen, Aristotle thinks that if someone is *eudaimon,* then he has a highly affirmative attitude towards his life, and his deepest desires are being satisfied. Aristotle differs from us only in that he thinks a *eudaimon* life must come very close to the ideal, whereas our judgments of happiness rely on a subjective standard. And as I have just argued, this sort of difference is not plausibly viewed as a difference in meaning.

VI

We can get a clearer picture of the objectivist's proposal if we ask what it is to wish someone future happiness. More specifically, what are we wishing for when we say of a new-born baby, "I hope he has a happy life"? The subjectivist might be tempted to reply: "We are wishing the child success in attaining the things he will come to value, whatever these things are; and we are hoping he will find these goals, whatever they are, fulfilling." But I do not think this is the right account. For think of all the terrible things that would not be excluded by the wish for happiness, if this were all it amounted to. A newborn child might become retarded—yet still live happily; he might be enslaved, or blinded, or severely incapacitated in other ways—yet still live happily. Even though these are awful misfortunes, they do not so restrict us that a happy life becomes impossible, given the subjective account of happiness. Yet when we wish a happy life to a new-born baby, we are wishing for something better than such lives as these. The child's parents, upon hearing

---

and a person cannot be happy if his nature is totally unsuited for the situation in which he finds himself. In general, we speak of happiness only when there is a fit between a thing and its context. This fact is surely connected with our commonsense view that if a human being is happy then he is satisfying his major desires. Happiness requires a fit between a thing's nature and its surroundings, and since our desires form an important part of our nature, we cannot be happy unless they are fulfilled. The objectivist goes one step further and claims that a life can be unsuitable for someone's nature even if he satisfies his deepest desires. There is no absurdity or linguistic impropriety here.

our wishes, do not respond: "But why are you being so ungenerous? Why don't you wish our baby all the best, rather than a merely happy life? You've said nothing so far to exclude the major misfortunes—things one should not wish even upon one's enemies!"

Why don't parents make this accusation of ungenerosity? To answer this question, it will be useful to remind ourselves that there is a close linguistic connection between happiness and good fortune. "Hap" means chance; a hapless person is luckless; a happy turn of events is always good news; the first dictionary definition of "happy" is: "characterized by luck or good fortune."[30] I suggest that when we wish a child a life of happiness, we are tacitly relying on this connection between hap and happiness. We hope that the child will achieve the things he values, and find these things rewarding; but we also hope that the child's range of choices will not be restricted by unfortunate—that is, unhappy—circumstances. This explains why we do not react in different ways to the wish that a baby have all the best and the wish that he lead a life of happiness.[31]

[30] See, e.g., *The American Heritage Dictionary* (Boston, 1969) and *Webster's New International Dictionary* (Springfield, Mass., 1966), *s.v.*

[31] I think this connection between hap and happiness sheds light on some earlier points: (*A*) I claimed that the deceived man is not leading a happy life (Section III); in a parallel case, I said (n. 22) that when someone looks back at a day on which he was deceived into euphoria, he could sensibly call it the unhappiest day of his life. In both cases, we take note of the individual's values (friendship, popularity) and judge him unfortunate in the light of those values. And then we justifiably slide from talk of an unfortunate person or an unfortunate day to talk of an unhappy person and an unhappy day. (*B*) I also said (Section IV) that if individuals live in impoverished conditions, they can be happy, though not as happy as they might otherwise have been. The connection between hap and happiness helps explain why we think this way: impoverished conditions are a misfortune, and a life lived in happier circumstances is a happier life. To say that someone might have been happier in different conditions is not always to say that a certain psychological state might have been more intense. Notice that I have left unanswered the question of what makes something a misfortune. Why, for example, is blindness an objective misfortune, as I claim in n. 25, whereas the lack of perfect pitch is not? Is it because sight is so much more valuable as a means to further practical ends? I suspect that this is not the whole story. A blind person is cut off from a significant part of the real world, and so is worse off even if his practical aims do not require vision. A philosopher who denies the reality of the physical world has less reason to consider blindness a misfortune.

As children grow up and their lives take on a definite shape, their parents and others will employ our usual subjective test for determining whether they are happy. A parent might judge that his children are very distant from the best life that was available to them, but that they are nonetheless happy. We are objective in our early hopes and subjective in our later judgments. That is, when we wish someone a happy life, we hope he comes as close as possible to one of the best lives available to him; yet later our assessments of happiness abandon any reference to an ideal. The objectivist's proposal is that we bring our judgments of happiness into line with our early wishes. He says that we should only judge a person happy if he is leading the kind of life we should have wished for him when he was a new-born baby. Some explanation is needed of why we do not adopt this practice.

Notice, by the way, how silly it would be to say that "happiness" has two different meanings: one when we wish children a happy life, and another when we assess the happiness of adults. Quite clearly what is happening is not a change in meaning but a change in standards. We include more in a happy life, when we wish it to the new-born, than we require of such a life, when we judge that someone has achieved it. All the more reason, then, to think that objectivists and subjectivists mean the same by "happiness," and that Aristotle's *eudaimon* is properly rendered, "leading a happy life."

VII

The objectivist wants us to change our linguistic habits and use his test for determining whether people are happy. To convince us, he must give us a definite idea of how to use that test. That is, he must tell us how to determine what the ideal life (or set of ideals) is for each person. We must have a fairly complete picture of what must be included in such lives and of what can safely be left out. Further, the objectivist must convince us that the lives he calls ideal really deserve that name. When people engage in the activities he calls ideal, and refrain from the ones he thinks unimportant, they must find their lives more rewarding than they were before. Conversely, when people move away from lives the objectivist considers ideal, and try different alternatives, they must come to regret their decisions. And the objectivist ought to have some explanation of why people prefer the kind of life which he says is best for them. He must point to certain deep-seated facts of human nature and social organization which incline people to find a certain way of life best from their own point of view. Without such an explanation we may suspect that the objectivist merely has acquired a powerful hold over people who cannot consider themselves happy unless they do what he tells them. Furthermore, the objectivist must say something about what it is for a person to come *reasonably* close to leading his ideal life. Obviously, he cannot require that a happy life be absolutely perfect—there are no such lives. But unless we have some idea of what deviations from the ideal are compatible with happiness, it would be pointless to try to judge whether anyone is living happily. It would be like trying to decide whether London is reasonably close to Bristol.[32]

The trouble with objectivism is that no one has worked out a detailed and plausible theory that satisfies these demands. And so even if we are attracted by the objectivist's proposal,

[32] It might be thought that the subjective conception of happiness must tackle this same difficult problem. After all, it says that a happy person attains the important things he values, or *comes reasonably close* to this standard. But what is it to come reasonably close? The subjectivist, fortunately, can get himself off the hook in most cases by leaving it up to the individual to make the decision. There is no reason to establish a uniform way of measuring each person's distance from his ideal. Of course, a subjectivist cannot say that people are living happily so long as they believe they are coming reasonably close to attaining what they value. That would mean that even the deceived man is leading a happy life. But what the subjectivist can say is this: when a person has a good idea of how close he is to meeting his goals, then it is up to him to determine whether his distance from these goals is so large as to make him unhappy. What one person considers reasonably close another may not, and the subjectivist need not be bothered by this. Nor need he be disturbed by the fact that many individuals are unsure whether to call themselves happy. Though they may know how close or far they are from attaining the things they value, they may not know whether their distance from their ideals is such as to deprive them of happiness. In these cases, the individual simply has to decide whether or not he should be happy with his life. That is not something the subjectivist can decide for him. The objectivist, however, is in a more difficult position, since *he* is the one to decide *in all* cases whether a person is leading a happy life.

we have very little idea of how to put it into practice.[33] For example, suppose we read Aristotle's discussion of *eudaimonia* as a recommendation about how to determine whether people are living happily. (This is how he should be read, if *eudaimonia* means "leading a happy life.") The idea that the best life is philosophical seems much too narrow, so let us leave this aside and consider Aristotle's claim that the best life must make an excellent use of reason. Two questions arise: First, might someone make a poor use of his reasoning abilities, but make such excellent use of other capacities and talents that he comes reasonably close to leading one of the lives that could be ideal for him? Aristotle does not give any convincing reason for believing that this cannot happen. Second, there is the question of what constitutes an excellent use of reason. Here Aristotle has a lot to say. Using reason in an excellent way about practical matters requires exercising the virtues as he interprets them: one must be temperate in matters of physical pleasure, rather than a sensualist or an ascetic; one must be courageous, chiefly on the battlefield; and so on. Here too, Aristotle has worked out his theory too narrowly. There is no reason to believe that a person fully realizes his capacities only if he adopts Aristotle's attitudes towards physical pleasure and the use of force. Any objective theory of happiness which tries to do better than Aristotle's conception of *eudaimonia* will have to avoid his narrowness, without becoming so vague and general as to be useless.

I want to emphasize that I am making a limited point against objectivism. I do not claim that in principle such a theory can-

[33] I said earlier that when we wish a child a happy life, we are expressing the hope that he will come as close as possible to one of the best lives available to him. (See Section VI.) But now I say that we have no defensible method of determining what the class of best lives is. If this is an obstacle to making objective *judgments* of happiness, shouldn't it equally be an obstacle to making objective *wishes* for happiness? Should the subjectivist stop wishing someone all the best (i.e., wishing someone a happy life), since he doesn't know what that involves? To both of these questions, the answer is no. The fact that you can't tell whether someone will have achieved a certain goal does not argue against wishing for it. But if it is important to know whether someone has achieved that goal—and I assume we have a deep interest in knowing whether we are happy (see n. 24)—then we need a workable method for deciding when it has been attained. Our ignorance is no bar to wishing for an objectively happy life, but it does discredit our judgment that someone's life is objectively happy or unhappy.

not be found.[34] Great figures have claimed to see what the ideal life is for each individual, and the only rational response to these philosophies is to examine them case by case. Perhaps with more work we can provide objectivism with the philosophical foundations it requires. My point is that at present we have no defensible method for discovering each person's distance from his ideal lives. And so if we drop our subjective judgments of happiness, we have no workable and systematic alternative to put in their place.[35] Unless some incoherence can be found in our subjective conception of happiness—and so far none has—we have good reason to continue our present practice. Even so, our interest in the alternative provided by objectivism is bound to continue. For subjectivism says so little about how we should lead our lives: it tells us that if we want to be happy we should make up our minds about what we value most, and this is of little help to those who are uncertain about what kind of life to lead. Subjectivism requires less of a philosophical foundation than objectivism, but as a result it is, from a practical standpoint, the less informative theory.

VIII

One final complaint must be lodged against Aristotle's particular brand of objectivism: the standard by which he evaluates lives is too rigid. To see this, consider his doctrine of natural

---

[34] Here I am in disagreement with G. von Wright, as I understand him. He says, "Whether a person is happy or not depends on *his own* attitude to his circumstances of life. The supreme judge of the case *must be* the subject himself. To think that it could be otherwise is false objectivism." *The Varieties of Goodness* (New York, 1963), pp. 100-101, his emphasis. I take this to mean that our way of judging people happy cannot change so that the supreme judge of happiness becomes a wise observer, rather than the subject himself. I have been arguing that this is false, when "happy person" is equated with "person leading a happy life." If our question is, "Does this person feel happy with his life?", then von Wright is correct in saying that the supreme judge is the subject who is not deceiving himself.

[35] The objectivist might reply that we should abandon our subjective conception of happiness, and withhold judgments about the happiness of people's lives until we have developed a workable objective theory. But this proposal is quite weak. If we have an adequate theory, we justifiably continue to use it until a better one comes along. We don't drop it merely because a superior view might be developed.

slavery.[36] He thinks there are individuals who are constitutionally incapable of rational deliberation (1260*a*12, 1280*a*32–34), and for whom the best life is one of docile subordination to a wise master (1254*b*16–20, 1278*b*34–35). These natural slaves are not wholly devoid of reason (1254*b*22–23). Like all human beings, and unlike other animals, they are capable of emotions and desires which are persuaded and therefore altered by rational argument. But since they cannot rationally plan their lives on their own, they need to attach themselves to a benevolent superior who will regularly do this for them. If natural slaves discipline themselves so that their emotions and desires conform with their masters' correct conception of the good, they will achieve a low-grade form of virtue (1260*a*34–36). But even so—and this is the point I want to emphasize—Aristotle says that they can never attain *eudaimonia,* no matter how well they do within their limits (1280*a*33–34). Evidently, his test for *eudaimonia* is not how well one is doing, given one's limitations, but how close one comes to a perfect human life. Since the best a slave can do still falls far short of the ideal available to some, he can never be *eudaimon.* An objective theory of happiness that follows Aristotle on this point will say that a mentally retarded person can never live happily, even in the best of circumstances. Is there something wrong with this uncompromising form of objectivism?

Aristotle's inflexibility might be defended in this way: even if a slave cannot achieve *eudaimonia,* he nonetheless has every reason to try to come as near as he possibly can to that ultimate end. Certain ways of life will move him closer to this ideal and others will move him farther away, so his conception of *eudaimonia* will influence him as much as it influences those who can actually achieve it. What harm is done, then, if Aristotle's rigid standard makes the slave incapable of *eudaimonia*?

The answer is that Aristotle's inflexibility makes it difficult, if not impossible, for seriously handicapped individuals to maintain their self-esteem and vitality. On his view, only a *eudaimon* life is well lived (1095*a*18–20), and so slaves cannot justifiably believe that they are doing a good job of living their lives. The most favorable point they can make about their existence is

[36] All references in this paragraph are to the *Politics*. My interpretation follows that of W. Fortenbaugh, *Aristotle on Emotion* (London, 1975), pp. 53-55.

that among the bad lives theirs are not the worst: quite a negative judgment about the worth of being alive. Similarly, a slave is never justified in congratulating himself on the way he is living, nor can others justifiably congratulate him. For to congratulate someone on his life is to call him *eudaimon*[37]—and the slave is utterly distant from that end. Now, just as a dedicated singer would find it hard to live with the public recognition that he sings poorly, so a person who wants to see some good in his being alive will find it hard to do so if he and others judge that his life can never be well lived. The singer, at least, can try to change his role, but one cannot turn to some other activity besides living one's life. The slave is kept going by the biological urge for survival and can develop no justified confidence that his existence is preferable to death. Aristotle himself suggests that when we ask what *eudaimonia* is, we are asking what makes life worth living, that is, what reasons there are to choose to stay alive (*Eudemian Ethics* I 5). Since the slave has such a small sampling of those goods that make life worthwhile, he can never be *eudaimon,* and can find little reason to be glad that he is alive. Aristotle's conception of self-love (*NE* IX 4) yields the same dismal conclusion: the less virtuous one is, the less one can justifiably love oneself, and so, since the slave can at best achieve a reduced form of virtue, he is entitled to little self-regard.

I suggest that there is something inhumane about Aristotle's doctrine, and that an objective theory of happiness should depart from his lead in some way. Objectivism, as I have described it, takes happiness to be a highly valuable goal, and it urges us to be dissatisfied with our lives if they are not objectively happy. But if a person is permanently handicapped, there is no reason why we should persuade him to be unhappy with his life, distant though it may be from the ideal he might have achieved. Rather, objectivism will be a more humane doctrine if it evaluates each person's life by a standard which reflects his unalterable capacities and circumstances.[38] What an objectivist

[37] This is a point made by Austin, op. cit. at n. 19, p. 280. Cf. H. Liddell and R. Scott, *A Greek-English Lexicon*, 9th edn. (Oxford, 1940), *s.v. eudaimonisma.*

[38] An objectivist could choose to depart from Aristotle in a different way: he might claim that the permanent absence of happiness is a minor disadvantage, since there are many other goods. On this view, there is nothing

should say is this: Happy individuals can fall far short of the ideal they might have achieved, but they must do reasonably well with whatever restrictions currently surround their lives. A person is happy only if: (1) he meets the standards he has set for himself, and finds his life highly desirable; and (2) nothing he can now do would make his life significantly better.[39]

Notice that the objectivist who takes this line must give up a claim made earlier, in Section VI. He said that we ought to call someone happy only if he is leading the kind of life we should have wished for him when he was a new-born baby. But what happens when a normal baby later receives severe physical injuries which cause some retardation? Humane objectivists would not have wished such a life upon this unfortunate person, but they will nonetheless judge him happy if he is doing his best under the circumstances. So flexible objectivists, no less than subjectivists, allow for a discrepancy between early wishes and later judgments. When they wish a baby a happy life, they mean to exclude certain events which, if they occur at a later time, do not prevent them from calling that life happy.

By tailoring each person's ideal to fit his current limitations, and thus departing from Aristotle's conception of *eudaimonia,* objectivism can be a humane outlook. But its main difficulty still remains. It requires us to judge someone happy only if his

---

objectionable about inflexible standards of happiness, since the unavailability of happiness should mean little to us. I think, however, that this way of modifying Aristotle results in a less defensible theory. Normally we think that if a person gives up his chances to lead a happy life, he is making a great sacrifice. But if there are many other goods available to the unhappy person, has he really given up that much? The objectivist cannot easily combine these ideas: (*A*) a life that is not happy can still contain many good things; (*B*) if one's life contains many good things, then one should be happy with it; (*C*) if one's life is not happy, then it is inappropriate to be happy with it. Objectivism must affirm (*C*), and since (*B*) is more plausible than (*A*), the latter should be rejected. I see no reason why the objectivist should adopt (*A*) rather than the position I urge on him in the text.

[39] Objectivism, thus modified, claims that a person is not living happily if his conception of the good is both alterable and radically defective. For such an individual fails to satisfy condition (2). Objectivists who think that defective conceptions of the good are unchangeable—and perhaps Aristotle is one of these—might find this amended version of their theory unattractive. But I am inclined to think that we can and often do revise our notions of what is worth pursuing.

life cannot be significantly better; but we do not know how to determine this, in so many cases. Of course, all of our lives, or nearly all, could be somewhat better—but could they be significantly better?[40] To answer this question, the objectivist will have to say what the best attainable life is for each of us, and he must provide some reasonable way of measuring our distance from this reachable ideal.

To summarize, let me turn back once more to Aristotle: his differences with us stem from the fact that he calls someone *eudaimon* only if that person comes fairly close to the ideal life for all human beings, whereas our standard of happiness is more subjective and flexible. We do not have a defensible theory about which lives are ideal, and even if we did, we would not want to judge people happy only if they come close to the best life a human being can lead. So, when Aristotle says that a slave cannot be *eudaimon,* and we say that in certain conditions he can be happy, we are not, strictly speaking, contradicting each other. He is measuring the slave's distance from the ideal for all human beings, while we are saying that the slave's life can meet his own reduced standards. But even though we are

[40] There may be a few isolated cases in which we can already answer yes, without doing further philosophical work. For example, suppose sight could be restored to a certain blind person, who nonetheless willingly chooses to remain blind. Then even a subjectivist should admit that this individual's life could be significantly better, i.e., that he is far from an attainable life that is much happier. See n. 25. (I am assuming in this example that the restoration of sight would not bring with it countervailing misfortunes.) Even so, we may be reluctant to say that this person, in his blindness, is necessarily leading an unhappy life. For in so many other cases, we justifiably use a subjective standard of happiness, and this blind man may in fact meet that standard. Wouldn't we be picking on him, if we switched to an objective test and denied him the happiness we attribute to others on subjective grounds? Looking at the matter in this way, it may seem that objectivism has to work in a great many cases, or it won't work at all. But the point is debatable. We could also say that this blind man ought to be made dissatisfied with his present life, since a much better one is available. Why should we encourage him in his error by agreeing that his life is happy? Objectivism is supposed to help people view their lives correctly, and surely we are allowed to help a few even though we can't help everyone. On this view, there is nothing wrong with piecemeal objectivism. I am unable to decide between these two alternatives. But notice that even piecemeal objectivism, since it accepts subjective standards in many cases, is a far cry from the objective conception of happiness discussed throughout this paper. See n. 28.

not contradicting Aristotle on this point, we still have something to argue about. He would accuse us, and we should accuse him, of measuring people's lives by an inappropriate standard.[41]

University of Illinois, Chicago Circle

[41] I am grateful to D. Blumenfeld, C. Chastain, G. Dworkin, R. Meerbote, G. Watson, and two anonymous referees, for their comments on earlier drafts. I also profited from reading this paper to the Philosophy Departments at Northwestern University and the University of Wisconsin at Milwaukee.

Is Aristotelian *Eudaimonia* Happiness?

"WE NEED NOT hesitate to translate the word *eudaimonia* by the English 'happiness'" (my transliteration). So Burnet wrote in 1900,[1] but the hardening consensus is that he was wrong.[2] The differences between the two notions, it is now commonly supposed, are too many and too deep to think that happiness and *eudaimonia* are very closely related; and consequently "happiness", the long-established conventional translation, will seriously mislead us in understanding the nature of Aristotelian *eudaimonia*.

The arguments supporting this popular view are usually stated briefly in notes or by the way. They would benefit from a more extended airing than they have had so far. The results of this examination, I believe, will leave the tradition looking stronger than it has recently seemed.

The tradition, even if it is finally judged to be mistaken, one should note, is not based simply on scholarly wilfulness. For Aristotle it is a commonplace that *eudaimonia* is the supreme good (*N.E.* 1095a18–9); for many modern philosophers the same holds for happiness.[3] The candidates Aristotle reviews for what *eudaimonia* consists in including pleasure, honour, contemplation, virtue, and money-making (*N.E.* 1,5) are equally plausibly taken as candidates for what someone might think happiness – at least in part – consists in.[4] And when Aristotle, summarising the conventional wisdom, notes that being *eudaimon* can be adversely affected by what happens to family and friends, and by whether one is financially strapped or even ugly (see, *inter alia*, *N.E.* 1099a31–b8), these remarks are recognizable as statements which might also be made about a person's happiness. Points of resemblance like these constitute a *prima facie* case supporting the tradition.

One preliminary qualification needs to be made, however, in order to forestall possible misunderstanding. It must be immediately conceded that there are some ways in which we use "happiness" which do not correspond to anything Aristotle, and most likely other Greeks,[5] would have accepted about *eudaimonia*. There is no Greek expression, for instance, which corresponds to the heavily psychological English phrase "to feel happy". Nor again is Aristotle prepared to predicate *eudaimonia* of someone in virtue of a very brief period, as happiness readily can be.[6] Even if differences such as these are allowed to colour "happiness" as the translation of *eudaimonia*, it could still be true that a close resemblance exists between *eudaimonia* and some uses of "happiness" as illustrated in expressions like "happy life" or "happy person". The arguments which I wish to consider deny even such a resemblance.

Objection 1: John Ackrill argues forcefully: "It may be true ... that happiness is not everything, that not everyone seeks it and that it can be renounced in favour of other goals. What Aristotle says, however, is that *eudaimonia* is the one final goal that all men seek; and he would not find intelligible the suggestion that man might renounce it in favour of some other goal. Nor is Aristotle here expressing a personal view about what is worthwhile or about human nature. It is in elucidation of the very *concept* that he asserts and emphasises the unique and supreme value of *eudaimonia* ... there can be plenty of disagreement as to what form of life is *eudaimonia*, but no disagreement that *eudaimonia* is what we all want."[7] Happiness, it would seem, is a more highly coloured concept than is *eudaimonia* and, on that account, cannot function in the same way as does *eudaimonia*.

Bernard Williams has recently supplied some useful illustrations which can be used to support Ackrill's claim that not everyone seeks happiness.[8] He cites as examples a certain kind of Protestant who finds value in suffering itself or a Romantic who is determined to stay true to his deepest impulses despite their possible self-destructive character or the risks to others. These individuals have outlooks on life which are at least intelligible, but it would certainly be wrong to characterise them as having possible, if eccentric, conceptions of happiness. As outlooks they seem rather to have turned their backs on happiness.

Reply: This objection crucially depends on separating "a personal view about what is worthwhile or about human nature", on the one hand, from the elucidation of a concept, on the other. Is this separation so neatly achieved for Aristotle's account of *eudaimonia*? I believe not.

Just how much disagreement can there be about what form of life is *eudaimon*? Ackrill rightly says there can be plenty, but how far can this "plenty" be stretched? Can it be made to extend as far as Williams' Protestant or his Romantic? On Ackrill's view it must, since no one can renounce *eudaimonia*. But, against this, Aristotle would seem to be no more prepared to grant that the Protestant or Romantic have an eccentric picture of *eudaimonia* than we are that they have an eccentric view about happiness. For a life to be conceived as *eudaimon*, apart from being seen as the final good, it must also satisfy some further constraints deriving from commonly accepted beliefs, which Aristotle is not prepared to abandon, but which such lives deliberately forswear. In particular, a *eudaimon* life must be conceived as pleasant and reasonably equipped with external goods. Only someone wishing to defend a thesis at all costs would wish to deny this (*N.E.* 1091a1–2). It would seem that Aristotle could only claim that *eudaimonia* is what we all want and that it also satisfies the traditional constraints if he is committed to a view about human nature and, in particular, the character of human wants. The Protestant and the Romantic constitute a challenge to that view and it seems safe to conclude that Aristotle could not have made much sense of their outlooks. Certainly the range of actual disagreements about how it is best to conduct one's life that Aristotle mentions is quite narrow. So while Ackrill rightly alerts us to certain discrepancies between Aristotle's philosophical commitments and our ordinary concept of happiness, the analysis of these differences on further scrutiny reflects less on any supposed difference between *eudaimonia* and happiness than on the relation between Aristotle's philosophical claims about *eudaimonia* and the view of human nature against whose background they were formulated. *Eudaimonia* has much more coloration than the objection had imagined.

Objection 2: Happiness designates a state. It is akin in this respect to comfort, prosperity or content, if not actually identical to any one of them. *Eudaimonia*, by contrast, is the name of an *energeia* or activity, as Aristotle insists. But where "comfort and prosperity may be goals secured by action, ... *eudaimonia* is precisely not such a goal. It is doing well (*eupraxia*), not the result of doing well; a life, not the reward of a life" (my transliteration of *eupraxia*).[9] The upshot is that goals like acting virtuously cannot be the whole or even parts of what happiness is, whereas nothing prevents them from being the whole or parts of *eudaimonia*. It would seem, therefore, that such goals and happiness easily conflict whereas they are readily assimilable to *eudaimonia*.

Reply: While the objection makes important use of the distinction between states and activities, there is no need to become embroiled in the many difficulties attending its philosophical analysis.[10] We can work well enough from the intuitive idea that activities like contemplating, stroking and listening are identifiable as actions whereas states like existing are not. It can also be granted that happiness is a state and likewise that when, in the *Nicomachean Ethics* at least, Aristotle says that *eudaimonia* is an *energeia*, he should be understood as asserting it to be an activity. His use of *energeia* as correlative to *praxis* (action) in the *N.E.* (see, e.g., 1098a3–4) sets this last point beyond doubt.

There are two parenthetical points worth noting, however, which set this last admission into some perspective. First, consider Aristotle's remark in the *E.E.* (1218b35–6) that of those things in the soul there are, on the one hand, *hexeis* (dispositional states) or *dunameis* (potentialities) and, on the other, *energeiai* and *kineseis* (movements or performances). This classification appears to claim completeness, but there is no place within it for occurrent states, if the identification of *energeiai* as activities is granted. While the distinction between *hexeis* and *energeiai* has occasionally been claimed to correspond to that between states and activities, *hexeis* seem to constitute no more than a subclass of states.[11] Second, if we closely examine those passages where Aristotle attempts to provide a philosophical analysis of *energeiai*, it would seem that his analysis fails to distinguish activities from states. In *Meta.* θ.6 he remarks of some illustrative *energeiai*: "at the same time one sees and has seen, understands and has understood, thinks and has thought ...".[12] He probably should only be construed as claiming that the present tense of *energeiai*-verbs is compatible with the perfect, since the contrast he goes on to draw is with *kineseis*-verbs where the present is incompatible with the perfect. There are other passages, however, which strengthen Aristotle's claim (most notably *De Sensu* 446b2): the present entails the perfect. Aristotle does not suggest that the justification for these claims rests upon an appeal to our linguistic intuitions. Ackrill has given the best explanation so far for Aristotle's insistence upon the entailment. The explanation turns on Aristotle's view that there is no first instant of change or motion. For if whenever I say that I am seeing, there must be an interval, no matter how small, in respect of which I have been seeing, this interval insures that for *energeiai* the perfect holds when the present does. Evidently, however, this whole line of argument will apply to states as much as to activities so that the analysis of *energeiai* will fail to distinguish between them. It seems that in these passages Aristotle either overlooks states or shows no inclination to distinguish activities from them. So much by way of preliminaries.

How clear is it – first of all – that Aristotle is justified in concluding as he does in *N.E.* I and elsewhere that *eudaimonia* is an *energeia*? If Aristotle is not entitled to draw such a conclusion, it cannot be very confidently exploited in making the objection.

At *E.E.* 1,2 Aristotle emphasises how important it is to observe the distinction between what something is and what is merely indispensable for its existence. Eating well and taking exercise, for example, are not what health is, not even in part, but health would not exist without them. Similarly Aristotle insists that it would be difficult, not to say impossible, to be *eudaimon* without such external goods as good birth, good looks, friends and good children, but it is not in these that *eudaimonia* consists. It consists rather in an *energeia* in accordance with virtue.

In the *N.E.* Aristotle returns to this distinction and he further subdivides the goods merely indispensable for *eudaimonia* (1099a31–b6; 1099b26–8). Some like wealth are naturally collaborative with, and instrumentally necessary for promoting, such an *energeia*. It is very easy to see how the *E.E.*'s distinction applies to them. They stand to *eudaimonia* rather like taking exercise stands to health. The others, like having good looks, must exist beforehand as preconditions for *eudaimonia*. The relation between them and the *energeia* that *eudaimonia* is held to be, however, is rather puzzling. For if their contribution to that *energeia* is not to be explained instrumentally (any attempt to do so would in any case seem implausible or at least to fall short of explaining the importance evidently attached to them), what stops us from claiming that they are further parts of what *eudaimonia* is? But, in that case, since Aristotle in the *N.E.* would not wish to say that having good looks or good birth counts as an *energeia* (not being a *praxis*), his claim that *eudaimonia* just is an *energeia* would be in trouble.

A further difficulty points to much the same conclusion. Aristotle contrasts *energeiai* with *hexeis* (dispositional states). *Hexeis*, unlike *energeiai*, are compatible with inactivity whether temporary as in sleep or permanent when the occasion for actualizing them fails to arise (see *N.E.* 1098b31–1099a7 together with 1095b31–1096a1). But if *eudaimonia* must be an *energeia* rather than a *hexis* (since the latter can exist without achieving any good), it would seem reasonable that *eudaimonia* should only be predicated in the duration of the *energeia*. *Eudaimonia*, therefore, would not belong to a sleeping person or someone otherwise inactive. But since Aristotle also believes the *eudaimonia* is something enduring and hard to take away from a person (1100b1–3), it would seem absurd that merely dozing off for a moment should be sufficient to interrupt it. The difficulty can be easily solved if *eudaimonia* is allowed to be a rather complicated state (the discussion below bears on this point) specified in such a way that it lacks the disadvantage of *hexeis* of being compatible with total or protracted inactivity.

Even if we choose to disregard these arguments, however, a further question still arises about the interpretation of the "is" in *eudaimonia* is a (certain) *energeia*"? Must we understand it as the "is" if identity?[13]

Let us shift for the moment to the case of happiness. Suppose that I believe that real happiness is contemplating God. Contemplating evidently counts as an activity, whereas being happy has been conceded to be a state. If so, am I mistakenly identifying a state as an activity in expressing my belief as I have? There is no need to suppose so, for the "is" may be interpreted as the "is" of constitution as illustrated in Wiggins' example: "The soufflé you are eating is simply eggs and milk".[14] In Aristotelian terminology we can regard the soufflé as a substance (although it is not a particularly good example of one); the eggs and milk, as its matter. And just as the material constituents of a substance need not themselves be substances (for instance, the milk would not count as an Aristotelian substance), so it is hard to see why anyone should insist, as the question apparently does, that states can only be constituted or composed from further states. A state of siege, for example, is constituted if certain kinds of events and activities are taking place, the enemy preventing supplies from entering the city for example. When such activities cease, the siege is lifted and the state no longer exists. But the relation of such activities to the state is not merely that of instrumental means to end (even though it might well be in the case of other states like prosperity), but rather of constituent to constituted condition. The objection's claim about happiness, therefore, would seem to misfire: goals such as acting virtuously are not debarred from serving as constituent parts of happiness just because they are activities.

While the way is now clear for entertaining the suggestion that the "is" in the *N.E.*'s claim that "*eudaimonia* is an *energeia*" should be interpreted constitutively, the argument clearing the way obviates the need to defend this suggestion very strenuously. For even if happiness is a state and *eudaimonia* is identical to a certain activity, this difference alone is not critical from the point of view of moral philosophy. For the activity, which is *eudaimonia*, could well be constitutive of happiness. The objection would thus collapse into impotence.

To summarise, it seems that (1) Aristotle shows no clear awareness of the distinction between states and activities in his philosophical analysis of *energeiai*; (2) he had no clear philosophical entitlement for claiming that *eudaimonia* is an *energeia* if the latter is understood to correspond to an activity; (3) the "is" could be interpreted constitutively; and (4) even if it were not, the mere difference between a state and an activity is not all that significant for the moral philosopher. I conclude, therefore, that the objection can be safely ignored.

Objection 3: *Eudaimonia* is not just an *energeia*, but one in a complete life. Austin elaborates on the significance of this qualification as follows: "... what is important ... is, that, though of course we can speak of a man as *eudaimon*, the substantive with which *eudaimon* naturally goes is *bios* [life] or a similar word: a man is only called *eudaimon* because his life is so. Hence the discussion ... of the various *bioi* which lay claim to being *eudaimonia*. And hence the saying 'call no man *eudaimon* until he is dead'" (my transliterations).[15] But while we can and do predicate happiness of a life, we also predicate it of a person in virtue of periods within that life. Our judgment about those periods isn't overturned by the miseries of subsequent periods. The misadventures of adult life do not cancel the happiness of a good childhood. The advice "call no man happy until he is dead" simply doesn't make sense. The principle that a person is *eudaimon* if and only if his life is does not translate out for happiness.
Reply: Aristotle's thesis that *eudaimonia* is predicated primarily of a life seems to be offered as his explanation for the claimed Greek refusal to attribute *eudaimonia* to a person in virtue of a day or even longer periods, most notably childhood, as well as such sombre Greek commonplaces as "Call no man *eudaimon* until he is dead".

It is worth remarking, however, that Aristotle derives this thesis from *eudaimonia*'s status as a final end (*teleion telos*). The argument is fullest perhaps in the *Magna Moralia* (1185a1–13), if indeed this work is Aristotle's[16] but a version of it is also to be found in the *Eudemian Ethics* (1219a40–b7). What makes *eudaimonia teleion* is that unlike most other ends it is not also pursued for the sake of something else (*N.E.* 1097a25–30) or that it is complete inasmuch as it does not require the addition of any further component (like justice) (*M.M.* 1184a7–14).[17] But since it is *teleion*, it will have to be found in what is itself *teleion*, and that is nothing less than the complete (*teleion*) term of a life. This argument, like its cousin in the *E.E.*, fails, however, because its plausibility is gained at the cost of treating *teleion* equivocally. Neither explanation of *eudaimonia*'s status as *teleion* sanctions the inference that it must also be complete in relation to life's full term. But – now setting aside philosophical criticism of Aristotle's argument – if he justifies the thesis that *eudaimonia* is predicated primarily of a life through the principle that *eudaimonia* is a final end of action (or that it is complete with respect to its component parts), then evidently we should also be entitled to use the same argument with equal justice if we can conceive of happiness in the same way. There is no obstacle, however, to conceiving it thus and so the alleged difference between the two notions which is exploited by the objection would disappear.

Perhaps, however, this is too short a way with the objection. For quite apart from the argument Aristotle uses to arrive at the thesis that *eudaimonia* is predicated primarily of a life, he is motivated by the need to explain certain features of the *received* concept of *eudaimonia*. We do not stand in the same position, however, relative to happiness.

Something has already been conceded to this argument in the introductory remarks to this essay. But is Aristotle clearly right in all the reporting he does on the received concept of *eudaimonia*? Consider, for example, Aristotle's claim in the *E.E.* (1219b5) that the received concept does not permit *eudaimonia* to be predicated of a young person. In the *N.E.* he weakens the claim by allowing that it sometimes is so predicated (1100a2–3), but such predication, he says, should be analysed as no more than an expression of our hopes for the person. Such an analysis, however, will not work for the example of such a predication found in *Euripides' Heracles* where the chorus expresses regret over the loss of youth's *eudaimonia* (1.441). They are evidently looking back with regret to more than the defeat of youth's promise. It seems clear, therefore, that *eudaimonia* on some occasions, like this one, was predicated in virtue of a period.[18] In fact, Aristotle himself at least once implies that it can be. For he remarks that someone like Priam who has once lost his *eudaimonia* due to great misfortune will find it difficult, although not impossible, to become *eudaimon* again (1101a9–13). Even if Aristotle were to rule out the possiblity of regaining it, he concedes at least that *eudaimonia* was once possessed. Such a concession is not consistent with the doctrine that a person is *eudaimon* if any only if his life is.

These remarks, however, may only seem to have deflected the objection rather than to have fully met it. After all Aristotle and other Greeks thought they could make sense of "Count no man *eudaimon* ...' But can we make sense of "Count no man happy ..."? I think we can, but the defence of this claim is best postponed until we come to the fifth and final objection.

Objection 4: We believe that a person's happiness is closely bound up with how he sees his life and with his psychological states. His life might seem enviable to us judging from without, but if he looks upon it as disappointing and lack-lustre, we would not regard him as happy.

Greek philosophical discussions of *eudaimonia*, by contrast, might seem not to attach sufficient, if any, weight to the individual's own point of view. The exchange between Socrates and Polus in Plato's *Gorgias* (470c9 ff.) is an especially apt illustration. Polus is protesting that one need look no further than to Archelaus, who has just become tyrant of Macedon by particularly outrageous means, for an unjust man who is demonstrably *eudaimon*. Socrates, however, will not presume to judge since he has never met Archelaus. Polus objects: Why should that be necessary? What more need one know other than that his power can be compared with that of the Great King of Persia himself? Socrates still refuses to judge. He first wants to know how Archelaus stands to *paideia* (education) and *dikaiosune* (justice). Polus then asks: Is that what we are to believe that *eudaimonia* consists in? Yes, Socrates answers, poker-faced.

Socrates' initial reticence is motivated apparently not by any desire to ask Archelaus quite simply whether his life satisfies him, but by the need to assure himself about his alleged injustice. That knowledge, and apparently it alone, will settle the question. For Polus, on the other hand, it is enough to know that Archelaus can act as his fancy moves him. While Polus' view is familiar enough if it is construed as a view about happiness, Socrates' certainly seems bizarre.

We turn next to the extension of this idea to Aristotle. About him Bernard Suits has claimed: "Aristotle wants to argue that just because morality and metaphysics are proper functions of men, they and they alone will produce happiness worthy of the name, no matter how miserable they may seem to make us."[19] This last clause is the crucial one: one's functions and one's psychological states are regarded as independent of each other. The proper performance of one's function is compatible with the full range of psychological states directable at that performance. Admittedly Suits is arguing that Aristotle makes an exceptionally silly point about happiness. But we might try to defend him against this charge. The mistake really lies in thinking that Aristotle is talking about happiness.

Reply: The flaw in this objection is its assumption that for Aristotle (and Plato alike) performing one's function or *ergon* properly, on the one hand, and one's point of view and psychological states, on the other, are independent of each other. In particular, it overlooks the central fact that

Aristotle's as well as Plato's theorising about moral virtue and philosophical contemplation are embedded in a theory of human activities which closely connects their proper performance to the agent's psychological states as well as his attitude towards their performance (and towards their place in his life generally). If, for example, a person's supposed virtue makes him feel miserable, then, on Aristotle's account, he does not have a properly virtuous disposition. To have such a disposition he must act with enjoyment or, at least, gladly (*N.E.* 1104b4 ff.). A person who feels wretched about doing what a virtuous person does can come no closer to virtue than "continence". A similar point holds for contemplation. For Aristotle's general theory is that when the best human powers are directed towards their best objects, as they are in philosophical contemplation most notably, the activity should be enjoyable (*N.E.* 1174b20–4). So if a would-be metaphysician reports his misery, Aristotle needn't count him as *eudaimon*, as Suits implies that he must. Instead Aristotle could use the reported misery as an indication that something had gone wrong so as to interfere with proper performance: that a relevant capacity was missing or perhaps that it had been improperly nurtured. The attitudes one would expect to find in those properly engaged in their *ergon* are no different from those we would expect to see in those finding happiness in what they did.

Objection 5: Happiness, however, does not simply depend on one's subjective psychological states; it precisely is one. Yet Aristotle seriously credits the common belief that what happens after a person's death has an impact on his *eudaimonia*. Since what happens after a person no longer exists can have no bearing on his subjectively felt condition, happiness and *eudaimonia* must be quite different from each other.[20]
Reply: The force of this objection depends entirely on what it too easily assumes must be true about happiness. It can readily be granted that "happiness" often is used as the objection has it. The issue is whether it always is or must be.

It should be observed that Aristotle's view about *eudaimonia* does not rely simply on an appeal to common belief. He takes that belief to be supported by argument (*N.E.* 1100a14 ff.). *Eudaimonia*'s vulnerability to events following death occurs because death, while it ends a person's existence, does not finally set him beyond the reach of evils and misfortunes. For if, say, the loss of reputation or the loss of someone a person deeply cares about are misfortunes and evils for the person affected even though he is unaware of their occurrence, their status as evils is thereby rendered independent of his awareness of them whatever else may be true of other evils and misfortunes. But if we are prepared to grant this much, why chafe against the supposition that they may equally be evils and misfortunes for the person once he is dead? Nagel has recently given an especially clear statement of the underlying position: "There are goods and evils which are irreducibly relational; they are features of the relations between a person, with spatial and temporal boundaries of the usual sort, and circumstances, which may not coincide with him either in space or in time. A man's life includes much that does not take place within the boundaries of his body and his mind, and what happens to him can include much that does not take place within the boundaries of his life."[21] Aristotle's argument, therefore, simply overlays the conceptual point that evil and misfortune threaten *eudaimonia* with a thesis about the nature of evils and misfortunes. This thesis should be recognized as the basis of Aristotle's view.

A first thought is that a connection parallel to the one Aristotle exploits between *eudaimonia* and evil and misfortune is readily drawn for happiness. There may be some temptation, however, to hold back and to refine this first thought. Perhaps it is only the discovery of evil which threatens happiness and not evil as such. Before we too easily yield to this temptation, however, we should take note of a related, but different consideration.

Happiness is commonly connected to the realisation of at least the most important among one's major desires.[22] Their gratification and the prospects thereof are taken to be a necessary, although not a sufficient, condition of happiness. But what matters, often desperately, is that they really should be, and not merely that they should seem to be, satisfied. If their seeming satisfaction would do, then the character of the original desire would often call for redescription.[23] The retention of the connection between happiness and the realisation of desire, granting the character of many of our desires, therefore, offers one powerful motivation for a less thoroughly subjective account of happiness than the objection demands. It may sufficiently weaken any contrary temptations over the case of evil and misfortune at least to see how it is possible to arrive at an Aristotelian view while starting from what is recognizably a notion of happiness.

A low-keyed illustration drawn from an unfinished short story by Katherine Mansfield entitled "All Serene" may reinforce these considerations. We enter directly into the consciousness of Mona, recently married, still very much in love with her husband, taking delight in his appearance and manner as he comes down for breakfast. She regards herself as deliciously happy. Her relationship to her husband, the central part of her life now, is so good. A letter arrives for him. She notes casually that the handwriting looks to be a woman's as she passes the letter over to him. So it does, he readily agrees, but it is actually from a mining engineer. Alas, he will have to be late home that evening. Business, he remarks.

The story, or what exists of it, relies on a sustained ambiguity and irony. We suspect, although we never know for certain, that the letter really is from another woman whom her husband will be seeing that very evening. But Mona, feeling as she does, is incapable of entertaining such a suspicion. This difference creates an increasing distance between her and us as readers. It makes it difficult by the end for us to ratify the thoughts she has about her relationship with her husband and her well-being, even though at the outset we had been inevitably drawn into identifying with her moods and feelings. Her happiness, we suspect, is not what she takes it to be. The fact that we harbour such powerful suspicions is sufficient indication in itself of our underlying doubt that happiness must invariably be regarded as simply a subjective psychological state. We are in no doubt about her on that score after all. Our sense of her actual circumstances taken together with our knowledge of what really does matter to her ground our suspicions.

This example can be brought to bear on some unfinished business, notably will the advice "Count no man *eudaimon* ..." translate into a remark about happiness. Consider in this light the following remark made by Roger Montague:

> We must not take 'goal' so as to postpone indefinitely most instances of happiness. In one way a person has, and in another he has not, achieved his goal of marrying and staying married to someone when he has stayed married to her for five years. The way in which he has not achieved it is nonetheless compatible with happiness provided the prospect remains fair. Many of life's goals involve this kind of partly achieved and partly prospective continuity.[24]

Montague clearly wishes to block a path which could lead us in the direction of "Count no man happy ...". But when we apply his remark to less homespun examples than his, we also find ourselves edging away from the robust common-sense he intends to defend. Consider Mona some time later retrospectively reviewing her early married life which she has since discovered was based upon a deception. Not only have her hopes suffered a reverse now that she can see that part of her life clearly, but, more disturbingly, a backward shadow may be cast over that period. While we know that she would have said that her life was a happy one if she had been asked earlier on, is it certain that she should still grant that it was in her retrospective review? Montague's interpretation refers to goals "partly achieved", but in Mona's case they were merely thought to be.[25]

Next consider Oedipus from whose example the chorus was led to assert "Count no man *olbios* ..." (here essentially equivalent to *eudaimon*) (1.1528–30). Again Oedipus is not simply a person who in middle age happens to suffer a great and very probably irremediable reverse in fortune. He is someone who as a young man sought the help of the Pythian Apollo and heard dreadful prophesies about the deeds he would perform. To escape the fate which had been apparently settled for him, he leaves his home in Corinth and the adoptive parents whom he had come to believe were his biological parents as well. At first he seems to prosper, solving the sphinx's riddle and coming to the throne of Thebes as well as marrying the widow of his predecessor. Far from escaping his fate, however, that fate has been working itself out through his seeming achievements.

The play's fatalistic setting in a world where human achievement counts for little beside the awesome power of fate and the Gods allows the chorus to treat Oedipus as representative of the human situation. Hence their "Call no man ...". But wouldn't we equally find ourselves thinking in such a world "count no man happy ..." just as in our own we might arrive at a more circumscribed moral from the life of Mona? Remember that we are not required to agree to "count no man happy ...", only to make sense of it. And that seems possible.

Conclusion: It seems ironic that when some contemporary philosophers have looked to Aristotle for a more interestingly rich conception of happiness than glows of feeling or feelings of comfort and prosperity, others, partly under the influence of this pedestrian picture of it, have done their best to set this project beyond reach.[26] But the selling short of the possible riches of happiness has also been complemented by pictures of *eudaimonia* which wrest it from Aristotle's larger theories about human nature and the cast of mind proper to it.

No doubt our own concept of happiness has been and will continue to be shaped by historical factors including the philosophical theories that are believed from time to time. Part of the utilitarian heritage, for example, has been the difficulty illustrated by some of conceiving of happiness as anything but pleasure which, on the traditional utilitarian account, is a sensation only contingently related to the activities giving rise to it. But while all this is properly noted, it would be a pity if Aristotle's reflections on *eudaimonia* were placed beyond our reach whenever we tried seriously to think about happiness.

The largest obstacle standing in the way of thinking of *eudaimonia* in the light of happiness – from the perspective of our common understanding of happiness at least – is the view that we must think of happiness as no more than a subjective psychological state. What I have suggested is that while we conceive of it as a state, we need not think of it as totally determined by our subjective feelings. Such feelings do matter importantly of course, but they may not be the whole story. This is a suggestion we may find ourselves accepting not only by reflection on our reactions to particular cases like Mona's, but, more theoretically, through the deep and lingering connections we feel to exist between happiness, on the one hand, and notions like the fulfilment of desire, and the achievement of our goals, on the other. If we agree to this much, the way is largely clear for transforming the *prima facie* case from which we started into a reasonably settled conviction. *Eudaimonia*, after all, has a deep kinship with happiness.[27]

J.C. DYBIKOWSKI
The University of British Columbia

NOTES

1 Burnet, *The Ethics of Aristotle*, p. 1.

2 Apart from those cited in the paper, the view is supported, among others, by Joachim, *Aristotle: The Nicomachean Ethics*, p. 28; and J. Gosling, *Plato: Philebus*, p. 140. Gosling uses an etymological argument. He says: "Originally [*eudaimon*] was a word for remarking on what a good guardian spirit a man was blessed with. It leaves open how we should judge the work of guardian spirits. Their ability to supply us with happy or pleasant lives is obviously one possible criterion, but for that very reason 'happiness' cannot be the meaning". Not only are arguments from origins weak, but a parallel argument can be run for happiness. It derives from hap, meaning luck. What we would characterize as a happy or pleasant life might be a possible criterion for good luck. "Happiness", therefore, cannot mean what we take it to mean, which is evidently absurd.

3 See, for example, R. Brandt, article on Happiness, *Encyclopedia of Philosophy*; and A. Kenny, "Happiness", *Proceedings of the Aristotelian Society* (1965–6), p. 93.

4 J.S. Mill, for example, considered many of these as parts of happiness. See *Utilitarianism*, Ch. 4.

5 The most comprehensive review of literary uses of *eudaimonia* may be found in C. de Heer, *Makar, Eudaimon, Olbios, Eutuches: A Study of the Semantic Field Denoting Happiness in Ancient Greek to the End of the 5th Century B.C.*

6 A nice example is provided by Jane Austen's narrator who at one point remarks – one

would have wished ironically – of Emma: "To be in company, nicely dressed herself, and seeing others nicely dressed, to sit and smile and look pretty, and say nothing, was enough for the happiness of the present hour."

7 J. Ackrill, "Aristotle on *Eudaimonia*", British Academy Lecture (1974), pp. 12–13; see also his *Aristotle's Ethics*, p. 242.

8 B. Williams, *Morality: An Introduction to Ethics*, (Harper Torchbooks) pp. 81 ff.

9 J. Ackrill, "Aristotle on *Eudaimonia*", p. 13. As stated in this passage Ackrill's argument, which is only partly quoted here, relies on actually identifying happiness as comfort or prosperity. For on the basis of an admission about the latter he draws his conclusion about the former. See also A. Kenny's "Happiness" whose arguments against Aristotle's account of happiness Ackrill recasts as arguments against identifying *eudaimonia* with happiness.

10 Among recent discussions see: Z. Vendler, "Times and Tenses", *Philosophical Review* (1957), pp. 143–60; A. Kenny, *Action, Emotion and the Will*, Ch. 8; J. Ackrill, "Aristotle's Distinction Between *Energeia* and *Kinesis*", in R. Bambrough (ed.), *New Essays on Plato and Aristotle*, pp. 121–41.

11 Notably by A. Kenny, *Action, Emotion and the Will*, p. 173, n. 2.

12 Ackrill's translation. See Ackrill, Ibid., p. 122.

13 Following this suggestion helps us over a difficulty. In *Meta.* θ.6 an *energeia*, on my interpretation, can be either an activity or a state whereas in *N.E.* 1 it must be an activity. Yet both works assert that *eudaimonia* is a (certain) *energeia*. If the 'is', however, is that of identity in *Meta.* θ.6, then *N.E.* 1 is asserting a different thesis. This account is lent some color by the fact that tense-relations are at the heart of the *Metaphysics* thesis, but a *di*fferent set of arguments supports *N.E.* 1's thesis. While this account is admittedly awkward, at least it is not impossible and I persist in believing that it is true.

14 D. Wiggins, *Identity and Spatio-Temporal Continuity*, p. 10.

15 J.L. Austin, "*Agathon* and *Eudaimonia* in the *Ethics* of Aristotle", *Aristotle: A Collection of Critical Essays*, (ed.) J. Moravcsik, p. 280. Austin's initial hostility to "happiness" as a translation of *eudaimonia* is really directed at Prichard's equating of happiness with pleasure. Once he sees this (p. 283), he reconciles himself to the translation. Austin's point "hence the discussion ... of the various *bioi* which lay claim to being *eudaimonia*" doesn't take us very far because these *bioi* are very probably only abstractions of aspects of a person's total life and such aspects need only characterise a person for periods within his life's full term. This point is forcefully made by David Keyt in a forthcoming paper, "Intellectualism in Aristotle".

16 The authenticity of the *M.M.* has been defended most recently by J. Cooper, "The *Magna Moralia* and Aristotle's Moral Philosophy", *American Journal of Philology* (1973), pp. 327–49; and compare C. Rowe, "A Reply to John Cooper on the *Magna Moralia*", *American Journal of Philology* (1975), pp. 160–72.

17 A similar equivocation would seem to underpin Aristotle's linkage of *eudaimonia* as an *energeia* (*energeiai* being *tele* or ends) and *eudaimonia* as belonging primarily to a life. The link is made at *Rhet.* 1450a15 ff.

18 For some further references, although admittedly there are not many, see the tables in de Heer.

19 B. Suits, "Aristotle on the Function of Man: Fallacies, Heresies and Other Entertainments", *Canadian Journal of Philosophy* (1974), pp. 39–40.

20 J. Cooper, *Reason and Human Good in Aristotle*, p. 89, n. 1; see also A. MacC.

Armstrong, "Aristotle's Conception of Human Good", *Philosophical Quarterly* (1958), pp. 259–60, who says "*eudaimonia* is usually translated 'happiness', but this rendering suggests a glow of contentment ..." (my transliteration). Cooper recommends "human flourishing" as a preferable translation to "happiness". Since this suggestion has been widely and sympathetically received, it deserves some brief comment. First, "human flourishing" fails as a translation because it makes nonsense of *eudaimonia*'s predicability of the Gods. (Nor is there any retreat to "flourishing" because that would license *eudaimonia*'s predication to plants and animals.) Second, Cooper asserts that "flourishing implies the possession and use of one's *mature* powers over, at any rate, *a considerable period of time*" (my emphases), but this simply seems not true. Third, Cooper argues: "... it is plausible to suppose that a man's flourishing partly consists in his having good grounds for a good prognosis for his children's lives, and if after his death he turns out to have been deceived in this regard it does seem natural to say that his life was not so flourishing as it had seemed." But in what regard is he said to be deceived? Is his prognosis false or is it false that he had good reason to make it? If only the latter, the inference about the diminishment in his flourishing seems to collapse; but if the former, the position fails to match up to Aristotle's since his suggestion is that what happens to the children weakens the claim to *eudaimonia* whether or not it would have been antecedently reasonable for the parent to expect such an outcome.

21 T. Nagel, "Death", *Noûs* (1970), pp. 77–78.

22 See, among others, R. Brandt's *Encyclopedia* entry and R. Montague, "Happiness", *Proceedings of the Aristotelian Society* (1966–7), pp. 87–102.

23 See further R. Solomon, "Is There Happiness After Death?', *Philosophy* (1976), pp. 189–93.

24 R. Montague, "Happiness", p. 90.

25 See further D.A. Lloyd-Thomas, "Happiness", *Philosophical Quarterly* (1968), pp. 97 ff. and esp. 106–7, although he does not consider retrospective first-person assessments.

26 See, e.g., R. Scruton, "Reason and Happiness", *Nature and Conduct* Royal Institute of Philosophy Lectures, Vol. 8 (1975), pp. 139–61.

27 I have accumulated many debts in writing this paper, but most especially to Myles Burnyea, Mohan Matthen and Richard Sorabji and, more recently, Alan Code.

For Goodness' Sake: More on *Nicomachean Ethics* I vii 5*

by Troels Engberg-Pedersen (Copenhagen)

"Honour, pleasure, rationality and any type of virtue we choose, admittedly, for their own sake (for if nothing should result from them we would still choose each of them), but we also choose them for the sake of happiness, believing that by means of them we shall be happy."

My aim in this paper is to contribute to the clarification of certain concepts in the quoted passage: choosing something 'for its own sake', choosing it 'for the sake of happiness or *eudaimonia*[1]', and indeed the concept of *eudaimonia* itself. The more general topic of the paper is that of the relation in Aristotle's ethics between the value of 'acts proper' (*praxeis*), as opposed to 'production' (*poiesis*), and the supreme value in his ethical system: *eudaimonia*. *praxeis* are often understood as identical with what we should call moral acts. This is false, I believe: *praxeis* form a wider class of acts, which *includes* Aristotelian moral acts, whether good or bad. Nonetheless, through a discussion of the relation between the value of *praxeis* and *eudaimonia* light should be thrown on the crucial question of the relation to *eudaimonia* of the value of *moral* acts: are moral acts good because they contribute to *eudaimonia* and if so, how can they retain their property of being intrinsically good?

My remarks have been prompted by recent developments in the answer to be given to this question. Independently of each other J. L. Ackrill[2] and J. M. Cooper[3] have suggested revisions of the tradi-

---

* I have benefited from discussion of the matters treated with J. L. Ackrill (Oxford), Lesley Brown (Oxford), Myles Burnyeat (Cambridge), David Charles (Oxford). Johnny Christensen, Sten Ebbesen and Karsten Friis Johansen (Copenhagen). A version of the paper was presented at the bi-ennial meeting of the Scandinavian Plato Society in Copenhagen, June 1979.

[1] As far as I can see there is no reason not to translate *eudaimonia* as 'happiness'. But since people who know English better than I do consistently have qualms about that translation I stick to transliteration of the Greek word.

[2] J. L. Ackrill, 'Aristotle on *eudaimonia*', Proceedings of the British Academy 60 (1974) 3–23.

[3] J. M. Cooper, 'Reason and Human Good in Aristotle', Harvard UP (1975).

0003-9101/81/0631-0002$2.00

tional answer which go in the same direction. And many of the conceptual tools they have introduced play a crucial role in Terence Irwin's recent book on *Plato*'s moral theory[4]. As will be seen, my comments are heavily indebted to the contributions of these scholars. At the same time it is my contention that at a fairly central point, concerning the understanding of the concept of *eudaimonia* itself, the three commentators do not go far enough in the direction in which they have rightly pointed.

1.1 What may fairly be called *the traditional answer* to the question of the goodness of moral action in Aristotle detects a fundamental inconsistency in his views. On the one hand he seems to insist that moral acts are intrinsically good or good in themselves. On the other hand his doctrine of certain connected concepts is such that as a consequence moral acts must be considered good due to their being means to *eudaimonia*.

In support of the former claim one may point to two passages in *EN* VI where Aristotle distinguishes sharply between *praxis* and *poiesis*: VI v 3–4 and ii 5. The distinction may vaguely be stated to be the one between acts that are good in themselves and acts that are good because they produce something other than the act itself. But moral acts are *praxeis*. Hence their value cannot lie in their being means to *eudaimonia*.

On the other hand certain passages that discuss deliberation imply a different view. The truly good man is a man who is able to deliberate correctly with a view to "living well in general", i.e. to *eudaimonia* (*EN* VI v 1–2). But in his analysis of deliberation (in *EN* III iii) Aristotle uses as his model *technical* sciences and they characteristically either possess or look for *means*, in the normal causal sense of the term, to an end which is regarded as settled. So if, as must be the case, what the truly good man finds as a result of deliberation are morally good acts, they must be considered good as a result of being means to *eudaimonia*.

1.2 This, the traditional, diagnosis of an Aristotelian dilemma has been challenged by Ackrill and Cooper.

Cooper bases his attack on a consideration of Aristotle's account of deliberation[5]. Deliberation is not just concerned with means in a strictly

---

4 Terence Irwin, 'Plato's Moral Theory. The Early and Middle Dialogues', Oxford UP (1977).

5 Cooper pp. 19–20.

causal sense, but with 'things that contribute to the end' (*ta pros to telos*) and these may also be constituent parts of complex ends or particular things that a given end may be seen to consist in. Thus, to take an un-Cooperian but Aristotelian example that illustrates Cooper's point, a doctor may decide to rub a patient's limb in order to heal it, and both the rubbing, which is a means proper, and the resulting warmth of the limb, which is an element in its health, may be said to be things that 'contribute' to the end. But then, if we say of the ultimate end, or *eudaimonia*, that it is something desired for its own sake we may say the same of morally good action if we take the way in which morally good action 'contributes' to *eudaimonia* to be that of its being a *constituent part* thereof[6]. By this move the dilemma seems solved.

Ackrill takes as his starting-point a puzzling remark of Aristotle's on the very first page of the *Ethics*[7]. Here Aristotle is concerned to subordinate ends of acts to other ends and in the final outcome, as is clear from ii 1, to a single, truly final end. However, he has also distinguished between acts which are their own ends and acts which have ends other than themselves. And then, when it comes to subordinating either type of end he rather oddly remarks that it makes no difference as far as subordination is concerned whether a given end is of the one type or of the other. This *is* odd: in what way can an act which is its own end be subordinated to any further end? The puzzle is solved, according to Ackrill, by the introduction of the relation part to whole. Acts which are their own end may at the same time be constituents of or ingredients in or, for short, *parts* of a certain whole. The relation is illustrated by two examples: as putting is to playing golf and as golfing is to having a good holiday. By means of this conceptual tool, Ackrill further suggests, we may solve the problem of the relation of moral acts to *eudaimonia*. For we may now sensibly say that moral acts are done for their own sake and at the same time for the sake of *eudaimonia*, viz. as parts of that whole.

Finally *Irwin* makes extensive use of the idea that moral virtue may be said to be good both in itself and because of its contribution to the final good for the reason that moral virtue should be seen as a *component* of the final good[8]. And when he introduces the distinction between 'instrumental' and 'component' means he explicitly refers to

[6] *id.* p. 82.
[7] Ackrill pp. 6–7.
[8] Irwin, e.g. pp. 188, 225.

2*

the Aristotelian context[9]: to Greenwood, who introduced the distinction in connection with a certain passage in *EN* VI[10], and to Cooper and D. Wiggins[11], who have recently made use of it in connection with Aristotle's *ta pros to telos*.

2 So, should we say, and in what sense should we say, that in Aristotle a moral act, and generally a *praxis*, is considered good both in itself and also as a component, part or constituent of *eudaimonia*?

For an answer we should turn to the passage I quoted at the beginning (*EN* I vii 5). The passage itself speaks of things as chosen both 'for their own sake' and 'for the sake of *eudaimonia*', and it forms the conclusion of a sustained argument (in vii 1–4) and is followed by further elucidation (in vii 6–8) of the concept of *eudaimonia* that is expressed in § 5: perhaps renewed analysis of what comes before and after will throw light on the point of the passage itself.

3.1 First, however, we must consider the context and the point of the whole section referred to: vii 1–8[12].

Right at the start of the *Ethics* (i–ii 1) Aristotle works out the idea of a single end of all acts which is 'the good' or 'the highest good'. I shall consider the passage in more detail at the end of this paper. He then asks (in ii 3) what that single end may be and what science is concerned with it. The latter question is immediately answered (in ii 4–8): the science is politics. The former question, of course, is the one that guides the development of the rest of the work. It is taken up in iv 1, following remarks (in iii) on method and addressee of the work: 'what is the thing that we claim to be what politics strives towards and what is the highest of all practical goods?' In terms of its name, Aristotle continues (iv 2–3), there is general agreement: everybody speaks of *eudaimonia* and understands living well and doing well as synonymous with being

---

9 *id.* p. 83 note 53 (p. 300).

10 L. H. G. Greenwood, 'Aristotle, Nicomachean Ethics Book Six' (1909). I believe severe damage has been caused by Greenwood's application of his distinction, which makes perfectly good sense in connection with the passage he refers to (*EN* VI xii 5, 1144a3–6), to the passages and problems of *EN* I that I shall discuss. In VI xii 5 Aristotle is talking of the relationship of a certain good to a certain whole that *eudaimonia* is taken to consist in, not to *eudaimonia* itself. In the passages of *EN* I, as we shall see, he is totally reticent on what *eudaimonia* consists in and only interested in the relationship of goods to *eudaimonia* itself.

11 D. Wiggins, 'Deliberation and Practical Reason', Proceedings of the Aristotelian Society 76 (1975–76) 29–51.

12 Highly relevant to these two questions is J. L. Austin, '*Agathon* and *eudaimonia* in the *Ethics* of Aristotle', in J. M. E. Moravcsik (ed.), 'Aristotle' (1967) 261–296, especially pp. 274–279.

eudaimon. But people disagree about *what eudaimonia* is, and often even the same person will at different times have different views.

It has been noted more than once, and it *is* noteworthy, that the concept from which Aristotle takes his starting–point in the Nicomachean Ethics is not that of *eudaimonia* but that of 'the good' in the form of the highest practical good. *eudaimonia* is the term people normally use when talking of these matters, and when they disagree about what to go for they disagree about what *eudaimonia* is; but the basic concept is that of the good as the end of acts: *eudaimonia* is not introduced until the passage I paraphrased from chapter iv and then only as the more familiar concept.

So people talk of *eudaimonia*. They will agree that when the philosopher talks instead of 'what politics strives towards' and 'the highest of all practical goods' he is really talking of what they think of when they use the term *eudaimonia*. But they will disagree about *what* the philosopher's highest good, or their own *eudaimonia*, is.

There can be no doubt that as *eudaimonia* is used here it is to be understood as an 'indeterminate' end, viz. something which has properties that are formal in the sense that knowledge of them will not necessarily result in agreement among different people about what things or activities fall under the thing. The reason for such indeterminacy will often be that the definition of the indeterminate thing contains predicates on whose application to particular cases each individual is the final arbiter. Thus if the definition of some type of state we should wish to talk of contained the predicates *frightening* or *threatening*, there might well be universal agreement about what it is for a thing to be frightening or threatening. But such agreement would not always result in agreement about what things *are* frightening or threatening and hence fall under the state. And I take it to be a fact that this is because the properties that are referred to by these predicates, as opposed e.g. to the property referred to by the predicate *dangerous*, are essentially relative to the individual who talks about them, in the sense that his judgement as to what things possess those properties cannot be overruled. It is true that "the man who is by nature apt to fear everything, even the squeak of a mouse, is cowardly with a (sub-human or) brutish cowardice" (*EN* VII v 6, 1149a7–8), but still fully human beings in fact do fear different things and in the case of both human and sub-human fears, while we may rightly claim people to be wrong in considering the things they fear *dangerous* we cannot deny them the right to consider the things *frightening*.

Aristotle was keenly aware of this special feature of certain predicates. He makes the point when he observes that the same thing may appear in different ways to different people: sweet or bitter, warm or cold, pleasant or unpleasant. The fact that he always insists that the thing *is* as it appears to be to the 'sane' man does not militate against this interpretation.

Next (chapter v), following further remarks on method and addressee of the work (iv 5–7), Aristotle returns to his quest for "the good and *eudaimonia*". He mentions the three or four things that people normally suggest, on the basis of the well-known three 'lives'[13], to be what *eudaimonia* consists in. There is pleasure, for the life of enjoyment;

[13] Against tradition I translate 1095b14–19 as follows: "For people seem reasonably enough to understand the good and *eudaimonia* on the basis of the (well-known)

there is, for the political life, honour or perhaps rather the virtue that a man is honoured for; and similarly there will presumably be, for the contemplative life, some kind of theoretical activity – though Aristotle defers further consideration of that till later.

These are suggestions as to what particular types of thing or activity should be taken to fill in the concept of *eudaimonia*. The following chapter (vi), on Platonic views of the good, is clearly indicated by Aristotle, at the start of chapter vii, to be a digression. Hence when, in vii 1, he announces a return to the question what the good that is sought may be, one naively expects to get his own view of the substantial content of *eudaimonia*. As is well known, however, this expectation is not fulfilled until very much later in the work. What, then, is the answer of chapter vii to the question of what the good that is sought may be?

3.2 vii 9 is relevant. The claim, says Aristotle, that the highest good is *eudaimonia* may seem unenlightening[14]: we want a clearer suggestion as to what it is; but this we may perhaps get if we consider man's proper activity (*ergon*). According to this paragraph chapter vii divides into two. In vii 10ff. Aristotle defines the highest good, and consequently *eudaimonia*, in terms of the concept of man's proper activity. In vii 1–8 he has defined the highest good as – *eudaimonia*.

The latter point may seem surprising: has not the relationship of the good and *eudaimonia* been sufficiently determined already in chapter iv? Nevertheless there can be no doubt that Aristotle's most overt purpose in vii 1–8 is precisely to identify the good as *eudaimonia*. (a) Consider the line of thought in the argument of §§ 1–5: the good that is sought, or the practical good, is that-for-the-sake-of-which or end; there are several types of end; so the good is most final or final without qualification: it is what is always choiceworthy for its own sake and never for the sake of anything else – "but that sort of thing *eudaimonia* seems precisely (*malista*) to be" (1097a34). So, we may infer, the good is *eudaimonia*. (b) "The same seems also to follow from its self-sufficiency", i.e. from the fact that it, viz. the good, is self-sufficient (1097b5–6)[15]. §§ 6–7 repeat the pattern of argument of §§ 1–5: the good is self-sufficient; the self-sufficient is this and that – "but that sort of thing we take *eudaimonia* to be" (1097b15–16). So, the good is *eudaimonia*.

However, it seems clear that Aristotle also has a less overt purpose in vii 1–8, which is that of defining the two properties of being final and self-sufficient and of suggesting that

---

lives: the many, who are the most vulgar, (judge it to be) pleasure – that's precisely why they love the life of enjoyment; for the prominent lives are *three* (in number), no more no less (*malista*), viz. the one just mentioned, the political one and thirdly the contemplative one". The *lives* are what people immediately know of. When asked what they take *eudaimonia* to consist in, people will answer by extrapolation from the lives. Cf. lines 22–23.

[14] In the Greek text *ten . . . eudaimonian* must be the grammatical predicate and *to ariston* the grammatical subject. Otherwise it will be impossible to draw out a consistent line of thought for the whole of §§ 1–9. Ramsauer and Gauthier/Jolif take it thus.

[15] In the quotation 'its' is a translation of *tēs*. That it is *the good* (not *eudaimonia*) whose self-sufficiency is the starting-point of the argument is, once more, clear from the structure of the section as a whole.

they both belong to *eudaimonia*. Thus he sums up the whole section in this way (vii 8, 1097b20–21): "So *eudaimonia* appears to be something final and self-sufficient, being end of acts".

We may make sense of this seeming crisscross of purposes if we take Aristotle's basic aim to be that of bringing out certain formal properties, viz. those of being final and self-sufficient, that belong to the concept people normally use: *eudaimonia*. Aristotle seemingly, and most overtly, argues thus: the good (*his* concept) has certain properties; but look, they are precisely the properties we take *eudaimonia* to have – so the good is *eudaimonia*. But the point of the argument, in spite of its overt conclusion, lies in bringing out *that eudaimonia has* those properties. By starting from his own concept and developing *that*, he forces upon the person who is only operating with the more familiar concept of *eudaimonia* a realisation of certain properties that are had by *that* concept.

4.1 What, then, are the two properties that are ascribed to the good and *eudaimonia* in vii 1–8? The good and *eudaimonia* is something final (*teleion*) and self-sufficient (*autarkes*). Before turning to the paragraphs themselves it is worth considering Aristotle's general use of those two concepts. Although they are evidently closely related, it seems possible to maintain a certain difference between them.

The final, according to Aristotle, is 'that beyond which one cannot lay hand on anything'[16]. It seems clear that Aristotle intends this definition in the following sense: the final is that beyond which one can *no longer* lay hand on anything. In other words, the final is to be understood as the terminus of a chain that consists in constantly going beyond what was first taken as final. Thus the final is essentially relative to what lies 'before' the thing that is called final.

The case is different, I believe, for the concept of the self-sufficient. What is self-sufficient is 'what lacks nothing in addition'[17]. Here too there will be something relative to which the self-sufficient will be so called. But the former thing will not be something that lies 'before' the self-sufficient. Rather it is some demand that is raised by the context into which the concept of the self-sufficient is introduced. Thus when Aristotle describes certain types of practical science as exact and self-sufficient (*EN* III iii 8, 1112a34–b1), he means that they contain the answer to all the questions that may be asked concerning how to bring about something that falls under the given practical area. In this context there is a demand for a type of knowledge that will enable a person to answer all practical questions in a certain area: when the self-sufficient is there, there is knowledge that satisfies that demand.

The important point for the general use of the two concepts is, then, that the final is, but the self-sufficient is not, relative to something that lies 'before' itself[18].

---

[16] See, e.g., *Metaph.* 1021b12–13 and 1021b32–1022a1 in the chapter (16) in *Metaph.* Delta on the concept. And cf. *Metaph.* Iota 4, 1055a11–16.

[17] See, e.g., *EN* IX ix 1, 1169b5–6 and X vi 2, 1176b5–6.

[18] I do not wish to be dogmatic here. It is sufficient for my purpose that 'final' and 'self-sufficient' are *sometimes* used in this slightly different way.

4.2 Let us now turn to vii 1–8. It will be convenient to start from §§ 6–7.

We know the direction of Aristotle's argument. That 'the good' is *eudaimonia* may be seen to follow from its self-sufficiency; for the final good *is* self-sufficient; now the self-sufficient is "that which when taken alone makes a life choiceworthy and lacking in nothing" – "and that is the sort of thing we take *eudaimonia* to be"; so the good is *eudaimonia*.

Let us consider the definition of the self-sufficient. The self-sufficient makes a *life choiceworthy*. Aristotle is talking of a whole life, not just of living: but what does he mean by his claim that in being self-sufficient a whole life will be choiceworthy? We may make use of the fact that in his definition Aristotle glosses 'choiceworthy' as 'lacking in nothing'. If a life is lacking in nothing there will be no desires which are not satisfied. Perhaps, then, Aristotle's idea is that the value of living lies in the satisfaction of desires: the feeling of need, in so far as this is the only thing that fills a person's consciousness, will necessarily make non-living preferable to living. But if in this way for the self-sufficient to be there the whole life must be choiceworthy or such as to leave no desires unsatisfied, then since a life is a stretch of time that is made up by smaller stretches of time and since it seems likely that Aristotle means what holds of the whole life to hold of the smaller stretches too, the consequence will be that at any particular moment during the life that is self-sufficient living will be in all respects preferable to non-living: there will be no desire which is not satisfied.

This may seem a strange conception. How, if at any particular moment all the desires of a given person are satisfied may he 'move' from one situation to another: there will be no desires to guide such a move? Nor will it be at all possible for human beings to come to lead such a life; for they do in fact get desires for things which are not immediately present. However, I insist that this *is* precisely Aristotle's conception of a state which is properly called self-sufficient. What the two oddities point to is just that human beings shall never attain to the self-sufficient state: they do not show that the concept of that state is incoherent.

The self-sufficient, then, is the state that satisfies all the desires of a given person, and hence makes him want to live, during the whole of his life. It is, furthermore, a state of a person during the whole of his life which is such that at any particular moment during that life all of his desires are satisfied and he prefers living to non-living. This state cannot in fact be attained by human beings, but that does not render the concept of the state incoherent. It hardly could be incoherent without severe consequences, since it is the concept of the *point* of all the desires of a given person.

Aristotle also claims the self-sufficient to be what when *taken alone* makes a life choiceworthy etc. His point is simply that the self-sufficient is, logically speaking, sufficient to make a whole life choiceworthy and lacking in nothing in the manner I have explained.

So, the self-sufficient is a state with the formal property of being the point of all the desires of a given person. Therefore, since it is relative to what desires the person in fact has, it is indeterminate with respect to its substantial content.

"- and that is the sort of thing we take *eudaimonia* to be": on the account I have given of the self-sufficient, what Aristotle has done in §§ 6–7 is to define in more precise terms the understanding of the concept of *eudaimonia* that seemed implied in his remarks in chapter iv concerning the role of the concept in everyday usage.

It is worth pointing out already at this stage that Aristotle's definition of *eudaimonia* as the self-sufficient leaves absolutely open the question whether just one thing or more things than one fall under the state that it is. Nor is there any implication in his definition that if more things than one fall under the state they either will or will not form some ordered compound. The self-sufficient is a state that satisfies all the desires of a given person and there is absolutely no restriction on how many, or how few, desires a person may have, nor on what type of object they may be for.

In what follows I shall speak of the 'eudaimonic' state and mean thereby a state of a person during the whole of his life which is such that if a person is in it all his desires will be satisfied and he will at any time prefer living to non-living.

4.3 Let us now turn to Aristotle's account in §§ 1–5 of the good that is sought.

§ 1 starts from the question what the good that is sought may be and suggests, in a careful progression of thought, first that it is that-for-the-sake-of-which other things are done and then that it is the end – for the end *is* that-for-the-sake-of-which other things are done (1097a21–22). "So if there is a single end of all acts, that will be the practical good, if there are more than one, they will be that good" (a22–24).

§ 3 distinguishes between types of end. Some ends are subordinate: though ends of other things they are themselves chosen for some further end. Other ends are truly end-like or final. "So if there is only one final thing, that will be the good that is sought, if there are more than one, the most final among them will be that good" (a28–30). Two questions should concern us here. If the good is the *most* final among final things what has happened to those other things which *are truly* final though not the *most* final thing? And what sense should be given to the claim that among things which are themselves truly final something may be most final?

§ 4 is clearly intended by Aristotle to help clear up these questions. The important distinction that is introduced here is the one between on the one hand things that are choiceworthy both in themselves and for the sake of something else and on the other hand what is always choiceworthy in itself and never for the sake of something else: the latter is *implied* to be that *most* final thing and *stated* to be final "without qualification".

§ 5: "and that is precisely the sort of thing *eudaimonia* seems to be; for . . ." (a34–b1).

4.4 What is the good, and *eudaimonia*, if it is the most final thing or the thing which is final without qualification, i.e. what is always choiceworthy in itself and never for the sake of something else?

I take it for granted that Aristotle wishes to give expression, in §§ 1–5, to the conception of the good and *eudaimonia* that is also expressed in §§ 6–7 by the introduction of the concept of the self-sufficient. In §§ 1–5 he wishes to bring out that same conception by the use of other concepts.

He glosses 'the good that is sought' as 'the practical good' and suggests that it is an *end* of *acts*. So we are in the realm of *acting*, which immediately brings in the concept of an *end*: any act is for an end, according to Aristotle. Now a concept that is closely connected with those of acting and an end is that of choosing (*haireisthai*). Choosing is a bad translation for Aristotle's concept, which is that of 'doing something with a view to having something else'. There is something one wants to have, one takes steps to get it: one 'chooses'. Thus when there is choice (*hairesis*) there is some *end* and some *act* that is supposed to bring about the end. And when one 'chooses' one *wants* to do the *act* with a view to bringing about the *end*. I wish to suggest that when Aristotle glosses 'the good that is sought' as 'the practical good', when he introduces the concept of an end, and when he draws the crucial distinction between ends that have, and ends that do not have, other things as their end, he is wishing to define the good in relation to the concept of 'choosing'. And I suggest that when he defines the good as the most final thing or the thing which is final without qualification, and hence as what is always choiceworthy in itself and never for the sake of something else, he is claiming the good to be the point of all choice. Any choice has as its 'ideal' object the state where its end has been reached. When this state is present the choice has made itself superfluous. But then, once more, we may introduce the idea of a state of a person during the whole of his life in which all the choices that he makes have made themselves superfluous. This, the eudaimonic state, is the point of all his choices.

4.5 I am evidently relying here on my interpretation of the self-sufficient. More important, however, is it to observe that the suggested interpretation throws light on the crucial stages of the argument of §§ 1–5.

First, of course, it explains why Aristotle connects the good that is sought with acts and ends thereof: he is construing the good that is sought as something that may be brought about by choice, *i.e.* by purposeful activity.

Secondly one can see why Aristotle introduces the distinction between ends that are and ends that are not subordinate to other ends. The distinction may seem natural enough once the concept of an end has been introduced. But note that Aristotle's aim in drawing it is not so much to discard ends that are subordinate to other ends from qualifying as the good that is sought. Rather it is to discard even ends which in the dichotomy as it is first drawn are *not* subordinate to other ends, in favour of some even higher end. Thus by his use of the distinction Aristotle may now be seen to turn the reader's attention in the direction of his peculiar conception of the good as not just *an* end among others but *the* end, the point of *all* the choices of a given person.

Thirdly we can see why Aristotle restricts the good to being the *most* final among final ends, and what he means by the phrase 'most final among final ends'. The eudaimonic state is different from ends that are final since while the latter are the point of each their particular chain of choices the former is the point of all the choices that a person will make during the whole of his life. This means that all particular final ends will *fall under* the eudaimonic state. There is therefore no problem about Aristotle's restricting the good to being the *most* final among final ends: the final ends have not been accidentally left out.

Nor is it difficult to see what he means when he talks of the most final among final ends. The eudaimonic state is an end that belongs at a different level from that of particular final ends, in as much as they *fall under* the state, and the point of Aristotle's use of the superlative form is to bring out that difference of level. Similarly the point of 'without qualification' and, in the definition of the end that is final without qualification, 'always' and 'never' is to bring out that the good is *the* choiceworthy thing, the thing or state which puts an end to the activity of choosing since all the things that are the objects of the choices of a given person have been acquired when he is in that state. And *the* choiceworthy thing, thus understood, belongs at a different level from particular choiceworthy things in as much as the latter fall under the former.

4.6 It is noteworthy that it is precisely this force of the superlative form that Aristotle strives to bring out in § 8. *eudaimonia* is there stated to be the most choiceworthy of all things – without being counted among them; for were it so counted it would clearly become *more* choiceworthy by having added to it even the slightest of those other goods – and, we may conclude the argument, if *eudaimonia* is such a thing that it will become *more* choiceworthy by having goods added to it, it will not be the *most* choiceworthy of all things in the sense intended. *eudaimonia*, then, is most choiceworthy in the sense of absolutely or perfectly so: it belongs at a different level from that of particular choiceworthy things.

4.7 In §§ 1–5, then, Aristotle defines the good and *eudaimonia* as the point of all the choices of a given person; in §§ 6–7 he defines it as the state where all the person's desires are satisfied. Thus interpreted the two definitions look similar. But note that they differ in a way that is consonant with the general difference between the concepts of being final and being self-sufficient that I brought out in section 4.1. *eudaimonia* as final without qualification is precisely the terminus of a chain or chains of things, viz. choices and their (particular) ends whether themselves subordinate or not, that lie 'below' the absolutely final end. *eudaimonia* as final without qualification is at the top of a hierarchy (whether one-stringed or not is irrelevant) of things that are subordinate to it.

Not so for *eudaimonia* when it is defined as the self-sufficient. Here *eudaimonia* is simply relative to the desires that the person has at any particular moment and there is no implication that these desires are connected with other desires in a chain or hierarchy. *eudaimonia* as self-sufficient is the state that satisfies the person's desires at any particular moment during the whole of his life, just as a practical science which is self-sufficient is one that contains the answer to any question one may be forced to raise as one goes through life.

The difference between the two accounts lies in the fact that while they both make use of the concept of desire, the definition of the self-sufficient does just that while the definition of the final uses desire in connection with the realm of action; and this area is in fact such that one must introduce first, a distinction between what is done and what it is done for (the end) and next, a distinction between ends that are and ends that are not subordinate to other things as their end. *eudaimonia* as the final without qualification is the point of all choice and action, but the area of choosing and acting is itself articulated in terms of the distinction I mentioned. *eudaimonia* as the self-sufficient, on the other hand, is just the state where all desires are satisfied and in itself the area of desire is not articulated in any specific way.

5.1 I have been concerned, till now, to bring out the sense of the two definitions of the good and *eudaimonia*, as absolutely final and as self-sufficient. Two questions in connection with vii 5 have not been discussed. First, what is the sense of choosing something for the sake of *eudaimonia*? And secondly what is meant when we are stated to choose something, e.g. honour, *both* for its *own* sake *and* for the sake of *eudaimonia*?

For the moment I shall concentrate on the former question. On my reading of *eudaimonia* as the point of all choice and the state where all desires are satisfied, *eudaimonia* is an indeterminate state with a certain formal property. It is indeterminate because it is dependent for its substantial content on what choices a given person will in fact make and what desires he will in fact have. What, then, can be meant when something is stated to be chosen *for the sake of* that indeterminate end?

If we are to maintain, and we are, the exact force of *eudaimonia* as an indeterminate end, the point of the phrase 'for the sake of *eudaimonia*' cannot be to introduce something that will explain *why* the thing that is referred to *eudaimonia* is considered choiceworthy. The reference to *eudaimonia* cannot in any way *add* to the value that the thing is taken to have whether it is referred to *eudaimonia* or not. For this would presuppose that *eudaimonia* is considered something determinate and we have decided to keep it an indeterminate end. So the explanatory value of the reference to *eudaimonia* will not be the one of 'conferring value' on the thing that is referred to *eudaimonia*. When, e.g., honour is chosen for the sake of *eudaimonia* the reference to *eudaimonia* does not confer additional value on honour. Honour is considered choiceworthy and it is *also* stated to stand in a certain relationship to *eudaimonia*.

But then it is not difficult to see what that relationship must be. It is that of 'falling under' the eudaimonic state, of being one thing that makes determinate (so far) that indeterminate state. Thus understood the reference to *eudaimonia* does have explanatory value. It introduces the concept of a very wide state, viz. the state of a person during the whole of his life, and a state which though indeterminate for its substantial content nevertheless exhibits a certain precise formal property. When honour is related to this concept we do become wiser concerning the description under which the given person considers honour choiceworthy, but our enlightenment is not due to fact that we can now see more clearly *why* the person values honour as he does, but to the fact that the person's estimation of honour has now been inserted into a wider conceptual framework. He is now seen as a person who operates with the notion of *eudaimonia* and who is apparently prepared to mention honour as one thing that goes into *eudaimonia*. When we know that we know more about the person's attitude to honour. But still we do not know more about *why* he considers honour choiceworthy in the first place.

Observe here that when honour is referred to *eudaimonia* as that for the sake of which it is chosen there is absolutely no hint or implication that there either are or are not other things that fall under *eudaimonia* in addition to honour. The reference to *eudaimonia* is a reference to a purely indeterminate state, which is the point of all choice and the state where all desires are satisfied. It is not a reference to any considered view of what things make up that state. One may of course attempt to relate honour to other such things: this, however, is not what is done when honour is referred to *eudaimonia* as what it is chosen for.

5.2 This is the point where my account of the relation 'for the sake of *eudaimonia*' differs from those I mentioned earlier. For in these accounts it does seem to be presupposed that the reference to *eudaimonia* will *add* to the value of the thing that is referred to *eudaimonia*.

Thus, to take a single example from Irwin's book, when, in connection with Plato's *Republic*, he discusses the idea that justice is good both in itself and for the sake of the final good, or *eudaimonia*, Irwin insists that the final good is "an ordered compound"[19]. Here the underlying idea seems to be that only thus will the reference to *eudaimonia* have any point. But this, of course, is only so if one expects that point to be the one of 'conferring value' on the thing that is referred to *eudaimonia*, of adding to the value which it is anyway taken to have.

A similar expectation seems to be entertained by Ackrill when he remarks that if *eudaimonia* is viewed as an aggregate instead of an organised system the move, i.e. the

---

[19] Irwin p. 225.

reference, to *eudaimonia* will be trivial[20]. The reference to an aggregate *eudaimonia* will only be trivial if one expects it to do more than it is intended to do, viz. to provide a reason *why* the thing that is referred to *eudaimonia* is considered choiceworthy.

Why do Ackrill and Irwin take the reference to *eudaimonia* to have 'substantial' explanatory value in this way? The reason seems to be that though they have introduced and stressed the importance of certain points I have made use of in the above account of *eudaimonia*, e.g. that it is an indeterminate end[21] and that it may be glossed as 'the perfectly satisfying life'[22], they do not always keep in view the difference between eudaimonia as an indeterminate state and the, in all probability, inclusive determinate conception of that state that we shall in the end come out with as *our* view of what the state consists in. But these two types of end must be kept apart; for the explanatory value of referring something to either is different.

It will not do, therefore, to explicate the relationship between a thing and *eudaimonia*, where the former is referred to the latter, by means of the following two examples: as putting is to playing golf or as golfing is to having a good holiday. In the former case the thing is referred to a whole which is equivalent to what I called an inclusive *determinate* conception of *eudaimonia*. In the latter case, however, the thing is referred to something which is equivalent to the indeterminate eudaimonic state: in fact having a good holiday *is* being *eudaimon* – during one's holiday.

Cooper too wants to *infer* the intrinsic value of the components of the ultimate end from the intrinsic value of that end itself. *Because* the ultimate end is something, in fact the only thing, which is desired for its own sake, *therefore* the components of that end are themselves desired for their own sake (and, of course, for the sake of the ultimate end too)[23]. It would presumably be unjust to charge Cooper with the claim that the reference to the ultimate end *adds* to the value of the component. But still it is clear that in the passage I have just referred to, and elsewhere, when Cooper talks of the ultimate end he is talking of some *conception* of that end, not of the entirely formal state that it is. Thus in an important section[24] he states that the ultimate end is "an inclusive second-order end". This looks promising. But what he is really thinking of is a certain "*conception* of human flourishing" (my emphasis), which though it is claimed, validly enough, to allow for the independent value of a number of different activities and interests is also described as "an orderly scheme" and "an overall plan of life".

As against this, I claim that when something is referred to *eudaimonia* it is referred not to some (inclusive or dominant) conception of what *eudaimonia* consists in, but to the state itself which has the single property of being the point of all the choices and desires of a given person, and none in addition.

---

20 Ackrill p. 11.
21 Irwin *passim*.
22 Ackrill p. 15.
23 Cooper p. 82 with footnote.
24 *id.* pp. 96–99.

6.1 I have discussed, in connection with vii 1–8, the sense of the concept of *eudamonia* and the sense of referring a thing to *eudaimonia* by means of the phrase 'for the sake of *eudaimonia*'. However, Aristotle also says that one may choose something, e.g. honour, *both* for its own sake and (at the same time, I take it) *also* for the sake of *eudaimonia*. What is meant here? What is the relationship between 'for its own sake' and 'for the sake of *eudaimonia*'?

If one accepts the interpretation I have given of *eudaimonia* and the sense of referring something to *eudaimonia* one might contend that the latter reference adds nothing significant to the claim that the thing is choiceworthy for its own sake. The eudaimonic state will consist of all the things that are considered choiceworthy in themselves, but then could we not altogether dispense with the concept of that state?

This is not to say that Aristotle is wrong to spend time on elucidating the concept. For, as we have seen, people do talk of *eudaimonia*, hence it is well worth bringing out what they mean. However, I shall contend that the concept of *eudaimonia* has a much more important role to play. The concept is put to use at a theoretically central point.

6.2 There are good grounds for ascribing to Aristotle a view of the concept of rational want (in effect his notion of *prohairesis*) according to which it is a necessary condition for a want to be rational that the person who has it is able to mention something that he considers the wanted object to be good *for*. He must, in Aristotelian terms, be able to mention some *telos* (end) or other. A paradigm case is the want which is had by a technician for an act which is considered a means proper to some end. His want is rationalised by being referred to the end and the expression that is used to bring about this reference is the phrase 'for the sake of' where what is for the sake of is a different thing from what it is for the sake of. It also seems clear that Aristotle is prepared to use the phrase 'for the sake of' not only where what is related are two different *things* but also where the phrase brings in some other *description* of the one initial thing. Thus, e.g., when something is stated to be choiceworthy or good 'for the sake of the noble'.

When, however, the two things that are brought into relation with each other by means of 'for the sake of' are one and the same thing under the same description it is much less easy to see how the want is rationalised by means of that phrase. 'x is good for its own sake or because of itself', 'x has as its end itself': one might think that these sentences are unproblematic in the way in which talk of a mathematical set as being empty is unproblematic. However, when the point of talking of an 'end' of something and of using the phrase 'for the sake of' is to rationalise or make intelligible some want, it can hardly be sufficient just to use the concepts of an end and for the sake of: the wanted object must be connected *by means of* those concepts with other things, whether it be truly different things or just different descriptions under which the one initial thing is seen. So the sentence 'x is choiceworthy or good for its own sake' is problematic as an expression that is intended to rationalise the want for x.

However we cannot dispense with the phrase 'good for its own sake'. People do or bring about certain things for the sake of others, but the chain of explanation cannot go on for ever. Any chain must stop *some*where, otherwise the initial desire will be pointless. And in fact, people do stop chains by stating of something that they choose *that* thing for its *own* sake. Moreover since the function of that statement is to put a stop to chains of explanation that *rationalise* wants, by the use of the phrase 'for the sake of something else', the statement must itself rationalise or make intelligible the want for the thing that is claimed to stop the given chain. But we saw that precisely as a rationalising concept it is problematic[25].

6.3 This is where the concept of *eudaimonia* comes in. The problem about the phrase 'for its own sake' is that we want it to put a stop to chains of explanation, but that it is not fully intelligible as a concept that rationalises a want. The concept of *eudaimonia* is both sufficient to rationalise a want and eminently suited to put a stop to chains of explanations. It is sufficient to rationalise a want since being the concept of the state whose existence is implied in the very notion of choosing (it is the concept of a state which is the point of all choice) it is itself so eminently rational. And it is well suited to put a stop to chains of explanation since it is the concept of a state where all chains of explanation come to a stop. It seems, therefore, that we may make use of the concept of *eudaimonia* to put a stop to any *particular* chain of explanation at the point at which we *do* wish to stop and that the way in which we may use the concept is by saying that we choose this thing not for the sake of anything else but 'for the sake of *eudai-*

[25] Relevant to this section are, in each their different ways, G. E. M. Anscombe, 'Intention' (1957) and Jaakko Hintikka, 'Remarks on praxis, poiesis, and ergon in Plato and in Aristotle', in 'Studia philosophica in honorem Sven Krohn', Annales universitatis turkuensis, series B, tom. 126 (1973) 53–62.

monia', i.e. as one thing that has the role of filling in that indeterminate concept or of falling under the by itself indeterminate eudaimonic state.

However, what we in fact normally say is not immediately that we choose the thing for the sake of *eudaimonia*, but that we choose it for its own sake: I suggest that we take the phrase 'for the sake of *eudaimonia*' as an *explication* of the phrase 'for its own sake' or, in other words, that we take the reference to the state where there is room for nor no more choices at all to rationalise the suggestion of some particular thing as something that puts a stop to *one* set of choices. We may say, then, that properly understood the phrase 'for its own sake' *introduces* the concept of *eudaimonia*. The latter concept is the one that renders the phrase sufficiently informative for it to rationalise the want for the given thing.

So the concept of *eudaimonia* has a most important role to play at a crucial point for our understanding of the system of concepts that are implied by the concept of choice. The latter concept implies the notion of an *end* of something and the notion of an end implies the distinction between ends that are themselves related to *other* things as their end and ends which are not themselves so related. But in order to make sufficiently rational sense of the latter type of end we must introduce the concept that is basic to the concept of choice, viz. that of the 'ideal object' or point of all choice: the state where all choice has made itself superfluous since the ends of all choices have been reached. When the phrase 'for its own sake' is seen to introduce *this* concept we shall be rationally satisfied by a claim that makes use of the phrase and states that something is chosen as an end which is not related to *other* things as its end but is its own end.

6.4 But is this view of the theoretical role of the reference to *eudaimonia* in its relation to the phrase 'for its own sake' Aristotle's? What he says, in vii 1–8, is just that we may choose, e.g., honour *both* for its own sake *and* for the sake of *eudaimonia*. I shall come back to the question whether I am in fact right to ascribe to Aristotle the view of the theoretical use of the reference to *eudaimonia* that I have presented.

At present we should note that there is no danger of circularity in that view. It is true that in vii 1–5 Aristotle brings out his conception of *eudaimonia* by means of the distinction between ends that are chosen for the sake of other things and ends that are chosen for their own sake. But the conception of *eudaimonia*, as the point of all choice, that he brings out in this way does not rely for its intelligibility on the notion of a thing's being choiceworthy for its own sake. The definition of *eudaimonia* as the point of all choice makes use of the following two conceptual connections: that choosing implies the existence of some *end* and that choosing *qua* a type of desire, viz. a desire for *acts*, implies the existence of a state where all desire is satisfied and made superfluous. Aristotle makes use of the distinction between subordinate and non-subordinate ends as a *way* of bringing out his conception of *eudaimonia*, but the distinction plays no role in that conception itself.

7.1 Before I turn to the question whether I am right to ascribe to Aristotle the view I have introduced of the relationship between choosing something for its own sake and choosing it for the sake of *eudaimonia*, I will, for the sake of completeness, comment briefly on the lines that conclude the section we have been discussing. "So *eudaimonia* seems to be something final and self-sufficient, being end of acts" (vii 8, 1097b20–21). What is the exact force of the participle? Commentators suggest that the sense is: "*and* it is the end of acts"[26]. This is, of course, a possible interpretation of the Greek form, and it may well be right. By itself, however, it does not settle the question of the precise point of those last four words: what message are they intended to convey?

It is not very likely that the participle has a causal sense: "because it is the end of acts". Aristotle is entitled to conclude from the preceding section that *eudaimonia* is something final and self-sufficient, but hardly that it is so *because* it is the end of acts. Rather, that it is the end of acts is something that might seem, if anything, to *follow* from the definition of it as final as that definition was reached through the argument of §§ 1–5. However, I am not quite happy about this suggestion either. §§ 1–5 are the crucial paragraphs in as much as they *do* talk, as §§ 6–7 do not, of *acts* and *ends* thereof. They do so, as we know, because they attempt to define the good and *eudaimonia* relative to the concept of choice, and that concept involves the other concepts. Hence when, in § 5, *eudaimonia* is identified with the absolutely final *as defined in § 4*, *eudaimonia* is identified as the absolutely final *end of acts*. But in that case it is unlikely that Aristotle should have wanted in the closing words of the passage to sever the connection between *eudaimonia*'s being something final and its being an end of acts and to intimate that its being the latter *follows* from its being the former.

If this view of the connection, in § 4, between the definition of the absolutely final and its being an end of acts is correct, a third interpretation of the concluding four words suggests itself. We have seen that being final, and for that matter being self-sufficient, are general concepts that may be used in very different areas. We have also just seen that in §§ 1–5 being final is used in connection with the realm of acts. I suggest, therefore, that when Aristotle adds his four last words his aim is to spell out that when he sums up *eudaimonia* as being something final (and self-sufficient) he is using the term in connection with the end of *acts*: "*Final*, then, in some way and self-sufficient is what *eudaimonia* seems to be and (when I say it is *final* I mean that) it is the end of *acts*". This reading gives satisfactory sense to the emphatic position in the

[26] E.g. Burnet.

Greek of 'acts' (*tōn praktōn*), and it suits perfectly the use of the participial form: *eudaimonia* is final (and self-sufficient) *in the way that* it is the end of *acts*.

7.2 One more word on Aristotle's summary of the whole passage. We know that Aristotle concludes that *eudaimonia* is *both* something final *and* something self-sufficient, and it is of course wholly appropriate that he should do so. However, if the above remarks on the summary are correct, it will still be the case that the main emphasis lies on the point that *eudaimonia* is something *final*, and final in the realm of acts – witness, once more, the position of 'final' in the Greek sentence. This is worth a few comments.

I have suggested that though closely connected the two concepts of being final and being self-sufficient differ in an important respect. Being final involves a reference to something that lies 'before' the final thing, being self-sufficient does not. I have also suggested that the concept of being self-sufficient has an important role to play in the passage as a whole. First, it helps us to make sense of Aristotle's definition of the most final or final without qualification. And secondly, it is of vital importance for my suggestion that while the idea of being choiceworthy for its own sake is problematic, the problem that it raises will disappear with the introduction of the concept of *eudaimonia*. For if it were not possible to define *eudaimonia* in other ways than by making use of the idea I take to be problematic, my whole suggestion would evidently be wrecked: due to the way it influences our understanding of the definition of *eudaimonia* as final, viz. as the point of all choice, the concept of self-sufficiency saves my suggestion from that wreck.

But now, though the definition of *eudaimonia* as self-sufficient it important in these ways, it remains the case that the basic consideration by which Aristotle reaches his definition of *eudaimonia* is the one that connects the concept with that of choice and consequently talks of *acts*, of their goodness in terms of their *ends*, and of ends of acts in terms of their being choiceworthy for the sake of something else for their own sake. In section 9 we shall see an illustration that this *is* the basic consideration.

8.1 What argument, then, can I bring for my suggestion that the relationship between the phrases 'for its own sake' and 'for the sake of *eudaimonia*' is more complex than the simple one of *both* one thing *and* the other?

A passage I have already alluded to will provide material for an argument: *EN* VI v 4, 1140b6–7. Here Aristotle defines the difference between *praxis* and *poiesis* in the following way: "- in the case of *poiesis* the end is different (from then act which is the *poiesis*): in the case of *praxis* it is not; for its very (being) 'acting well' (*eupraxia*) is end."

I shall assume the concept of *eupraxia* to be basically equivalent to that of *eudaimonia*, but suggest that there is the following point to operating with both concepts. *eudaimonia* is a state of a person during the whole of his life in which all of his desires are satisfied. This state will consist in one or more concrete things or activities, viz. those that do satisfy the person's desires. In fact, however, it is an Aristotelian point that the state which has the *proper* claim to being the eudaimonic state, viz. the state where all the desires are satisfied that are had by man *as he truly is* – that this state is one of *activity* (see *EN* I vii 10ff.). I believe that when in passages where he is really working with the concept of the eudaimonic state Aristotle uses *eupraxia* instead of *eudaimonia* he is smuggling into the concept of that state the idea that the state will be one of *activity*. And if it be questioned whether in *eupraxia*– passages Aristotle really *is* working with the concept of the eudaimonic state, I believe that the connection between *EN* VI v 4, 1140b6–7 and VI ii 5, 1139b1–4 on the one hand and between the latter passage and I vii 1–5 and i–ii 1 on the other hand is sufficient to settle any doubts. *eupraxia is eudaimonia*, in the realm of acts. So, when something is done with *eupraxia* as its end or for the sake of *eupraxia*, it is done as one thing that falls under the eudaimonic state of activity.

8.2 But if this is accepted I may use the account of *praxis* at 1140b6–7 in support of my suggestion concerning the phrase 'for its own sake'. For what Aristotle will then be saying of a *praxis* is this: the end of a *praxis* is the *praxis* itself (it is its own end or done for its own sake), *for* its end is *eupraxia* (it is done for the sake of *eupraxia* or as one thing that falls under the eudaimonic state of activity). Here the crucial point for present purposes lies in Aristotle's use of 'for'. While in I vii 5 he stated that honour and a number of other things, including moral virtue, are chosen *both* for their own sake *and* for the sake of *eudaimonia*, in the present passage he is claiming *praxeis* to be chosen for their own sake *because* they are chosen for the sake of *eupraxia*. With the sense that we should give to the phrase 'for the sake of *eupraxia*', i.e. when it is remembered that *eupraxia* is the purely indeterminate eudaimonic state of activity, this can only mean that the very sense of the claim that a *praxis* is its own end or is done for its own sake lies in the fact that by these locutions the act is seen as falling under the state of *eupraxia*. *eupraxia* is the concept under which the phrase 'its own end' makes rationally satisfactory sense.

So if I am right in my assumption concerning the relationship of *eudaimonia* and *eupraxia*, the passage we have considered strongly supports my earlier suggestion concerning the relationship of the phrases 'for its own sake' and 'for the sake of *eudaimonia*'. It is not just that things may be said to be chosen or done *both* for their *own* sake and *also*, more or less gratuitously, for the sake of *eudaimonia* or, in connection with acts, because they are acting well: rather the *reason* why they may be satisfactorily said to be chosen or done for their *own* sake is that they are referred to *eudaimonia* and *eupraxia* and seen to fall under those states.

8.3 One more point should be noted about the definition of *praxis*. Aristotle is saying, in my contorted translation, that in the case of a *praxis* "its very (being) 'acting well' is end". The point of 'its' (ἡ) and 'very' (αὐτή) may be seen if we consider the other passage that helps to define the difference between *praxis* and *poiesis*: *EN* VI ii 5, 1139b1–4. Practical thought, says Aristotle, rules productive knowledge too; "for everybody who produces produces some end, and end without qualification is not the result that is produced – *that* thing is (good) relative to some *other* thing and (result) of some *particular* (process) –: no, end without qualification is the result of *praxis* (*to prakton*) – for the *eupraxia* is end – and the desire (viz. the one that guides even the *poiesis*) is for *this* (viz. *to prakton*)."

I will not argue for the details of this translation. Aristotle's main point is clear: in the final resort the end even of an act which is a *poiesis* is 'the result of *praxis*' or *eupraxia*.

But then the point of 'its' and 'very' in the former passage will be that in the case of a *praxis*, as opposed to *poiesis*, there are no intermediaries between the act and *eupraxia*. *eupraxia* is directly the end of an act which is a *praxis*.

We may sum up these remarks on 1140b6–7 in the following definition of an Aristotelian *praxis*. A *praxis* is an act which is done for its own sake, *i.e.* which is *itself* considered as one thing that falls under the eudaimonic state of *eupraxia*. This is my answer to the question I formulated at the beginning of section 2.

9.1 I now wish to go back to the very first page of the *Ethics*. I shall try to show that the conception of *eudaimonia* I have argued to be Aristotle's helps to solve a problem that has puzzled commentators, and that the passage provides support for the truth of my claim that this conception *is* Aristotle's.

The passage is i–ii 1. The division into chapters is unfortunate here. Chapter ii ought, if anywhere, to start between what is now ii 1 and ii 2. For ii 1 forms the conclusion of the argument of i.

Aristotle is introducing the basic concept of his ethical system: 'the good'. The good is what is aimed at (i 1). But there are different types of end; some are (the) activities (themselves), others are certain results of the activities (i 2). And there are *many* ends (i 3). But then some are subordinate to others (i 4). And here, with respect to subordination, "it makes no difference whether the ends are the activities themselves that the acts are or whether the ends are something else beyond the acts" (i 5, 1094a16–17). We have already been puzzled by this remark. But Aristotle crowns his argument in this way (ii 1, 1094a18–22): "If, then, there is a (single) end of acts which we want for its own sake, while we want the rest for *it*, and (if) we do not choose everything for some *further* thing (for in that case the chain will continue *ad infinitum* with the consequence that the desire becomes empty and pointless), it is clear that *that* will be the good or (rather) the highest good."

9.2 This paragraph has puzzled commentators[27]. Is it not the case that Aristotle concludes, invalidly, from the point (in the second part of the *protasis*) that any chain of choice must stop *some*where to the claim (in the first part of the *protasis*) that there must be some *one* place where *all* chains of choice come to a stop?

I agree that it is most natural to take Aristotle to be arguing from the latter to the former part of the *protasis*. But with the conception of *eudaimonia* and the good that I have argued for we can see that it is in fact quite legitimate for him to do so. I have suggested that *eudaimonia* is the state which is the point of all choice and that in vii 1–5 Aristotle reaches this concept via the concept of an end, the idea of subordination of some ends to others, and finally via the concept of an end which is *not* subordinate to any other end. The same line of thought runs through the whole of chapter i and the first part of the *protasis* of ii 1[28]. It seems, then, that this line of thought *is* the basic one for the development of Aristotle's peculiar conception of the good and *eudaimonia*. But I have also suggested that Aristotle needs the concept of the good and *eudaimonia* as the state that is the point of all choice, in order to make sufficiently rational sense of the idea of stopping *particular* chains of choice each at its own particular place.

[27] See, e.g., *Anscombe* p. 34; Bernard *Williams*, 'Aristotle on the Good: a Formal Sketch', Philosophical Quarterly 12 (1962) 289–296, p. 292; Anthony *Kenny*, 'Aristotle on Happiness', Proceedings of the Aristotelian Society 66 (1965–66) 93–102, pp. 94–95; Christopher *Kirwan*, 'Logic and the Good in Aristotle', Philosophical Quarterly 17 (1967) 97–114, pp. 107–111; *Ackrill* pp. 13–15; *Irwin* p. 52.

[28] I suggest that when, in I vii 2, Aristotle states that "the argument has come round to its starting-point" he is drawing attention to the fact that by introducing, in vii 1, the concepts of that-for-the-sake-of-which and end of acts he now finds himself in the position from which he began right at the start of chapter i. From this position he argued, via the notion of subordination of ends to others, to the formulation, in ii 1, of the concept of the single end of all acts; and in an exactly similar way he starts, in vii *3*, by considering the notion of subordination and eventually reaches, in vii 4 and 5, his concept of the single end of all acts. Thus vii 2 does not, as it is normally taken, refer directly back to ii 1, but to the very beginning of the work.

And this is precisely the logical relationship that Aristotle implies to hold between the latter and the former part of the *protasis* of ii 1. *Because* we cannot choose everything for the sake of some further thing, i.e. because any particular chain of choice must come to an end *some*where (– and this must be so since otherwise the desire will become empty and vain), *therefore* there must be a single end of all choice, *viz. the eudaimonic state*. Without the concept of this end we could not make sufficient sense of stopping any particular chain at any particular place.

I conclude that the conception of *eudaimonia* I have argued to be Aristotle's does help to solve the puzzle of ii 1. Furthermore ii 1 itself supports my point concerning the logical role of the concept of *eudaimonia* vis-a-vis the phrase 'for its own sake'.

It is perhaps worth pointing out that in the argument of i–ii 1 for the existence of the single ultimate end it is left absolutely open whether just one thing or activity or more things or activities than one should in the end be said to fill in *eudaimonia*. The answer may of course be, and presumably will be: more than one; but it might equally well be: just one thing or activity. Just at this question was not raised in vii 1–8, so it is totally irrelevant to the logical point concerning the concept of *eudaimonia* that Aristotle wants to make in i–ii 1. For even if it were the case that only one thing should be taken to fill in *eudaimonia*, that thing, which would then be *the* thing that everything else is done for, would still be different from the eudaimonic state. It would be the only thing that falls under, but would not be identical with, the state which is the point of all of a man's choices and desires: the satisfactory life[29].

[29] The final version of this paper was written in July 1979. In a paper entitled 'Aristoteles' Einführung des Begriffs *eudaimonia* im I. Buch der "Nikomachischen Ethik", Eine Antwort auf einige neuere Inkonsistenzkritiken', which was published in Philosophisches Jahrbuch 86, 2. Halbband (1979) 300–325, Mr. K. Jacobi suggests, among other things, an interpretation of *EN* I vii 5 and the point of Aristotle's concept of *eudaimonia* which is closely similar to the one presented here. Moreover Mr. Jacobi bases his interpretation on the two points that have also been introduced here, viz. the self-sufficiency of *eudaimonia* (Jacobi pp. 317–318, cf. here sections 4.2, 4.4, 7.2) and the suggestion that the concept of *eudaimonia explains* the idea of choosing something for its own sake (Jacobi pp. 319–320, cf. here sections 6.1–6.4). The solution to the problem of *EN* I ii 1 that I have propounded in sections 9.1–9.2 above is not suggested in Mr. Jacobi's paper. It comes to mind as a direct consequence of emphasising, as I have done throughout the paper, the importance for Aristotle's concept of *eudaimonia* of the nexus of concepts that surround the one of (rational) choice, e.g. in my sections on the notion of being final and the role this notion plays in *EN* I vii 1–5.

Aristotle on the Best Life for a Man

W. F. R. HARDIE

The sketch of well-doing in Book I

Does Aristotle in the *Nicomachean Ethics* give one consistent answer to the question what life is best or two (at least) mutually inconsistent answers? In the First Book (*E.N.* I) he says that we can agree to say that the best life is *eudaimonia* or *eupraxia* (well-being or well-doing) but must go on to say in what *eudaimonia* consists (1097b22–24). By considering the specific nature of man as a thinking animal he reaches a conclusion: *eudaimonia*, the human good (*agathon*), is the activity of soul (*psuchē*) in accordance with virtue (*aretē*), and if there are more than one virtue in accordance with the best and most complete (*teleia*), and (since one swallow does not make a summer) in a complete life (1098a16–20). Aristotle states that his formula is no more than a sketch or outline (*perigraphē*), but that a good sketch is important since, if the outline is right, anyone can articulate it and supply details. He seems to be thinking here not just of the rest of his own treatise but of the work of pupils and successors; he speaks, as at the end of the *Topics*, of progress in a science.

This statement about *eudaimonia* is at the centre of our question. Commentators refer to it as a 'definition'. But a definition does not usually incorporate disjunctive alternatives. Aristotle does not tell us here, or anywhere else in I, whether human excellence is in fact one or many or, if many is suggested, which particular virtue is the one which is 'best and most final'. 'Definition' suggests determinate outlines in an architect's plan. Perhaps we should think rather of preliminary sketches made by an artist before he determinately creates the work of art to which the sketches point. It may seem easy to say that, of course, there are many virtues; we might extract from the Books of the *E.N.* which follow names for at least eleven ethical and eight intellectual virtues or excellences. But the corresponding passage in the *Eudemian Ethics* defines *eudaimonia* as the activity of a complete life in accordance with complete virtue (1219a38–9); the context suggests that virtue is a whole of parts rather than a genus containing species. Modern editors of the *E.N.* do not comment on Aristotle's silence at this point on the number of the virtues and on the criterion for affirming or denying that the different names of the members of a set of virtues correspond to a set of mutually separable, or at least different, human qualities.

The two kinds of excellence in man as a rational animal in VI and X

In *E.N.* VI, which deals with the intellectual virtues, we are told that a man who has practical wisdom (*phronēsis*) necessarily has all the ethical virtues and that, unless he has *phronēsis*, a man cannot have any ethical virtue (Chs. 12 and 13). In VI 1, 2 we learn that there are two intellectual truth-finding virtues: practical wisdom shown in deliberation and action and theoretical wisdom (*sophia*) shown in contemplation (*theōria*). Thus, if mutual conditionality is our criterion for the unity of virtue, the names of the various ethical virtues will refer to the different spheres or different ways in which a single virtue, for which *phronēsis* would be the appropriate name, is exercised. Is *sophia* separable, and alone in being separable, from the rest? *Prima facie* not all philosophers are good men, and not all good men are philosophers. Neither in VI nor in X does Aristotle explicitly assert or deny a two-way conditionality between the two rational virtues. In VI 12 each is intrinsically choice-worthy (1144a1–6; cf. X 1178a9f.); and in VI 13 we are told that it is the business, clearly not the whole business, of *phronēsis* to promote the attainment of *sophia* (1145a6–11). That *sophia* is the capacity for theoretical knowledge has been implied by its definition in VI (1141a18–b3). The sentences which reintroduce us to *sophia* in X 7 run as follows in the Oxford translation (Ross). 'If happiness is activity in accordance with virtue, it is reasonable that it should be in accordance with the highest virtue; and this will be that of the best thing in us. Whether it be reason (*nous*) or something else that is this element which is thought to be our natural ruler and guide and to take thought of things noble and divine or only the most divine element in us, the activity of this in accordance with its proper virtue will be perfect happiness. That this activity is contemplative we have already said' (1177a12–18). Here the phrase translated 'our natural ruler and guide' surprises us by seeming to suggest that, at the highest level, practical and theoretical wisdom can be viewed as aspects of a single Platonic excellence of reason. We are surprised; for, while it is natural to ascribe to Aristotle the view that philosophers, being men, have practical as well as theoretical wisdom, we cannot suppose him to have thought that the *phronimos* is necessarily *sophos*.

The familiar and crucial passages which I have recalled remind us that Aristotle's manner and method in approaching his answer to his important question is exploratory and tentative. In I the theoretic life is barely mentioned; but we learn that it will be considered later (1096a4–5). The enigmatic question whether there is more than one virtue is unexplained and unanswered; the possible 'best virtue' is unnamed. On the relations between *sophia* and *phronēsis* we are offered no neat thought-saving analogy as in the *Magna Moralia*: the steward who so arranges things that his master can give his whole mind to his own high concerns

(1198b9–20). We are allowed to entertain the suspicion that philosophizing may be less other-worldly and planning less pedestrian than such a formula would suggest.

Recent contributions to the discussion of the question

I must now explain what has prompted me to write more on this much discussed, although still unsettled, problem of interpretation. In the past year I have read three important recent contributions, one lecture and two books, to the study of Aristotle's ethical theory: J. L. Ackrill, 'Dawes Hicks British Academy Lecture on Philosophy 1974', *Aristotle on 'Eudaimonia'*, (OUP, London); Stephen R. L. Clark, *Aristotle's Man* (Clarendon Press, Oxford); John M. Cooper, *Reason and Human Good in Aristotle* (Harvard University Press). All three were published in 1975. In all three, as their titles indicate, Aristotle's doctrine of the final end or human good is a central interest. Do they claim to find in Aristotle a doctrine which is single and systematic? Clark does; Ackrill and Cooper do not.

For Aristotle, as Clark's 'speculations' or 'meditations' expound him, the understanding of man's end, or *ergon* (function), a concept earlier explored by Clark in an article in *Ethics* (1972), is part of an 'intuition of Being', 'the crown of our metaphysical and our ethical thinking alike' and of our biological thinking as well (189–90; cf. xi). 'We practise virtue, we concern ourselves with what is worthwhile, in order to clear the way to the knowledge of the good, and having reached that end we act correctly in the world. We act as the knowledgeable man would in order to become knowledgeable' (197). 'It is the Aristotelian saint who is most especially human, in that it is his life which gives sense to human structure and society —and also, as I shall argue, to the world' (27, and on 'the Aristotelian saint' cf. ix, 12, 172, 189, 200). Clark's energy and critical acumen encourage the opinion that he has reached the saint's synoptic point of view. In any event his speculations deserve to be closely studied. His interpretation of the doctrine of the final end may be described as unitarian: 'Civil and theoretic good meet in this, that both are a service of the divine in man' (xi). 'This whole inclusive/dominant dichotomy in fact serves only to darken counsel: there is indeed room for many different sorts of activity in the good life, though not literally for all sorts; this does not prevent there being one activity which is central' (156; cf. 160). I shall discuss later the 'inclusive/dominant' dichotomy. The interpretation reminds us of Stewart's insistence that, in the best activity (*theoria*), other activities are 'not lost but co-ordinated' (note on 1099a29; cf. his notes on 1098a17 and 1094a1).

Ackrill and Cooper differ from Clark in not combing the whole Aristotelian corpus and cosmos in a search for Aristotle's man. They prefer to pursue a study in depth of familiar texts in the *Nicomachean* and *Eudemian Ethics*. Both find in *E.N.* X, and in *E.N.* X alone, a doctrine which elevates the *eudaimonia* of the theoretic life to a position of enormously and incomparably superior attractiveness to the *eudaimonia* of the householder, citizen and politician. Neither indeed is inclined to praise what they regard as Aristotle's second, not his better, thoughts.

Cooper gives the name 'intellectualism' to this development and, at the end of his book (180), states his preference for 'the moral theory of the *Eudemian Ethics*' with its 'mixed ideal' of *eudaimonia* in which theoretical contemplation may be one element. Sometimes he seems inclined to say that it is the emphasis of the two treatments which is different, that the difference is not a chasm. But he digs, or deepens, the chasm himself when he propounds the idea that Aristotle, when he says that the philosopher, as a man among men, 'chooses to act in accordance with virtue' (1178b5–6), means that the philosopher does not himself possess the ethical virtues but merely 'conforms his conduct' to their requirements (164–5). I do not find this interpretation acceptable. I do not think that *kata aretēn* ('in accordance with virtue') can have this meaning here, if indeed it could have it anywhere in Aristotle. But I shall not argue the point here as I have stated my objections elsewhere in a notice of Cooper's book. For the same reason it would be superfluous and irrelevant to comment here on much that is both original and acceptable in Cooper's treatment of what he calls the 'theoretical backbone' of Aristotle's ethics, his theories of practical reasoning and of *eudaimonia* (or 'human flourishing' as Cooper renders the term) (ix).

I have said that Ackrill seems to share the opinion of Cooper that Aristotle's doctrine in *E.N.* X is not easy to defend. The difficulty for Ackrill, is that, while there must be 'trading between *theoria*' and the secondary *eudaimonia* which is expressive of social and ethical virtues, there can be no such trading if the two kinds of *eudaimonia* are incomparable or incommensurable. 'Aristotle's theology and anthropology make it inevitable that his answer to the question about *eudaimonia* should be broken-backed' (22). The difficulty, or complex of difficulties, is familiar and serious, and it is right that it should be stated strongly. I shall return to the issue later. But we have first to consider a way in which Ackrill is more radically opposed than Cooper to a unitarian or single-doctrine interpretation of the *E.N.*

Ackrill's 'inclusive' interpretation of 'the best and most final excellence' in Book I

Aristotle's two explicit treatments of *eudaimonia* (well-doing), the most final end, are at the beginning and at the end of the *E.N.* When he returns to the subject in X 6 he refers to his earlier statement of the doctrine, and in particular to the distinction between the acquired dispositional capacity or propensity (*hexis*) to perform an activity (*energeia*) and the activity itself, and the division of activities into those desirable in themselves and those desirable for the sake of something else (1176a30–b6). I have quoted above the passage in X 7 which affirms that is is reasonable to think that *eudaimonia* is 'in accordance with the highest virtue' (1177a12–18). This sentence is commonly, and very naturally, taken as retrospective to the 'best and most final virtue' in the 'definition' of *eudaimonia* in I 7 (1098a-16–18; cf. 1099a29–31, 1097a28–30, and VII 1153b10–12). Ackrill rejects the identification of these two summit excellences: the 'highest virtue' of X 6–8 is indeed *sophia* (theoretical wisdom); but 'the best and most final virtue' of I 7 is not one particular virtue among others but 'total virtue, the combination of all virtues' (17). His argument for this interpretation contains three main constituents.

(1) The meaning of 'best and most final virtue' is 'not perfectly obvious' (17). But can the ambiguity of this expression belong to it as it occurs in this sentence, especially if we consider along with it the sentence in I 8 where Aristotle distinguishes 'the best activities' from 'the one of those which is the best' (1099a29–31)? It is not clear whether or how, in Ackrill's view, a translator should exhibit the ambiguity and suggest the 'total virtue' interpretation. I have found only in the Everyman version a translator who takes the bold course, which must be deliberate, of mistranslating; in D. P. Chase's rendering 'if there are more than one excellences' becomes 'if excellence admits of degrees'.

(2) Ackrill claims that his interpretation is not only compatible with scrupulous translation but is rendered natural and even inevitable by the fact, as he claims, that, earlier in the chapter, Aristotle has 'told' the reader to understand 'the most final end' as referring to 'the comprehensive end that includes all partial ends' (17). But this claim leads the reader to expect something more explicit and obviously relevant about the superlative of *teleion* (final) than he will find anywhere in the earlier part of the chapter (1097a15–b21). Moreover it is not clear why an instruction for the use of 'most final', or of any other eulogistic superlative, as applied to 'end' should be assumed to determine its meaning when applied to 'virtue' or to 'activity'.

What is contained in the earlier section of I 7 may be summarized as follows. (a) Different actions and arts have different ends (*telē*), aim at different goods (*agatha*). Some ends are pursued only as means to other ends, and such ends are not 'final ends' (*teleia*) (a21–8). (b) What is best is final. Hence, if there is only one final end, this will be what we are seeking; if more, the most final of these (*to teleiotaton toutōn*) (a28–30). (c) An end (E1) is more final (*teleioteron*) than another (E2) if either (i) E1 is desirable for itself and E2 for something else, or (ii) E1 is desirable only for itself and E2 both for itself and for something else (a30–2). (d) An end is final without qualification (*haplōs*) if it is desirable only for itself (a33–4). Aristotle then states that *eudaimonia* is final without qualification and mentions a number of goods (honour, pleasure, reason, virtues) which are chosen both for themselves and for the sake of *eudaimonia* but for the sake of which no one chooses *eudaimonia* (a34–b6). The argument is reinforced by what he goes on to say about the sufficiency (*autarkeia*) of *eudaimonia* (the logical impossibility of making it any better by any addition) (b6–21). I shall return to *autarkeia*, the treatment of which by Ackrill I cannot follow. For the rest, the section contains no explicit instruction on what *teleiotaton* (most final) is to mean when applied to an end. If it did contain the instruction which Ackrill claims to find, I have suggested that it would not be applicable to the superlatives in 1098a17–18. Moreover we need not suppose that Aristotle's instruction for the use of *teleioteron* (more final) is meant to be exhaustive: E1 might simply have a higher degree of intrinsic desirability than E2. Thus I do not see that the earlier passage would incline even the most diligently attentive and retentive reader to assume an inclusive interpretation of the superlatives in 1098a-17–18.

(3) Finally Ackrill argues that the reader 'will find that this interpretation gives a sense to the *ergon* argument that is exactly what the argument itself requires' (17). For it is to the power of thought, not specifically of theoretical thought, that the argument has pointed as being 'distinctive of man' (16). But, unless Ackrill's argument under (1) is successful, this last argument can do nothing to help his case: perhaps Aristotle is inconsequent. But, at this stage, Aristotle is not pressing his argument to final conclusions; his approach, as I have suggested, is tentative; so far, at least, he has not divided the 'power of thought' into two distinct and separable intellectual excellences; we do not at this point know whether we are to say that human excellence is single or dual or plural.

In thus insulating Books I and X from each other Ackrill disrupts the *E.N.* as by intention and essentially a single treatise in a way which is unacceptable to Cooper. It is, perhaps, unlikely that Cooper knew what Ackrill was saying in his Lecture about 'the best and most final virtue'. But he reports, as a suggestion made to him by T. Irwin, that the expression might be taken as meaning 'all the human excellences, moral and intellectual, taken together as a whole' and he rejects the suggestion in a full and careful footnote (100–1). He argues that the superlative here has its natural 'exclusionary' force (also in 1099a29, as he might have added) and that the earlier part of the chapter supports this conclusion; finally he suggests, as a reason which Aristotle might have had for not naming *sophia*, theoretical wisdom, the need to leave room for determinate doctrinal developments in later books. If we agree with Cooper on the linguistic point, we have to say that any counter-argument based on what is required by the dialectic of I is out of order from the start.

The meanings of 'inclusive', 'dominant', 'paramount' as applied to an end *(telos)*

The main conclusion of Ackrill's examination of Aristotle's argument in *E.N.* I is that in it Aristotle's account of *eudaimonia* is decidedly 'inclusive' (18). What does he mean by this? '*Eudaimonia* is the most desirable sort of life, the life that contains all intrinsically worthwhile activities' (9). '*Eudaimonia*, being absolutely final and genuinely self-sufficient, is more desirable than anything else in that it *includes* everything desirable in itself . . . in the way that bacon, eggs, and tomatoes is a better breakfast than either bacon or eggs or tomatoes—and is indeed the best breakfast without qualification' (10). Again he speaks of the end (*telos*) which is 'most final' or 'final absolutely' as 'the comprehensive end which includes all partial ends' (17). This concept of the omni-inclusive end or life, like that of the progressively diversified breakfast, has no constructive application. What is needed is the narrower concept of the life-plan, constructed or taken for granted by the individual as suited to his/her capacities and desires, circumstances and obligations; an end constructed, as Ackrill says in one place, 'from any plurality of separate ends' (15). The terminology which distinguishes 'inclusive end' from 'dominant end' was introduced, I believe, into recent discussion by my article, 'The Final Good in Aristotle's Ethics', in *Philosophy* **40**, No. 154 (October 1965). In the article (291), and later in *Aristotle's Ethical Theory* (Oxford: Clarendon Press, 1968), I defined what I came to prefer to call the 'comprehensive plan' (as opposed to any 'paramount object' within the plan) as being 'inclusive in the sense that there is no desire or interest which cannot be regarded as a candidate, however unpromising, for a place in the pattern of a life' (329).

The scope of the present article allows me only the briefest reference to what I wrote ten or more years ago. But without minimal citation I could not deal with two points which are clearly proper to this article. (1) I wish to say that I accept up to a point the sharp criticism of my 1965 article in Ackrill's Lecture. (2) I wish to suggest that, in his radical defence of an inclusivist interpretation of *E.N.* I, Ackrill offends against his own important and useful insistence on the difference between *kinds* of question which interest Aristotle here; between 'linguistic' or 'conceptual' questions and 'evaluative' questions (5, cf. 9). It will be convenient if I refer to my article (1965) as A and to my book (1968) as B.

The concept of the end as 'monolithic'

(1) When in A (278–9) I introduced the terminology of 'inclusive' and 'dominant' end, I suggested that Aristotle's doctrine 'confused or con-

flated' affirmative answers to two questions. I suggested, as the correct answers (a) that all men are in some degree planners of their own lives but (b) that not all give a central and dominant place in their plans to one ruling interest (278). I did not say that to say of someone that he lived under the 'dominance' of a single interest was to deny that he had an 'inclusive' end containing also other interests. Later in A, as Ackrill notes, I said that an inclusive end might include a dominant end (287). But unfortunately what I said in the context of the earlier passage suggested a denial of this compatibility: Aristotle's 'explicit view' made 'the supreme end not inclusive but dominant, the object of one prime desire, philosophy' (279). Commenting on this Ackrill rightly distinguished a weak and a strong sense of 'dominant end', the former but not the latter being compatible with co-presence in the inclusive end of 'two or more independently valued goods' (5). Thus he attributes to me an interpretation of *E.N.* I as affirming that the final end is 'monolithic' and inclusive only of theoretical activities. Ackrill quotes only from A. But a general reference to B in a footnote suggests that he finds the same confusion, or traces of it, in B (4). He may be right. I wish to make only the following comments. (a) The motive of my change of terminology from 'inclusive' and 'dominant' ends in A to 'comprehensive plan' and 'paramount objects' in B was a desire to rule out a 'monolithic' interpretation of 'dominant'. (b) In commenting on Aristotle's application of 'practical' to man's rational way of life (1098a3), I argue that this does not exclude theoretical activity (25), thus implying that, of course, it includes the more narrowly practical activities of the citizen and householder. But (c) I do indeed speak of Aristotle as 'hesitating' (23) and as 'straddling' (25) between 'an inclusive and an exclusive formulation' (23). He straddles at the beginning of I 4: 'what it is that we say political science aims at and what is the highest (*akrotaton*) of all goods achievable by action' (1095a15–17). The political end, as expounded in *E.N.* I 1, is inclusive but 'highest good' suggests a paramount object. He hesitates, as we have seen, when he defines *eudaimonia* (1098a16–18). But this is not to say that Aristotle's mind when he wrote *E.N.* I was in confusion or doubt. It is natural that a 'sketch' should be indeterminate, but that *eudaimonia* embraces non-theoretic activities is made clear, as we have seen, in VI and X.

A monolithic end is not a conceptual absurdity

(2) 'In claiming that Aristotle expounds in I an inclusive and not a monolithic doctrine of *eudaimonia* I was referring both to his account of the concept itself—or what one might call in a broad sense the meaning of the word—and to his view about the life that satisfies the concept and deserves the name' (6). Ackrill is referring to the division in I 7 (at 1097b22)

between the linguistic or conceptual and the evaluative parts of Aristotle's treatment. That the best possible life would be made better by the possible addition of some extra constituent is a conceptual absurdity. But a monolithic doctrine of *eudaimonia*, if absurd, is not a conceptual absurdity. For the proposal to include any second constituent would be an evaluative judgment. Ackrill implies this a few pages later when he says that there is nothing in 'the logical force of the word *eudaimonia*' which is 'capable of provoking moral or practical dispute' (10). To the seeker of the best life the word is not a sign-post pointing between too much of too few kinds of activity and too little of too many. The man who values only Aristotelian contemplation or only Buddhist meditation, or only music or poetry, may be eccentric or fanatical but is not necessarily incoherent; just as someone who likes tomatoes can reject them as an addendum to eggs and bacon. Ackrill's hospitable descriptions of inclusive ends leads him to make suggestions remote from Aristotle. Thus he seems to imply that, if a man's inclusive end embraces philosophy and crossword puzzles, Aristotle might say that he pursues philosophy both for itself and (for the inclusive end) because it goes well with crossword puzzles (15). This is not what Aristotle actually says about pleasant amusements in X 6 (1176b9–1177a11). They are scarcely regarded as even candidates for inclusion in the best life except as means; no doubt an excessively austere doctrine. It is, of course, true that *ta pros to telos*, the things which contribute to the end, may be constituents of its present, not means to its future, realization. But they may be just means.

Conclusions so far reached

We started by asking whether Aristotle in the *E.N.* gives a single consistent answer to the question what is the best life for a man. Did Aristotle conceive the later Books, including X, as a consistent development of his 'outline' in I? If so, was he right in supposing them to be in general consistent? I have proposed affirmative answers to both questions but shall have more to say about the second. I have shaped my discussion with an eye on the interpretations which I have found, if I have not misunderstood them, in the recent works of Ackrill, Clark and Cooper. Passages I have quoted from Clark imply affirmative answers to both questions. I agree with these answers, but this is not to claim that I can follow his arguments far or deep. I disagree with Ackrill's interpretation of the 'most final' virtue in *E.N.* I and generally with his rejection of what most commentators have taken to be cross-references or allusions connecting I and X. On this point I note my agreement with Cooper. But I do not, as Cooper does, find in X an 'intellectualist' doctrine in the sense of the recommendation of a fanatical self-dedication to metaphysics, a dedication which can do without the virtues and satisfactions of the family man and the citizen. It is true that two kinds of well-doing are indicated in X, with one ranked above the other. The two differ as they include, or do not include, *theoria* as their paramount concern. I agree with Cooper that what he calls the 'Eudemian' ideal or the 'mixed life' does not exclude theoretical interests as not necessarily paramount constituents of *eudaimonia* (see his index under '*Eudemian Ethics*' and 'mixed life'). But a life in which theory is paramount has Aristotle's recommendation for any human person whose capacity for thought and the circumstances of whose life bring the summit of happiness within reach.

Some criticisms of Aristotle's view

So far my main effort has been to make as clear as I can what Aristotle actually says in answer to the perhaps central, but by no means the only, question on which the *E.N.* is an illuminating work. I shall try now to make a tentative move towards an appreciation of that central answer. Again I find it helpful to indicate the general direction of this move by reference to the recent work of Ackrill, Clark and Cooper. All three, in their different ways, seem to me to attach catastrophic importance to the influence of Aristotle's theism, or rather deism, on his ethical thinking. My prejudice against this consensus, if I am right in claiming to detect it, is based on the belief (a) that any attempt to explain a relationship between man and his aspirations on the one hand and the nature of all that is on the other faces dangers of which (b) one is that of representing the latter entity as more cosy than we can see it to be. If this is so, (c) we should not without clear evidence set limits to Aristotle's capacity for rational scepticism. I apologize for my stenographic use of 'catastrophic' and 'cosy'. I hope that what I mean by these words is clear. I could not withdraw either. I shall now, from this point of view, consider briefly some standard criticisms of Aristotle's doctrine on *eudaimonia*.

(1) Man's specific nature is to be inquisitive and thoughtful; but Aristotle's concept of mind and thought is too narrow, even if his 'theory' embraces mathematics and 'physics' as well as first philosophy. Claims similar to some of those made for philosophy can be made for the activities of the poet, the musician, the artist, the statesman. For, under favourable circumstances, all these vocations can attract and fill a lifetime of continuous and absorbing interest centred on a paramount end. I shall not here discuss this criticism, having little to add to what I have said on the matter elsewhere.

(2) Aristotle's 'best life' is 'mixed', a complex of interests and activities, with theoretical interests paramount in the best life of all. But, complains the critic, Aristotle evades the questions on what principle or principles the complex is composed, what makes rational the deter-

mination of priorities by the man of practical wisdom, what is the basis of the claim to paramountcy of the theoretic life.

(3) The criticism may take a more aggressive form. If Aristotle has a principle, it is said, it is one that he derives from his psychology, his cosmology, his doctrine of divine being. The doctrine requires him to say that a man is his reason (*nous*), his capacity to come to know the highest objects. Hence Cooper's final attribution of 'intellectualism'; hence Ackrill's conclusion that for Aristotle *theoria* is incommensurably more valuable than virtuous living (21), that 'Aristotle's theology and cosmology make it inevitable that his answer to the question about *eudaimonia* should be broken-backed' (22). It is not difficult to feel force in these comments, this reaction. Clark, perhaps, is reacting against such a reaction when, by conducting us all round Aristotle's world and showing us the works, he seeks to persuade us that, for Aristotle at least, there is no such conflict between his theology and 'anthropology' on the one hand and his ethics on the other.

The demand for rationality in the determination of priorities

Critics who demand rational principle in the determination of priorities, or the resolution of conflicting values, do not always make it clear how their demand itself is rational. Thus at one place Clark seems to suggest that, when ideals conflict, we decide between them on the basis either of 'immediate impulse' or of 'some overriding value', a value which is 'the reasonable man's reason for his ordering of ends' (148–9). Do we, then, look for a still further value to justify the decision that the overriding value overrides? And so on? The pros and cons may be complex, but a practical decision which takes them all in, including the relative probabilities of success or failure, while immediate in the sense of not being based on any further value, is not an 'impulse'. It is the termination of an intellectual appraisal; 'it is difficult sometimes to determine what should be chosen at what cost, and what should be endured in return for what gain' (1110a29–30).

Ackrill, holding rightly that, in Aristotle's view, a man does well, if he can, to combine in his life two 'independently though not equally valuable' forms of activity, confronts Aristotle with the question 'what really is in full the recipe?' (21). Aristotle, he says, 'signally fails to attempt an answer'. 'Recipe' suggests cookery; not an apt analogy. It is true that cookery books may allow for variations 'according to taste'. But the differences between one man and another relevant to the pursuit of happiness are deeper. Aristotle was clearly aware that, if abilities are defective, resources inadequate, or fortune adverse, a man has to make the best of a bad job (1101a1–5). But Ackrill's recipe is for 'the best possible human life' and here 'best' can be taken as postulating intellectual capacity, health and the best of luck. What makes it impossible, in Ackrill's view, for Aristotle to accept any recipe is the fact, to be taken as evident, that '*theoria* is the incommensurably more valuable activity' (21). 'Incommensurably' (*asummetrōs*)? The word is Ackrill's metaphor for incomparable in value: 'incomparable' by definition excludes 'compromise and trading between *theoria* and virtuous action' (22), as 'incommensurable' excludes measurement as a ratio between whole numbers. So Ackrill implies that, in Aristotle's view, weighing and deciding between one form of activity and another is possible if, but only if, either both are theoretic or neither is. And the paragraph as a whole suggests that here the line between what is and is not *theoria* coincides, in Ackrill's view, with the line between 'separable reason' (as in the *De Anima*) and the soul which is 'the form of a body' (22).

The difficulty which Ackrill is pressing is real and troubles many readers of the *E.N.* It is the declared basis of Cooper's 'intellectualist' interpretation of *E.N.* X: Cooper follows Rodier 'in appealing to the *De Anima*'s theory of the soul' (180). But Cooper has more to say than Ackrill about the difficulty of understanding the doctrine of the *De Anima* (Γ 4 and 5) and of using it for the elucidaton of the *Ethics*. Can separable reason be equated with the capacity for *theōria* (413b25) or with an intuitive element in that capacity? (175–6). In Γ 5 what is primarily ascribed to the separable faculty is causal efficacy. 'The question is further complicated by the theory of the *nous pathētikos* (passive reason) which seems to connect even some intuitive thinking with the body' (176). I cannot discuss these difficulties here; but I wish to suggest that in the *E.N.* the priority ascribed to *theoria* is not so 'absolute' as to make comparison and compromise impossible. How does Aristotle himself speak of the appraisals which precede life-determining, or death-determining, decisions?

I have quoted the general formula in which Aristotle uses two senses of the preposition *anti*—at what cost, for what gain (1110a29–30). In V 5 he speaks of transactions which are literally commercial, where money functions as a measure of demand. 'Now in truth it is impossible that things so different should become commensurate (*summetra*), but with reference to demand they may become so sufficiently' (1133b18–20). Happiness requires a complete life, since one swallow or one day does not make a summer (1098a18–19). Yet a great man can be unsparing of life itself; he knows that survival can be too dearly bought (1124b8–9). Such courage is 'beyond' ordinary men, and is honoured as 'heroic and divine' (1145a18–22). In IX 8 the self-sacrifice of the good man for his friends or his country is described as obedience to reason (*nous*), as a 'great beauty': he prefers 'one year of noble life to many of humdrum existence' (1169a17–26). But Aristotle does not, of course, suppose that heroism is easy, even if sometimes it is easy to see that it is called for (cf. 1153b19–21).

Along with these passages in the *E.N.* we should place, when we consider the conflicts of ends, the famous passage in the *Parts of Animals* (I 5) in which Aristotle exhibits the rival attractions of 'the philosophy which contemplates the things that are divine' (of which we have only fleeting if precious glimpses) and the study of plants and animals, the things that perish (about which anyone who takes enough trouble can learn much). Each has its own power to attract (*charis*): 'detail and certitude, nearness and affinity to us, balance somewhat the loftier interest' (644b22–645a4). Aristotle's judicious appraisal seems here to be uninhibited by mysteries concerning divine self-contemplation and the efficacy of a separable soul in man. Our sense faculties and bodily organs are deeply and continuously involved in the study of plants and animals; in theology hardly so but for the fact that, for Aristotle, part of theology is astronomy. Aristotle seems to face quite calmly the question which Ackrill thinks he should find unanswerable. 'But how can there be a trading relation between the divine and the merely human?' (22). Somewhat similarly, in the strictly practical province of eudaimonics, Aristotle shows a restrained enthusiasm for the choice, in some circumstances, of certain or probable death, when the choice is required by reason (*nous*) and such virtue is divine. One year of noble life is better than many that are mediocre (IX 8). 'One day in thy courts is better than a thousand'.

As we read what Cooper and Ackrill say about Aristotle's elevation of 'theory' in *E.N.* X we notice a similarity in their responses. Aristotle's voyage ends in stormy confusion; if the ship does not sink, it is only because at the last moment the steersman turns a blind eye towards his guiding light. Cooper decides that Aristotle's philosopher cannot really prize and possess ethical virtue or care for his family and his neighbours. That must be a mere show to avert black looks. Ackrill insists on the 'monstrous' implications of saying that the priority of theoretical intellect is 'absolute' and 'incommensurable'. Yet the texts do not demand, or even perhaps permit, these horrific speculations. If everything Aristotle says about the separable soul and the activity of reason, in God and in man, were known to be true, should this prevent us from calmly considering, as Aristotle does, in what respects the contemplation of fishes, birds, earthworms might be more satisfying than first philosophy? Should these revelations impair our admiration for heroic human courage? Why? Both Ackrill and Cooper seem to feel that Aristotle somehow failed to face his own convictions. Ackrill suspects that 'a man who really believed in the supreme importance of some absolute could not continue to live in much the same way as others' (23). Could Aristotle? Did Hermias? Cooper's conclusion is thet Aristotle finally preferred the 'superhuman ideal', but that a more 'down-to-earth' ideal persisted, like cheerfulness, in 'breaking in' (179–80).

Is there a bridge between primary and secondary *eudaimonia*?

Clark, as we saw earlier, would agree with Cooper and with Ackrill in the opinion that the student of the *E.N.* would have (has) a right to feel dissatisfied if he were not (is not) given an explanation of the connections between primary and secondary *eudaimonia*; both, as Aristotle (*pace* Cooper) holds, are ingredients in the happiness of the 'Aristotelian saint' (Clark). But Clark differs from Ackrill and Cooper in holding that Aristotle does convey to his readers the required explanation: the practice of virtue 'clears the way to the knowledge of the god' and knowing the god enables us to 'act correctly in the world' (197). This formula postulates a bridge between the self-knowledge of the self-knowing god and our knowledge of our world. The bridge is crossed in principle when we know that, where what is known is the form, knower and known are one and the same; God is not a 'self-gnawing mouth' (178). 'The Prime thinks itself not because it introspects, but because it is knowingly the World' (187). For man too 'to practise *theoria* is to be aware of the world' (186). This formulation of one crucial part of the argument leaves us, of course, with many questions to answer and, if they can be answered, much detail to fill in. The project of constructing such a bridge from materials extracted from Aristotle's works must strike us as surprising in view of his liking for a tentative and exploratory approach to particular problems. What is required is indicated by Clark's comments on the passage, considered above, in the *De Partibus Animalium* where Aristotle contrasts our glimpses of divine objects with the detailed study of the natures and forms of every kind of animal. He quotes Aristotle's claim that the study of the humblest animal 'will reveal to us something natural and something beautiful' (645a15f.), and then speaks of such study as undertaken 'in our pursuit of the intuition of the whole (V 3.27), to fill in the details of that intuition, and to be able to act in the world with due awareness of the way it works' (190). But does Aristotle anywhere offer this as the (or a) justification of biological research? If not, why not? When we try to follow up Clark's interlocking references to other paragraphs of his book we do not, I think, find answers to such obvious questions.

It should be said that the above comment is one of a kind which Clark anticipates, and seeks to disarm, in his lively first chapter, 'Introduction: Methods and Interpretation' (1–13). The objector who 'declares urgently' 'But that is not what the text says' is met by a volley of half-truths: '. . . strictly the text says nothing at all' (1); 'the choice is not between scholarship and guess-work but between two varieties of guess-work' (2); 'convinced that their own language maps the world in the only possible way they translate other doctrines into their own terms and then hold the results up to derision' (3). Clark suggests 'the semantic sneer' as the 'best label' for the 'argument form' against which he is protesting. His six examples show that what he has in mind is the argument from 'paradigm' cases. For example: when everyone is killed in an air-crash we say that there are no 'survivors'; so personal 'survival' of death is nonsense. The form of argument (no longer fashionable) is one the validity of which has to be assessed separately for every application; it is not a 'sneer'.

In only one of his examples is Clark attacking perversity in critics of Aristotle: 'Aristotelianism implies that men are tools' (4). The reference is to a point in Clark's chapter (II 1), 'The Ergon Argument' (15). But here, as sometimes, Clark spoils a possibly good point by overstating it. For the critics to whom he refers do not depreciate the argument connecting *eudaimonia* with the fullest development of the capacities, peculiar to the human animal, to think, to plan, to choose. They merely wish to deny that the obviousness of the fact that the *erga* (functions) of pruning hooks, cart-horses and cabinet-makers are respectively to prune, to draw carts and to make cabinets should condition us into admitting as obvious that man has an *ergon*. For this reason 'the *ergon* argument', if a convenient, is not a felicitous, label for what Plato and Aristotle are propounding in familiar passages.

But Clark's purpose in his Introduction is not to attack others but to explain what kind of book he has himself written. His aim is perhaps best expressed in his quotation from Peirce: 'I have read and deeply pondered upon all the main systems, never being satisfied until I was able to think about them as their own advocates thought' (4–5). 'What is required is an openness, an empathy, a concern that seeks windows rather than mirrors . . . ' (4). For Clark this empathy is to be sought in the close reading of the Aristotelian corpus, including the biological works. ' . . . I have assumed that Aristotle's biological works may fairly be combed for helpful addenda to his ethics and metaphysics' (69) He has made himself familiar also with contemporary work on meta-biological issues. More provocatively he suggests that, to counteract ill-grounded assumptions about feelings and beliefs in Aristotle's day, 'we should perhaps occasionally allow ourselves to think of Aristotle as a Zen Buddhist, a Neo-Confucian, an existentialist, or a disciple of Pindar' (8). Many readers will wish that Clark had allowed himself to enlarge more freely on Neo-Confucian doctrines and on the world-view of Pindar.

For the student of Aristotle's ethics Clark's book is a valuable supplement to less enterprising, and less laborious, approaches. But it does not seem to me that his ways of bringing together the well-doing of the philosopher and the well-doing or right-doing of the citizen can be accepted or even made plausible. How can man's brief vision, in a 'good minute', of the divine nature, single simple and unchanging, be an intellectual intuition of the world somehow containing or implying complexities to be filled in by the labours of the biologist or of the statesman and political philosopher? Moreover Clark himself, when he gives us in three pages (ix-xii) the 'summary' of his book, seems to loosen his grip on this unifying doctrine. The 'complete realization of the paramount good' is only 'momentary'. His formula emerges as: 'Civil and theoretic good meet in this, that both are a service of the divine in man' (xi). As at other 'summits' nothing definite or disputable is revealed about the terms of the meeting. This judicious vagueness seems closer than any systematic doctrine could be to memorable but brief remarks dropped by Aristotle.

As we have noted, Clark nowhere elucidates his suggestion that Aristotle can be viewed as a 'disciple of Pindar' (8). But a paragraph near the end of his chapter on *Eudaimonia* is a quotation from the poet's 'last extant poem' (162): 'Man's pleasure is a short time growing and falls to the ground as quickly, when an unlucky twist of thought loosens its roots. Man's life is a day. What is he? What is he not? A shadow in a dream is man, but when God sheds a brightness, shining light is on earth and life is as sweet as honey'. In another 'last extant poem', published on the day of the poet's death, Robert Browning speaks of greeting the unseen with a cheer; but he is content that what is cheered should not be seen. Browning is sometimes accused of optimism. But he can say memorably, like Pindar, that happiness, if as real as anything we know, is elusive and insecure:

Just when I seemed about to learn!
  Where is the thread now? Off again!
The old trick! Only I discern—
  Infinite passion and the pain
Of finite hearts that yearn.

Corpus Christi College, Oxford

INTELLECTUALISM IN ARISTOTLE

David Keyt

I

When Aristotle returns to the topic of happiness at the end of the *Nicomachean Ethics* (X.6-8) presumably to give us his final and best thoughts on the matter, he says that perfect happiness (*hē teleia eudaimonia*) is theoretical activity (*theōrētikē energeia*), that happiness and contemplation (*theōria*) are coextensive, and that the life of reason (*ho kata ton noun bios*), also called the philosophic or theoretical life (I.5.1095b19,[1] *E.E.* I.4.1215b1-2, *et. passim*), is the happiest life (X.7.1177a12-18, 1178a4-8, 8.1178b7-32). He goes on to say that the life in accordance with the other excellence (*ho kata tēn allēn aretēn bios*)–namely, the life in accordance with practical wisdom and moral virtue, elsewhere called the political or practical life (I.5.1095b18, *Pol.* VII.2.1324a40)–is the second happiest life (X.8.1178a9-22). And he draws a sharp contrast between the activities that characterize the two lives: theoretical activity is leisured, aims at no end beyond itself, and is loved for its own sake whereas practical activity is unleisured, aims at an end (other than itself), and is not chosen for its own sake (X.7.1177b1-26). As for the relation between the two sorts of activity, Aristotle implies that practical activity is merely a means to theoretical activity: ". . . we work in order that we may have leisure and wage war in order that we may have peace" (X.7.1177b4-6).

These remarks raise a major and well-known interpretive problem about Aristotle's ethical ideal and his conception of the best life for a man, for they seem to conflict with things he says earlier in the *Nicomachean Ethics* and elsewhere. They seem to conflict, in particular, with his account of the distinction between making (*poiēsis*) and doing (*praxis*) and with the conclusion of the function argument. In distinguishing making and doing, Aristotle says that "the end of making is something different from the making, but not the end of doing; for *good action* (*eupraxia*) *itself is an end*" (VI.5.1140b6-7); and in arguing that the goodness of an action is unlike the goodness of a product of one of the arts, he insists that for an act to be good it must be chosen for its own sake. The goodness of a product of one of the arts (a shoe or a statue) is a quality of the work itself; but, Aristotle argues, the goodness of an act is not a quality of the act itself. One must also consider the agent's state of knowledge, his motive, and his character. For an act to be good it must be done with knowledge, it must be chosen and *chosen for its own sake*, and it must issue from a stable character (II.4.1105a26-b9). This account of good action appears to directly contradict Aristotle's statement in the tenth book of the *Nicomachean Ethics* that practical activity, in contrast to theoretical, aims at an end (other than itself) and is not chosen for its own sake.

The conclusion of the function argument is that "the good for man turns out to be activity of soul in accordance with virtue (*kat' aretēn*), and if there are several virtues, in accordance with the best and most final" (or "most complete," *teleiotatēn*) (I.7.1098a16-18). There are two interpretations of *teleiotatē aretē*. According to the exclusionary interpretation,[2] Aristotle uses the expression to single out the highest excellence, theoretical wisdom, from among the rest; and the conclusion of the argument thus foreshadows the view of the tenth book that perfect happiness (*hē teleia eudaimonia*) is theoretical activity. According to the inclusive interpretation,[3] Aristotle uses the expression to refer to complete virtue–that is to say, to the combination of all the virtues, both moral and intellectual–and the conclusion of the argument conflicts, at least prima facie, with the view of the tenth book. The latter interpretation must be the correct one, for both the conceptual analysis that immediately precedes the function argument and the force of the argument itself require it.

In the passage immediately preceding the function argument Aristotle distinguishes three types of end (*telos*) (I.7.1097a25-b6). First, there are ends such as wealth, flutes, and instruments in general that are chosen only for the sake of other things. Secondly, there are ends such as honor, pleasure, and reason that are chosen for their own sake and for the sake of other things. And, finally, there are ends such as happiness that are always chosen for their own sake and never for the sake of anything else. I shall call an end of the first type a "subservient" end, of the second type a "subordinate" end, and of the third type an "ultimate" end. An ultimate end is more final (*teleioteron*) than a subordinate end, and a subordinate end than a subservient end. Furthermore, an ultimate end cannot be made more worthy of choice by the addition of anything. For if two ends are each chosen for their own sake but both together are more worthy of choice than either separately, then there is a compound end that embraces both to which each is subordinate (see X.2.1172b23-34, and compare *Top.* III.2.117a16-24 and *Rhet.* I.7.1363b12-21). Happiness is such an inclusive end (I.7.1097b17-20) and as such is the most final (*teleiotaton*) end (1097a30). The subordinate ends mentioned by Aristotle—honor, pleasure, and reason (*nous*)—are the ends of the three lives, the political, the apolaustic, and the philosophic respectively (see I.5, 6.1096b23-24, and *E.E.* 1.4). The thrust of the entire passage is thus that theoretical activity, the activity of *nous*, is a subordinate end that is included as one component among others of the ultimate end, happiness. It would seem, then, that the activity in accordance with the most final virtue referred to in the conclusion of the function argument must be the activity that constitutes the most final end—namely, activity in accordance with all the virtues, moral and intellectual.[4]

A second reason for favoring an inclusive rather than an exclusionary interpretation of the conclusion of the function argument is that the argument itself entails that the good for man is activity, not only in accordance with philosophical wisdom, but also in accordance with moral virtue and practical wisdom. In interpreting this argument I have attempted, by supplying its implicit premisses, to cast it into the form of a valid deductive argument.

Aristotle distinguishes four general functions in the animate world: to reproduce and to use food, to perceive, to move from one place to another, and to think (see *De An.* I.1.402b12-13, II.4.415a26, III.9.432a15-17). These four functions define three general forms of life: the nutritive and reproductive life, which is shared by all (mortal) living things (*zōnta*); the perceptive life, which is shared by all animals (zō(i)a); and "the practical life of that which has a rational principle," which is special to man (I.7.1098a1-4, *G.A.* I.23.731a24-b8, *Pol.* VII.13.1332b3-5). In describing this third life as a *praktikē zōē*, a practical life, Aristotle is presumable using the word *praktike* in a generic sense that includes theoretical activity as well as practical activity in the specific sense (see *Pol.* VII.3.1325b14-21). Practical activity in the specific sense must be included since "man alone of animals is capable of deliberation" (*H.A.* I.1.488b24-25), and theoretical activity is implied since that which has a rational principle (*ho logon echōn*) is part practical and part theoretical (*Pol.* VII.14.1333a25-27). Aristotle does not distinguish a locomotive life since, except for a few immobile marine animals such as the oyster (*P.A.* IV.7.683b4-11, *H.A.* I.1.487b6-15), locomotion and perception are coextensive (*De An.* III.9.432a15-17).

That there are these four general functions in the animate world so distributed is the material premiss of the function argument. The conclusion follows when this premiss is combined with four general principles. First, one kind of mortal[5] living thing is *lower* than another if, and only if, normal members of the one kind lack a function that normal members of the other possess (*De An.* II.2. 413a20-b13, III.12); moreover, mortal living things are *lower* than immortal (*Met.* Θ.8.1050b6-7). Thus plants are lower than animals; animals with fewer sense modalities (say, touch alone) lower than those with more (say, touch and sight); and animals other than man lower than man. Secondly, a form of life or an activity of the soul[6] is the *distinctive function*[7] of a kind of living thing if, and only if, every normal member of this kind and no member of a lower kind can perform it (see I.7.1097b33-34). Thus to reproduce and use food is the distinctive function of plants; to perceive, that of the lower animals; and "activity of soul in accordance with rational principle (*kata logon*) or not without rational principle" (I.7.1098a 7-8), that of man. It would seem to follow from this second general principle that God has no distinctive function since God's life consists entirely of theoretical activity, an activity in which man can share (X.8.1178b7-23, *Met.* Λ.7.1072b13-30). This is a problem that needs to be addressed, and I will return to it below. Thirdly, a *good member* of a kind is one that performs the distinctive function of its kind well (compared with other members of its kind) (I.7.1098a8-12). Thus a good man (*spoudaios anēr*) is one whose rule governed activity accords with excellence (1098a12-15). Finally, *the good for*—that is to say, *the ultimate end of*—a member of a kind is to be a good member of its kind. Thus the good for a particular man, his most choice-worthy end, is to be a good man. This is a consequence about which one might be sceptical[8] since there are occasions when a good man might be called upon to sacrifice his life (see IX.8.1169a18-26). But the last principle, though problematic, is absolutely crucial to the argument. For the function argument is introduced to give content to the characterization of happiness as "something final and self-sufficient, being the end of action" (I.7.1097b20-25), and without this final principle there will be no connection between the argument and this characterization. The conclusion now follows that the good for man is practical and theoretical activity that accords with excellence. Aristotle's own statement of the conclusion—"the good for man turns out to be activity of soul in accordance with excellence, and if there are several excellences, in accordance with the best and most final" (1098a16-18)—should, if possible, be interpreted as saying this; for Aristotle obviously intended the conclusion of his argument to be entailed by its premisses. Since, as we have seen, it is possible to take Aristotle to be referring in the last phrase to the combination of all the virtues or excellences and since Aristotle does intend to assert that there are several virtues, his conclusion must be that the good for man is activity of soul in accordance with the best and most complete (*teleiotatēn*) virtue—namely, the combination of all the virtues, moral and intellectual. To return now to the point that led to this lengthy discussion of the function argument, this seems to contradict Aristotle's assertion in the tenth book that perfect happiness (*hē teleia eudaimonia*) is theoretical activity alone.

II

The issue raised by the apparent conflict of Aristotle's remarks in the tenth book of the *Nicomachean Ethics* with those expressed earlier in the treatise and in other works[9] is that of the relation of the life of practical wisdom and moral virtue to the best life for a man–the relation of moral action to happiness. Does Aristotle abandon in Book X the view of Book I and elsewhere that moral activity is a subordinate end, a component of happiness, in favor of the view that it is merely a subservient end, only a means to happiness?

The difference between a *component* and a *means* may be illustrated by the difference between the activity of an ancient choregus in selecting the members of a chorus, outfitting it with costumes and masks, and providing for its training, which is one of the means to a dramatic performance, and the activity of the chorus in the performance of a play, which is a component, though perhaps a secondary component, of the dramatic performance itself.[10] This distinction is similar to one that Aristotle himself draws between a part (*meros*) and a necessary condition[11] that is not a part (*E.E.* I.2.1214b11-27, *Pol.* VII.8.1328a21-b4, 9.1329a34-39). A citizen, for example, is a part of a polis (*Pol.* III.1.1274b38-41) whereas property is not a part but only a necessary condition (*Pol.* VII.8.1328a33-35). Eating meat and taking a walk after dinner are for some people necessary conditions of health without being themselves parts of health (*E.E.* I.2.1214b14-24).

In Book X Aristotle seems to be espousing the view, which I shall call "strict intellectualism," that theoretical activity is the sole component of the best life for a man and that practical activity has value only as a means to theoretical activity. Some scholars have attributed this view to him without hesitation: Alexander Grant,[12] for example, in the nineteenth century and John Cooper[13] today. But some hesitation is in order. For strict intellectualism, as is well known,[14] in addition to being inconsistent with the doctrine of Book I, has unpalatable moral consequences, which Aristotle (at least in his more worldly moments) would not accept. According to strict intellectualism it would be right for one person to steal from or to defraud another in order to obtain the wealth required to have the leisure for theoretical activity, for on this view the end justifies the means. But Aristotle says that theft is always wrong: "It is not possible ever to be right with regard to these things [namely, such things as adultery, theft, and murder], but to do them is always to be wrong" (II.6.1107a14-15). Aristotle may be espousing strict intellectualism in Book X without being aware of its unpalatable consequences or in spite of them. Still, it may be worthwhile to try once more to rescue Aristotle's ethical philosophy from inconsistency and immorality.

One possibility is that Aristotle is embracing a moderate rather than a strict intellectualism in Book X. By "moderate intellectualism" I mean the view that theoretical activity is the primary but not the sole component of the best life for a man, moral action being a secondary component. Moderate, unlike strict, intellectualism is consistent with the doctrine of Book I. But there are several versions of moderate intellectualism corresponding to the various ways of combining moral and intellectual activity while preserving the primacy of the latter. And some of these have consequences almost as unpalatable as those of strict intellectualism. So it will be well before turning to Book X to sort and grade the various possibilities.

Suppose that moral action, as moderate intellectualism affirms, has value in itself and not simply as a means to theoretical activity. The value it has independently will then either be commensurable[15] with the value of theoretical activity or not. Suppose it is commensurable. In this case the independent value of moral action can always be weighed against the value of theoretical activity; and when a situation arises in which one must choose between engaging in contemplative activity and performing some moral action, the activity of lesser value can be sacrificed for that of greater value with the aim of maximizing the total value in one's life. I shall call this the "trade-off" view. According to it, the value of theoretical activity, which for Aristotle resembles the activity of God, is related to the independent value of moral activity, activity that is wholly human, as the value of gold is to silver. The details of this view—namely, how to measure the value of moral and theoretical activity and how to balance the value of the one activity against the value of the other—are difficult to envisage, but the view is sufficiently precise for one to see some of its consequences. Since on the trade-off view the value of a moral action can sometimes exceed that of a competing theoretical activity, an adherent of the view will sometimes sacrifice theoretical for moral activity. He might, for example, trade an hour of contemplative activity for an act of liberality or munificence. Similarly, the owner of a silver mine might pay his workers in gold. On the other hand, it would be right according to the trade-off view for a person who is poor but intelligent to steal from or to defraud another person if this were the only means he had to obtain the wealth required to have the leisure for theoretical activity. For the value of an act of honesty (in this case refraining from theft or fraud) can, on this view, be outweighed by the value of a certain amount of theoretical activity. An adherent of the trade-off view will, of course, have scruples in many cases where the strict intellectualist will not since the former, unlike the latter, needs always to consider whether the end of theoretical activity can be achieved without acting contrary to the moral virtues and, if not, whether the theoretical activity sought is worth the moral cost.

Suppose, to take the other alternative, that moral action has value in itself and not simply as a means to theoretical activity but that the value it has independently is incommensurable with (and thus cannot be weighed against) the value of theoretical activity. One will want to consider in this case whether theoretical activity is absolutely prior to moral activity or not. If it is, we have the "absolute priority" view. An adherent of this view will act on the precept, Maximize theoretical activity first; then maximize moral activity. Thus he will perform moral actions for their own sake but only when they do not interfere with his theoretical activity. He will never, for example, sacrifice a moment of theoretical activity, however uninspired, for a disinterested moral action, however noble. The consequences of this view are only slightly less unpalatable than those of strict intellectualism. Unlike the strict intellectualist, whose attitude toward any action that neither promotes nor hinders his theoretical activity is indifference, an adherent of the absolute priority view will act in accordance with the moral virtues when unable to contemplate or to do anything that will promote his theoretical activity; but, like the strict intellectualist, he will do anything, however base, that promotes his theoretical activity.

Suppose, to take the final case, that theoretical activity is the primary and moral action a secondary component of the best life for a man, that the value that moral action has in itself is incommensurable with the value of theoretical activity, but that theoretical activity is not absolutely prior to moral action. There *is* a view that fits this description. According to it, theoretical activity is more desirable than moral activity—one would spend all of one's time engaged in it if that were humanly possible—andis in this sense the primary component of happiness. But what is more desirable must be pursued within the constraints placed upon a person by his bodily nature, by his family and friends, and by his polis. The idea is that theoretical activity is to be maximized but only within the constraints of the life of practical wisdom and moral virtue. Moral activity is the foundation and theoretical activity the superstructure of the best life for a man. Moral action will not, on this view, be absolutely prior to theoretical activity. This view is not simply the converse of the preceding one. The demands of civic and domestic life are so indefinite and potentially so all consuming that there would be few, if any, opportunities for contemplation if moral activity were given absolute priority over theoretical. Such a priority would violate the primacy of theoretical activity. According to the "superstructure" view, the moral life sets certain minimum requirements that must be satisfied before one is to engage in theoretical activity; but the view does not demand that one should never shirk a duty, however trivial, for an opportunity to contemplate. Where the line is drawn will presumably be determined by the moral intuition of the practically wise man (*ho phronimos*).

The following table displays the various possibilities:

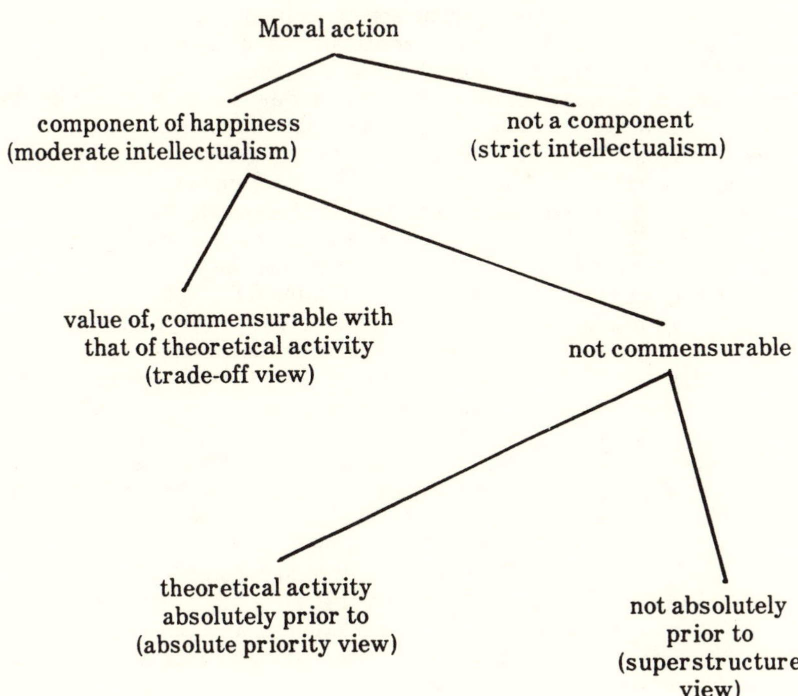

143

III

Ackrill's and Cooper's acute but divergent discussions of Aristotle's account of *eudaimonia* exemplify in various ways each of the four specific possibilities.

Ackrill maintains that "the question [how *theoria* and virtuous action would combine in the best human life] is incapable of even an outline answer that Aristotle could accept" ("*Eudaimonia*," p. 357). Ackrill reaches this conclusion because it seems to him that Aristotle's theology and anthropology together yield a consequence that is irreconcilable with his respect for ordinary moral views. Ackrill's argument, as I interpret him, goes like this. According to Aristotle's theology, the divine is incommensurably more valuable than the merely human. And, according to his anthropology, man is "a compound of 'something divine' and much that is not divine" (p. 358). *Theoria* is the activity of man's divine component while virtuous action belongs to his earthly nature. Therefore, *theoria* is "incommensurably more valuable" than virtuous action (p. 357) and in the best life for man must be given absolute priority over it (pp. 357-58). Aristotle's anthropology and theology thus lead to what I called the "absolute priority" view. But this view, Ackrill points out, has the consequence "that one should do anything however monstrous if doing it has the slightest tendency to promote *theoria*. . ." (p. 358)—a consequence that Aristotle must find "paradoxical" (*ibid.*) since he wishes to adhere "reasonably closely to ordinary moral views" (p. 357).

"The only way to avoid such paradoxical and inhuman consequences," Ackrill believes, "would be to allow a certain amount of compromise and trading between *theoria* and virtuous action, treating the one as more important but not incomparably more important than the other" (p. 358). Ackrill thus for his own part endorses the trade-off view. But he seems to be mistaken in supposing that this view does not share some of the paradoxical consequences of the absolute priority view and in supposing that the trade-off view is the only alternative available.

Cooper, in fact, attributes to Aristotle a view different from any that Ackrill considers. He finds what I have called the "superstructure" view in the *Eudemian Ethics*, in Books VII and VIII of the *Politics*, and in the middle books of the *Nicomachean Ethics*—namely, "a conception of human flourishing [*eudaimonia*] that makes provision for two fundamental ends--morally virtuous activity and intellectual activity of the highest kind. Neither of these is subordinate to the other; moral virtue comes first, in the sense that it must be provided for first, but once moral virtue is securely entrenched, then intellectual goods are allowed to predominate" (*op. cit.*, pp. 142-43). Cooper believes, however, that Aristotle adopts an intellectualist ideal of the best life in Book X of the *Nicomachean Ethics* and that he paves the way for this ideal in Book I (pp. 100, 147-48, *et passim*). By "intellectualism" Cooper means "the view that human flourishing consists exclusively in pure intellectual activity of the best kind" (p. 90)—the view that I have called "strict intellectualism." What leads Aristotle to embrace strict intellectualism, according to Cooper, is his doctrine that "one *is* his theoretical mind" (p. 168). Aristotle does not, on Cooper's interpretation, completely abandon the superstructure view; the life described by this view is simply downgraded in the final book of the *Nicomachean Ethics* from best to second best (pp. 177-80).

Cooper is led to this interpretation of Book X partly by a philological consideration—namely,by what he thinks Aristotle can and cannot mean by the Greek word *bios* ("life"). This matter needs to be examined since it raises a fundamental issue of how Aristotle is to be read.

IV

What does Aristotle mean by a "life," a *bios?* The traditional answer is that each of the various "lives" that Aristotle mentions–the apolaustic,[16] the political,[17] the philosophic,[18] the agricultural,[19] the military,[20] and so forth–is a personification of an abstraction.[21] On this interpretation none of these lives need be more than one aspect of the total life led by some particular person. Thus the life of a person like Xenophon might combine the military, the political, the agricultural, and the literary.[22]

Cooper has challenged this idea (*op. cit.* pp. 159-60). He denies that the word *bios* can be used in Greek to refer to an aspect or phase of a person's total life. According to Cooper, the word "means always '(mode of) life,' and in any one period of time one can only have one mode of life." "Hence," he concludes, "when Aristotle contrasts an 'intellectual life (*bios*)' with a 'moral life (*bios*),' he cannot mean . . . the intellectual life and the moral life of a single person. The Greek expression can only mean two different lives led by two different kinds of persons." Cooper here is making two distinct claims. The first and weaker claim denies that one person can live two or more distinct *bioi* synchronously but does not rule out the possibility that a person might lead one *bios* at one time and another *bios* at another time–that a person might, for example, lead an agricultural life during one part of the year and a military life during another. The second and stronger claim denies, or seems to deny, that one person can live two or more distinct *bioi* either synchronously or successively.

There are passages in Plato and Aristotle that refute both claims. In his discussion of domestic economy in the first book of the *Politics* Aristotle lists five lives (*bioi*) that procure their sustenance through their own work rather than through the exchange of goods–the pastoral, the agricultural, the piratical, the life of fishing, and the life of hunting (I.8.1256a40-b1). Aristotle goes on to say that some people combine one mode of life with another when the one is insufficient for their needs–for example, "some live a pastoral and piratical life at the same time (*hama*), others an agricultural and hunting life, and similarly with the others" (1256b2-6). This passage shows that the stronger claim about the word *bios*, that one person cannot live two or more distinct *bioi* either synchronously or successively, is clearly false. But in spite of the occurrence of the word *hama*, it probably does not refute the weaker claim as well. For Aristotle presumably does not mean to say that some people hunt while they plow but rather that within some interval of time–a year, say–they both hunt and plow.

That the weaker claim is also false is demonstrated by a passage in Plato's *Laws* (V.733D7-734E2). Plato considers four lives (*bioi*)—the temperate, the brave, the wise, and the healthy—and their opposites—the profligate, the cowardly, the foolish, and the diseased—and maintains that each of the first four is pleasanter than its opposite. He concludes from this that the life of excellence with respect to the body or the soul—that is to say, the life that combines, and of course combines synchronously, the first four lives—is pleasanter than the life of depravity, which combines the four opposite lives.

Thus it is clear that the Greek word *bios* can be used to signify, not only a person's total life, but also one particular phase or aspect of it. Furthermore, there are positive indications that Aristotle intended, at least in *Nicomachean Ethics* X.7-8, to signify two distinct aspects of a total life by "the life of reason" (*ho kata ton noun bios*) (1178a6-7) and "the life in accordance with the other excellence" (*ho kata tēn allēn bios*) (1178a9). For he says that a person lives the one life "as possessor of something divine" (*hē*(*i*) *theiōn ti en auto*(*i*) *huparchei*) (1177b28)—that is to say, as demigod—whereas he lives the other "as he is man" (*hē*(*i*) *anthropos estin*) (1177b27, 1178b5). And Aristotle uses this *hē*(*i*) ('as,' 'qua') locution as part of his standard terminology to signify one aspect of a thing in abstraction from all others. He says, to take a simple example, that "the infinite qua infinite is unknowable (*Phys.* I.4.187b7; see also III.6.207a25-26) meaning by this that an infinite object need not be completely unknowable but only in the respect in which it is infinite: if a surface were infinitely long but only an inch wide, one could know its width but not its length. Or, to consider another example, speaking of natural science Aristotle says that "there are many statements about things merely qua moving (*hē*(*i*) *kinoumena*), apart from what each thing is and from their incidental properties" (*Met.* M.3.1077b23-24).

There is now an answer, or a sort of answer, to a puzzle that arose in analyzing the function argument. It seemed that of all living things God alone lacked a distinctive function since his only activity, contemplation, is an activity in which man can share. The answer is that man does not engage in this activity as man but only as possessor of something divine—namely, reason or *nous*.[23] In so far as man can contemplate he is a god himself.

V

The way is now clear for an interpretation of *Nicomachean Ethics* X.6-8 that minimizes the conflict between it and the rest of the work. Aristotle begins his final and consummative discussion of happiness by considering whether happiness lies in play (X.6). This preliminary discussion raises at least two interpretive questions. First, what exactly is the view that Aristotle is considering? And, secondly, what contribution, if any, does this discussion make to Aristotle's ultimate conclusion that perfect happiness is theoretical activity?

The word *paidia*, along with two other words that figure in the discussion in chapter 6, *paidikos* ('childish') (1176b33) and *paizein* ('to play like a child'—then: 'to play,' 'to jest,' 'to dance,' 'to sing,' 'to play at a game') (1176b30, 33), is derived from the word *pais* ('child') (1176b22, 23). This derivation undoubtedly assists the conclusion of chapter 6 that happiness does not lie in play (1176b27-28): since a *pais* is *ateles* (undeveloped) (see *Pol.* I.12.1259b3-4). *paidia* can hardly be the *telos* (end) of a man (see *E.E.* II.1.1219b4-8).

The range of application of the word *paidia* is very wide. In Plato, for example, *paidia* covers among other things children's games (*Polit.* 30bD3-4, *Laws* 643B4-D4, 793E3-794A4), war games (*Laws* 829B7-C1), singing and dancing (*Laws* 803E1-2), the mimetic arts from dancing to drama (*Soph.* 234B1ff., Rep. 602B6-10, *Polit.* 288C1-10), religious sacrifices (*Laws* 803E1), puns (*Crat.* 406C3-4), and carousing (*Prot.* 347D6, *Laws* 673E8ff.). Human life for Plato is divided into just two phases—play (*paidia*) and seriousness (spoudē) (for the dichotomy see *Rep.* 602B8, *Polit.* 288C9-10, *Laws* 643B6, 647D6-7, 732D6, 797A7ff., 942A8)—play being a preparation for, a means to, or a relaxation from serious endeavors (*Laws* 643B4-D4, 796A1-D5, *Phil.* 30E6-7). It is not so clear what activities Aristotle counts as *paidiai*, for he is not as lavish with examples as Plato. But a few examples may be gleaned from the *Nicomachean Ethics* and the *Politics*. He mentions children's games (*Pol.* VII.17.1336a21-30) and urbane and witty conversation (*eutrapelia*) (*E.N.* II.7.1108a23-26 and IV.8) and reports the common view that the purpose of sleep, drink, music, and dance is play and relaxation (*Pol.* VIII.5.1339a14-21). Interestingly, in chapter 6 Aristotle alludes to the things valued among boys (1176b22), to those who are ready-witted (*eutrapeloi*) in the pastimes of tyrants (1176b12-16), and to the bodily pleasures (1176b19-21, 1177a6-7) (under which would fall the pleasures of sleeping, drinking, and dancing).

The association of play with the bodily pleasures connects the discussion in chapter 6 with that of the apolaustic life in I.5.[24] The two discussions are also connected by one of Aristotle's reasons for considering the view that happiness lies in play—namely, that the pleasures of play seem to be chosen for their own sake (1176b9-11). For it is Aristotle's view that the apolaustic life is the only life besides the political and the philosophic that is chosen for its own sake. Aristotle notes in the *Eudemian Ethics* that there are other modes of life besides these three--for example, that of the laborer, the artisan, and the trader--but he believes that they are always entered into for the sake of the necessities of life (*E.E.* I.4.1215a25-32), not for their own sake (see I.5.1096a5-7). All who happen to have the means, he remarks, choose to live either a political, a philosophic, or an apolaustic life (*E.E.* I.4.1215a35-36). It seems, therefore, that the life of play and the apolaustic life are the same.

Aristotle offers two reasons for supposing that happiness lies in the pleasures of play: the one just mentioned, that they seem to be chosen for their own sake, not for the sake of anything else; and, secondly, that they are pursued by persons deemed happy such as tyrants and others in positions of power (1176b9-17). Both reasons are rejected: tyrants are not trustworthy judges any more than (immature) boys (1176b17-27); and in the proper ordering of life, play is a relaxation from toil and a means to further exertion, not an end in itself (1176b28-1177 a1).[25] Aristotle rounds off his discussion of play with the following argument, the major premisses of which play a leading role in the discussion in chapters 7 and 8. "The happy life seems to be a life in accordance with excellence." The activity of one's higher faculties accords more with excellence and is thus more conducive to happiness than that of one's lower faculties. But play does not engage one's higher faculties. Therefore, happiness cannot lie in play (1177a1-11).

The stage is now set for the discussion of chapters 7 and 8. One of the three nominees for happiest life has been eliminated. Thus if one of the two remaining candidates can be shown to be happier than the other, it will follow that this one is also the happiest life possible.

VI

In chapter 7 Aristotle considers in turn six attributes that seem (*dokei*) to characterize the activity that constitutes happiness or the happy life. (For the form of the various conjuncts of the major premiss of Aristotle's argument see 1177a1-2, b4). The six are collected from different sources. The first comes from the conclusion of the function argument and reflects a philosophical thesis; the others reflect various common opinions (*endoxa*) about happiness and goodness. Thus the activity that constitutes happiness seems to be:

(1) in accordance with excellence (*kat' aretēn*) (1177a1-2, 12; compare I.7. 1098a16-17).

(2) continuous (*sunechēs*) (1177a21-22; compare I.10.1100b11-12, IX.9.1170a 4-8, and *Rhet.* I.7.1364b30-31).
(3) pleasurable (*hēdus*) (1177a22-23; compare I.8.1099a7-31, VII.1153b14-15, IX.9.1170a4, and *Rhet.* I.7.1364b23, 1365b11-13).
(4) self-sufficient (*autarkēs*) (1177a27-28; compare I.7.1097b6-16, IX.9. 1169b 4-5, and *Rhet.* I.7.1364a5-9).
(5) loved for itself (*di' hautēn agapasthai*) (1176b2-5, 1177b1-2; compare 1097a 34-b6 and *Rhet.* I.6.1362a21-22, 7.1364a1-5).
(6) leisured (*scholastikon*) (1177b4, 22).

If the attribute under consideration admits of degrees, Aristotle argues that theoretical activity (*theoria*) possesses it to a higher degree than practical (that is, moral and political) activity (*praxis*) (1177a12-b1). If the attribute does not admit of degrees, he argues that it characterizes theoretical but not practical activity (1177b1-15).[26] Aristotle then infers (1177b16-26) that perfect (or complete) happiness (*hē teleia eudaimonia*) is theoretical activity or, alternatively expressed, that the life of reason—the theoretical life—is the happiest life.[27]

As it stands, this is not a valid argument. For one thing it does not rule out the possibility that some third kind of activity–making pots, writing dramas, or reveling in the bodily pleasures–is superior to both theoretical and practical activity in respect of the six attributes under consideration. For another it allows the possibility that the list of attributes is incomplete, that the six considered do not include all that are essential to an activity that constitutes happiness. Furthermore, the conclusion is categorical–"The life of reason *is* the happiest life" (1178a7-8)–whereas the conjuncts of the major premiss are qualified–"The happy life *seems* to be a life in accordance with excellence" (1177a1-2). The solution of the first weakness is to add the implicit conclusion of chapter 6, that happiness consists of either theoretical or practical activity, as an additional premiss. As for the other two weaknesses, I shall simply assume, in order to raise a more interesting question about the argument, that Aristotle intended his major premiss to be read in a strengthened form–that he intended to assert that the attributes he considers actually do characterize, rather than merely seem to characterize, any activity that constitutes happiness and that the six he considers include all that are essential to an activity that constitutes happiness.

The more interesting question concerns the interpretation of Aristotle's conclusion—that *hē teleia eudaimonia* is theoretical activity or, alternatively expressed, that the theoretical *bios* is the happiest *bios*. What exactly is the force of this assertion? Does Aristotle mean to assert, as Cooper claims, "that the best plan of life is to pursue constantly the single end of theoretical contemplation in preference to all else" (*op. cit.*, p. 156)? Does he mean that the best total life for a man is one in which theoretical activity is constantly, exclusively, and (of course) successfully pursued? Or is he making the more modest assertion, as Stewart and Gauthier claim, that the best *element* of the nest total life for a man is its theoretical activity?[28] As I have argued in section IV above, Aristotle's use of the word *bios* coupled with *hē(i)* not only permits but supports the latter interpretation. The word *teleia* in *hē teleia eudaimonia*, on the other hand, is perfectly ambiguous and allows either interpretation. In *Metaphysics* Δ.16 Aristotle distinguishes three senses of *teleios:*

(1) having all of its parts: captured in English by the word 'complete,' as the complete time (*chronos teleios*) of a thing (1021b12-14).
(2) being best of its kind: captured in English by the word 'perfect,' as a perfect doctor (*teleios iatros*), perfect thief, or perfect circle (1021b14-23, *Phys*. VII.3.246a13-16).
(3) having reached its end (*telos*): captured in English by such expressions as 'fully realized' and 'fully developed' and predicated, for example, of an adult in contrast to a child (1021b23-30, *Pol.* I.12.1259b3-4).[29]

If *teleia* has sense (1) in the expression *hē teleia eudaimonia*, then Aristotle's conclusion expresses the strict intellectualist view that complete (or total) happiness is theoretical activity. If *teleia* has either sense (2) or sense (3), then his conclusion can be given a weaker, moderate intellectualist interpretation–that perfect or fully realized, as distinct from complete, happiness is theoretical activity.

Both formulations of Aristotle's conclusion will thus bear a moderate intellectualist interpretation. Although such an interpretation even seems indicated for one of the two, the perfect ambiguity of the other makes one hesitate to claim on the basis of an analysis of the verbal formulations alone that such an interpretation of Aristotle's conclusion is demanded. One must also consider Aristotle's argument. What sort of intellectualism does it entail–moderate or strict? If Aristotle's argument entails one view but not the other, this is a good reason for attributing the one rather than the other to him.[30]

On one interpretation strict intellectualism is entailed by that part of Aristotle's argument which is based on the philosophical idea that the activity that constitutes happiness is activity in accordance with excellence. This subargument opens (1177a12-21) and closes (1177b26-1178a8) chapter 7, though its leading ideas are introduced at the end of Aristotle's discussion of play (6.1177a1-11). Most English translations of these passages obscure the simple relations between the key terms of the argument and make it almost unintelligible, so a few elementary comments about its terminology are in order. The argument is based on the noun *aretē* ('goodness,' 'excellence,' 'virtue') (see 1177a2, 10, 12, 17, b29) and three forms of the comparative and superlative of its simple adjective *agathos* ('good'):

comparative: 'better'	superlative: 'best'
beltiōn (1177a3, 4, 6)	*beltistos*
kreittōn (1177a6, b26)	*kratistos* (1177a13, 19, b34, 1178a5-6)
ameinōn (1178a3)	*aristos* (1177a13)

Rendered literally, the argument of 1177a1-21 runs as follows:

1. Happiness is activity in accordance with goodness (a1-2, 12).
2. And the activity of the better part of a man is better and hence more conducive to happiness (a5-6).
3. So the activity of the best part is best and most conducive to happiness (see a12-13).
4. Reason (*nous*) is the best thing in us, and its objects are the best of knowable objects (a20-21, see Stewart, *ad loc.*).
5. Therefore, the activity of reason is the best activity and the one most conducive to happiness. As Aristotle expresses it, ". . . the activity [of reason] in accordance with its proper goodness will be *hē teleia eudaimonia*" (a16-17).

The premisses of this argument entail, not that theoretical activity is complete happiness, but only that it is perfect or fully realized happiness.

But when Aristotle returns to this theme at the end of chapter 7, he seems to advance beyond his earlier claim that reason is the best (but not the only) thing in us and to claim now that a man and his reason are identical: "This [*viz.* reason] would also seem *to be* each man, since it is the authoritative and better part. Thus it would be odd if he were to choose not his own life but that of someone else" (1178a2-4). Similar assertions occur in two earlier passages in Book IX (4.1166a10-23, 8.1168b28-1169a18). However, the element or faculty with which a man is (or seems to be) identified is not the same in the two books. In Book IX the thinking or reasoning element (*to dianoetikon, to nooun, nous*] with which a man seems to be identified (1166a16-17, 22-23, 1168b35), since it has the ability to guide action and to control the passions, must be either his practical reason[31] or his intellect as a whole[32]-practical, productive, and theoretical. In Book X, on the other hand, the reason in question must be the theoretical reason alone.[33] For its activity is said to be theoretical (1177a17-18 *et passim*], and practical wisdom (*pronēsis*) is explicitly distinguished from it (8.1178a16-22).[34] But, in spite of these differences, the passages in Book IX, as we shall see, provide the clue to the proper interpretation of 1178a2-4.

Now, if a man is strictly identical with his theoretical reason and if practical reason is not a part of theoretical reason, then practical reason is not a part of a man. On the strict-identity hypothesis practical reason will be merely something without which a man cannot exist, like food (*Met.*Δ.5.1015b20-22)—not a part of a man but only a necessary condition of his existence.[35] Practical and theoretical reason will be related as the lower and higher order in Aristotle's ideal state (see *Pol.* VI.4.1291a24-28 and VII.8-9). The warriors, officeholders, and priests who compose its higher order are its parts. The farmers, craftsmen, and tradesmen who compose its lower order, though the state cannot exist without them, are not parts of it: their role is to serve the members of the higher order. On the strict-identity hypothesis practical reason will be subservient to theoretical in just the same way; and Aristotle will, as Cooper claims (*op. cit.* pp. 162-63), be embracing strict intellectualism.

But does Aristotle really mean to claim that a man is strictly identical with his theoretical reason? There is good reason for thinking not since his statement that reason "would also seem *to be* each man" (1178a2) is immediately qualified: ". ". . for man, then, the life according to reason [is best and pleasantest], since this [*viz.* reason] *most of all* (*malista*) is man" (a6-7). To be most of all man is to be less than, and so nonidentical with, man.[36] That this reservation is seriously intended is indicated by its earlier appearance in the two passages in Book IX where a man is identified with his thinking faculty. In the first of these Aristotle says that "the reasoning element would seem to be, or to be *most of all* (*ē malista*), each man" (4.1166a22-23); and the reservation is repeated in almost the same words in the second–"That this [*viz.* reason] is, or is *most of all* (*ē malista*), each man is clear" (8.1169a2). But to claim that reason is the most important, but not the sole, part of a man is simply to reiterate a premiss–namely, line(4)—of the argument of 1177a1-21, an argument that does not entail strict intellectualism.

Other parts of the overall argument of chapter 7 that need to be examined are those in which Aristotle tries to show that theoretical activity is leisured and alone loved for its own sake whereas military and political activities (the pre-eminent practical activities) are not chosen for their own sakes and are unleisured (1177b1-24). Aristotle offers the same consideration in support of both conclusions—namely, that military and political activities aim at an external end but theoretical activity does not, a claim that seems to conflict with his earlier assertion that "good action itself is an end" (VI.5.1140b7).[37] The conclusion that theoretical activity alone is loved for its own sake in conjunction with Aristotle's earlier requirement that the activity that constitutes happiness must be chosen for its own sake (X.6.1176b2-5) entails that theoretical activity is the sole component of happiness (strict intellectualism). Given the association of theoretical activity with leisure and military and political activities with work, Aristotle's statement that "we work in order that we may have leisure and wage war in order that we may have peace" (1177b4-6) points to the same interpretation; for it seems to imply that practical activity has value only as a means to theoretical.

In examining these two subarguments the first thing to notice is that the conflict between Aristotle's various remarks on action is only apparent. Good action on Aristotle's theory is typically double-barreled, the target of one barrel being different from that of the other. A man may act in accordance with a particular virtue such as temperance, bravery, or justice for the sake of the particular temperate, brave, or just act itself; and he may also at the same time seek an end apart from the action--*a telos para tēn praxin*--such as health or victory or the reform of a wrongdoer. Although this distinction between an *internal* and an *external* end is never drawn explicitly by Aristotle, it underlies his treatment of bravery[38] and once drawn provides a key to several puzzles in Aristotle's ethics. The brave man on the field of battle wishes to do two things: to attain the morally beautiful (*to kalon*) while avoiding the morally ugly (*to aischron*)[39] and to defeat his enemy while avoiding death and wounds.[40] And like Hector facing Achilles he may attain the one goal but not the other.[41] (Failure to attain the external goal may mean, as it did to Hector and his family, the destruction of happiness [see I.10. 1100b22-1101a8].) Aristotle's remarks on action appear to conflict because some refer to the internal, some to the external end.[42]

Unfortunately, Aristotle does not always keep this distinction clearly in mind. Otherwise he would not have inferred that theoretical activity "alone[43] would seem to be loved for its own sake" from the premiss that "nothing arises from it apart from the theorizing, whereas from practical activities we gain more or less apart from the action" (1177b1-4). That an action has an external end does not prevent it from being loved for its own sake. What follows from Aristotle's premiss, as Hardie points out, is that theoretical activity "alone is loved for its own sake alone."[44] Thus even though the conclusion of this subargument in conjunction with the requirement that the activity that constitutes happiness must be chosen for its own sake entails strict intellectualism, Aristotle's reason for accepting the conclusion itself is inadequate. To my mind, the invalid conclusion of this subargument is the only basis Aristotle provides for a strict intellectualist interpretation of chapter 7.[45]

The distinction between an internal and an external end of action is also helpful in interpreting Aristotle's remark that "we work in order that we may have leisure and wage war in order that we may have peace" (1177b4-6). If an action can be performed for its own sake as well as for an end apart from the action, then work can have value both in itself and as a means to peace and leisure. The munificent man who uses his wealth to outfit a trireme (IV.2.1122a24, b23), though he wishes to help secure the safety of his polis, acts also for the sake of the morally beautiful (1122b6-7, 1123a24-27).[46] Moreover, Aristotle's distinction between work and leisure does not correspond to his distinction between practical and theoretical activity. The moral virtues have a role to play in both phases of life: "Bravery and endurance are needed for work, philosophy for leisure, temperance and justice at both times, and more especially when men observe peace and have leisure; for war compels men to be just and temperate, whereas the enjoyment of good fortune and the possession of leisure accompanied by peace makes them rather insolent" (*Pol.* VII.15.1334a22-28). Aristotle's remark that work is for the sake of leisure thus does not imply strict intellectualism.

VII

Chapter 8 contains three additional arguments for the conclusion that perfect happines is theoretical activity. (1) The gods are paradigms of happiness but their lives consist entirely of theoretical, rather than practical or productive, activity; "so of human activities that which is most akin to this is the most conducive to happiness" (1178b7-23). (2) The whole of the life of the gods, consisting as it does of ceaseless contemplation, is blessed (*markarios*); so too is the life of man in so far as it is spent in such activity; but none of the lower animals are happy since they in no way share in contemplation. "As far, then, as contemplation extends, so also does happiness; and to those to whom contemplation more fully belongs happiness also more fully belongs, not incidentally but in virtue of the contemplation." Therefore, happiness is a kind of contemplation (b24-32). (3) He who exercises his (theoretical) reason is most loved by the gods; those most loved by the gods are the happiest; therefore, the wise man is the happiest (1179a22-32).

The second argument requires examination, for the part of it that is directly quoted seems to identify happiness and contemplation straightforwardly and, consequently, to be an unambiguous expression of strict intellectualism. But the argument will, I think, bear another interpretation. The second argument follows directly upon the first and begins with the words "A proof, too, is that . . ."(*sêmeion de kai . . .*). This indicates that it is intended to establish the same conclusion as the first—namely, that *hē teleia eudaimonia* is theoretical activity (1178b7-8). Now, if *hē teleia eudaimonia* means, as it seems to, perfect or fully realized rather than complete happiness throughout X.7-8 and if *makarios* and *eudaimonia* mean *teleia eudaimonia* in argument (2), then Aristotle's statement that happiness and contemplation are coextensive will mean simply that perfect or fully realized happiness is coextensive with contemplation. But this assertion is compatible with a moderate intellectualism that allows a place for the secondary happiness of moral and political activity. This interpretation also resolves a small puzzle about the argument–namely, that Aristotle's explanation of the fact that happiness is not attributed to the lower animals seems inadequate. They are incapable of happiness, one would suppose, not simply because they are incapable of contemplating but also because they are incapable of practical thinking.[47] But if Aristotle is thinking only of perfect or fully realized happiness, his explanation is completely adequate.

VIII

Thus with the exception of the one statement that theoretical activity "alone would seem to be loved for its own sake" (1177b1-2) there seems to be nothing in

X.6-8 that is inconsistent with a moderate intellectualism and with the rest of the *Nicomachean Ethics*. This is a fairly weak conclusion. Can it be strengthened? Is there anything in these three chapters that can be taken to be an expression of moderate intellectualism? In particular, can anything be taken to be an expression of the only reasonable version of moderate intellectualism—namely, the superstructure view according to which theoretical activity is to be maximized within the constraints of the life of practical wisdom and moral virtue?

Aristotle's famous injunction "as far as possible to immortalize oneself and to do everything with a view to living in accordance with the best thing in oneself [*viz.* the theoretical reason]" (7.1177b33-34) is an expression of the superstructure view if the restriction signified by the words "as far as possible" includes moral restrictions as well as those of mind, body, and estate. Does it? The answer to this question can be inferred, I think, from a passage in chapter 8 where Aristotle is discussing the extent to which the theoretical life and the life in accordance with practical wisdom and moral virtue need extenal equipment and where he seems for once to combine the two lives: "The person who contemplates has no need of such things (*viz.* external goods) for his activity; but they are so to speak even impediments, at least to contemplation; however, as he is a man and lives with a number of others, he chooses to do those things that are in accordance with [*scil.* moral] virtue; he will therefore need such things with a view to living as a man" (1178b3-7). Here Aristotle states explicitly that the person who contemplates (*ho theōrōn*), qua man, *chooses* to act in accordance with moral virtue.[48] It has been denied, however, that Aristotle intends by this statement to imply that the person who contemplates will be a morally virtuous person. Cooper in defending his strict intellectualist interpretation of Book X claims that Aristotle "says only that the theorizer may *perform* various virtuous actions" and that "Aristotle conspicuously avoids saying that his theorizer will *be* a virtuous person" (*op. cit.* p. 164). "This is easily understood," Cooper explains, "since it is clear that however often [the theorizer] may perform the just or the temperate or the liberal deed, anyone who organizes his life from the [strict] intellectualist outlook cannot care about such actions in the way a truly just or temperate or liberal man does" (*ibid.*). But unless one can find strict intellectualism elsewhere in Book X this is not a plausible reading of the passage. The correct explanation of Aristotle's formulation is much simpler than the one Cooper offers. Aristotle says that the person who contemplates "chooses to do those things that are in accordance with virtue" (*haireitai ta kata tēn aretēn prattein*) because he is considering whether the person who contemplates will need very much external equipment and, as the immediately preceding passage makes plain, it is moral actions, not moral dispositions (*hexeis*), that require such equipment (1178a28-b3). Arthur Adkins in a recent article concedes that the person who contemplates will on Aristotle's theory be a morally virtuous person: "[t]he *theoretikos* will indeed possess all the *aretai*. ."[49] But he remarks on the passage before us that Aristotle "does not tell us *when* [the *theoretikos*] chooses: he may well mean 'chooses when *theoria* is not available' " (*ibid.*). On Adkins' interpretation the author of this passage might without inconsistency condone the conduct of a man who refused to interrupt his theoretical activity in order to rescue a neighbor from a burning building. Thus Adkins believes the passage to be consistent with what I have called the "absolute priority"view—the view whose precept is, Maximize theoretical activity first; then maximize moral activity. There are at least two reasons for rejecting Adkins' interpretation. First, Aristotle says that the person who contemplates, *qua man*, chooses to act in accordance with moral virtue. But a person is not a man–that is to say, a human being (*anthrōpos*)—at one moment and at another not. He is a human being all of his life just as he is always an animal and always a living thing. Thus once the moral virtues are acquired he is *always* prepared to act in accordance with them. Secondly, possession of the moral virtues would seem to be inconsistent with their erratic exercise. The brave man defends his polis whenever the enemy attacks, not just at his convenience. Thus if the person who contemplates, qua man, chooses to act in accordance with bravery, he must always be prepared to sacrifice theoretical activity for battle. So this passage does not seem to be consistent with the absolute priority view. It seems better to take it as picking up the theme of the function argument, the centerpiece of Book I: namely, that the various aspects of a person's total life–his life as a living thing, as an animal, as a man, and as a demigod–form a hierarchy with the higher aspects resting on and presupposing the lower.

If my interpretation is correct, Aristotle does indeed subscribe to the superstructure view: one should seek to immortalize oneself but only within the bounds of the life of practical wisdom and moral virtue.[50]

Footnotes

1. All Aristotelian references are to the *Nicomachean Ethics* unless otherwise identified.
2. W. F. R. Hardie, "The Final Good in Aristotle's Ethics," *Philosophy*, XL (1965), p. 280 and John M. Cooper, *Reason and Human Good in Aristotle* (Cambridge, Massachusetts, 1975), pp. 99-100.
3. J. L. Ackrill, "Aristotle on *Eudaimonia*," *Proceedings of the British Academy*, LX (1974), pp. 351-354.
4. In this paragraph I am following Ackrill's lead.
5. For the restriction see *De An.* II.2.413a31-32, 3.415a7-11.
6. For the equation of *zōē* and *psuchēs energeia* see I.7.1098a13.
7. Its *ergon idion* (*Pol.* II.5.1263a40) as distinct from its *koina erga* (*G.A.* I.23. 731a30-31).
8. See P. Glassen, "A Fallacy in Aristotle's Argument about the Good," *The Philosophical Quarterly*, 7 (1957), and J. L. Ackrill, *Aristotle's Ethics* (New York, 1973), pp. 20, 244.
9. Most notably in *E.E.* II.1 especially 1219a35-39. See Cooper, *op. cit.*, pp. 116-118.
10. For other illustrations of the distinction see L. H. G. Greenwood's commentary on Book VI of the *Nicomachean Ethics* (Cambridge, 1909), pp. 46-47.
11. *hou aneu ouk endechetai*, literally: "that without which it is not possible."
12. "*sophia*, while producing happiness, is identical with it: but *politikē* is to happiness as means to end" (*The Ethics of Aristotle* [London, 1885], vol. II, p. 336).
13. See below.
14. See Ackrill,"Aristotle on *Eudaimonia*," p. 358 and Cooper, *op. cit.*, pp. 149-50.

15. *sumblētos*, compare *Pol.* III.12.1283a3ff.
16. *ho apolaustikos bios*, I.5.1095b17.
17. *ho politikos bios*, I.5.1095b18.
18. *ho philosophos bios*, *E.E.* I.4.1215b1.
19. *ho geōrgikos bios*, *Pol.* I.8.1256b5.
20. *ho stratiōtikos bios*, *Pol.* II.9.1270a5.
21. See J. A. Stewart, *Notes on the Nicomachean Ethics* (Oxford, 1892), vol. II, pp. 443-445.
22. This last life is not mentioned by Aristotle.
23. For the divinity or quasi-divinity of *nous* see X.7.1177a13-17, b30-31 and *De An.* I.4.408b18-31.
24. See the note to 1177a6-9 in R. A. Gauthier and J. Y. Jolif, *Aristote: l'Éthique à Nicomaque* (Louvain and Paris, 1970).
25. But for Aristotle, unlike Plato, life has three phases, not two: *work* [*ascholia*] relieved by *play*, and *leisure* (*scholē*). Play is for the sake of work, which is in turn for the sake of leisure (X.7.1177b4-6; *Pol.* VII.14.1333a30-36, 15.1334a 14-16, VIII.3.1337b28-1338a1, 5.1339b15-17). See also Friedrich Solmsen's perceptive article "Leisure and Play in Aristotle's Ideal State" in *Kleine Schriften* (Hildesheim, 1968), vol. II.
26. For the comparison of theoretical and practical activity, which runs throughout the argument, see 1177a21-22 (*theōrein-prattein*), a28-34 (*ho sophos* versus *ho dikaios*, *ho sōphrōn*, and so forth), b2-4, 16-24, 29; and in chapter 8 see especially 1178b20-21.
27. For the various formulations of Aristotle's conclusion see 1177a16-18, b24-26, 1178a7-8, b7-8, b32, 1179a31-32.
28. ". . . la vie contemplative est pour Aristote un élément de la vie idéale, elle n'est pas, à elle seule, *toute* la vie idéale" (Gauthier-Jolif, *op. cit.*, tome II, p. 862). See also Stewart, *op. cit.*, vol. I, pp. 59-62, vol. II, pp. 443-445.
29. It has often been pointed out that when Aristotle says that happiness requires a *teleios bios* or a *teleios chronos* or a *mēkos biou teleion* (I.7.1098 a18-20, 10.1101a8-16, X.7.1177b24-26), he must be using *teleios* in this third sense. If happiness can be lost and regained (1101a8-16), the *mēkos biou teleion* required for happiness must be somewhat less than the span of life from birth to death–the *teleios bios* required for happiness cannot be a *complete* life. It seems rather to be a span of life that is sufficient to attain the *telos* of human life. See Stewart and Gauthier-Jolif, *ad. loc.*
30. Cooper complains that the six reasons Aristotle gives at 1177a18-b26 do "not tend to show that [contemplative] activity would reasonably be pursued as a dominant end in anyone's life" even though, according to Cooper, this is just what Aristotle infers from them (*op. cit.*, pp. 156-57). Cooper thinks, however, that the immediately succeeding passage, 1177b26-1178a22, contains a more intelligible reason for endorsing strict intellectualism (pp. 157ff.).
31. *ho praktikos nous* (*De An.* III.10.433a13-15).
32. This possibility is suggested by Aristotle's use of *to dianoētikon* to describe it, *dianoia* being Aristotle's generic term for thinking in general (see VI.2. 1139a26-31 and *Met.* E.1.1025b25).
33. *ho theōrētikos nous* (*De An.* III.9.432b26-28, 10.433a14-15).
34. For a detailed analysis of the differences between the passage in Book X and the two in Book IX see Cooper's excellent discussion, *op. cit.*, pp. 169-175.

35. See p. 4 above.
36. See Daniel T. Devereux, "Aristotle on the Active and Contemplative Lives," *Philosophical Research Archives* III (1977), pp. 840-1.
37. See p. 1 above.
38. See D. F. Pears, Aristotle's Analysis of Courage," *Midwest Studies in Philosophy,* III (1978).
39. On *to kalon* as an end of action and *to aischron* as an object of avoidance see III.7.1115b11-13, 23-24, 1116a11-12, 15; 8.1116a28-32, b2-3, 19, 30-31, 1117a8, 16-17; 9.1117b9, 14-15; 12.1119b16; IV.1.1120a23-24, 1121b4-5; 2.1122b6-7, 1123a24-25; IX.8.1169a21-22, 28, 32, 35; X.8.1178b13; and *E.E.* III.1.1229a2, 1230a29-33.
40. See I.1.1094a6-9 and III.9.1117b7-8. When Aristotle says in speaking of bravery that "it is not the case, then, with all the virtues that their exercise is pleasant, except in so far as one attains the end" (III.9.1117b15-16), the end in question is the external end. See also III.3.1112b33.
41. On Hector's motivation see III.8.1116a21-29.
42. On this topic see also Ackrill's notes on 1139b1, 1176b7, and 1177b1-26 in *Aristotle's Ethics.*
43. *scil.* of the two pre-eminent human activities. *Happiness*, of course, is loved for its own sake.
44. *Aristotle's Ethical Theory* (Oxford, 1968), p. 356.
45. Aristotle's assertion that "from practical activities we gain more or less apart from the action" seems itself to be an overstatement, for there are actions such as bravely facing death from a terminal illness that have no external end but are performed entirely for their own sakes (see Pears, *op. cit.*, p. 274).
46. If it be objected that Aristotle, in giving his final account of happiness in X.6-9, seems to have forgotten his (implicit) distinction between an internal and an external end of action, the reply is that the internal end of action is alluded to twice in the course of these chapters: see X.6.1176b6-9 and 8.1178a 12-13.
47. See Ackrill, *Aristotle's Ethics, ad. loc.*
48. Stewart, *ad. loc.*
49. "*Theoria* versus *Praxis* in the *Nicomachean Ethics* and the *Republic*," *Classical Philology,* 73 (1978), p. 301.
50. In writing this paper I profited from a number of discussions with Fred Miller.

References

J. L. Ackrill, *Aristotle's Ethics* (New York, 1973).

J. L. Ackrill, "Aristotle on *Eudaimonia,*" *Proceedings of the British Academy,* LX (1974).

A. W. H. Adkins, "*Theoria* versus *Praxis* in the *Nicomachean Ethics* and the *Republic,*" *Classical Philology,* 73 (1978).

John M. Cooper, *Reason and Human Good in Aristotle* (Cambridge, Massachusetts, 1975).

Daniel T. Devereux, "Aristotle on the Active and Contemplative Lives," *Philosophical Research Archives*, III (1977).

R. A. Gauthier and J. Y. Jolif, *Aristote: l'Éthique a Nicomaque*; (Louvain and Paris, 1970).

P. Glassen, "A Fallacy in Aristotle's Argument about the Good," *The Philosophical Quarterly*, 7 (1957).

Alexander Grant, *The Ethics of Aristotle* (London, 1885).

L. H. G. Greenwood, *Aristotle; Nicomachean Ethics* VI (Cambridge, 1909).

W. F. R. Hardie, "The Final Good in Aristotle's *Ethics*," *Philosophy*, XL (1965).

W. F. R. Hardie, *Aristotle's Ethical Theory* (Oxford, 1968).

D. F. Pears, "Aristotle's Analysis of Courage," *Midwest Studies in Philosophy*, III, (1978).

Friedrich Solmsen, "Leisure and Play in Aristotle's Ideal State," *Kleine Schriften* (Hildesheim, 1968), vol. II.

J. A. Stewart, *Notes on the Nicomachean Ethics* (Oxford, 1892).

Ancient Philosophy 8

Aristotle's Function Argument: A Defense

Jennifer Whiting

Aristotle thinks it is uncontroversial that *eudaimonia* is the highest good, or ultimate end, of human action (*EN* 1095a14-20).[1] He thinks that we all desire *eudaimonia* only for its own sake and not for the sake of anything else, and also, that *eudaimonia* is that for the sake of which we do all things (*EN* 1097a30-b6; 1102a1-4). But Aristotle also thinks that this is uninformative; it does not tell us what the components of *eudaimonia* are and this is something about which there is much dispute (*EN* 1095a20-28).[2]

Some of Aristotle's contemporaries (and many of ours) are so impressed by the fact that different people enjoy different things that they follow Protagoras and adopt a subjectivist conception of *eudaimonia* according to which what seems best to each person *is* best for him. Others adopt an objectivist conception according to which what is good for a person is at least partly independent of his beliefs about what is good for him. On this objectivist view (but not on the subjectivist one) a person can mistakenly believe that something is good for him. So within the objectivist camp there are further disputes about which particular conception of *eudaimonia* is correct—some objectivists identifying *eudaimonia* with pleasure, others identifying it with honor, and yet others with contemplation or some combination of these goods.[3]

Aristotle claims that we can resolve these disputes and give a clearer account of what *eudaimonia* is, if we appeal to the human ἔργον (or function). He argues that the good and the (doing well) (τἀγαθὸν καὶ τὸ εὖ) of a flute player or a sculptor or of anything which has a function is determined by that thing's function—a function which Aristotle says is peculiar to it (*EN* 1097b23-35). A good flute player has the virtue or ability which enables him to perform well; a good knife is sharp and able to cut well.[4] Similarly, Aristotle thinks that a good man has the virtues and abilities which enable him to do well whatever it is the function of a man to do. Furthermore, Aristotle thinks that it is *good for* a man to have these virtues and to do these things; in fact, that man's *eudaimonia* depends on it (*EN* 1098a12-18).

Many commentators have thought this argument obviously mistaken and wrongheaded—primarily on the grounds that men do not have functions, and that even if they did, nothing about their good or *eudaimonia* would follow from their having these functions. But I will argue that these objections are based on misinterpretations of Aristotle, and that properly interpreted he presents an interesting and defensible (though admittedly controversial) account of the relationship between *eudaimonia* and human nature. If Aristotle's account *is* mistaken, it is mistaken in more interesting and ultimately more informative ways than commentators have traditionally thought.

I

In general, Aristotle attempts to argue from claims about what it is to be a man (or the function of a man)[5] to conclusions about what is *good for* a man. Because he does so by appeal to the notion of a good man, commentators have often viewed his argument as consisting of two moves—first, the move from (a) what it is to be a *man* (or the function of a man) to (b) what it is to be a *good man*; and second, the move from (b) what it is to be a *good man* to (c) what is *good for* a man.[6]

The legitimacy of these moves is typically challenged by appeal to the following sort of examples. From an understanding of the function of a knife, it *may* follow that being sharp and cutting well make something a good knife; but it does not follow that being sharp and cutting well is *good for* a knife. Similarly, from an understanding of what it is to be a flute player, it *may* follow that some things (e.g., perfect pitch and a sense of rhythm) make someone a good flute player; but it does not follow that these things are *good for* someone who plays the flute. In a depressed economy, an unemployed virtuoso may wish that he had been tone deaf and had instead become a doctor.

So the fundamental challenge to Aristotle runs as follows. From an understanding of what it is to be a man, it *may* follow that a good man is one who has the virtues and abilities which enable him to perform characteristically human activities, though even this much is doubted. But it does not follow that having these virtues or engaging in these activities is *good for* any individual. Just as what makes someone a good flute player may fail to benefit him, so also what makes someone a good man may not be good for him. Suppose, e.g., that men are characteristically social or political animals. It does not follow that joining clubs or running for office is good for me, if I prefer to spend all my time reading Aristotle's *Metaphysics*.

Aristotle, however, does not agree. He thinks that *if* men are characteristically social or political animals, then my exclusive preference for reading his *Metaphysics* reflects a mistaken judgment about what is good for me.[7] Our current problem is to see whether Aristotle can defend this objectivist view against the foregoing challenge. That challenge rests on three common, but I think mistaken, objections to Aristotle's argument.

The first objection attacks the move from (a) (the function of a man or what it is to be a man) to (b) (what it is to be a *good* man) on the ground that this requires that men, like bodily parts or craftsmen and their tools, have instrumental functions or virtues which presuppose their being good or useful for some further ends or purposes. But, the objection continues, men as such do not have instrumental functions or purposes, so the move from (a) to (b) is unwarranted.[8]

The second and third objections grant that men may have functions, not in the instrumental sense, but rather in the sense that there is some capacity (or set of capacities) which is peculiar to men and which distinguishes them from other animals. The second objection then attacks Aristotle's moves from (a) to (b) and from (b) to (c) on the ground that peculiarity is no recommendation. From the fact that some capacity (e.g., the capacity for prostitution) is peculiar to the human kind, it does not follow that a good man is one who exercises that capacity. Nor does it follow that it is *good for* men to exercise that capacity.[9]

The third objection allows the move from (a) to (b), and so allows that there may be a distinctively human set of capacities (including, e.g., the capacities for courage and justice) which determine what makes someone a good man. It then objects to the move from (b) to (c) on the ground that *even if* a good man is one who exercises these capacities, it does not follow that it is *good for* any individual man to exercise these capacities; in situations of danger and scarcity, cowardly and unjust behavior may in fact benefit a man. The idea is that what makes someone a good instance of his kind is not necessarily good for *him*.[10]

Behind these objections lies a more general worry—namely, that Aristotle is attempting to move from purely descriptive and non-evaluative claims about what the human function *is* to explicitly normative conclusions about what is good for men and about how men *ought* to live—very roughly, the worry that Aristotle attempts to move from an 'is' to an 'ought'.

We have seen that these objections are typically supported by substituting references to things like knives and prostitutes for Aristotle's references to men in (a) to (c). The legitimacy of the moves from (a) to (c) in the man-instance is then challenged by appeal to their illegitimacy in these substitution instances. But these substitutions are unwarranted. Aristotle explicitly makes distinctions which rule out the inferences from (a) to (c) in the substitution instances, while allowing them in the man-instance. Once we see how these distinctions rule out the illegitimate inferences, we will see that the foregoing objections are based on misinterpretations of Aristotle's fundamental project. Aristotle does not suppose that men have instrumental functions or virtues. Nor does he attempt to move from a purely descriptive and non-evaluative account of the human function to normative conclusions. As we shall see, Aristotle's account is normative 'all the way down'.

II

First, Aristotle distinguishes two senses in which we say one thing is for the sake of another (*DA* 415b20-21). One is the beneficial sense in which x's occurring benefits someone. The other is the instrumental sense in which x is instrumental (or a means) to bringing it about that y, and it is a further question whether or not anyone is benefited in the process; it is simply a matter of causal efficacy. For example, hemlock may be instrumental (or a means) to killing someone. If no one is benefited by his death, we can say that his taking hemlock is *merely instrumental* to bringing it about that he dies. But if anyone is benefited by his death, we can say that his taking the hemlock is not merely instrumentally but also beneficially good for whomever it benefits.[11]

This distinction between the merely instrumental and the beneficial senses in which we say that one thing is for the sake of another is important because Aristotle claims that the notion of benefit is appropriately applied *only* to living creatures. He explicitly distinguishes love for friends from love for inanimate objects and says that while it is a necessary condition of friendship that I wish good to another for his own sake, it would be ridiculous for me to wish good to a bottle of wine; for it is only possible to wish that a bottle of wine be good in order to have it for oneself (*EN* 1155b29-31). A certain kind of sugar may be instrumentally good for fermentation; and a lengthy aging process instrumentally good for producing a mellow wine. But unless we introduce reference to the desires and interests of living creatures, these things will be merely instrumentally, and not also beneficially, good.

Restricting the class of beneficiaries to the class of living things rules out the inferences from (b) to (c) in those substitutions involving inanimate objects such as knives. But this does not show that Aristotle will allow the inference in *all* substitutions involving animate creatures. He may want to rule out *some* inferences from (b) to (c) where living creatures are involved—namely, in the sort of inference from (b) what it is to be a good flute player (or a good prostitute) to (c) what is *good for* a flute player (or a prostitute).[12]

Now the class of flute players and the class of prostitutes do not constitute natural kinds. So Aristotle can rule out such inferences by claiming that the move from (b) to (c) is warranted only in substitutions involving natural kinds. But in order to show that this is not *ad hoc*, Aristotle must establish some connection between a thing's membership in a natural kind and what is beneficially good for that thing—or, since Aristotle takes membership in a natural kind to be an essential property (*Topics* 101b26-30), some connection between a thing's essential properties and what is beneficial for that thing. And this must be a connection which is lacking between a thing's membership in a non-natural kind (or a thing's accidental properties) and what is beneficially good for it. In other words, Aristotle must show that my belonging essentially to the human species determines at least something about what is beneficially good for me in a way in which my belonging accidentally to the class of flute players does not.

It is not hard to see that nothing about what is beneficially good for me follows simply from my playing the flute. Whether or not the characteristics which make me a good flute player benefit me will depend upon on the other desires and interests I happen to have. These characteristics may in fact benefit me, not simply *qua* flute player but also *qua* man, if playing is my sole source of support or personal fulfillment. But it will not follow *simply* from my being a flute player that these things benefit *me*. If I despise the flute, I may wish that I had been tone deaf so that my parents would not have encouraged me to develop this talent and I would not now be stuck giving music lessons when I would rather be doing philosophy instead. Because the potential benefits of playing the flute depend on what desires and interests I happen to have, they belong to the class of goods which Aristotle calls relative or conditional (τινί) and contrasts with unconditional or categorical (ἁπλῶς) goods.[13] And it is because the characteristics which make someone a good specimen of a non-natural kind tend to confer only conditional or relative benefits, that the inference from (b) to (c) is unwarranted in substitutions involving members of non-natural kinds.

If this interpretation is correct, then Aristotle suggests a connection between something's membership in a natural kind (or its essential properties) and what is unconditionally or categorically good for that thing. These unconditional goods are not unconditional in the sense that they are fixed entirely independently of the characteristics of the kind to which they are attached, but rather in the sense that they are fixed by characteristics which belong to each member of that kind simply in virtue of its being a member of that kind and not on characteristics such as particular desires and interests which may vary from one individual to another. These categorical goods are fundamental to Aristotle's project. Very roughly, his view is that for each species there is an ultimate end such that realizing that end (which Aristotle identifies with living a certain sort of life) is categorically or unconditionally good for any normal member of that species—that is, good for it whatever its actual interests and desires.[14]

Furthermore, Aristotle's account of friendship suggests that he regards these categorical goods as intrinsic and non-instrumental in a way in which conditional goods are not. He claims that only virtuous persons wish well to one another for the other's own sake because they wish one another well for the sake of what each is essentially, and not (as in friendships for advantage or pleasure) for the sake of what each is accidentally (*EN* 1156a10-19, b7-24). This suggests that these categorical goods are independent of further ends and purposes, and so, intrinsically and non-instrumentally good in a way in which conditional goods are not. Now this is certainly a controversial view. But it is not the easy target that our initial objections take it to be.

III

The first objection was that the inferences from (a) to (c) require that men have instrumental functions which presuppose their being good or useful for further ends or purposes. But we have just seen that this is not so. Aristotle can argue that the inferences from (a) to (c) hold only for individual members of (living) natural kinds to which categorical goods are attached. In other words, Aristotle can argue that these inferences depend upon there being some activities associated with each natural kind such that engaging in these activities is intrinsically and non-instrumentally beneficial for any normal member of that kind. So Aristotle's moves from (a) to (c) not only fail to require that men be viewed instrumentally; they actually require that men *not* be viewed instrumentally.

The inferences from (a) to (c) in those substitutions involving non-natural kinds fail precisely because the goods involved are merely instrumental and dependent upon the further purposes and ends of the members of those kinds. So it is the notion of an intrinsic or categorical good associated with each species which allows Aristotle to say that my belonging to the human species determines something about what is good for me in a way in which my belonging to the class of flute players does not. Of course, other things besides categorical goods may in fact benefit me—either because I have essential properties additional to those belonging to me as a member of this kind or because of certain accidental features of my environment or constitution.[15] But the fact that *some* claims about what is beneficially good for an individual *do not follow* from her belonging to a certain kind is no counterexample to the view that *some* claims about what is good for an individual *do follow* from her belonging to that kind.

We can now see that the second objection—that peculiarity is no recommendation—is also based on a misunderstanding of the term 'peculiar' (or ἴδιον) and its role in Aristotle's argument. In *Topics* i 4, Aristotle says that ἴδιον is sometimes used to refer to the essence (τὸ τί ἦν εἶναι) of a thing, and sometimes to refer to the necessary but non-essential properties of thing. Although Aristotle rarely uses ἴδιος to refer to the essence of a thing, this seems to be how he uses it in the function argument. For in that argument Aristotle talks exclusively about activities (especially rational activities) of the human soul. And Aristotle takes the soul of an organism to be its *essence* and not simply one of its necessary but non-essential properties.[16] In any case, Aristotle is not using ἴδιος as we would ordinarily use the word 'peculiar' to identify properties which are peculiar (in the sense of being unique) to the human species. If he were, he could not allow that contemplation is part of our good, for the capacity to contemplate is not unique to us; it belongs most of all to the gods. And similarly, he could not allow that *we* also share in contemplation, for then contemplation would not be peculiar (in the ordinary sense of the word) to the gods either.[17] Only if we interpret ἴδιος as referring to the human essence as a whole can we allow that contemplation belongs both to human and to divine welfare. On this interpretation, human and divine welfare will differ in so far as each is determined by a different conjunction of essential properties. But any individual conjunct of one may be shared by the other as long as there is at least one conjunct which belongs to one and not to the other. This interpretation of ἴδιος as referring to the human essence as a whole enables Aristotle to rule out proposed counterexamples which involve capacities (like the capacity for prostitution) which are peculiar to us in the ordinary sense, but which are not parts of the human essence.[18]

I have now argued that Aristotle has the resources to rule out the illegitimate inferences from (a) to (c) in those substitutions involving inanimate objects and members of non-natural kinds. But this does *not* show that the inferences from (a) to (c) *are* warranted in substitutions involving living members of natural kinds. Aristotle must defend his claim that something's membership in a natural kind at least partly determines what is beneficial for that thing; he must, that is, answer the third objection.

IV

At this point, Aristotle might appeal to his view that membership in a natural kind is an essential property which an individual cannot lose without ceasing to exist. So the connection between membership in a natural kind and the capacity for benefit may simply be a consequence of Aristotle's view that there must be some stable and enduring entity which survives any change involved in coming to be benefited—i.e., something which sticks around to receive the benefit.[19] But Aristotle is not claiming simply that something must remain what it is essentially in order for it to be benefited. He is making the stronger claim that the ways in which a thing can be benefited are at least partly determined by the kind of thing it is and what its essential properties are.

Aristotle might defend this claim by appeal to the claim that the psychological structures and characteristic functions of a natural kind largely determine what is healthy for members of that kind. For example, the physiological structures and characteristic activities of a plant determine that exercising the capacity for photosynthesis is consti tutive of a plant's health. So if we allow that healthy functioning is *good for* an individual, then these examples may show that at least *some* things about what is good for an individual are determined simply by the kind of thing it is. These things are what I have been calling the unconditional or categorical goods associated with natural kinds. Aristotle wants to argue that just as the characteristic structures and functions of plants determine that some things are categorically good for plants, so the characteristic structures and functions of men determine that some things are categorically good for men.

At this point, however, it is important to stop and examine Aristotle's argument with care. For this is the point at which many commentators suspect that Aristotle attempts to move from a purely descriptive and non-evaluative account of the function of an organism to explicitly normative conclusions about what is good for that organism. But that is not Aristotle's argument; he does not think that we can identify the characteristic structures and functions of an organism without introducing normative considerations. In other words, Aristotle does not think that we can give an account of the essence or the function of a kind without introducing some notion of what is beneficial for members of that kind. This is what I had in mind whan I said that Aristotle's account was normative 'all the way down'.

The primary evidence for this comes from Aristotle's teleology. As is well known, Aristotle distinguishes four types of cause—material, efficient, formal, and final—and argues that in the case of many things (especially natural ones) the formal and final cause coincide.[20] His idea here is not difficult.

The final cause of a thing is what that thing is for—the end (τέλος) for the sake of which it exists. This is usually some activity. For example, the final cause of an axe is the activity of chopping. The formal cause is the capacity (or set of capacities) which enables a thing to engage in that activity constitutive of its final cause or end. In the case of an axe, this is the capacity to chop. This capacity is the essence of a thing or what makes that thing a thing of its kind. So the formal and final cause of a thing coincide in the sense that the formal cause of a thing is the capacity (or set of capacities) which enables that thing to perform those activities constitutive of its end—i.e., the capacity to perform those activities for the sake of which it exists. So we cannot say what the formal cause (or essence) of something is without reference to its final cause or end.

The fact that formal and final causes coincide in this way is important. For Aristotle generally associates the final cause with the good of the organism (*Meta.* 983a30-b1, 1013b25-27) or with what is better for the organism (*Physics* 198b4-9), and hence, with something explicitly normative. So if we cannot identify or define the formal cause (or essence) of a thing without reference to its end or final cause, we cannot identify or define the formal cause (or essence) of a thing without introducing explicitly normative considerations.[21] These, of course, will help to answer the question about which of the many characteristics (or sets of characteristics) peculiar (in the ordinary sense of the word) to men constitute the human essence, and so determine what it is to be a good man. They will be those characteristics which are essentially related to the activities constitutive of our end. But this only serves to relocate the problem at the point where we ask which of the many activities (or sets of activities) peculiar to men constitute our end. If Aristotle has no independent method of answering this question—independent, that is, of what seems best to each person—then he is going to have a tough time defeating the subjectivist. His strategy of appealing to an objectively determined essence to generate an objective end or good will be undermined if there is no objective essence and each person's end is just what it seems to him to be.

V

The fundamental claims on which Aristotle's position rests should by now be clear, even if controversial. They are first, that there are objective essences belonging to members of natural kinds, and second, that these essences (at least partly) determine what is beneficial for members of those kinds. In other words, Aristotle attempts to defeat the subjectivist by arguing that our essence is objective and not whatever it seems to us to be, and so, that our *eudaimonia* is objective and not whatever it seems to us to be. And Aristotle thinks that determining precisely what our essence is will also enable him to reject mistaken objectivist conceptions of *eudaimonia* such as hedonism and (in my view) Strict Intellectualism.[22] It is because he thinks that we are neither beasts nor gods that Aristotle denies that our *eudaimonia* consists solely in the pursuit of pleasure or exclusively in contemplation.

An adequate defense of Aristotle's position thus involves three tasks. First, he must argue that there are objective essences belonging to members of natural kinds. Second, he must defend the alleged connection between the essence of a kind and what benefits members of that kind. And third, he must give an account of the human essence. Moreover, since Aristotle wants to appeal to that essence to resolve disputes about *eudaimonia* and human welfare, he must have some method for determining what our essence is which is (at least partly) independent of our beliefs about human welfare.

Aristotle attempts his first task (that of defending essentialism) in several contexts—most notably, in *Metaphysics* iv 4 (where he attempts a dialectical argument against someone who denies the principle of non-contradiction) and also in his defense of the distinction between generation (or destruction) *simpliciter* and mere alteration. I cannot now evaluate the success of the arguments. Nor, barring the presence of a radically subjectivist opponent, do I think that necessary. The relevance of these arguments here is simply that they rest on *general* considerations about the possibility of rational discourse and change—considerations which are independent of our moral beliefs. So these arguments provide independent and non-moral support for Aristotle's ethical argument.

I have already suggested that Aristotle can attempt his second task by appealing to the life sciences where facts about the natures of various species are supposed to justify *some* claims about what is good or bad (in the sense of being healthy or unhealthy) for members of those species. For we are less inclined to be skeptical about biological benefit and harm. And even if we think that we must introduce *some* normative notions in order to determine what constitutes healthy functioning for a plant or animal, we need not deny the existence of a connection between the characteristic structures and activities of a living organism and what benefits and harms that organism. Here again, there is independent and non-moral (though not necessarily non-evaluative) support for Aristotle's ethical conclusions.[23]

Now what I want to suggest is that Aristotle can achieve some of the independence from our beliefs about *human* welfare necessary for his third task, if he applies to humans the *general* methods he uses to determine which of a plant's (or animal's) characteristics are essential to it, and which of a plant's (or animal's) activities constitute its end. That is, Aristotle must apply to humans, methods which are similar to (or the same as) those used to determine that, e.g., photosynthesizing is constitutive of a plant's health. These methods will presumably include the observation of behavior and the attempt to explain such behavior within his general teleological framework, an attempt which admittedly appeals to beliefs about the ways in which such behavior is related to the welfare of the relevant organism.[24] *If* Aristotle can use these *general* methods to establish that the exercise of some capacities is essentially human, then he can claim that the exercise of these capacities is essentially related to human welfare or *eudaimonia* in much the same way that exercising the capacity for photosynthesis is related to a plant's health. These capacities may turn out to be rational, linguistic, social or otherwise. But whatever they are, Aristotle can view the *method* of establishing what is good for rational beings as no less objective than that of establishing what is good for plants and non-rational animals.

So Aristotle need not rely on a mere analogy between a plant's health and a man's welfare. He can argue that each is a special case of the general notion of εὖ ζῆν (or living well). *Eudaimonia* is simply the εὖ ζῆν of essentially rational animals, and so, is strictly parallel to the εὖ ζῆν of any other plant or animal.[25]

VI

At this point, someone might object to Aristotle's assimilation of *eudaimonia* to the εὖ ζῆν (or welfare) of plants and animals. He might object that we can derive an adequate conception of a plant's welfare simply from an understanding of its physiological structures and activities only because we *identify* a plant primarily—or exclusively—with those physiological structures and activities which are definitive of health; these things exhaust the essence of a plant. So contributing to (or damaging) the health of a plant is the only way to benefit (or harm) it. The same presumably goes for most animals. But we do not think that contributing to (or damaging) a man's health exhausts the ways in which we might benefit (or harm) him. That is because we do not *identify* men primarily with the physiological characteristics definitive of health and Aristotle may not identify men with these at all.[26] Something else is thought to be essential to human nature—namely, rationality.

So far, Aristotle agrees. He thinks that men are essentially rational animals whose characteristic activity or *ergon* is to pursue intentionally their own good—or at least their own apparent or conceived good. But Aristotle denies that this undermines his attempt to assimilate *eudaimonia* or human welfare to the welfare of plants and other animals. Given the connection between a thing's essence and the ways in which it can be benefited, Aristotle thinks that a man's rationality (at least partly) determines what is beneficial for him.

But someone who accepts the main points of Aristotle's argument *and* his characterization of men as essentially rational animals may still be dissatisfied. He may object that this characterization of men as essentially rational is not sufficient to yield any interesting or substantive conclusions about human welfare, and so, will not help us to discover the components of *eudaimonia* He may think that these components will be contingent on which goals and desires rational creatures happen to have and that these goals and desires can vary from one individual to the next. He may say that whatever we think about the welfare of non-rational creatures, the welfare of rational ones is subjective in the sense that a rational agent's welfare is determined by the beliefs and desires an agent happens to have.

We have seen, however, that Aristotle does not entirely agree.[27] He thinks that there are objective components of *eudaimonia* which are determined by human nature without being entirely dependent on the particular goals and desires individuals happen to have. Aristotle might defend this claim by arguing that whatever goals and desires a man happens to have, he has reason to cultivate rational agency by developing those virtues which enable him to pursue his goals (whatever they are) most effectively. For example, practical wisdom or the ability to identify the best available means to his ends will contribute to the effective pursuit of his goals. And temperance or the capacity to control his appetites and passions will make a similar contribution. Just as someone can perform certain actions which undermine a heart or a kidney's capacity to function effectively (by, e.g., eating and drinking too much or exercising too little), so also someone can undermine his capacity to pursue his goals effectively if he fails to develop temperance and practical reason. And Aristotle is entitled to claim that establishing the connection between these virtues and effective rational agency is no less a matter of empirical inquiry than that of establishing the connection between the former actions and their effects on hearts and kidneys.

Similarly, Aristotle can appeal to the connection between a thing's essence and the conditions for its survival in order to argue that any essentially rational agent (whatever his actual goals and desires) has reason to preserve his capacity for rational agency. For remaining what he is essentially is a condition of *his* attaining those goals, or indeed, of *his* receiving any benefits at all. On Aristotle's view, someone who destroys his capacity for rational agency (by, e.g., taking excessive doses of hallucinogenic drugs) literally destroys himself. For even if someone else takes over and manages his life for 'him', Aristotle would say that it is not *he*, but rather someone else, who receives the apparent benefits of this overseer's efforts.

This case—or the case of someone who becomes what we call 'a human vegetable'—is analogous to the case where my friend who 'becomes' a god fails to survive that change, and so, is not strictly the beneficiary of any goods accruing to that newly existing deity. This analogy is important *if* practical intellect is part of the human essence. For practical intellect is essentially concerned with psycho-physical affections such as desire and anger. This means that even if my theoretical intellect could survive in a disembodied state, I (who am essentially human and so essentially composed of practical intellect) could not. So however singlemindedly Aristotle thinks I ought to pursue contemplation, he cannot recommend that I 'become' a disembodied intellect in order to do so. For there is a sense in which *I* would be no better off 'becoming' a god, than if I were to 'become' a beast or a vegetable. The general point is that *if* we are essentially rational agents, we have reason to preserve our rational agency simply as a necessary condition of attaining any of our goals, whatever they happen to be.

Of course this argument will not convince absolutely everyone. It will not convince a present-aim theorist whose goal is to live for the moment because he does not think of himself as existing over extended periods of time. Nor will it convince someone whose *goal* is to be intemperate or irrational. But Aristotle can reasonably reply that this goal is one that a rational agent, in so far as he thinks of himself as such, cannot coherently have. On Aristotle's view, each of these men—the intemperate man and the present-aim theorist—makes a mistake about who or what he is, and so, about what is good for him. Of course, if these men turn out to be right and Aristotle wrong about what we are, then Aristotle may have to abandon his own conception of *eudaimonia*. But the fact that he cannot convince people who do not think of themselves as rational agents existing over time that temperance and prudence are good for them is not an objection to Aristotle's view.

So far then, our objector may agree that any essentially rational agent has reasons to preserve and to cultivate his rational agency, whatever goals and desires he happens to have. But this shows only that temperance and practical wisdom are instrumentally valuable to any rational agent and these instrumental connections are not enough for Aristotle. For they do not show what the *components* of *eudaimonia* are. Nor do they justify the independent value Aristotle attaches to a man's own rational pursuit of his final good. In order to explain this, we must invoke Aristotle's conception of *eudaimonia* as a special case of the kind of welfare attributable to any plant or animal.

A merely instrumental connection between a heart's strength and its capacity to pump blood does not show why a heart is better off beating on its own if a pacemaker could be doing its work instead. Nor does a merely instrumental connection between practical wisdom and *eudaimonia* show why *I* am better off running my own life, if someone else could do it for me. Suppose that my powers of practical reasoning are modest and that I occasionally suffer from weakness of will. Why should I not turn my deliberations over to a highly efficient life planning agency and then commit myself to the care of someone empowered to enforce its decisions? This might seem especially prudent, if I am thus able to satisfy a larger proportion of my first order aims and desires than I would otherwise do—or than most of my admittedly more self-reliant friends do.

But Aristotle would not agree. He does not view *eudaimonia* (as we might view happiness) simply as the satisfaction of all (or of a reasonable portion) of a person's various first order desires and aims. That person's role in bringing it about that his desires are satisfied or his aims attained is of fundamental importance.[28] We might put this point by saying that *eudaimonia* does not simply require that my desires *be* satisfied or that my ends *be* attained; *eudaimonia* requires that *I* satisfy my desires and that *I* attain these ends.[29] This explains why Aristotle says that *eudaimonia* is an *activity* of soul in accordance with virtue, and refuses to call a person *eudaimôn* if her various first order ends and desires are satisfied simply as a matter of luck or chance.[30] While *we* might be willing to say that such a person is *happy* and perhaps even that she lives well, Aristotle's conception of *eudaimonia* as a special case of the welfare of living things shows why he would not agree.[31]

Aristotle is relying on a conception of attaining one's ends which is fundamentally natural. A heart which, owing to some deficiency in its natural capacities, cannot beat on its own but is made to beat by means of a pacemaker is not a healthy heart. For *it*, the heart, is not strictly performing its function. Similarly a man who, owing to some deficiency in his natural capacities, cannot manage his own life but is managed by means of another's deliberating and ordering him is not *eudaimôn*—not even if he possesses the same goods and engages in the same first order activities as does a *eudaimôn* man. For *he*, the man, is not strictly performing his function. This is why Aristotle refuses to call slaves, who lack the capacity for deliberation, *eudaimôn* (*Pol.* 1260a12-14, 1280a31-35; *EN* 1177a8-9). On this naturalistic view, the connection between *eudaimonia* and rational agency is not merely instrumental. Aristotle's claim that *eudaimonia* is an activity of soul in accordance with virtue shows that he thinks that *eudaimonia consists in* exercising rational agency.

VII

So far our objector, if he adopts Aristotle's naturalistic framework, may agree. But he is likely to complain that this still tells us very little about what *eudaimonia* or human welfare is. Surely it consists in the rational pursuit of one's own goals, but which goals are these? Could my *eudaimonia* consist in the deliberate pursuit of evil ends (e.g., in torturing children)? Or could it consist in the rational and calculating pursuit of sensual pleasure?

Aristotle does not think so. He thinks that a full account of human nature can show us not only that *eudaimonia* consists in the rational pursuit of our own conceived ends, but also something about what these ends are or ought to be. This is clear from Aristotle's discussion of friendship and self-love.

Aristotle thinks that only virtuous friends wish well to one another for the other's own sake. They do so because they wish well to one another for the sake of what each is essentially and not (as in friendships for advantage and pleasure) for the sake of what each is accidentally (*EN* 1156a10-19, b7-24). What does Aristotle mean by this?

Business associations are typical cases of friendship for advantage. Suppose that my friend and I are stockbrokers who wish well to one another in that respect in which we are friends. We each hope that the other will be successful in his pursuit of profit. But this does not show that each wishes well to the other *for his own sake*. For that depends not only on why each of us pursues profit, but also on each of us understanding where profit fits into the other's aims. Suppose that my friend values the money only instrumentally and as means to things which he values for their own sakes—e.g., as tuition for a philosophy course so that he can achieve contemplation. It is only if I wish him well in pursuing these ultimate ends and not simply as a profiteer that I wish him well for his own sake.

But there is a problem here. What if I, unlike my friend, make profit my ultimate end? Does this mean that any true friend who wishes me well for my own sake must wish me well in my pursuit of profit? Aristotle does not think so, for he thinks that when I pursue profit as an ultimate end, I do not even wish *myself* well for my own sake. This is clear from Aristotle's distinction between two kinds of self-love.

Aristotle says that the person who loves and gratifies the dominant part of himself—that is, his intellect (or rational part) is most truly a lover of self. But someone who places too high a value on money, honor, or pleasure, and so gratifies his affections and the irrational part of himself, is less truly a lover of self. For he assigns goods to the irrational part which is less truly him than the rational part, which is most of all (and perhaps even exclusively) who or what he is (*EN* 1168b25-1169a6). Aristotle thinks that like the intemperate man and the present-aim theorist, this person makes a mistake about who he is, and so, about what is good for him.

Aristotle thinks that we are essentially creatures who intentionally pursue our own good (or our own conceived good). So he thinks that there is a sense in which we must be pursuing what is really or objectively good for us, even when we deliberately pursue specific ends which are not in fact good for us. In such cases, we desire the good and are simply mistaken about what it is.

Suppose, e.g., that I believe that sensual pleasure is good (for me) and on the basis of this belief, make pleasure my ultimate end. Because I pursue pleasure *as good* (or on the basis of that belief) Aristotle thinks that *if* pleasure is not really good for me, then there is a sense in which I do not get what I am after, no matter how much pleasure I achieve in the process. It is as though I have captured Oswald believing that he is the killer of JFK. If someone else killed JFK, then whether or not I know it, I have not got what I want. And this, Aristotle says, is like getting nothing at all (*EN* 1164a13-16). Aristotle thinks it is like this with pleasure and the good.

In this sense, Aristotle may allow that a person can sincerely believe that he is *eudaimôn* and still be mistaken in that belief—something we would not be very likely to say about happiness. He believes that someone whose desires rest on mistaken beliefs about what is good for him will be better off if his beliefs (and desires) are corrected so that he has true beliefs about what is good for him, and so desires what is really good for him (*EN* 1129b4-6). And Aristotle thinks that this is true, no matter how subjectively satisfied he is with his present lot.

Now these things which are objectively good for a person, whatever his actual beliefs and desires, are the categorical goods which Aristotle thinks will benefit him simply in so far as he is essentially human. What these things are will depend on what the human essence is. If, as some commentators think, Aristotle identifies us exclusively with our theoretical intellects, then contemplation alone will be categorically good for us. And this is true even if virtues such as temperance and prudence are instrumentally valuable in our pursuit of contemplation. But if (as I think Aristotle believes) practical intellect is also part of our essence, then moral virtue will also be categorically good for us. Similarly, if the irrational desires are part of the human essence, then even certain sensual pleasures may also be categorically good for us. And these things will be categorically good for us and components of our *eudaimonia* in the same way in which photosynthesis is categorically good for plants. The fundamental difference between us and plants is that we intentionally pursue our categorical good and they do not.

VIII

Before concluding, I want to point out just how ambitious Aristotle's project really is. He initially appeals to the human function in order to give content to our uncontroversial but uninformative account of *eudaimonia* as the ultimate end of human action. But much of his success depends on how much he is willing or able to build into his account of human nature in the first place. For as we saw, the specification of man simply as a rational agent does not get him very far. It may (given Aristotle's naturalistic framework) show that *eudaimonia* consists in the rational pursuit of one's own goals. But it does not show much about what these goals ought to be.

If Aristotle wants to show more about these goals, he needs a fuller account of human nature. For example, if (as Aristotle says) man is by nature a social or political animal, then this may show that friendship and political activity are components of *eudaimonia* (*EN* 1097b8-11, 1169b18-19; *Pol.* 1253a8-9). Similarly, if theoretical intellect is part of human nature, then contemplation will also be a component of *eudaimonia*. But Aristotle needs to be careful here—especially if he wants to argue against Thrasymachus, Callicles, and Co. that all the traditional virtues benefit a man. For Aristotle then needs some independent means of deciding which things are, and which are not, parts of human nature—that is, means which are not entirely dependent on views about what the traditional virtues or the components of *eudaimonia* are. This is crucial, if Aristotle's appeal to human nature is supposed to provide a way of *discovering* what *eudaimonia* is.

This is why it is important that in *EN* i, Aristotle appeals to his general teleology and to the independently plausible psychological theory of the *De Anima* in order to establish that man is essentially a rational animal. But the further Aristotle strays from these independently plausible teleological and psychological theories, and the more he tries to restrict the contents of *eudaimonia* by filling in the account of human nature, the more suspect his conclusions become. We may not agree that reading Aristotle's *Metaphysics* is good for me if I prefer to spend my time playing basketball—or that an occasional cocktail party or political appointment is good for me if I prefer to devote all of my time to Aristotle's *Metaphysics*. But whatever we think of these more specific conclusions, Aristotle's general identification of what it is to be human with rational agency is not altogether implausible—at least not to those of us who would prefer to trust our hearts to pacemakers than our deliberations and the pursuit of our ends to another, no matter how benevolent and wise he happens to be.[32]

University of Pittsburgh

NOTES

[1] Although I believe that 'happiness' is an appropriate translation of *eudaimonia* in the sense that each refers to the ultimate end of human action and allows for both subjective and objective conceptions of that end, I leave *eudaimonia* untranslated because I believe that contemporary conceptions of happiness tend to be subjectivist in a way in which Aristotle's conception of *eudaimonia* is not. On this point, see Kraut, 1979b, 167-197.

[2] On Aristotle's distinction between the components of a thing and the necessary conditions for its existence, see *EE* 1214b6-28; *Pol.* 1328a21-b4 and 1239a34-39, and Greenwood 1909, 46-47.

[3] I include hedonism (and other conceptions of *eudaimonia* which identify *eudaimonia* with some subjective psychological state such as pleasure) among objectivist conceptions of *eudaimonia* in so far as they claim that pleasure (or some other subjective psychological state) is good for us independently of our belief that it is so—that is, in so far as they allow that someone may (like Antisthenes) mistakenly believe that pleasure is not in fact good for him, and so, mistakenly avoid pleasure. The fact that different things please different people does not undermine the claim that pleasure, whatever its source, is objectively good.

[4] Aristotle does not explicitly mention the function of a knife or of any other artifact in the Nicomachean version of the function argument, but he argues by induction from the functions of artifacts to the function of the soul in the Eudemian version (*EE* 1219a1-5). This may support the view that the Eudemian version is earlier and that by the time he wrote the *EN* Aristotle was aware of, and sought to avoid, some of the objections discussed in this paper. But we must suspend judgment on this issue for now. (For a brief comparison of the Nicomachean and Eudemian versions of the function argument, see Cooper 1975, 145-146n.) I introduce the knife example at this point because many commentators believe that Aristotle is explicitly committed to it, and, indeed, relying on it.

[5] For the view that what a thing is is determined by its function, see *Meteor.* 390a10-13 where, incidentally, Aristotle uses the example of a saw.

[6] Although I will eventually argue that Aristotle thinks that there is really only one move here, i.e., the move directly from (a) to (c), commentators have often represented Aristotle as making two moves here, and so, have attacked the general move from (a) to (c) in different ways—some by attacking the move from (a) to (b), others by attacking the move from (b) to (c). So for the sake of argument, I will begin by speaking as if there are two distinct moves here, even though I doubt that Aristotle distinguished them in this way. On Aristotle's view, there is no real distinction between (a) and (b) because what it is to be an F (or the function of an F) and what it is to be a *good* F (or the function of a *good* F) are the same.

[7] These examples are not intended to suggest that Aristotle takes the function argument to yield results at this level of specificity; the activities of joining clubs and reading the *Metaphysics* should be regarded as determinate examples of the more general determinable types of activity in which *eudaimonia* consists. On this point, see Irwin 1985, 98-99.

[8] See, e.g., Hardie 1980, 23-24. For statements (though not explicit endorsements) of this objection, see also Suits 1974, 23-25 and Siegler 1967, 37.

[9] See, e.g., Clark 1972, 273, Clark 1975, 14-17, and Nozick 1971, 288-289. (Nozick does not explicitly discuss Aristotle.)

[10] See, e.g., Glassen 1957, 319-322 and Wilkes 1978, 555-556.

[11] 'x' and 'y' can be taken as referring to events or activities. The idea here is that only in the case of living organisms is the good performance of the function for the sake of (i.e., beneficial for) the performer of that function.

[12] Here Aristotle can allow that something is good for x *qua* flute player, but not good for x *qua* man. So if x is essentially a man and only accidentally a flute player, that thing will be only accidentally (and not essentially) good for x. In this case, x will belong to the class of what Aristotle calls 'conditional' or 'relative' (τινί) goods and distinguishes from unconditional (ἁπλῶς) goods. See next note.

[13] See, e.g., *EN* 1152b26-27, 1155b23-27, 1157b26-28 with 1148b15-19; *EE* 1235b30-34, 1228b18-22. Cooper 1980, 317, describes this distinction as follows: 'A thing is good absolutely if it is good for human beings as such, taken in abstraction from special and contingent peculiarities of particular persons: these peculiar-

ities may provide additional interests, needs, and wants and on the basis of them one can speak of additional, possibly divergent, things as good for this or that particular person.'

[14] If Aristotle admits the possibility that there are members of natural kinds which are defective in the sense that they lack certain essential properties of that kind (e.g., mentally defective and non-rational members of the human species) then these categorical goods may not be good for them. He can say, as he does about pleasure at *EN* 1148b15-19, that because of such defects, what is good (or pleasant) *for them* does not coincide with what is unconditionally good (or pleasant). On the issue of essential properties which do not necessarily belong to any member of the species, see Irwin 1980, n5.

[15] It is worth noting that if Aristotle allows that there are qualitatively distinct individual essences which, however, belong to a single kind, then he may be able to argue that individual members of a single species can be benefited in substantially different ways without abandoning the connection between a thing's essence and the ways in which it can be benefited. But nothing in my argument depends on attributing this controversial view to Aristotle.

[16] Here it is important to note that I am not claiming that ἴδιος *means* 'essential', but only that it is used here to refer to what is essential. Perhaps 'proper' would be a less misleading translation than 'peculiar'.

[17] See Kraut 1979a, 469-471.

[18] At this point, someone may object that taking what is ἴδιος to man as referring to the human essence as a whole conflicts with Aristotle's explicit claim that nourishment and growth are not parts of our good. But Aristotle can deny that there is any conflict here, if he appeals to his distinction between necessary but non-essential properties and essential properties, or alternatively, between the necessary conditions and the components of a thing. (See n2.) He can then argue that our nutritive and reproductive capacities are necessary but non-essential properties of us, while our capacities for moral virtue and contemplation are components of our essence.

[19] Aristotle clearly regards this point about change as relevant to the capacity for receiving benefit. For he argues that it is possible to wish someone well for his own sake and out of concern for what he is (οἷός ποτ' ἐστίν) only on the condition of his remaining who (or what) he essentially is (*EN* 1159a8-12). Just as one can wish the greatest goods for one's friend only in so far as he remains a man, one can wish goods for oneself only on the condition of remaining oneself. For no one would choose to possess all goods on the condition of becoming another—not even if he were to become a god (*EN* 1166a20-24). For he would not survive that change and these goods would accrue rather to some newly existing deity.

[20] See *Phys*. ii 3; and *De Anima* ii 4 where Aristotle argues that the soul is the formal, final and efficient cause of the living body.

[21] See Sorabji 1964, 289-302.

[22] Following Keyt 1980, 138-157, I take 'Strict Intellectualism' to be the view that contemplation is the sole component (as opposed to necessary condition) for *eudaimonia*. I argue that Aristotle rejects this view in Whiting 1986, 70-95. But nothing in my present argument depends on which particular objectivist conception of *eudaimonia* Aristotle adopts.

[23] This argument will not work against someone who rejects Aristotle's general teleological views. It will not, e.g., convince someone who restricts the notion of benefit to rational evaluators and makes all benefits relative to the attitudes of such evaluators. But that does not mean that this is not Aristotle's view. There is no reason to assume that he expected his argument to convince opponents who rejected his teleological and essentialist premisses. What is important for Aristotle is that some people do accept these premisses and others can be persuaded to accept them on grounds which are independent of their views about morality.

[24] See Irwin 1980, 35-53 and 1981, 193-223.

[25] Aristotle sometimes seems to restrict the capacity for εὖ ζῆν to rational, or at least to higher animals. See *PA* 656a5-10; and *Pol.* 1280a31-34, where he denies εὖ ζῆν even to slaves. If this is his considered view, then εὖ ζῆν is not a general conception of living well applicable to *all* living things. Nonetheless, there does seem to be some notion of what is beneficial for any living thing and *eudaimonia* can still be viewed as a special case of that—i.e., as a special case of the general notion of welfare applicable to any living thing.

[26] See Cooper 1975, 144-180.

[27] Aristotle may allow that some of what benefits a rational agent may be contingent on what goals and desires she happens to have and that these goals and desires can vary from one creature to the next. This will presumably occur as our descriptions of what benefits individuals become increasingly specific and is compatible with there being things which benefit *any* rational agent at higher levels of description.

[28] Nagel 1972, 252-259 (rep. in Rorty 1980) calls this 'the condition of autonomy'. (See *EN* 1099b18-25

and *Pol.* 1323b24-29.) The importance of autonomy stems not so much from the practical benefits of self-sufficiency as from Aristotle's conception of *eudaimonia* as an *activity* of the agent's soul.

[29] If these desires or goals are personal (as opposed to impersonal) then it may be conceptually true that the *only* way for them to be satisfied or attained is by *me*.

[30] This does not mean that someone cannot be deprived of *eudaimonia* by luck or by chance. Even if someone must be responsible for his *eudaimonia*, he may not be responsible for his failure to achieve *eudaimonia*. This asymmetry of responsibility is not necessarily objectionable; we often attribute responsibility to people for acquired skills which, however, can be lost through accidents, as in the case of the young pianist who was pushed in front of an oncoming subway train. But this leaves Aristotle a problem of explaining why someone should cultivate his powers of rational agency even if, as a result of misfortune, his own *eudaimonia* should fail to result.

[31] See n1 above.

[32] I am grateful to audiences at Rice University, UCLA, and the University of Pennsylvania—and to Richard Boyd, David Brink, Leon Galis, Phil Mitsis, Steve Strange, Gisela Striker, and the referees of this journal—for their comments on previous versions of this paper. I would like especially to thank Terry Irwin for repeated criticism and encouragement.

BIBLIOGRAPHY

Aristotle. *De Anima*. W.D. Ross ed. 1956. Oxford Classical Texts. Oxford: Clarendon Press.

Aristotle. *The Eudemian Ethics*. H. Rackham ed. and trans. 1935. Loeb Classical Library xx. London: William Heinemann Ltd..

Aristotle. *Ethica Nicomachea*. I. Bywater ed. 1894. Oxford Classical Texts. Oxford: Clarendon Press.

Aristotle. *Metaphysica*. W. Jaeger ed. 1957. Oxford Classical Texts. Oxford: Clarendon Press.

Aristotle. *Meterologica*. H.D.P. Lee ed. and trans. 1952. Loeb Classical Library vii. London: William Heinemann Ltd.

Aristotle. *Nicomachean Ethics Book VI*. L.H.G. Greenwood ed. 1909. Cambridge: Cambridge University Press.

Aristotle. *Parts of Animals*. A.L. Peck ed. and trans. 1937. Loeb Classical Library xii. London: William Heinemann Ltd.

Aristotle. *Physica*. W.D. Ross ed. 1950. Oxford Classical Texts. Oxford: Clarendon Press.

Aristotle. *Politica*. W.D. Ross ed. 1957. Oxford Classical Texts. Oxford: Clarendon Press.

Aristotle. *Topica*. F.S. Forster ed. and trans. 1960. Loeb Classical Library ii. London: William Heinemann Ltd.

Clark, S. 1972. 'The Use of "Man's Function" in Aristotle' *Ethics* **82** 269-283.

Clark, S. 1975. *Aristotle's Man*. Oxford: Clarendon Press.

Cooper, J. 1975. *Reason and Human Good in Aristotle*. Cambridge: Harvard University Press.

Cooper, J. 1980. 'Aristotle on Friendship' in Rorty 1980, 301-340.

Glassen, P. 1957. *Philosophical Quarterly* **66** 319-322.

Hardie, W.F.R. 1980. *Aristotle's Ethical Theory*. Oxford: Clarendon Press.

Irwin, T.H. 1981. 'Aristotle's Methods of Ethics' 193-223 in D.J. O'Meara ed. 1981. *Studies on Aristotle*. Washington: Catholic University Press.

Irwin, T.H. 1985. 'Permanent Happiness: Aristotle and Solon' *Oxford Studies in Ancient Philosophy* **3** 89-124.

Irwin, T.H. 1980. 'The Metaphysical and Psychological Basis of Aristotle's Ethics' in Rorty 1980, 35-53.

Keyt, D. 1978. 'Intellectualism in Aristotle' *Paideia* Special Aristotle Issue 138-157.

Kraut, R. 1979a. 'The Peculiar Function of Human Beings' *Canadian Journal of Philosophy* **9** 467-478.

Kraut, R. 1979b. 'Two Conceptions of Happiness' *Philosophical Review* **88** 167-197.

Nagel, T. 1972. 'Aristotle on *Eudaimonia*' *Phronesis* **17** 252-259: rep. in Rorty 1980.

Nozick, R. 1971. 'On the Randian Argument' *Personalist* **52** 282-304.

Rorty, A. ed. 1980. *Essays on Aristotle's Ethics*. Berkeley: University of California Press.

Siegler, F. 1967. 'Reason, Happiness and Goodness' 30-47 in J.J. Walsh and H.L. Shapiro eds. 1967 Belmont: Wadsworth Publishing Company.

Sorabji, R. 1964. 'Function' *Philosophical Quarterly* **14** 289-302.

Suits, B. 1974. 'Aristotle on the Function of Man: Fallacies, Heresies and other Entertainments' *Canadian Journal of Philosophy* **4** 23-40.

Whiting, J. 1986. 'Human Nature and Intellectualism in Aristotle' *Archiv für Geschichte der Philosophie* **68** 70-95.

Wilkes, K.V. 1978. 'The Good Man and the Good for Man in Aristotle's Ethics' *Mind* **87** 553-571: rep. 341-357 in Rorty 1980.

The Philosophical Review, XCIV, No. 2 (April 1985)

ARISTOTLE ON THE GOODS OF FORTUNE

John M. Cooper

In this paper I discuss one aspect of Aristotle's theory in the *Nicomachean Ethics* of *eudaimonia* ("happiness," or, more illuminatingly, "a humanly flourishing life" or simply "a good life"). The question I want to raise concerns the relation Aristotle establishes in the *Nicomachean Ethics* between *eudaimonia* and those goods that he describes as external (*ta ektos agatha*).

Though this is little remarked on by commentators, Aristotle's theory of *eudaimonia* in the *Nicomachean Ethics* differs importantly from what one finds in the corresponding passages of the *Eudemian Ethics* and the *Magna Moralia*. All three accounts agree in making *eudaimonia* consist in completely virtuous living (*MM*) or (what comes to the same) in completely virtuous activity (*EE*, *NE*) over a complete lifetime.[1] This is what is sometimes referred to as the "definition" that Aristotle reaches in the *NE* as the conclusion of his famous argument starting from the idea that human beings, as such, have an *ergon* or essential work (*NE* I 7, 1098a 16–18). But only in the *NE* does he go on to say (in the next chapter, Chapter 8) that *eudaimonia* requires in addition[2] being sufficiently equipped

[1]See *MM* I 4, 1184b 28–1185a 1 (completeness of life is added at a 4-9); *EE* II 1, 1219a 35–39; *NE* I 7, 1098a 16–18. *MM* does not make a point of saying explicitly that the virtuous living or activity in question is living or activity in accordance with *all* the virtues (what *EE* calls "complete virtue"), but this is implicit in its repeated references here simply to living in accordance with *the* virtues (1184b 30, 34, 36, 38). I ignore for present purposes the complications caused by the *NE*'s introduction at 1098a 17–18 of a ranking of the virtues on some scale of goodness and completeness (on this see John M. Cooper, *Reason and Human Good in Aristotle*, pp. 99–100 with n. 10). I take it we can speak loosely but fairly enough of the "definition" in *NE* I 7 as amounting to the same as the *EE* and *MM* definitions, since it is not until book X, i.e. retrospectively, that the potentialities of the *NE*'s formulation for a more restrictive interpretation are ever exploited (and see 1100a 4 and 1101a 14 where in repeating and expanding on his "definition" Aristotle speaks of "complete virtue," obviously in the *EE*'s sense of "all the virtues").

[2]That this is an *additional* requirement, and not just another way of saying, or a direct implication of, completely virtuous activity over a complete lifetime, is made clear by the language of 1101a 14–16, discussed just

with "external goods" (1099a 31 ff; cf. 1098b 26). And it appears that Aristotle's intention in the *NE* is actually to imbed this further requirement in a revised statement of what human happiness or flourishing essentially is. For in *NE* I 10, he concludes his defense of the account of *eudaimonia* developed in Chapters 7 and 8 against a certain objection by asking rhetorically, "What then prevents one from saying that that person is *eudaimōn* (flourishes, is happy) who is active in accordance with complete virtue and sufficiently equipped with the external goods not for just any old period of time but for a complete life?" (1101a 14–16). Here he reaffirms his theory of what *eudaimonia* is, and this time the requirement of equipment with sufficient external goods is given an explicit place in the "definition" itself. The final and considered *Nicomachean* theory of what it is for a human being to flourish is, therefore, (a) to live a complete life (b) in the active exercise of the human virtues, of both mind and character, (c) equipped with sufficient external goods. My main purpose is to consider carefully exactly why Aristotle thinks having external goods *is* necessary for a flourishing life, what effects their inclusion as actual constituents of *eudaimonia* has on the character of his ethical theory, and the position that in consequence his theory occupies in the Greek philosophical tradition.

The fact that it is only in the *Nicomachean Ethics* that Aristotle explicitly includes the possession of external goods in his "definition" of *eudaimonia* has important implications about the history of Aristotle's writings. For already in the first century B.C., which is as far back as our more or less first-hand knowledge of the state of Aristotle-interpretation in antiquity goes, there is clear evidence that it was accepted as uncontroversial that Aristotle had advanced precisely this *Nicomachean* theory of what human flourishing consists in. Cicero in *de Finibus* II 19 says that in his account of the final good *Aristoteles virtutis usum cum vitae perfectae prosperitate coniunxit* ("Aristotle combined the exercise of virtue with prosperity over a complete lifetime"): here we find the same three conditions as in the *NE*, since *prosperitas,* though no simple translation of the Greek

below. But this is already implied at 1099a 31ff., where the natural supplementation of the *pros-* ("(needs) in addition") at a 31 and b 6 is: in addition to completely virtuous activity over a complete lifetime.

for "external goods" or "goods of fortune," is obviously intended to cover the same ground. And Arius Didymus, who became court philosopher to the emperor Augustus, in a survey of philosophical theories of the final end assigns to Aristotle what is (despite some unAristotelian terminology) plainly the same three-part theory,[3] and he repeats and elaborates it later on in his epitome of Peripatetic ethical theory.[4] Such formulaic statements are pretty certain to derive ultimately, either by these authors' own inspection or by that of previous authors whose word they take for it, from explicit formulations in appropriate places in Aristotle's own texts. And although in both *MM* and *EE* one *can* find statements about the necessity of external goods for the happy life, there are not many such statements and they occur only in contexts far removed from the official discussions of the nature of *eudaimonia*.[5] In the official discussions in *MM* and *EE*, the external goods are omitted altogether. So the formulas in Cicero and Arius almost certainly derive from *Nicomachean Ethics* I, and not from the *Eudemian Ethics* or *Magna Moralia*. If so, then contrary to what Anthony Kenny has recently argued,[6] the *Nicomachean Ethics* was not only read during

---

[3]*Apud* Stobaeus, *Eclogae* II, p. 51. 12 Wachsmuth; cf. below pp. 184–186.

[4]Stob. p. 126. 18–20 Wachs.

[5]See *MM* II 8, 1206b 33–4 (in the chapter on *eutuchia*). The divisions of goods set out in I 2–3 list the external goods under two headings (as *dunameis*, 1183b 27–35; as bodily and—in the narrow sense—external goods, 1184b 1–6), and in between these two passages, where Aristotle spends some little time (1184a 15–38) discussing the sense in which *eudaimonia* is the best good and a complete good, it is said that *eudaimonia* is a complex composed of many goods (1184a 18–19, 26–7, 30–1), but there is no distinct indication of what these are, and no explicit mention of external goods (the whole discussion is highly abstract, focussing on questions about the structure of *eudaimonia*, not about its content). References to the external goods in the *EE* are even more meagre: apart from IV–VI, which are of course also *Nicomachean* books, there are only two passing references (1218b 32, 1249a 15), and in neither of these is there any basis for concluding that Aristotle thinks *eudaimonia* requires possession of such goods. This implication *is* found in *EE* VI=*NE* VII, 1153b 17–19 (on which see below, pp. 180–181), but again this is very remote from the book II official discussion of what *eudaimonia* is and requires. (It is also found in *Pol.* VII 1, 1323b 40–1324a 2, but that cannot be Cicero's or Arius' principal source.)

[6]See A. Kenny, *The Aristotelian Ethics* (Oxford: The Clarendon Press, 1978). The evidence I cite in this paragraph against Kenny's view should be added to that already assembled in my critical review of his book, *Nôus* 15 (1981), pp. 388–390.

Hellenistic times, but was even uncontroversially treated as the authoritative text for Aristotle's answer to what the ancients regarded as the crucial question of ethical theory, what human flourishing actually consists in.[7] Plainly, our practice of assigning priority on the central questions of philosophical theory to the *Nicomachean Ethics* over the other treatises was standard among philosophers already by the beginning of the first century B.C. at latest.

Let us turn then to the *Nicomachean* definition, and Aristotle's reasons for including external goods as a component of *eudaimonia*. First we need to see more closely what class of goods is in question. Aristotle uses the phrase "external goods" (*ta ektos agatha*) in two different but easily distinguishable ways, depending on which of two understandings he intends of what the goods in question are external to. There is a narrower usage according to which what they are external to is the person, that is (for Aristotle) an embod-

---

[7]The fifth book of Cicero's *de Fin.* offers valuable evidence on this point, too. For, as is well known (cf. *de Fin.* V 6–8, 75), Cicero claims to reproduce there the views of Antiochus of Ascalon, who wrote and lectured on ethics at Athens in the first quarter of the 1st c. B.C. The account of Peripatetic ethics Cicero gives in *de Fin.* V is, not surprisingly, not very faithful to the Aristotle we know from the three ethical treatises. Since Antiochus' intention was to prove that, where sound, Stoic ethical theory repeats in other and less intelligible words the views of Plato and Aristotle and their immediate successors, it is inevitable that his account of Aristotle should show a significant overlay of Stoic doctrine and Stoicising interpretation. According to Antiochus the Stoics wrongly departed from these "ancients" in holding that virtue is the only good and, in consequence, that virtue by itself (without the addition of Aristotle's "external goods") is not just sufficient for happiness but the only thing that has any effect whatsoever on the goodness of a person's life (see V 20–21). Much of the latter half of *de Fin.* V is occupied with an attack on the Stoics on this point and a defense of the Peripatetic view. It is very hard not to believe that the solution Antiochus finally gives (V 79–95) to the problem of the relation of external and bodily goods to *eudaimonia* rests partly on an interpretation of *NE* I 10–11, taking Aristotle (cf. 1101a 6–8) to have drawn a distinction between (mere) happiness (*vita beata*), something that virtue is by itself sufficient to guarantee, and blessedness (*vita beatissima*), a higher degree of happiness that requires, besides virtue, the external goods. Certainly Antiochus could have found nothing to suggest this idea anywhere else in the Aristotelian corpus as we know it than these *NE* chapters. Cicero's evidence suggests, therefore, that Antiochus used *NE* I, and not *EE* or *MM*, as his source for Aristotle's theory of *eudaimonia*.

ied soul (cf. *Rhet.* I 5, 1360b 25–6); and in fact the first mention of "external goods" in *NE* I, at 1098b 12–14, contrasts them with *two* other kinds of goods, goods of the soul (such as the virtues and pleasure) and goods of the body.[8] But when Aristotle, shortly thereafter, mentions and then adopts the view that *eudaimonia* requires what he again calls external goods (1099a 31; cf. 1098b 26) he has a broader usage in mind, according to which what these goods are external to is the *soul* (cf. *EE* II 1, 1218b 32, *Pol.* VII 1, 1323b 24–6); he mentions good looks (*kallos,* standardly listed as a good of the body where those are distinguished from external goods, e.g., 1360b 22, 1184b 4) as well as external goods according to the *narrow* usage (things like good birth, wealth, political power and friends) in listing the external goods that *eudaimonia* requires a sufficient supply of.[9] So it is according to the broader usage that Aristotle means in this passage, and others like it, to say that *eudaimonia* requires external goods: he means that *eudaimonia* requires goods of the body together with external goods according to the narrower usage, i.e., good things one can possess that lie outside one's own mind, character, and physical make-up and constitution.

Aristotle's examples, here and elsewhere, of external goods in the broader usage are limited to a somewhat conventional illustrative list: wealth, political position, friends, good birth, (good) children, good looks (often health, absent here, gets added, and sometimes also honor), so it is important to emphasize what I have just said, that the external goods we are talking about are *all* the good things a person can acquire or enjoy that lie outside his own mind and character (his soul). In fact the only goods that are *not* external are the virtues of intellect and character themselves, innate endowments of mind and personality such as cheerfulness or

---

[8]So also *MM* I 3, 1184b 1–4, in the (more or less) corresponding passage. Curiously, *EE* II 1, 1218b 31–35, the passage that corresponds precisely to the *MM* passage just cited and more loosely to *NE* 1098b 12–14, gives a two-fold division of goods into those in the soul and those outside, thus using the phrase "external goods" with the broader reference I distinguish just below.

[9]Similarly the two passages of *NE* X where *ektos chorēgia* recurs, 1178a 23–b 7, b 33–1179a 13; in the second of these bodily health is counted as part of *ektos chorēgia*. *NE* VII 13, 1153b 17–19 uses the threefold division, saying that what the *eudaimōn* needs is *ta en sōmati agatha kai ta ektos.*

a good memory, pleasure, and knowledge. Now anything one aims at producing or getting through one's action will, if the decision to aim at it is a correct one, be something good in one way or another for oneself. Any *correct* object of pursuit, therefore, that one achieves by one's action and that is other than one's own virtue, pleasure or knowledge will be an external good. If for example I decide, and am correct to decide, to try to further another person's moral development, then, if my action is successful, his improved soul will be a good, external to me, that I aimed at and got. Likewise if I correctly decide that a certain diet is best for me, then the items of food on that diet, being objects of pursuit in my actions, are goods at which I aim, and being external to me they are external goods. Thus it is clear that Aristotle is talking here about a very wide range of potential and actual good things. It is important to bear this in mind as we consider the reasons he gives for thinking that external goods are needed if one is to lead a flourishing life. He is talking about a wider range of potential goods than his conventional list might suggest.

At the end of our passage Aristotle remarks that the fact that a flourishing life requires external goods, as well as the goods of mind and character, leads some people actually to identify *eudaimonia* with good fortune (*eutuchia*) (1099b 7–8, cf. also 1153b 21–3). That is presumably because, as he remarks at *Politics* 1323b 27–9, "the goods external to the soul come of themselves and by luck (*tuchē*), whereas no one is just or temperate from or on account of luck." Hence Aristotle himself sometimes describes external goods also as goods of fortune.

But why does Aristotle think that *eudaimonia* requires a sufficient supply of external goods? He gives two different reasons, one for each of two groups of external goods. First, some external goods serve as necessary or especially effective instruments in and for the doing of some virtuous actions (1099a 32–3). For example, he says, in order to do *some* virtuous actions one needs a good deal of money. Presumably this money would have to be inherited, and so would come to the virtuous man by luck—to have to work long and hard to accumulate it will itself already preclude one from being fully virtuous and living in the exercise of complete virtue, since to devote oneself to making lots of money betrays a false evaluation of its actual importance, in comparison with other things one might devote oneself to instead. One can perhaps most easily understand why such money is needed by reflecting that, as Aristotle conceives him, the person who possesses the human excellences in fully developed form ought to occupy a position of visible leadership among men. He must be active in advancing the moral and intellectual culture of his community and one important way of doing this is to possess and use financial resources for public and private philanthropy. He should sponsor public performances of artistically and morally significant works, support other people who show promise of intellectual and moral excellence but who unluckily are not well enough off to devote themselves adequately to the pursuits necessary to their full development, and in other ways contribute to the general awareness and prestige among his fellow-citizens of the right scheme of values. In much the same way, I take it, we can understand political position and *philoi* (translated "friends"—but Aristotle means more generally, as we say, one's personal and family connections) as instruments used by the virtuous and flourishing person in his moral projects. Unlike inherited wealth it is presumably not totally a matter of luck whether one has these or not; still, luck plays an important part even here, and it seems reasonable to think, as Aristotle apparently does, that political office and good social connections can and will be used by the virtuous person in the same sort of way that wealth can be. Through all these means—wealth, political office and good connections—the virtuous person is able to influence in significant ways the tastes and the practices of his society, and further the careers of like-minded people, thereby contributing importantly to the spread and flowering within his society of the right scheme of values, the scheme of values he himself holds to, with its special emphasis on things of the mind, respect for every kind of significant human accomplishment, and good will towards other people generally.

The second reason Aristotle gives for thinking that *eudaimonia* requires external goods is not so easy to construe. What he says is this: "lacking certain things people find their blessedness disfigured—e.g. good birth, good children, good looks. For someone who is utterly repulsive in appearance or low-born or solitary and childless is certainly not a very good candidate for happiness; and presumably even less so is one whose children or friends are totally bad or were good but died" (1099b 2–6). It is not at first sight clear what Aristotle means by finding one's blessedness disfigured. One might suppose that the way having bad children, or good children who died young, would disfigure even the virtuous man's happiness would be by frustrating efforts that, as a virtuous man, he would have made to produce, educate and protect his offspring. A virtuous man knows the value to himself of having good children, who grow to maturity and live fine lives in close mutual dependence with his own, and will, just because he *is* virtuous, devote considerable effort to procreating and raising such a family. If, by blows of bad fortune he is deprived of the fruits of these labors he would certainly lack some important good things, and good things, moreover, he had wanted and worked to achieve. The failure to have children would be a bad thing for him, and as such must be counted as detracting from the overall value of his life. In addition, one might expect the virtuous person, in reflecting on these facts, to *feel* frustrated and disappointed, and that psychological response might be counted as a second debit against his happiness. Somewhat similarly, being low-born or ugly might be thought to disfigure his blessedness because good birth and good looks are things that he, like any reasonable person, prizes, although in these cases the failure to have them could not even partly be regarded as the result of failures of his own efforts to secure them.[10] So one might conjecture that the disfigurement of one's blessedness in all these cases might be a matter of simply lacking or being deprived of something one very much prized and wanted to have, together perhaps with a consequent sense of frustration and disappointment.

In fact, however, I believe this is not what Aristotle has in mind. To see this one needs to consider a passage of book VII that may refer back to this discussion and in any event seems intended as repeating the same doctrine.[11] Here Aristotle lumps together *all*

[10]Good birth and good looks belong to the goods John Rawls describes as assigned by the "natural lottery." See *A Theory of Justice* (Cambridge, Mass.: Harvard University Press, 1971), p. 74.

[11]The similarity of language at 1153b 17–18, 21–23, to that at 1099a 31–2, b 6–8, makes this passage rather seem to be implicitly referring back to that one; certainly, if read as part of the *NE* that is how an attentive reader would take it. If read as part of the *EE* it might, by contrast, seem to introduce a rather surprising change of view (at least an important supple-

the external goods as making, anyhow generically, the *same* kind of contribution to the happy life. He is discussing the way that pleasure is necessarily involved in the happy life: on the view of pleasure he has argued for, a pleasure is an unimpeded activity of a natural capacity, and of course the happy life is a life of unimpeded activity of natural capacities, including prominently the capacity to know and choose various objects of pursuit in accordance with their true value. He adds (1153b 17–19): "That is why the happy person needs in addition the goods of the body and external goods or goods of fortune, so that these activities will not be impeded." So the happy man needs external goods, both the ones Aristotle earlier classified as like instruments and those whose lack he said disfigured our blessedness, in order that his virtuous activities not be impeded.

It is certainly easy to see how the lack of necessary instruments impedes an activity. Think of a carpenter faced with the task of making a table from unsawn wood with hammer and nails but no saw: he may decide the thing cannot be done at all, and if he does undertake it his work will certainly be more difficult and less in any standard way carpenterlike, and also more risky (since it will be to some degree uncertain whether a satisfactory table *can* be made under these conditions). Similarly, Aristotle reasonably implies, the happy man's virtuous activities, in engaging in which his happiness actually consists, will be impeded—perhaps by being actually blocked altogether, perhaps only by being much harder to do or more uncertain of their outcomes—if he lacks an ample supply of money, or political influence or social connections. But Aristotle suggests here that something similar may hold for the other external goods he mentions in the book I passage (good birth, good

mentation of what was said in bk. II that one might think ought therefore to have been argued there, not slipped thus offhand into a discussion of pleasure). One must bear in mind that even if, as seems likely, the common books were originally composed as part of the *EE* they may have been somewhat revised later on for inclusion into the *NE* (on this see my review of Kenny, n. 6 above, pp. 387–388); it seems that 1153b 14–25 may be one such passage. If so, the original *EE* may well not have contained *any* clear statement of the good and flourishing person's need for external goods. (We have no way of knowing how this part of the *EE* read in the version available to Antiochus, Cicero and others in the first century B.C.: did it have the revised versions of the common books?)

looks, good children). So apparently the disfiguring of the virtuous man's happiness that the lack of these goods causes is traceable to some way in which his virtuous activities are impeded if he lives without them. How is this to be understood?

Aristotle's thought, I believe, is this. Some external conditions (being good-looking, having good children, coming from a good family), while not used by the virtuous person as means to achieve his purposes (as e.g., his money or personal influence might be), put him in the position where the options for action that are presented to him by his circumstances allow him to exercise his virtues fully and in ways that one might describe as normal for the virtues. Thus if one is physically quite unattractive not only will one's sex life, and so one's opportunities for exercising the virtue of temperance, be limited in undesirable ways (you may still have sex, given the circumstances, with whom you ought, and when, and to the right extent, and so retain and exercise the virtue of temperance, but the effects of this kind of control will not be as grand as they would be if you really had a normally full range of options);[12] something similar will happen all across the board. People will tend to avoid you, so that you will not be able to enter into the normally wide range of relationships that pose for the virtuous person the particular challenges that his virtue responds to with its correct assessments and right decisions. Such a person, let us assume,[13] may in fact develop all the virtues in their fully perfected form and actually exercise them in ways that respond appropriately and correctly to his circumstances; but the circumstances themselves are

[12]This is now I would interpret Aristotle's reference to the temperate person's need for *exousiai* (opportunities), *NE* X 8, 1178a 33.

[13]This assumption is unrealistic, of course. As Aristotle himself elsewhere insists, the development of the virtues requires practice, and someone whose circumstances prevented him from facing a normally wide range of opportunities in the course of his preliminary practice of virtuous behavior would presumably not be expected to develop the virtues, at least not in their fully perfected forms. *Perfect* (or complete) virtue must fit a person to deal correctly and sensitively with *all* the types of problems and opportunities a normally equipped normal human being might meet. But it is important to make this assumption here, in order to set firmly aside one possible misunderstanding of what Aristotle is saying. He is *not* saying that the external goods are needed by anyone if he is to *develop* (fully) the virtues; his point is rather that no one can *exercise* fully the (full) virtues he already possesses, if he lacks these further goods.

restricted by his ugliness and the effects this has on others, so that his virtue is not called upon to regulate his responses and choices in all the sorts of circumstances that the more normally attractive person would face, and so its exercise is not as full and fine a thing as that more normally attractive person's would be. Something similar could be said (though its limiting effects would seem more obvious to a Greek of Aristotle's time than to us) for coming from a bad family (the second century A.D. commentator, Aspasius, mentions as an example having a male prostitute for a father). Having good children, Aristotle's third example, can easily be seen to contribute to the exercise of the virtues in the same way.[14] A childless person or one whose children are bad people will find his virtuous activities impeded, even though he retains a firm grasp on those qualities of character that constitute the virtues, because, again, he is forced to put them into effect in circumstances that do not give his virtues their normal scope. One central context for the exercise of the virtues is in the raising of children and the subsequent common life one spends with them, once adult, in the morally productive common pursuit of morally significant ends. If this context is not realized in one's life then, Aristotle would be saying, one's virtuous activities are diminished and restricted.

Aristotle distinguishes, then, between those external goods that provide the normal and expected contexts for the exercise of the

[14]One might suppose that the way that being childless or without good children would disfigure one's blessedness would be by making one disappointed and embittered with life, and so be impeded in one's virtuous activities by losing one's zest and commitment for them. But this cannot be what Aristotle has in mind: such a disappointed person is someone who allows the way things have gone for him actually to affect his character for the worse, but Aristotle clearly has it in mind that the disfigurement should be something that happens although one's character remains intact and unaffected. In the next chapters after the mention of the external goods in Bk. I (I 9–10) Aristotle discusses the person who falls into disasters, as King Priam in the story of Troy did in old age (his fine children are all killed off, or driven mad, his city is razed to the ground, and so on), and insists that such a person is not a happy man—*not*, however, because his character is affected for the worse, by embitterment, loss of enthusiasm, etc., but because *though* he remains a noble and fine person, and takes what happens to him gracefully and acts nobly and virtuously in the circumstances, his activities, or many of them, are (he repeats) "impeded" (1100b 29).

virtues, and external goods that are used instrumentally as means to the ends aimed at in virtuous activities. Even without goods of either of these types a person might, we may assume, possess all the virtues in their fully perfected forms, but without them he would not be able to engage *fully* in virtuous action. When Aristotle says that without the sorts of goods that provide the appropriate contexts for the normal exercise of the virtues the virtuous person will find his happiness disfigured, he does not mean simply that he will fail, even if non-culpably, to achieve goals at which, being virtuous, he aimed, or will lack conditions (e.g., good birth or good looks) that he simply wanted for their own sakes (whether or not it was at all up to him to secure them). When he considers these goods, as also the more strictly instrumental goods, as making a contribution to our happiness he abstracts from the fact that in some cases the virtuous agent's own choices and actions have been aimed in the first instance at achieving and preserving them, and from the fact that they may be wished for by him for their own sakes. The contribution of the external goods to happiness which Aristotle has in mind only begins once, to whatever extent the virtuous person may himself have aimed at getting and preserving these goods, he actually *has* them. It is the virtuous actions that he is able to go on to do that constitute this contribution. So we can continue to speak of all these goods as goods of fortune—goods one either has or doesn't have by luck—since in every case, even those where the virtuous person himself is concerned in his actions to obtain or preserve them, the contribution they make to happiness, on Aristotle's theory, is not made immediately by the success of these efforts, but instead by the effects that they have on the good person's *further* action and activity. And their presence, as context for or instruments to be used in these further actions, is not something the agent controls in the way that, according to Aristotle's theory, he controls the virtuous state itself—the other salient source of the actions.

In working out this suggestion I have been following the interpretation that one finds in three very old and authoritative accounts of Aristotle's theory that have not been given proper notice in modern discussions. It will help to bring out the significance of the theory I am attributing to Aristotle if I indicate briefly what these three sources have to say. They are, first, Arius Didymus' epitome of Peripatetic ethics (end of the 1st century B.C. or beginning of the 1st A.D.); second, our oldest surviving Greek commentator on the *Nicomachean Ethics* (or, for that matter, on any other work), Aspasius (2nd century A.D.); and, thirdly, his successor the great commentator Alexander of Aphrodisias (end of the 2nd century A.D.). It seems clear that these authors all rely partly on a living tradition of Aristotle-interpretation that must go back to Aristotle himself, and that is good reason to take seriously what they say. I mentioned earlier that Arius Didymus includes external goods as components of *eudaimonia* according to Aristotle. But that this is so has to be inferred, since in stating Aristotle's view he does not use the expression "external goods" or any close relative familiar to us from Aristotle's own writings. His language in the crucial place is in fact unparalleled anywhere in Aristotle, and for that reason the editor of the standard modern edition has emended the text to bring it more closely into line with Aristotle's own usage.[15] But that the text is correct as the manuscripts have it is shown by the fact that both Aspasius in presenting Aristotle's view and Alexander in discussion use precisely the same language; and, moreover, both these later authors give the evidence needed to interpret its meaning, confirming that it *amounts to* Aristotle's own requirement of external goods as one element in *eudaimonia.*

The definition in Arius Didymus runs (Stob. 51. 12 Wachsmuth): "the *proēgoumenē* use of complete virtue in a complete life." *Proēgoumenē* is a participle meaning literally "taking the lead" or "coming first"; there is an adverb *proēgoumenōs* that appears in later Greek that often means "by preference," and this may give a hint as

[15]Wachsmuth emends *proēgoumenē* (etc.) at 51.12 and elsewhere in the Arius part of Stobaeus to *chorēgoumenē* (etc.), relying e.g., on *Pol.* IV 2, 1289a 33, VII 1, 1323b 41 f. (Cf. *NE* 1098b 33, 1101a 15). On the correctness of the manuscripts and the significance of the passages I cite from Aspasius and Alexander see Paul Moraux, *Der Aristotelismus bei d. Griechen* (Berlin, 1973), p. 353n.; see also the full discussion of F. Dirlmeier, *Die Oikeiosis-Lehre Theophrasts, Philologus* Supp. XXX.1 (1937), pp. 15–19. Dirlmeier's attempt to link this usage of *proēgoumenos* specifically to Theophrastus, so that the definitions containing it can be claimed as his, is quite arbitrary. We do not know at what point in the tradition this word began to be used in this connection. In *sense,* even if not in terminology, the definitions Arius cites certainly express Aristotle's own view in the *NE* and that is the crucial point.

to what Arius means here by a use of virtue that "comes first." But literally what Arius says is that happiness according to Aristotle is *that* use of complete virtue in a complete life that "comes first." Aspasius' phraseology is that happiness is activity according to complete virtue in a complete life in conditions that "come first" (or, possibly, in actions that "come first").[16] Now the use of this participle elsewhere in Aspasius shows that this "coming first" is coming first in the estimation and choice of the virtuous man himself—in effect, happiness is virtuous activity in *preferred* circumstances, or what comes to the same, the *preferred* virtuous activities falling under each of the virtues. For in discussing the virtue of liberality Aspasius says (52. 32–35) that the liberal person has to do with both giving and taking money, "but more with giving; the primary activity (the *proēgoumenē* one—the one that "comes first") of the liberal person is in connection with that, whereas taking money is characteristic of him on an hypothesis, namely *if* he is in great need."

Alexander confirms and sharpens this interpretation in a passage in book II of his *De Anima* where he is arguing, from the Peripatetic point of view, against the Stoic doctrine that virtue all by itself suffices for happiness. One argument he gives against the Stoic view is the following (160. 31–161. 3): "further, activity in accordance with a craft (*technē*) covers in each case two things. On the one hand there is activity in primary circumstances (*en proēgoumenois,* lit., circumstances that "come first"), as for the flute-player if he is healthy in body and has flutes of the kind he wishes for and nothing external troubles him; on the other hand there is activity in circumstances he does not wish for (*en aboulētois*), that is, in circumstances the opposite of those just mentioned. So, just as the ends of the other crafts lie in activities with wished for things and in primary circumstances,[17] so also for virtue, supposing it too is a craft [as the Stoics do]." Alexander's implication is that for virtue to achieve its end, namely *eudaimonia,* it must be exercised in primary circumstances, the ones the virtuous agent himself, qua

[16]I cite here Aspasius 19. 10–11, as supplemented in accordance with his remark at 22. 34–5 that we must everywhere supply in thought *en proēgoumenois* when dealing with Aristotle's theory of *eudaimonia*. See also 22. 25–6.

[17]Reading *proēgoumenois* for *-ais* of the manuscript at 161. 2.

virtuous, wishes for.[18] And since, as Alexander's comments make clear, the primary circumstances and activities are the ones where appropriate external goods are present, one is justified in understanding him, together with Aspasius and Arius Didymus in their formal accounts of the Aristotelian theory of happiness, as representing the Peripatetics as making the possession of external goods a part of *eudaimonia*—as indeed we have seen Aristotle does in the *Nicomachean Ethics*.

The important point for my present argument is the way in which these authors introduce the requirement of external goods. They do this *via* the requirement that in order to be happy a person must not just have and exercise the virtues through a complete life, but exercise them in the primary and preferred circumstances for each virtue. For this puts into a perspective that would not be very easy to capture from reading Aristotle's text alone a consequence of the fact that for Aristotle the virtues (anyhow the virtues of character and practical reason) are broadly based:[19] each of them equips a person to deal effectively, correctly and with discrimination and moral sensitivity, with a very wide variety of circumstances and conditions of life. The temperate person knows the proper value to place on food, drink and sex and the associated pleasures, in comparison with other values. This means that whatever circumstances he finds himself in (whether in conditions of plenty or of deprivation, whether by spending time eating and drinking he will or won't affect significantly other things he values) he will act temperately so far as the use of food and drink go. And likewise for courage, and justice, and good temper, and liberality, and most of the rest (it is true that certain virtues on Aristotle's list,

---

[18]Alexander confirms that this is his view in a passage of the *Quaest. Eth.* (p. 148. 23–33) where he explains the Aristotelian theory of *eudaimonia*. The nub of his account makes *eudaimonia* "activity in accordance with the virtue of the rational soul, there being added, of course, 'in a complete life' . . . and furthermore 'in primary (*proēgoumenois*) circumstances'—for the primary (*proēgoumenas*) and wished for activities require instruments" (148. 30–33). (I retain the manuscript reading *boulētas* in the next to last line, and reject Spengel's emendation, kept by Bruns, to *bouleutas*. Comparison with Alex. *de An.* II 160.34, cited above, suffices to defend the manuscript tradition: if *aboulēta* can at *de An.* II 160.34 be set in contrast with *proēgoumena*, then the latter can be glossed, as here, by *boulēta*.)

[19]Compare Rawls, *op. cit.* pp. 435ff.

most notably the virtue of magnificence, are less broadly based—but the essential point is little affected by such partial exceptions). Aristotle maintains that the virtuous person even in adversity will use his virtues, and will act nobly and well. If a person has many great strokes of ill-fortune, as Priam did, "they pinch and tend to spoil his blessedness; for they inflict pains on him and impede many of his activities. And yet even in these circumstances fine character shines through, when someone bears many great misfortunes with a good temper, not because he does not feel distress but because he is noble and great in soul. . . . For we think a truly good person, a person of sound understanding, will bear strokes of fortune gracefully, and, whatever his resources at any time, do the finest actions he can, just as we think a good general, too, will use the forces he has in the best way for war . . ." (1100b 28–1101a 4). But plainly, in each virtue there is a more or less clearly marked out range of circumstances within which, for that virtue, the *preferred* exercises of the virtue come. The thought is this: one needs to be *basically* healthy physically and mentally, *reasonably* well-off financially, *reasonably* well-liked by others, and to have available to one a *reasonably* good supply of other things one needs by way of food, drink and so on, *most* of the time in one's life; for the human virtues consist essentially and in the first place in the proper use of this normally expected (or anyhow reasonably hoped-for) array of goods. Clearly, of course, this does not mean that the preferred exercise of the virtues should presuppose perfect good health, or a constant supply of everything one needs—that would itself be abnormal, and would actually deprive the virtues of one normal context for their employment, namely in temporary deprivation and distress. On Aristotle's view, in some vaguely marked out middle ground lies the active life of the virtuous person that deserves to be counted, for a human being, the happy and flourishing one; get very far outside it, on either side, and, even though the virtues and their constant exercise remain central to the life someone might lead, such a life is nonetheless not a happy one.

Now on this interpretation, in integrating the external goods into *eudaimonia* Aristotle is treating them all as if their only value lies in the contribution they make to virtuous actions in which *they* are not the, or a, goal of action. It is true that, as we have seen, he distinguishes between those, like money, that are used only as instruments in the virtuous man's projects, and others like health and good looks, but even these latter, according to Aristotle's account, are needed as antecedently existing conditions that make possible the full exercise of the happy man's virtuous qualities of mind and character. In each case the value to the happy man consists in what the external goods make it possible for him, as a result of having them, to do. Any value goods other than virtuous action itself might have just for their own sakes is denied, or at least left out of account, on this theory. The seriousness of this omission comes out clearly in examples like the following. The virtuous man will in a certain situation, if he has money available, give some of it to a promising young friend so that he can study philosophy. Here money makes possible a certain exercise of the virtue of liberality, namely giving the right amount of money to the right person for the right purpose. And that is something Aristotle's theory takes account of. But notice that the virtuous man's purpose in this case is to enable the young man to become a philosopher. Suppose he suddenly takes sick and dies not long afterwards, with the result that the money is lost without this goal being achieved. Suppose also (as might well be the case) that this does not cast doubt on the correctness of the decision. After all, decision has to be made in the light of the best information available, and it may well be that neither the formation of the liberal man's information base, nor his deliberation leading from it to the decision, can be faulted. On Aristotle's account *this* way that external goods might be thought to contribute to someone's life—by being objects of pursuit aimed at in his virtuous actions *and* achieved partly as a result of them—gets left out of account. Similarly, as I mentioned above, Aristotle does not count the failure of the virtuous man to have good children who grow to maturity as disfiguring his happiness because it frustrates plans he conceived and acted on precisely *as* a virtuous man. The failure to have good children only affects his happiness insofar as it prevents the subsequent activities he might have engaged in together with them; it does not affect it by rendering his earlier actions aimed at producing and educating his children ineffective.

Why does Aristotle apparently neglect this further way goods other than virtue itself contribute to a happy life? Why, when he speaks of the contribution that goods other than the virtues make to happiness, does he not count the good the virtuous man achieves for himself by obtaining the outcomes that *qua* virtuous he aims at from time to time, as a second way that these goods contribute to his happiness? I think there are two separate considerations that help to explain his failure to mention this further contribution in this context. The first is a historical point.

It seems clear that in his remarks on the external goods Aristotle is strongly influenced by views about these goods that Socrates in early dialogues of Plato prominently flaunts. Socrates argues in two related passages of the *Euthydemus* (278e–282d) and the *Meno* (87d–89a) that virtue, which he identifies with a certain kind of knowledge, is the *only* thing that deserves, strictly speaking, to be called good. Socrates relies on the basic axiom that there is an essential connection between something's being good and its benefitting (and not harming) the person for whom it is good. But, he argues, any other so-called good besides virtue, construed as knowledge, *will* sometimes harm a person; its harming or, instead, benefitting him, depends on the circumstances. Socrates' discussion in these passages seems to be the origin of Aristotle's and later Greek philosophy's tripartition of (so-called) goods into external goods, bodily goods and goods of soul: Socrates' claim is that external goods in Aristotle's broad sense, and goods of the soul other than virtue-knowledge, are not *really* goods at all, because whether they benefit or not, which is what a good must do, does not depend on them, but on something else—the circumstances. If they benefit it is not because of *their* nature, and that shows that they are not good to begin with. What makes the difference, Socrates claims, is virtue or knowledge: the virtuous person knows how to use external goods and the other goods of his soul, and the benefit he gets from them is always ultimately due to his knowledge—his knowledge how, when, for what purpose to use them. It is the nature of knowledge or virtue, and, among supposed goods, *only* of knowledge or virtue, to benefit; only it always and necessarily benefits its possessor; so only knowledge or virtue is, strictly speaking, a good at all.[20]

[20]See especially *Meno* 87e 1–2 (a good must benefit); *Euthyd.* 281d 2–e 5 (the external goods are not in themselves good at all; in fact only wisdom is a good, since it is needed to guide us to use the external goods to our benefit.)

These passages of *Euthydemus* and *Meno* are crucial texts for the whole later development of Greek moral philosophy, and not merely for the Aristotelian theory of the external goods and their place in *eudaimonia*. They are plainly the source, or prominent among the sources, for the Stoic theory that only virtue is good and that, in consequence, *eudaimonia* consists simply in the possession of virtue, and does not require as well the Aristotelian external goods. The Stoics accepted Socrates' reasons for saying that only virtue is good, and devoted themselves to elaborating the distinctions necessary to defend successfully the Socratic theory. Now unlike the Stoics, Aristotle rejected the idea, fundamental to Socrates' argument, that what is really good must by its very nature, and so necessarily and always, benefit whoever has it.[21] This idea rests on the Eleatic confusions that Aristotle found at the core of Plato's theory of Forms and that caused him to reject Platonic metaphysics altogether. But he was, as were the Stoics too, deeply influenced by Socrates' treatment of the external goods, and indeed all goods other than virtue, as having only a use-value in relation to virtue. His response to Socrates consists in emphasizing (surely correctly) the distinction between *possessing* a virtue and exercising it. The benefit that, according to Socrates, virtue does one consists in its exercise. But that puts us in a position to see, and I have discussed how Aristotle developed this point, that the exercise in question, in which the benefit that virtue entails is actually and fully realized, itself depends upon the presence of external goods, either as part of the context of action or as instruments to be used in it. Even if their value is not independent of the value of virtuous action, that does not mean that the good that virtue does is available without them. Socrates, then, was wrong to say or imply that happiness is possible without these goods.

When one takes into account the Socratic background of Aristotle's discussion it is easy enough to see how it happens that in his account of *eudaimonia* it is only as contributing to the virtuous person's subsequent activities that the external goods figure. He is in effect taking over the Socratic view of the central and determinative role of virtue as a constituent of happiness, but insisting that,

[21]See for example *NE* I 3, 1094b 16–19.

even so, external goods, since they are essential for the exercise of the virtues that constitutes happiness, must be counted in as constituents of *eudaimonia* as well.[22]

Yet in other places in his ethical writings it is clear that Aristotle did take notice of the fact that for the virtuous person these goods also play the other role I specified, as objects of pursuit or goals of action in virtuous activity. We can see this by considering the chapter on *eutuchia* (good fortune) in the *Eudemian Ethics* (VIII 2). By "good fortune" here and the "person of good fortune" (*ho eutuchēs*) Aristotle does not mean occasional good luck, such as affects all of us, virtuous as well as vicious, and the person who occasionally benefits from such good luck. He means good fortune as a settled and permanent feature of someone's way of life. He contrasts such a person with the person who acts as he does from *phronēsis* (sound understanding, actual knowledge how to act) (1246b 37–1247a 2). Aristotle entertains the thought that perhaps a person might mimic the same sort of life as the virtuous person, on the basis of his understanding and his trained character, leads. He would live that way by some kind of sheer luck, not as the result of his own understanding and not as the result of a fixed view of what is proper to do being imbedded in his habitual ways of feeling about and reacting to things.

In what, then, does the fortunate person, by sheer luck, mimic the virtuous man? No doubt he has all the requisite external goods that the virtuous man has and uses in his activities; but Aristotle

---

[22]In a well-known passage of *EE* (I 2) Aristotle distinguishes between what amounts to necessary conditions of happiness and its actual parts, and says that it is a grave mistake to treat what is merely a necessary condition (of happiness, or whatever else) as actually a constituent part of it. Of course, it is not easy to know how to apply this distinction, which is clear enough in the abstract, to particular cases. Nonetheless, it seems clear that Aristotle is not guilty, in counting external goods as parts of *eudaimonia*, of violating it. For, as we have seen, in his view the external goods are not conditions necessary either for (the exercise of) complete virtue or for a complete span of life (the other two constituents of *eudaimonia* that Aristotle recognizes); they are necessary for a *certain* exercise of the virtues, and the necessity in question is not an externally causal one. The external goods are circumstances and conditions reference to which is actually part of the essential characterization of the virtuous activities that constitute *eudaimonia*, on Aristotle's theory.

implies that whoever has external goods, even the virtuous person himself, has them by good luck (see 1099b 7–8, 1153b 18, 21–2). So that is not a kind of good luck that the fortunate man has that distinguishes him from the virtuous. Perhaps Aristotle thinks that, in addition, the fortunate person acts in the context of, or uses, these external goods in just the ways the virtuous person would in the same circumstances—not, of course, that he acts for the same reasons and from the same deliberated desires as the virtuous person does, but at any rate (whatever in him produces them) he does the same actions. That would mean that his actions are the result of luck, not of his own forethought and character. But, however that may be, it is clear that Aristotle thinks of the fortunate man as mimicking the virtuous and practically wise man in yet a further way. His actions, whatever they are (and whether they are the same the virtuous man would have done), succeed in achieving the results the virtuous man, in the various situations he finds himself in, would have tried to achieve.

That this is the crucial kind of good luck that distinguishes the fortunate man from the virtuous becomes clear when near the beginning of the chapter Aristotle insists that such a kind of person really exists: "though foolish," he says (1247a 4–23),

> "many people are successful in matters in which luck is decisive, others also in matters where skill is involved, but there is a large element of luck, for example in generalship and navigation. . . . [T]hat it is not by practical wisdom that they succeed, is evident. For practical wisdom is not irrational but has a principle on account of which it acts thus and so, but these people would not be able to say why they succeed; for ⟨if they could⟩, it would be skill. For it is clear . . . that they are foolish even about those matters in which they enjoy good fortune. For in navigation, it is not the most skillful who are fortunate, but, as in dice-throwing, one man scores nothing, another throws a naturally fortunate man's throw."[23]

The good fortune of the fortunate person, then, consists primarily in his regularly achieving by his actions the more particular goals that the virtuous man too would aim at were he in the same situa-

[23]Text and translation as in M. Woods, *Aristotle's Eudemian Ethics* (Oxford: The Clarendon Press, 1982).

tions—whatever corresponds for the virtuous man to the navigator's goal of arriving in port.

Now this implies that in Aristotle's view the corresponding successes will also be achieved by the virtuous man. For the governing assumption has been that the fortunate man's life mimics that of the virtuous. The virtuous man's successes are not, however, the result of good luck. Why not? Precisely because when he achieves them, that is due to the knowledge that he possesses, but the fortunate man does not, *how* to act in those situations. No doubt this knowledge does not guarantee success (the one who has it can *fail* in his projects, by *bad* luck), but plainly Aristotle thinks that it would not count as knowledge at all, unless it made it likely that he would succeed. It is, among other things, knowledge how the world runs, and so if it is regularly applied correctly, as of course the virtuous man does apply it, the looked-for results can be expected, anyhow a large percentage of the time.

The contrast Aristotle draws in *EE* VIII 2 between the morally virtuous person and the man of good fortune thus brings out two aspects of moral virtue as he conceives it that are not much emphasized elsewhere. The practical knowledge that is the leading component of the virtuous state of mind and character does not involve merely a correct assessment of the relative values of the various things that are good for human beings and knowledge of the (morally) right thing to do in whatever conditions one finds oneself in.[24] The virtuous person's knowledge how to act includes knowing how, if things go as they normally and usually do, actually to bring about the results that he aims at in his actions. And since it is usually the acquisition or maintenance of external goods (goods lying outside his own mind and character) that the virtuous man aims at in his actions, it follows that the regular success of the virtuous man's efforts to acquire, or to maintain, external goods is itself already implied by his having that knowledge how to act that his virtue involves. It should come as no surprise, therefore, that Aristotle does not mention the attainment of external goods, insofar as they are objects of pursuit in virtuous action, as something the virtuous person needs in *addition* to virtue in order to be happy.

[24]Cf. *NE* 1140a 25–29, b 4–6, and Cooper, *op. cit.* pp. 120–133.

The virtuous person will generally and regularly get these goods as an immediate consequence of his being virtuous, so that they should not be counted as goods that he needs as *supplements* to virtue if he is to be happy.

Of course, Aristotle recognizes that bad luck can cause even the virtuous person to fail occasionally to attain such goods despite his efforts to do so. And sometimes (as when his children turn out bad or die young) such bad luck can be no trivial matter, something to be made good later by trying again. Aristotle's view, if I am right, is that such occasional failures (even these most serious ones) will not be such as to detract from his happiness insofar as the missing goods were wished-for outcomes of prior action, but only insofar as their absence deprives him of conditions he needs if he is to go on living in the full exercise of his virtues. Is this a reasonable view? It ought to seem so to anyone who shares (as presumably not everyone will) Aristotle's central conviction that what determines the character of a person's life is what *he does.* On the one hand, a virtuous person who suffers such reverses acted knowing both that his choice of action was the, or one of the, best available in the circumstances, and that human beings never do completely control the outcomes of their actions, since nature is such that unpredictable irregularities and accidental results are simply always possible. Since he has done the best he or anyone in the circumstances could do, he should not count his own actions as in any way defective just because they did not lead to the wished-for outcomes. Insofar as happiness consists in deciding and doing what is best, his happiness has not been diminished by such failures. And on the other hand Aristotle pictures the happy person's life as a forward-looking progress from virtuous activity to virtuous activity, so that it is natural that he should regard the contribution to the virtuous man's happiness of external goods not in this backward-looking way, as crowning earlier activities with success, but as making possible continued virtuous activity in the future.

When, therefore, one takes into account Aristotle's conception of the virtuous man's practical knowledge, one sees readily enough why he integrates the external goods into *eudaimonia* in the way we saw he does. Though he recognizes that external goods are very often objects of pursuit in the virtuous man's activities, and things therefore that he values for themselves, Aristotle has good reasons for thinking that external goods are a *second* component of *eudaimonia,* alongside virtuous activity, only because of the effect they have in enabling the virtuous person to live, and go on living, a fully virtuous life.[25]

Princeton University

[25]I wish to thank Cynthia Freeland and Nicholas White for commentaries on this paper presented at colloquia at Boston University and the University of Michigan, respectively. David Sachs read a version of it and gave me detailed and very valuable criticisms. Written comments of T. H. Irwin enabled me to make a number of improvements in preparing the final version. I thank also the National Endowment for the Humanities for fellowship support during the period I was working on this paper.

The Southern Journal of Philosophy (1988) Vol. XXVII, Suppplement

SOME REMARKS ON ARISTOTLE'S MORAL PSYCHOLOGY

John M. Cooper
Princeton University

I.

Aristotle the moral philosopher seems very much in vogue these days. Among the philosophers of the traditional pantheon he, alongside perhaps only Thomas Aquinas, has been adopted as patron of the increasingly prominent philosophical movement toward moral theory based on the virtues, rather than on moral rules or other principles of behavior. Yet Aristotle and medieval Aristotelians such as Aquinas are by no means the only important philosophers of the past who regarded the acquisition and constant employment of the virtues as the center both of morality itself and of a correct theory of what morality demands of us. Aristotle does not differ at all in *this* respect from the whole of the main tradition in ancient Greek moral theory, descending from Socrates and including Plato, the Stoics Zeno and Chrysippus and their followers, and the many Aristotelian and Platonist philosophers of later antiquity. And quite a few post-Renaissance moralists, both Christian and secular, shared this much of Aristotle's outlook. To mention only the most celebrated, one can think, for example, of Spinoza, of Butler and Hume, all of whom treat morality as the possession of certain personal qualities, in fact a set of virtues, rather than conformance to some set of moral rules. Presumably, then, Aristotle's position as patron owes something to special features of *his* understanding of what the virtues are and how they shape and are otherwise connected to the truly moral life—features that give his theory greater appeal than those of these other philosophers. Nor in very gross terms is it difficult to see, or to guess at, some of the special attractions of Aristotle's theory. A virtue for Aristotle is a matter of one's character, where that is understood as a certain *unified condition* of both feeling and reasoned judgment, and both reasoned judgment and trained sensitivity and perceptiveness with regard to significant features of actual situations as they arise or are anticipated. Aristotle's conception of virtues makes them properties of great psychological complexity and depth, and partly in consequence it is easy to see why, if he is right about what a virtue is, virtues might deserve to be regarded as central to morality.

On the other hand, when it comes to the detail of Aristotle's theory, where its interest and supposed philosophical strengths will either be confirmed or, perhaps, proven illusory, those who invoke Aristotle's authority often say little, and what they do say is so obviously selective as to leave one doubtful whether they have a properly balanced appreciation of all the actual complexities of Aristotle's theory. At a number of important places, in fact, I believe Aristotle's theory of the virtues is not correctly represented in the recent philosophical literature, or for that matter in the more scholarly literature, either.

In the time available I will obviously not be able to set out and argue properly for a complete interpretation of Aristotle's theory of what a virtue of character, such as justice or courage or generosity, regarded as psychological properties of individual persons, is. Instead, I will begin by listing what I take to be the seven central claims Aristotle makes in this psychological connection about the virtues of character. This will at least give a summary of what would need to be worked out in detail in order to get a complete and properly balanced understanding of his theory. (See the Appendix.) You will notice from this list that at the center of Aristotle's understanding of what it is to have a character, and what it is to have a good or virtuous character, lies a certain distinction between reason (or, more properly, practical reason), on the one hand, and non-rational or non-reasoning desires, on the other. According to Aristotle, having a character at all, and a fortiori having a good character *consists* in a settled, trained disposition of a person's capacity and tendency to experience some range of *non*-rational desires, or other non-rational feelings, and, partly in consequence of those desires or feelings, to act in certain characteristic ways.

Now Aristotle's fundamental thesis in this whole area, that human beings do have non-rational desires and other feelings that need to be disciplined and controlled, and that to have a character is, precisely, to be in some particular settled condition with respect to non-rational feelings, was by no means universally accepted by philosophers in antiquity. The ancient Stoics, who correctly thought that Socrates as represented in Plato's early dialogues held, even took it for obvious, that adult human beings have *no* non-rational desires, developed an elaborate and complex theory of the virtues of character (one at least as complex as Aristotle's own) that strenuously and apparently rather persuasively maintained that these virtues are settled conditions of practical reason itself, and not of non-rational desire, for the simple reason that there were no non-rational desires (that is, none in any adult human being). Now obviously the Stoics were not denying such facts of everyday experience as that human beings sometimes feel anger or fear or sexual arousal or grief (things that Aristotle counts as non-rational desires and feelings); *they* held rather that these psychological phenomena are *not* non-rational feelings, in the relevant, Aristotelian sense, at all, but states of our rational minds. If we are to understand Aristotle's theory adequately, either from the historical or the philosophical point of view, it seems to me crucial that we understand as clearly as we can Aristotle's theory of the human desires, which counts anger, fear, and other such feelings as non-rational, precisely as one alternative to the account of these phenomena provided by the Stoics. If instead, as I suspect most contemporary readers of Aristotle do, we simply accept Aristotle's view of these matters, without seriously entertaining the Stoic alternative, we will certainly miss much of the force and interest of Aristotle's position.

In what follows I am going to concentrate on Aristotle's distinction, which as I have said is central to his theory of the virtues of character, between non-rational desires and reason itself in the generation of human action. I will have the contrast with the Stoic theory in mind throughout, but will only turn explicitly to the Stoics at the end of the paper, where I will offer some brief comparative remarks that I hope will help to sharpen our understanding of both the historical and the philosophical significance of Aristotle's theory.

II.

To begin with it is necessary to understand clearly how Aristotle uses the word "desire" (*orexis*) when he speaks, as he does in the contexts which will interest us, of occurrent desires, desires that are actively influencing in some way an agent's behavior on some occasion. Such a desire is taken by Aristotle (and in this the Stoics are in complete agreement) as more than merely an *inclination* to want to have or experience or do something; it is a fully-fledged, completed such want—an active psychological movement toward getting in an appropriate way, or experiencing or doing, whatever it is the desire for. Aristotle says at one place in discussing weakness of will (*NE* VII-*EE* VI, 1147a 34-5) that *epithumiai* or appetitive desires like thirst, understood not as a set of uncomfortable bodily feelings but as a desire *for drink*, actually have the power to set the bodily limbs themselves in movement. And the same holds for all other desires: they are fully realized psychological movements that move the limbs and so initiate action, unless some other similar psychological movements outweigh them or add some weight of their own so as to diminish or deflect their influence on the relevant bodily parts. So in maintaining that human beings have *non*-rational desires, Aristotle is maintaining that human beings are capable of being set in movement and action in ways that are completely independent of the use of their rational capacities—that is, as I will explain more fully below, independently of any rational, i.e., reasoned *thoughts* they may have about what *to do*, about what is *to be done*. On Aristotle's view, to be desiring food or drink, where these are appetitive desires, or to have an angry desire to retaliate against some supposed offense, is, as such, both to be moving psychologically toward relevant action *and* to be so moving without thinking, in one's rational mind, that these things *are to be done*—in fact, one might be thinking, quite on the contrary, that they are definitely *not* to be done. When the Stoics deny that human beings have any non-rational desires at all, precisely that is what they are denying. According to them, appetitive and angry desires, whatever else they involve, involve centrally the rational, i.e., reasoned thought that the actions they are moving the agent to do are *to be done*. These are mistaken, erroneous thoughts, the Stoics hold, but the errors are errors of reasoning, not some other kind of errors.

Now in coming to grips with Aristotle's theory, the first thing to notice is that, in common with Socrates, Plato, the Stoics and Epicurus, Aristotle held what is for us the strange-seeming view that reason is *itself* the source of a certain sort of desire, of a certain sort of psychological impulse or movement toward action. This way of thinking is strikingly evident in Plato's *Republic* IV, but equally and in a precisely parallel way in *NE* I 13 (to which I will turn in a moment). As you remember, Socrates in the *Republic* wants to show that there are three parts of the soul. He argues from cases of *akrasia*, first that there are appetites (in addition to reason), then that there are spirited impulses (in addition to both reason and appetite). It is worthy of notice that in his arguments Socrates *assumes* as something that does not need discussion that reason is a source of motivating force of some sort. Assuming that, his question then is whether there are other sources of motivation distinct from reason. As just noted, he argues this first for appetites. He claims that sometimes when a person's reason declares that some action is not to be done he nonetheless feels an impulse (an appetite, in fact), opposed to reason, and sometimes even acts on it. Here the opposition is clearly being conceived as an opposition of impulses or psychological movements, one coming from reason and pulling the agent back from the action, the other coming from appetite and moving him for and toward the action.[1] (Hence he can conclude we have two parts of the soul at work here, not one.) Plato's way of developing Socrates' argument, by making him *assume* that reason has its own impulses, makes perfectly good sense if one reflects that Socrates in earlier dialogues, notably the *Meno* and *Protagoras*, was himself thoroughly convinced that reason alone was responsible for our decisions and actions: that presupposes that reason is a source of motivation, of impulses to movement and action. Plato has Socrates in the *Republic* take that for granted, and argue that reason is not the *only* source of movements in the soul toward action. The Platonic view, as introduced in *Republic* IV, begins by accepting Socrates' earlier account of reason as a source of action, and goes on to recognize two *other* sources of action (two other parts of the soul). In other words, Plato saw the need to argue that we experience appetitive and spirited desires, where these have to be construed as non-rational, but not that we have rational desires (or whatever one is to call reason-derived psychological movements toward action). That seemed to him perfectly clear and not to need argument.

Aristotle, too, just like the Socrates of the *Republic*, when introducing the division of the human soul in *NE* I 13, takes for granted the motive-power of reason (which is why, as with Socrates in the *Republic*, that it has so often escaped people's notice). He, too, argues tht there are *other* motive forces, as well, the non-rational ones. He appeals (1102b 13-25), just as Socrates in the *Republic* does, to the phenomenon of *akrasia* (but also to that of self-control). The *hormai* or impulses, he says, of people acting akratically go in opposite directions: *epi tanantia hai hormai ton akraton* (the same is true of course for the self-controlled too).[2] That is, they experience a rational desire (*horme*)—a desire coming from their reasoned view of what to do—together with a non-rational desire of some sort, and these desires are opposed to one another. One moves them toward an action that the other moves them away from. The weak agent acts on the non-rational desire, the self-controlled person on the rational one.

Aristotle has a name for this rational impulse. It is *boulesis* (what Ross translates "rational wish"; or more simply, just "wish," as Irwin and others translate it). In many places (in *EE* and *MM*, in *de An.*, in *de Motu*, and in the *Rhetoric* and *Politics*),[3] but, curiously, none in the *NE*, Aristotle explicitly divides *orexis* (that seems to be his established word for movements of the soul toward or away from action) into three kinds: *epithumia* or appetite, *thumos* or spirited, competitive impulse, and *boulesis*. And he repeatedly makes it clear that *epithumia* and *thumos* are the two genera of non-rational desire, while *boulesis* is his preferred name for the movement toward action produced by the use of reason itself, on its own.

III.

Now this theory that there are three forms of *orexis*, two non-rational and one rational (in the sense that one comes from what Aristotle calls the reasoning part of the soul and two from the part or parts that do not reason) has very important implications for how Aristotle is conceiving reason itself, and correlatively for how he is conceiving the non-reasoning desires.

First of all, when he says, as he does, e.g., at *NE* VI-*EE* V, 1139a 35 and again at *de An.* III 10, 433a 23 that *nous* or *dianoia* by itself does not produce movement (i.e., any psychological movement toward or away from action), one must not assume that this means that reasoning about what to do does not lead to any movement toward acting *except* when it is coupled with some or other *non*-rational desire. There is also the rational *orexis*, and Aristotle's theory of the three kinds of *orexis* shows that *one* movement toward action that such reasoning might lead to is precisely a *boulesis*. In fact this is what he says explicitly at *de An.* 433a 22-25: "*nous* plainly does not produce movement without *orexis*, for *boulesis* is an *orexis* and whenever a person is moved by reasoning he is in fact (or: also) moved by *boulesis*."[4]

Secondly, one must be careful to bear in mind the *sense* in which a wish is a *rational* desire and, correspondingly, the sense in which the non-rational desires are *non*-rational. In *NE* VI-*EE* V 2, 1139b 12, Aristotle says that of both theoretical and practical reason the function (*ergon*) is (to pursue and attain) the truth. One part of what he asserts in this passage about practical reason is that its function is, not just to hold views to the effect that something or other is good for us, but to do so, whether we are self-conscious about this or not, as somehow part of or the result of a process of investigation *into* the truth about what is good. That is, a rational desire or *boulesis* is the practical expression of a course of thought about what is good for oneself, that is aimed at working out the truth about what *is* in fact good. Of course, in speaking thus about the *function* of *logos* (reason) he is describing how it operates when fully developed. He does not mean that whenever in any person a thought occurs that derives from or expresses his *logos* or reason, or whenever in consequence he has a *boulesis*, the person has actually done any such investigating into the truth about what is good. All it means is that a *logos*-thought and a *logos*-desire are about the good in a way that lays claim to there being a reason for thinking this, and to thinking it for that reason. (This will become clearer as I proceed, when we see how similar thoughts about the good occur differently from this in the non-reasoning desires.)

This means that the non-rational desires, as such, can be conceived simply as ones that lack these special features that their origin in reason gives to the rational desires. Accordingly, non-rational desires will be desires no part of the causal history of which is ever any process (self-conscious or not) of investigation into the truth about what is good for oneself; whatever the cause of the value-judgment such a desire may nonetheless contain may be, the cause is never any reason the agent might think there is for *making* this judgment. Non-rational desires have other causes than reason, and these are the origin of whatever value-thoughts the desires may contain. (I'll explain this further as I go on.) Accordingly, non-rational desires (say, a desire for something because it is pleasant, or an angry desire to strike back at someone) may on Aristotle's theory perfectly well be propositional and conceptual in structure (they may be or involve the thought *that* something is pleasant or that someone has acted against oneself in an intolerable manner): *that* is not a feature reserved to rational desires, given the conception Aristotle is working with of reason. But they can also even contain thoughts about what is good or bad for oneself—the thought, e.g., that pleasure, or this particular pleasure, is a good thing, or the thought that vengeance is not just sweet but entirely proper, even required if one is to be a person of any worth at all.

Aristotle is clear about this last point when he says in *NE* VII-*EE* VI, 1149a 25 ff. that *thumos* or spirit sometimes hears reason but mishears what it says. For example, reasoning about what to do in the face of an apparent insult, someone's reason declares that it was in fact an insult, and his *thumos* immediately boils up, as if, Aristotle says, inferring that someone who acts in that insolent way must be punished at once (i.e., that it is right or good *to* punish such a person). And the same thing is implied about *epithumia* or appetite by his frequent claim that its object, the pleasant, is the apparent good: to experience an appetite for something is, on Aristotle's view, to find it pleasant, i.e., to take it to be good.[5] The use here of what *we* might call reason (the power to think with concepts, even with the concepts of good and bad) does not make these desires rational desires in Aristotle's sense of the word "rational"; these desires, and so the thoughts that they contain, do not occur as parts of any process of reasoning for the purpose of figuring out what one should do, i.e., what one has the best reasons for doing; nor do those value-judgments rest upon reasons. One's appetitive desire, let us assume, is a more or less immediate response to the way the thing desired appeals to one's senses; though arousal for it partly consists in the thought that it would be a good thing to have it in whatever way one desires it, that opinion is not based on any *course* of thought purporting to reveal any reason for thinking it good (even if at the time one does think one has such a reason), nor is it the holding of any reason, or even the holding that there *is* any reason, for so valuing it. Likewise for the anger: although, as in Aristotle's example of the anger that mishears or half-hears, it may be aroused by a thought occurring within such a course of reasoning, viz. the thought that some person has insulted you, the further thought contained in the anger, that this kind of thing must be combatted forthwith, is not based on any *reason* for thinking this (even if at the time one has, or thinks one has, some reason for thinking it). You get angry because that is how you feel about insults, whether or not that is also how you think you have reason to act in relation to them.[6]

IV.

Aristotle's distinction, then, between rational and non-rational parts of the soul has nothing to do with the modern distinction between reason (regarded as *the* faculty of concept-formation and the manipulation of concepts), on the one hand, and desire (regarded on its own as a concept-free faculty of urges), on the other hand. There are both conceptual thoughts and (if you like) "urges" on both sides of Aristotle's distinction between *logos* and the *alogon*—reason and the non-rational. But it also has nothing to do with the subtler distinction between thoughts about, and desires that involve thoughts about, the good, and thoughts and desires that involve no reference to the good, that has recently been used to interpret the views argued for by the Socrates of the *Republic*.[7] All three of the types of desire Aristotle distinguishes involve (as he thinks) not just thoughts, but thoughts about what is good or bad: the difference between the two non-rational types of desire and the rational one consists solely in whether or not the source of these thoughts lies in *reasons* one thinks there are for having them.

This is crucially important for understanding how Aristotle thinks reason can obtain control of the non-reasoning desires, despite the independence from reason that essentially characterizes them. Aristotle holds that reason controls them not just by getting them to "follow" its directions (somehow or other), but by *persuading* them: the ideal is to persuade the non-rational desires to obey.[8] Now this persuasion is only possible because the very same terms in which reason thinks about the circumstances of action and about the relative values of things in the world in general, are also employed by each of the types of non-rational desire as well. When you are angry, for example, the anger you feel contains the thought that (e.g.) some other person has done you an injury, i.e., has not only done you some *harm* but has done it deliberately or anyhow without paying the heed to your desires or needs that he ought to have paid, and that such a person ought to be made to suffer in return. If your reason thinks differently at any of the places where value-terms connected with good, right, ought and so on occur in this angry thought, you are internally not just pulled in different directions; you are thinking ultimately contradictory thoughts, one through your anger the other through your reason. For reason to *persuade* anger (in this particular case, or in general) is for it to get its own view of what is good to prevail, in the sense that this conception comes to be adopted by the non-rational part itself, as well. To cause this to happen, even intermittently, may require practice and training, of course, but in that process reason is not just exercising brute force, as one might in training an animal. It is, among other things, addressing one's anger, trying to direct its attention to features of the situation that will show one's anger, by getting it to respond not just to some narrow, admittedly anger-arousing, range of features, but at the same time to a wider and more comprehensive view of the facts, that it would be, or was, wrong to feel in that way. If anger that springs up in you on some particular occasion obeys reason and is persuaded to obey it by being persuaded thus to feel about the situation as reason, on its own grounds, thinks best, that will mean that your rational thought about the goods and bads in that situation comes to be accepted by the non-rational part, and its own responses will then be adjusted accordingly. If you judge on rational grounds (or with the claim that there *are* rational grounds) that there was no injury at all, or that, though there was an injury, there is no good reason in this case to retaliate, and your anger is persuaded, then you simply cease to be angry (anyhow, at this person). Or it might be that you judge, on reflection, that it was not a very great injury, and/or that only a small retaliation is justified; then your anger dies down to the levels appropriate to those evaluations. The way you then feel about what has happened and about what should be done about it, is exactly also the way you think, for reasons, about it.

In the general case, where one habituates one's tendency to become angry to control by one's reason, reason persuades the source of anger in the soul (that from which it boils up) to adopt in general as a fixed and settled outlook on things the system of ideas about what is and is not an injury, and about what does and does not merit retaliation, etc., that reason itself has worked out by trying to discover the correct and rationally grounded considerations that reveal the actual truth about these matters. In that case, one's tendency to respond with anger comes to be always or regularly responsive to the full range of facts about situations as they arise that (and as) reason thinks relevant.

Now because Aristotle thinks that the truth about such matters—matters of value in general—is properly settled by reasoning, he thinks that this is the direction that the resolution of such contradictions *should* take. Your anger was caused not by what you rationally thought, nor by what you would rationally think if you gave reason a chance, but by (possibly obscure) causes lying in your recent or distant past experience: maybe on the occasion in question you are in an irritable frame of mind because of events earlier in the day, and that frame of mind now causes you to find fault where there was none. And so on. In any event, your *having* these thoughts about injury, justified retaliation and so on is caused ultimately not by any views you may hold that were worked out by rational reflection (or that claim to have a rational justification) but simply by this history of your experiences and the development in relation to them of your innate tendencies to feel in reaction to what happens to you. So where there is a contradiction it is your anger that ought to yield, not your reason. There is no good reason to think that your anger reflects the truth about the matters about which it is making claims.

Furthermore, I take it (here I am speculating a bit), Aristotle thinks that part of what it means to be rational is to have the general tendency not just to resolve such contradictions (to be uncomfortable in the face of contradictions of attitude) but to resolve them in that direction: see *NE* II 1, 1103a 24-26, "the virtues (viz. of character) are formed in us not by (our) nature nor contrary to it; rather, it is natural to us to receive them, when we are brought to perfection by habits of feeling (and acting)," *pephukosi men hemin dexasthai autas, teleioumenois de dia tou ethous*. The virtues, which of course imply a resolution in reason's favor, are here said to involve the perfection of our nature as rational, i.e., human, beings.

However, it is also important to bear in mind that the resolution *can* go in the other direction, both in individual cases and in general orientation. Faced with a conflict between how you feel about things in some respect and how you think about them, especially if this persists for a long time despite efforts on your part to adjust the way you feel, you will, *faute de mieux*, tend to adjust it in the other direction, by adopting in your rational thoughts a view about good and bad and right and wrong that conforms to the way you habitually feel: it is as if, under pressure from your stubborn desires, you decide on reflection that the correct way to determine what is good is simply to accept as authoritative how you feel. (Perhaps you then figure out some reasons to suit.) What forces us to take one of these two alternatives is the central fact that being rational creatures we cannot very readily or contentedly let the contradiction stand. We are moved, because we are rational, to resolve it in one direction or the other.[9]

V.

One last point needs to be emphasized. As I have said, the non-rational desires carry with them value-judgments framed in (at least some of) the very same terms of good and bad, right and wrong, etc., that also reappear in our rational reflections about what to do and why, and can be trained by habituation to respond to events and circumstances, actual or anticipated, on the basis of the very same normative outlook that reason works out. But the non-rational desires are according to Aristotle's view a permanent fact of human life, grounded in human nature and not eliminable, even (*especially*, one is inclined rather to say) in the perfected, fully virtuous person. When a virtuous person acts on reasons, these reasons will (typically anyhow) be reflected in two distinct forms of *horme* or impulse toward that action. He or she will act from his or her rational desire to so act (a *boulesis,* i.e., a *prohairesis*), which explicitly rests on, is caused by, the reasons, as represented in deliberation and its conclusions, that he or she has for so acting. But he or she will also experience, and act from, some set of non-rational desires active at the moment, which also contribute their motive force in favor of this action. These do not rest on, and are not caused by, the deliberation and the reasons he or she thinks there are for the action, as they are represented in that deliberation. They are caused by the state of his or her capacity and tendency for non-rational desire (anger, pity, appetitive desire, fear, etc.), as these have developed over time in response to his or her experience of things, including of course the experience of self-discipline and training. Reason and the non-rational aspects of human nature both survive in the virtuous person, and each is called into play independently of the other, even although, by habituation, the non-rational desires have come not to diverge significantly from the rational ones and in fact not to represent to the virtuous agent any significantly different picture of what is valuable in life and worth exerting oneself for or against, from the one his reason presents.

So, on Aristotle's view, when a virtuous person loses a child in an accident he will feel grief, even be seriously affected by grief. He will act (say) in comforting others and being comforted by them, in burying the child, etc., both from his grief, and from his rational wishes to alleviate others' feelings, to accept their sympathy, and to show his devotion for his child. This is, in one way, one of the most attractive aspects of Aristotle's theory of virtue of character. Intuitively it certainly does not seem right that someone should be thought virtuous who behaved in all these ways (comforted others, accepted their comfort, etc.), judging these behaviors right and having and acting on the right reasons for so judging, but without feeling the grief. Aristotle's recognition of the independence from reason, and the permanence, of our tendencies to feel non-rational desire, can seem a decisive measure of the extent to which he really does take seriously the fact that we are *human* persons, and not (even potentially) some kind of gods. Having non-rational feelings, such as anger, grief, fear, etc., appropriate to the circumstances we find ourselves in is part of our fullest perfection, on his view.

It is at this point that the Stoic theory stands in most radical opposition to Aristotle's. The Stoics agree that what they and Aristotle both call *pathe* or passions essentially consist, anyhow in part, of judgments that one affirms: in an appetitive urge or an angry feeling one affirms the judgment that a pleasant experience or an act of vengeance, is good and worth having or doing. In feeling these desires one is asserting such a judgment, not just entertaining it: that is why, on both the Stoic and the Aristotelian view, these desires are *hormai*—"impulses," actual movements in the soul toward (or away from) action. Merely entertaining such a judgment, or even being *inclined* to assert it, would not, on either of their views, constitute a *horme*. Furthermore, the Stoics and Aristotle agree that we come to experience these *pathe* and in doing so to assert these judgments about what is good and bad (for ourselves and others) as a result of our experiences in life as we grow up—and, of course, in particular because in our culture (as in that of ancient Greece) it is the dominant view, which we all imbibe with our mother's milk (if not also in some way from our nature itself), that the things in question (pleasure, insults by others, etc., etc.) really are good or bad, as the case may be. Anger and appetitive urges are *strong* feelings, and having strong feelings about these things is just what one should expect of someone who did somehow think them really good or bad.

According to the Stoics, however, this view is false. Only one's inner state (the state of one's mind as one faces external things) is either a good or a bad thing for any human being. Accordingly, on the Stoic view, anyone who puts reason in control of his life, as of course both they and Aristotle thought was the road to virtue and to human perfection, will have eventually to repudiate, and to repudiate decisively, *all* the judgments about value that get affirmed in the experience of any *pathos*—anger, grief, appetitive desires such as ordinary hungry pursuit of food, ordinary sexual arousal, and so on. And by decisively repudiating these value-judgments one ceases to feel the passion too—in the absence of the thought that anything good or bad is present or in the offing, there is nothing to feel strongly about. Accordingly, on the Stoic theory, the full development of any human being from childhood to maturity to full moral perfection will pass through a phase during which passions will be experienced, but the final goal will be to cease to experience them altogether. So the virtuous person, on the Stoic view, who loses a child, may *act* very much as the Aristotelian virtuous person would act, comforting others, accepting comfort from them, and so on, but he will not feel any grief, however tiny an amount. He will only feel, and will only act from, his rational desire (his *boulesis*, a term the Stoics take over in this context from the

Platonists and Aristotle). He will have no non-rational desires or feelings, at all.

VI.

Now, as this rapid summary comparison should make you expect, the Stoics concentrated their opposition to the Aristotelian view on this question of what the nature of goodness is, and which things *are* actually good. It is easy to see why. If they could succeed in showing that only a person's internal state was either good or bad for him, that only his inner state could affect him for better or worse, then it would apparently follow directly that *pathe* would all of them disappear once virtue (which both sides agreed at least included knowledge of what truly *is* good and bad) was achieved. After all, *pathos* was agreed by Aristotle to include a judgment that certain external things or events were good or bad, and if when you *knew* the true theory of what is good or bad you could show decisively that none of these things were or could be good or bad, you could not continue to hold these false beliefs. Thus Aristotle would be hoist by his own petard, the petard of his own theory of the *pathe* as containing such judgments, once the correct theory of goodness and badness was established.

But this conclusion follows only if at the same time you also deny the permanence in human beings and the independence from reason, in the sense I have specified, of the non-rational desires. Aristotle will agree with the Stoics, though not for all the same reasons, that if their theory of goodness and badness is correct anyone who comes to *know* that theory (in the sense of having *phronesis*, or practical knowledge, of it) will also cease affirming in his thoughts, even in the thoughts contained in his non-reasoning desires, any judgment to the effect that any external thing or event is either good or bad. Practical knowledge necessarily involves bringing the non-rational desires to that extent into conformity with reason's settled judgments about the values of things. But that does not mean at all that the *pathe* will have to disappear. If the non-rational desires really are ways in which values get represented to us that are independent in origin from reason, then the developing history of the ways one is affected in one's feelings about things will include an extra last stage that Aristotle, since of course he did not in fact accept the Stoic theory of goods, did not envisage. This will be the stage at which one's tendency to become angry or to be affected appetitively will be educated so that *in* feeling those things one no longer thinks (what our culture has brought us up so that we do think) that the things one is affected by are bad or good, strictly speaking. This (as one might describe it) "refined" anger and "refined" appetitive desire will contain the thought, not that some external thing or event is or would be good or bad, but only that it has some positive or negative value of some other, lesser kind. But nonetheless it will still be anger or appetitive desire, because of its historical development from earlier versions of the underlying tendency to feel, to be affected by, the ways things *appear* to you (and not merely by the ways you think about them in pursuit of the truth about such matters). Virtue of character would still consist, on this semi-Stoicized Aristotelian view, in *feeling* passions of grief, anger, appetitive desire, and so on, but in conformity with one's fully educated rational judgments about what things are valuable, in what ways they are valuable, and why.

And that is why the Stoics conducted their argument against Aristotle simultaneously on a second front as well. Is there, after all, really any non-rational part or aspect of the human soul, in the sense in which Aristotle held that there was, i.e., as a source of desires independent of reasoning about what ought to be done? We are now in a position to see clearly that that is the really fundamental point of contention.

This brings us full circle and I cannot pursue the argument further here. But it should by now be clear that Aristotle pays a considerable price in order to maintain the independence of the human emotions from human reason which many of us nowadays find so attractive, even perhaps compelling, an idea. As we have seen, he has to assign to the emotions and non-rational desires quite a bit of what we, and the Stoics, would regard as aspects of the capacity for reason: not just conceptualization and evaluation, but, more seriously, even something perilously akin to decision. In experiencing full-fledged anger, as Aristotle thinks and we and the Stoics would insist, a person *assents* to the idea that some act of retribution is to be done, and it is only in consequence of that that she is actually moved to do it. Can one give an acceptable account of what this assent is, without being forced to admit that *it*, at least, comes from that very rational power that Aristotle wanted to set clearly apart from the non-rational desires as a separate, competing source of impulses to action? Anyone who wants to adopt an Aristotelian theory of the moral virtues or virtues of character, and so the Aristotelian psychology of action, must face this question. It must not simply be begged as it seems nowadays mostly to be. The best way to face this question is to think closely and carefully about the Stoics' objections against the very possibility of a non-rational part of the soul conceived as Aristotle conceived it.[10]

APPENDIX

1. Virtues of character belong to what Aristotle calls the non-rational part of the soul (*EE* II 1, 1220a 10; *NE* I 13, 1102b 13).

2. Virtues of character and traits of character in general (i.e., *ethe*) are qualities (*poiotetes)* (that is, relatively fixed and longlasting ways of being qualified) belonging to the non-rational part, *insofar as* that part is capable of following reason; in fact, these qualities require and depend essentially upon a *prescriptive judgment* of the reason of the person whose soul is in question (*EE* II 2, 1220 b 5-6; and cf. *NE* II 5 and *Cat.* 8b 25ff. on *hexeis*).[11]

3. Virtues of character are in *some* way connected essentially with decisions (*prohaireseis*), and so with actions (*praxeis* in the narrower of the two senses that Aristotle's usage gives to this word): see *NE* VI-*EE* V 2, 1139a 31.[12]

4. Virtues of character essentially involve experiencing non-rational desires, i.e., *pathe*, in an intermediate degree, i.e., in a degree that precisely suits the circumstances (*NE* II 6, *EE* II 3).[13]

5. It is the practical knowledge possessed by the *phronimos* that determines what the virtuous and intermediate degree of *pathos* is (*NE* II 6, 1107a 1-2; *EE* II 3, 1220b 28 with II 5, 1222a 8 and b 7).

6. It is not possible to have a virtuous character without having practical knowledge, nor to have practical knowledge without having a virtuous character (*NE* VI-*EE* V 13, 1144b 30-32).

7. A virtue of character is brought into being by repeatedly feeling and acting precisely (or as nearly so as possible) as, in the given circumstances, the person having the virtue would feel and act (*NE* II 1, 1103b 6-25, *EE* II 1, 1220a 22-24; cf. *de Anima* II 5, 417a 22-b 2).

NOTES

[1] See John M. Cooper, "Plato's Theory of Human Motivation," *History of Philosophy Quarterly* I (1984), 3-21, at pp. 6-8.

[2] The *EE*, in a different context, agrees about this analysis of *akrasia* and self-control: 1224a 31-32, *enantias hormas echon autos hekastos hautoi prattei.*

[3] See, e.g., *EE* II 7, 1223a 26-27 and II 10, 1225b 24-26; *MM* I 12, 1187b 37; *de An.* II 3, 414b 2 and III 9, 432b 5-6 and 10, 433a 22-26; *de Motu* 6, 700b 19; *Rhet.* I 10, 1369a 1-4; *Pol.* VII 15, 1334b 17-25. Aristotle seems already in the *Topics* to have appropriated *boulesis* as the name for desire coming from reason: see IV 5, 126a 6-13, where he says roundly that *boulesis* (*=orexis agathou*, 146b 5-6) is *en toi logistikoi*, by contrast with *to epithumetikon* and *to thumoeides*. The nearest Aristotle comes in *NE* to dividing all *orexis* into these three types is III 2, 1111b 10-12, where he lists *epithumia*, *thumos* and *boulesis* alongside *doxa tis* as potential candidates for what *prohairesis* is, but without saying that they are candidates precisely because they are *the* forms of *orexis* (contrast *EE* II 10, 1225b 21-26).

[4] This has very important implications, which however I will not pursue in this paper, for what Aristotle means when he says that a *prohairesis* or decision is a union of deliberative reasoning and desire (i.e., *orexis*): the desire that is an element of a *prohairesis* need not be a non-rational desire (an appetite or any other passion), but may, given Aristotle's theory that there are three types of desire, be a form of *boulesis*. That he intends to adopt the view that it is a *boulesis*, and not any form of non-rational desire, is not perfectly clear in the *NE* (either in III or VI-*EE* V), but it *is* clear in *EE* II 10, 1226b 2-5 and 1227a 3-5. The *NE* texts permit this interpretation,

and in view of the exceptionally clear statements in the *EE*, I have no doubt that it is what Aristotle intended in the *NE* as well.

[5] Does Aristotle mean that *epithumia* in human beings is in this way for pleasure taken for good, without implying or meaning to imply the same for the other animals?

[6] It should be clear that the distinction I have sketched in the foregoing paragraphs, and develop further below, between rational and non-rational desires requires the rational "part" of the soul to be independent in a very strong way from all our other psychological capacities, including especially our capacities for non-rational desires. The reasons for doing things, and for valuing things, that issue from the exercise of reason in this sense must be construed as arrived at independently of one's acceptance of beliefs and other commitments in and through the exercise of other capacities (including the emotions and appetites). Reason is to be thought of as operating by stepping back completely from all such commitments and examining on grounds that it itself works out what is true or false in them. When I speak of a *boulesis*, but not, e.g., an angry desire, as resting on and being caused by (the holding of) reasons, I mean reasons so construed. We may say, truly enough, that in feeling anger we feel as we do for a reason, viz. (as it might be) that some person has insulted us, and that that is intolerable. To that extent, our anger is caused by (the holding of) that reason. But that does not count against the claim I mean to be making in the text when I say that only rational desires (*bouleseis*) rest on reasons. I do not undertake to defend this conception of reason here (I believe it is held in common by at least Plato, Aristotle and the Stoics), or, for that matter, to do much by way of defending my attribution of it to Aristotle. For present purposes all I require is that this conception should be intuitively clear enough, and have enough intuitive initial appeal, to allow us to proceed to examine and evaluate the theory of the virtues of character that, if I am right, Aristotle constructs on this foundation.

[7] See T. H. Irwin, *Plato's Moral Theory* (Oxford: Clarendon Press, 1977), ch. VII. Irwin is mainly concerned with the distinction between thoughts about one's *overall* good and other thoughts, and I do not mean to say that Aristotle attributes thoughts about one's overall good to, for example, appetites. However, this should not be allowed to obscure the more important point, that for Aristotle, at any rate, even appetites essentially involve value judgments employing concepts of goodness.

[8] Cf. *NE* I 13, 1102b 31: non-rational desire is also, in a sense, rational, insofar as it is *katekoon autou kai peitharchikon*; b 33, *to alogon peithetai pos hupo logou.*

[9] Given the centrality of this fact about rational beings to much of what Aristotle says about virtues and vices of character and how they come into being, it is surprising that he nowhere in the ethical writings seems to state or draw attention explicitly to it.

[10] In revising this paper for publication I have benefitted from comments on earlier versions by T. H. Irwin, Heda Segvic and Gisela Striker, my commentator at the Conference.

[11] Here I give what seems to be the burden of a textually corrupt passage of *EE* II that gives a sort of definition of *ethos*; the *NE* nowhere gives such a definition.

[12] Here I rely on the first part of the passage that is usually cited as Aristotle's "definition" of virtue of character in the *NE*, at II 6, 1106b 36: virtue is a *hexis prohairetike*. Nothing exactly corresponds to this definition in the *EE*, but note 1230a 27, *pasa arete prohairetike.*

[13] Aristotle normally distinguishes just two types of non-rational desires (i.e., *orexeis*), *epithumia* and *thumos*, appetitive and spirited or competitive

desire, respectively. It is by reference to non-rational *orexis* so understood that he introduces the non-rational part of the soul in *NE* I 13 and *EE* II 1, 1219b 16-1220a 4 (cf. *to orektikon*, b 23, with II 4, 1221b 30-32; but NE that already at 1220a 1-2 he mentions not *orexis* but *orexeis kai pathemata* as what reason controls); and in the *NE* contexts, at any rate, virtue of character itself is introduced as the virtue that controls non-rational desire. However, when in *NE* II 5-6 he defines virtue of character as a *hexis*, he explains *hexeis* as conditions on our capacity to feel *pathe* (*not* non-rational *orexeis*), and gives a list of *pathe* (at 1105b 21-23) that includes the two sorts of non-rational *orexis* as only two instances of a wider class: fear, grief, pity, envy, etc., as well as *epithumia* and *orge* (anger—I assume that *orge* is intended here as a variant for *thumos,* as at *Rhet.* I 10, 1369a 4; compare the shorter list of *pathe* in the corresponding passage of *EE,* II 2, 1220b 12-13, where we get *thumos* instead of the *NE*'s *orge*). It is an interesting question exactly how Aristotle intends (or indeed whether he has any worked-out intention at all in this regard) to bring together these two somewhat different characterizations of what it is that the virtues of character control. I do not pursue these questions further in this paper, but loosely interchange "non-rational desire" with "passion."

Aristotle and the Emotions

STEPHEN R. LEIGHTON

Since the object of rhetoric is judgment (*Rhetoric* 1377b21) and since what appears does vary with the emotions (ibid, 1378a1), a concern for rhetoric provided Aristotle with the opportunity to develop his most sustained thoughts on emotions; not only does he define, explicate, compare and contrast various emotions, but also he characterizes emotions themselves.[1] His observation is quite striking.

> Emotions are the things on account of which the ones altered differ with respect to their judgments, and are accompanied by pleasure and pain: such are anger, pity, fear, and all similar emotions and their contraries. (ibid, 1378a20-23)

Here a number of things provoke thought. First, how did Aristotle take the altering of judgments to occur? Second, what does Aristotle mean by speaking of the 'accompaniment' of pleasure and pain? Last, and resolvable only after the above questions are answered, is the conception of emotion like our own?[2] These questions are worth answering not only for their value in understanding Aristotle, but also insofar as they shed light on our own understanding of emotion. Let us begin with the matter of altering judgment.

I

We would agree that emotions may alter our judgments. Love's flame flaring, we view a beloved, and sometimes the whole world, through rose colored glasses; our blood boiling, these same things are viewed rather differently.

> For it does not seem the same according as men love or hate, are wrathful or mild, but things appear altogether different, or different in degree; for when a man loves one on whom he is passing judgment, he either thinks the accused has committed no wrong at all or that his offense is trifling; but if he hates him, the reverse is the case. And if a man desires anything, and has good hopes of getting it, if what is to come is pleasant, it seems to him that it is sure to come to pass and will be good; but if a man is unemotional or in a bad humour, it is quite the reverse. (ibid, 1377b30-78a4, based on a translation by Freese)

From this and the previous quotation we can infer that emotions may move one to a particular judgment, may alter the severity of a judgment, or may change a judgment entirely. The field in which emotion operates is not restricted. Although the judgments altered which are foremost in Aristotle's mind are formal verdicts given at the end of proceedings, there is no reason to doubt emotion's effect on judgments on the way to a formal verdict, or for that matter on any other judgment. Thus the range of things to be included under affected judgment is quite general, forming, from our point of view, a rather heterogeneous group. For, so far, there is no requirement of belief in the judgment. Yet, as the passage immediately above suggests, belief may be present. Again, the group is not simply restricted to stated judgment, or even terminating judgment of any sort. Also, the sorts of changes Aristotle includes can be quite dramatic.[3] Nevertheless, that such changes occur sits rather well with our own intuitions on the matter. What, then, is (are) the explanation(s) of changes of judgment involving emotion?

Aristotle nowhere explicitly reports on this matter. However, he does provide for a number of solutions.

1. An obvious place to begin is with the definitions of each of the emotions. The aim or end of an emotion could explain a change of judgments. In anger's definition Aristotle speaks of seeking revenge (ibid, 1378a31-34). It is easy to see that one way of seeking revenge in a court room would be to return an unfavorable verdict. In more pedestrian settings one could achieve the same end by, say, slandering the person. Similarly, in love's definition, Aristotle speaks of seeking the beloved's good for his own sake (ibid, 1380b35-81a2). Again, it is easy to see that one way of seeking his good in a court room would be by bringing down a favorable verdict. In more pedestrian settings one could sing the beloved's praises (though not really deserved) and thereby alter one's judgments.

Similar considerations apply to other emotions Aristotle considers. Pity and indignation require a sense of justice. We are moved to pity because the misfortune suffered is undeserved (ibid, 1386b11); we are roused to indignation because the good fortune enjoyed is undeserved (ibid, 1386b10). Thus we can suppose that our judgments concerning those we pity would become lenient and generous, while our judgements concerning those with whom we are indignant would be severe and mean-spirited. In both cases one would be compensating for the injustice that roused the emotion. This compensation takes the form of an alteration in judgment.[4]

In all likelihood one is well aware of what one is doing in such cases. We make certain judgments in public which are at odds with what we really believe.[5] We are like the person who forms the right opinion, but through viciousness or lack of good will does not say what he really thinks (ibid, 1378a12-15). Just how this works is fairly transparent. One holds view A, but because one wants to do well or poorly by another, says B. This, then, is our first explanation of emotions altering judgments.

It is most unlikely that Aristotle intends this sort of insincerity to bear much of the burden of explaining how emotions alter judgments. For though this can explain why one's pronouncements vary and to that extent how judgments are altered, it is not helpful with Aristotle's remark that things appear differently through emotion (ibid, 1377b30). Moreover, unless we suppose Aristotle to hold a rather eccentric, and suspiciously unacknowledged theory of self-deception, his theory has not yet begun to account for the interesting cases of emotions altering judgment: cases in which one is like the man who lacks good sense rather than like the vicious or those without good will (ibid, 1378a8-16); cases in which the change of judgment has to be a matter of belief. Thus we must seek a further explanation of emotion's effect.

2. A different sort of explanation is implicit in Aristotle's remark about the speaker who rouses the judges' indignation towards those pleading for forgiveness.

> If then the speech puts the judges into such a frame of mind and proves that those who claim our pity (and the reasons why they do so) are unworthy to obtain it and deserve that it should be refused them, the pity will be impossible. (ibid, 1378b17-21, based on Freese's translation)

The same sort of explanation is implicit in Aristotle's remarks concerning one made envious.

> So that if the judges are brought into that frame of mind, and those who claim their pity or any other boon are such as we have stated, it is plain that they will not obtain pity from those with whom the decision rests. (ibid, 1388a26-29, based on Freese's translation)

The defendant vainly struggles to move the judges to one emotion while they are in the grips of another. The point seems to be that emotions have certain judgments connected with them such that certain other emotions, their judgments, and other judgments too are excluded. For example, John's indignation with Mary involves John making a judgment of Mary's unmerited good fortune (ibid, 1386b10) which thereby precludes John making the judgment of Mary's undeserved misfortune (ibid, 1385b14) that he would have made were he roused to pity her. Again, Mary's envy of John involves, for example, Mary making a judgment of reproach concerning herself through John's successes (ibid, 1388a17) which thereby precludes Mary making a judgment of John's undeserved misfortune that she would have made were she roused to pity him (ibid, 1385b14). This is not a matter of insincerity on John or Mary's part. Rather, being moved to one emotion with its judgments rules out being moved to another emotion with its judgments. Those judgments obtain which are connected with the emotion one is moved to. Thus, insofar as one moves to a given emotion one thereby alters one's judgments; and this is underlined by the consequent exclusion of other emotions and their judgments.

We can see the same sort of alteration with other emotions as well. Should one be moved to anger, one thereby views the object of anger as having insulted one (ibid, 1378a31-33). Becoming ashamed of a person involves being brought to view the person as involved in misdeeds that bring dishonor (ibid, 1383b15-16). Again, to the extent one is moved to these emotions one's judgments are thereby altered. Similar points can be made for all the emotions Aristotle discusses.

How this works is transparent also. To be moved to emotion A involves making judgments A; to be moved to emotion B involves making judgments B, etc. Thus, 'things do not seem the same' as one finds oneself in one emotional state as opposed to another, or none at all. Moreover, the judgments in any given complex may logically exclude those of another complex, or any other judgments.

The most obvious contrast between the two cases considered is that while the former is a matter of insincerity, the latter is not. An equally striking contrast is that while the former is an example of emotion altering judgments, the latter is actually a matter of emotion itself being an alteration of judgments. In the second case, emotions are complexes involving judgments, each complex possibly excluding other emotion complexes, their judgments, and other judgments as well. It is not that envy brings about a change of judgments such that one does not show or feel pity; rather, to be moved to envy involves being moved to a particular set of judgments which excludes those of pity. Similarly, it is not that being angry makes us view the object of emotion as insulting, but being angry involves viewing the object as insulting.

This sophisticated thesis sits very well with many modern analyses of emotion in which changes of emotion are, in part at least, changes in judgments. Although this is not what we began searching for, given the passages quoted above and Aristotle's understanding of shame, anger, etc., and given how well this suits his claim that things do not seem the same when one is in different emotional states (ibid, 1377b30), we have no reason to doubt that the thesis is Aristotle's. However, it does mean that we have not exhausted Aristotle's thoughts on emotions and changes of judgments. For the characterization of emotion quoted at the outset of this paper speaks of emotions being that on account of which judgments change, not emotions themselves being changes of judgments. Since, as we have seen, the matter of insincerity cannot be the whole of this explanation, there must be more to the account. Thus we must search for further explanations of emotions altering our judgments. So far, our study has revealed two species of the genus changes of judgment involving emotion: i) change of judgment as a consequence of emotion; ii) change of judgment as a constituent of emotion. The latter we have just considered. It will not be further subdivided; it works by means of emotions involving particular sets of judgments, judgments which may exclude the judgments constitutive of other emotions. The former will subdivide into four species, one of which is the matter of insincerity (method one).

3. Another way in which emotion might affect judgment is like our first explanation (1) insofar as it depends upon the aim or end of the emotion, but is like the second (2) insofar as it is not disingenuous, but rather a seduction by emotion. Consider again the angry person. We have seen that he seeks revenge. A change of judgment may result here only because one is disposed to give an unfavorable interpretation where the case is ambiguous. One never grants the benefit of the doubt, quite the opposite. In this way one would not only say that the person was worthless, but would have come to believe it, one's anger having seduced one's judgment. Again, in love's seeking the benefit of a beloved, where circumstances are unclear, one would be inclined to give the beloved a favorable interpretation because one is 'favorably disposed'. One thereby arrives at a far more charitable judgment than one would have had one been more rigorous and critical when considering the matter.

As with the previous explanations, how this favor/disfavor method works is fairly transparent. Of a certain case, A, one is unsure how to evaluate it. But since the emotion disposes us and makes us desirous to favor or disfavor that to which the emotion relates, and since we do need to form some opinion of the case, we correspondingly judge the case harshly or favorably. Thus, emotion alters judgment.[6] Should there be a number of related cases, one's judgment not just of each particular case, but of the person will be likewise swayed. For example, we shall tend to be charitable about the motives of a beloved, judging ambiguous cases in this light. Should we be faced with a number of such cases, this will strengthen our charitable interpretation not only of the cases, but also of him. This, then, is a third and twofold way in which emotion changes judgment.

Although our ability to account for emotion changing judgments is increasing, further explanations are still needed. For the explanations appropriate do not seem at all helpful in the cases of fear, shame and shamelessness, given Aristotle's definitions of these. For, on his view, these have no aim towards the realization of which our judgments might be bent. Of course, instead of searching for further explanations, this might lead some to think that the *Rhetoric*'s characterization of these emotions is inadequate. They too should have an aim in their definitions, or at least the general characterization of these emotions should include an aim. For example, it would be plausible to say that fear aims at flight. Now, if this sort of move could be made for all emotions, then we could say that all emotions could affect judgment in each of these three ways. However, this is not the position of the *Rhetoric*; and so it does not resolve the problems here. Nor is it plausible. What does sadness or shame aim at? If we disagree about Aristotle's characterization of fear, I do not think we want to dispute that some emotions have no aim. That leaves us needing to search for further explanations. Moreover, where we do think emotions seduce our judgment, we do not always want to construe it in any of the above fashions. For example, consider Aristotle's own example at 1378a1. It is plausible that one could explain, in the favorable interpretation manner, the person who hopes for something good, and thus supposes it will come to pass. He desires its occurrence; and it is likely that he would give himself the benefit of the doubt concerning the many hurdles he has to face, but does not really know whether he can leap or not. Likewise, one without hope would be disposed to underestimate his prospects. However, if the case is unambiguous, if the hurdles to be faced are insurmountable, then any seduction of judgment seems inadequately explained in terms of a favorable interpretation. Because of this, and because certain emotions lack an aim, we must look for further explanations.

4. The *Nicomachean Ethics* (1149a24-31) is helpful.[7]

> Anger seems to listen to argument to some extent, but to mishear it, as do hasty servants who run out before they have heard the whole of what one says, and then muddle the order, or as dogs bark if there is a knock at the door before looking to see if it is a friend. So anger by reason of the warmth and hastiness of its nature, when it hears, though not hearing an order, springs to revenge. (Ackrill's revision of Ross's translation)

The position here is not that there is something particularly ambiguous; it is not just that one does not know how to take something, and so throws it in with one's other judgments through the aim of one's emotion. Neither is it a matter of conniving, nor of anger being a change in judgments. Rather, through the emotion one mishears, i.e., does not hear an order. Here the seduction arises from a mishearing, a misperception of what may be very clear evidence. This misperception in its turn results in faulty judgment.

This is quite insightful, covering certain cases more plausibly. For emotion can alter perception and consequently the judgments based on these perceptions. Excited supporters of opposing tennis players often see rather different things. Their judgments based on these perceptions are accordingly influenced. Thus the seduction of the hopeful person facing nearly insurmountable hurdles can be explained by the misperception of those hurdles and the consequent misjudgment. However, even though we might like to agree that something along these lines is surely right, the account needs to be articulated more clearly. For the precise operation of emotion, especially upon perception, is not yet clear. Until it is clear, we do not know if Aristotle has adequately provided an additional way in which emotion alters judgment.

To see how Aristotle can suppose this to work, we need to begin with a passage in *De Somniis* and then reflect upon the theory of objects of perception in *De Anima*.

> With regard to our original inquiry, one fact, which is clear from what we have said, may be laid down – that the percept still remains perceptible even after the external object perceived is gone, and moreover that we are easily deceived about our perceptions when we are in emotional states, some in one state and others in another; e.g. the coward in his fear, the lover in his love; so that even from a very faint resemblance the coward expects to see his enemy, and the lover his loved one; and the more one is under the influence of emotion, the less similarity is required to give these impressions. Similarly, in fits of anger and in all forms of desire all are easily deceived, and the more easily the more they are under the influence of emotions. So to those in a fever, animals sometimes appear on the wall from a slight resemblance of lines put together. Sometimes the illusion corresponds to the degree of emotion so that those who are not very ill are aware that the impression is false, but if the malady is more severe, they actually move in accordance with appearances. (460b1-16, based on Hett's translation)

Like the passage from the *Nicomachean Ethics* and unlike the first three explanations, this concerns the perceptual level of emotions affecting perceptions rather than the epistemic level of emotions affecting beliefs and knowledge. Aristotle claims that deception occurs readily when we are excited by the emotions – the coward by his fear, the lover by his love. With little basis the coward will see his foes; the lover, the beloved. Moreover, the more deeply the emotion is felt the more remote a resemblance may be which gives rise to illusory impressions. However, this is not to hold that we always get it wrong when in an emotional state: Aristotle suggests that we may recognize the illusion if the emotion is slight.

In addition to concurring with the view of the *Nicomachean Ethics*, this provides part of the explanation we seek. Emotion is meant to alter perception through the expectation of emotion and the 'putting together' (*suntithemenōn*) of things accordingly. If this occurs, then, having the wrong perceptions, we are likely to go on to make inadequate judgments. Still, how emotion can operate in this way on what we perceive is unclear, even if we grant, say, that the fearful would expect and put things together differently from the amorous.

If we recall the distinction between objects of perception *per se* and objects of perception *per accidens* in *De Anima* (book two, chapter six), we can make good sense of putting together through the expectation of emotion. An object of perception *per se* is a white thing; *per accidens*, Socrates. We are meant to perceive both sorts of objects.[8] And what is noteworthy for us is that while the former object has little or no room for misperception or difference in perception, the latter object has a good deal of room. Thus, with this latter object error can occur; emotion can create illusions and alter perception.

To explain exactly how this occurs, let me begin with the differences of perception that may occur without involving error or emotion. The object of perception that we all see (the object *per se*) is a black, circular, flat thing.[9] If it is a record, a piece of plastic, and something different as well, then according to Aristotle, those things are perceived *per accidens*, even though the perceiver may not perceive it as those things and they may not, therefore, be 'his object'. Although with my knowledge of records what I perceive it as is a record, and with another's knowledge of the mysteries of Lil what he perceives it as is the sacred God, etc., still what is perceived *per accidens* is the record and the sacred God. While what is seen *per se* and even *per accidens* remains the same, the object *per accidens* that it is perceived as need not be the same. We can say 'our objects' of perception are different.

As plausible as this may be, we need the case of misperception, and misperception through emotion.[10] We have noted that the object of perception *per se* is not subject to misperception, while the object *per accidens* is. The sorts of error involved here includes misperception of what the object of perception *per accidens* is (*De Anima* 418a15), and illusion (*De Somniis* 460b19). Thus, here, the object of perception *per accidens* that it is perceived as is not in fact the same as the object of perception *per accidens*. Given that emotion is held to be responsible for misperception, its means of influence is through the expectation and consequent putting together of a given object of perception. Let me illustrate these points.

Suppose we have two people. George is swept by fear; Harry is exceedingly calm and confident. Both hear a loud sound (object *per se*); George hears a gun firing (object *per accidens*); Harry hears the backfiring of a car (object *per accidens*). Suppose, in fact, a car did make the loud sound. Then we say that through his fear George is expecting (*dokein, De Somniis* 460b6) fearful events to occur. The object *per se* can be taken for the firing of a gun; and, through the expectation, the loud sound is heard, though misheard, by being put together (*suntithemenōn*, ibid, 460b13) as a gun firing. The emotion involves certain expectations by which what the object of perception *per accidens* is perceived as can be put together erroneously. Suppose now it was a gun firing. What we say of Harry is that he is not expecting anything untoward, that his confidence precludes any such thing. Hearing the loud sound (object *per se*), he puts it together differently – here misperceives – and this is what he hears. Turning to the example in *De Somniis*, we find that even where the resemblance is very faint, the coward is meant, through expectation, to put together an enemy that is not there as an object of perception *per accidens*. Turning to the examples of the *Nicomachean Ethics*, the servant hears a sound, is expecting something, and through the haste and warmth of the emotion puts it together accordingly, thereby misperceiving. Without further ado, he springs to action. Likewise, the dog hears a sound, is expecting some evil, and through the warmth and hastiness of the emotion puts together the knock of a friend as that of an enemy. Without further ado, it springs to action.

Thus the distinction in *De Anima* helps to explain the suggestion of both *De Somniis* and the *Nicomachean Ethics*. Moreover, we can understand why Aristotle says in this latter work that the servant hears but does not hear an order (1149a31). For he hears the object *per se*, the sound, but through his emotion he is expecting something, and does not hear (does not put together) the object *per accidens*, the order issued. Thus far, we can explain how Aristotle takes misperception to arise through emotion. That the emotion controlling us is seen to predispose us to see things in terms of it through expectation, is, I believe, a plausible suggestion on Aristotle's part: emotion is supposed to be part of our way of viewing the world. Our way of viewing the world is the way we put things together, and thus brings about an alteration of perception.

That the emotion controlling someone affects his perception is a good part of the explanation of how a person is seduced to dissent from what is, for others, unambiguous. What it is perceived as (*per accidens*) differs for one moved by a particular emotion. The judgments based on this perception would be askew correspondingly. But this does not yet seem adequate to explain how, say, the lover gets all wrong what is plain to others, and never catches on. Of course, one should maintain that he constantly misconstrues, so long as the emotion is present. This must be part of the answer. But we should also recall the warmth and hastiness both of the dog and the servant mentioned in the *Nicomachean Ehics*. That warmth and hastiness helped to explain that and how he mishears what he hears. In addition, it helps to explain why neither the dog nor the servant takes in all the relevant information. Rather, they spring to action. Remember, the wary dog hears but does not look to see, so immediate is its reaction. Likewise, the amorous .person hears a little but through his emotion mishears, and springs to action (here, misjudges). But he has not listened to all the evidence, fastening on to some only, and that misheard and misjudged. All the rest he judges in terms of it.

There can, therefore, be a variety of reasons why the lover seems to be able to misjudge even in light of what appears to be insurmountable evidence to the contrary. What he takes in, he misconstrues. To the extent he continues to take in, he continues to misconstrue. Through his warmth and hastiness, and the expectation of emotion, he stops considering further evidence, and instead views the entire matter in terms of what he has already taken in and determined. This completes the fourth explanation of emotion altering judgments – though one should add that it may well be augmented by any of those methods discussed so far, the favor/disfavor method seeming very likely to be involved here.[11]

What spurred us on to search for a fourth explanation has been found: we have an explanation that does not rely on emotion having an aim or goal, and one that can account for the seduction of judgment though the evidence to the contrary is clear enough. Rather than rely on the end of the emotion, this explanation relies on the emotion having a certain expectation and a person's putting together what something is perceived as *per accidens* in light of this. This may be plausibly said of all emotions; and thus this explanation applies most generally.

5. Although the need to search for additional explanations has been fulfilled, this does not exhaust all the answers implicit in Aristotle for the ways in which emotion alters judgments. In the characterization of emotion at 1378a20-23, we find that pleasure and pain play a key part. Pleasure and pain can provide us with a further, albeit very general, explanation of the effect of emotion upon judgment. According to *De Anima* (431a8-10), as something is painful or pleasant it is avoided or pursued. Thus, the person experiencing a pleasant emotion (e.g. love) will be moved to focus on the matter more than he who is not in a state of pleasure. Contrariwise, the person experiencing a painful emotion (e.g. anger) will be moved to avoid

the matter, unlike the person not in a state of pain. Hence, the lover is better able to understand the beloved insofar as the pleasure of his emotion moves him to more attention to the beloved; and the one angry is less able to understand the object of his anger insofar as the distress of his emotion moves him to shun that object. Through attention or its opposite, one's judgments may be influenced. To this extent, things do not seem the same; and this is a fifth way in which emotion alters judgments.

Clearly this is a very general explanation, relating to emotions only insofar as they are pleasant or painful. Although a change in judgment is brought on by the pleasure or the pain of the emotion, the operation of that change is a result of attention or its lack. Moreover, it should be added that other considerations may alter the effect of pleasure and pain. Indeed, in the case of love, insofar as the previous explanations are appropriate, they tend to counteract the force of this explanation. So we should retain a readiness to admit that it could be overridden by other factors. Nevertheless, insofar as one feels pleasure or pain, one has a better or worse opportunity to understand. Insofar as one is so influenced, emotion alters judgment.

These different methods answer our question as to how well equipped Aristotle is to explain emotion's ability to alter judgment. He is very well equipped. Doubtless, there can be other answers consistent with the Aristotelian framework, and some of these we can anticipate. (For example, we might expect an explanation parallel with the fourth, but having expectation and 'putting together' alter judgment directly.) Nevertheless, it is these five that are implicit in Aristotle's works. Their complexity varies from the simplicity of the fifth to the intricacies of the fourth. All, I think, provide plausible solutions to the problem addressed. To this, it should be added, what has been hinted at before, namely that when we come to account for instances of emotions affecting judgment, often we shall find that more than one explanation is involved. They need not be separate. Still, the principles remain distinct; indeed, as the examples illustrate, cases can be imagined in which only one need apply. Thus we end with the following two species of the genus changes of judgment involving emotion: i) change of judgment as a consequence of emotion; ii) change of judgment as a constituent of emotion. The former has the following species: a) connivance, b) seduction through favor and disfavor, c) seduction of perception, d) seduction through pleasure and pain.

Having dealt with the first of our tasks, let us now consider the second aspect of Aristotle's characterization of emotion: pleasure and pain accompanying emotion. Some points may be readily stated. The definition of anger holds that it is with pain; contemplating, dwelling upon and achieving its revenge is pleasant (*Rhetoric*, 1378b1-5, 1370b29); those disposed to be angry are those in pain (ibid, 1379a10-21, cf. *De Anima* 403a18-20). And one can go on to cite similar information regarding the different *pathē*. But to do so would not go very far to explain what Aristotle means by pleasure and pain accompanying *ta pathē*.

What could Aristotle mean by saying that emotions are accompanied by pleasure and pain?[12] A number of interpretations are possible. This might have the status of an observation of a frequent concurrence, much like 'mothers accompany their daughters to new schools'. There is no necessity here: it is just that the two often or always concur. Alternatively, it could be a conceptual point. If so, there are at least two ways this might go. 'Accompanying' might suggest a link between two separate concepts, 'accompanying' relating the two; or the point might be that the concept of emotion includes within it an accompanying pleasure or pain. In addition, we must enquire into the nature of that which accompanies. Is the pain, for example, that accompanies shame an instance of pain of the same kind that accompanies anger? Or is the pain peculiar to shame and of a different sort from that which accompanies anger?

The thought that the accompaniment by pleasure and pain with emotion is like mothers and their daughters need not delay us very long. After all, the point is not stated in terms of 'it is often found that' or 'it is usually the case that' or 'it will be observed that'. Instead, the claim is stated as though a point were being made about the concept of emotion. Moreover, had the point been one of simple concurrence, then one would expect the language to reflect an analogous discussion in Plato's *Philebus*, using '*meta*' only and not '*hepetai*' to make the point about *ta pathē*.[13]

Although we should understand Aristotle to be making a conceptual point, an oddity remains. When contrasting hatred and anger (*Rhetoric*, 1382a11-13), Aristotle goes out of his way to point out that hatred, unlike anger, has no pain. Since the implication is not that hatred is a pleasure, the point must be that hatred is without feeling, cold, accompanied by neither pleasure nor pain. This is definitely out of step with the thesis that the concept of emotion involves pleasures and pain. Mind you, with this oddity noted, we should reject any suggestion that emotion being accompanied by pleasure and pain is anything other than a conceptual point about emotion.[14]

If 'accompanying' introduces a conceptual link, what sort of link is it? Is it a link between two distinct concepts, one always attending the other (perhaps as do cause and effect), or is it that the concept of emotion includes within it pleasure and pain? Now, simply speaking of 'accompanying' might suggest the former to us, so that, for example, when the definition of anger is given as a certain sort of longing, the pain could be understood as something necessarily accompanying this longing but itself distinct from the emotion. If true, this would mean that the pain was not part of the emotion, and would not be required in the definition of the emotion – though it would need to be noted as a necessary accompaniment of the emotion. Since we find that the accompanying pain is placed within anger's definition, Aristotle means more than a necessary accompaniment; emotion includes the pleasure or pain. This conclusion is further confirmed when we observe that many of the emotions are defined as pains or disturbances (e.g. fear, shame). Thus Aristotle includes pleasure and pain within the concept of emotion when he speaks of 'accompanying'.[15]

The link between emotion and accompanying pleasure and pain is conceptual. Further, pleasure and pain are part of the emotion. Now, we must ask whether the pain felt in, say fear, is unique to fear, or is it interchangeable with the pain of shame? Do the relevant pains or pleasures differ only in number and intensity? Before dealing with this question we should notice that even if the relevant pains or pleasures do not differ in kind, the absurdity would not follow that if, say, the judgment appropriate to fear was made and at the same time a pain arose (say, in the foot), one would then be afraid. This does not follow because the linking together of the elements in the definition is done in a way stronger than simple concurrence. This, I have argued, is part of the force of 'accompany'. Moreover, if we look at the definitions of the various emotions, consider fear, we find that the pain is not just conjoined with a particular judgment, but caused by that judgment. 'Let fear be defined as a pain or troubled feeling caused by the impression of an imminent evil that causes destruction or pain' (ibid, 1382a20-22). Thus, for a variety of reasons, there is no possibility that such an absurdity could follow within the Aristotelian framework.

Having dismissed such a misunderstanding, let us turn to our alternatives: the pain or pleasure of an emotion being unique, or the pain or pleasure being different in number and intensity but never in kind. The definitions given in the *Rhetoric* are plausibly interpreted either way; and within that work I see no reason for confidence that Aristotle holds that there are kinds of pleasures and pains.[16] It is tempting, then, to restrict oneself to the modest conclusion: the pains and pleasures of different emotion types differ in number and intensity but not in kind. However, if we expand our horizons somewhat, I think we shall see the stronger position to be Aristotle's. The *Nicomachean Ethics* provides reason to think that the pleasure or pain is specific to a given emotion and not shared with other emotions.

> For this reason, pleasures seem, too, to differ in kind. For things different in kind are, we think, completed by different things (we see this to be true both of natural objects and of things produced by art, e.g. animals, trees, a painting, a sculpture, a house, an implement); and, similarly, we think that activities differing in kind are completed by things differing in kind. Now the activities of thought differ from those of the senses, and both differ among themselves in kind; so therefore do the pleasures that complete them. (1175a22-28, Ross translator)

Given that Aristotle goes on to talk about the pleasures of flute playing as opposed to those of argument, and given that the pleasures of the different senses vary, it is reasonable to conclude, concerning emotions, that the pleasure of love differs in kind from that of joy. Likewise, it is reasonable to conclude that the pain of anger differs in kind from that of shame. Thus the pain or pleasure of emotions differ from one to another in number, intensity, and kind. This means that the proper reading of the definitions, again taking fear as our example, is the following: 'Let fear be defined as a painful feeling caused by . . .' rather than 'Let fear be defined as a painful or troubled feeling, caused by . . .'. The pleasure that accompanies completes the emotion, rather than supervenes upon it.[17]

We can say the following about the accompaniment of emotion by pleasure and pain. The pleasure or pain is part of the concept of the emotion; neither is separable from the emotion. For each emotion type there is a type of pleasure or pain peculiar to that emotion. They complete the emotion.[18]

With this observed, it must be recalled that the role of pleasure and pain in emotion is not exhausted by the 'accompanying' relationship. As noted already, in addition to the pain or pleasure of the emotion, contemplating and achieving the aim of the emotion (where appropriate) is pleasant, the bodily precondition for the emotion may be pleasant or painful, and so on.

III

Concerning Aristotle's characterization of emotions, we have seen how emotions alter judgment, are an alteration of judgment, and what it means to say that emotions are accompanied by pleasure and pain. We now come to our third, and perhaps most difficult task. Throughout, we have spoken of *ta pathē* as the emotions. That is surely the right translation, given the examples Aristotle offers us. But does his notion match our own?

Implicit in Fortenbaugh (in his 'Aristotle's Rhetoric on Emotions') is an answer to this question. Fortenbaugh takes the concern here to be clearly that of the emotions because he believes Aristotle's characterization of *ta pathē* is implicitly qualified in terms of the *Philebus*'s 'psychic attributes'. Because of this, *ta pathē* are held to be quite distinct from desires such as hunger and thirst; and all doubts that by '*ta pathē*' Aristotle has grasped the emotions are dispelled. Although I find this conclusion agreeable, I do not think Fortenbaugh's argument is adequate. First, there seems to be no reason to be confident that Aristotle's characterization is so qualified: Aristotle never hints at this. Second, Aristotle does offer a list of what are emotions and takes them to involve the body (*De Anima* 403a16-19). Thus the suggestion that *ta pathē* are distinct from desires because Aristotle thinks that emotions are 'psychic' rather than 'bodily' is not an accurate portrayal of Aristotle's position. Again, when it is recalled that Aristotle often does include bodily desire (*epithumia*) in with *ta pathē* (cf. note 2), Fortenbaugh's proposal becomes more and more doubtful. Indeed, even if it were clear that the *Philebus*'s qualification was intended, and we did not have to worry about *epithumia* or Aristotle's claim of a bodily nature for emotion, it still would not be evident that *ta pathē* are the emotions. For included in the *Philebus*'s psychic attributes are *pothos* (yearning) and *erōs* (sexual desire), 47e1-2. As is especially clear concerning sexual desire, these are and are seen to be types of desire (cf. *Republic* 549c6-8, *Rhetoric* 1385a24, *Nicomachean Ethics* 1118b8ff.). Hence, even were Aristotle to be building upon Plato, it does not seem that this itself is to grasp the notion of emotion. Consequently, if Aristotle has grasped the notion, this is not to follow old blue prints, but to redraw the boundaries within the human soul.

My own position is that Aristotle is redrawing boundaries. Yet that he is doing so requires justification; how and why he is doing so requires explanation. To resolve these matters, we should begin by turning our attention back to the *Rhetoric*'s characterization of *ta pathē*, examining how the 'accompaniment' of *hēdonē* and *lupē* sharpen and refine this notion.[19] This will lead us to consider other ways in which the *Rhetoric* hones *ta pathē*. Examining these matters should provide insight into what Aristotle understands by '*ta pathē*' here and elsewhere, how well it matches our own notion of emotion, and how it contrasts with Aristotle's notion of desire.

Let us begin with our concepts. Were we to try to set forth all the elements of our 'inner life', we would wind up with an extensive list, including yearnings, moods, thoughts, wants, perceptions, pleasures, satisfactions, hankerings, and so forth. Obviously, a complete list would fill pages, but I think the following distinctions will serve here to mark off major areas: 1. sensations, 2. desires, 3. emotions, 4. thoughts, 5. perceptions, 6. attitudes, 7. pleasure and pain. We shall examine the first six in light of the seventh. The object is to see what work the accompaniment of pleasure and pain accomplishes. This, I think, will provide some insight into Aristotle's notion of *ta pathē* with its accompaniment by *hēdonē* and *lupē*.

It seems to be the case that desires and emotions require pleasure and pain in a way sensations, attitudes, perceptions, and thoughts do not. Take thinking. As I think about how best to put my point, the process is neither pleasant nor painful; as I think about a vacation to France, the thought is pleasant. Thus, while pleasure or pain may attend my thoughts, there is no necessity to it.[20] Sensation too may be pleasant or painful: the warming of the sun is pleasant; its burning is painful. But sensation need not be either pleasant or painful, just as the sensation of a gurgling stomach or twitching eye is neither pleasant nor painful. Parallel considerations apply to perceptions and attitudes.[21] But emotions and desires (and here we are thinking of their occurrent manifestation) do not seem like this. My desire for a drink is something disturbing to me: its 'satisfaction' is just that, a pleasure. And this would seem to be so for all desires. Of emotion, it seems that it must in some way involve pleasure or pain. Anger, shame, sadness are themselves painful or distressing; love, joy are pleasant. The pleasure or pain of these is not just coincident, but necessary to the emotion or desire.

By speaking of what must involve pleasure and pain, we limit ourselves to emotions and desires. Turning to Aristotle, that is an interesting consequence. For, likewise, by speaking of *hēdonē*'s and *lupē*'s 'accompaniment', since that accompaniment is understood as a necessary and conceptual claim (cf. section II), Aristotle thereby limits himself to what we call emotions and desires. Moreover, all this seems to fit in with Aristotle's theorizing. For that Aristotle does take pleasure and pain to do this work concerning emotions is clear both through his claim that *ta pathē* (which, at least, include the emotions) are accompanied by pleasure and pain, and through his definitions of various emotions as types of pleasure and pain. That he takes pleasure and pain to be central to desire (*orexis*), and its other face, aversion, we see in *De Anima*, 431a8-16. What is pleasant is pursued;

what is painful is avoided. Again, in the *Rhetoric*, 1385a23-25, we see that desire (*orexis*) is a discomfort seeking satisfaction.

But how far does this get us?

We are seeking to understand what sort of notion Aristotle develops with *ta pathē* in the *Rhetoric*'s characterization of them. We have looked at the necessary accompaniment of pleasure and pain, finding that through this accompaniment we understand how a realm exhausted by emotions and desires is delimited. Yet the examples mentioned in the *Rhetoric*'s initial characterization of *ta pathē*, as well as the examples hegoes on to discuss, concern emotions only and not desires. We are, then, puzzled on our own terms as well as on Aristotle's by this exclusion.

There is the possibility that desire's exclusion from the *Rhetoric* is just an omission on Aristotle's part. Here it is worth recalling that lists of *ta pathē* in other works do include desire (e.g. *Nicomachean Ethics* 1105b21). Alternatively, the *Rhetoric* may develop in *ta pathē* a notion like that of emotion. But if this is so, the basis upon which Aristotle has excluded desire remains mysterious. These matters may be cleared up somewhat if we inspect Aristotle's analysis of desire, and try to find its proper place in Aristotle's psychology.[22]

I begin by observing that Aristotle's notion of desire (*orexis*) is not some one, homogeneous, all encompassing entity, rather it includes: 1. spiritedness, *thumos*; 2. wish, *boulēsis*; and 3. appetite, *epithumia* (*De Motu Animalium* 700b22, *De Anima* 414b2, *Eudemian Ethics* 1223a25-27).[23] The differences between these must be noted; and the exclusion or inclusion of any one of these from the *Rhetoric*'s notion of *ta pathē* must be considered and explained.

The characterization given of *thumos* is very much like that of anger, *orgē*. It too seems painful, while the prospect and achievement of its aim is a pleasant thing, revenge (*Eudemian Ethics* 1229b31, *Nicomachean Ethics* 1116b23-1117a9). Indeed, *thumos* is sometimes offered as an example of a *pathos* in the *Rhetoric*. However, this inclusion does not expand the notion of *ta pathē* beyond that of emotion, since when '*thumos*' is included, it is included as a synonomous expression for '*orgē*' (*Rhetoric* 1378b4, 1379a4).

Aristotle is not tempted to include *boulēsis* as a *pathos*; and this exclusion is quite appropriate. Pleasure and pain do not seem to characterize the desire. Moreover, *boulēsis*'s first aim is *to on kalon* (*Metaphysics* 1072a27, cf. *Rhetoric* 1369a2). *If* it relates to pleasure and pain at all in terms of its aim, it does so incidentally (cf. *Topics* 146b3, 147a1-4, *Rhetoric* 1381a1-4). Thus *boulēsis* does not satisfy the pleasure/pain test as emotion does, but, at most, as perception or thought does.[24] This is to say that *boulēsis* does not satisfy Aristotle's first test for *ta pathē*. Hence, this type of desire is not to be confused with emotion; and Aristotle has good reason to exclude *boulēsis* from his list of *ta pathē* in the *Rhetoric* and elsewhere (*Nicomachean Ethics* 1105b21, *Eudemian Ethics* 1220b12).

One might object that this last argument argues too much. Shame, *aischunē*, like *boulēsis*, does not aim at pleasure or pain, yet remains a *pathos*. Thus my argument that *boulēsis* does not aim at pleasure or pain is not a reason for its exclusion as a *pathos*. However, the cases are dramatically different. For while *boulēsis* only relates incidentally to pleasure or pain, shame is defined as a pain (*Rhetoric*, 1383b15). Thus this latter, but not the former, satisfies the pleasure/pain test; and *boulēsis* has rightfully been excluded as a *pathos*.

So far, so good. Aristotle does seem to be developing a notion like that of emotion. We have seen why neither *boulēsis* nor *thumos* create difficulties; we have only *epithumia* to contend with. Since *epithumia* is not mentioned in the passage from the *Rhetoric* we are concerned with, this development seems quite likely. However, we still have to find justification for *epithumia*'s exclusion. In addition, we need an account of why *epithumia* is not counted as a *pathos* here when it has been elsewhere (*Nicomachean Ethics* 1105b21, *Eudemian Ethics* 1220b12).[25]

First, we need look at *epithumia*. *Epithumia* (appetite or sensual appetite) is a desire for the pleasant (*Rhetoric* 1370a17, *De Anima* 414a5-6, *Topics* 147a2); like anger and other painful emotions it is characterized as painful (*Nicomachean Ethics* 1119a4). *Epithumiai* include and are explained in terms of the desires for food, drink, sex (*Nicomachean Ethics* 1118b8ff., cf. *De Anima* 414b13).[26] As something itself unpleasant craving the pleasure of satisfying its lack, movement as a result of appetite is not very mysterious (*De Anima* 433a25, cf. *Rhetoric* 1369b15, 1379a10-11). It is taken to be contrary to choice (*Nicomachean Ethics* 1111b16), a wild beast (*Politics* 1287a31). Its operation occurs without involving reason: 'But appetite leads without persuading, being devoid of reason' (*Eudemian Ethics* 1224b2). We have here something well suited to causal analysis.

From this characterization, we can see that *epithumia*'s exclusion (unlike *boulēsis*'s) cannot be accounted for through failing to satisfy the pleasure/pain test. Moreover, there is no indication (as there was concerning *thumos*) that '*epithumia*' is but another name for an emotion. What, then, accounts for its absence from the *Rhetoric*? I suggest that what justifies this desire's exclusion is the *Rhetoric*'s other major characterization of *ta pathē*: emotions being the things on account of which the ones altered differ with respect to their judgments. If I am right in saying that *epithumia* is excluded because it does not meet this demand, then the *Rhetoric* delimits what we mean by emotions, offers a justification of this, and advances beyond Plato's spirited realm. A fascinating and perceptive development. But one that requires some argument before we grant it. Although *epithumiai* do not seem to be emotions, and the *Rhetoric*'s exclusion of them as *pathē* seems to be a recognition of this, we cannot really be sure that it is this until we see that that part of the characterization of *ta pathē* which speaks of altering judgments does properly exclude *epithumiai*.

I think that it does. There is no need for a difference in judgment between one thirsty and one hungry: they may hold all the same judgments, but the former seeks food while the latter seeks drink. Indeed, being hungry or thirsty does not require the holding of any particular judgments, or any judgments at all. Moreover, it is not itself a reasonable or unreasonable state. As Aristotle suggests, it is devoid of reason (*Eudemian Ethics* 1224b2). However, as Aristotle recognizes, emotions are rather different from this. Those in a different emotional state do differ with respect to judgment, e.g. whereas the envious man will view another's good fortune as undeserved, the emulous will not. Being in an emotional state requires judgments, particular judgments. Moreover, it is itself reasonable (fear of a formidable enemy) or unreasonable (fear of a mouse).

Thus the two, epithumetic desire and emotion, do seem importantly different with regard to the role of judgments. It would seem, then, that Aristotle has noted the difference, distinguished the realms, and provided justification for this.

Still, one might doubt that what Aristotle has set forth is really adequate, even though right-headed. After all, is there not a sense in which an *epithumia* might bring about a change of judgments? For example, hunger's pang could make one so irritable that one comes to a very harsh view of someone who interferes with one's attempt to acquire food. Again, the alcoholic's thirst may be so strong that the person decides that the wood alcohol is not so bad. However, it is not the hunger or the thirst that alters judgment. For, as we have seen, what these desires do is seek out their own satisfaction. Rather, the difference in judgment that may arise in such situations will arise through one's anger, irritation, despair, or reflections upon these matters. And Aristotle follows this up by noting that emotions often arise when desire is present.

> Men are angry when they are pained, because one who is pained aims at something; if then anyone directly opposes him in anything, as for instance, prevents him from drinking when thirsty, or not directly, but seems to be doing just the same; and if anyone goes against him or refuses to assist him, or troubles him in any other way

> when he is in this frame of mind, he is angry with all such persons. Wherefore the sick, the necessitous, the love-sick, the thirsty, in a word, all who desire something and cannot obtain it, are prone to anger and easily excited . . . (*Rhetoric*, 1379a10-17, translated by Freese)

Any change of judgment here is only an incidental result of hunger or thirst, and quite remote from it. Epithumetic desire is not sufficiently complex to speak of it as altering judgments. The changes of judgments are to be explained by emotions or reflections upon these matters.

Aristotle is right in thinking that emotions are quite different from these desires, *epithumiai*; and he is able to locate just what accounts for the difference. Like epithumetic desire emotions too have an object, involve pleasure and pain, and through this latter are involved in pursuit and avoidance. However, in addition, emotions have a much more wide-ranging aim. Through expectation, they alter the way we put things together. Moreover, they require judgments. And because of this emotions are themselves alterations of judgments (anger views its object as having insulted one, *Rhetoric* 1378a31), and alter judgments (hope leads to a better view of one's prospects, ibid 1378a1-4). In contrast, because *epithumia* has only the satisfaction of eating, drinking, etc., what counts as satisfaction here is much more restricted; and it will not involve changes of judgment. That Aristotle excludes *epithumia* from the list in the *Rhetoric* is justified; *epithumia* as an emotion does not belong.[27]

The thesis that Aristotle is delimiting a realm of emotions finds further confirmation. For not only does Aristotle recognize the difference between *epithumiai* and emotions, but also he utilizes this difference. Aristotle discusses the nature of *epithumia*, making the point that it is not subject to rational principle (is not reasonable or unreasonable). Moreover, when strong and violent it can expel the power of calculation (*Nicomachean Ethics* 1119b5-15). Thus the angry man may reason poorly in deciding to wreak a terrible vengeance; the man of unquenchable thirst does not reason at all, but simply seeks the object of his desire.

This role for *epithumia* is utilized elsewhere. For example, in a discussion of incontinence Aristotle's position is not that the desire for the sweet alters one's universal opinion forbidding tasting. Rather, one follows one's desire to taste and loses sight of the universal opinion. Once more, desire seems to *expel* rather than alter reasoning (*Nicomachean Ethics* 1147a25-b17). All this is rather different from the way, say, hope brings about a favorable interpretation of what is ambiguous or envy views the good fortune of another as undeserved.

Yet another utilization of the difference between *epithumia* and emotion has to do with the obedience of emotion, but not *epithumia,* to reason. If emotions are the sorts of things that rationally alter our judgments, one can expect them to be open to reason. Similarly, if *epithumia* does not rationally alter judgments, one would not expect it to be open to reason. Aristotle appreciates this when he says:

> Therefore anger obeys the argument in a sense, but appetite does not. It is therefore more disgraceful; for the man who is incontinent in respect of anger is in a sense conquered by argument, while the other is conquered by appetite and not argument. (*Nicomachean Ethics*, 1149b1-4, Ross' translation, cf. 1119b7)

This contrast is fairly drawn between *epithumia* and emotions in general. Thus while you might convince a person not to act on his *epithumia*, say, for food, you cannot talk him out of feeling hungry. Hence, we find Aristotle observing: '. . . it is assumed that there is no gain in being persuaded not to be hot or in pain or hungry or the like, since we shall experience these feelings none the less' (*Nicomachean Ethics* 1113b27-30). In contrast, not only might you convince a person not to act on his emotion, say fear, but also you might talk him right out of it. This latter you might do by convincing him that one of his judgments whence his fear arose was wrong, or you might convince him that even though all is as he judged, the object he fears is not worth fearing. And by convincing him you also move him.[28] The contrast between the two is that while we give grounds for emotions, we only give causes for thirst and other *epithumiai.* Thus the former, but not the latter, is, in this sense, conquered by argument. Thus it is the former, but not the latter, that Aristotle concerns himself with and explains the grounds upon which they are felt (*Rhetoric* 1378a28).

In view of the interaction between the rational soul and desire, we must digress to notice that the contrast between epithumetic desire and emotion becomes more complicated in certain instances. Epithumetic desires, we have seen, are the sorts of things that get set in motion, halted, stemmed, suppressed, expelled, etc. The causal chains for any particular desire can be quite diverse. Consider sexual desire. Gestures, clothing, movement, glances, pictures – all these may serve to 'turn one on or off'. A causal conception is in operation here in a clearcut way. However, it may seem a little less clearcut when we consider that reading certain passages from novels may have the same effect. For here it seems as though epithumetic desire is available to reason. However, there are two objections to this conclusion. First, the case remains one of being 'turned on' or 'off', of causation. Although reading the novel may dampen or arouse one's ardour, still one has been turned off or on, shocked or titillated. One has not been reasoned into anything or persuaded, in the way one may be moved to anger by being persuaded that Fred has insulted you or by deliberating upon Fred's character. So whereas emotion admits of rational persuasion, epithumetic desire still is not available to reason. The complication here has been that, as an animal capable of reason, the means of turning on and off epithumetic desire are that much richer, involving the rational soul, but still not in a way to be confused with emotion's involvement with the rational soul. Second, to the extent one still wants to say: 'No, my desire really has been rationally altered here', that we can quite happily accommodate by the operation of *boulēsis*, not *epithumia*. That is to say, in the example above, we have not only epithumetic desire in operation, but also rational desire. For that the desires are distinct has no implication about forced separability or lack of interplay amongst them. And it is possible that deliberative desire could enter into the picture here.[29] Thus the contrast between *epithumia* and emotion stands.[30]

Hence, not only is the exclusion of *epithumia* and all desire from the list in the *Rhetoric* reasonable, but also the implications are appreciated and utilized elsewhere.

What I have just argued is that in the *Rhetoric* and elsewhere Aristotle shows a perceptive awareness of the differences of operation of epithumetic desire and emotion. Before that I argued that other sorts of desire (*thumos* and *boulēsis*) do not interfere with the suggestion that Aristotle is delimiting the realm of emotion in the *Rhetoric*. My conclusion is that the characterization of *ta pathē* in the *Rhetoric* distinguishes emotion from other elements of our inner life: the pleasure/pain test setting emotion and certain desires quite apart from the other elements, the alteration of judgment setting emotion quite apart from *epithumia*.[32] That the *Rhetoric* does not mention or expand upon the *pathos epithumia* is not an oversight or error, but a recognition that *epithumia* is not an emotion.[32]

Setting forth the notion of emotion is a sophisticated advance within the realm of philosophical psychology. However, at least one problem lingers. Why is *epithumia* here excluded from the list of of *ta pathē*, while elsewhere included? Historical explanations are often employed in this sort of situation, arguing, for example, that here Aristotle abandons the Platonic psychology that mesmerized him elsewhere. However, we cannot be certain that the *Rhetoric* is Aristotle's last word in this area of psychology; and since Aristotle utilizes these distinctions at some points in his ethical works (see above), but does not utilize them at other points (*Nicomachean Ethics* 1105b21, *Eudemian Ethics* 1120b12), an historical explanation cannot resolve this problem. We must search for some other sort of explanation. There are a number of possibilities.

The most radical one suggests that the picture of *ta pathē* that has emerged is all wrong. In the *Rhetoric* Aristotle simply chose not to use *epithumia* as an example; and we have made a mountain from what is not even a mole hill. But too much has been gained; there is too much rigor, too much perceptiveness, too much following out of consequences on Aristotle's part for this explanation to be seriously entertained.

A different explanation urges that sometimes Aristotle wrongly includes *epithumia* (*Nicomachean Ethics* 1105b21, *Eudemian Ethics* 1220b12). There are the differences noted between *epithumia* and *ta pathē*; he is aware of them; yet his inclusion of *epithumia* in the lists of *ta pathē* in the ethical works is a lapse, a failure to appreciate fully and mark out adequately what he does elsewhere. Alternatively, one can suggest that Aristotle is driving at a slightly different point than our analysis of the *Rhetoric* suggests. What he really wants to do is to note a group of things that a) relate to pleasure and pain, and b) 'in one way or another', however remotely, alter judgment. These all *ta pathē* do, including *epithumia*. *Epithumia*'s absence from the *Rhetoric* is just a failure to list fully. That we find very important differences between the 'one way' and the 'other' is interesting and important to us, but does not signify for Aristotle's analysis of *ta pathē*. He may be dividing the cake differently from us, but not therefore mistakenly.

These two approaches are not really that far apart. The latter tries to claim that Aristotle's conceptions when brought forth on his own terms are somewhat different from our own – though it admits that at certain points he does draw the contrasts as we do. The former views Aristotle in terms of distinctions we make (accusing him, in parallel and quite important passages in his ethical works, of failing to appreciate adequately what he at other times takes to be important). Neither of these ways of resolving the matter is as satisfactory as we might want. Both interpretations make Aristotle's analysis of *ta pathē* broken backed and admit that he should have been aware of the broken nature. The former view's contention that in the ethical works Aristotle is simply guilty of a glaring error through his inclusion of *epithumia* as a *pathos* is difficult to believe. Equally difficult to believe is the latter view's contention that though Aristotle is aware that emotions as such alter judgments, while epithumetic desires do not, he nevertheless ignores this in the *Rhetoric* opting for an 'in one way or another' – especially since *epithumia* is not listed or discussed there. Also difficult to believe on the latter interpretation is Aristotle's silence about his own thesis that emotions but not *epithumiai* are altered by reason. In addition, this interpretation by supposing *epithumia* as a legitimate candidate for a *pathos* in the *Rhetoric* fails to appreciate that whereas the *pathē* Aristotle does mention and discuss do have a 'with whom', *epithumia* does not. Thus neither of these explanations can be accepted. Moreover, when we look at the much greater scope given to *ta pathē* in *De Anima* 403a1-7, 17-19, and the *Categories* 9b9-10a10, we realize that something different might be occurring than has been suggested so far.

The clue to a more satisfactory explanation (not without its own difficulties) is found in the last observation. Rather than trying to find a unified or developing (though broken backed) theory of *ta pathē*, let us look carefully at the different contexts in which Aristotle deals with *ta pathē*; and let us allow that Aristotle's use of '*ta pathē*' may vary in extension and intension with the purposes at hand. We shall focus on the relevant discussions in the *Rhetoric, Eudemian Ethics*, and *Nicomachean Ethics*.

We have seen that the two criteria present in the *Rhetoric* distinguish in an insightful way the emotions from the other elements of one's inner life. The examples Aristotle chooses, develops, and excludes bear this out. Turning to the lists of *ta pathē* in the ethical works, we find similar lists, though *epithumia* is included. Hence these are not lists of the emotions. Moreover, we should notice that though we do find the pleasure/pain test, we do *not* find anything about altering judgments.[33] Consequently, the lists with their inclusion of *epithumia* match perfectly with the single pleasure/pain test. Viewed in this way, Aristotle seems to wield the two principles with great sensitivity to their implications both in the *Rhetoric*, the *Eudemian Ethics*, and the *Nicomachean Ethics*.

Well and good, we might think, but still it remains puzzling in its way. Why does Aristotle speak of *ta pathē* in these similar, but importantly different ways? Why not stick with one, preferably the most subtle?

These differences in intension and extension can be explained, I believe, by noticing the issues Aristotle is addressing at a given time. At the appropriate places in the ethical works, Aristotle is trying to discover where virtue lies. The alternatives he offers are: *pathē, dunameis, hexeis*. In light of these contrasts and the goals sought, it seems quite reasonable that *ta pathē* should include more than emotion. The distinction between epithumetic desire and emotion does not matter to his ongoing discussion. Whether *ta pathē* are subject to reason will not matter to the discovery that virtue is a *hexis*. Indeed, given that Aristotle wants to hold that virtue concerns the *pathē*, he means it to concern epithumetic desire as well as the emotions. For virtue concerns those occurrent rumblings which may lead us astray, whether they be rumblings subject to reason or not.[34] Hence, Aristotle does not bother about the second criterion; and *epithumia* is rightly included. Here '*ta pathē*' resemble what Hume and others call 'the passions'. However, when Aristotle's purposes are different – when he is trying to offer a theory of those affections relevant to rhetorical purposes, when he is trying to avoid the Platonic tendency of seeing rhetoric as sophistical, and when, as in certain parts of the ethical works, he is trying to illustrate the differences between *epithumia* and anger – then the differences between things that do and do not influence judgment, are and are not influenced by judgment is crucial. The *Rhetoric*'s interest in *ta pathē* has to do with persuasion and as a result Aristotle sharpens the notion to those things that do affect judgment. Thus Aristotle excludes *epithumia* which does not similarly affect judgment. Moreover, this explains the introduction of his second criterion, a criterion not introduced elsewhere.[35]

Aristotle does not hold a broken backed theory with all its awkwardnesses. Moreover, we appreciate how skilfully Aristotle uses the different senses of '*ta pathē*'. Where he is concerned to speak of the role of judgments concerning affection, he adequately gives the notion of *ta pathē* as emotion. Where his interest is not so specific, he includes *epithumia* in with emotions, but there correctly excludes the judgment criterion. And where his concern, as in *De Anima*, is with any affection of the soul, he properly drops the pleasure/pain criterion. In all these cases the theory is adequate, skilful, and is not subject to the above complaints.[36]

This completes our third task. If the arguments are right, the consequences are impressive. In the *Rhetoric* Aristotle develops a notion of emotion to which he turns elsewhere. As well as coming to this notion, he isolates those features that set emotion apart from other elements of the human soul. We have come to see what it means to say that *ta pathē* are accompanied by *hēdonē* and *lupē*, as well as how these help to refine the notion of emotion. We have come to see the ways in which *ta pathē* can alter judgment, as well as how this also helps to refine the notion of emotion. In addition, we have seen that Aristotle is quite able to call upon the notion of emotion when needed, and related notions when they are needed. By this ability to wield the features that distinguish these notions, by his sensitivity to the different notions and their place, we see an extremely subtle philosopher at work.

University of Texas.

NOTES

[1] I should like to take this opportunity to thank Professor J. L. Ackrill, J. Barnes, D. Browning, L. Judson, P. Mitchell, and the Euthyphrones Discussion Group for their criticisms and suggestions. Where I have not profitted as I should, the fault is mine alone.

[2] One might think that the concern is so obviously that of emotion that this question hardly bears investigation. Given the examples he offers, given that *ta pathē* are meant to be occurrent phenomena, given that 'the emotions' is a reasonable translation of '*ta pathē*', Aristotle has surely grasped the notion of emotion here. However, we need to be a little more cautious before drawing this conclusion. For there are more occurrent phenomena than emotions; and Aristotle often includes as a *pathos epithumia*, a type of desire which includes hunger and thirst (*Nicomachean Ethics* 1105b21, *Eudemian Ethics* 1120b12). This plus doubts that Plato ever clearly distinguishes emotion and desire should lead us to take this question very seriously. Should it turn out that Aristotle does develop the notion of emotion, he has redrawn psychic boundaries in a very insightful way.

[3] How dramatic is very apparent in the case of Ergophilus. Concerning the exhausting of anger and consequent growing mild, Aristotle observes:

> For although the Athenians were more indignant with him than with Callisthenes, they aquitted him, because they had condemned Callisthenes to death on the previous day. (*Rhetoric* 1380b11-14, Freese translator)

[4] In his stated definitions of pity and indignation an aim is not explicitly announced. Rather, it is part of the larger concept of these emotions. We find the same thing in envy and emulation. Part of the concept of envy involves preventing one's neighbour from possessing certain goods, while emulation strives to make oneself fit for such goods (*Rhetoric* 1388a35-37). From these aims, which are part of the concept of emotion (but not part of their stated definitions), we still can explain certain changes of judgment.

[5] It is plausible that there will be certain cases in which there is no such discrepancy. Someone might forget what he did believe and so come to be persuaded by his own pronouncement.

[6] The alteration is a seduction unless one is simultaneously aware of the presence and workings of the disposition and desire. Such awareness is not typical, though it is certainly possible.

[7] I assume that *thumos* is meant to be an emotion. This seems to accord with most translations and with the *Rhetoric*, in which Aristotle happily switches from *thumos* to *orgē*. This point, I comment on later.

[8] If J. Cooper is right (in an unpublished paper "Aristotle on the Ontology of the Senses"), then contrary to Hamlyn's translation of *De Anima*, '*krinein*' means 'distinguish', not 'judge'; and the perceiving of both types of objects is, properly speaking, a matter of perception.

[9] This is a variation of an example of Cooper's.

[10] Concerning the plausibility of the thesis, modern theorists would be inclined to reject different types of objects of perception, speaking instead of differences in perception. However one chooses to characterize the difference, there is here an additional, distinct way in which emotion alters judgment.

[11] Under the favor/disfavor case I include what is objectively ambiguous. In the case of misperception I have spoken of what is not itself ambiguous. An interesting case is one in which something is not itself ambiguous, but seems so due to carelessness or inattention. This sounds very much like the case of the hasty servant. When the carelessness concerns perception, it is. However, where something seems ambiguous through inattention in evaluation, then we have a second version of the favor/disfavor case: one version explicable by the ambiguity of the phenomena; the other explicable by ambiguity arising through inattention.

[12] K. J. J. Hintikka, "On the Interpretation of 'De Interpretatione' XII-XIII", in his *Time and Necessity* (Oxford, 1973), pp. 53-5, speaks of the meaning of '*hepesthai*'. Unfortunately, his conclusions are meant to be restricted to that text, and will not help us here.

[13] The problems that arise in the *Philebus* through using '*meta*' to explain the place of pleasure and pain, and Aristotle's appreciation of this in his *Topics* with respect to the emotions is nicely illustrated by W. W. Fortenbaugh, "Aristotle's Rhetoric on Emotions", *AGP* 52, 1970, 40-70, at pp. 55-6.

[14] One attempt to resolve this apparent anomaly would be to observe that hatred should take pleasure in the destruction of the hated. Even if true, it is to be explained by the fact that contemplating and achieving one's aim is pleasant (*Rhetoric* 1370b29, 1378b1-5). It is no more a matter of hatred being a pleasure than the sweetness of anger's revenge is a matter of anger being a pleasure.

I suspect that part of the reason for this anomaly is that the description of hatred in the *Rhetoric* is similar to what is elsewhere called a *hexis*. Since a *hexis* has more a dispositional than occurrent tone, the need to speak of pleasure or pain is that much weaker. But this is only partially satisfying. For hatred remains classed as a *pathos*.

[15] If this is right, then although we find Aristotle using '*meta*' in his definition of anger, the '*hepetai*' controls the '*meta*'. The accompaniment of pleasure and pain does not suddenly become contingent here.

[16] That being pained disposes one to emotion (*Rhetoric*, 1379a10-21), and that the point seems to be about pain in general, rather than a matching between a certain sort of pain predisposing one and a corresponding emotion disposed to might suggest that there are not kinds of pains and pleasures in emotion. However, that the pains that predispose one do not divide into kinds is no reason to doubt that the pain of the emotion does so divide. After all, the pain of anger is not the pain in one's tooth that has disposed one to anger.

[17] Actually, Aristotle does not offer a full analysis of pain in the *Nicomachean Ethics*. But he often considers pleasure and pain in terms of health and disease. If pain is like disease, then it is a privation of pleasure; and as a divergence from a pleasant condition, separating pains into kinds becomes messy. More serious problems in applying an analysis of pain implicit in the *Nicomachean Ethics* to emotion occur insofar as a pleasure proper to each activity would imply that the activity of being angry or being ashamed would be a pleasure. This is both absurd and contrary to Aristotle's analysis of these emotions. Hence, the analysis of pain in the *Nicomachean Ethics* is unsuited in some respects to account for painful emotions.

The problem could be resolved by giving pain its own character (not simply a privation), and admitting that pains complete certain activities. Thus pain would as much complete anger as pleasure completes love. However, to the extent that the *Nicomachean Ethics* offers an account of pain, this is not it (but see note 20).

[18] It is not the case that the completion in the case of flute playing or argument is just like the completion in the case of the emotions. For while flute playing can occur without being completed, the emotions do not. Anger is not anger unless it is painful.

[19] To avoid confusion I will use Greek terms for Aristotle's concepts, and English terms for modern concepts.

[20] One might object that by Aristotle's analysis of *hēdonē* and *lupē* in the *Nicomachean Ethics*, this claim could not be made. For any unhindered activity should be pleasant, including thinking. Thus an attempt to see what is behind the notion of *ta pathē* in the *Rhetoric* is doomed if one continues in this way. However, we have already seen that some thoughts on pleasure and pain in the *Nicomachean Ethics* are out of step with the analysis

in the *Rhetoric*. Ttus I am not assuming Aristotle to be bound in every detail to the theory in the *Nicomachean Ethics*; I am allowing that in thinking out a different problem Aristotle might not depend upon or be loyal to some of his conclusions elsewhere. This may be to skate on rather thin ice, but it is not unusual for Aristotle to forgo theoretical consistency for observations closer to the truth. Moreover, there is evidence to suggest that some of the thoughts on pleasure and pain are different in the *Rhetoric*. Many of the emotions are defined as types of pain. It seems implausible that by this each is meant to be a lack of something. A lack of what? Thus the disease model is inappropriate here. Pain seems to be understood as having a character of its own; and that is why it is sufficient for the definitions of the various emotions. Not every unhindered activity is pleasant. Elsewhere (*Eudemian Ethics* 1220b13), Aristotle speaks of perceptible pleasure and pain. Here too the disease model is unlikely. Thus we can expect some unhindered activities to be pleasant, others to be painful, others still to be neither pleasant nor painful.

21 At one point in *De Anima*, 413b23, Aristotle speaks of *aisthēsis*, including pleasure and pain (cf. *De Sensu* 436a8-11). This does not disturb my thesis, since I take his point there to be that where we speak of *aisthēsis*, the possibility of pleasure or pain is introduced, and not that *aisthēsis* must be pleasant or painful, i.e. not that it must be accompanied by pleasure or pain. That this is the right way to interpret Aristotle is suggested by the erroneous nature of the alternative interpretation. It finds further confirmation in the fact that where Aristotle speaks of *ta pathē* and explicates this with 'accompanying pleasure and pain', he does not introduce *aisthēsis* as an example (*Rhetoric* 1378a20, *Eudemian Ethics* 1220b12, *Nicomachean Ethics* 1105b21), whereas when *ta pathē* have been expanded and *aisthēsis* is included, the claim of an accompaniment by *hēdonē* and *lupē* is dropped (*De Anima* 403a1-7).

22 That desire is not an emotion may need some argument. Its inclusion is counter-intuitive; and I shall advance arguments shortly, one consequence of which is to distinguish emotion from desire.

23 For a somewhat different analysis of the desires than the one to follow see M. C. Nussbaum's edition of *De Motu Animalium*, pp. 334-337.

24 Aristotle's earlier claim that desire is a discomfort seeking satisfaction is, effectively, modified in the case of *boulēsis*. This, in part, is an appreciation of the point that the intellectual desires do not run along the same lines of distress and pleasure in the way bodily desires do.

25 It is noteworthy that Fortenbaugh supposes that '*ta pathē*' in the passages from the *Ethics* means 'the emotions' (cf. "Aristotle and the Questionable Mean-Dispositions", *TAPA* 99, 1968, 203-31, at p. 207). Here too the reference to the 'psychic attributes' from Plato's *Philebus* is thought to be implicit. Earlier, I suggested, concerning the *Rhetoric*, that this reference to the *Philebus* was both questionable, and, if true, still does not provide us with the notion of emotion. Thus, I argued that care is needed when claiming that the concern of the *Rhetoric* was that of emotions. These considerations apply to the passages from the *Ethics* as well. More importantly, the inclusion of *epithumia* (which for Aristotle is to include desires such as hunger and thirst) in the *Ethics* precludes the idea that here Aristotle is implicitly referring to the *Philebus*'s 'psychic attributes' and bars the claim that by '*ta pathē*' in the relevant passage from the *Ethics* Aristotle means 'the emotions'. What it does mean, we shall see shortly.

It must be emphasized that this dispute about the *Ethics* (and the *Rhetoric*) cannot be dismissed as 'quibbling'. For, as Fortenbaugh himself is keen to show, there is a world of difference for Aristotle between the operation and nature of shame or fear versus hunger or thirst. Where Aristotle includes or excludes these latter is significant.

[26] I am not here concerned to compare and contrast each sort of desire. However, I would like to emphasize one point of contrast between *epithumia* and *boulēsis*. While *epithumia* aims at the pleasure of food or drink, *boulēsis* may take pleasure in achieving its aim (*to on kalon*) but does not act for the sake of such pleasure (cf. *Eudemian Ethics* 1235b19-24).

[27] A quite different and less central consideration for the distinction between *epithumia* and *ta pathē* arises when we consider one of the headings under which *ta pathē* are analyzed, the person before whom one typically feels the *pathos* (*Rhetoric* 1378a24). *Ta pathē* seem to involve one with others: the person loved, hated, angry with, ashamed before, etc. *Epithumia* is not like this. Thirst is not bound up with others, but with the seeking of drink. So, similarly, hunger, and the desires of the senses. Erotic desire seems out of tune with this insofar as the object typically is another person. Short of withdrawing the point of contrast, one might urge that erotic desire can be satisfied without the existence of another, but *philia* cannot. Second, there need be no social involvement with another in the case of *erōs*, while there is with *philia* and other emotions. Thus while *ta pathē* require others, *epithumia* does not.

[28] This latter would be a matter of convincing a person to change his values. So by converting to Buddhism one might lose one's fear of dying.

It is important that emotions only 'listen to argument to some extent' (*Nicomachean Ethics* 1149a25, cf. *De Memoria et Reminiscentia* 453a25-30). The thesis is not so strong that the relevant change about the facts or values is or forces a change of emotion. Rather, emotion is available to reason. Aristotle leaves room for what we call irrational emotions, be they so from lack of foundation in the first place (fear of a mouse) or loss of a foundation. Hence, to convince is not necessarily to move. (Here we have a further contrast between *boulēsis* and *ta pathē*. In addition to failing to satisfy the pleasure/pain test, *boulēsis* does not just listen to some extent.)

[29] That *boulēsis* is available to reason is not in question. Its exclusion from the realm of emotion has been accounted for on other grounds. It is also worth emphasizing here that the attempt has not been to say that Aristotle's distinctions within desire match our own. Rather, the attempt has been to say that Aristotle's characterization of *ta pathē* excludes desire; and *ta pathē* matches our notion of emotion.

[30] But is not there still a sense in which one can and does speak of having 'reasonable appetites'? Yes, but this sense is the following: one's appetites are well brought up so that what they desire is in conformity with rational principle. Unlike rational principle or emotions, *epithumia* is not itself rational, but spoken of so only insofar as it happens to conform to *logos*. The truly virtuous have such *epithumiai*; the continent and incontinent do not. As a result, these latter have to control their *epithumiai*, though, as we have seen, sometimes *epithumia* will expel any reasoning present.

[31] That part of *thumos* which is not to be seen as equivalent to *orgē* is excluded from the realm of emotion by this second test. Moreover, were one dissatisfied with the exclusion of *aisthēsis* (cf. note 21) its exclusion from *ta pathē* is supported by this test.

[32] There are two spots in Aristotle that might present difficulties for this understanding of desire, and consequently the distinction between it and emotion. First, *Rhetoric* 1370a19-25 distinguishes desire into rational and irrational desire, instead of the typical triad. The rational desires seem to be more sophisticated. Such desires do not present serious problems for my analysis. For though this is a different way of examining desire, it can be dealt with in much the same fashion I dealt with the sophistication within erotic desire, and the sense of 'reasonable appetites' spoken of in note 30. Second, a discussion

of the soul in the *Nicomachean Ethics* (book one, chapter thirteen) may seem to present problems. There Aristotle talks of *hormai*, impulses. These seem to be available to reason, yet they do seem to be *boulēsis*. Still, this is not too troublesome. They are said to be reasonable and listen to reason as does the son to the father. Now, this seems to be a matter of a certain sort of habituation. If so, this is a 'reasonable' appetite of the sort mentioned in note 30. Moreover, the discussion of *hormai* is unique and very difficult to square with the earlier discussion of the soul in chapter nine, as well as with the discussions in *De Anima*. So, at worst, this passaga can be dealt with as a matter of Aristotle wandering from his normal path. Most importantly, Aristotle makes it perfectly clear that this discussion lacks precision (1102a22-32). That Aristotle himself does not take this way of dividing the soul too seriously means that we need not be bothered if it conflicts with more serious attempts to understand distinctions within the human soul. It is these latter that are the important ones.

[33] The absence of this criterion is further evidence that Aristotle is up to something very different in the *Ethics* than he is in the *Rhetoric*; and that '*ta pathē*' in the *Ethics* cannot be 'the emotions'.

[34] This is another reason why Fortenbaugh cannot be right in his understanding of '*ta pathē*' from the relevant passages in the *Ethics* (cf. his "Aristotle, Virtue and Emotion", *Arethusa* 2, 1969, 163-85, esp. note 24). Virtue is not just a preparation and control regarding emotions and actions, but also *epithumiai*. The inclusion of these desires is more in the Aristotelian spirit. For, as we observed in note 30, the man of perfect virtue has trained his desires so as to be moderate in them, while the continent man is not moderate in them, but has control over them. Indeed, Aristotle's whole picture of moral education has to do with the training of the emotions and desires. Not only does this way of understanding what *ta pathē* are in the *Ethics* create a more Aristotelian view, but also a more accurate one. For the inclusion of the control of one's desires seems to help create a better description of virtue's place in our moral life.

[35] I shall not here deal with the passages from the *Categories* or *De Anima* in detail. They are interesting, but a full analysis would take us far afield; and would not help us with the issues here. Let me only say that a similar approach to these passages will explain the use of '*ta pathē*' there. The general direction would seem to be the following. In *De Anima* the concern is whether attributes of the soul involve the body. '*Ta pathē*' is used to collect these attributes; and hence the list is much expanded from any so far examined (ibid, 403a1-7). A second list 403a17-19 more closely resembles that of the *Rhetoric*, because emotions are more obviously bodily than perception, thought and other such attributes mentioned in the first list. But it must be said of both lists that the remarks are problem-initiating rather than problem-solving. Hence Aristotle uses a very non-technical and non-refined sense of '*ta pathē*'. Indeed, he provides no criterion for them. In the *Categories* a general interest in *ta pathē* brings Aristotle to speak of those of the soul. These seem to be occurrent rather than dispositional features; and their temporary nature is featured. Again, a rather non-technical conception is in use. Aristotle is roughly mapping the area, rather than sharpening a philosophical tool with which to resolve a particular problem. As we have seen, matters are rather different in the *Rhetoric* and the *Ethics*.

[36] Although this does solve our problems, I mentioned that even this proposal has a difficulty. In the *Rhetoric* (1388b33), having completed his analysis of *ta pathē* Aristotle reviews his progress. At this point he does include *epithumia* as a *pathos*. This runs contrary to Aristotle's development here. Indeed, given Aristotle's understanding of *epithumia* (see above), this inclusion must be seen either as an uncareful moment, or as

the destruction of all that Aristotle has sought to achieve in his characterization and explanation of *ta pathē* in the *Rhetoric*. Thus I would suggest that it be seen as an uncareful moment.

I should add that one alternative explanation of what Aristotle has done in the *Rhetoric* yet remains. Instead of seeing Aristotle as defining a notion of emotion which is distinct from desire, one might suggest that what Aristotle has done is to refine a subset within desire (*orexis*); the subset is emotion. Evidence for this view would include Aristotle's inclusion of *thumos* as one of the key notions of *orexis*, yet his willingness to understand '*thumos*' as synonymous with '*orgē*'. Evidence consistent with this includes both the exclusion of *epithumia* as a *pathos*, and the inclusion of *orexis* within the definition of anger. What seems to count against this is that Aristotle does not ever say that a type of desire is a *pathos*. More importantly, many of the emotions are defined without reference to desire, and without reinterpretation as a desire. It seems as though we must wait for another thinker within the tradition of Aristotle, Aquinas, to offer a motivational analysis of emotion.

IV*—A FALSE DOCTRINE OF THE MEAN

by Rosalind Hursthouse

Introduction. Aristotle says that *ethikē aretē,* excellence of character, is a disposition in virtue of which we are well disposed in respect of feelings (*pathê*). Feelings are said to be such things as appetites, emotions such as anger and fear, and, in general, all conditions that are attended by pleasure or pain. (1105b19ff) Taken in isolation, this might sound as though Aristotle makes excellence of character a merely inner matter, but this is not so. Most feelings involve a desire to perform certain actions, so being well disposed in respect of feelings involves being well disposed in respect of actions too. The occasions on which the two come apart are not relevant to anything I say in this paper so let us concentrate on feelings for the moment.

What it is to be *well* disposed in respect of feelings is, apparently, specified by saying that excellence of character is a disposition (concerned with feelings) which is in a *mean.* The thesis that virtue (excellence of character) is a disposition in a mean is Aristotle's doctrine of the mean.

Whether you think of the doctrine as empty, or interesting, bold, and (roughly) true, is partly determined by what you think it is. J. O. Urmson[1] has defended it as the latter, and it is his account of what the doctrine is that provides the main stalking-horse in this paper.

When Urmson gives a summary of Aristotle's account of excellence of character, he begins it like this. (Note that he is using 'emotion' as his translation of *pathos.*)

> (1) For each specific excellence of character that we recognise there will be some specific emotion whose field it is.
> (2) In the case of each such emotion it is possible to be disposed to exhibit it to the right amount, which is excellence.[2]

---

* Meeting of the Aristotelian Society held at 5/7 Tavistock Place, London WC1 on Monday November 24 1980 at 6.30 p.m.

E

We should note one objection here, which is that Aristotle nowhere commits himself to the thesis that to each specific excellence of character or virtue there corresponds just *one* emotion (*pathos*) whose field it is. Indeed, much of his discussion shows that he denies this. I shall return to this point later.

So far, we have some account of virtue, and it is already quite strong. It is at least strong enough to be falsified. The virtue of *megalopsuchia* (magnanimity), although it no doubt involves exhibiting a variety of feelings 'to the right amount' consists, according to what Aristotle himself says, in correct *judgement*. To be magnanimous is to be well-disposed in respect of *judgements* of one's own worth, neither over- nor under-estimating it. Only consequentially is it a matter of being well-disposed in respect of feelings, but it is a disposition in respect of feelings that virtue is supposed to be.[3]

Similarly, the virtue of *megalopropeia,* magnificence, which is contrasted with vulgarity and pettiness, is a virtue which consists in correct *judgement*. The magnificent man judges correctly that the expense is worthy of the result and the result of the expense; the vulgar and the petty constantly get this judgement wrong.

So the account even so far is not true of all the virtues. For all that, it might be true of most of them, and, if it were, it would be an interesting account. But it is not yet an account that could be called a doctrine of a *mean*. For we could add to (1) and (2) no more than

> (3a) In the case of each such emotion (feeling) it is possible to be disposed to exhibit or feel it to a wrong extent, as one should not, which is a vice, a defect

and claim no more than that to each virtue there corresponds at least one vice.

This claim itself is a strong one and we should pause to consider it. Suppose that it is true—isn't it a surprising truth that calls for some explanation? Why *should* there be at least one vice corresponding to each virtue? If we found that, as a matter of fact, when we drew up a list of virtue words, we could draw up a list of corresponding vice words, that itself would be a sufficiently striking fact to call for explanation. If, in line with Aristotle's own procedure, we maintained that vices do not necessarily have names, and sometimes said that there *is* a certain vice even if there is no word for it and no-one (or no-one sane) ever has the vice, the call for an explanation seems even more pressing. What makes us so sure?

A sketch of the explanation of the fact (for I think it is a fact) that to each virtue there corresponds at least one vice, has recently been given, in a different context, by Philippa Foot. She has argued that

> the virtues are *corrective*, each one standing at a point at which there is some temptation to be resisted or deficiency to be made good.[4]

Courage and temperance, she says, exist as virtues because human nature happens to be such that fear, and the desire for pleasure, often operate as temptations. Justice and charity exist as virtues because there is a deficiency of motivation in most of us to be made good. We happen not to be as much attached to the good of others, or their rights, as we are to our own.

Mrs. Foot's thesis is not restricted to those vices that clearly consist in being disposed to exhibit or feel an emotion to the wrong extent, as one should not, but it clearly applies to them. The thesis is still tentative and sketchy but I think it is very promising and just the sort of thesis one needs to explain why to each virtue there corresponds at least one vice. The explanation is located in exactly the right place—in facts about human nature, about how we go on. A particularly attractive aspect of the thesis is that it suggests an explanation of why, in some cases, several vices might correspond to one virtue. One virtue, upheld as an ideal, might serve to correct several dangerous tendencies all at once.

I have spent a little time on this point in order to make the next point clearer. I said that (3a) does not yield anything that deserves to be called a doctrine of a *mean*. *This* comes in only when we add something like

> (3b) One's character may err in *two opposed* ways

as Urmson does.[5] Now this is, I think, definitely false, but the point I want to make here is that, if it *were* true, its truth would be a deeply mysterious fact. That to each virtue there corresponds at least one vice is an odd fact, but one for which we can imagine an explanation. But that to each virtue there should correspond precisely two vices, neither more nor less—what kind of explanation could there be of this extraordinary mathematical symmetry? What could there be about our lives and the way we conduct them, about our feelings and our dispositions to have those feelings, that necessitated such a symmetry?

The problem is made even worse by the idea that each pair of vices is a pair of *opposed* vices. I haven't yet said in what way they are meant to be opposed, and to complete the Urmsonian view of Aristotle's doctrine of the mean, (3b) should be replaced by something which specifies the opposition (and also preserves the connexion with emotion or feeling). Hence

> (3c) In the case of each such emotion it is possible to have an excessive or deficient disposition with respect to it: (or perhaps—in the case of each such emotion it is possible to be disposed to exhibit or feel it either too much, excessively, or too little, deficiently).

I am not sure whether Aristotle does maintain the thesis of (3b) and (3c). Much of Book 2 suggests that he does; but there he disarmingly says that he is talking in outline only, and much of the *detailed* discussion of the particular virtues in Books 3 and 4 shows that he is aware that both (3b) and (3c) are, in fact, false. However, there are more elaborate versions of the doctrine of the mean which are not merely false but extremely silly, and I am sure that Aristotle did not always hold *them*.

More elaborate versions arise from filling out 'excess' and 'deficiency', 'too much' and 'too little'. It is worth noting that we cannot find any detailed specification of how to fill them out in Aristotle. To get such a specification we must leave him and turn to, for example, Urmson, who unhesitatingly commits himself to the following:

> (4) 'Too much' includes 'on too many occasions' and similar possibilities as well as 'too violently'; 'too little' includes 'on too few occasions' and similar possibilities as well as 'too weakly'.[6]

The 'similar possibilities' are given earlier.

> . . . one may exhibit an emotion too often or too rarely;

> about too many or too few things; toward too many or too few people; for too many or too few reasons . . .[7]

I take it that, given that he holds (4), Urmson would specify what it is to have a disposition in a mean in the following way:

> (5) To have a disposition regarding a certain emotion in a mean is to be disposed to exhibit or feel that emotion neither too often nor too rarely; about or toward neither too many nor too few objects or people, for neither too many nor too few reasons, neither too strongly nor too weakly

and that he would regard that as being *equivalent* to Aristotle's statement of what it is to have a disposition in a mean, namely

> (5a) To have a disposition regarding a certain emotion in a mean is to be disposed to exhibit or feel that emotion on the right occasions, about or towards the right objects or people, for the right reasons, in the right manner.

It may be that Urmson's way is the only way to fill out 'too much' and 'too little'; about that I am not sure. If it *is* the only way then in so far as Aristotle committed himself to (3c) he committed himself to nonsense. His saving grace will then be inconsistency, for he very rarely lapses into the nonsensical (4) and (5), and, even when he does, does not do so whole-heartedly. What he usually does is operate straightforwardly within the terms of (5a), using the concept *dei*—*right* object, *right* occasion, *right* reason, or the very general *hos dei,* as one should, without any suggestion that this concept can either be captured by, or can necessarily generate, concepts of too much or too little.

The idea that the concept of the *right reason* could be captured by specifying it as a mean between too many and too few reasons has only to be stated to be seen as absurd. What I want to illustrate in what follows is that *right object* and *right occasion* similarly cannot be specified as means, and that, more generally, some vices that correspond to the virtues of temperance, courage, and what is usually translated as 'patience' or 'gentleness'—the right disposition with respect to anger—cannot be understood as dispositions to exhibit or feel an emotion (a *pathos*) too much or too little.

Temperance. There is a fairly obvious quibble to be made about there being *a* specific emotion or feeling to be the field of temperance, namely that *the* appetite for physical pleasure need not be an appetite for food *and* drink *and* sex. Some people are temperate with respect to sex but not with respect to food and drink and *vice versa*: some people are intemperate only with respect to drink and so on.

Though I think this is an unimportant quibble in this context, I want to discuss temperance with respect to food and drink by itself first because it raises problems that become especially acute when we turn to temperance with respect to sex.

Temperance with respect to food and drink. 'In the case of natural desires, few people go wrong, and only in one way, in the direction of too much' (1118b16–17). 'The licentious display excess in every form' (1118b24–5). How literal is the talk of 'excess' and 'too much' here? Aristotle says licentious people go wrong 'in enjoying the wrong objects' (1118b23–4), that 'they enjoy things it is wrong to enjoy' (1118b25–6). Are we to understand this as saying that they enjoy too many objects?

Some things are naturally wrong objects for appetite, for example foetuses, raw meat, human flesh, charcoal and earth. (Book 7, chap. v.) But the licentious man does not err in virtue of enjoying these sorts of things; only the brutish and the mad eat them. What else could wrong objects be?

It is initially very plausible to say that 'wrong objects' just are 'too many objects'. The licentious man enjoys too many courses, too many pints; he eats and drinks until he is full to bursting, thus *exceeding* his natural limit (1118b17–18), that is, he eats the right amount and then some. Moreover, he does not do this only on the rare occasions when it is necessary (as it might be if one wasn't going to eat again for forty-eight hours) but on all those occasions and then some—on too many occasions. And whenever he does it he enjoys it more than he should —too much. Moreover, all these excesses seem to be the natural outcome of not desiring physical pleasure to the right extent but too much.

So far, so good. 'Wrong objects', 'wrong occasions', 'wrong

manner' are all captured by 'too . . .' and the Urmsonian doctrine of the mean applies.

But so far temperance seems important for preserving health and not particularly important otherwise. A licentious person, one who desires physical pleasure too much, will simply be a greedy person who, if not forced to be sensible, will make himself fat and alcoholic. But it is clear that Aristotle thinks licentiousness leads, not merely to ill health but to other vices. *Sophrosune,* thought which saves, saves one not merely from the defect of ill health but from vice in general. (1140b12) Why is this so?

The significant difference between the temperate and the licentious seems to be this. The temperate man not only avoids pleasures which are incompatible with health, but also pleasures which are dishonourable (contrary to what is *kalos,* 1119a15–18). The licentious man disregards these limitations (1119a19) and enjoys not only unhealthy excessive guzzling but also things which are odious (*misēta*) (1118b26).

Odious things are presumably contrary to what is *kalos,* and are things it is wrong to enjoy. But what can these wrong objects be, given that they are something other than unhealthily excessive extra helpings, and presumably not unnatural objects such as foetuses and earth? Aristotle does not tell us but I think we can easily imagine examples. The best way to recognise this particular sort of wrong object is to distinguish, as Aristotle does not, two quite different ways in which someone might become and be licentious. Let us imagine the likely effects of two different sorts of upbringing.

Suppose we have one person who was brought up by greedy, gourmand parents who encouraged their child to eat too much, but who also brought him up to be polite, considerate, unselfish and fair. That is, they brought him up to delight in food and drink (though not in health) but also to delight in acting fairly, generously and considerately. Now I imagine that someone brought up this way is likely to turn out to be one of those fat, jovial, generous, scrupulously fair people who are indeed the despair of their doctors, but the delight of their friends.

Now let us think of another person, brought up, say, by a dietician and a doctor, who believe in the law of the jungle and arming their child to fight in it. They taught him how to preserve his health, but nothing about being fair, generous or considerate. I imagine that he is likely to turn out to be slim, healthy and wicked. He will not scruple to take my food if he has a (healthily moderate) desire for it, even if I am starving; he will happily cheat fellow soldiers out of their rations on campaign. He does such things in pursuit of physical pleasure, having been taught to delight in nothing but health and satisfying his own desires where these are not incompatible with it.

Both these people are licentious according to what Aristotle says about licentiousness, but it is clear that they are licentious in very different ways. The fat jovial person does indeed have an 'excessive disposition'; he eats and drinks too much, too often, enjoys it too much. His 'wrong objects' are 'too many objects'. But he is not disposed to pursue pleasures that are dishonourable, or odious. The slim wicked person on the other hand, does *not* have an excessive disposition but nevertheless he is licentious and enjoys things it is wrong to enjoy—not wrong because they are excessive and unhealthy, but just plain wrong, dishonourable, what one should not enjoy.[8]

I think Aristotle overlooked the possibility of being brought up to be healthily moderate but wicked. Moreover, I think he assumes that anyone who has been brought up greedy must inevitably become greedier and greedier until, almost maddened by the desire for physical pleasure, he will cease to care about the limitations imposed by the other virtues and get out of the habit of being generous, fair and so on. (cf. 1119b8–12) But even if this assumption were true, it would guarantee that licentiousness was an excess, and that 'a wrong object' was 'at least one object too many' only by fortuitous overlap. Some of the wrong objects which the greedy and wicked person enjoyed would still be wrong simply in so far as they were contrary to what is honourable; if they were cases of excess this would be accidental.

It might be thought that there is something perverse, or at least very un-Aristotelian about calling 'the food someone else needs' or 'other people's rations' wrong objects which the licentious man goes wrong in enjoying. But it seems to me they are exactly the sorts of examples we need in order to capture the idea that the licentious man disregards the limits set by what is honourable. Moreover, we find that this sort of idea of a wrong object becomes essential when we turn to temperance with respect to sex.

Temperance with respect to sex. When Aristotle actually specifies the wrong actions that licentiousness disposes one to commit, he specifies (unhealthy) excessive guzzling with respect to food and drink, and adultery with respect to sex. This is mentioned four times (1117a2, 1129b21, 1130a24f, 1130a29f) and I used to find this odd—I mean, why *adultery* in particular? But then I found that:

> It was *moikheia,* 'adultery' to seduce the wife, widowed mother, unmarried daughter, sister or niece of a citizen;[9]

And then it made more sense.

One might plausibly say that any man who seduced the wives and widowed mothers and unmarried daughters etc. of citizens must be a man greedy for sexual pleasures, and, as in the case of greed with respect to food and drink, we can maintain that such a man will be disposed to enjoy too many women, too often, too intensely—more than the temperate man—and all because he desires sexual pleasure too much. (There is probably the same connexion with health; it seems likely that Aristotle would believe that there is an excess of sexual activity which is unhealthy.)

Some people are greedy for sexual pleasure, and in such cases we can make good sense of licentiousness being a form of excess. There is a corresponding deficiency, for we may speak of people as being unnaturally or unhealthily indifferent to sexual pleasure. But cases of excess may well be rare though licentiousness with respect to sex be common. A man who commits 'adultery' just *once* has done an act which 'connotes depravity' and is 'simply wrong'. (1107a10ff). He goes wrong in enjoying something it is wrong to enjoy, and this wrong object is not 'unhealthily excessive sexual activity' or one woman over the eight, but intercourse with someone it is 'adulterous', and hence dishonourable, to have intercourse with. (Of course, someone might commit adultery for gain not for pleasure; but *if* he does it for pleasure (however minimal) rather than for gain, he counts as licentious, (1130a25–30).)

No doubt it is often the case that excessively lustful people are impelled by their excessive desire to commit 'adultery'. And then, perhaps, by fortuitous overlap, each 'wrong object' will happen to be 'at least one object too many'. But it is certain that excessive lust is not necessary. It might be that one had moderate, or even unnaturally low, sexual drive. But if one has any sexual drive at all *and* cares naught for what is honourable, then one will be disposed to commit licentious acts of 'adultery'. So having a licentious disposition is not necessarily a matter of having excessive sexual desire; someone could have his disposition with respect to sexual desire in a mean, or deficient, and *still* be licentious. He will be licentious just in so far as, for example, he sees sex solely in terms of satisfying his own healthy desires, or in terms of fun, as if it were not connected to anything else in life. And when he enjoys something it is wrong to enjoy, this wrong object will not be one object too many, nor (assuming he *is* licentious, not brutish) an unnatural object, but an object which the temperate man would not pursue in similar circumstances because the pleasure would be dishonourable.

Courage. As with temperance, there is a fairly obvious quibble to be made about there being *one* specific emotion or feeling which is the field of courage, namely that Aristotle himself specifies two—fear and confidence. One can attempt to preserve the thesis by maintaining that Aristotle has confused two distinct virtues, courage and caution, and Urmson, in support of his own position, and in line with several other commentators[10] does just this. For reasons too lengthy to go into here (but see David Pears, 'Aristotle's Analysis of Courage', *Midwest Studies in Philosophy,* III 1978), I think this is a mistake. But I can make the points I want to make without begging this question, so I shall follow Urmson in discussing only fear, in relation to courage.

The cowardly err on the side of 'excess'; they are disposed to exhibit fear 'too much'. Once again, how literal is this talk of 'excess' and 'too much' here? Is fearing the wrong objects on the wrong occasions a matter of fearing too many too often?

It is noteworthy that Aristotle begins his discussion of courage by stating baldly that fearing the *right* objects as part of being upright and decent is a matter of fearing e.g. disgrace. He goes on to specify the other things it is *right* to fear which are the concern of the courageous man, and these right objects are picked out without any reference or covert appeal to any notion of the mean. There are some things it is natural for men to fear and a kind of thing that we describe as being beyond human endurance; these things are the ones it is right to fear and they are these three—death, great pain and fairly extensive physical damage.

So fearing the right objects is fearing just those three things and fearing the wrong objects is fearing anything else. It is true that most cowards will fear those three things and then some; that is, they will fear some wrong things just in so far as they fear *more* things than the courageous man does, i.e. too many. But, as in the case of temperance, this is a matter of fortuitous overlap. Just suppose that although I fear the dark, enclosed spaces and mice, I do not fear death, pain or physical damage. (This is not an entirely silly supposition given the phobias people genuinely have.) Then, given that it is death and so on, rather than mice and so on, that create the problem on the battlefield, it seems that whatever defect or vice I have, it is not cowardice. On the contrary, despite my fear of mice and so on, my defect is more like fearlessness—not because I fear too few objects (I fear as many as the courageous man), but because I do not fear the *right* ones.

Fearing the right objects is not a matter of fearing, say, three, some figure in a mean between two or less and four or more; it is a matter of fearing death, pain and physical damage. Hence, a corresponding vice is not a matter of fearing too many or too few objects, but simply a matter of fearing anything other than the right ones, or not fearing the right ones. The imaginary 'fearless phobic' certainly fails to fear the right objects, but he is neither excessive nor deficient. (Or, if you like, he is both.)

What about fearing things 'on the wrong occasions'? Is this a matter of fearing things too often or too seldom? Only accidentally. *Any* time you fear a wrong object you have felt fear on a wrong occasion. By fortuitous overlap, a coward who fears the three right things and then some (the dark, mice) will indeed feel fear more often than the courageous man, i.e. too often. But without the fortuitous overlap, this is not guaranteed.

If I spend my life safely in the well-lit, mouse-free battlefield I may, if I do *not* fear the three right things, hardly ever feel fear at all. But I shall still do so 'on the wrong occasion' if I do.

Mutatis mutandis, the same can be said for 'wrong amount'. Any time I feel *any* fear towards a wrong object I have felt a wrong amount; this is not because there is a right amount of fear to feel which I overshoot, but simply because wrong object guarantees both wrong occasion and wrong amount.

What about fearing the *right* things the right or wrong amount? I submit that we cannot maintain that fearing death etc. 'the right amount' is fearing them somewhere between too much and too little. What fearing death 'the right amount' comes to is fearing death the right way, and what *that* comes to is fearing an ignoble dishonourable death but not fearing an honourable one. And the same, I think, applies to fearing great pain or damage 'the right amount'.

The background assumptions. Why does Aristotle talk in terms of excess and deficiency, too . . . and too . . . at all? Why should he not rest content with saying that men may go wrong in *countless* ways, but hit the target and achieve excellence in only one (1106b30ff) rather than even suggesting that, for each virtue, there are just two opposed ways of going wrong?

I think the explanation of this lies in the fact that, in some cases, he is making certain background assumptions about how we are.

The assumption in the case of courage is, roughly, that all (sane) human beings fall somewhere on a range that goes from fearing almost everything, to fearing almost nothing, and passes through sensibly fearing death, pain and damage. Now, as a matter of fact, this assumption is generally true—the sorts of phobias I mentioned are rare and even more rarely, if ever, combined with a lack of fear of death etc. This rather general fact about us provides the explanation I said earlier was needed of why, to the virtue of courage, there correspond just two vices. The explanation is—that's just the way we happen to be; we just do go wrong in these two ways. Similarly, the explanation of why the two vices should be opposed, as excess to deficiency is—that's just the way things happen to turn out;

fear works that way with us. The possibility of the 'fearless phobic' shows that things might have been otherwise. If he were as common as the cowardly and the fearless, there would be three vices not two; if he and the cowardly were common and no-one was fearless, there would be two vices but they would not be *opposed* ones.

Since the assumption is roughly true, it is roughly true that to have the virtue of courage is to have one's disposition regarding fear in a mean. But courage is not a virtue *because* it is a disposition in a mean; and cowardice and fearlessness are not vices because they are excessive or deficient dispositions. This is to get the order of explanation the wrong way round. Courage is a virtue because it is having the right disposition with respect to fear; cowardice and fearlessness are vices because they are both wrong dispositions with respect to fear. And it so happens that they can be called excessive or deficient; it so happens that they involve exhibiting fear too . . . .

Aristotle's assumption in the case of temperance is roughly, that all sane human beings fall on a range that goes (in theory) from being utterly indifferent to the pleasures of food, drink and sex, to being utterly consumed by the desire for them, and conveniently passes through being healthily interested *and* sensible about the relative importance of satisfying our own physical desires and other considerations.

If we *were* like that, then indeed temperance would have exactly two corresponding opposed vices, and that we were this way would explain why. But, as I have suggested, this assumption is manifestly false. The way we are guarantees that to the virtue of temperance there correspond at least the following vices—ordinary gluttony, drunkenness, lasciviousness, and a particular lack of scruple. The former may be called excesses: the latter is neither an excess nor a deficiency.

Patience. Now although Aristotle makes this sort of assumption about human beings in the case of courage and temperance, he does not do so in the case of all the other virtues. Interestingly enough it is Urmson, not Aristotle, who makes the (as it happens) false assumption about human beings which is required to guarantee that the right disposition with respect to anger is a disposition in a mean. Urmson says:

> The man whose character is such that he feels only mild annoyance at a trivial slight and is enraged by torture (of his wife?) has a character which is in a mean between one which exhibits rage on trivial *as well as important occasions* and one which can coolly contemplate the greatest outrages.[11] (My italics)

Note that here we must assume that the man who can coolly contemplate the greatest outrages is also someone who coolly contemplates trivial slights, in order to make sense of the first man's character as being in a mean. But there is the rub—why should we assume any such thing?

If we assume that human beings mostly fall on a range that goes from being angered by nearly everything (the trivial *and* the important) to being angered by hardly anything (neither the trivial nor the important) and conveniently passes through being angered by the important but not by the trivial, then we could indeed say that *praotes,* patience, like courage, is a disposition that lies in a mean between excess and deficiency. But the assumption is false. The defect many of us have is to be angered by the trivial and *not* by the important, or by the trivial and just those few important things that touch us very nearly.

As Urmson's own use of 'trivial' and 'important' implicitly recognises, Aristotle's talk about getting angry at the right (or wrong) objects is quite independent of any notion of excess and deficiency. Someone who gets angry about the wrong objects can *easily* be someone who fails to get angry about the right ones. Someone who is bad tempered might well be angry less often with fewer objects than someone who is constantly enraged by say injustices, but because these objects are wrong objects, such as tin openers and people disagreeing with him, we call him bad tempered. A person who hasn't grasped the idea of the *right* objects of anger, will, like the 'fearless phobic', be neither excessive nor deficient, or, if you like, both.

As in the case of fear, getting angry about a wrong object will automatically guarantee that one is angry on a wrong occasion, to a wrong extent, and only fortuitous overlap will guarantee that each wrong occasion is a case of at least once too often. Similarly, failing to get angry about a wrong object will be not getting angry on a right occasion, and only fortuitous overlap will guarantee that this is a case of once too seldom.

Conclusion. Urmson says that 'Aristotle . . . fails to notice that it is possible, if unlikely, that one's character should exhibit deficiency in some respect, the mean in others, and excess in others, even with regard to a single specific excellence',[12] and I find this an odd remark for two reasons.

One is that it is so clearly false. Regarding anger, Aristotle says 'the excess occurs in respect of all the circumstances, with the wrong people, for the wrong reasons, more than is right . . . ; but *of course these conditions do not all attach to the same subject.*' (1126a9ff) and he explicitly contrasts the irascible, who stop quickly, with the bitter, who keep up their anger too long. He also acknowledges the same complexity when he discusses liberality (which Urmson does not mention); the prodigal, he says, go too far in giving and fall short in receiving . . . thus the faults of prodigality are hardly ever found together. (1121a12ff)[13]

The other thing I find odd about Urmson's remark is that he does not seem to realise that, according to him, it must amount to 'Aristotle fails to notice that the doctrine of the mean is false.' For according to him, the doctrine of the mean requires at least the mysterious 3b, that one's character may err in two, exactly two, opposed ways, and this is admitted to be false as soon as one admits more than two vices corresponding to a virtue.

Of course it is true that, even if, like Aristotle, one does recognise more than two vices corresponding to a virtue, one could try to describe them all in terms of 'too . . .'. The irascible are too violent; the bitter are angry for too long; the irritable are angered too often (by too many objects?). Perhaps it is the apparent possibility of doing this that continues to entice people into believing that there is some truth in some quasi-Urmsonian doctrine of the mean. But this is an illusion. To many of the virtues there correspond vices which consist simply in being disposed to feelings about wrong objects, as I have illustrated. The objects are not 'too many' or 'too few', but just plain wrong; the vices are not excesses or deficiencies but just ways of going wrong. The fact that many vices can be characterised in terms of 'too . . .', is a fact that has its own interest, but it does not serve to support the doctrine of the mean.

NOTES

[1] In 'Aristotle's Doctrine of the Mean', *American Philosophical Quarterly,* 1973.

[2] Urmson, *op. cit.* 226.

[3] *Cp.* W. F. R. Hardie, '"Magnanimity" in Aristotle's Ethics', *Phronesis,* 1978.

[4] Philippa Foot, *Virtues and Vices* (1978), 8.

[5] *Op. cit.* 225.

[6] *Op. cit.* 226.

[7] *Op. cit.* 225.

[8] And it is clearly this second sort of licentiousness that inevitably brings the other vices in its train.

[9] K. J. Dover, *Greek Popular Morality* (1974), 209.

[10] E.g. Ross.

[11] *Op. cit.* 225.

[12] *Op. cit.* 225.

[13] And see also the *Eudemian Ethics,* 1232a10–15 where Aristotle goes even further and rightly distinguishes the man who has strong feelings about small amounts as a special case of meanness, thus admitting at least three sorts of illiberality.

ARISTOTLE: ONTOLOGY AND MORAL REASONING*

DAVID CHARLES

1. Introduction

IN this paper, I wish to consider some topics which are central to Aristotle's account of moral reasoning and moral action: praxeis, productions (*poiēseis*), and the goals of moral action. In the major part of the paper (sections 2–5), I will argue that two specific difficulties which have troubled Aristotelian commentators have an ontological basis, and can be resolved once one has grasped Aristotle's account of actions, processes, and their results. However, while a proper appreciation of Aristotle's ontology may help to resolve these specific difficulties, their resolution serves only to raise further, and more intractable, philosophical questions about the nature and value of several of his basic moral concepts. Once the ontological basis of Aristotle's theory is more fully understood, we will be better placed to evaluate and be properly troubled by his account of ethical reasoning and moral action (section 6).

2. The problems

Two exegetical puzzles arise in any discussion of Aristotle's account of moral action.

(1) Aristotle, it appears, held that praxeis and productions are distinct and exclusive sets of occurrence (*genomena*). Moral actions are chosen for their own sake, and are distinct from productions. However, in many cases, praxeis and productions co-occur as when, for example, a mechanic, in his spare-time, and without asking for financial reward, repairs the electrical petrol pump on a stranger's car which has broken down near his home. But if virtuous actions are praxeis, and productions and praxeis are mutually exclusive classes of actions, we seem compelled to conclude that the mechanic who

performs this production does not act virtuously in Aristotle's account. This consequence is most paradoxical; for there will be few, if any, virtuous acts if the agent's desire to produce some future goal excludes the possibility of his performing a moral praxis. It seems rather that, in Aristotle's account, a paradigm example of a moral praxis fails to be one.

(2) It is a central feature of Aristotle's ethical theory that virtuous actions are chosen 'for their own sake' (*di'autas*).[1] It is a central feature of his account of choice,[2] that the agent must choose to do an act for the sake of something separate from the act. But these statements are incompatible, if the latter requires that virtuous acts be chosen for the sake of something beyond themselves. Praxeis differ from productions precisely because praxeis are their own ends (*NE/Eudemian Ethics* (*EE*) 1140b2–7; *Magna Moralia* (*MM*) 1197a3–6). But if the praxis too is itself chosen for the sake of a separate end, why isn't it now a production, namely, something not chosen for its own sake? Doesn't this lead to a collapse of the praxis/production distinction? This problem will apply also in the case of eudaimonistic activity, if all such praxeis are chosen for the sake of an end (namely, *eudaimonia*) separate from the action.

These two specific puzzles give rise to two more general problems.

(*a*) Which action is the moral praxis, and which the production? Is there one event which is a praxis under one description, and a production under another? Or are praxeis and productions (or actions chosen for their own sake and those chosen for the sake of something else) distinct actions?

(*b*) What is the relation between actions and the results of actions (or goals of actions) which are not themselves actions, but are achieved by acting? This also depends on an ontological issue, namely, what types of entity are the results of actions in these cases, and how are they related to actions? For all actions appear to be means to results which are other than actions (e.g. *NE* 1111a5–6, 18–19).

John Ackrill showed that these two general problems arise out of difficulties in Aristotle's ontology, but thought that he had reached an impasse:[3]

[1] *Nicomachean Ethics* (*NE*) 1105a32ff.
[2] *NE* 1111b26–8.
[3] J. L. Ackrill, 'Aristotle on Action', *Mind*, LXXXVII (1978), 601.

I conclude that ... Aristotle does not direct his gaze steadily upon the questions 'What *is* an action?' and 'What is *an* action?' ... It seems likely that this failure is itself the reason for many of the 'incoherences' and 'contradictions' to be found in these passages.

I wish to support Ackrill's basic and important insight that these and other related difficulties in Aristotle's ethical theory require a proper understanding of his ontology for their resolution, but to argue that Aristotle did pay sufficient attention to questions of action-individuation to provide an answer (although not in all respects a satisfying one) to both these general problems ((*a*) and (*b*) above).

3. Similar ontological issues elsewhere in Aristotle's ethical theory

The two specific puzzles raised at the beginning of section 1 seem strongly analogous to two issues that arise in Aristotle's discussion of pleasure.

(1) Aristotle, it appears, held that pleasures are activities (or intimately connected with activities)[4] and, as such, distinct from processes. Thus, for example, contemplating would be a pleasure for S at t_1, and be distinct from any related process such as reading a book. But in certain cases activities and processes co-occur. Take the case of a spectator who enjoys listening to a symphony which consists in four movements. It is plausible to say of him that 'he cannot have enjoyed listening to all the symphony' until the symphony is completed, and hence to conclude that he cannot *have* enjoyed listening to all of the symphony and still continue thereafter listening to it. But if enjoying is taken as the same occurrence as listening, it appears that enjoying cannot be (after all) an activity, as it does not pass (in this case) the tense-test for activities set out in the *Metaphysics*: and so Aristotle's paradigm example of an activity fails his favoured test for being an activity.

The problem (also raised by John Ackrill)[5] seems precisely parallel to the first one raised in section 1: activities and processes co-occur, but are apparently taken by Aristotle to be distinct and exclusive

[4] See problem (2) below.

[5] It is one of several problems raised in his paper 'Aristotle's Distinction Between *energia* and *kinesis*', in *New Essays on Plato and Aristotle*, ed R. Bamborough (London, 1965), 12–41.

classes of occurrence. How can this be the case? Substitute 'praxeis' for 'activities' and 'productions' for 'processes', and one has exegetical puzzle (1) of section 1.

(2) In *Nicomachean/Eudemian Ethics* VII it appears that Aristotle characterized pleasures as unimpeded activities, namely as activities of a given kind (*NE/EE* 1153a10, 14–15); but in *Nicomachean Ethics* X, he takes pleasure to be a supervenient goal or result which *completes* the activity, and as such is not *identical* with the activity (*NE* 1174b31–3, 1175b32–5). This gives rise to the classical exegetical problem of the consistency of *Nicomachean/Eudemian Ethics* VII and *Nicomachean Ethics* X.[6] Miss Anscombe suggested that this problem had a philosophical basis in the difficulties of analysing pleasure successfully. She wrote: 'Its difficulty, astonishingly, reduced Aristotle to babble, since for good reasons he both wanted pleasure to be identical with and to be different from the activity that it is pleasure in.'[7] The exegetical difficulty is this. What is the ontological status of the *end* of the activity in these cases, and how is it related to the *activity* itself? Is its relation to the activity compatible with activities of a given kind (e.g. listening to music) being chosen for their own sake and for the sake of the pleasure which is the result of the activity? For if the activity is chosen for the sake of a separate end, why isn't it now a process—namely something with an end beyond the action, for the sake of which the action is done? Substitute 'praxis' for 'activity' and 'production' for 'process' in the last sentence, and one has exegetical puzzle (2) of section 1.

In this paper, I am not able to discuss these two ontological issues concerning Aristotle's discussion of pleasure directly or in detail.[8] But

[6] For recent treatment of this problem see G. E. L. Owen, 'Aristotelian Pleasures', *Proceedings of the Aristotelian Society* (*PAS*), LXXII (1971/2); J. C. B. Gosling, 'More Aristotelian Pleasures', *PAS* LXXIV (1973/4), 15–34; J. C. B. Gosling and C. C. W. Taylor, *The Greeks on Pleasure* (Oxford, 1982), chs 11, 12, and 13. The problem survives Gosling and Taylor's discussion of it. They hold that in *NE/EE* VII, pleasure is an *activity* of a given kind, while in *NE* X it is a *condition* (cf. 248) which perfects the activity (namely, its formal cause), and dismiss the apparent ontological difference as 'terminological' (250ff) and philosophically insubstantial (251–2). While there are, no doubt, many issues to which these two accounts will give comparable answers (on the interpretation offered by Gosling and Taylor), they will not do so for the ontological question: 'What is pleasure? Is it a *condition* achieved by action, or is it the *action* which achieves that condition?' Since it is difficult to give an analysis of pleasure without answering ontological questions such as 'Is pleasure to be analysed adverbially as a way of doing an action, or is it rather an agreeable state which results from action?', the interpretation offered by Gosling and Taylor cannot fully illuminate Aristotle's analysis of pleasure.

[7] G. E. M. Anscombe, *Intention* (Oxford, 1957), 77.

[*See opposite page for n 8*]

I will seek to indicate in outline how the proposed resolutions of the two specific puzzles concerning praxeis and productions apply to these related problems in the theory of pleasure.

4. Exegetical puzle (*A*): praxeis/productions (*poiēseis*)

To fix the questions at issue more clearly let us take a concrete example. Bethan is doing a generous action: she is tying together a broad bean framework for an elderly acquaintance, Mr Jones, who is crippled by arthritis and so cannot do it himself. She is doing this to ensure that he has sufficient fresh vegetables to eat, as she knows that he is loath to spend his old-age pension on protein. She is under no specific obligation to Mr Jones, and cannot expect any financial reward for her labour (although she knows that Mr Jones will be grateful). Which is the praxis, chosen for its own sake, in this case and which the *poiēsis*, chosen for the sake of another? How are they related? What is their ontological status?

In the example described, there are good grounds for attributing to Aristotle the view that neither tying together the bean framework nor providing Mr Jones with winter vegetables is the praxis, chosen for its own sake.[9]

(1) In this case, in tying together the bean framework Bethan aims—as one might in politics and warfare—at a goal which is over and above (*para*) the action (*NE* 1177b2–12): for example, giving Mr Jones winter vegetables. Hence, her tying together the bean framework cannot be the action chosen for its own sake. Bethan wouldn't knock down the framework after she had finished it to do the same type of action again (cf. *NE* 1110a19).

(2) Tying together bean frameworks—like fighting and killing—is for many regularly unpleasant (even when done for a noble goal) and disagreeable (*NE* 1117b7–9); and let us assume that is also so, in this case, for Bethan. But moral actions are characterized as pleasant

[8] I have discussed the first of these problems in *Aristotle's Philosophy of Action* (London, 1984), 35–40, and in 'Aristotle's Distinction Between Energia and Kinesis: Inference, Explanation and Ontology', *Language and Reality in Greek Philosophy*, Proceedings of the Greek Philosophical Society (1984/5). These issues are further discussed by Pascal Engel, *Structure sémantique et forme logique d'après l'analyse aristotelicienne des phrases d'action* (forthcoming).

[9] These arguments apply also to Bethan's basic action at t_1 of moving her hands in a given way so as to tie the framework. For a discussion of 'basic' actions in Aristotle's theory, see *Aristotle's Philosophy of Action*, 70–8.

activity (*NE* 1117b15–16). Hence her tying together the framework cannot be the action chosen for its own sake or her moral praxis.

(3) Bethan's providing Mr Jones with autumn vegetables is not her praxis, chosen for its own sake, either. In *Nicomachean Ethics* 1177b12–15, Aristotle writes that the politician, in pursuing the goal of power, glory, or welfare, pursues something which is over and above (*para*) political activity itself. But in *Nicomachean Ethics* 1094a5–6, Aristotle holds that if the goal is over and above the action, the consequential result is better than the activity. Praxeis are defined (*NE* 1176b6–8, *NE/EE* 1140b6–8) as activities in which nothing is sought *over and above* the action. Since in producing peace or autumn vegetables the agent aims at producing the product: peace/autumn vegetables, *over and above* the action, neither can be praxeis.

(4) Both tying together bean frameworks and providing Mr Jones with autumn vegetables are processes, and not activities, as the past tense ('She has provided autumn vegetables') is applicable only at the end of the action. But praxeis are activities—a subset of those in which nothing is sought beyond the activity (*NE* 1176b2–10). Thus, Bethan's providing autumn vegetables and her tying together bean frameworks cannot be praxeis, since they are not activities.

These four arguments strongly support taking Bethan's acting generously to be the praxis which she chooses for its own sake in the example above. They also show that winning Mr Jones's gratitude cannot be her praxis. For if the definitions of production and process presupposed here are correct, winning Mr Jones's gratitude will be a production and a process, and hence cannot be a praxis. Hence, of the four acts specified only acting generously can be the praxis; thus, if a praxis is the moral agent's goal, she chooses acting generously as her goal for its own sake.

What is the ontological status of the praxeis and productions in these cases? There is strong evidence that they form distinct and exclusive classes of actions.

(1) In *Nicomachean/Eudemian Ethics* 1140b2–4, praxeis and productions are said to constitute distinct genera.[10] But in *Physics* 226a26–33,

[10] This premiss seems plausible to Ebert ('Praxis und Poiesis', *Zeitschrift für philosophische Forschung*, XXX (1976), 12–30) who writes of this passage: 'Auf ersten Blick mag die Behauptung dass Poiesis und Praxis keine einander ausschiessenden Begriffe sind befremdliche erscheinen'. Ebert however thinks that *NE/EE* 1140a3–5 requires the alternative ontology of extensional (Davidsonian) events with different descriptions true of them. However, in analysing 1140a3ff below, I argue that Aristotle's argument

difference in genus (e.g. quality/spatial change) is sufficient to show that there is no occurrence which is both a quality and spatial change. If so, there is reason to believe that productions and praxeis form distinct and exclusive classes of occurrence. This is further supported by Aristotle's argument in this passage. It runs as follows:

P (*a*) praxeis and productions constitute distinct genera (*NE/EE* 1140b3–4);
P (*b*) skill is concerned with production (exclusively);
P (*c*) the goals of production and praxeis are different;
P (*d*) skill is different from practical wisdom;
So, (*e*) practical wisdom is concerned with praxeis (exclusively).

The assumptions behind this argument seem to be:

[Assm I] practical wisdom and skill have no common objects;
[Assm II] skill is concerned with productions;
[Assm III] productions and praxeis are different genera in the class of what can be otherwise;
[Assm IV] production and praxeis are the only relevant genera for practical wisdom.

From these assumptions, Aristotle can draw his conclusion: practical wisdom is concerned with praxeis, and not with productions. For this conclusion to be valid, he requires a way of ruling out the possibility that there is one thing in the relevant class which is both a praxis and a production.[11] If this is not excluded, there could be something in this

demands that *productions* and *praxeis* form exclusive classes of occurrence; nor do I see that the syntax of 1140a3ff supports Ebert's conclusion. Ebert is led to this view by two considerations, neither of which is conclusive:

(*a*) that he cannot see how the aim of a praxis can fail to be separate from the action, if Aristotle's discussions of politicians in 1140b5–6 and *NE* 1177b10–15 are to be consistent. Hence, he proposes that 1140b6–7 be interpreted so that '*x* is a praxis if its aim is itself a praxis'. Given this, he concludes that there may be an event which is a praxis under one description, and a production under another. Below I argue for a different solution to the problem of the consistency of 1140b5–6 and 1177b10 which does not require either of Ebert's proposals;

(*b*) that Terry Penner ('Verbs and Identity of Actions: a philosophical exercise in the Interpretation of Aristotle', *Ryle: A Collection of Critical Essays*, ed O. P. Wood and G. Pitcher (London, 1971), 37–8) has shown Aristotle's treatment of processes to involve (Davidsonian) extensional events. I have criticized Penner's arguments on other grounds elsewhere: see *Aristotle's Philosophy of Action*, 37–8; and 'Aristotle's Distinction Between *Energeia* and *Kinesis*', *passim*. However, Aristotle's account of the praxis/production distinction, if correctly given here, also tells against Penner's analysis.

[11] A similar result could also be achieved by weakening [Assm I] to [I ′]: practical wisdom and skill have different objects, and strengthening [III] to [III ′]: productions

class of occurrence which is both a production and a praxis–and a possible object for practical wisdom (contrary to the conclusion). But this can only be excluded if praxeis and productions form exclusive classes of occurrences. It is not enough for them to be merely different descriptions of such occurrences; for if this was the case, there could be occurrences which were both praxeis and productions, and practical wisdom could be concerned with these. The argument of the previous paragraph rests on the assumption that:

(*a*) occurrences that can be otherwise are specifed in this context independently of the descriptions held true of them; and
(*b*) skill and practical wisdom are directed towards such occurrences, and not to such occurrences under these descriptions.

(*a*) is supported by passages in *Nicomachean/Eudemian Ethics* VI. 4 and 5 in which Aristotle focuses on to occurrences in the world (1140a12, 14, 35, b1–3), and not on to such occurrences appropriately described. Thus, in discussing skill he writes:

All skill is concerned with coming into being: that is, with the skilled production and with the consideration of how something may come into existence which is capable of existing or not existing, and whose starting point lies in the maker and not the object made; for it is not concerned with what is or comes to be of necessity nor with what comes into existence by nature: for the latter contain in themselves the cause of their existence. (1140a10–15)

Here he seems concerned with what the skilled agent can produce, without reference to how it is described: whether essentially or accidentally (contrast *Physics* (*Phys.*) 195a30–b5; *NE/EE* 1135a26–30). And these cases are contrasted with what occurs of necessity or by nature and have their cause within themselves: and this too is independent of how they are described. Since skill is focused on to the former occurrences (thus specified), the objects of skill are here occurrences in the world—no matter how they are described. Since the objects of skill and practical wisdom are treated in the same way, the first sentence of *Nicomachean/Eudemian Ethics* VI. 4:

The class of what can be other includes what is made and what is done . . . (1140a1–2)

and praxeis are mutually exclusive classes of phenomena in the class of what can be other. It is not clear which of these routes to his conclusion Aristotle 'had in mind' in this section of argument.

should be taken to show an extensional difference between what is made and what is done in the class of what can be other—specified independently of how these occurrences are described.

This conclusion is supported by a second argument from the immediately following section:

(2) In 1140a3–6, Aristotle argues as follows:
P (*a*) The reasoned capacity to act is different from the reasoned capacity to produce.
P (*b*) The action is not a production, and the production is not an action.
So (*c*) That is why they are not even included either of them by the other.

The problem in this passage is to explain how (*c*) follows from (*a*) and (*b*);[12] for (*a*), by itself, is compatible with productions and praxeis being related as part to whole. Hence, what is required in (*b*) is a premiss which serves to interpret (*a*) in such a way as to exclude this possibility. But if (*b*) is construed as 'there is no praxis which is a production, and no production which is a praxis', then it follows that there can be no member of the category praxis, which is included in the category production—and vice versa. Hence, if (*b*) is taken as indicating a difference between distinct and exclusive classes of praxeis and productions, the argument is valid and the truth of (*c*) is explained by the truth of (*a*) and (*b*). However, if there had been one occurrence[13] with separate praxis—and production—descriptions true of it, the latter could have been—even given (*a*) and (*b*)—a subset of the former. This is because production-descriptions might (for all that is said by (*a*) and (*b*)) be, for example, that subset of praxeis—descriptions which involve some skill. If Aristotle had wished to exclude this possibility he would have needed to add a further premiss

(*b'*) Production-descriptions and praxeis-descriptions are mutually exclusive,

to derive (*c*) validly. But there is no sign of a premiss like this in the text; nor should there be since if it were added, Aristotle would have

[12] As Greenwood remarks in *Aristotle, Nicomachean Ethics* VI. *Essays, Notes and Translation* (Cambridge, 1909), 181. Gauthier and Jolif (*Aristote. L'Éthique à Nicomaque* (Paris, 1958/9)) seek to avoid this difficulty by reading '*kai*' not '*dio*' in 1140a5 with L^b and M^b (i.e. against the majority of the Manuscripts K^b, N^b, O^b, Γ, etc.) but do so only because they do not see the point of '*dio*'.

[13] As for example if Aristotle had adopted an ontology of events of the type favoured by Davidson, *Essays on Actions and Events* (Oxford, 1980), 102–203.

failed to explain the truth of (*c*) by means of (*a*), (*b*), and (*b'*), but would have merely built the conclusion explicitly, and in an *ad hoc* way, into the premisses: for (*b'*) would have been equivalent to (*c*), and so could not have explained its truth.

These two arguments from the immediate context of *Nicomachean/ Eudemian Ethics* VI. 4–5 support the conclusion that:

(1) the praxis chosen by the moral agent as his goal is a separate action from any production he undertakes as a means;
(2) if the moral agent chooses a praxis as his goal, this act will be distinct from any process or production which he undertakes as a means to that goal.

These conclusions are strongly supported by Aristotle's discussion elsewhere.

(1) In *Metaphysics* 1050a30–b2, he distinguishes productions from certain praxeis (e.g. living well, contemplating) as follows:

In the case of those things where something occurs over and above the activity, in these cases the activity is to be found in what is made (e.g. building in what is built . . .); in the case of those things in which there is no result over and above the activity, the activity occurs in the agent (e.g. seeing in the seer, contemplating in the contemplator; life in the soul—and this is why living well is in the soul—for it is a kind of life).

The crucial difference here appears to lie in the *location* of the relevant productions and praxeis: productions occur in the product, praxeis in the agent.[14] But things that occur in different places cannot be the same; for to be the same numerically, Aristotle requires the same (e.g. particular spatial or quantity) beginning and end points (*Phys.* 242a67–8; cf. also 224b7–8); and things in different places with different

[14] See also *Phys.* 202b5–7. I construe *Metaphysics* (*Metaph.*) 1050a30–b2 as specifying the *location* of the production in the product, and not as making the (more pedestrian) point that the production merely involves some change in the product for the following reasons: (i) the pedestrian point is obvious, and would not require ten lines to make (a24–34); nor could it even seem strange (see *Phys.* 202a31–3); (ii) Aristotle appears to move beyond the pedestrian point to a further claim in a30–1, when he writes: 'in the case of those things in which something occurs beyond the activity, in these the activity is in the product'. If he had intended only the pedestrian point, and its obvious extension, he should have said: 'what occurs, occurs in the product', and not said: 'the activity occurs in the product'. So the obvious explanation of the form of words used is that Aristotle intends the further (less pedestrian) point: the activity, in these cases, is actually *in* the product. And this is the point whose apparent paradoxicality requires some explanation (*Phys.* 202b5–8, 19–22).

intrinsic features cannot fulfil this condition. So praxeis and productions must be exclusive classes of phenomenon.

(2) Aristotle held that praxeis are activities, and productions are not[15]—but are a special case of processes. Activities and processes are distinct and mutually exclusive sets of entity (*Metaph.* 1048b25–7). No process can be an activity, and no activity a process since Aristotle refers to distinct classes of cases (*tas men* . . . *tas de*), whose particular instances are of a different kind (b34–5) and distinct (*tēn men*. . . *ekeinēn de*). Nor is this construal of the tense-test for activity- and process-verbs surprising; processes and activities have distinct goals: one is immanent throughout the activity, the other is the final point of the process. Since difference in goal yields difference in capacity, these will be distinct entities as they are the realization of distinct capacities (with distinct goals). Hence, Aristotle's basis for the individuation of processes (by a theory of capacities and goals) strongly motivates his treating entities with distinct goals (such as activities and processes) as distinct particulars.[16]

[15] In the case of production, the product is better than the activity (*NE* 1094a5–6) and is the goal (*NE* 1140b5–7; cf. *NE* 1105a26–8). In the case of praxeis, the activity is better than the product and is the goal (*NE/EE* 1140b6–8). I take praxeis to be a subset of activities (*NE* 1176b2, 7; 1094a2–18) which are not chosen for a further goal over and above (*para*) the activity (1176b6–7). This is because praxeis, like activities (*energeiai*) in Aristotle's technical sense, have immanent internal results which are not over and above the activity (*Metaph.* 1048b22–3): 'the goal is immanent in the praxis'. In the case of processes, the goal is not immanent (1048b21–2) and in the subset of processes which are productions is in the object changed (1050a31–3). This suggests the following rough scheme.

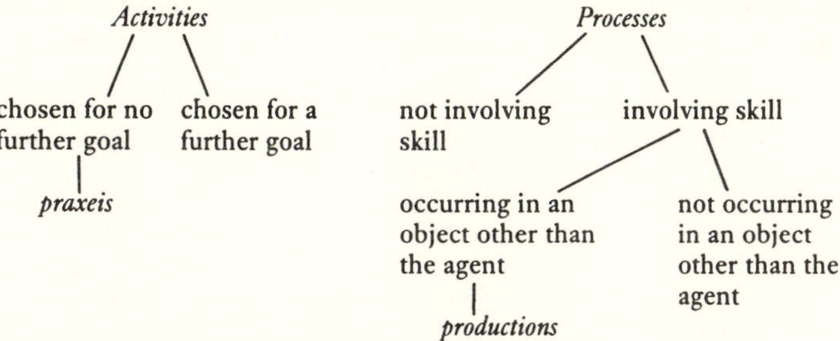

If so, the praxis/production distinction will be an exclusive one but not an exhaustive one. For a similar result, see C. C. W. Taylor's article, 'States, Activities and Performances', *PAS* Supp. vol 39 (1965), 85–102.

[16] Difference in goals between praxeis and productions (*NE* 1140b6–7; 1139b1–4) serves to distinguish them ontologically, if it is correct to see the difference in goal (in general) as spelling difference in action/process/activity and capacity in Aristotle's ontology. I argue for this general thesis on the basis of *Phys.* V. 4 and III. 1–3 in *Aristotle's*

One value of this result (namely, that praxeis and productions are mutually distinct entities) lies in its power of showing coherence at points of Aristotelian exegesis where others have found confusion and incoherence. Thus, John Ackrill[17] derived an inconsistency in Aristotle's account of moral action by an argument which rests essentially on its denial. He argued, in effect, as follows:

P (1) tying the bean framework is the generous act;
P (2) Bethan chooses to tie the bean framework not *qua* tying the bean framework, but *qua* the generous act;
P (3) there are not two things done: tying the bean framework and acting generously.
(4) Therefore, there is only one thing done (tying the bean framework = acting generously).
But (5) for Aristotle, Bethan's tying the bean framework is not done for its own sake but for its generosity, and the just act is done for itself.

However, if the arguments sketched above are correct, Bethan's tying the bean framework and her acting generously will be distinct actions as one is a process and the latter an activity. And if Ackrill's premiss (3) is rejected, tying the bean framework may be chosen as a means to acting justly right now, and acting justly right now chosen for its own sake without contradiction.[18] Thus, taking *a* to be Bethan's tying the

Philosophy of Action, 6–28. My present aim is to show, on grounds apart from those provided by *Phys.* II and V, that praxeis and productions form separate classes of phenomenon. However, I do take the *Phys.* passages to support the argument of this paper as there Aristotle discusses actions amongst other processes: see 201a16–19, b10–15, 202a32–b29. They show Aristotle at work giving general answers to questions like 'what is *an* action?' while considering also 'what is *a* process?'

[17] *Mind*, LXXXVIII (1979), 600–2. Gauthier and Jolif spot a similar 'incoherence' in *NE* 1112b32–3, but do not note its ontological basis.

[18] John Ackrill gives no specific Aristotelian motivation for (4), but comments only: 'it does not seem natural to say in such cases that the agent has done two things at the same time' (op cit 596). If the arguments above are correct, Aristotle would have had strong theoretical motivations to accept that there are *two* things done by Bethan in this case: one a praxis (activity) and the second a production (process), the first of which reflects her moral character, while the second does not. However, it is not clear to me that the Davidsonian event/ontology is actually 'more natural' than the alternative (apparently favoured by Aristotle) in which there is *one action-episode* made up of numerically distinct individual actions such as praxeis and productions. Do our intuitions really force us to say that Bethan's tying the bean framework *is identical* with her acting generously, rather than these two actions co-occur and are closely related (e.g. under an equivalence relation)? For in the latter case, Aristotle would hold that the two distinct actions are 'the same ... but different in essence' (if my analysis of *Phys.* 202b5–22 is

bean framework at t_1, and *b* to be her acting justly then, she will pursue *a* as a means to *b*, and *b* for its own sake. As Aristotle writes in 1151a35–b2:

If an agent chooses this (*a*) for the sake of that (*b*), he chooses the latter (*b*) for its own sake, and the former (*a*) accidentally—as a means; we call non-accidental what is for its own sake.

Thus, (*b*)—the specific act of acting generously now—will be an object of Bethan's preferential choice, as such choices are of the form: this for the sake of that (*EE* 1225a10–14; 1226a12–14; 1228a1–4), and may even be classified as *the* final, or non-accidental, object of her choice (*NE* 1105a28–33).

This account allows the following solution to the initial problem. The moral motor mechanic, who repairs the petrol pump in your car, performs a production for the sake of a praxis (for example doing you a good turn). The presence of a production thus related to a praxis in no way excludes the possibility of a moral praxis. Indeed, the reverse is true: the moral agent may repair your petrol pump in order to ensure that you get home safely (and thereby act generously) without the value of his generous act residing in its remote consequential benefits.[19] He would have acted generously even if these benefits did

correct: see *Aristotle's Philosophy of Action*, 11–18, 27–9). The occurrence of the basic act (Bethan's moving her hands) would in the circumstances (i.e. with this goal) be sufficient for (but not the efficient cause of) her acting generously:

$$O(a) \wedge O(c') \; \Box\!\!\rightarrow \; O(b)$$

where *a* stands to *b* as matter to form. Their relation will exemplify a general pattern which is not confined to the case of agency, but extends also to the relation of physical and psychological processes in perception and desire. This is, of course, compatible with Aristotle's allowing that by doing *a*, Bethan did *b*, and with her seeing that by doing *a* in those conditions she was acting generously. It just means that the relations specific to agency do not define the relevant equivalence class. For a differing view, see Cynthia Freeland's 'Aristotelian Actions', *Nous*, 1986.

[19] In even the best discussions uninfluenced by Ackrill's paper one finds vagueness at crucial points of Aristotle's ethical theory arising from a lack of concern with his account of act-individuation. I cite a few examples:

(*a*) Allan, 'The Practical Syllogism', *Autour d'Aristote* (Louvain, 1955), 339, commenting on *NE* 1169a22: 'laying claim to the noble for himself' writes: 'evidently this denotes the intrinsic goodness of the act apart from its consequence'. *Which* act?

(*b*) Cooper, *Reason and Human Good* (Harvard, 1975), 78: 'Aristotle insists . . . that in cases of acting or doing (praxis), as distinguished from making or producing something, the end in view is eupraxia.' *Which* act is the praxis? *How* is it related to production?

(*c*) Irwin, 'Aristotle on Reason, Desire and Virtue', *Journal of Philosophy*, LXXII (1975), 570: 'Productions aim to make some product independent of their own existence, but activities do not—for good activity is its own end'. *Which* activity is this? *How* is it related to the production?

not follow: subsequent failure of the transmission system might prevent you from getting home, but would not lessen the moral value of his generous act. For Aristotle, the value of this act would not lie in its actual consequences; but this did not prevent him from allowing the moral agent to consider, when acting, the consequences of his action or require the agent to focus exclusively on the action itself—shorn of all its consequences. His generous act retains its value even if done for the sake of consequences which do not actually occur.[20] Its moral value, although it rests on the presence of a prospective good of this type (namely, helping you home), is immune to the failure of the planned consequences.

The plausibility of this account is to be assessed below; before we can do this, there is a further exegetical puzzle which survives the 'resolution' of the first.

5. Exegetical puzzle (*B*): praxeis and their results

Praxeis differ from productions precisely because praxeis are their own ends (*NE/EE* 1140b6–7) and chosen for their own sake (*NE* 1176b6–7); however, elsewhere Aristotle holds (*NE* 1112b32–3) that:

> Deliberation is concerned with what is done by the agent, actions are done for the sake of *other* things; for the goal is not the object of deliberation, but things done for the sake of the goals the objects of deliberation.

In the first sentence, Aristotle appears to insist that his model is that of *actions* done for the sake of something else. If the something else is also an *action*, it too must presumably be done for the sake of something else.[21] If action for an end is to be possible (not vain), it must be that at some point there is a *goal of action*, which is not itself an action (whatever its ontological category). And this explains the second sentence in an obvious way: 'praxeis are deliberated as means to a goal which is not a praxis and not deliberated'. So the means to an end are actions,

[20] Moral praxeis may, but need not, directly express the moral character of the agent in the way that acting generously affects Bethan's generous character. Alternative praxeis in this case might be helping Mr Jones in his difficulties or lending Mr Jones a hand.

[21] Nor need there always be a further praxis, since basic actions need not all be processes or productions. For example, a basic action may be reflecting on one's prayers (an activity) and need involve no further praxis (I owe this point to Cynthia Freeland). In my earlier discussion of Aristotle's basic actions (*Aristotle's Philosophy of Action*, 70ff) I focused exclusively on that subset of basic actions which are movements of one's limbs or 'detached' limbs. But not all basic actions (in Aristotle's teleological conception) need be of this type.

but the end is something other than an action (*NE* 1111a5–6, 1118a18–19). But this is hard to reconcile with Aristotle's insistence in *Nicomachean/Eudemian Ethics* 1140b6–7 that praxeis are their own goal. Of this passage, Gauthier and Jolif wrote (Commentary ii, 204) of Aristotle:

> il arrive ici à se contradire formellement, en deniant à l'action (*praxis*) l'immanence dans laquelle il avait reconnu sa caractéristique propre, et en lui attributant une fin exterieure à elle-même, ce qui partout ailleurs est la caractéristique propre de la production (*poiēsis*).

There are two separate roots of this apparent incoherence.

(1) *The goal of action is not itself an action*

In *Nicomachean Ethics* III, it appears, Aristotle is concerned in his discussion of practical reasoning with means–ends reasoning only. That is, the agent is pictured as asking 'Given what I have decided, how shall I achieve the end I have set myself?' Hence, successful deliberation consists in the agent's devising a route consisting of means to achieve his goal. The goals in these cases are specified as *objects* or *objects in certain conditions*: for example, safety (*NE* 1110a10, 1111a14), health (*NE* 1111a31; *Metaph.* 1032b6–9; *Phys.* 202a24–7; *EE* 1227a13–35), a house (*Phys.* 200a24–7), wealth (*EE* 1227a13–15). In these cases, the goals of action seem to be states, for example being safe etc., and not *actions*.

Further, in *Nicomachean/Eudemian Ethics* VI. 9 Aristotle's discussion of deliberation is, it appears, of the same model. Thus, in 1142b22–4, in discussing 'good deliberation' he writes that the goal is made by incorrect means. But if the goal in question is 'made', it should be a product of some type: a state (or object in a certain condition) and not an action. Since the account of deliberation in VI. 9 is intended to cover both making and doing, the goal should be of the same ontological type in both cases, and hence must be an object or a state in both cases and not an action. Further, in *Nicomachean/Eudemian Ethics* 1142b27–9, Aristotle sees good deliberation as consisting in finding correct means to particular or to more general goals. But particular ends will include health and strength (1140a27–8), in addition to cases which involve skill. Since such cases have (as their goals) states and objects, the relevant reasoning must take these as its goals and not actions. If so, deliberation appears here to be concerned exclusively with means to producing objects and states

(1142b27–9). But since practical wisdom is defined as excellence in deliberation (1142b31–2), moral deliberation must be conceived here also as the finding of means to bring about products which are states. And this is why in 1140a25–30 Aristotle (while concluding that the practically wise calculate well towards a good end, which is not the object of skill) treats the distinct ends of skill and practical wisdom as falling within the same ontological category, namely, states, and not actions (see also 1140a10–14). But this seems difficult to reconcile with Aristotle's insistence elsewhere that good actions are chosen for their own sake and not for the sake of anything beyond the action, when one adds a further point (2):

(2) *The goal of an action is distinct from, and over and above, the action.*

If these reflections about the goals of action in *Nicomachean Ethics* III and *Nicomachean/Eudemian Ethics* VI are accepted, Aristotle is correct to say in *Nicomachean Ethics* 1112b32–3 that the goal of a praxis is distinct from (*allo ti*) the praxis, as it is a state. If the result is distinct from the action (*allo*), then (it might seem) it is over and above (*para*) the action. Thus, a praxis, if done for the sake of a state of this kind, will be done for the sake of something over and above the action. But then there will be no difference between praxeis and productions: for it is assumed as definitive of the latter that their result, unlike that of praxeis, is over and above the action (cf. 1050a30ff). The result of these considerations is well known: it appears that Aristotle's preferred theory of practical reasoning is inconsistent with his central moral insight: namely, praxeis are chosen for their *own* sake and not for the sake of a further goal. Gauthier and Jolif express this inconsistency as follows (Commentary ii, 5–7):

> C'est là une de ces incohérences foncières . . .: d'une part il a le sentiment tres vif de ce caractère d'absolu qui fait l'originalité des valeurs morales . . . mais d'autre part il applique à l'action morale des analyses conçues pour rendre compte de la production. (7; see also ii, 199, 203–4, 574–5)

Hintikka emphasizes a similar point elsewhere[22] when he argues that Aristotle remained enslaved to a general Greek way of thought about practical reasoning conceived of as directed towards the production of a concrete goal, and concludes that this 'does not sit very happily with some of the kinds of human action which he considers most impor-

[22] Hintikka, 'Remarks on Praxis, Poiesis and Ergon in Plato and Aristotle', *Annales Universitatis Turkuensis Sarja*, Series B (Osa-Tom, 1973).

tant'. Nor is this inconsistency properly removed by postulating a different account of reasoning (Rule-Subsumption Reasoning) in moral cases. For, as has been pointed out by both Hintikka and Wiggins,[23] the texts on which it depends fail clearly to articulate the different type of reasoning at issue. And, as we have seen, Aristotle's discussion in *Nicomachean/Eudemian Ethics* VI. 9 appears to rely on the goal-directed view of practical reasoning in analysing moral reasoning.

Attention to Aristotle's ontology provides a basis for resolving these difficulties, and one which Aristotle himself was happy to apply in relevant cases. His crucial move is as follows: moral praxeis have as results (*erga*) states (or conditions) which are distinct (*allo*) from the actions which bring them about, but which are not over and above (*para*) them in that, for example, they do not 'go beyond' the actions (in a sense to be explained). This move has two ingredients:

(*a*) moral actions have results which they bring about;
(*b*) these results are distinct from the actions but are not over and above them (*allo* $\neq$ *para*).

I want to give grounds for favourable consideration of both (*a*) and (*b*).

(*a*) *Moral actions have results which they 'bring about': the act/result ambiguity*

Aristotle is aware that two of his crucial terms: 'activity' (*energeia*) and 'what is done' (*to prakton*) are *act/result* ambiguous. Thus, '*energeia*' may refer either to the result of an activity or to the activity which leads to that result. In *Metaphysics* 1050a21 ff he notes:

> The result (*ergon*) is the goal (*telos*), the activity (*energeia*) is the result, and this is why the term '*energeia*' is predicated/said by reference to the result and is extended to the actualization (*entelechia*).

That is, an *energeia* may be either the *result* of an activity or the *activity* which leads to that result. In the first use, '*energeia*' is the substance, that is, form, which makes the activity the activity it is. Thus, when in *Metaphysics* 1048a22 ff, he writes: 'that in which the goal is present throughout is a praxis' the goal which is present throughout the

[23] Hintikka, op cit; Wiggins, 'Deliberation and Practical Reason', *PAS* LXXVI (1975/6), 29–51. The problem on which I focus here survives the realization (which I fully endorse) that *charin* and *dia* may be understood as pointing to both causal and non-causal means to a given result.

actualization is what makes the actualization the one it is. Thus, for example, the result for the contemplator is the contemplation, and for the seer the seeing (i.e., that contemplation is done or that seeing is done) which are the internal, and logically necessary, results of his contemplating or his seeing. If the state of contemplation was not achieved, there would be no action of contemplating. And this parallels the way in which the change of the window's opening, in Von Wright's ontology,[24] is the logically necessary internal result of the action of opening the window. The result, in the case of some activities is an immanent state (*hexis enhuparchousa*) which makes the activity the activity it is. In the case of being healthy, the internal good would be health (or health being achieved/maintained); in the case of living well, it would be the good life (or the good life being lived), conceived of as the condition achieved if one lives well.[25]

Aristotle emphasizes that '*what is done*' is act/result ambiguous in precisely this way elsewhere. Thus, in *Eudemian Ethics* 1217a35–7, he writes:

[24] See Von Wright, *Explanation and Understanding* (London, 1971), 66ff, 75, 87ff, 92.

[25] The act/result ambiguity in the case of '*energeia*' suggests a solution to the second puzzle concerning Aristotle's discussion of pleasure raised in section 3 above. If '*energeia*' is act/result ambiguous, there is no ground for insisting that *energeia* in *NE/EE* 1153a10–15 must be the actualization/action rather than the result of the activity (as was supposed when the puzzle was raised). Indeed, there is ground for taking '*energeia*' to refer to the result of the activity in 1153a10 where Aristotle writes: '... pleasures are *energeiai* (activities), that is, a goal' (taking the '*kai*' as epexegetic), and continues with the goal-usage in a11–12 leading to his conclusion: 'this is why ... pleasure is said rather to be an activity of a disposition in line with nature ...' (a13–14). If '*energeia*' is unequivocal in this passage, it must mean throughout the result/goal of the activity and not the actualization; for Aristotle has gone to some length to get the former usage to the forefront of our attention in a10. If so, the result of the activity in *NE/EE* VII can be that which makes the perfect activity perfect: i.e. the condition which in *NE* X perfects the activity. There need be no residual inconsistency between *NE/EE* VII and *NE* X in this respect; for in both, pleasure may be the result of the activity and not the activity itself (or only derivatively the activity: see *Metaph.* 1050a23). *Pace* Miss Anscombe (in the passage cited above), Aristotle need not be seen as identifying pleasure *both* with the activity *and* with something other than the activity in VII and X respectively. In both discussions, pleasure would be best seen as what is sought in doing the action, and need not be identified with the action itself. Of course, there is still need for an analysis of the type of phenomenon which this result is. But that is Aristotle's major philosophical difficulty which we can see more clearly once we have resolved the ontologically-based exegetical puzzles which are our present concern. If what has been said is correct, the result could in some cases—e.g. when smelling roses—be a pleasant sensation which makes the activity a perfect one of its kind. Contrast the view taken by Urmson, 'Aristotle on Pleasure', in *Aristotle. Critical Studies*, ed Moravcsik (New York, 1967), 323–33. Urmson, and Ryle whose account he follows, construe *energeia* as actualization rather than result throughout *NE/EE* VII and *NE* X.

Since 'what is done' is said in more than one way—for it is said both of the results (*hou heneka*) of action and the actions done for these results: for example we say that health and wealth are in the category of what is done (achieved), as are what is done for the sake of these: maintaining health, taking healthy exercise and doing lucrative business—it is clear that well-being (*eudaimonia*) is to be placed as the best of the things done by man.

A similar distinction is present in *de Caelo* 292b6 applying to '*the action*' (praxis): 'This is said in two ways—the result (*hou heneka*) and what is done for the sake of it.' If '*what is done*' and '*the action*' are act/result ambiguous, both may, in the case of maintaining health, refer *either* to health (health being maintained) conceived of as the internal and immanent state which makes the activity the one it is (*NE* 1174b31–2) *or* to the action which brings about this state.

If 'activities', 'actions', and 'what is done' are ambiguous and may refer either to actualizations (bringings about) or to the state brought about (e.g. *hexis*/condition, *NE* 1174b31–3), actions may be done for the sake of something other than the action (namely, the state they bring about) even when they are done for the sake of their internal result. Thus, we may do actions which are health-maintaining for the sake of health (i.e. that health be maintained) or actions which are eudaimonistic for the sake of eudaimonia (the good life *or* that the good life be lived), or contemplate for the sake of contemplation (that contemplation be done). If these results are states distinct from, but not over and above (*para*), the actions which bring them about, an action done for the sake of its logically necessary internal result may be characterized as done for its own sake rather than for the sake of anything over and above the action.

(*b*) *Internal results of activities are distinct from activities (*allo*), but are not over and above them (*para*)*

Aristotle distinguished sharply between types of results in several passages. In *Metaphysics* 1050a30ff he writes:

In those cases in which there is an occurrence beyond (*para*) the actual use, in these the actuality is in what is made (e.g. building is in what is built, weaving is in what is woven . . .); in those cases in which there is no result beyond (*para*) the activity, in these the actuality is in the agent (e.g. seeing in the seer, contemplation in the contemplator, life in the soul, and thus well-being: for this is a kind of life).

Thus, he separates as results over and above (*para*) the action those which occur in what is made, and distinguishes these from what occurs when the goal is immanent in the actualization. Thus, there are some results (*erga*) which are over and above the action, and these occur in paradigm cases of activity. Such results will be distinct (*qua* immanent states or actualities, 1050a21) from the actions (or actualizations, 1050a22ff) which produce them, but will not be over and above these actions.[26] And this is because results of this type are not changes in other objects brought about by the action, but are immanent in the action (i.e., present while the agent acts)[27] and occur without any change being produced in another object.

This passage is echoed in Aristotle's distinction between types of results in *Eudemian Ethics* 1219a12–17:

'Result' is said in two ways: of some the result is something over and above (*para*) the employment (e.g. the house of house-building) . . . of others the result is the employment itself (e.g. sight in the case of seeing, contemplation in the case of mathematical knowledge).

Only the former set of results are over and above the action; the latter are not. Hence, there may be conditions or states which serve as results of action, but which are not over and above the action, although they are distinct (ontologically) from the action. In both cases, the action can be done *for the sake* of these results; but the results

[26] Such results will be *different* from the praxeis (*allo*, *NE* 1112b33) as they are goals of the action and not the action itself (*NE* 1094a17; *EE* 1217a37ff; *Metaph.* 1050a21–3), in the way that health differs from actions done for the sake of health and from being healthy (*NE* 1174b32–3). But they are not over and above (*para*) the actions (*NE* 1094a4, 5, 1176b5–7, 1177b1–3, see also *Metaph.* 1050a30ff) since they do not occur in anything else (*Metaph.* 1050a31–5) and cannot exist apart from the activity itself (*NE* 1175a32, 35). Thus, they are distinct from the activity, but inseparable from it (*NE* 1175a32–5). A full discussion of all cases (not involving actions) where *a* is different from *b* (*allo*), but is not over and above (*para*) *b* lies outside the scope of the present paper. It would involve discussion of Aristotle's account of the relation of, e.g., universals and particulars, wholes and parts, matter and form. I am indebted to Jennifer Whiting for noting the possibility of a wider application of this distinction.

[27] In *NE* 1176b6–8 and 1177b3ff Aristotle defends the following bi-conditional claim: *x* is chosen for its own sake (*di'hautēn*, *kath'hautēn*) if and only if nothing is sought over and above (*para*) *x*. And this allows that the result may be other than *x* (*allo*) and *x* be chosen for its own sake, provided that the result is not over and above (*para*) *x*. But it rules out the possibility that in these cases *x* actually is chosen for its own sake and for the sake of a result *over and above x* (see also *NE/EE* 1151b1–3). If *eudaimonia* is not (in this specific sense) over and above virtuous action, the latter may on occasion be chosen for its own sake and for the sake of eudaimonia which results from it (*NE* 1097b2–5), even though eudaimonia is other than (*allo*) virtuous actions. (I intend to develop this point further elsewhere.)

will differ depending on whether or not they essentially involve changes in others beyond the agent (*NE* 1094a15–17).

These two claims:

(*a*) moral actions have results which they bring about,
(*b*) these results are not *over and above* the actions, but are distinct from them,

allow Aristotle to reconcile the result-directed account of practical reasoning with his emphasis on moral action being chosen for its own sake. A courageous action may be chosen for the sake of its internal result: for example, courage (*NE* 1115b21), that is, the actuality of courage (that courage be exemplified), which is brought about by acting courageously. But the presence of a result of this type would not turn the action into a production, or debar it from being a praxis. Provided that the relevant result is an internal state of the action of this type (and essentially involves no change in others), the action may be a praxis and done for the sake of its resultant state. There is no conflict between φ'ing being a courageous action, chosen for its own sake, and φ'ing being done in order that courage be exemplified. Indeed, being done so that courage be exemplified just is choosing φ'ing for its own sake and not for the sake of anything over and above the action (see *NE* 1176b6–8).

If this is correct, there is no incompatibility between Aristotle's talk of practical reasoning as aiming at results distinct from actions, and his insistence on the production/praxis distinction. Given the plurality of types of result he allows, he can employ an act/result model for all cases of practical and productive reasoning, while at the same time allowing that praxeis are done for their own sake. In using the act–result model of reasoning, Aristotle—so far from showing himself wedded to an outdated telic element of the Greek conceptual scheme—was employing a model which could apply equally, and without distinction, to all cases of practical reasoning. Once one is clear on Aristotle's act–result ontology, and the *variety* of results he envisages, the apparent 'incoherences' which so troubled Gauthier and Jolif and Hintikka disappear.[28]

[28] Failure to appreciate the variety of results possible in Aristotle's ontology leads Troels Engberg-Pederson astray. He poses the following difficulty: 'If the act-description contains a reference to the result of the action ... this is what gives the act value; but in that case it seems impossible to distinguish an act under such a description from an act which is a *poiēsis*' (*Aristotle's Theory of Moral Insight* (Oxford, 1983), 32). His 'solution' runs as follows: 'in the case of *kinēseis* (such as building a house

6. Philosophical problems of the *poiēsis*/praxis distinction

At the outset, we considered two exegetical issues which threatened the coherence of the production/praxis distinction: the co-occurrence of productions and praxeis, and Aristotle's insistence on praxeis being done for a distinct goal. I have argued that these two puzzles arise from a failure to grasp Aristotle's ontology of actions, and that this (with its distinctions between praxeis, their results and co-occurring *poiēseis*) provides the basis for their resolution. Is this enough to vindicate Aristotle's insistence that moral actions are praxeis? And what does the account tell us about his general views on moral action and practical reasoning? I wish to raise two problems only.

Aristotle's position, as it emerges from these considerations, seems to be as follows: if Bethan ties the bean framework for a good end (e.g. providing Mr Jones with autumn vegetables), this is sufficient for her to act generously. However, the value of her moral action, namely, acting generously, does not depend on whether the good consequences actually occur, even though she would not have done this fine action had she not aimed at a good end. The moral action is a praxis, whose moral worth is immune to the failure of Bethan's desired consequences. As a praxis, it is an activity chosen for its own sake which Bethan may enjoy doing (namely, the acting generously) at a time before the good consequences, at which she aims, occur. Although consequences are relevant to Bethan's deliberation, their occurrence does not determine the moral value of her action. So why is it important for Aristotle to establish the presence of a praxis of this type in the cases of moral action? Is his claim a substantial thesis?

Immunity to the failure of planned consequences can be achieved in

or trying to rescue a drowning child) we cannot sever the act from the intended act-result, since no act will be left once the logical operation has been performed. The definition of *poiēsis*, on the other hand, relies on the possibility of such severance' (34). But this solution seems paradoxical since building, like weaving, is one of Aristotle's paradigm cases of a *poiēsis* (*Metaph.* 1050a31 ff). Indeed, in any case of a *poiēsis*, if we subtract the intended result (viz., a house, a woollen garment), it is not clear that what survives is a *poiēsis* (e.g. making a house/woollen garment) rather than, e.g., a moving of one's hands with the aim of making a garment (i.e. a failed *poiēsis*). Nor is this surprising: in Von Wright's scheme, subtraction of *intended act-resuls* undermines the relevant *poiēsis* or praxis (cf. *Explanation and Understanding* (London, 1971), 87–9). Aristotle's actual way of distinguishing results in the case of praxeis (*Metaph.* 1050a31 ff) depends on the *immanence of the result in the activity* and its separability from the effects it produces in others. If so, bringing about maximal welfare will not be a praxis since its effects are generally located in others.

ways different from Aristotle's. One could ascribe value to Bethan's basic action (namely, moving her hands so as to tie the bean framework) on the basis of either the value of the state of affairs she actually produced *or* the state she would have produced had her plan succeeded. The value of her trying to φ could be determined by the value of the state, if it occurs. There is no need to ascribe value to the separate moral praxis of acting generously in order to achieve Aristotle's degree of immunity to future failure of one's plan. So why did Aristotle insist that the prime bearer of moral value was the *praxis*: an activity cotemporaneous with, but distinct from, Bethan's tying up Mr Jones's bean framework? Why posit a separate *activity* over and above the process of tying, done for a good end? What is the actual motivation for doing so?

It seems possible, in general, to posit (or detect) a relevant praxis—even in the least promising cases. Suppose that Bethan is making a pot for money, but also that she enjoys doing this and is happy to do it for its own sake. In such a case, there could be a separate activity, namely, exercising her manual skills (doing some pot-making), which is the praxis different from the *poiēsis* of making the pot.[29] Suppose that Farooq is walking up K2, and derives his enjoyment both from walking and from approaching the summit (i.e. from seeing each step as contributing to reaching his goal).[30] In this case, the confirmed 'praxis-hunter' could spot the following activities:

Farooq's walking: his doing some exercise of his ambulatory abilities;
Farooq's seeing that his walking is leading to the end he has set for himself;

as well as the process of his walking up to the summit. So he can save Aristotle's thesis that activities and praxeis are present in cases like

[29] Taylor and Gosling emphasize the importance of such cases in *The Greeks on Pleasure*, 313.

[30] Aristotle needs to be circumspect in his description of the proper aspects of activities such as seeing or hearing. For if the proper object of *S'* seeing was, e.g., the fleet going by, or of *S'* hearing was a four-part symphony, it would be plausible to regard both the seeing and the hearing as processes, incomplete until the goal is reached. Hence, in order to preserve their status as *activities*, Aristotle needs to characterize their objects differently, e.g. as sights and sounds (*NE* 1174b27–8), which are the internal objects of seeing and hearing. This seems to be in line with his characterization of the proper objects of the senses in *de Anima* 418a10ff: what is specific to each sense, as colour is to sight and sound is to hearing. This he distinguishes from incidental perception, namely, that these colours belong to the fleet or that these sounds belong to the symphony (418a21–4). Thus, he is able to treat *seeing* as an activity, as we may have seen colours and go on seeing them, even though these colours belong to a spectacle which one cannot have seen until it was over.

this where, for example, *enjoyment* seems essentially to involve a stage-by-stage goal-directed process, by adding separate psychological activities, for example seeing. But what is his motivation for doing so?

The two questions raised in the preceding paragraphs are related. One motivation for insisting that the prime bearer of moral value is the praxis is that, for example, Bethan can *enjoy* the activity of acting morally while tying the bean framework—independently of whether (or not) the good consequences at which she aims occurs. So if the proper objects of enjoyment are activities, then Aristotle has good reason to posit a separate activity in such cases. But if this latter thesis itself depends on no more than the praxis (activity)-hunter's ability to detect an activity whenever a subject enjoys his actions, Aristotle's preference for praxeis as the central feature of his moral theory appears to be unmotivated. Why couldn't what is appropriately enjoyed just be the process of tying up the bean framework for a good end (winter vegetables)? Why generate a further activity, namely acting generously, as the prime bearer of enjoyment or moral value?

Full discussion of Aristotle's account of pleasure lies beyond the present paper. But what is clear is that if Aristotle's praxis-thesis is to be a substantial one, he will need to provide a strong and theoretically interesting connection between activity and pleasure in order to safeguard it. It is not enough that one is able to 'rig up' an activity whenever there is a plausible case of enjoyment or moral praxis. What is required is a strong conceptual connection between pleasure and activity which justifies this procedure. Gosling and Taylor in effect despair of this when they write:

> [Aristotle's] arguments themselves provide no refutation of the theories [i.e. the process theories] against which they are directed.[31]

If their despair is justified, the need for a substantial defence of the thesis that moral praxeis are the prime bearers of moral value is the more pressing. Without such a defence, the thesis appears trivial, and cannot sustain the weight which Aristotle places on it. For what of value would be lost if there were no praxeis and all occurrences were processes—provided that the time for moral assessment, or for being satisfied, was distinguished from the time at which the goal of the process was achieved?

Aristotle's account, if it can be sustained,[32] puts pressure on our

[31] above n 6, 317.

[32] A question which calls for immediate philosophical attention is the following: is

own concepts as well. Is his moral theory consequentialist (and teleological) or not? This depends on whether the internal result of acting courageously (the state of courage being exemplified) is to be counted as a consequence of acting courageously. For many, the answer is obvious: 'No'. But this is because they confine consequences exclusively to causal consequences (as in utilitarian ethical theories). While one may legitimately define *one* species of consequentialism (e.g. welfarism) in this way, it is not clear that all consequentialists must confine their attention exclusively to causal consequences. If Evans had climbed to the top of Everest in 1953 and thereby become the first man to scale that mountain, why should the latter valuable state (a non-causal consequence of his reaching the summit) not be a consequence of his action? Of course, utilitarian consequentialists have been, in general, causal consequentialists; but that is a different matter. Aristotle may have been a non-utilitarian consequentialist.

Precise, and illuminating, characterizations of consequentialist (teleological)[33] theories are hard to find. Frankena's definition is adopted by Rawls and Irwin. He wrote:

> A teleological theory says that the basic or ultimate criterion of what is right is the value that is brought into being. The final appeal must be to the comparative amount of good brought about.[34]

Aristotle entitled to assume that there are conditions or states such as the *actuality of courage*, which is the internal result of courageous action, or *pleasure* and the *life of well-being*, which are the internal results of enjoyment and living well? What type of entities are these? Are they theoretically defensible? These are some of the genuine philosophical questions about Aristotle's theory which should properly trouble us once we have cleared away the ontologically based exegetical puzzles with which this paper is principally concerned. For if there can be, e.g., no actualities of courage or states which exemplify courage, Aristotle cannot legitimately use the act–result model to analyse moral action and moral reasoning. He will have no ground for postulating *results* in the case of *praxeis* to parallel those in the case of productions. Detailed philosophical appraisal of this feature of Aristotle's thought requires a separate paper; but two considerations have already been given which constitute a *prima facie* defence of Aristotle's view:

(i) the possibility in natural language of characterizing internal results of praxeis, such as occur when the agent brings it about that there is (*a*) a *courageous deed*, (*b*) *a deed which exemplifies courage*, (*c*) *a state which exemplifies courage*, (*d*) *a state which reflects his courage*;

(ii) the theoretical use of these internal results (states) in characterizing both moral and technical practical reasoning in a common ontological model.

[33] Most writers introduce the term without detailed definition. Thus, Julia Annas once wrote, 'A consequentialist holds that moral justification is provided by pointing to desirable consequences' (*Introduction to Plato's Republic* (Oxford, 1981), 62–3). But this leaves it unclear under what conditions something (whether action or state) is to count as a *consequence* of an action. Similarly, Elizabeth Anscombe, *en route* to her famous

[*See p 144 for n 33 cont. and n 34*]

But if it is sufficient for being a consequentialist that one sees courageous actions as valuable because they bring about a given state of affairs (the exemplification of courage) which is the internal result of acting courageously, then Aristotle is a type of consequentialist—one who holds that these internal results are of more moral worth than the causal consequences of the action (e.g. autumnal vegetables for Mr Jones/general well-being). Why should these internal results be excluded when one considers the states of affairs brought about in the world by doing the action? Provided that all the morally relevant states which result from our actions can be unified (e.g. as exemplifying properties which exemplify well-being), why not assess both the internal and external results brought about by our actions?

It is not my intention to maintain that Aristotle was a consequentialist. It is rather to note that unless we obtain a clearer grasp of what *consequentialism* is, discussion of whether Aristotle or Plato, or we ourselves, are consequentialists or anti-consequentialists (e.g. deontologists) will prove idle. The study of Aristotle shows that there is much unoccupied ethical space between the position of the causal consequentialist and that of the theorist who considers only the agent's intentions or motives. But without a proper understanding of *consequentialism*, we will not be able to grasp the alternatives in this area. Nor is it sufficient to distinguish those ethical theories which emphasize right actions from those which emphasize good results. For in Aristotle's theory, there can be no right actions without good internal results, and no good internal results without right actions. What is required, and is not on the surface of either Aristotle's or, for example, Rawls's ethical theory, is an argument for the priority of the one over the other.[35] It is a major merit of Aristotle's ontological account that it contains the resources to raise this central question in a clear and cogent way.[36]

Oriel College, Oxford

conclusion that 'it is a necessary feature of consequentialism that it is a shallow philosophy' ('Contemporary Moral Philosophy', repr. in *Is/Ought Question*, ed W. D. Hudson (London, 1969), 187) does not tarry to define precisely what consequentialism is.

[34] Frankena, *Ethics* (Englewood Cliffs, NJ, 1968), 13. Rawls, *A Theory of Justice* (Oxford, 1971), 24ff. Irwin, *Plato's Moral Theory* (Oxford, 1977), 340.

[35] Or an argument that no such priority is required.

[36] My major debt to John Ackrill's writings on these topics should be clear thoughout this paper. His high scholarly standards and philosophical acumen give a paradigm of the successful study of classical philosophy. I have also gained from his criticisms of an earlier version of this paper, and from discussing these issues with Jonathan Barnes, Cynthia Freeland, Gavin Lawrence, Michael Morris, and Barry Taylor.

Aristotle on Choosing Virtue for Itself

by Richard Kraut (University of Illinois at Chicago Circle)

In this paper, I will be taking a close look at four groups of passages in the *Nicomachean Ethics*[1]. All make similar claims, and all have a Kantian ring: we choose virtue for itself, virtuous activity is desirable in itself, good action is an end, a good person chooses virtuous acts for themselves. What does Aristotle mean by these statements? Are they inconsistent with the rest of his moral philosophy, as some have thought?[2] Do they reflect significant agreement with Kant? So it has been said[3]. However, my own answer to these last two questions will be negative. I will argue that the passages in question neither anticipate Kant nor indicate inconsistency in Aristotle's thought.

To avoid confusion, I want to separate the issue I will be discussing from another important one. Some assert that Aristotle lacks such concepts as moral duty and moral goodness, so that his framework for ethics differs radically from our own rather Kantian outlook. As G. E. M. Anscombe puts it, "... The term 'moral' ... just doesn't seem to fit, in its modern sense, into an account of Aristotelian ethics."[4] By contrast, R. A. Gauthier claims that "... Aristotle placed the distinct idea of moral 'duty' at the very

---

[1] Unless otherwise indicated, all references will be to this work. I have consulted the translations of W. D. Ross (London, 1915) and M. Ostwald (Indianapolis, 1962).

[2] See W. D. Ross, *Aristotle*, 5th edn. (London, 1949), pp. 188 and 233—234; H. A. Prichard, "The Meaning of *Agathon* in the *Ethics* of Aristotle," in J. M. E. Moravcsik (ed.), *Aristotle* (Garden City, N. Y., 1967), pp. 241—242, 247—248, and 258—259. Compare R. A. Gauthier, *La Morale d'Aristote* (Paris, 1963), pp. 33—37 and 79. Gauthier's position can be found in translation in J. Walsh and H. Shapiro (eds.), *Aristotle's Ethics* (Belmont, Cal., 1967), p. 19.

[3] See Roger J. Sullivan, "The Kantian Critique of Aristotle's Moral Philosophy: An Appraisal," in *The Review of Metaphysics* XXVIII (September, 1974), pp. 31 and 43—44. W. D. Ross (ibid., p. 188) also says that certain statements of Aristotle's suggest agreement with Kant, though Ross take these statements to be incompatible with the rest of Aristotle's ethics.

[4] See her "Modern Moral Pihlosophy," *Philosophy* 33 (1958), pp. 1—2. D. J. Allan also asserts that Aristotle "takes little or no account of the motive of moral obligation". See *The Philosophy of Aristotle*, 2nd. ed. (London, 1970), p. 140.

center of his ethics."[5] I will not address myself to this complex issue of what the modern, or Kantian, concept of moral duty is, and whether it applies to Aristotle's philosophy. It seems plausible to me that when Aristotle says that an act is in accordance with virtue, and Kant calls that same act a duty, they are making different claims. But I will not argue the point or assume it. Rather, the question I am concerned with has to do with motivation. According to Kant, performing a duty for its own sake is incompatible with acting solely in order to be happy. As I interpret Aristotle, however, to choose virtuous acts for themselves is to choose them only because they are principal ingredients in a happy life. Though both Aristotle and Kant believe that we must perform good acts from pure motives, they differ over what this purity involves. For Aristotle, it means recognizing one's good actions as parts of a happy life. For Kant, it means not caring whether they contribute to one's own happiness.

A cautionary note about vocabulary: Instead of continually using "virtuous" and "non-virtuous" to describe Aristotle's theory, I sometimes use such substitutes as "moral" and "immoral", "ethical" and "unethical". I do this only for the sake of variation, and not to imply that Anscombe is wrong.

I

I begin by sketching an interpretation of the *Nicomachean Ethics* according to which the contrast between Aristotle and Kant is extreme and obvious. Then in the following sections I will examine the four passages in which Aristotle says that the virtues and virtuous acts are desirable for themselves. We will see that these four passages, so far from reflecting agreement with Kant, are entirely consistent with the anti-Kantian interpretation I describe in this section.

[5] See *La Morale d'Aristote* (Paris, 1963), p. 88. The entire section of this book, "La Sagesse: Conscience du Devoir" (pp. 86—91), is relevant to this question. For an English translation, see Walsh and Shapiro, *op. cit.*, pp. 20—23. Sullivan's paper, cited in n. 2, sides with Gauthier; see especially pp. 35—36. Also relevant here is W. K. Frankena's distinction between an ethics of virtue and an ethics of duty. See his "Prichard and the Ethics of Virtue," *Monist* 54 (1970), pp. 1—17. Notice that Frankena holds back from attributing to Aristotle what he calls a pure ethics of virtue (p. 15). On this issue, I am most in agreement with W. F. R. Hardie's statement: "Moral obligation is not a simple concept of which there is an agreed account, so that we can ask whether Aristotle had the concept, yes or no." See *Aristotle's Ethical Theory* (Oxford, 1968), p. 335.

Consider a soldier who knows that a battle to defend his just and well-governed state will soon take place. He reflects, in a moment of quiet, on what reasons there are for the two alternatives uppermost in his mind: remaining to fight, and running away. What advice does Aristotle's ethics give him? According to the anti-Kantian interpretation, Aristotle would argue as follows: "Your strongest rational desire is to lead a happy life; this is the highest priority of every human being, good and bad. You should therefore perform that action which best fits in with your desire to be happy. Now, if someone could convince me that the unethical act, running away, is required for you to be happy, then I would urge you to perform this act of cowardice. But no such thing can be shown, and in fact the very opposite is true. For reasons presented in the *Nicomachean Ethics*, you will be happy only if you courageously remain in battle."

The crux of the anti-Kantian interpretation is that Aristotle recommends performing the virtuous act *only if* this, rather than the immoral alternative, is necessary for happiness. The contrast with Kant is obvious, for although Kant would agree that the soldier ought to remain at his station, he would insist that the soldier must stay regardless of whether this action detracts from or constitutes part of his happiness. For Aristotle, but not for Kant, we must ask what happiness is before we can know whether to lead a moral or an immoral life.

I take the anti-Kantian interpretation to be a common and plausible reading of Aristotle's ethics[6]. It may not be the only possible way of understanding him, but it is nevertheless strongly suggested by a number of passages. For example, the *Nicomachean Ethics* assigns to politics the all-embracing task of determining what must be done and what left undone in any polis; it determines which skills and sciences should be learned, and to what extent (Book I, Ch. 2). To decide such questions, politics uses the touchstone of happiness: the value of all human pursuits depends on how much they are needed in order to achieve this highest of all goals. Now, this implies that virtuous activity must be assessed by the same standard. If it really is true that we ought to be courageous rather than cowardly, generous rather than stingy, and so on, then

[6] It can be found in Prichard, *op. cit.*, p. 241: "... When a man does an action deliberately ... he does it simply in order to ... become happy, this being so even when he does what is virtuous ..." D. J. Allan, *op. cit.*, p. 126, suggests the same point: "Happiness ... is ... the ultimate standard of reference for all our moral judgments." Also see W. D. Ross, *op. cit.*, p. 188.

these qualities must be shown to make a larger contribution to happiness than their opposites.

Furthermore, this interpretation is supported by the fact that for Aristotle "What is happiness?" is a momentous question. It is, in other words, a question motivated not by mere intellectual curiosity, but by the desire to know how to live (1094a18—26). Aristotle therefore could not be saying, "From a practical standpoint, it does not matter where our argument leads, for we shall continue to live virtuously whatever happiness turns out to be — whether it be wealth, or physical pleasure, or virtuous activity, etc." For if this were his approach, his question, "What is happiness?", *would* be purely academic. Instead, Aristotle must be taken to mean, "Whichever life our arguments point to, that is the life we should try to lead." And this entails that one should cultivate the ethical virtues only because such qualities are more needed for happiness than the corresponding vices[7].

Nonetheless, in spite of the plausibility of the anti-Kantian interpretation, it does seem to be contradicted by all those passages which say that the virtues and virtuous behavior are desirable for themselves. To take one of the most striking of these passages: ". . . We choose every virtue for itself, for if nothing resulted from them we would still choose each one; but we also choose them for the sake of happiness . . ." (1097b2—4). Aristotle endorses this choice, as the statement's context indicates. He believes, in other words, that we *should* choose every virtue even if none resulted in happiness. Yet the anti-Kantian interpretation says that, according to Aristotle, virtuous actions should be preferred to immoral alternatives only because of their importance for happiness.

My aim is to show that this contradiction is only apparent. When we look carefully at this and other passages in which Aristotle says that virtuous activity is desirable or chosen for itself, we will see that none contradicts the anti-Kantian interpretation. In none of them is Aristotle anticipating or agreeing with Kant.

[7] Of course, the happiest life, Aristotle argues in Book X, Ch. 7—8, is the contemplative life, and so this is the life one should try, above all, to lead. But this in no way interferes with Aristotle's believing that a person who has the moral virtues (justice, courage, etc.) to a high degree is, so far forth, happier than one who has them to a low degree. In other words, Aristotle believes both that a contemplative moral life should be chosen over a non-contemplative moral life, and that a non-contemplative moral life should be chosen over a non-contemplative immoral life. These choices are correct *only* because in each case the first kind of life is happier than the second.

Before proceeding to these passages, however, I want to make two further remarks about the anti-Kantian interpretation, so that no misunderstanding of it takes place.

First, this interpretation does not claim that according to Aristotle happiness somehow comes to a person *after* he performs virtuous acts. Clearly, Aristotle's view is that actions in accordance with virtue are among the necessary and principal *ingredients*, not *antecedent causes*, of a happy life[8]. What the anti-Kantian interpretation holds is that virtuous acts are more desirable than their immoral alternatives only because they can be shown to be necessary and principal ingredients of happiness.

Second, this interpretation presupposes that for Aristotle the concept of happiness and the concept of virtuous activity are different. That this is presupposed is obvious, for if they were the same concept, then the desire for happiness would be the same desire as the desire to act virtuously, and the former could not be sensibly said to have any priority over the latter. And it should also be obvious that this assumption is correct. After all, if "What is happiness?" were for Aristotle just another way of asking, "What is activity in accordance with virtue?", then he would not be giving us a very informative answer when he finally arrives at the conclusion, in Book I, Ch. 7, that happiness is, in large part, activity in accordance with virtue. His "answer" would be an empty tautology.

Nonetheless, "activity in accordance with virtue" is at least part of Aristotle's definition of *eudaimonia*[9]; though the two concepts are not the same, one appears in the definition of the other. And this may seem to present a problem for the anti-Kantian interpretation. For how can happiness be the standard by which we judge the value of virtuous activity, if the very definition of *eudaimonia* refers to such activity?

To answer this question, we must distinguish two sorts of beliefs Aristotle has about happiness. First, there are his substantive con-

[8] I say "necessary and principal" ingredients and not merely "necessary" ingredients in order to distinguish activity in accordance with virtue from external goods (wealth, power, friends, etc.). The latter, Aristotle insists, are necessary to some degree for a good life (1099 a 31—1099 b 8), but they differ from virtuous behavior in that they are not principal ingredients (*kyriai*), but only necessary accessories, of happiness (1100 b 8—11, using Ostwald's translation of *prosdeitai*).

[9] At 1098 b 10, 1098 b 20, 1098 b 31, 1099 b 25 and 1100 b 11, Aristotle applies the word *logos* to his conclusion that happiness is virtuous activity. It does not matter, for my present purposes, whether he also means to include in the definition a reference to external goods.

clusions about what goods a happy life should include: the contemplative life is best; but since we are human we will be happy only if we act from the moral virtues; and as accessories we need the external goods. Second, there are the criteria he uses to establish and confirm his substantive conclusions. To take some examples: whatever happiness turns out to be, it must be something that belongs to a person in such an intimate way that it can be taken from him only with great difficulty (1095b25—26). Furthermore, happiness must consist in using a capacity that is distinctive of human beings, whatever that capacity turns out to be (1097b22—1098a18). And it would be very odd if happiness came to us purely by chance (1099b20—25), or if it did not require hard work (1176b28—30).

Now, according to the anti-Kantian interpretation, Aristotle's belief that we should pursue happiness above all else is independent of his substantive conclusions concerning which lives are happy. He is convinced that the criteria he uses in his search for happiness are such that, whichever life they point to, one ought to lead that kind of life. It is true that these criteria are not built into the definition of *eudaimonia* he eventually gives. Rather, that definition refers only to his substantive results: happiness turns out to be activity in accordance with virtue. Nonetheless, the fact remains that Aristotle's unconditional allegiance to happiness is independent of his conclusion that happiness is virtuous activity. In view of what the criteria of happiness are, we should lead that kind of life, whatever it turns out to be.

There is therefore no circularity in Aristotle's procedure. Happiness is the standard by which virtuous activity is judged; such activity has its prominence only because it meets the criteria Aristotle uses in his search for happiness. It is not as though Aristotle is measuring the value of virtuous activity by means of a yardstick which has already been defined in terms of that activity. For the builds a reference to such activity into his definition of *eudaimonia* only after he has arrived at the conclusion that virtuous acts are among the principal ingredients of a happy life.

So much by way of elucidation of the anti-Kantian interpretation. Whether or not it proves to be the best way of understanding Aristotle, it certainly is a coherent and plausible candidate. For the remainder of the paper, I will try to show that, appearances to the contrary, nothing in Aristotle is inconsistent with it.

II

Honor, pleasure, intelligence (*nous*), and every virtue we also choose for themselves, for if nothing resulted from them we would still choose each one. But we choose them too for the sake of happiness, since we suppose that because of them we will be happy. (1097 b 2—5)

This statement contains important ambiguities[10], and contradicts the anti-Kantian interpretation if they are resolved in one particular way. As we will see, however, there is a plausible way of understanding the passage which makes it entirely compatible with that interpretation.

The ambiguities are these: First, to whom does "we" refer? Is Aristotle trying to characterize the attitude of all human beings in this passage, or is he instead describing only the views of himself and his virtuous listeners? The *Nicomachean Ethics* is addressed to those who have already been brought up properly (1095 b 4—6), and Aristotle may have this special audience in mind when he says ". . . we choose . . ." On the other hand, nothing in this statement or its context indicates that "we" must be narrowly construed. It is quite possible that what Aristotle says here is intended to hold true of everyone.

Second, when Aristotle says that we choose honor, pleasure, intelligence and every virtue, what does he mean these goods are chosen over? After all, there is no such thing as simply choosing; to choose something is to prefer it to, to want it more than, something else[11]. There are a number of ways of filling in this ellipsis, but the most important, I think are these: (a) We choose these goods in the sense that we want to have all of them to a high rather than

[10] These ambiguities are not noticed by the commentaries I have consulted: J. Burnet, *The Ethics of Aristotle* (London, 1900); R. A. Gauthier and J. Jolif, *L'Ethique a Nicomaque* (Louvain, 1970); A. Grant, *The Ethics of Aristotle* (London, 1874); H. Joachim, *The Nicomachean Ethics* (Oxford, 1951). The first two of these works observe that the goods named in this passage correspond to the types of lives mentioned in Book I, Ch. 5 as the main candidates for happiness. Now these candidates are rivals, since no individual adheres to more than one of these conceptions of happiness at any one time. And this suggests that Burnet, Gauthier and Jolif take both the first and second *hairoumetha* ("we choose") to mean that *some* human beings choose pleasure, *some* choose honor, etc., no person choosing more than one of these. As will be seen, the interpretation I favor is a different one, for I take the first *hairoumetha* (though not the second) to mean that all human beings make the same choice: they all want some of these goods rather than none.

[11] Aristotle is sensitive to this point, for he says that choice is the result of preceding deliberation, and that deliberation necessarily involves considering alternatives, accepting one option and rejecting others (1112 a 15—17 and 1112 b 11—19). Joachim, *ibid.*, pp. 100—101, is helpful here.

a low degree (i. e. the more of each the better); (b) We choose these goods in the sense that we want to have some rather than none of each. Again, there is nothing in the passage or its immediate context to indicate which construal is correct.

The statement contradicts the anti-Kantian interpretation only if Aristotle is using "we" narrowly and is asserting (a) rather than (b). For in that case he means: "We virtuous ones choose a high degree of virtue over a low degree; that is we would rather be good than bad. And in preferring this, we are choosing the virtues for themselves, for we want to be virtuous rather than immoral regardless of the connection between virtue and happiness or any other good." If this is what Aristotle means, then no doubt he would also say that one should choose a virtuous *act* over any immoral alternatives, regardless of the connection between happiness and virtuous activity: a remarkable anticipation of Kant's ethics, and a direct denial of the anti-Kantian interpretation.

But, as I have said, it is open to us to construe "we" broadly, and to choose reading (b) rather than (a). In this case, Aristotle is saying: "We human beings choose to have some honor, pleasure, intelligence and virtue rather than none, and in so doing we are choosing these things for themselves. That is, even if nothing, not even happiness, resulted from these things, we would still rather have some of each than none[12]. But in fact, we human beings do choose these goods for the sake of happiness, for some of us say that happiness is honor, some that it is pleasure, some that it is intelligence, and others that it is virtue."[13]

---

[12] See Book VII of the *Politics* for Aristotle's claim that whatever one's view about happiness, one will in any case want some degree of physical, external, and psychological goods (such as intelligence and virtue). His statement is worth quoting in full: "Nobody would deny that the ideally happy (*makarioi*) are bound to possess a" three (external goods, goods of the soul, and goods of the body). For nobody would call ideally happy a man who does not have a particle of courage, temperance, justice or wisdom (*phronēsis*), who is afraid of the flies that flutter by him, cannot refrain from any of the most outrageous actions in order to gratify a desire to eat or drink, ruins his dearest friends for the sake of a farthing, and similarly in matters of the intellect (*dianoia*) is as senseless and mistaken as any child or lunatic. But although everyone would agree with these propositions, they differ about amount and degrees of value. They think it is enough to possess however small a quantity of virtue, but of wealth, riches, power, glory and everything of that kind they seek a larger and larger amount without limit" (1323 a 24—38). I have adapted H. Rackham's translation (London, 1932).

[13] "We suppose that because of *a*, *b*, *c*, and *d*, we will be happy" can mean "Some of us suppose that because of *a* we will be happy, others suppose that because of *b*

On this interpretation, Aristotle is considering four different answers to the question, "What is happiness?"[14], and he is telling us that even if all four were wrong, they would still name goods that we want to some extent, whatever their connection with other goods. If this is what he is saying, then our passage does not reveal any significant agreement between him and Kant. For Aristotle would not be claiming that whether virtue is important for happiness or not, we should still strive to be virtuous people. Rather, he would only be saying that whatever the connection between virtue and happiness, we would in any case strive to have *some* degree — not necessarily a high degree — of virtue.

Now, as I have said, nothing in the text indicates which of these two readings is correct. But we have nonetheless arrived at a significant conclusion: Contrary to our first impressions, the passage under examination does not show that the anti-Kantian interpretation should be rejected. That interpretation is entirely consistent with Aristotle's claim that we choose every virtue for itself. (Recall that in this and the following sections I am not offering further evidence for the anti-Kantian interpretation. Rather, I am arguing that what seems to be evidence against it really is not.)

III

> Of activities, some are necessary and desirable for the sake of other things, while others are desirable in themselves. Obviously, happiness must be considered one of the activities that are desirable in themselves, and is not among those that are desirable for the sake of something else . . . Activities that are desirable in themselves

we will be happy, etc.", just as "In 1973, we Americans visited every country in the world" can mean "Every country in the world was visited by some American."

[14] The four goods named in our passage (1097 b 1—5) correspond to four of the five goods briefly mentioned earlier in Book I, Ch. 5. (The fifth, wealth, is dismissed because it is not desirable for its own sake.) However, notice this important change: whereas in Book I, Ch. 5, Aristotle says that some take happiness to be the contemplative life (1096 a 4—5), the corresponding good in our passage is intelligence (*nous*), not contemplation. My interpretation provides an explanation for the shift: Aristotle is saying that certain goods are wanted by all people to some extent. But not everyone has some desire to contemplate, and so Aristotle shifts to the very reasonable claim that everyone wants to have at least some intelligence. Here my interpretation departs from those of Burnet and of Gauthier and Jolif (*op. cit.* in n. 10). They simply assume that *nous* in the present context represents the contemplative life, not realizing that this presupposes without argument a definite interpretation of the passage. For if *nous* means "philosophical contemplation", then "we choose . . . *nous*" can hardly mean "all human beings choose . . . *nous*."

are those from which nothing is sought beyond the activity. Actions in accordance with virtue are thought to be of this sort, for noble and good acts are among the things that are desirable in themselves. (1176 b 2—9)

This is put forward by Aristotle as a restatement of points made earlier. As a partial summary, however, the passage suffers from a major fault: strictly speaking, its characterization of what it is for an activity to be desirable in itself conflicts with what Aristotle has already said in Book I. For when he introduces the notion of a good in itself, he says that even if we pursue something for the sake of something else, it can still be good in itself (1096 b 16—19)[15]. Yet now, in the present passage, he contradicts this by saying, "activities that are desirable in themselves are those from which nothing is sought beyond the activity."[16]

It is hard to believe, however, that Aristotle is seriously revising his theory or his terminology at this point; and to my knowledge, no interpreter of the *Nicomachean Ethics* has ever suggested this. It is more likely that he is simply omitting his word for "only", for he does the same elsewhere. He says, for example, that wealth cannot be the good, since it is useful and desirable for the sake of something else (1096 a 6—7). He means, of course, that it is *only* useful, and *only* desirable for the sake of something else[17]. Similarly, in this passage, he is again dropping a word: he means that activities that are desirable in themselves are those which are not sought *only* for the sake of something beyond the activity.

Properly understood, then, our passage is distinguishing two kinds of activities: (a) those that are *only* necessary and desirable *only* for the sake of other things, and (b) those that are desirable in themselves. Both happiness and virtuous actions are placed in the second category.

---

[15] This point is reaffirmed a page later, at 1097 b 1—5: the fact that certain goods (honor, pleasure, intelligence, and virtue) are desired for the sake of happiness does not interfere with their being desired for themselves.

[16] Curiously, the commentaries referred to in n. 10 do not notice this careless contradiction. Burnet says that Aristotle merely commits a sin of omission, since he neglects to mention the category of goods that are both desirable in themselves and for the sake of other things. But the sin is somewhat greater, since Aristotle's statement, taken strictly, obliterates this category.

[17] Both W. D. Ross and M. Ostwald supply an "only" or a "merely" in their translations of this passage, even though nothing corresponds to it in the Greek. Other passages in which "only" could be supplied to make Aristotle's meaning more clear are 1147 b 23—25 and 1177 b 1—2. (In the latter passage, Aristotle means that contemplation is the only activity that is loved *only* for its own sake.)

We know from what Aristotle says elsewhere that happiness is never sought by anyone for the sake of anything else (1097 a 25—1097 b 1, 1176 b 30—31); whereas everything else is sought for the sake of happiness (1102 a 2—3, 1176 b 30—31). Now, this entails that virtuous actions are chosen for the sake of happiness[18]. The passage we are now discussing certainly does not deny this — as we have just seen, it merely denies that virtuous activity is desirable *only* for the sake of other things.

Virtuous actions, then, are both desirable in themselves and also desirable for the sake of happiness. I will assume that this commits Aristotle to the view that virtuous actions would remain desirable even if they were not principal ingredients of a happy life. Does this contradict the anti-Kantian interpretation? Obviously not. To say that something is valuable is not to say how valuable it is; and to say that virtuous actions would remain desirable even if they weren't principal ingredients of happiness is not to say how desirable they would remain. Therefore, even an immoral person could agree with Aristotle's claim that virtuous activity is desirable in itself. The immoralist need only maintain that when all considerations (including happiness) are taken into account, some alternative to virtuous activity (the unbridled pursuit of external goods, for example) is even more valuable than ethical behavior.

The point, then, is that there is a great difference between (a) saying that virtuous activity is *desirable*, regardless of its importance for happiness; and (b) saying that such activity is *more desirable* than immoral behavior, regardless of their relative importance for happiness. Aristotle makes the former claim, but only the latter would conflict with the anti-Kantian interpretation. For that interpretation is a thesis about why Aristotle believes virtuous acts to be *more desirable* than their immoral alternatives. It says they are more desirable, according to Aristotle, only because a man who acts virtuously will be happier than a man who does not. This is consistent with Aristotle's believing that even if he were wrong

[18] Recall my earlier point that for Aristotle the concept of virtuous activity is different from the concept of happiness. To support this point further: Aristotle insists that happiness is never chosen for the sake of anything else, whereas he asserts at 1177 b 2—4 that virtuous activities are desirable for the sake of other goods. So although a happy life is one and the same as a life that includes actions proceeding from a virtuous disposition, such actions are desirable for the sake of happiness, and not *vice versa*. For these actions to be desirable for the sake of happiness is simply for there to be arguments that establish their high importance for happiness.

about how important virtuous activity is for happiness, such activity would still be desirable to some extent[19].

IV

Everyone who produces does so for the sake of something else, and his product . . . is not an end in an unqualified way (*haplōs*). But in the case of action it is different. For good action (*eupraxia*)[20] is an end . . . (1139 b 1—4)

Producing has an end other than itself, but action cannot. For good action (*eupraxia*) is itself an end. (1140 b 6—7)

Do these statements contradict the anti-Kantian interpretation? Some would say so. W. D. Ross, for example, writes that if Aristotle "had held fast to that distinction (between action and production) he would have reached a more Kantian type of theory."[21] And more recently, Roger Sullivan has claimed that Kant wrongly "implies that his classification of practical rules into hypothetical and categorical is original with him."[22] These categories, Sullivan says, would be no news to Aristotle, since the *Nicomachean Ethics* already contains the distinction between action and production.

These writers, I will argue, are badly mistaken, for the above passages are entirely consistent with the anti-Kantian interpretation.

What, after all, does Aristotle mean by saying that good actions, unlike physical products, are themselves ends in an unqualified way (*haplōs*)? Surely he has in mind his earlier distinction between those ends that are final or complete (*teleion*) and those that are not (1097 a 25—34). Such ends as "wealth, flutes, and all instruments" fail to be final, Aristotle says, because they are desired only for the sake of other things; final ends are those that are desired for themselves. (And the most final end, happiness, is one which is always desired for itself, and never for the sake of something else.)

---

[19] Recall the passage quoted in note 12, which says that immoral men, who disagree with Aristotle about what happiness is, nonetheless admit that virtue is to some extent desirable. So, Aristotle is making a very weak claim when he says that virtuous activity is desirable in itself.

[20] I follow Ross in taking *eupraxia* to mean "good action" in both of these passages. Ostwald, however, takes it to mean "the good life" at 1139 b 3, and "good action" at 1140 b 7. Now, if "the good life" (i. e. "happiness") is the proper translation of *eupraxia* in either of these two statements, then obviously that statement could not possibly contradict the anti-Kantian interpretation. Such a contradiction is possible only if Aristotle is taken to mean that good action, i. e., virtuous activity, is an end.

[21] *Op. cit.* in n. 2, p. 188.

[22] *Op. cit.* in n. 3, p. 43.

So, a physical product is not an "end in an unqualified way" in that it is never desired for its own sake. Good actions, by contrast, are desired for themselves. We have already seen in the preceding section that this latter claim is compatible with the anti-Kantian interpretation. There is no basis, therefore, for saying that his distinction between productive and practical thinking is equivalent to Kant's distinction between hypothetical and categorical imperatives. To adhere to a categorical imperative is to choose an action regardless of its connection with one's happiness. Aristotle's distinction between action and production, on the other hand, is completely consistent with the claim that we should choose virtuous actions over their alternatives only because such actions are principal ingredients of the good life.

V

The final passages we will be examining are, I think, the most important and interesting. Verbally, they hardly deviate from the ones we have already studied. But the point Aristotle is making in these new passages is quite different.

In Book II, Chapter 4, Aristotle asks what properties a good person must have, and he answers that performing virtuous acts is not enough. The motive underlying these acts is essential: virtuous acts must be chosen, and chosen for themselves (1105 a 31—32). The same point is made later, in Book VI (1144 a 13—20)[23].

What does Aristotle mean by this? Two points can be made immediately. First, however unclear we are about what kind of motivation is involved in choosing virtuous acts for themselves, we nonetheless have a good idea of what motives Aristotle means to *exclude*. A person cannot be courageous in the full sense, he tells us, if he chooses courageous acts merely for the sake of avoiding

[23] See too all of the passages in which Aristotle says that a good person performs virtuous acts for the sake of the noble (*tou kalou heneka*): 1115 b 12—13, 1116 b 30—31, 1117 a 8, 1120 a 23—25, 1122 b 6—7 and 1123 a 24—25. It seems likely that choosing an act for the sake of the noble is equivalent to choosing it because it is a virtuous act. In that case, to choose a virtuous act for the sake of the noble is to choose it for itself. The same point is made by Burnet (*op. cit.* in n. 10) in his notes on 1105 a 31—32, and I know of no interpreter of Aristotle who would deny it. The important controversy that surrounds the phrase *tou kalou heneka* is not whether this is equivalent to "for its own sake," but whether it is equivalent to "out of a sense of duty." The question is discussed, rather dogmatically I think, by Gauthier (see pp. 20—21 of the translation cited in n. 2) and Sullivan (see pp. 45—46 of the paper cited in n. 3).

reproach, disgrace, or punishment (1116 a 15—1116 b 3). Similarly, one cannot have the virtue of magnificence if one spends large amounts of money only to show off (1123 a 19—26). And Aristotle implies that if one tells the truth only in order to gain financially, then again one fails to display any virtue (1127 a 27—1127 b 6). In general, it seems that one cannot be virtuous if one chooses virtuous acts only because they bring one external goods (wealth, honor, etc.) or physical pleasures. To perform virtuous acts solely for these reasons is incompatible with choosing them for themselves.

The second point is that Aristotle clearly means that *only* the virtuous, and those striving to be virtuous, choose virtuous acts for themselves; immoral individuals may act like them, but no one else has their motives. Therefore, Aristotle cannot be saying, in the passages we are now considering, that it is the mark of a good person to believe that virtuous acts would remain to some extent desirable even if they were not highly important ingredients of happiness. For *that* attitude towards virtuous acts *could* be shared by all people, good and bad alike. The analysis we gave of earlier passages will not work for the ones we are considering now.

To understand these new passages, I think we must take a closer look at the way they use the words *di'auta* ("for themselves"). Now, these same words, or their equivalents (*di'hautous, kath'hautous*), play an important role in Aristotle's theory of love: he says that the best form of friendship is one in which each individual loves the other *for himself* (1156 b 7—11). I think that once we see what Aristotle means by loving others for themselves, we will have a clearer idea of what is involved in choosing virtuous acts for themselves.

To love another for himself, according to Aristotle, is to love him for his character; it is to respond to a person not simply because of his wealth, or his looks, or any other superficial qualities, but because of his deep-seated moral characteristics[24]. So, if Jones benefits Smith only because he hopes thereby to encourage Smith to give him money, he could not seriously claim that, since he loves Smith for one of his qualities (his ability to help Jones financially), he therefore loves him for himself. For loving someone for himself is not responding to just any arbitrary property; it must be a response

[24] See 1156 a 10—20; those who love for the sake of advantage or pleasure do not love another for the kind of person he is, and therefore these are "incidental" (*kata symbebēkos*) forms of friendship. See too 1156 b 7—11: To love another for himself is to love him for properties he has in himself, not properties he has incidentally.

to a particularly deep and relatively fixed trait. The ethical virtues, Aristotle claims, are just such qualities: of all the properties that distinguish human beings, none are so permanent and so difficult to change as one's moral character[25]. It is this fact that entitles Aristotle to equate the expressions, "loving someone for himself" (*di'hauton*) and "loving someone for his character" (*dia to ēthos*)[26]. He is presupposing a distinction between the intrinsic and extrinsic qualities of a human being, and he takes a person's character to be intrinsic and virtually unchangeable.

Now, Aristotle is not claiming that when *A* loves *B* for himself he is completely oblivious to all of *B*'s qualities besides his virtues. It is obvious throughout his discussion of love that a good friend is fully aware of the advantages and pleasures he will normally get as a result of loving someone of high moral character[27]. What Aristotle insists upon is that if the friendship is real, it will continue regardless of its incidental advantages and pleasures[28]. A true friend may know that his acts of friendship will bring him rewards and pleasures, and that will be one of his reasons for valuing the friendship. But that cannot be his sole or even his major reason for loving his friend.

I believe that this brief excursion into Aristotle's theory of love illuminates his claim that a virtuous person chooses virtuous acts for themselves. Just as his description of a true friend's motives rests on an explicit distinction between a person's incidental and inherent properties, so his characterization of a truly virtuous person implicitly presupposes a distinction between the superficial attractions of the moral life and its deep-seated, fixed nature. When he says that a good man chooses virtuous acts for themselves, he is assuming that certain properties of virtuous activity are intrinsic

[25] Throughout his discussion of friendship, Aristotle stresses the fact that since loving someone for his character is loving him for properties that rarely change, such relationships are highly stable (1156 b 11—12, 1156 b 33—34, 1158 b 6—11). By contrast, "incidental" friendships are based on characteristics that can easily be lost, and so Aristotle emphasizes their inherent instability (1156 a 19—24, 1164 a 8—13, 1165 b 1—6). See too 1100 b 12—22 for the claim that no qualities of human beings are as stable as character traits. Aristotle's point is supported by the fact that we are most tempted to say that someone is no longer himself, and has become a different person, when his character changes.

[26] See 1164 a 12, 1165 b 5—6, 1165 b 9.

[27] See, for example, 1156 b 33—35: in a perfect friendship, each gives and *receives* the same things.

[28] See 1167 b 30—33: those who love others perform services even when they know that their beneficiaries are not and will not be able to repay. The same point is made at 1159 a 27—33 and 1162 b 35—1163 a 6.

and others extrinsic. Moreover, it is not difficult to say which features fall into each category.

The superficial attractions are the honors that are often bestowed upon the virtuous, the avoidance of disgrace and punishment, and all of the other external goods (favors, wealth) that a person might receive because others consider him virtuous. A good person will be attracted by these features of the moral life, but he cannot be attracted primarily or solely by them. Rather, he performs virtuous acts because of the intrinsic and unalterable features of the virtuous life. Which qualities are these? A large number of them are mentioned in Book I of the *Nicomachean Ethics*: Virtuous behavior is an activity rather than a state (1098 b 30—1099 a 7), an activity of the soul rather than of the body (1098 b 12—16), an activity that is in accordance with reason (1097 b 22—1098 a 18). It is something that we can master through our own efforts (1095 b 25—26, 1099 b 18—25), and once mastered it can be enjoyed (1099 a 7—1099 a 31). Many different people have a capacity for it (1099 b 19—25), and once acquired it is not easily lost (1100 b 12—22). All of these are properties that indicate, for Aristotle, the desirability of virtuous activity, and they are all permanent. There is no danger that tomorrow the virtues will become irrational, unenjoyable, beyond our control, etc. By contrast, the superficial features of the virtues could, in certain circumstances, be lost. A good man can be falsely accused, punished, and disgraced.

One further intrinsic feature of the virtuous life remains to be mentioned: virtuous actions are principal components of a happy life. Certainly, Aristotle believes that if something has the other deep-seated properties that I have mentioned just above, then it must also have this further characteristic. If, in other words, something is an activity in accordance with reason that is enjoyable once mastered, widely available, etc., then that thing must be a highly significant factor in a happy life[29]. And this fact has an important consequence: it means that there is no incompatibility, in Aristotle's ethics, between choosing virtuous acts for themselves and choosing them only on condition that they are principal ingredients of happiness[30].

---

[29] Here I am relying on the general principle that if *a*, *b*, and *c* are intrinsic features of *X*, and if anything that has *a*, *b*, and *c* must also have *d*, then *d* is an intrinsic feature of *X*.

[30] Notice that this interpretation accords with both points made earlier: First, choosing virtuous acts for themselves is incompatible with acting virtuously only

I conclude that Aristotle, in claiming that a good person chooses virtuous acts for themselves, is not anticipating or agreeing with Kant — quite the contrary, in fact[31]. According to Kant, virtuous acts must be chosen regardless of their relation to happiness. For Aristotle, however, virtuous acts must be chosen for what they are in themselves, that is, for their inherent properties, one of which is their being principal components of happiness. This deep difference between the two philosophers is masked by verbal similarity: both tell us that virtue must be its own end.

Recall, finally, the limited aims of this paper. I have not sought to adduce all the evidence there is for the anti-Kantian interpretation. Rather, I have attributed an initial plausibility to this approach, and have argued that it is compatible with passages that seem to go against it. In this way I have tried to highlight an important difference between Aristotle and Kant. We have seen that, for Aristotle, happiness and virtuous activity are indeed intimately connected: the definition of *eudaimonia* refers to virtuous activity, and one of the intrinsic features of ethical behavior is its important place in a happy life. Certainly, Aristotle is very far from those philosophers who make virtuous acts desirable merely as means to the production of certain states of mind. Nonetheless, this close connection between virtuous activity and happiness should not blind us to the latter's priority. Aristotle's ultimate allegiance is to the good life, and he urges us to perform virtuous acts only because they, and not their immoral alternatives, are among the principal ingredients of happiness[32].

---

for the sake of external goods or physical pleasures. And second, only the virtuous (and those trying to be virtuous) choose virtuous acts for themselves. For only they realize that one of the inherent properties of virtuous activity is its important place in a good life, and only they would continue to act ethically even in circumstances in which such acts do not have their normal extrinsic features.

[31] This conclusion contradicts Roger Sullivan's claim that there is an important agreement between Aristotle and Kant, since both believe that "a man must act rightly because it is the right way to act" (*op. cit.* in n. 3, p. 31). Of course, I am not denying that there is this much in common between Aristotle and Kant: both believe that a good person must not only act in a certain way, but must also have a certain motive. My point is that the motive is different for each philosopher. The conclusion I have reached is also in opposition to W. D. Ross' assertion that Aristotle's description of a good person's motivation ins inconsistent with the rest of his moral philosophy (*op. cit.* in n. 2, pp. 233—234).

[32] I thank Amelie Rorty and Howard McGary for their comments on an early draft. I am also grateful to Daniel Berger for his criticism of a later version of this paper.

The Philosophical Review, Vol. XCVII, No. 4 (October 1988)

ARISTOTLE ON TEMPERANCE[1]

Charles M. Young

> When we were cut off from our supplies and forced to go without food, as is common on military campaigns, no one else endured it well. But when there was plenty to eat, he alone was really able to enjoy it.[2]

For Aristotle, practical wisdom and the virtues of character—courage, temperance, liberality, and the rest—are intimately bound up with one another. Virtue of character, he says, consists "in a mean state . . . that is defined by principle (*logos*), that is, by the principle by which the practically wise person would define it" (*Nicomachean Ethics* II.6,[3] 1106b36–1107a2). Further, since "vice corrupts one, and makes one hold false views about the starting points of action" (VI.12, 1144a34–36), "it is not possible to be practically wise without being good" (a36–b1). When Aristotle discusses individual virtues of character in Books III through V, however, he does not address the question of their connections with practical wisdom. His concern is rather with demarcating their respective spheres of application, describing their correlative vices,

---

[1]I adopt the most usual translation of *sōphrosunē*, despite its inadequacies, because the alternatives—"self-control" and "self-restraint"—are even less acceptable. Either of these alternatives carries the strong suggestion that a display of *sōphrosunē*, requires reason to defeat appetite in a struggle within the temperate agent, a struggle the existence of which Aristotle denies (see, for example, *Nicomachean Ethics* II.3, 1104b3–7). Etymologically, *sōphrosunē* means something like "mental health"—being of sound (*sōs*) mind (*phrēn*)—and an ideal translation would capture this idea. At *Cratylus* 411e4–412a1, Socrates says that *sōphrosunē* is so-called because it involves the preservation of practical wisdom (*sōtēria . . . phronēseōs*), an etymology Aristotle apparently knows (*EN* VI.5, 1140b11–20; see also VII.8, 1151a15–20). The standard general treatment of the Greek notion is H. North's *Sophrosune: Self-Knowledge and Self-Restraint in Greek Literature* (Ithaca, N.Y.: Cornell University Press, 1966).

[2]Alcibiades describing Socrates at Potidaea, in Plato's *Symposium* (219e8–220a2).

[3]Henceforth I refer to the *Nicomachean Ethics* with "*EN*" and to the *Eudemian Ethics* with "*EE*," to books with Roman numerals and to chapters with Arabic ones. Thus the first sentence of the *Nicomachean Ethics* is *EN* I.1, 1094a1–3.

and defending the idea that they are mean states. Furthermore, when Aristotle does expressly raise the issue of the connections between virtue and practical wisdom in Book VI, he concerns himself only with virtue generally, and not with individual virtues.

Aristotle thus leaves it to his interpreters to explicate the connections he sees between particular virtues of character and practical wisdom. In the hope of discovering these connections, I have been working through the details of his discussions of the various virtues and vices in *EN* III–V and *EE* III. This paper presents a portion of that work: an account of Aristotle's view of temperance.

I.

It will be useful to begin with the doctrine of the mean, Aristotle's idea that each virtue of character is a *mesotēs* or mean state.[4] According to this doctrine, there are two respects in which the virtues are mean states. First, each of the virtues is, Aristotle thinks, a member of a triad, and not (as Plato seems to have thought[5]) one of a pair of opposites. However natural it may be to think of courage as opposed to cowardice, or of temperance as opposed to profligacy, Aristotle tries to show in *EN* II.6 that each virtue is instead a mean state between two vices, one of excess and

[4]A source of confusion in dealing with the literature on the doctrine of the mean is that in explaining the doctrine Aristotle uses two words—the adjective *meson* and the noun *mesotēs*—both of which can be translated as "mean." Thus Rackham translates *mesotēs* as "mean state" and *meson* as "mean," while Ross renders *mesotēs* with "mean" and *meson* with "intermediate." As a result, it is not always clear whether, in discussing the doctrine of the mean, a commentator has in mind the idea (i) that a virtue is a *mesotēs* or (ii) that a virtue aims at what is *meson* in action and passion. When Urmson, for example, says "an emotion or action is in a mean if it exhibits a settled state that is in a mean," only confusion results: the first occurrence of "mean" comes from *meson*, the second from *mesotēs*. (See J. O. Urmson, "Aristotle's Doctrine of the Mean," in *Essays on Aristotle's Ethics*, ed. A. O. Rorty (Berkeley, California: University of California Press, 1980), p. 161, originally published in *American Philosophical Quarterly* 10 (1973), pp. 223–230.) Aristotle of course sees a clear difference between (i) and (ii); indeed, as we will see, he argues from one to the other. To avoid confusion on this point, I translate *mesotēs* with "mean state" and *meson* with "intermediate" throughout.

[5]See, for example, *Euthyphro* 5d, *Protagoras* 332a–333b, and *Republic* IV, 444e.

one of defect (1107a2–3).[6] Second, a virtue is a mean state in that it gives rise to actions and passions that are in some sense intermediate relative to the actions and passions characteristic of its associated vices. "While the vices fall short of, or go beyond, what is required in action and passion," Aristotle says, "the virtue finds and chooses what is intermediate" (1107a3–6),[7] and "a virtue is a mean state (*mesotēs*)," he says, "because it aims at what is intermediate (*to meson*)" (1106b27–28).[8]

Temperance might seem to fit this doctrine quite well. Since the appetites (*epithumiai*) temperance regulates—those for food, drink, and sex—clearly admit of excess and deficiency, it is easy to suppose that we will find one vice involving excess, another involving deficiency, and temperance in between.

Aristotle sometimes speaks as if he means to give an account of temperance as straightforward as this. In his preliminary sketches of the virtues in *EN* II.7, for example, he says:

> Temperance is a mean state concerned with pleasures and pains, though not with all of them, and less so with pains;[9] profligacy is an

---

[6]At *EN* II.8, 1108b35–1109a19, Aristotle argues that, although his doctrine of the mean matches each virtue with a pair of vices, it sometimes happens that one of the vices is "more opposed" to the virtue than is the other. Profligacy, for example, is more opposed to temperance than is insensibility, he holds, for the reason that human beings are naturally inclined towards pleasure. Here, I think, Aristotle is attempting to reconcile his doctrine of the mean with the appearance that virtues and vices are opposites. In the case of temperance, the problem facing him is to explain how insensibility could plausibly have escaped the notice of those who treated profligacy and temperance as opposites, and the fact that insensibility is rare is useful in this connection.

[7]Aristotle argues in *EN* V that, although justice is associated with only one vice (injustice), in all its forms justice aims at what is intermediate. Thus "it is a mean state, but not in the same way as the other virtues" (1133b32–33): it aims at what is intermediate, but it is not "between" two vices.

[8]Although I lack the space to argue it here, I believe that these are the only respects in which, for Aristotle, a virtue of character counts as a mean state, and that attempts to understand the doctrine of the mean in the light of other appeals by Aristotle to the notion of a mean state are, in consequence, misguided.

[9]*EN* III.10 differs interestingly from II.7 in its characterization of the sphere of temperance. II.7 says that temperance is "concerned with pleasures and pains, though not with all of them, and less so with pains" (1107b4–6). III.10 says, "We have said that temperance is a mean state

> excessive state. People deficient in relation to pleasure occur hardly at all, with the result that they have no name. Call them "insensible" (1107b4–8).

Furthermore, this is basically the account of temperance that we find in the *EE*. There, after some observations on equivocity, Aristotle argues in III.2 that temperance and profligacy are concerned with tactile pleasures (1230b21–1231a26). He next notes that insensible people are deficient with respect to these pleasures while profligates are excessive (1231a26–29). Then he claims that the presence of excess and deficiency implies the existence of a middle state (1231a34–35), and he concludes that this middle state is temperance (1231a35–b4). Thus we have excess, deficiency, and temperance in between.

In the *EN*, however, matters are much more complicated. In the first place, the *EN* stresses very heavily the idea that temperance concerns those pleasures that human beings share with animals (see especially III.10, 1118b2–3, and III.11, 1119a6–10). The *EE* does note this fact (III.2, 1230b36–1231a17), but it makes nothing of it; the *EN* seems to turn it into a point of theory. A second complication has to do with the manner in which the *EN* demarcates the sphere of temperance. It draws a difficult distinction—one not found at all in the *EE*—between "common" (*koinai*) or "natural" (*phusikai*) appetites and "peculiar" (*idioi*) or "adventitious" (*epithetoi*) ones (III.11, 1118b8–15), and it restricts temperance to appetites of the latter sort (1118b15–28). Yet another complication is that the *EN* makes an attempt, albeit a brief one, to ground temperance in human well-being, connecting it with health and

---

concerned with pleasures, for it is concerned less so, and in a different way, with pains" (1117b24–26). Thus II.7 includes pains within the sphere of temperance, while III.10 takes them out and suggests a reason why. Aristotle is reluctant in III.10 to include pain in the sphere of temperance perhaps because temperance regulates appetite and appetite has pleasure, not pain, as its object (see, for example, *EN* III.1, 1111a32–33). When he discusses the topic of temperance and pain in III.11, he says only that profligates feel more pain than they should when they are deprived of the pleasures of food and drink, while temperate people are not bothered (1118b30–33). The pain here is simply the pain of vicious people unable to indulge their vice and would be involved in the account of any virtue (see II.3, 1104b3–8); it is not peculiar to temperance. Strictly speaking, then, the statement of II.7, 1107b4–6, is an error, and III.10 does well to correct it.

fitness (1119a16–17); no such attempt is found in the *EE*. Finally, in the *EN*, temperance is not symmetrically related to the two vices with which it is correlated. The *EE* says that insensibility is rare (III.2, 1230b15–16), a point the *EN* also makes (II.7, 1107b6–7, and III.11, 1119a5–6). Usually, Aristotle explains why insensibility is rare by reference to human propensities: because we incline towards the pleasures of food and drink, he thinks, we will err on the side of profligacy if we err at all (*EE* III.2, 1230b16–18; *EN* II.8, 1109a13–19). But *EN* III.11 goes further than this, claiming that insensibility is not only rare but unnatural as well. "Insensibility is not human" (1119a6–7), Aristotle says. "A creature to whom nothing is pleasant, or to whom nothing is more pleasant than anything else, is very far from a human being" (1119a9–10).

In summary, then, the *EN* stresses a connection between temperance and animality; it deploys a difficult distinction between common and peculiar appetites; it connects temperance to health and fitness; and, in suggesting that insensibility is not a human possibility, it arguably represents temperance as a counterexample to the doctrine of the mean.[10] The straightforward account of temperance sketched earlier is clearly inadequate to these complications, and a subtler account of Aristotle's view of temperance is accordingly to be sought.

II.

We can begin to work towards a better account by trying to understand Aristotle's restriction of temperance to the pleasures that human beings share with animals. He argues for this restriction in *EN* III.10 as follows. First he distinguishes between pleasures of the body and those of the soul, and argues that temperance has to do only with the former: "People are not called temperate," he says, "in relation to the pleasures of learning, nor profligate in relation to the pleasures of learning" (1117b28–1118a1). Next he

[10]That insensibility is rare (or even non-existent) would not make temperance a counterexample to the doctrine of the mean (*pace* W. D. Ross, *Aristotle*, 5th ed. (London, England: Methuen, 1949), p. 207). But Aristotle says that insensibility is not human (1119a6–7), and this may mean that it is not a human possibility.

sorts bodily pleasures into types by reference to the sensory modalities they involve, and, claiming that temperance is not concerned with the pleasures of sight, hearing, or smell,[11] he concludes that it is restricted to the pleasures of touch and taste, senses that human beings share with the other animals[12] (1118a1–26). Surprisingly, Aristotle goes on to exclude even the pleasures of taste from temperance. Tasting involves discrimination, he asserts, and the pleasures of discrimination are not what profligates enjoy; they seek rather the pleasure that comes from touch, whether in eating, drinking, or sexual activity (1118a26–32).[13] Because of this, profligacy—and temperance too—is restricted to pleasures that derive from the sense of touch[14] (1118b1–4).

How are we to understand Aristotle's restriction of temperance to animal pleasures and to the sense of touch? Usually, when Aristotle connects temperance to animal pleasures, his point is the simple one that the class of pleasures with which temperance is concerned happens to coincide with the class of pleasures to which the other animals are sensitive. He actually argues for this coincidence in the *EE*,[15] and he makes the point in the *EN* as well, saying that "temperance and profligacy are concerned with the sorts of

[11]It is interesting that the *EN* allows for excess and deficiency with respect to the pleasures of sight, hearing, and smell, while the *EE* does not. Perhaps the *EE* is silent on this point because it typically assumes that the presence of excess and deficiency implies, by itself, the existence of a virtuous mean state (see, for example, III.2, 1231a34–36, on temperance, and III.3, 1231b15–21, on gentleness). On this assumption, the mention of excess and deficiency with respect to the pleasures of sight, say, would have inclined the *EE*, implausibly, to recognize a virtue with respect to these pleasures. Because the *EN* makes no comparable assumption, it can mention such pleasures safely.

[12]Aristotle may go too far in his confidence that non-human animals take no pleasure in senses other than these. If pleasure is (found in) the unimpeded activity of a natural state, as Aristotle holds (see *EN* VII.12, 1153a14–15), there seems to be no good reason for thinking that animals' sensory pleasures are restricted to touch and taste.

[13]I will have more to say in Section VII about Aristotle's argument for eliminating the pleasures of taste from the sphere of temperance.

[14]According to *EN* III.10, 1118b4–8, not even all tactile pleasures—notably not the "refined" pleasures of the gymnasium—are regulated by temperance.

[15]*EE* III.2, 1230b22–35, isolates the class of pleasures with which temperance is concerned; 1230b38–1231a7 isolates the class of pleasures to which animals are sensitive; and 1230b36–38 notes that the two classes coincide.

pleasures in which the other animals also share" (III.10, 1118a23–25). But with the concluding remarks of III.10 he breaks new ground:

> Profligacy, then, corresponds to the most common (*koinotatē*) of the senses, and it would seem that it is rightly reproached, because it belongs to us not insofar as we are human beings but insofar as we are animals. To revel in such pleasures, or to like them most of all, is bestial (1118b1–4).

The claims here that profligacy "corresponds to the most common of the senses" and that it belongs to us "insofar as we are animals" should be understood in light of the psychology of the *De Anima*, which argues that sense perception (*aisthēsis*) in general[16] and the sense of touch in particular are definitive of animality. Plants, as Aristotle understands them, can absorb nourishment directly from the environment. Animals lack this ability, and in consequence they need to be able to seize nourishment from their surroundings if they are to stay alive. This ability, Aristotle thinks, requires sense perception and especially the sense of touch. Touch is the crucial sense, in Aristotle's view, because the properties of nourishment—hotness, coldness, wetness, dryness—are the proper objects of that sense (*De Anima* II.3, 414b6–14). The sense of touch, then, is part of what makes an organism an animal, and because it alone is common to all animals (see *De Anima* III.11, 433b31–434a2, and III.12, 434b18–25) Aristotle can describe it in the *EN* as the "most common" of the senses. But, since Aristotle counts human beings among the animals, touch for him is not simply a sense that human beings just happen to share with the other animals. It is rather a distinctively animal sense, and, in consequence, a sense that we human beings have "insofar as we are animals."

In connecting temperance with animal pleasures, then, Aristotle does not mean simply that the pleasures with which temperance is concerned happen, as a mere matter of fact, to be pleasures to which the other animals are also sensitive. He has in mind the deeper point that temperance is concerned with the pleasures to

---

[16]The bluntest statement of this idea occurs at *De Sensu* 1, 436b10–12: "Each animal insofar as it is an animal has to have sense perception, for it is by this that we distinguish between what is and what is not an animal." See also *De Anima* II.2, 413b1–4.

which we human beings are sensitive precisely because we are animals, too. He means us to understand temperance as a virtue that regulates our relation to our animality.

III.

With this point in hand, let us now turn to the heart of Aristotle's account of temperance: his distinction in *EN* III.11 between common and peculiar appetites. Aristotle draws this distinction because he means to restrict the sphere of temperance to peculiar appetites. He does allow for error on the side of excess with respect to common appetites, but he thinks that the nature of these appetites makes such excess rare: common appetites are appetites for nourishment and repletion, and thus tend to vanish when repletion is achieved (1118b15–19). There is also some evidence that he thinks that error regarding these appetites is a pathological condition, and not a moral failing, for he calls those who err to excess "mad-bellies," *gastrimargoi* (1118b19).[17] Temperance and its correlative vices, for Aristotle, have to do not with these common appetites but instead with peculiar ones. "Regarding peculiar pleasures," Aristotle says, "many people go wrong, and they go wrong in many ways" (1118b21–22). Those who err on the side of excess with respect to such appetites are the profligates (1118b25–27). Those who err on the side of deficiency are rare and have no name; Aristotle coins the label "insensible" for them (1119a5–11). The people who get it right with respect to peculiar appetites are of course the temperate (1119a11–12).

Despite the importance of this division in appetite to Aristotle's account of temperance, he does not say as much about it as one would like. He says that common appetites are universal to human beings: "Everyone who needs it desires solid or liquid nourishment, and sometimes both, while the young and lusty want sex, as Homer says" (1118b10–11). They are also natural (1118b9), and they are, as we have seen, directed towards nourishment and repletion (1118b9–11). None of these points holds for peculiar appetites. In the first place, such appetites are not universal: "Not everyone desires this or that sort of nourishment, nor does ev-

[17]Aristotle seems not to know about anorexia. No doubt he would treat it too as pathological.

eryone desire the same things" (1118b12). Second, while it is natural to have preferences for certain foods rather than others (1118b13–15), the preferences themselves are individual peculiarities: "our own," as Aristotle puts it (1118b13). Finally, peculiar appetites are not directed simply towards nourishment and repletion. If they were, error with respect to them would be as rare as error with respect to common appetites. But Aristotle believes that error with respect to peculiar appetites is frequent: "Regarding peculiar pleasures," he says, "many people go wrong, and they go wrong in many ways" (1118b21–22).

To understand what Aristotle has in mind in speaking of common appetites, we need a brief look at his theory of nutrition, as put forward in the *De Anima.*[18] According to this theory, if a species is to propagate, its members must stay alive long enough to reproduce. This requires that they take in nourishment, which Aristotle explains as what is hot, cold, wet, and dry. In the case of animals, the need for nourishment is registered in the psychic states of hunger and thirst, the former being an appetite for what is dry and hot, the latter for what is cold and wet. Prompted by these appetites, an animal is led to seek repletion by eating and drinking appropriate substances. The ingested matter is then broken down by the process of digestion and built back up into the body of the organism by metabolism. In this way the animal's body is maintained, so that it can reproduce.

The common appetites referred to in *EN* III.11 are clearly the hungers and thirsts mentioned in this account of nutrition. Aristotle connects common appetites with physical needs (1118b10), and he says that they are directed simply towards nourishment, not towards particular sorts of nourishment (1118b9–12). Furthermore, his calling these appetites "natural" (1118b9) suggests that he takes them to have their origin in the bodily or animal nature of human beings, a suggestion buttressed by his calling these appetites "common" (1118b8) just after calling the characteristically animal sense, touch, the "most common" of the senses (III.10, 1118b1). That common appetites are grounded in our animal nature, finally, explains why they are universal to human

[18]The remainder of this paragraph freely summarizes the relevant portions of *De Anima* II.3–4.

beings (1118b10–11). We may take it, then, that common appetites are simply hungers and thirsts.[19]

Peculiar appetites are another matter. They differ from common appetites first in being more finely focused: a common appetite is directed simply at nourishment, while a peculiar appetite is directed at a particular sort of nourishment. They also differ in what they require for explanation. Since common appetites are simply the psychic manifestations of physical needs, our having them can be explained physiologically. But, because peculiar appetites are more finely focused than common ones, our possessing them requires more by way of explanation. My needing food may explain why I want to eat something, but it cannot explain why I want to eat Athenian pastries rather than broccoli.

Where is the fuller explanation of our possession of peculiar appetites to be found? Surely in the fact that different people like to eat—take physical pleasure in eating—different sorts of foods. Consider this passage from III.11:

> Regarding peculiar pleasures many people go wrong, and they go wrong in many ways. For when people are said to be fond of such-and-such, it is either because they enjoy things they should not, or because they enjoy them more than most people do, or because they don't enjoy them as they should; and profligates exceed in all these ways. For they enjoy things they should not (because the things are hateful); and if they do enjoy the things they should, they enjoy them more than they should, and more than most people (1118b21–27).

Here Aristotle is clearly not talking about the pleasures we get simply from repletion; such pleasures could come from any sort of food. He is talking instead about the physical pleasure we get from eating certain sorts of foods.

The distinction between common and peculiar appetites, then, is the distinction between appetites we have simply in virtue of needing food and drink and those we have in virtue of deriving physical pleasure from eating foods of certain sorts. Aristotle's presentation of this distinction as one between two kinds of appetite may well be misleading. Suppose I am hungry and am eating

[19]Aristotle's "mad-bellies" (*EN* III.11, 1118b19) apparently have common appetites even without physical needs; anorexics have the needs without the appetites.

my favorite food, Athenian pastries. Aristotle will refer my eating at all to a common appetite and my eating Athenian pastries (rather than, say, broccoli) to a peculiar one. This makes it sound as if I have two appetites, one in respect of my need and another in respect of my preference. But, since the object of my common appetite is the same as the object of my peculiar appetite, though under a different description, Aristotle might want to say that my common appetite is the same as my peculiar appetite, also under a different description.[20] If so, his distinction between common and peculiar appetites is better seen, not as a distinction between two different kinds of appetite, but rather as a distinction between different grounds for our having the appetites we do. In the case at hand, I have a single appetite, but I have it for two reasons. I want to eat the Athenian pastries before me both because I am hungry and because I like to eat Athenian pastries.

IV.

What philosophical work does the distinction between common and peculiar appetites do for Aristotle? The easiest way to see the distinction's importance is to look briefly at the *EE*, where it is not found. Here is how the *EE* tries to characterize the objects of temperance, profligacy, and insensibility:

> One who is so disposed as to fall short of such things as nearly everyone must share in and take pleasure in is insensible, or whatever label is appropriate; and one who is excessive is profligate. For everyone by nature enjoys these things and has appetites for them, and not everyone is called profligate. The reason for this is that they do not feel more pleasure than they should when they get them, nor more pain than they should when they do not. Nor are they unfeeling, for they do not fall short in feeling pleasure or pain; if anything they exceed (III.2, 1231a26–34).

According to the *EE*, then, temperance and its correlative vices are concerned with things that "everyone must share in," that

[20]Aristotle would express this point by saying that, while my common appetite and my peculiar appetite are "incidentally" or "accidentally" (*kata sumbebēkos*) the same (see *Metaphysics* V.9), they are different in "being," *to einai* (see, for example, *Topics* V.4, 133b15–25).

"everyone must take pleasure in," that "everyone by nature enjoys," and that "everyone by nature has appetites for."

These can only be the objects of what the *EN* calls common appetites. But the *EN* sees clearly what the *EE* does not, that common appetites cannot define the sphere of temperance, since their very nature is such as to make over-indulgence in them problematic:

> Eating and drinking simple food until one is over-replete goes beyond what is natural in amount. For the natural appetite is for the repletion of a need (III.11, 1118b16–19).

It is crucial to appreciate this fact about common appetites. Temperance is a virtue that regulates appetites occasioned by physical needs, and this much the *EE* sees. But it does not see what is problematic about temperance: if the appetites with which it is concerned arise in this way, why is a virtue needed for their regulation? Why don't the appetites simply vanish when the needs that occasion them are satisfied, at least in normal cases?[21] It is exactly this question that the *EN*'s distinction between common and peculiar appetites allows Aristotle to answer. The distinction drives a wedge between the physical bases of our appetites for food and drink, on the one hand, and the pleasures (beyond those of repletion) we may take in their satisfaction, on the other, permitting Aristotle to explain how over-indulgence can occur. The distinction allows for the possibility—indeed, the frequent circumstance—of one's wanting to eat something, even when one isn't hungry, because one likes to eat that sort of thing.

V.

We may now turn to Aristotle's account of temperance itself. Here again, what is distinctive in the *EN*'s account can be brought out by looking first at the *EE*. In characterizing temperance and its correlative vices, the *EE* says this:

---

[21]Common appetites need not correspond exactly, either in strength or in duration, to the physical needs that occasion them, but Aristotle seems to assume that they will correspond closely enough (except in pathological cases) that temperance plays no role in bringing them into correspondence.

> One who is so disposed as to fall short of such things as nearly everyone must share in and take pleasure in is insensible, or whatever label is appropriate; and one who is excessive is profligate. For everyone by nature enjoys these things and has appetites for them, and not everyone is called profligate. The reason for this is that they do not feel more pleasure than they should when they get them, nor more pain than they should when they do not. Nor are they unfeeling, for they do not fall short in feeling pleasure or pain; if anything they exceed. Since there is excess and deficiency concerning these objects, it is clear that there is also a mean state, and that this disposition is best, and that it is the opposite of both the others. Hence, if temperance is the best disposition concerning the things with which the profligate is concerned, the mean state regarding the pleasant sensible objects just mentioned will be temperance, a mean state between profligacy and insensibility (III.2, 1231a26–39).

The *EE* thus characterizes temperance by contrasting it with the vices of insensibility and profligacy. It observes, first, that insensible people are deficient while profligates are excessive regarding the pleasures of food and drink (1231a26–34). Then it locates temperance between insensibility and profligacy, claiming that the existence of excessive and deficient states implies the existence of a mean state (a34–35), that this mean state is the best state (a35–36), and that this best state is temperance (a36–39).

The point to notice is that the *EE* offers no positive account of temperance. Instead, it treats temperance as a privative motivational state, calling temperate those who avoid the errors of the profligate and the insensible.[22] To be sure, it does imply that temperate people enjoy the pleasures of eating and drinking "as they should," and that they do not feel more pain "than they should" when they fail to get them. But because it offers no explanation of what the proper enjoyment of food and drink consists in, it gives these fine phrases no real content.

The *EN*'s account of temperance begins in the same way:

> The temperate person is moderately disposed towards [the pleasures

[22]For the idea of a privative motivational state, see R. B. Brandt, "Traits of Character," *American Philosophical Quarterly* 7 (1970), pp. 23–37. For modern accounts of temperance that also make it a privative state, see J. D. Wallace, *Virtues and Vices* (Ithaca, N.Y. and London, England: Cornell University Press, 1978), Chapter 3; and P. Geach, *The Virtues* (Cambridge, England: Cambridge University Press, 1984), pp. 132–133.

> of eating and drinking]. For he does not enjoy the things that the profligate most enjoys; if anything he detests them. In general, he neither enjoys things that he should not, nor enjoys too much anything of this sort. When [such pleasures] are absent he feels neither pain nor appetite, except moderately, nor does he desire them more than he should, nor when he should not, and so on (III.11, 1119a11–15).

So far, we are no better off in the *EN* than we were in the *EE*—we have no idea of exactly what foods and drinks temperate people should and should not enjoy, or of how much they should enjoy them.

But where the *EE* comes up short, the *EN* goes on to describe more exactly the foods temperate people enjoy consuming:

> But such pleasures as conduce to health and fitness [the temperate person] will desire moderately and as he should, as well as other pleasures that do not get in the way of health and fitness, so long as they are neither ignoble nor beyond his means. He who is otherwise disposed cares for such pleasures more than they are worth. The temperate man is not like this; he cares for them as right reason prescribes (III.11, 1119a16–20).

Two kinds of foods are mentioned here: foods that contribute to health and fitness, and foods that are merely consistent with health and fitness (and that are neither base nor too expensive). It will be convenient to call foods that meet the first condition *healthful* foods, those that meet the second *treats*, and those that meet one or the other *wholesome* foods.

According to the *EN*, then, temperate people take physical pleasure in consuming wholesome foods. They are disposed to enjoy consuming what is healthful and not to enjoy what is unhealthful, and to this extent physical pleasure serves them as an index to the healthful. Had Aristotle restricted the enjoyments of temperate people to healthful foods, it would be reasonable to interpret his view of the temperate person's stance towards the pleasures of eating and drinking as one of mere acceptance: eating and drinking are activities in which, as animals, we must engage; we might as well enjoy the pleasures these activities naturally bring. But Aristotle's inclusion of treats within the category of wholesome foods complicates matters. Apparently his idea[23] is that a temperate person will on occasion eat or drink something solely for the sake of the pleasure it brings. And his holding that temperate people will indulge in treats seems to suggest that, in his view, temperate people do more than merely accept the pleasures of eating and drinking even healthful foods. It seems to be Aristotle's view that, while eating and drinking are activities in which, being animals, we must engage, temperate people welcome—delight in—the pleasures these activities bring.[24]

Now that we know which foods temperate people take pleasure in consuming, we are in a position to give an account of Aristotelian temperance that makes explicit its connection with practical reason. For, in fixing the appetites of temperate people by reference to his list of wholesome foods, Aristotle's point cannot be that these appetites merely happen to come to rest on such foods. Such coincidence would be the mark of what, using the language of *EN* VI.13, Aristotle would call "natural" temperance—the normal result of a proper upbringing with respect to the pleasures of food and drink. His point must rather be that, in the case of temperate people, practical reason fixes appetite. One has Aristotelian temperance, in other words, just in case one's judgments as to which foods are wholesome determine one's peculiar appetites for food and drink.[25]

VI.

The excessive state with respect to the pleasures of food and drink is profligacy. Profligates go to excess, Aristotle says, in enjoying "what they should not" (*EN* III.11, 1118b25) and in enjoying even what they should "more than they should or more than most people" (1118b26). Since the foods one "should" enjoy

[23]Shared by G. H. von Wright, *The Varieties of Goodness* (London, England: Routledge and Kegan Paul, 1963), p. 148, and N. J. H. Dent, *The Moral Psychology of the Virtues* (Cambridge, England: Cambridge University Press, 1984), pp. 132–133.

[24]For a modern account of temperance with similarities to Aristotle's, see Dent, *op. cit.*, Chapter 5.

[25]I ignore the difficult question of the extent to which these judgments need to be correct.

are wholesome foods, part of Aristotle's point here is that, unlike the appetites of temperate people, the appetites of profligates are not fixed by Aristotle's list of wholesome foods. But why, exactly, are the appetites of profligates undetermined in this way, and why do they go to excess even in their enjoyment of wholesome foods? Aristotle does not answer these questions directly, but he says enough, I think, to allow us to see what he has in mind. For he regularly associates profligacy with a view about the worth of the pleasures of eating and drinking in human life. Profligates, he says, "choose [the pleasures of food and drink] instead of other things" (1119a2–3); they "like such pleasures more than they are worth" (1119a19–20); indeed, they "like [these pleasures] most of all," *agapan malista* (1118b4). The clear suggestion of these remarks is that the errors of excess characteristic of profligates derive from a mistaken view they hold of the value of the pleasures of eating and drinking. Profligates enjoy consuming what they should not, and derive more pleasure than they should from consuming what they should, because they take it that physical pleasure is worthy of serious pursuit.

Aristotle invents the term "insensible" for those who are deficient with respect to the pleasures of food and drink. Such people "enjoy the pleasures [of eating and drinking] less than they should" (III.11, 1119a5–6); they find "nothing pleasant, or more pleasant than anything else" (1119a9). Since Aristotle limits temperance to peculiar appetites, his point here must be that insensible people are deficient with respect to these appetites, and not, or not necessarily, with respect to common appetites. Thus we may presume, I think, that insensible people eat and drink what is necessary to maintain their bodies, but that they take little or no pleasure (beyond the pleasures of repletion) in doing so. Insensible people, then, are not to be confused with anorexics. Their problem is not that they eat and drink too little, but that they partake too little of the pleasures that eating and drinking naturally bring. They are insensitive to the pleasures temperate people welcome.

VII.

Before summing up, I should deal with a few loose ends: taste, sex, and wine. Earlier I noted in passing that one curious aspect of

Aristotle's account of temperance is that he excludes the pleasures of taste from its sphere. This idea is common to the *EE* and the *EN*, but the *EN* offers a more effective defense of it. The *EE* offers us only the unargued claim that the other animals are insensitive to such pleasures, together with a point of folk wisdom to the effect that gluttons pray for long throats, not for long tongues (III.2, 1231a12–17). The *EN* does better, saying that taste involves the discrimination (*krisis*) of flavors, and arguing that it is cooks and wine-tasters who take pleasure in such discriminations, not profligates (III.10', 1118a26–30). The *EN*'s more effective exclusion of taste from the sphere of temperance is made possible, I think, by the greater stress the *EN* places on the connection between temperance and animality. Since, in the *EN*, temperance regulates pleasures that spring from our animality, Aristotle can argue with some plausibility that the pleasures of taste, because they involve discrimination, are too cerebral to rate inclusion.

Some plausibility, but not a lot. If Aristotle means to exclude taste altogether from the sphere of temperance, he surely goes too far.[26] In the first place, people are commonly led to eat or drink too much because they like the taste of certain foods. Aristotle appreciates this fact elsewhere—the case of incontinence analyzed at *EN* VII.3, 1147a24–b5, for example, makes taste the culprit—and it would be unfortunate if no place could be found for the pleasures of taste in his account of temperance. Second, it is only by restricting taste to the discriminations typical of cooks and wine-tasters that Aristotle is able to argue that the pleasures of taste are not the concern of temperance. But the proper object of taste is not the differences between flavors but the flavors themselves (see *De Anima* II.10, 422a17). And, while Aristotle is no doubt correct in supposing that profligates (as such) do not take pleasure in gustatory discrimination, this is not a sufficient reason for him to think that the pleasures of gustation itself play no role in profligacy.

The key to understanding Aristotle's exclusion of taste from temperance is the distinction between common and peculiar appetites. As we have seen, Aristotle grounds common appetites in

[26]And *epi mikron* at III.10, 1118a27, may show that he would stop short of this.

physical needs and peculiar appetites in individual preferences. But he is silent on the question why particular people have the preferences they do. One person may like Athenian pastries and another broccoli, but Aristotle offers no explanation of why this might be. His silence here is understandable, for it is not likely that there is any structure to the variety of explanations for why people like to eat the things they do.[27] They may like to eat certain foods because they were trained to eat them, because the foods are healthful, because they were forbidden those foods as children, because the foods have pleasant associations, or—crucially for our present purposes—because they like the taste of those foods. Thus there really is a place for the pleasures of taste in Aristotle's account of temperance, albeit a small one: they enter in as one of the explanations for why people like to eat and drink the things they do.[28] Still, Aristotle seems right to have excluded the pleasures of taste from the sphere of temperance proper. Taste may explain why we have some of the preferences we do, but it is in respect of the preferences themselves, and not their grounds, that temperance is displayed.

A second curious feature of Aristotle's official account of temperance in *EN* III.10–12 is that it slights sex and ignores alcohol altogether.[29] Sex is mentioned twice (III.10, 1118a31–32, and III.11, 1118b11), but it does not receive serious attention. Wine is mentioned once (III.10, 1118a28), but only to make the point that profligacy is not concerned with pleasures taken in discriminating flavors. The explanation for these curiosities is to be found in Aristotle's connecting temperance to physical needs. Aristotelian temperance is not concerned with alcohol, I suggest, because Aristotle sees no physical need for alcohol in normal human beings. So too with sex. We do have a natural appetite for sex, Aristotle concedes elsewhere,[30] but our appetites for sex, unlike our appetites

[27]Indeed, Aristotle says at *EN* III.11, 1118b9, that such pleasures are "adventitious" (*epithetoi*) and at *Metaphysics* VI.2, 1026b26–27, that "there is no science of the incidental."

[28]For the other animals, Aristotle thinks, taste serves as an index to the nutritious. See *De Anima*, III.13, 434b22–24, and *De Sensu* 1, 436b15–17.

[29]Elsewhere Aristotle does include both sexual activity and alcohol within the scope of temperance and profligacy. See, for example, *EN* VII.14, 1154a17–18.

[30]See, for example, *De Anima* II.4, 415a22–b7. Here Aristotle goes so far as to say that all of a living creature's activities, including nutrition, have as their end the propagation of its species.

for food and drink, do not spring from physical needs.[31] We can live without sex, but not without food and drink.[32] Aristotle ignores alcohol, then, because our appetite for it has no physical basis. And he treats sex uncertainly, because, although it does have a physical basis, it is not based in a physical need.[33]

VIII.

I have argued that, for Aristotle, temperate people are those whose judgments as to which foods are wholesome determine their appetites for food and drink. This is, I think, a plausible view of temperance. But it is worthwhile, in addition, to appreciate the special expression Aristotle gives to his view with the language of his metaphysical psychology.

The point to stress is his insistence on connecting temperance with animality. For Aristotle, human beings are animal in genus. As animals, we are naturally subject to appetites for food and drink, and we are sensitive to the various pleasures the satisfaction of these appetites can bring. Aristotelian temperance concerns the place of such pleasures in human life. Since our animality is not the distinguishing aspect of our humanity, the pleasures relating to it should not be of major concern to us. Still, our susceptibility to these pleasures is grounded in the sort of creature we are: our animality is part of our essence. The field of Aristotelian temperance, then, is the relation of a rational animal to its animality, as

[31]Note that even when Aristotle gives sex as an example of a common appetite he does not connect it with a need: "Everyone who needs it desires solid or liquid nourishment, and sometimes both, and the young and lusty want sex, as Homer says" (*EN* III.10, 1118b10–11).

[32]*De Anima* II.4, 415a23–26, and especially 416a19, treat nutrition and reproduction as strictly parallel in their contribution to propagation, and *EN* VII.4, 1147b24–28, describes both activities as necessary. But, while it may be true that the ultimate purpose of nutrition is the preservation of species, the fact remains that nutrition also preserves individual organisms, and this is not true of sexual activity.

[33]There are, of course, various ways in which Aristotle could bring sexual activity and the consumption of alcohol into the scope of temperance. He might say, for example, that it would be characteristic of temperate people to enjoy these activities properly, even though such enjoyment does not exhibit temperance proper—as it would be characteristic of courageous persons to bear up well in a prisoner of war camp, even though this does not (on Aristotle's account) exhibit courage proper.

expressed in the pleasures it takes in the animal activities of eating and drinking.

Profligates over-value these pleasures. Such pleasures do, on Aristotle's account, have value—temperate people, as we saw, do take pleasure in eating and drinking, and they will even consume certain foods solely for the sake of pleasure. But the value of these pleasures is strictly limited. As activities we engage in because we are animals, eating and drinking are not distinctively human activities, and the pleasures these activities bring are not distinctively human pleasures. The distinctively human pleasures are rather found, Aristotle thinks, in activities he associates with rationality,[34] the human differentia, and it is these activities, according to him, that should fill our lives, so far as possible (X.7, 1177b26–1178a8). It may therefore be said that, in the importance they attach to the pleasures of eating and drinking, profligates in effect submit to their animality. And to call them bestial is a fair and accurate reproach (III.10, 1118b1–4; see also *EE* I.5, 1215b30–36).

Insensible people err in the contrary direction. The pleasures of eating and drinking are not worth as much as profligates think, but they are worth something, and insensible people go wrong in taking little or no pleasure in food and drink. Their error, like that of profligates, reflects a more serious one. Although not the most important part, our animality is a real part of our humanity.[35] It is our genus, and in taking little or no pleasure in food and drink, insensible people in effect repudiate this aspect of their humanity. As Aristotle puts it, "insensibility is not human" (III.11, 1119a6–7); "a creature to whom nothing is pleasant, and to whom nothing is more pleasant than anything else is very far from a human being" (1119a9–10). Profligates may submit to their animality, but insensible people disown theirs altogether. The name Aristotle coins for their condition, *anaisthēsia* (insensibility), is singularly apt: *anaisthēsia* is the lack of *aisthēsis* (sensation), which the *De Anima* makes definitive of animality.

---

[34]In *EN* X.5, Aristotle makes pleasure relative to the activity in which it is taken and uses this idea to define the class of characteristically human pleasures as those that perfect or complete the characteristically human activity or activities.

[35]Cf. *Parts of Animals* I.5, 645a26–28: "If anyone supposes the study of the other animals to be worthless, he ought to hold the same opinion also about himself."

Temperate persons avoid either extreme. Unlike insensible people, they do take pleasure in food and drink; unlike profligates, they take only limited pleasure. What limits their appetites, moreover, is what gives rise to the appetites in the first place: animality. For temperate people take physical pleasure only in eating and drinking what is good for their bodies, or at least not harmful to them. In their relation to their animality, then, temperate people differ both from profligates and from insensible people. Profligates submit to their animality; insensible people repudiate theirs. The achievement of temperate people is that they acknowledge their animality without submitting to it.

IX.

I conclude by locating Aristotle's conception of temperance, and Plato's too, in relation to the Greek ideal each seeks to articulate. Greek temperance has two distinguishable aspects, one intellectual and one moral.[36] Intellectual temperance is a matter of self-knowledge. It contrasts with *hubris*, arrogance, and consists in a consciousness of one's place and of the limits that this implies. It is intellectual temperance, mainly, that Plato seeks to define in the *Charmides*. Moral temperance is a matter of self-control, not self-knowledge. It contrasts with *akolasia*, profligacy, and involves the control of spirit, and especially of appetite, by reason. This is the state Plato tries to define in *Republic* IV, and what concerns Aristotle in the *EE* and the *EN*.[37] But both Plato and Aristotle—each in his own way—manage to combine the two aspects of the Greek ideal in their accounts of moral temperance. For Plato in the *Republic*, reason controls appetite only when appetite accepts the hegemony of reason: a person is temperate, Socrates says, "when the ruling element [reason] and the ruled elements [spirit and appetite] agree in the belief that reason ought to rule, and the latter two do not rebel" (*Republic* 442c11–d1). Thus Plato represents moral temperance as the product of a kind of intellectual temper-

[36]See North, *op. cit.*

[37]Aristotle alludes to intellectual temperance at least twice in the *EN*. In IV.3, he contrasts the magnanimous man, who rightly considers himself worthy of great things, with the *sōphrōn* or unassuming man, who is worth little and knows it (1123b5). And at IV.4, 1125b12–13, he notes that we praise the unambitious man as *sōphrōn*.

ance: reason controls appetite when appetite knows its place in the community that is the soul. Aristotle makes moral temperance the product of a different kind of intellectual temperance. For him, people properly control their appetites when they are properly inflected towards their animality—when they acknowledge it without submitting to it. To have Aristotelian temperance, then, is to embody the recognition that one is animal in genus and rational in species. It is to know one's place in the community of souls.[38]

The Claremont Graduate School

[38]Earlier versions of this paper were presented to the March 1985 meeting of the Society for Ancient Greek Philosophy, to the philosophy department at the University of California at Irvine, and to Caltech's Tuesday Group; I am grateful to these audiences for helpful discussion. For their comments on earlier drafts, I am also pleased to thank Norval Anderson, Eugene Garver, David Glidden, Marcia Homiak, W. T. Jones, Miles Morgan, Gerasimos Santas, Michael Stocker, Frank Whigham, Steve White, Kay Wicker, Terry Winant, the referees and editors of *The Philosophical Review*, and especially Nancy Atkinson.

"Magnanimity" in Aristotle's Ethics

W. F. R. HARDIE

The ethical virtues

At the beginning of his survey of the particular ethical virtues and vices (*EN* III 6 to the end of V) Aristotle says that his purpose is to show what they are (τίνες) and also what sort of things they are concerned with and the manner of this concern (περὶ ποῖα καὶ πῶς). He adds a claim that the survey will also make clear that the list of virtues is exhaustive (καὶ πόσαι) (1115 a 4-5). In hs general account of ethical virtue (II-III 5) it has been shown that a virtue is concerned with ranges of passions (πάθη) and actions (πράξεις) and is a mean between extremes (1106 b 16-24). Thus his further programme is (1) to assign to each virtue its proper sphere or range of passions and/or actions and (2) to decide in what way each is a mean. The hint that not all ethical virtues are means in the same way is confirmed at least in the case of justice which is found not to be a mean "in the same way as the other virtues" (1133 b 32-3). In another passage Aristotle adds (3) as a further reason for making an exhaustive survey of ethical virtues and ethical vices (for some of which ordinary language does not have names) that, in addition to confirming the doctrine of the mean, it will enable us to know better "the facts about character", τὰ περὶ τὸ ἦθος (1127 a 15-17).

Magnanimity as a particular virtue and as a mean

The treatment in *EN* IV 3 (1123 a 34-1125 a 35) and *EE* III 5 (1232 a 19-1233 a 30) of the particular virtue which he calls "greatness of soul" (μεγαλοψυχία) does not exactly answer to the expectations evoked by the programme. Even to speak of greatness as a distinct particular virtue raises difficulties. That it is found only in conjunction with the other virtues (1124 a 2-3) is indeed consistent with its being distinct from them. For it is Aristotle's doctrine in *EN* VI (= *EE* V) that the ethical virtues are all inseparable from each other and from practical wisdom (1144 b 36-1145 a 6; 1178 a 16-19). But Aristotle does not merely deny separateness. He says that magnanimity is "a sort of crown" (Ross), with the suggestion that it is a beautifully ordered pattern (κόσμος), of the virtues (1124 a 1-2) and a few lines earlier that the magnanimous man has "what is great in every virtue"

(1123 b 30). From the first sentence of the chapter greatness or grandeur is the note of the great-souled man. So there is a suggestion that to say of someone that he has this virtue is to say that his practice of the virtues generally is on a grand scale and in a grand manner. But Aristotle does at least go through the motions of assigning a particular province to greatness: it is concerned with honours (τιμαί) and dishonours (ἀτιμίαι) (1123 b 21-2). Now honour, as Aristotle says, is something which "may be desired more than is right, or less, or from the right sources and in the right way" (1125 b 6-8). This remark, however, is made not with reference to magnanimity but in the following chapter where the range of desire for honour is assigned to the lesser nameless virtue concerned with lesser honours, standing to magnanimity as liberality to magnificence (1125 b 1-4). It is true that the great-souled man is said to take moderate pleasure (μετρίως) in great honours from good men (1124 a 5-7; cf. a 12-16). But Aristotle does not connect this remark with the doctrine of the mean. His account of the way in which greatness is a mean is in terms of the deserts, which must be great, of the great man and of his avoidance alike of excessive and of defective self-esteem. Thus Aristotle does not relate magnanimity, as he has related courage (III 6-9) and temperance (III 10-12), to a range of feeling; nor does he relate it, as he has related liberality (IV 1) and magnificence (IV 2), to a range of actions involving quantities of money or other measurable goods. By hiving off the lesser of the two virtues concerned with honour and honours Aristotle has eliminated the obvious account of the way in which magnanimity is a mean. He is led to do so by his recognition that the interest of the great man in honours is qualified and fastidious, if not a vanishing quantity. Aristotle has said in *EN* I that honour is the end (τέλος) of the "political life" (1095 b 23), and in X that of actions which exhibit the practical virtues those which are political and military are outstanding in nobility and greatness (1177 b 6-17). But he has also said that men pursue honour "in order to convince themselves of their own virtue" (1095 b 26-8; cf. 1159 a 17-25); they desire to be honoured for virtue by men of practical wisdom (1095 b 28-9). The great man, because he knows that he has complete virtue, feels no need even for this superior kind of honour (1124 a 5-9). The same doctrine is implied in the *EE:* the magnanimous man cares more for the good opinion of one good man than for any popular acclaim.[1]

The paradoxes in the portrait

We have seen that Aristotle's account of magnanimity as a mean does not confirm the doctrine expounded in II 6. This is hardly surprising if to be magnanimous is to possess, as a sort of crowning ornament, what is great in every virtue. It is not simply one particular virtue among other particular virtues. What Aristotle says about the ways in which the two vices deviate from a mean raises questions to which clear answers are not given. Why is a man not necessarily vain (χαῦνος) if he thinks his own merits greater than they are (1123 b 9)? How can the deserts of the mean-spirited man (μικρόψυχος) be great if he lacks self-knowledge and is harmed by this lack (1123 b 9-11, 1125 a 21, 24-7)? Other sets of difficulties are felt when we view the chapter as a contribution to knowledge of "the facts about character" (1127 a 15-17). Roughly a third of the chapter in the EN consists of a sometimes graphic description of the attributes and demeanour of the magnanimous man (1124 b 6-1125 a 16 with 1123 b 31-4), a description which concludes by telling us that he has a deep voice, level utterance and unhurried gait (1125 a 12-16). Burnet finds humorous touches in the portrait; Aristotle is explaining "what the average Athenian understood" by nobility (καλοκἀγαθία).[2] Can we attribute to Aristotle the moral feelings of the "average Athenian" or of "cultivated Greeks" (Ross)? Some of the realism seems inappropriate in a chapter professing to portray a great and good man. Modern readers are sometimes repelled: the magnanimous man is one for whom "nothing is great" (1123 b 32, 1124 a 19, 1125 a 3); he gives the impression of looking down on human affairs and on most of his fellow men — ὑπερόπτης (1124 a 20), καταφρονητικός (1124 b 29); he has a better memory for what he does for others than for what they do for him; he receives benefits with shame and does not like to hear them mentioned (1124 b 9-15). Ross complains that he is "self-absorbed" and "as a whole unpleasing" (208). Russell thinks that in his ethical ideals Aristotle shows "emotional poverty".[3] Professor MacIntyre is "appalled"; Aristotle cannot have been "a nice or a good man .[4] One of the most disconcerting of the traits ascribed to the great man is inactivity; he holds back "except when a great honour or great work is at stake"; his actions, while great and notable, are "few" (1124 b 24-6). It is a picture of remoteness where we might expect persistent devotion to the public good, the pursuit of personal happiness in promoting the happiness of fellow citizens (1177 b 14). That a man who has reason to esteem highly his own deserts should be inactive is a paradox: he can deserve to be honoured only for his actions and why should these, however great, be few? Opportunities for spectacular actions are rare; he would be even more deserving, and more greatly honoured, if he were less intermittently active.

How far is it possible to answer the questions and allay the qualms evoked by Aristotle's portrait of the man who has "greatness of soul"? Much has been written on the matter by contemporary scholars. In what follows I shall attempt a brief, and necessarily selective, review and offer suggestions for the further treatment of the problem. First, of course, we have had the sentence by sentence commentary of R. A. Gauthier and J. Y. Jolif on the *EN* (1958-9) and the commentaries of F. Dirlmeier on the *EN* (1956) the *MM* (1958) and the *EE* (1962). We can learn from them how much learning is needed to determine the precise shade or shades of meaning conveyed by Aristotelian sentences which seem to tell us, for example, that the great man thinks much of and about his own merits, that he is blasé ungrateful inert, that his manners exhibit contemptuous superiority, that it would not be fitting for him to be seen running away or at least jerking his arms when he runs.[5] Much light is thrown on numerous passages; but to be enlightened is not necessarily to be convinced.

Gauthier had published earlier a major work, *Magnanimité* (1951), on the treatment of the concept, or comparable concepts, not only in Aristotle (55-118) but generally in pagan philosophy and Christian theology. He maintains that in IV 3 Aristotle is drawing the portrait of a philosopher; I shall examine his reasons for this interpretation. Dirlmeier notes that, while some have found in the chapter a masterly account of supreme virtue, others have read it as a half-ironical rendering of the sentiments of the average Greek (370). He himself finds "less error" in the depreciators than in the high-minded (371). He finds "anticlimax" in the descent from the ideal to echoes of Isocrates and Xenophon and to the conclusion with its string of external traits in the manner of Theophrastus (379). Dirlmeier is no doubt right. But he leaves us to find, if we can, our own answers to the question why Aristotle, having claimed supreme merit for the magnanimous man, lets us down, if he does, by offering us this careful collection of mainly negative, and sometimes unattractive, attributes: the character of the μεγαλόψυχος is such that he does *not* seek danger, has *few* needs, is *rarely* moved to action, is *not* given to praise or admiration or the pursuit of grudges, *eschews* gossip or personal talk. Why tell us only what he does *not* talk about? Aspasius is driven to suggest that he talks theology, that he is not ἀνθρωπόλογος but θεόλογος (114. 24-9). Dirlmeier rightly dismisses this curious suggestion – darüber ist kein Wort zu verlieren (379).

An interpretation very different from Gauthier's and less sceptical than

Dirlmeier's is given by E. A. Schmidt.[6] He argues with impressive detail for a difference of doctrine between the *EE* and the *EN:* in the *EE* honour but in the *EN* virtue is the "central concept" (163-4). The *EE* presents to us an aristocrat whose concept of value (Wertbegriff) postulates that virtue and external goods, including honour and status as a ruler, "belong to each other" (163, cf. 168).[7] This conceptual blending binds the individual to his society and his world (163). In the *EN* on the other hand the magnanimous man knows that virtue alone deserves to be honoured; other goods have lost their honourable status and are merely gifts of fortune, εὐτυχήματα (162). A transformation (168), an interiorization (167), of virtue has occurred or is occurring, a cleft between the individual and the world (163, 168); virtue is manifested not in prize-winning feats of leadership (167) but in "ethical self-consciousness" (166). That there is a real difference, at least of emphasis, between the two treatises is apparent in the fact that in the *EN* the pursuit of honour, except that which consists in the good opinion of a man's equals or superiors, is relegated to a second virtue. But it is a mistake, as I shall argue, to deny that in the *EN* the virtue of magnanimity needs, and is enhanced by, the possession of external goods.[8]

Magnanimity and theoretical wisdom: Gauthier's thesis

Gauthier maintains that what makes most things, even honour (1124 a 16-19), seem small to Aristotle's magnanimous man is that, like Plato's ideal ruler, he is "a spectator of all time and all existence" (*Resp.* 486a; cf. *Tht.* 172c-176a). He commits himself to this thesis in a precise and unambiguous form in a section of *Magnanimité* (henceforth M) which answers affirmatively the question whether the philosopher is the only magnanimous man (114, 116), in the *Commentary* (henceforth C) (272-3, 290-1) and in *La Morale d'Aristote* (122).[9] Gauthier's interpretation may be considered under three heads: (1) the argument that, if the magnanimous man has perfect virtue, he must have the most perfect of the virtues, theoretical eisdom (M 106, C 291); (2) the suggestion that numerous passages in the account of the magnanimous man can only be understood as showing that he is a devotee of the theoretic life; (3) Gauthier's answer to Dirlmeier's objection (370) that, if Aristotle had intended to portray a philosopher, he could not have been "completely silent" on the point.

(1) According to the *EN* magnanimity is not found without the other virtues (1124 a 1-3; cf. 1123 b 29-30) and the great man's virtue is complete, παντελὴς (1124 a 7-8, 28-9). Similarly in the *EE* magnanimity accompanies all the virtues (1232 a 1-3) and reference is made to the commands of

practical wisdom and virtue (a 35-8). What these passages suggest is the doctrine developed in *EN* VI (= *EE* V) that practical wisdom and ethical virtue, the conjunction of all the ethical virtues, are inseparable as involved in right choice (1144 b 36-1145 a 6, cf. 1178 a 16-19). Theoretical wisdom is a further end which the good man should seek to promote (1145 a 8-9). In *EN* X theoretical wisdom is connected with a divine element and distinguished from the virtue and happiness of man *qua* man (1177 b 27-9; cf 1178 a 19-21, b 5-7). Thus Aristotle might well speak of the magnanimous man's virtue as complete without implying the inclusion of theoretical wisdom. If he were a statesman he might not know how to seek the happiness of all the citizens (1177 b 12-15) if he did not himself possess some capacity for the exercise of theoretical abilities; but it is not Aristotle's view that a statesman must be a philosopher.

(2) In his comments on at least the following passages Gauthier differs from other interpretations in seeing references to the theoretic life.

(a) Aristotle says that the great man accepts great honours from good men but despises the honours awarded by the casual crowd (1124 a 5-12). Gauthier thinks that Aristotle dismisses as small all honours awarded for services to the state (M 61-4, 113-14), and refers to the doctrine in X that practical activities are "unworthy of the gods" (1178 b 17-18). But Aristotle also says in X that "political and military actions" are distinguished by "nobility and greatness" (1177 b 16-17). The "great and notable" actions of the great man (1124 b 25-6) are not to be understood as philosophical achievements applauded by other philosophers.

(b) The great man, while ready to face great dangers and to give his life, is no lover of danger and does not seek it for slight reasons (1124 b 6-9). Gauthier strangely suggests that this puts the great man on the side of Amphion in Euripides who argues against his brother Zethus the case for culture and contemplation as opposed to sport war and politics (fr. 194).

(c) The great man is idle and prone to delay "except when the honour or the deed is great" (1124 b 24-5). Gauthier remarks that lack of employment (ἀργία) is the "classic reproach" levelled against the theorist (cf. 1177 b 4-5, M 108-9). But the use of this word alone is insufficient evidence for the suggestion that it is preoccupation with philosophy that explains the disposition of the great man to reserve himself for great occasions.

(d) The great man does not delight in personal talk (1125 a 5). But the fact that Plato regards this as a trait of philosophers (*Tht.* 173c-175b, *Resp.* 500 b-c) does not show that Aristotle mentions it as a philosophical peculiarity.[10] Dirlmeier refers to Gauthier's arguments for his thesis as "ingenious" (370). The adjective seems to be a fair comment on the above interpretations.

(3) How does Gauthier explain the fact that Aristotle in his account of magnanimity does not mention theoretical wisdom or the supreme value of the contemplative life? He points out that, while it is only in *EN* X that the doctrine is formulated and defended, there are passages in I which must be taken as alluding to it: in particular the reference in the definition of happiness to the possibility that there is a special virtue which is "best and most perfect" and the references to the possibility of a plurality of ultimate ends.[11] But these passages plainly indicate a question which may have to be further considered. There are no comparable passages in the account of magnanimity. There are references to "complete virtue". But, as we have seen, this complete virtue need not, and should not, be understood as embracing theoretical wisdom.

Honour and Virtue in the EE and the EN: Schmidt's thesis

I turn now to the view of E.A. Schmidt that in the EN the virtue of magnanimity is an "inner greatness" which is independent of external goods (167). An article at least as long as his would be needed for a critical analysis of his whole argument. But, in order to make my disagreement clear, it will be sufficient to direct attention to his interpretation (161 with n. 70) of 1124 a 20-9 and in particular of 1124 a 25-6. Aristotle here states *(a)* that "only the good man is to be honoured" (a 25), but *(b)* that the man who both is virtuous and has the good fortune to possess external goods (power and money) is thought the more worthy of honour – μᾶλλον ἀξιοῦται τιμῆς (a 26; cf. a 23-4). Schmidt takes *(b)* as Aristotle's report of a vulgarly held opinion which he rejects himself as false.[12] He does not reject it explicitly. The only proposition which he rejects here explicitly is that external goods constitute a claim to honour for a man who is not virtuous (a 26-9). But that the claim to honour of a man who is virtuous is enhanced by his possession of external goods which give him opportunities for virtuous actions is entailed by two propositions both firmly built into Aristotle's doctrine concerning virtue honour and happiness: (1) that external goods are tools indispensable to the practice of virtue and (2) that virtue is to be honoured on account of the virtuous actions in which it is realized.[13] Aspasius is clear about this: if noble activities rightly attract honour and good fortune promotes such activities, then a man's claim to honour is increased by good fortune (112.16-20).

If I am right Schmidt construes a difference of emphasis between the two treatises as involving a major difference of doctrine, a major development if the EE is earlier. The difference of emphasis is illustrated by their treatments of the vice of defect, smallness of soul. The definition of the vice involves both treatises in the paradox noted by Aspasius when he asks how the same man (the μικρόψυχος) can be both greatly deserving and vicious (110.10-11). What are the merits the existence of which falsifies his disbelie in himself? Aspasius suggests that, in addition to noble birth and the chance, not taken, of a political career, he may have abilities which, but for the radical mistake about himself which causes him to turn to a humble way of life, might have enabled him to achieve some honourable success (11-15). As he is and as things are he at best does nothing in particular and does it very well. Confronted with the paradox of the vicious man who is more deserving than he thinks the *EN* does not dwell on his supposed merits and remarks that his wrong opinion of himself has a bad effect on his character (1125 a 20, 24). The *EE* stresses his possession of the "powers" which, when well used, contribute indispensably to honourable activity (1233 a 25-6; cf. 1232 b 39-33 a 1). But it is a mistake to read the *EE* as suggesting that these powers, even when unused or misused, "deserve honour" and have "objective worth" (156-7). For the great man in the *EE*, as in the *EN*, this would be a vulgar error; as in the *EN* he is interested, as we have seen, only in the honour rendered for virtuous activity by the virtuous.[14]

Higher and lower levels of practical activity and ethical excellence

The interpetations of Gauthier and Schmidt are attempts to account for the lofty detachment of the magnanimous or greatly virtuous man. If these interpretations both fail, we have to accept as a conclusion the assumption, natural in view of the place of the section in Aristotle's work, that the sphere of the great man is practical activity, and particularly those "political and military actions" of which Aristotle says that they are "distinguished by nobility and greatness" (1177 b 16-17). Greatness and nobility (beauty) are the key notes which Aristotle strikes firmly at the beginning of the chapter: magnanimity requires greatness as beauty a good-sized body (1123 b 6-7). But, if we agree that Aristotle's intention is to describe a great man dedicated to great actions, we are faced by the question how he came to give us a description which has produced perplexity, and even dismay, in so many of his readers. This is a real question but one the difficulty of which must not be exaggerated. We exaggerate if we follow Gauthier in the use he makes of every phrase which, in another context, might be part of a description of a dedicated professor of philosophy. We exaggerate if we accept Schmidt's claim to find evidence that

Aristotle has moved away from his doctrine that the practice of human (non-theoretic) virtue at a high level demands a large equipment of "external goods". Moreover the passages which suggest a life of activity and leadership are in fact numerous: his actions are of a kind which attract honour and honours (1123 b 17-22); he has what is "great in every virtue" (b 30), not least courage since he faces great dangers and is ready to give his life (1124 b 8-9); it may embarrass him to receive benefits but he confers greater benefits in return (b 9-11); he is eager to give help (b 18); his deeds are great and notable (b 25-6). In the *Politics* Aristotle insists that the highest level of practical virtue is not attained by those who take no part in ruling, in caring for the public good (1278 b 1-5). Subjects have only true opinion not wisdom (1277 b 25-9). A man who is not a ruler knows only an imperfect kind of justice (b 16-20). This doctrine is not explicit in the account of magnanimity. But it is implied, or at least suggested, by the insistence on greatness and by the fact that political power always has a place in references to the class of external goods (1124 a 14, 17, 22).

Aristotle's references to a scale or scales of ethical virtue are usually brief and are nowhere co-ordinated. This makes it difficult to know what lies behind the striking expressions applied to the magnanimous man: "what is great in every virtue" (1123 b 30) and "a sort of ornament" of the virtues (1124 a 1-2). It is natural to think of the difference between the virtue of the ruler and the virtue of the subject. Another clue may be found in the scheme of six ethical states (ἕξεις), three which are to be shunned and correspondingly three which are to be pursued, which Aristotle lays down at the beginning of EN VII (1145 a 15-33). On the side of good "a virtue heroic and divine" is above, while continence (ἐγκράτεια) is below, the level of ordinary virtue. The scheme has received less attention than it deserves for its own sake; it is viewed as an archpectonic framework for Aristotle's celebrated confrontation of Socratic paradoxes. On the difference of level between virtue and continence considered as dispositional states the crucial passage is one in which Aristotle defines the difference between the man who is temperate and the man who is continent:[15] neither is such as to act contrary to reason (λόγος) on account of bodily pleasures, but the continent man has "bad desires" (φαύλας ἐπιθυμίας) while the temperate man has no bad desires; the temperate man does not feel pleasure contrary to reason but the continent man, while not yielding to temptation, does (1151 b 34-1152 a 3). Progress from the level of continence to the level of virtue is promoted by ethical training and "right education" (1104 b 11-13). A virtuous person is one in whom nature and training have together produced dispositions to like and dislike, neither more nor less than is right, what it is right to like and dislike. Not all situations evoke different responses from virtue and continence. The difference is revealed when actions which for the virtuous are easy effortless and pleasant are for the merely continent made difficult effortful and distressing by his bad or excessive desires. With this difference in mind Aristotle says that the life of virtue is "in itself pleasant" (1099 a 7, a 16, a 18-20).

It is important to notice what Aristotle does not say or imply when he distinguishes virtue from continence: he does not say that the desires of the continent man *always* make it difficult for him to act as the rule of reason (λόγος) prescribes; he does not say that the desires of the virtuous man *never* make right actions difficult for him. Both these propositions are obviously false and both are denied by Aristotle. It is false that the man who is continent, self-controlled but at a level below virtue, never eats or drinks without having to fight the impulse to eat or drink unwisely. Aristotle implies that it is false when he says that an action freely chosen may fall short of being a manifestation of virtue *only* because the disposition which it manifests is not firm and stable (1105 a 28-33). Does the virtuous man have desires which sometimes make it difficult and distressing for him to act with rectitude? What Aristotle says, when he distinguishes virtue from continence, is that for the virtuous man right actions are never made difficult by bad desires; for he has none. But he does not hesitate to say that the practice of virtue may be hindered and made difficult by desires which are not bad but are an element in normal and virtuous human nature. In the case of the brave man, facing wounds and death, his very virtue and deep desire for happiness aggravate the distress (1117 a 33-b 20). The same is true of the person in the power of a tyrant; for such a person it is difficult to abide by (ἐμμεῖναι) the right choice (1110 a 23-31; cf. a 4-8).[16]

In Aristotle's scheme bestiality (θηριότης) is below vice (κακία), and one way of being bestial is just to be exceedingly vicious (1145 a 32-3). To have heroic virtue is to be exceedingly virtuous. Aristotle's examples are the valour of Hector and the endurance of Priam. Thus, when we try to explain Aristotle;s "heroic virtue", we are bound to take account of his description of courage as well as of his doctrine on the difference between temperance and continence. The hero shares the superiority of virtue to continence in having "no bad desires", and has the additional excellence of rising to heights of courage and endurance in circumstances of exceptional strain and difficulty; a sort of synthesis of what is praiseworthy in both continence and virtue. Such heroism is one of the attributes of the magnanimous man (1124 b 8-9) and must be one of the ways in which he has "what is great in every virtue" (1123 b 30).[17]

I have argued that the difficulty has been overstated of accepting Aristotle's chapter on the magnanimous man as an account of the character and personality of a man who lives, at the highest level of virtue, the life of a citizen seeking to promote the general good. If this is Aristotle's intention much of his account matches the intention. But there are also reasons for perplexity and surprise. The magnanimous man is not described as active or dedicated in seeking the general good. He is made to seem self-admiring, contemptuous and aloof, detached and uninvolved, ungrateful, inactive. Careful analysis of the text modifies, but cannot remove, these impressions.[18] Perhaps it should not surprise us that the assessment of character traits and patterns of conduct as admirable or repulsive which Aristotle conveys, and appears to accept, does not coincide with ours. But I think also that the inevitably restricted scope of what Aristotle is doing in this part of the *Ethics* raises barriers to our understanding. In particular he is silent on two issues on which he explains his doubts or defends his conclusions in other parts of the treatise. (1) Aristotle was critically aware of the difference between praise and blame on the one hand, felicitation and commiseration on the other, and of the difficulties which arise when we reflect on this difference or attempt to trace the indeterminate boundary between merit and luck. Yet these complexities do not seem to disturb the self-appraisal of the magnanimous man. The face of practical virtue which he presents would be more acceptable if they did. (2) Aristtle thought that the satisfactions gained from practical and political activities were inferior to those offered by the "contemplative life". But, as we have seen, the detailed account of the magnanimous man makes no reference to theoretical activities.

The worth of the magnanimous man

In the first thirty lines of the chapter (1123 a 34-b28) two words, greatness (μέγεθος) and worth (ἀξία) with their variants, each occur in almost every line; the man who has greatness of soul is worthy of great honours and knows his own worth. But what is it in the great man that deserves to be honoured? His virtue (1124 a 25). But virtue is honoured on account of the activities which flow from it (1101 b 14-16). So the great man earns honours by his active services to his friends and his country in great matters. For the rendering of such services the tools of political power and wealth may be indispensable, and fortune gives access to such tools only to the few. As we have seen, Aristotle in his portrayal of the great man takes in his stride this dependance of virtue on luck (1124 a 20ff.; cf. 1099 b 24-5), but elsewhere he faces and discusses the awkward fact (*EN* III 5, *EE* VIII 2; cf. *[MM]* B8). The difficulty has a wide range. Aristotle points out that a man is not blamed for his physical defects unless they are attributable to his own slackness (1114 a 23-8). The athlete needs the right sort of physical endowment, and similarly a man "must be born *(phunai)*, with an eye, as it were, by which to judge rightly and choose what is truly good" (1114 b 5-8); this is the "perfect and true excellence of natural endowment", εὐφυία (b 10-12). The concepts of nature and chance, in contrast with agency which is deliberate, are brought together in the chapter in the *EE* (VIII 2) and in the similar chapter of the *MM* (B8): "good luck is nature without reason; for the lucky man is he who without reason has an impulse towards good things and obtains them, and this comes from nature" (*MM* 1207 a 35-7; cf. *EE* 1247 b 18-20, b 26-8, 1248 a 15-17). Such reflections suggest the idea that we should honour not those who win but those who most deserve to win. The answer to this notion is *(a)* that there are no agreed criteria for picking out the most deserving and *(b)* that our interest in competitions and pleasure in victories, whether for ourselves or others, is unaffected by our awareness that natural winners are lucky. The boxing champion who claims to be "the greatest" is acceptable if he does not expect to be taken solemnly. Aristotle describes the magnanimous man as thinking that no honour is adequate for his perfect virtue; he will accept honours from good men "since they have nothing greater to bestow" (1124 a 5-9). But, if he ignores the contribution of luck and nature to his achievement, if he thinks of it as all his own doing, he falls into fatuity below the level of common sense, and far below the level of Aristotle's critical reflection and unanswered questions about the human situation. Perhaps there is something in the opinion of Burnet that Aristotle did not mean us to take solemnly, or even seriously, some of the detail in his account of the great and good man.

Magnanimity and contemplation

"For him to whom even honour is a small thing other things must be too" (1124 a 19). Why should "the political and practical life" (*Pol.* 1324 a 27) seem small to the man who lives it? According to Gauthier's interpretation Aristotle's magnanimous man *(a)* does not choose and does not live the political life, and *(b)* regards such a life as small in comparison with the theoretic life which is the only one for a philosopher. The reasons for rejecting *(a)* do not require the rejection of *(b)*. Aristotle does not say that magnanimity and theoretical wisdom are incompatible excellences; he says that the philosopher, as a man among men, chooses to practise the ethical virtues (1178 b 5-7). Nor does Aristotle deny that a philosopher may have a call to rule or that a ruler may have leisure for philosophy. Thus Aristotle might well feel it natural to assume that a man of political wisdom will be capable of understanding and appreciating the reasons for preferring the theoretic life. But this is not all. It is involved in the function of statesmanship, as Aristotle conceives it, that the statesman should have a just estimate of the comparative attractions and intrinsic worth of the "two lives", the political and the contemplative (1324 a 30). This doctrine is at least implicit in the *Ethics* and is stated explicitly in Book VII of the *Politics.* In *EN* X we learn that the political man aims at happiness for himself and his fellow-citizens (1177 b 14); and at the end of VI that the promotion of theoretical wisdom is an aim of practical wisdom (1145 a 6-11). In the *Politics* he makes much of the well known difference of view on the question whether the political or the philosophic life is supremely excellent and happy (1324 a 23-35), and states that the active happiness which it is the business of the good legislator to promote (1325 a 7-10) must include above all the activities of contemplation (b 14-23). "If this were otherwise, God and the universe, who have no external actions over and above their own energies, would be far enough from perfection" (b 28-30).

I have argued that, although the account of magnanimity makes no mention of contemplation, it would not be surprising (and this should be conceded to Gauthier) if the account reflected Aristotle's conviction that theoretical activity is the supreme kind of human happiness. Aristotle's concept of "contemplative" happiness is for us in some respects remote and strange. As we have seen, the *Politics* reminds us that the doctrine is bound up with the theological cosmology which Aristotle presents as a great and demonstrable truth ("the divine embraces the whole of nature") attained in many or innumerable past civilizations (*Met.* 1074 a 38-b14; *Cael.* 270 b 16-20; cf. *Meteor.* 339 b 19ff.). Man is happiest when, or so far as, his activity resembles, or is akin to, the contemplative activity of God (1178 b 21-7), "an activity of immobility" — ἐνέργεια ἀκινησίας (1154 b 26-8). It is difficult to give a human content to this formula. We also find strange, if not foolish, the idea that in some sciences, and not only in the theory of the First Mover, final results have been achieved or are to be expected soon.[19] Cicero tells us that Aristotle accused the old philosophers of being "either very stupid or very conceited" in thinking of their own speculations as the last word but claimed himself, in view of the rapid advances made in a few years, that philosophy would soon be completed (*Tusc. Disp.* 3.28.69, *Protr.* fr.8, Ross). At the end of the *Topics* Aristotle claims that his treatment of "syllogising" has brought the science from its first fumblings to a stage of development when there is no serious obstacle to final completion (183 b 22-8, 184 b 1). A science, like the art of tragedy, starts from tentative improvization and stops when it has found its natural form (*Poet.* 1149 a 9-15). Perhaps the final form for the exposition of any theoretical science should be some kind of deductive system. But Aristotle speaks in similar terms of political science where we would not expect him to envisage this kind of finality. He suggests at the end of *EN* that "the philosophy of human affairs" is nearing completion.[20] An effort is needed to reach Aristotle's point of view. It is true that, even in this century, there have been philosophers claiming finality for their solutions, of, for example, the problem of induction or of the freedom of the will. Perhaps Newton's natural philosophy seemed, although not to Newton, to have achieved finality. But developments in philosophy, in logic and in the natural and social sciences have made optimistic declarations about whole sciences sound foolish. That final insight is attainable is part of Aristotle's concept of theoretical wisdom. It is hardly surprising that, in comparison with wisdom so conceived, "nothing great" should be found in other human activities.

Oxford

[1] In the *EE* the magnanimous man is represented as concerned about and caring for honour (1232 b 11-12) and this interest is represented as prima facie inconsistent with his contempt for the casual crowd (b 14-16). As in the EN the solution lies in distinguishing between two kinds of honour, the great and the small: the former is the good opinion which one good and wise man has of another; the latter is the tribute foolishly rendered by "the many" to power and wealth even when dissociated from virtue (1232 b 17-19; cf. b 6-7). That power and wealth and the honour which they attract are useless or harmful to their possessors if they are without practical wisdom and virtue is stated explicitly later in the *EE* (1248 b 27-34) in the chapter (θ 3) on the complete virtue (καλοκἀγαθία) in which particular virtues are elements.

[2] p. 163 and notes on 1123 b 1 and 31, 1124 b 12, 1125 a 12. Cf. Ross, *Aristotle* 202.

[3] *History of Western Philosophy*, 206.

[4] *A Short History of Ethics*, 66. For a different view see M. Plezia, "The human face of Aristotle" in *Classica et Mediavalia* 22 (1961). Cf. Zeller II ch. 1; Jaeger *Aristotle*, tr. R. Robinson, 320-3; Düring, *Aristoteles*, 14-16.

[5] 1123 b 29-32 . . . φεύγειν παρασείσαντι . . . It is not clear to what example or examples of "base conduct" this passage refers. The interpretations of commentators cover a wide field: "ridiculous cowardice" (Gauthier – Jolif), blackmail (M. J. MacInnes in *CR* 1910), bad sportmanship in track athletics (J. A. Smith i *CQ* 1920). See the notes of Rackham (Loeb), Gauthier – Jolif, Dirlmeier. In two other passages in Aristotle (*Part. An* 705 a 16-19, [*Pr.*] 881 b 3-6) παρασείειν describes a technique used by athletes to increase their speed in running. J. A. Smith's detailed argument for his suggestion deserves closer consideration than it appears to have received.

76

[6] "Ehre und Tugend. Zur Megalopsychie der aristotelischen Ethik", *Archiv für Geschichte der Philosophie* 49 (1967).

[7] In at least two passages Schmidt defines in a more extreme and less satisfactory way the sense in which in the *EE* (as he thinks) honour is the central concept: honour is the foundation of (begründet) the worth of both virtue and the external goods (157; cf. 164). But, as we have already seen, the doctrine of the *EN* that for the virtuous man the value of honour is secondary to that of virtue (1095 b 26-8) is implicit in the *EE* (1232 b 5-7, 17-19).

[8] I have space here only for a brief mention of two works each of which makes an interesting contribution to the interpretation of Aristotle's account of magnanimity. The first is H.V. Jaffa's *Thomism and Aristotelianism. A Study of the Commentary by Thomas Aquinas on the Nicomachean Ethics*, Chicago, 1952. Jaffa maintains that Thomas's assumption of a harmony between philosophy and revealed theology causes him to "impute non-Aristotelian principles to Aristotle" (187). The book contains lively discussion of Aristotle's doctrines, particularly in three central chapters: V "Heroic Virtue" (67-115), VI "Magnanimity and the Limits of Morality" (116-141) and VII „The Ambiguity of Man and the Limits of Human Happiness" (142-166). The following sentence describes one of his lines of approach: "Aristotle, in accordance with his uniform aim of presenting the various moral phenomena on their own levels (as well as the various levels of moral phenomena), is in *EN* IV presenting the magnanimous man in his own terms"(138-9, cf. 143-4). Jaffa thus encounters the question whether, in Aristotle's thinking, "the full development of moral goodness requires the untrue opinion that happiness is to be found in moral excellence" (224, n. 40); a good question. The second work is H. G. Kirsche's *Megalopsychia*: Beiträge zur griechischen Ethik im 4. Jahrhundert vor Christus, Diss. Göttingen 1952 (maschinenschriftlich). This dissertation is noticed by Dirlmeier (370) and quoted by Schmidt. Kirsche's analysis of the doctrine follows the lead of N. Hartmann: "Wertkonflikt Wertantinomie Wertsynthese" (62-85). But he also notes resemblances and differences between the portrait of the μεγαλόψυχος and the ideal ruler (ideale Herrscherpersönlichkeit) as celebrated by Xenophon (Agesilaos, Cyrus) and Isocrates (Euagoras, Nicocles). These writers praise the altruism (φιλανθρωπία) of rulers actively devoted to the welfare of their subjects. By comparison Aristotle's great man appears "detached from political and social obligations" (53-57).

[9] In *La Morale d'Aristote* (1963) magnanimity is discussed not in the chapter on virtue and practical wisdom but in a later chapter (after a chapter on the philosophic life) on magnanimity and friendship. The magnanimous man and the philosopher are "the same man" (122). In M the virtue is confined "à l'étroite élite de philosophes" (116); in C the philosopher is "le seul à pouvoir être magnanime" (290). In other passages Gauthier is much less definite. He speaks of magnanimity and theoretical activity as converging (M 107) and again, answering Dirlmeier, of a bringing together (rapprochement) of the proud man and the philosopher (272-3). Such passages might mean only that the portrait of the magnanimous man has some traditionally philosophic, or Socratic, features.

[10] The case for Gauthier's thesis is not helped by the fact that, in a passage in the *An. Post.*)97 b 15-25), Socrates, along with Lysander, is mentioned as an example of magnanimity in one of its senses, indifference to good and bad fortune (cf. *EN* 1124 a 14-16). Socrates was known for his courage in miary and political action and not only as a philosopher. The references in Aristotle to Socrates as an historical person are assembled and discussed by Th. Deman, *Le témoignage d'Aristote sur Socrate* (Paris 1942), who finds a number of Socratic attributes in the magnanimous man but does not claim that this makes it a portrait. The attributes he reviews include attitude to honours (1124 a 4-10; cf.

Plato, *Apology* 36B), indifference to danger (1124 b 6-9; cf. *Symposium* 220B-221B), response to benefits received (1124 b 9-12; cf. *Rhet.* 1398 a 24-6), irony (1124 b 30; cf. 1127 b 22-6). On the reference to μεγαλοψυχία in *An. Post.* see Dirlmeier, *MM* 293; Gauthier C 273; D. A. Rees in *Untersuchungen zur Eudemishen Ethik*, ed. P. Moraux and D. Harlfinger (1971).

[11] 1098 a 16-18 and 1097 a 22-4, 30; cf. 1099 a 29-31, 1153 b 9-12. These passages are adduced by Gauthier as showing calculated reticence, a policy of silence; C on 1097 a 30 and 1124 b 24, M 105-6.

[12] This interpretation is also that of Stewart and Gauthier-Jolif. I think that Gauthier-Jolif are wrong in claiming the support of Aspasius. Stewart (on 1124 a 20) distinguishes "true" greatness from greatness "as popularly conceived": only the latter depends on "fortuitous aid". But actions expressive of true greatness need goods supplied by fortune as much as do the performances of those who ape true greatness (1124 b 2). Aristotle does indeed feel qualms when he is confronted with the idea that luck can help to make a man good (e.g. 1099 b 9-25). But his qualms do not stop him from accepting as a fact of life that a virtuous disposition, although a necessary, is not a sufficient condition of honourable achievement.

[13] (1) External goods as tools (δι' ὀργάνων): 1099 a 31-b 2, 1101 14-16, 1153 b 16-19.
(2) Actions versus disposition as honourable: 1101 b 14-16; cf. 1099 a 3-7, 1122 b 1-2.

[14] D. A. Rees ("Magnanimity in the Eudemian and Nicomachean Ethics" in *Untersuchungen zur Eudemischen Ethik* ed. P. Moraux and D. Harlfinger) and C. J. Rowe (in *The Eudemian and Nicomachean Ethics: a Study in the Development of Aristotle's Thought;* Proceedings of the Cambridge Philological Society, Suppleent No. 3 (1971)) both mention Schmidt's article and commend his study of the differences between Aristotle's treatments of μεγαλοψυχία in the two works. Rees quotes with approval Schmidt's observation that the „central concepts" are different, honour in the *EE* and virtue in the *EN* (231n); but he does not examine this alleged difference in detail. Rowe refers to Schmidt's "complete analysis of the two treatments" and himself expresses the view that in the *EE* the magnanimous man is concerned with the honour which attaches to the position of a ruler while in the *EN* he is interested, and that only mildly, in the honour accorded to virtue and is uninterested in external goods (50-1). It is true that, in the view of the μεχαλόψυχος in the *EN*, "honour is a small thing" (1124 a 19). But in such passages what is being considered and depreciated is the claim of wealth and power to be honoured and valued for themselves and when not associated with virtue and virtuous activities. This indifference is consistent with a firm interest in external goods when these are viewed as instrumental to virtuous activity and enhancements of its value. The man who chooses actions in accordance with virtue (1178 b 5-6) "needs many things"; the greater and nobler the actions the more extensive are his needs (b 1-3). Rowe asserts that external goods "do not matter" to the μεγαλόψυχος: "At any rate he does not actively pursue them" (51). He does not have to: they come to him as gifts of fortune, εὐτυχήματα (1124 a 20).

[15] Continence in its primary sense is opposed to temperance (σωφροσύνη), i.e. moderation in the province of bodily appetites. But the concept is extended by analogy to the provinces of other virtues and vices (1145 b 19-20; cf. 1148 b 9-14, 1149 a 1-4, b 23-6).

[16] The same word (ἐμμένειν, ἐμμενετικός) is used in describing the moral strength of the continent man, ἐγκράτεια (1150 b 19-25 and see Bywater's index for other references). But the quality shown in self-sacrificial death is not, as is ἐγκράτεια, below the level of virtue. It might be objected that Aristotle's account of the highest kind of courage, while it may

be true to fact, is not consistent with the doctrine that virtue is a mean. For the virtuous man's feelings are not only within the right range of intensity but are manifested at the right times (ὅτε δεῖ) ... etc. – (1106 b 18-24, cf. 1119 a 14-18). But Aristotle is here speaking of a different range of facts. In the normal circumstances of an organised life desires to eat and drink, for example, have their places and times; they do not trouble us between meals. But in a battle, or in waiting for a battle, the desire to survive cannot be latent, and concern for children cannot fail to show itself as a strong propensity when their lives depend on the tyrant's will; the greater the virtue the greater the distress.

[17] Other references in the *EN* to heroic conduct: 1110 a 4-8, 19-31; 1117 a 33-b 16; 1169 a 18-26. Cf. 1100 b 22-1101 a 8. The few commentators who show interest in Aristotle's "virtue heroic and divine" are mainly negative in their comments. Ross says that, if ordinary virtue involves "the entire absence of bad desires", Aristotle has left "no room" for anything higher (222). But, if the desires and aversions which make virtue difficult are not all "bad", there is room and need at the top for positive effort and not just the absence of hindrances. As we have seen, the passage which defines the difference between temperance and continence (1151 b 34-1152 a 3) does not support so negative a view of ethical excellence. Grant identifies heroic virtue with "divine virtue or pure reason", which implies that it is a quality not rare (1145 a 27) but *non-existent* "in men" (a 30). Gauthier-Jolif say in effect that heroic virtue is merely posited as the counterpart of brutishness: "the whole passage, far from being an appeal in favour of heroic virtue, on the contrary invites man to be truly himself". The passage states the fact that some men are extraordinarily virtuous; it is not an "appeal". But that Aristotle was "in favour of heroic virtue" was shown when he wrote his Hymn to Virtue in honour of Hermias of Atarneus. On Hermias and Aristotle's hymn see C. M. Bowra, *CQ* 32 (1938) with its references to earlier literature and Düring *Aristotle in the Ancient Biographical Tradition* (1957). On the "heroism of Hermias" compare also the comments of F. E. Sparshott, "The Central Problem of Philosophy", *University of Toronto Quarterly*, 31 (1961) 7.

[18] Cf. R. L. Ottley writing on humility in Hastings' *Encyclopaedia of Religion and Ethics:* 'It is true that even in Aristotle's conception of the *megalopsuchos* there may possibly be discerned some elements of good: truthfulness of character and speech, magnanimity in overlooking offences, self-respect and indifference to death'.

[19] See Jonathan Barnes, Aristotle's Theory of Demonstration, *Phronesis* 14 (1969) 147 and the references give in n. 107.

[20] 1181 b 14-15. . .ἡ περὶ τὰ ἀνθρώπεια φιλοσοφία. . . cf. 1098 a 20-6. I see no reason for translating φιλοσοφία with Ross as "our" not "the" philosophy. Aristotle is surely speaking of the completion of a science not of the end of a book.

ARISTOTLE'S LEGACY TO STOIC ETHICS [1]

by A. A. Long

I

In his life of Zeno Diogenes Laertius (vii, 2; 25) makes the founder of Stoicism a pupil of Crates the Cynic, Stilpo the Megarian, Xenocrates and Polemo of the Academy, and Diodorus Cronus. The same teachers, except Diodorus, are mentioned by Numenius (*Stoicorum Veterum Fragmenta* = *SVF* i, 11) and Strabo and Cicero also cite Polemo (*ibid.* 10 and 13). Tradition does not credit Chrysippus with such a varied formal education, but he did apparently go beyond the Stoa to hear Arcesilaus at the Academy (Diog. Laert. vii, 183-4). No ancient authority mentions the Peripatetics, Theophrastus, Strato and Lyco, as having any direct influence on the early Stoics. Plutarch (*Comm. not.* 1069e) asserts that Zeno agreed with Aristotle and Theophrastus, as well as Polemo and Xenocrates, in taking φύσις and τὸ κατὰ φύσιν as the 'elements of happiness'. This enigmatic remark, which I will attempt to explain later, is the nearest Plutarch comes to suggesting a Peripatetic influence - and a shared one at that - on the Stoics, though Aristotle is mentioned several times in his anti-Stoic treatises. Cicero, on the other hand, cites Carneades (*De fin.* iii, 41) for the view that only terminology distinguished Stoic ethics from that taught in the Lyceum, and Piso, the spokesman for Antiochus (*ibid.* v, 74), claims essential agreement between the 'Old Academy' and the Stoics, after expounding a system allegedly based on Aristotle and Theophrastus (*ibid.* 9-13). But the polemic of the sceptic and the over-simplification of the eclectic have been sufficient grounds for discrediting these statements, though it remains to ask why they could have been made at all.

What then do we say about the antecedents of Stoicism? For Zeller, Socrates and the Cynics had the primary claim to influence Stoic ethical theory. Aristotle inspired much in logic and physics, but his influence on ethics is "restricted to the formal treatment of the material. . . and the psychological analysis of individual moral faculties".[2] We should look rather to Polemo and Xenocrates. Professor Brink has recently given somewhat similar instructions.[3] Unfortunately, the ethical theories of these Academics are desperately elusive. In most cases they are cited by eclectic sources not for independent moral positions but for positions which they shared with the Peripatetics. Von Fritz's attempts to explain away the references in such passages to Aristotle and give Polemo the credit are not convincing.[4] Strangely enough, he omits Cicero *De fin.* iv, 45, *Polemone. . .a quo quae essent principia naturae acceperat* (*sc.* Zeno). On the basis of this evidence Philippson and Brink reasonably concluded that Polemo influenced the Stoic concept of πρῶτα κατὰ φύσιν.[5] Not even so much can be said safely about Xenocrates.

Partly perhaps because of this paucity of evidence a racialist theory about some of the influences on Stoicism was born. I do not know who was the first to build hypotheses on the semitic origins of the early Stoics, but Grant in his edition of Aristotle's *Ethics* (1874, p. 307) speaks of them as "established", and Pohlenz built on the theory.[6] It is not clear that anything in Stoicism requires exotic sources, nor that such sources actually explain anything, and to-day they are probably quite discredited. Now one can read in Edelstein that Stoicism belongs within the tradition of Greek philosophy, and it is gratifying to find him opposing Bevan's extravagant claim that "it was a system put together hastily, violently, to meet a bewildered world".[7] But Edelstein has not developed his points, and like many scholars finds the differences from Aristotle more marked than the resemblances.

I am persuaded that the direct influence of Aristotle on Stoic ethics has been greatly underrated. It cannot be proved by documentary evidence, and if proved it would not rule out the important influence of Heraclitus (and perhaps Empedocles), Socrates and the Academy, and the Cynics. But I believe it can be shown that Stoic ethics owes more than some of its formal treatment and terminology to Aristotle; that the Stoics borrowed many concepts, sometimes altering their language, from the Peripatetics, and consciously developed or diverged from others. The subject is too large to be treated fully here, but I hope to prove the general point by discussing a selection of concepts in detail. This is not merely a matter of *Quellenforschung*. If the thesis is sound, Stoic ethics cannot be completely understood without reference to Aristotle, and this might suggest it as a worthier subject than modern English scholarship has been inclined to admit.

In seeking to establish Aristotle's influence on Stoic ethics I recognize that a place should also be assigned, perhaps a large one, to Theophrastus. Indeed, those scholars like von Arnim who have looked to the Lyceum for some interpretation of Stoicism, have concentrated on him.[8] This, I think, is a mistaken approach. It is probable that the Stoics knew Aristotle both through his own works and also through Theophrastus, but we have no sound means for establishing Theophrastus' independent contribution to ethics.[9] If Arius Didymus' *Epitome* and the *Magna Moralia* (abbreviated as *MM* hereafter) derive ultimately from Theophrastus, the form in which we possess these works shows unmistakable traces of Stoic influence and Stoic criticism.[10] Both present, as ostensibly Peripatetic, doctrines which are not paralleled in the Nichomachean or Eudemian ethics (e.g. *MM*'s restriction of ἀρετή to moral virtue and the theory of a μέσος βίος in Arius) but they cannot be safely fathered on Theophrastus, and are relevant more to the middle than the early Stoa.[11] In the present state of knowledge there is little reason to think that Theophrastus was a noteworthy innovator in ethics. He seems to have conceded more weight to externals than Aristotle, and thereby earned criticism from Antiochus.[12] But to establish a positive Peripatetic influence on early Stoic ethics we must go to the text of Aristotle.

A possible further objection may also be mentioned now. It could be argued that since so much of our information about the Stoics derives from eclectic sources who were influenced by Peripatetic terminology, correspondences between the two systems may merely *seem* close. By the time of Antiochus both Stoa and Lyceum had influenced the other, and controversy was limited to topics such as the αὐτάρκεια of ἀρετή which even eclecticism did not reconcile. Cleanthes' *Hymn to Zeus*, perhaps the longest piece of unadulterated Stoic writing which survives, looks so different from the summaries of ethics in writers like Stobaeus and Clement of Alexandria that we hardly seem to be dealing with the same system. But that hymn looks equally strange when set against some fragments of Chrysippus. It displays a religious feeling which is not recalled before Epictetus and Marcus, and some of its concepts seem scarcely compatible with evidence for other early Stoics. The correspondences with Aristotle which I will seek to show are major concepts which do not rely for their demonstration on purely verbal parallels.

We may begin with some fundamental (or apparently fundamental) differences in order to set the discussion in perspective. Stoic ethics is based upon understanding φύσις , a category both factual and moral which presents itself as the objective standard for moral action: the Stoic ought to *grow* into a good man. Aristotle's ethics prescribes the application of φρόνησις to those situations which provoke pleasure and pain: the Peripatetic learns to be a good man by habituating himself to be pleased and pained by those situations which a perfect man's practical reason prescribes. The Stoic concept of φύσις, which drew inspiration from the Cynics, backed a moral theory valid for all men in any social environment. Aristotle wrote for civilized Greeks, and this limitation is seen in his account of the particular virtues, though it does not, I think, affect the conceptual framework of his moral theory in general. To be irrational in Stoicism is to act viciously, contrary to reason. For Aristotle the moral virtues are dispositions of the irrational, emotional self. There are other major differences. But now we must set against them some evidence which makes the antithesis less sharp.

II εὐδαιμονία and external goods

One of the fundamental differences between the Aristotelian and Stoic accounts of εὐδαιμονία is thought to lie in their different assessments of external goods. The Stoics prided themselves on the αὐτάρκεια of their ἀρετή, while Aristotle found the moral life less adequate as a source of happiness than the contemplative life, partly because of its greater dependence on externals. When however we look closely at the two systems the differences, though persistent, appear less clear-cut, and it becomes reasonable to ask whether the Stoics have been partly prompted in their different thesis by Aristotle.

The passage in Aristotle most sharply distinguished from the Stoic appears in the *Rhetoric* (i, 1360^b 14-29). There Aristotle offers, almost casually, a number of candidates for εὐδαιμονία and finds that all require as their parts such external goods as εὐγένεια, πολυφιλία, πλοῦτος etc., as well as bodily goods. Now comes the interesting remark: "hence a man would be αὐταρκέστατος if he possessed both internal and external goods." The argument of *Nichomachean Ethics* (abbreviated as *EN* hereafter) x (1177^a27 ff.) about the superiority of θεωρία to moral action shows the same attitude. Claimants to εὐδαιμονία must satisfy, as far as possible, the condition of αὐτάρκεια. Aristotle of course fails in his quest for absolute αὐτάρκεια since even the θεωρητικὸς βίος is not entirely self-sufficient. He recognizes an aspect of δούλεια in human φύσις.[13] The Stoics succeed, because they insist on finding a solution. But that does not show, as some writers tend to imply, that αὐτάρκεια is a mainly Cynic-Stoic concept.[14] It is implicit in Plato and explicit in Aristotle.

The basis of this argument rests on what the Stoics call τὰ κατὰ φύσιν and what Aristotle calls τὰ ἐκτὸς ἀγαθά or τὰ ἁπλῶς ἀγαθά.[15] Whatever the influence of the Cynics may have been, it is essential to remember that Aristo, the most cynic of Stoics, was labelled a heretic just because he insisted on no concept of value outside ἀρετή and κακία.[16] For orthodox Stoics τὰ κατὰ φύσιν include and develop from the objects of instinctive choice.[17] Their value is natural, but not moral, and to possess them is no guarantee of εὐδαιμονία. They comprise health, wealth, mental and physical advantages, and indeed form the ἀρχή of καθήκοντα, miscalled 'duties'.[18] καθήκοντα are actions involving love of self, parents, fellow-men etc., based on natural and biological affiliation.[19] Now καθήκοντα are not in the strict sense 'moral actions'; but their *performance*, on the promptings of a consistent, rational disposition, is moral action.[20] And the Stoics pointed the distinction between the two types of action by making τὰ κατὰ φύσιν the ὕλη, not ἀρχή, of the latter (see note 18). Indeed, later definitions of the τέλος are formalized in terms of "rational selection of τὰ κατὰ φύσιν and rejection of their opposites".[21]

I say 'later definitions'. But it may be argued that these definitions are a product of the criticism which the Stoics encountered in the second century B.C. I have attempted to show elsewhere that "selection of τὰ κατὰ φύσιν" was implicit, if not explicit, in Chrysippus' definition of the τέλος.[22] And it is not a concept which requires reference to later, external influences on the Stoa. We have Plutarch's testimony, as I mentioned earlier (p. 72), for Zeno making φύσις and τὸ κατὰ φύσιν the στοιχεῖα τῆς εὐδαιμονίας, a position he is said to have shared with the Academics and Peripatetics. The meaning of this statement is not found in Plutarch (it occurs just after his quotation from Chrysippus about the ἀρχή and ὕλη of καθήκοντα and ἀρετή), but it is surely illustrated by Aristotle's discussion in *EN* i, 9.

Aristotle is considering the relation between τὰ ἐκτὸς ἀγαθά and εὐδαιμονία. Some, he says, are necessary as instruments (καθάπερ δι' ὀργάνων) such as friends, wealth, political power; others, such as noble birth, disfigure happiness if they are absent (1099^a31-1099^b8). Again we seem to be a long way from the Stoic position. But as he proceeds Aristotle widens the gap between εὐδαιμονία and εὐτυχία. Living εὖ or κακῶς does not depend upon the favours of fortune but on ἐνέργειαι κατ' ἀρετήν (1100^b8 ff.). The gifts of fortune are rather cosmetics which naturally add to or detract from εὐδαιμονία (1100^b25 ff.). "If", says Aristotle, "it is actions which determine the quality of a life, the truly good or wise man will never become unhappy, but will always make the best use of the materials available (τὰ ὑπάρχοντα) like the good general and the good cobbler" (1100^b33-1101^a8).

Here Aristotle is distinguishing between the goods which are necessary as instruments for performing good actions (friends, wealth etc.) and the gifts of fortune (noble birth, beauty etc.). He seems to argue that a man deprived of both cannot be happy, but changes of τύχη in later life will not easily or not necessarily affect the good man's εὐδαιμονία. This is a different concept from that offered in the *Rhetoric*, and a different one again is given in the *Politics* (vii. 1323^b21 ff.). There εὐδαιμονία and εὐτυχία are said to be "necessarily different". A man's εὐδαιμονία is a product of his φρόνησις and ἀρετή —witness God, who without any external goods is happy δι' αὑτὸν αὐτὸς καὶ τῷ ποιός τις εἶναι τὴν φύσιν. The best life is one furnished sufficiently to provide the means for virtuous action (ὁ μετ' ἀρετῆς κεχορηγμένης ἐπὶ τοσοῦτον ὥστε μετέχειν τῶν κατ' ἀρετὴν πράξεων, 1323^b40-1324^a2).[23]

Taking *EN* Book I and *Politics* VII together Aristotle's position seems to be this: there is a necessary connexion between εὐδαιμονία and τὰ ἐκτὸς ἀγαθά since the latter are materials or instruments for the exercise of ἀρετή; but there is no necessary connexion between εὐδαιμονία and the gifts of fortune since one can be unhappy with them and partly, if not completely, happy without them.

Is there a necessary connexion between τὰ κατὰ φύσιν (so far as these approximate to τὰ ἐκτὸς ἀγαθά) and ἀρετή in Stoic theory? The answer, I think, is an unequivocal 'yes'. To perform a κατόρθωμα, a morally right act, entails exercising φρόνησις in the sphere of 'natural advantages', i.e. knowing when to select/reject them etc.[24] In this sense τὰ κατὰ φύσιν might be called the ὧν οὐκ ἄνευ of moral action, as indeed they are by Clement (*SVF* iii, 114), but they are required only as ὕλη, not as things which the agent needs to possess for himself (as, so to say, gifts of fortune).[25] According to Cicero (*De fin.* iii, 60) it is because τὰ κατὰ φύσιν form the *materia sapientiae* that the decision to live / die must be determined by reference to them. A man would only die if his εὐδαιμονία were endangered, and the good man's εὐδαιμονία could only be endangered if his exercise of ἀρετή were uncertain – if he ran out of materials. We should also note that the Stoics did not define happiness as an ἐνέργεια but as a concomitant of the virtuous disposition.[26] Two conclusions emerge from all this, and both relate to Aristotle and αὐτάρκεια.

For the αὐτάρκεια of εὐδαιμονία to be guaranteed it is necessary to show that it cannot be assailed by anything. The Stoics satisfied this requirement by making εὐδαιμονία an internal state. But εὐδαιμονία must be defined in terms of something and the Stoics followed Plato, Aristotle and the Cynics in defining it in terms of ἀρετή. Stoic ἀρετή is purely moral; it requires a sphere of action. Aristotle found this in the situations which provoke pleasure and pain; the Stoics found it in the objects of our natural affiliation and aversion – in concrete terms, health, wealth, friendship etc. and their opposites. Aristotle's good man requires these in order to exercise his ἀρετή. The Stoic does not require *any one* of them for himself, but he too cannot exercise his ἀρετή in isolation from them. And this fact led Alexander of Aphrodisias (*SVF* iii, 64) to comment, not entirely unfairly, that "Stoic ἀρετή is not self-sufficient since it requires a sphere of action external to itself". But the Stoics tried to avoid this problem by making a distinction between 'possession' (τυγχάνειν) and 'selection or adoption' (ἐκλέγειν, λαμβάνειν). The good man aims not at possession of natural advantages, but to display ἀρετή in selecting them; and to avoid confusing εὐτυχία and εὐδαιμονία the value of τὰ κατὰ φύσιν is sharply distinguished from the value of a moral action. It is hard not to see the Stoics going consciously beyond Aristotle here, and this is equally true of their treating εὐδαιμονία as a concomitant of the virtuous διάθεσις rather than an ἐνέργεια. Even the good man cannot be active all the time. Both are moves to safeguard αὐτάρκεια, but the conceptual framework of the two theories is very close. When Aristotle says διαλάμπει τὸ καλόν in situations where a good man bears many great misfortunes lightly (*EN* i, 1100^{b}30 ff.) and asserts in the *Politics* (vii, 1323^{b}18-20) that τὰ ἐκτὸς and bodily goods τῆς ψυχῆς ἕνεκεν πέφυκεν αἱρετά, he is talking in different contexts but in Stoic terms. Aristotle found himself unable to formulate an entirely consistent position with regard to εὐδαιμονία and τὰ ἐκτὸς ἀγαθά, and his common sense stopped him short of the Stoic standpoint. But he prefigures much in theirs, and one can see why some ancient critics saw superficially little difference between the schools on this issue.

III

καθήκοντα and κατορθώματα compared with Aristotle's distinction between actions leading to and those proceeding from a virtuous disposition

The terms καθήκοντα and κατορθώματα are Stoic. Neither in itself reflects exactly a concept found in Aristotle, but the distinction between the terms, with respect to judgments about moral action, corresponds very closely to something in *EN* i.

I noted a moment ago that τὰ κατὰ φύσιν form the ἀρχή of καθήκοντα and the ὕλη of ἀρετή. ἀρετή is manifested in right actions, which are κατορθώματα. We also saw that Aristotle makes external goods the instruments of right action, though he does not base his argument upon a concept of biological affiliation, like the Stoics. Since the performance of certain καθήκοντα is *natural* to man (and indeed to animals and even plants) irrespective of his moral status, it follows that they denote a category of action wider than κατορθώματα.[27] A καθῆκον is an action "in conformity with life" (τὸ ἀκόλουθον ἐν τῇ ζωῇ, Diog. Laert. vii, 107); something which "when performed can be reasonably defended" (ὃ πραχθὲν εὔλογον ἴσχει ἀπολογισμόν, *ibid.*), though not necessarily (we may add) by the agent himself.[28] Thus we can say that it is reasonable in general that men should look after their health, their children, their parents etc., but they are not to be commended in a strictly moral sense *merely* for doing so. What then is a moral action? It is an action performed by a virtuous agent. That, however, does not get us very far, and the Stoics elucidated the concept by reference to καθήκοντα. Right actions are perfect or complete(d) καθήκοντα (τέλεια or τελειωθέντα), καθήκοντα "possessing all numbers".[29] What perfects a καθῆκον is its performance ἀπὸ φρονήσεως or *sapienter*.[30] We may say, I think, that the good man performs καθήκοντα not because, or not merely because, he has an instinct or training to do so, but because his φρόνησις tells him so to act. Unlike the man who merely performs καθήκοντα successfully, the good man performs them with his eye on a σκοπός, a fixed goal or plan of life, and in accordance with a καθῆκον λόγον.[31] Clement, who states this, goes on to show that it involves possessing γνῶσις and knowing how one should act throughout the whole of life. The wise man's actions are good not because they have a certain look about them or because they achieve certain external results (whether they do so is quite contingent), but because they follow from a consistently rational disposition (ἀπὸ ἕξεως καὶ διαθέσεως εὐλογίστου).[32] They are called τελικὰ ἀγαθά because they are parts of ἀρετή and ends in themselves.[33]

Both καθήκοντα then and κατορθώματα are *natural* actions, but the latter are peculiarly, though less universally, human, since they are the product of the peculiarly human quality, φρόνησις. By the evolution of his λόγος the Stoic intuits, or extrapolates, from τὰ κατὰ φύσιν, which he instinctively pursued as καθήκοντα, an *ordo* and *concordia rerum agendarum*, a *notio boni*, which is the standard and basis of moral action.[34] His task is to develop such a harmony within himself and thus 'flow smoothly' through life. Cicero and others imply clearly that the performance of καθήκοντα is a necessary antecedent to the performance of κατορθώματα.[35] Indeed, the man who is about to earn the title 'good' performs all καθήκοντα, but his disposition still lacks the firmness and infallibility required of the strictly moral agent.[36]

It appears then that the performance in Stoicism of natural, but morally neutral, actions should lead to the performance of natural moral actions if the former lead the agent to grasp the principle which makes them *appropriate*. The morally neutral actions are primarily instinctive or taught, and judged by external standards. They can be specified. The moral actions are thought out and fit a definite plan of life. They are judged by reference to the agent's disposition and intention. We have no detailed lists of specific κατορθώματα.

I turn now to Aristotle. At *EN* ii, 1105^{a}17 ff., Aristotle faces an *aporia*. If men become just by performing just actions must they not already be just (*sc.* in order to perform those actions)? No. A man might get something in grammar right by accident or assistance, but this would not entitle him to be called γραμματικός. His grammatical ability is something internal (κατὰ τὴν ἐν αὑτῷ). And this points the difference between ἀρεταί and τέχναι. Works of art contain their excellence in themselves. We do not make inquiries about the artist's disposition in making judgments about them. We are concerned exclusively with what the works of art are like (πως ἔχοντα). In the case of moral judgment we proceed differently. Here it *is* the agent's disposition (ἐὰν ὁ πράττων πῶς ἔχων πράττῃ) not the *look* of the action which determines its justice etc.

Aristotle now (1105^{a}31 ff.) stipulates three conditions of moral action which explain his stress on the agent's disposition:

1. A man must act εἰδώς. By 'knowingly' Aristotle means 'practical knowledge' (φρόνησις) of the right goals and how they are to be achieved. The wicked man does not know what he ought to do (1110^{b}28), and the involuntary wrong-doer gets the wrong view of a particular situation (1110^{a}33 ff.). Making moral mistakes in planning one's life (προαίρεσις) produces μοχθηρία (1110^{b}32). We have Plutarch's testimony (*SVF* i, 201) for Zeno equating ἐπιστήμη, in terms of which the Stoics defined ἀρετή, with φρόνησις.

2. A man must act προαιρούμενος, καὶ προαιρούμενος δι'αὐτά. The Stoics did not draw Aristotle's careful distinction between wishing the end and deliberating the means, but here Aristotle probably means that moral actions must be chosen for themselves because it is only by such actions that εὐδαιμονία, the goal of all action, can be actualized. For the Stoics too virtuous acts are τελικὰ ἀγαθά (Diog. Laert. vii, 96) since they are the activities of a virtuous disposition and manifestations of εὐδαιμονία. A Stoic would act deliberately for the sake of the action because all his actions are the result of a settled plan.

3. A man must act βεβαίως καὶ ἀμετακίνητως ἔχων. This condition is entirely Stoic. Both Aristotle's and the Stoics' good man must possess an inflexible moral character. βέβαιος is a common Stoic term, and along with ἀμετάπτωτος it characterizes the virtuous διάθεσις (Plut. *De virt. mor.* 441c). ἀμετάπτωτος is equivalent to Aristotle's ἀμετακίνητος.

The Stoics then accept all these conditions of the virtuous agent, though their precise sense in Stoicism must take account of the all-embracing concept of φύσις.

Aristotle goes on to show that men become just by repeatedly performing just acts. Actions are *called* just when they are the sort of actions performed by the just man (1105^b5 ff.). But a man is just not in virtue of performing them, but only if he performs them in the way that the good man does. Aristotle here has told us briefly what it is to be a virtuous agent, but his detailed discussion of φρόνησις is reserved for Book VI. In the light of his claim that a man must perform just actions in order to become just it is logically correct for Aristotle to consider what such actions are before establishing the intellectual element which is their basis.

We see then that the Stoics agree with Aristotle that men become virtuous by performing certain actions. But they do not claim that these preliminary actions are even homonymously virtuous. Actions performed by non-virtuous agents are necessarily not-good since the particular disposition (πως ἔχων) of the agent is the sole criterion for judging the moral status of his actions.[37] What is required of the good man is not infallible performance of καθήκοντα, but an infallibly virtuous disposition. To attain this, καθήκοντα are necessary since their consistent performance can lead to the grasp of ὁμολογία, the principle of moral action. Aristotle does not, I think, make explicit *how* consistent performance of virtuous acts leads to the qualities required of the φρόνιμος. Repetition and developing the right feelings are the means, but it is not clear (to me) how they produce the necessary intellectual conditions. The Stoics, by their concept of an evolving *logos*, show how the σκοπός required by both moral systems comes to be grasped.[38] What the Stoic φρόνιμος takes as his σκοπός is not of course τὸ ἀνθρώπινον ἀγαθόν, conceived as a mean between two extremes, but φύσις in the largest sense, and therefore what a Stoic actually does is fundamentally different. But φρόνησις in both systems consists in knowing and consistently doing what one ought to do, and it is acquired by consistently behaving in a certain way. The differences between Aristotle and the Stoics derive from different concepts of εὐδαιμονία, φύσις, ἀρετή, not from different ways of analysing moral action. (Having the right feelings, which I have only barely mentioned, is also common to both accounts, as I will shortly show.) The gulf between theory and practice in Stoicism, though strictly nil, is wider in fact than in Aristotle because the theory is so difficult to fulfil. When later Stoics tried to bridge the gap their modifications brought them closer still to Aristotle. Both Panaetius and Posidonius may have conceded some positive value to external goods.[39] Both again accepted the existence of an irrational faculty in the human ψυχή. One may surmise that part of the rigidity of early Stoicism stems from the adaptation of an Aristotelian framework to un-Aristotelian premises.

To conclude this section, it is important to notice that the distinction expressed by καθήκοντα and κατορθώματα could not be explained in Platonic terms as a distinction between true belief and knowledge. The performer of καθήκοντα does not perform the same actions as the good man, but fall short of the latter's ability to account for his moral principles. Moral actions in Stoicism are distinguished by the agent's disposition; hence only external appearance could strictly be shared by a καθῆκον and a κατόρθωμα. δόξα in Stoicism cannot be right or true because only ἐπιστήμη grasps truth.[40] True belief then, as John Rist has observed, would be indistinguishable from knowledge in Stoicism, and δόξα is actually defined as weak or false assent.[41] Bad men are probably not in a permanent state of δόξα since they can perceive truly by κατάληψις, and they can also make true statements.[42] But their doing so does not entitle them to any share in ἀλήθεια, which is firmly restricted to the good man.[43]

IV

Emotion and Virtue

Stoic ethics was calculated to promote ἀπάθεια, but this term does not mean freedom from *all* feeling, or insensibility; it means suppression of judgments based on false assessments of pleasure and pain (or good and bad). In a recent article, R. P. Haynes has examined the early Stoic theory of pleasure, and he concludes that "the Stoics followed Aristotle in maintaining that the virtuous man is the man who not only performs acts of virtue but performs them as the good man would, i.e. with pleasure".[44] Haynes did not make any detailed comparison of Stoic and Aristotelian attitudes on this question, but he was certainly right to point out the connexion between the two schools. I will conclude with some observations on the relation between emotion and goodness in the two systems.

After establishing that moral virtue is concerned with πρᾶξις Aristotle asserts that the pleasure or pain which accompanies our actions must serve as an index of dispositions (*EN* ii, 1104^{b}2 ff.). Pleasure and pain are causes of bad actions and the moral agent needs to be trained to find pleasure and pain in the right things. Since every πρᾶξις or πάθος is accompanied by pleasure or pain, virtue takes these as her material. Aristotle's insistence that the moral agent must have the right feelings about his actions is rightly related by David Furley to his discussion of the psychology of action in the *De anima* and *De motu animalium*.[45] Actions are motivated by desire (ὄρεξις) or choice (προαίρεσις) because some change has occurred through perception or imagination.[46] The perception or imagination of painful or pleasing objects causes changes in the animal's temperature and a mental reaction to pursue or avoid the object imagined or perceived.[47]

Now it is clearly part of Aristotle's doctrine that what a man finds painful or pleasant depends upon himself and how he has been brought up. The man of self-control finds pleasure in abstaining from physical pleasures; the courageous man feels pleasure, or no pain, in facing dangers (*EN* ii, 1104^{b}5-8). But pleasures and pains are not merely accompaniments of action. They are also, *qua* pleasing or painful objects, necessary factors in moral choice. ὄρεξις is a pleasurable response to the consciousness of something good.[48] It is by pursuing and avoiding pleasures and pains, either the wrong ones, or at the wrong time, or in the wrong way, that men become morally corrupt (*ibid.* 1104^{b}21-24).[49] A little later Aristotle distinguishes three factors which determine moral choice, καλόν, συμφέρον, and ἡδύ, but he makes it clear that the first two are not necessarily distinct from the last,

> κοινή τε γὰρ αὕτη (*sc.* ἡδονή) τοῖς ζῴοις, καὶ πᾶσι τοῖς ὑπὸ τὴν αἵρεσιν παρακολουθεῖ· καὶ γὰρ τὸ καλὸν καὶ τὸ συμφέρον ἡδὺ φαίνεται. (1104^{b}34-05^{a}1).[50]

In some sense all choice is concerned with pleasure (or the pleasant), and the morally good and expedient manifest themselves as ἡδύ. The judgment that it is good to abstain is pleasurable to the σώφρων and rouses the ὄρεξις to suppress his appetites; the pleasure of indulgence prompts the actions of the ἀκόλαστος. The psychological distinction between the two types of action rests not on the presence or absence of ἡδύ, but on the distinction between προαίρεσις and ἐπιθυμία or θυμός.[51] The σώφρων reaches an object of desire by βούλευσις which is καλόν *and* pleasing to him. The ἀκόλαστος pursues the pleasure prompted by his appetites and passions.

For Aristotle then ἡδονή is essential to πρᾶξις and the truly pleasurable is what seems to be so to the good man.[52] Since pleasure and pain are the general standards by which men regulate their conduct (κανονίζομεν τὰς πράξεις) it is fundamental that the moral agent should find virtuous activity pleasurable. Aristotle does not, I think, ever imply that the moral agent chooses to act virtuously *in order to acquire pleasure*. He holds rather that moral actions are inherently desirable, and the virtuous man finds the thought and generally the act of performing them pleasurable.

When we compare this thesis with the Stoic attitude to emotions and moral action it seems at first to be totally different. Stoic writers say nothing about pleasure and pain forming the material of virtue. In so far as they designate πάθη, ἡδονή and λύπη are always ἄλογος, contrary to right reason.[54] They are also both described as δόξαι, a term applied to the emotions in general. ἡδονή is the false belief that a good is present, and λύπη is the false belief that an evil is present.[55] Since the good man knows and never opines, it follows that he never has beliefs which can be called ἡδοναί or λῦπαι.[56] As terms describing irrational impulses pleasures and pains are the signs of κακία, and the Stoics could only say that virtue is concerned with them in the sense that it is concerned to remove them.

ἡδονή in itself, however, is not classified by the Stoics as bad, but indifferent.[57] It often denotes a physical feeling, and as such it is a sensation common to all creatures. Aulus Gellius (*NA* xii, 5, 7) makes *omnibus corporis sui commodis gaudere* a primary instinct, and Stobaeus (*SVF* iii, 136) makes bodily pleasure neither preferred nor rejected. We can probably take it then that ἡδονή in Stoicism is of no moral significance when it merely denotes bodily sensations, but acquires bad moral significance when it denotes the mental state of those who regard such sensations as good. Chalcidius, in a long discussion of the Stoic theory of moral corruption (*SVF* iii, 229), notes as primary the belief that pleasures are good and pains bad. Many other authorities confirm this.

But it is not the whole story. ἡδονή is also described by Diogenes Laertius in his life of Zeno as an ἐπιγέννημα:

> ἐπιγέννημα γάρ φασιν, εἰ ἄρα ἔστιν, ἡδονὴν εἶναι ὅταν αὐτὴ καθ'αὑτὴν ἡ φύσις ἐπιζητήσασα τὰ ἐναρμόζοντα τῇ συστάσει ἀπολάβῃ· ὃν τρόπον ἀφιλαρύνεται τὰ ζῷα καὶ θάλλει τὰ φυτά. (vii, 86)

This passage naturally prompts comparison with Aristotle's description of ἡδονή as something which crowns or perfects activities (*EN* x, 1174^{b}31-33), but how is it to be understood in Stoicism? A little later (94) Diogenes Laertius observes that "the good can be defined as the natural perfection of a rational being *qua* rational, and under this category we may put ἀρετή, αἱ πράξεις κατ' ἀρετήν, οἱ σπούδαιοι, and such ἐπιγεννήματα as χαρά and εὐφροσύνη". It seems therefore that at least in a derivative sense ἡδονή (equals χαρά) is a good, and this is certainly the view of Epictetus.[58] He distinguishes between physical pleasure and a mental pleasure which is εὔλογος ἔπαρσις and an accompaniment of τὸ ἀγαθόν (iii, 7, 7). Let us call this accompanying ἡδονή χαρά, and consider its relation to virtue.

χαρά, named as a τελικὸν ἀγαθόν by Stobaeus (*SVF* iii, 106), is one of the three so-called εὐπάθειαι peculiar to the good man.[59] The others are βούλησις and εὐλάβεια, and all three are defined as mental states which are εὔλογος, though only χαρά is an ἐπιγέννημα.

Diogenes Laertius states explicitly that χαρά is not a permanent feeling (vii, 98), and Stobaeus adds that it is not a necessary good (*SVF* iii, 113). If they are right (and the evidence elsewhere suggests they may not be) the Stoics would differ from Aristotle in not making the good man's feeling joy a necessary indication of his disposition, though a man's experiencing the πάθος of ἡδονή would guarantee his badness. But βούλησις, another 'good feeling', is defined as εὔλογος ὄρεξις, and ὄρεξις forms an aspect of ὁρμή which is a prerequisite for all action.[60] Galen, on the basis of Chrysippus, defines ὄρεξις as ὁρμὴ λογικὴ ἐπί τι ὅσον χρὴ ἧδον (*SVF* iii, 463), "rational impulse towards something pleasing, whatever it ought to be". I am not quite clear how ἧδον is to be interpreted here, but we get some help from Seneca: *ad summa pervenit qui scit quo gaudeat* (*Ep. mor.* xxiii, 2). This *gaudium* is explained as an internal condition which comes from *bona conscientia, honesta consilia, rectae actiones, contemptus fortuitibus, placidus vitae et continuus tenor* (7).[61] Putting the two passages together we may say that the good man is one who knows good conscience etc. to be pleasing and desires on the basis of his *logos* to attain them. This is not to say that he desires them because they please; he desires what he ought to find pleasing.

The Stoic concept of λογικὴ ὁρμή is closely analogous to Aristotle's βουλευτικὴ ὄρεξις (*EN* iii, 1113^{a}9 ff.). I suggested that this ὄρεξις in Aristotle is a pleasurable response to something καλόν, reached by the good man via βούλευσις. But the Stoics, I believe, have slightly modified Aristotle here. They subsume βούλησις under ὄρεξις, thus relating 'wish' to the particular object desired now, not the long-term objective. And ὄρεξις (ὁρμή) is itself subsumed under συγκατάθεσις, 'assent'.[62] Desiring or being motivated is an activity of the reason which follows from assent.[63] The Stoic does not deliberate. He assents to or withholds assent from presentations (φαντασίαι) and propositions (ἀξιώματα). His actions, like those of Aristotle's moral agent, are prompted by ὄρεξις, but the Stoic's ὄρεξις is not an irrational faculty under the control of reason, but the *logos* itself in its appetitive aspect.[64] Assent in Stoicism entails (perhaps simultaneously) the issue of an impulse or imperative. Aristotle too argues that in moral choice the ὄρεξις must pursue what the λόγος asserts (*EN* vi, 1139^{a}23-8), but his ὄρεξις, though necessarily associated with judgment, is not an aspect of λόγος itself.[65] It is the faculty which responds with a feeling of pleasure to τὸ ὀρεκτόν, the good or apparent good.[66] Again, in both systems ὄρεξις (or ὁρμή) is the means by which the mind gets the body (if we may use this misleading distinction) to execute its decisions; but in Stoicism, which wants to exclude the irrational at all costs, ὄρεξις is not a response to a pleasing stimulus but a movement, consciously articulated, towards the object of assent.[67] Since the objects of the good man's assents are always valid and entail morally right action χαρά, the ἐπιγέννημα of ἀρετή, is associated with them. It is this perhaps which makes the objects of his ὄρεξις 'whatever ought to be pleasing'. If he is a bad man his assents are weak or false, and issue impulses towards the wrong goals. His disposition expresses itself in πάθη, states of pleasure and pain, or false beliefs that he enjoys something good, or experiences something bad. Enjoyment in this sense, or suffering, are never conditions experienced by the good man; but he generally feels joy in acting virtuously, and he knows the objects which promote this condition, though his actions are never prompted by feelings.

The Stoics then agree with Aristotle that the feelings of the good man are utterly different from those of the bad man. And they might agree that some feeling is a normal accompaniment of any action. But it is not certain that χαρά is a necessary condition of ἀρετή. Seneca asserts that the good man always feels *gaudium* (*Ep. mor.* lix), but Diogenes Laertius denies the permanence of χαρά. One may be wrong, or the Stoics may have differed on the point. At least it seems clear that they have given it a different emphasis from Aristotle, though their position is very close to his. And the Stoics would certainly deny that the presence of χαρά perfects happiness. It is something like an aesthetic quality which the good man normally displays. Nor again does pleasure or the pleasant enter into the Stoic's moral choice. Having assented to (i.e. chosen) the morally good the Stoic commands himself to pursue this pleasing object. Unlike Aristotle's moral agent the Stoic does not need the objects of his moral choice to *present themselves as pleasing*, but he does, as a result of his χαρά, find what he actually pursues a source of joy. The Stoics have excluded all factors except ὀρθὸς λόγος from moral choice, but they permit the agent to derive some emotional satisfaction from his actions.

Since the Stoics differ fundamentally from Aristotle in regarding moral virtues as dispositions of a rational soul, not an irrational faculty, these modifications of his doctrine of pleasure are necessary and intelligible. What is remarkable is the closeness of the two accounts. The Stoics have eliminated pleasure as a factor in moral choice, but they have retained it as an accompaniment and description of the virtuous actions which are the objects of the good man's ὄρεξις. To avoid confusion they have also distinguished this pleasure from its pathological counterpart by different terms, but they accept that how a man feels is a normal, if not necessary, indication of his moral status.

V

No philosophical system is a creation *ex nihilo*, and Stoicism is more derivative than many. The indebtedness of Stoic ethics to pre-Aristotelian influences is generally acknowledged, but it does not rule out the direct influence of Aristotle himself. Time and again in Stoicism we meet the technical vocabulary which he established. In itself this does not prove that Zeno and his successors had read particular works of Aristotle, though we can hardly suppose that in Athens of all places they were not generally acquainted with his views. I have tried to show that the Peripatetic influence on Stoic ethics goes much deeper than this. My treatment has not been exhaustive, but it has, I hope, been sufficient to establish a close *rapport* on three basic moral doctrines. Considering the unsatisfactory nature of our sources for Stoicism it is surprising how precisely we can focus this relationship. The Stoics accept certain basic distinctions, first clearly drawn by Aristotle, and in some places they appear to be consciously correcting or modifying his arguments. These points of agreement or divergence belong to the core of both systems. They show that Stoic ethics belongs in important respects to the mainstream of Greek philosophy.

University College London

NOTES

1 This is an annotated version of a paper delivered to the Southern Society for Ancient Philosophy at Cambridge, September 1967.

2 *Philosophie der Griechen* (revised Wellman, Leipzig 1909) iii, 1, pp. 368-9. Some of these formal correspondences are noted by Dyroff, *Die Ethik der alten Stoa* (*Berl. Stud.* NF 2, 1898), especially pp. 16 f., 88 ff., 249 ff.

3 "Theophrastus and Zeno on Nature in moral theory", *Phronesis* 1 (1956) 142-45.

4 *RE s.v.* Polemon, xxi. 2, cols. 2524-2529.

5 Philippson, "Das erste Naturgemässe", *Philologus* 87 (1932) 447-50; Brink, *op. cit.*, 143.

6 *Die Stoa*[3] (Göttingen 1959), especially pp. 107, 134 f., 164 f. For a criticism of Pohlenz in this respect cf. the reviews of Edelstein, *AJPh* 72 (1951) 427 f.; Sandbach, *JHS* 71 (1951) 262.

7 Edelstein, *The Meaning of Stoicism* (Camb. Mass. 1966), p. 18; Bevan, *Stoics and Sceptics* (Oxford 1913), p. 32.

8 From his examination of Arius Didymus' *Epitome of Peripatetic Ethics* (*Sitzb. Wien*, 1926), pp. 157 ff., von Arnim concluded that many major Stoic moral principles derived from Theophrastus. His thesis has been forcefully rejected in general by Regenbogen (*RE s.v.* Theophrast, Suppl. vii, 1940, col. 1492) who showed that it rests on the improper assumption that all major divergences from Aristotle in Arius are due to Theophrastus. The epitome is an eclectic work which combines Peripatetic and Stoic teaching, cf. Walzer, *Magna Moralia und Arist. Ethik* (*Neue Phil. Unters.* vii, Berlin 1929). Brink, *Phronesis* 1 (1956) 123-45, has recently rejected von Arnim's attribution of Stoic οἰκείωσις to Theophrastus.

9 As sources for Theophrastus' ethics Regenbogen (*op. cit.*) cites Arius Didymus, the MM and Cic. *De fin.* v. It seems almost certain that Arius' source used the *MM* (cf. Dirlmeier, *RhM* 88 (1939) 214-43), and the MM is probably considerably later than Theophrastus (cf. the arguments and authorities cited by D. J. Allan, *JHS* 77 (1957) 7-11 and now also *Gnomon* 38 (1966) 142-144, criticizing Dirlmeier's latest claims for its Aristotelian authorship). The spokesman for Antiochus (*De fin.* v, 12) *claims* to follow Theophrastus on most points, but his assertion cannot be used as a reliable basis for deriving Theophrastus' ethics from Cicero, cf. Madvig's *De finibus*, Excursus vii; Luck, *Der Akademiker Antiochus* (Bern 1951), pp. 31 f., 55 ff.

10 e.g. in Arius (130, 21 Arnim), criticism of the Stoic distinction between σκοπός and τέλος; rejection of the view that the wise man's happiness is ἀναπόβλητον (133, 11); the use of the terms καθήκοντα and κατορθώματα (145, 6-10). For Stoic technical terms in *MM* cf. Dirlmeier, *RhM* 88 (1939) 218-228. Allan (*JHS op. cit.* p. 7) argues that the *MM* offers a selective version of Peripatetic ethics, perhaps designed to make converts from Stoicism. For Dirlmeier's new views see his *Aristotelis Magna Moralia* (Berlin 1958), 118-46.

11 cf. von Arnim, p. 145; on *MM*'s doctrine of moral virtue see Allan, 8-11. I would venture to suggest against Dirlmeier and others that the ὁρμή doctrine of *MM* reflects some Stoic influence.

12 cf. Cic. *De fin.* v, 12; *Ac.* i, 33; ii, 134; *Tusc. disp.* v, 85.

13 *Met.* A, 982^{b}29-34; *EN* x, 1178^{b}33 ff. cf. Schaerer in "La Politique d'Aristote" (*Entretiens de la Fondation Hardt* XI, Geneva 1964), pp. 91 f.

14 J. Léonard, *Le bonheur chez Aristote* (Brussels 1948), p. 54, distinguishes two broad senses of αὐτάρκεια: 1, sufficiency and independence (Cynic and Stoic); 2, mere sufficiency (Aristotle). Of some significance here is the anecdote about Zeno recorded by Stobaeus (*SVF* i, 62); Zeno approved of Crates for finding in a poor cobbler more of the necessary requirements πρὸς τὸ φιλοσοφῆσαι than Aristotle had found in the Cypriot king to whom he wrote the *Protreptikos*. For a valuable discussion of the pre-Platonic influences on Aristotle's theory of εὐδαιμονία see G. Müller, "Probleme der aristot. Eudaimonielehre", *Mus. Helv.* 17 (1960) 121-143.

15 On Stoic 'natural advantages' cf. I. G. Kidd, "The relation of Stoic Intermediates to the Summum Bonum" *CQ* NS 5 (1955) 181-94; A. A. Long, "Carneades and the Stoic Telos", *Phronesis* 12 (1967) 59-90.

16 *SVF* i, 361; 364-5.

17 cf. Stobaeus, *SVF* iii, 140-1; Aulus Gellius, *ibid.* 181.

18 Plutarch, *Comm. not.* 23, 1069e, πόθεν οὖν, φησίν (*sc.* Chrysippus), ἄρξωμαι; καὶ τίνα λάβω τοῦ καθήκοντος ἀρχὴν καὶ ὕλην τῆς ἀρετῆς, ἀφεὶς τὴν φύσιν καὶ τὸ κατὰ φύσιν;

19 Cicero, *De fin.* iii, 22, cum vero illa, quae officia esse dixi, proficiscantur ab initiis naturae, necesse est ea ad haec referri. . . They can of course be rationally justified, see p.76.

20 cf. Cic. *De fin.* iii, 59; Clement, *SVF* iii, 515; Sextus, *ibid.* 516; Stob. *ibid.* 510.

21 Diogenes of Babylon, *SVF* iii, 44-46; Antipater, *ibid.* 57-8.

22 *Phronesis* 12 (1967) 63-69.

23 *EN* x, 1178^{a}25 ff. appears to lay more stress on the quantity of goods required, but Léonard, *op. cit.* p. 47, warns against taking the remarks in too material a sense, cf. *ibid.* v, 1120^{b}7 ff., οὐ γὰρ ἐν τῷ πλήθει τῶν διδομένων τὸ ἐλευθέριον, ἀλλ' ἐν τῇ τοῦ διδόντος ἕξει, αὕτη δὲ κατὰ τὴν οὐσίαν δίδωσιν.

24 cf. Cic. *De fin.* iii, 31; Alex. Aphr. *SVF* iii, 766.

25 cf. Plut. *Comm. not.* 1071a: the τέλος is not obtaining τὰ κατὰ φύσιν, but these ὥσπερ ὕλη τις ὑπόκειται τὴν ἐκλεκτικὴν ἀξίαν ἔχουσα, cf. *Phronesis* 12 (1967) 69-71. Acc. Arius Didymus (129, 19) the ὧν οὐκ ἄνευ are not συμπληρωτικὰ τῆς εὐδαιμονίας, but they συνεργεῖν εἰς τὸ τέλος.

26 cf. Diog. Laert. vii, 89; Stob. *SVF* iii, 16. Contrast Arist. *EN* $1098^{b}31$-$1099^{a}7$.

27 cf. Diog. Laert. vii, 107; Cic. *De fin.* iii, 58, id officium nec in bonis ponamus, nec in malis; Philo, *SVF* iii, 512, ὁ φαῦλος ἔνια δρᾷ τῶν καθηκόντων. The fact that bad men can perform morally neutral καθήκοντα produces an apparent contradiction. Professor Sandbach, in a paper delivered at Cambridge (see n. 1), suggests that "an appropriate action viewed in isolation from the agent is neither good nor bad, but seen as the action of an agent acquires that agent's character".

28 cf. Stobaeus, *SVF* iii, 494. I am not here concerned with Panaetius' treatment of καθήκοντα.

29 Stobaeus, *SVF* iii, 499-500. On the queer phrase καθήκοντος ἀριθμοί see Farquharson's *Commentary to Marcus Aurelius*, iii, 1.

30 Sextus, *Adv. Math.* xi, 200, οὐ γὰρ τὸ ἐπιμελεῖσθαι γονέων καὶ ἄλλως τιμᾶν γονεῖς τοῦ σπουδαίου ἐστὶν ἔργον, ἀλλὰ σπουδαίου τὸ ἀπὸ φρονήσεως τοῦτο ποιεῖν. cf. Cic. *De fin.* iii, 32.

31 *SVF* iii, 515; cf. Marcus Aurelius, ii 7; 16.

32 Philo, *SVF* iii, 512; cf. Stobaeus, *ibid.* 510.

33 Cic. *De fin.* iii, 55; cf. Diog. Laert. vii, 96.

34 cf. Cic. *De fin.* iii, 21; 33.

35 *ibid.* 20; Stobaeus, *SVF* iii, 510; Epictet. *Ench.* xxx.

36 Stobaeus, *loc. cit.*

37 cf. Plut. *SVF* iii, 459; Stob. *SVF* iii, 560; 563; Galen, *SVF* iii, 471a. See further n. 27.

38 See n. 31, and Arist. *EN* vi, $1138^{b}21$ ff.; $1144^{a}23$ ff. At *EE* $1227^{b}24$ f. there is said to be no λόγος of the σκοπός.

39 The matter is controversial, cf. *Phronesis* 12 (1967), n. 75, 89-90. Panaetius was called φιλοπλάτων and φιλαριστοτέλης (*Ind. Herc.* col. 61).

40 cf. Sextus, *Adv. Math.* vii, 42.

41 *Eros and Psyche* (Toronto 1964), p. 164; cf. Sextus *ibid.* 151.

42 cf. Sextus, cited n. 40 and 41.

43 Sextus, *Hyp. Pyrrh.* ii, 83.

44 "The Theory of Pleasure of the Old Stoa", *AJPh* 83 (1962) 412-9.

45 *Two Studies in the Greek Atomists* (Princeton 1967), pp. 216-23.

46 *De motu an.* $701^{a}4$-6, cf. *De an.* iii, 10.

47 *De motu an.* $701^{b}13$-22; 33-$702^{a}1$. cf. also *Phys.* vii, $247^{a}7$ ff.

48 cf. *De an.* iii, $431^{a}8$-14. Hence the importance of its being controlled by λόγος (*EN* i, $1095^{a}10$) so that it becomes ὀρθή ($1139^{a}24$).

49 That is to say, *not* by pursuing pleasure as such, cf. vii $1153^{b}30$ f., οὐδ' ἡδονὴν διώκουσι τὴν αὐτὴν πάντες, ἡδονὴν μέντοι πάντες; *De hist. an.* $589^{a}8$ f.

50 cf. iii, $1110^{b}9$-11. For the necessary connexion of καλὰ and ἡδέα, cf. *ibid.* $1113^{a}31$ ff.

51 *EN* iii, 1111^{b}10 ff.

52 cf. *EN* x, 1176^{a}15 ff., esp. 25-28. At iii, 1117^{b}15 f. Aristotle observes that in the case of certain ἀρεταί (such as courage) the aspect of ἡδύ is associated with the τέλος rather than the ἐνέργεια.

53 cf. *EN* i, 1099^{a}11-21. Some modern commentators, in the stress they place on *EN* vi, 2, seem to me to underrate the place of τὸ ἡδύ in Aristotle's scheme. Confusion of course arises because ἡδονή and ἡδύ are frequently used to denote physical pleasure, which is to be suppressed in moral choice. But it is Aristotle's doctrine that genuine pleasures stimulate the actions of a particular φύσις (*EN* vii, 1154^{b}20). A just appraisal of Aristotle's views in this respect is given by Jelf in his commentary to *EN* (Oxford 1856), pp. 59, 153.

54 cf. Cic. *De fin.* iii, 35; Stob. *SVF* iii, 394; Andronicus, *ibid.* 391; Plut. *ibid.* 459.

55 Andronicus *loc. cit.*; Galen *SVF* iii, 463.

56 cf. Diog. Laert. vii, 121; Cic. *Tusc. disp.* iii, 19.

57 Diog. Laert. *ibid.* 102; Stob. *SVF* iii, 70.

58 cf. Bonhöffer, *Epictet und die Stoa* (Stuttgart 1890), pp. 293 f.

59 Diog. Laert. vii, 116. See in general Bonhöffer, *op. cit.*, pp. 284-98.

60 cf. Stob. *SVF* iii, 169.

61 In a later letter (lix), after observing that *gaudium* in the Stoic sense is peculiar to the good man, Seneca defines it as "animi elatio suis bonis verisque fidentis".

62 cf. Stob. *SVF* iii, 171; Plut. *ibid.* 177. What applies to ὁρμή in these passages applies also to ὄρεξις. See in general Dyroff (cited in n. 2), pp. 16-24.

63 For further discussion see "The Stoic concept of Evil", an article forthcoming in the *Philosophical Quarterly*, October 1968.

64 cf. Alex. Aphr. *SVF* ii, 823; Iamblichus, *ibid.* 826. Pohlenz "Zenon und Chrysipp", *NGG* 2 (1938) 181-99, argues that this "monistic psychology" was an invention by Chrysippus who "rationalized" Zeno's teaching on the πάθη. I am doubtful if the evidence gives Pohlenz his firm conclusion, but even if he is right there is no reason to think that human ὁρμή as such was irrational for Zeno. For the different theses of Panaetius and Posidonius cf. Galen, *Plac.* 457, 2-8; Cic. *De off.* i, 101; ii, 18.

65 cf. *De an.* iii, 431^{a}8-17; 434^{a}11-12; *EN* i, 1102^{b}29-31.

66 cf. *De an.* ii, 413^{b}21-4; iii, 433^{a}18-29; *De hist. an.* 589^{a}8 f.

67 cf. Chrysippus' definition or description of ὁρμή as λόγος προστακτικὸς αὐτῷ (*sc.* ἀνθρώπῳ) τοῦ ποιεῖν (Plut. *SVF* iii, 175). Clement attributes to the Stoics the description of ὄρεξις as λογικὴ κίνησις (*SVF* iii, 442).

THE HELLENISTIC VERSION OF ARISTOTLE'S ETHICS

From the Hellenistic period we have two extensive texts of great interest which draw on Aristotle's ethical works. One is Antiochus' system of ethics in Cicero's *De Finibus* V; the other is the long account of "the ethics of Aristotle and the other Peripatetics" in Stobaeus' *Eclogae* II, 116–152, plausibly ascribed to Arius Didymus.[1] Antiochus' ethics is consciously "eclectic" in the sense that he is using a variety of ethical material and approaches, Aristotelian and other, to create something of his own. Arius, however, professes to be telling us what Aristotelian ethics is, and scholars have been disconcerted to find something so different from any idea we have of Aristotelian ethics. We find a text in which material clearly taken from the ethical works and the *Politics* has been not just summarized but recast in terms that are clearly Stoic. Most strikingly, before we get to what we recognize as Aristotelian material we find a long section developing in an Aristotelian context what seems clearly to be the Stoic notion of *oikeiōsis*. Either Arius, or more likely the Peripatetic source he is following, has presented Aristotle's ethics in a very changed form. Since we have no hope of pinpointing a particular Peripatetic source for the passage, I shall for convenience refer to "Arius" or "the Arius passage," but the person or people with whom we are concerned are more likely to be, in fact, Arius' source or sources.[2]

When the text was first studied in a scholarly way, the initial reaction was that Arius was "eclectic" in something like Antiochus' way, producing a kind of eclectic synthesis of ethical theories.[3] Such "eclecticism" was assumed to be a mindless scissors-and-paste exercise, the product of unoriginal minds. Two monographs, by von Arnim and Dirlmeier,[4] introduced the exciting idea that the Stoic-looking material, particularly *oikeiōsis*, was not originally Stoic at all, but developed by Theophrastus. Arius would then be giving us a later version of an original development of Aristotelian ideas, from which the Stoics had borrowed. The exciting thesis was, however, definitively exploded by Pohlenz, who has been followed by Brink and Moraux, and to some extent by Giusta.[5] As Pohlenz made clear, *oikeiōsis*, and several other concepts prominent in the passage, are Stoic in origin, and what we have must be a Hellenistic attempt to recast Aristotelian ethics using some Stoic ideas. Pohlenz ascribed this to the tendency which is so manifest in Antiochus, to assume that different schools had basically the same ideas but put them in different terminology. On this scholarly debate I have nothing to add. What I would like to challenge is the widespread view that if what we find in Arius is not original untainted Peripatetic material, then it is an unintelligent mixture, of little or no interest for the study of Aristotelian ideas.

My approach here is in sympathy with a growing recent tendency to rehabilitate so-called "eclectic" philosophy and to find greater philosophical interest in "eclectic" Hellenistic texts than is often assumed.[6] In the case of the Arius passage, I would like to begin to explore the idea that it is not just a combination of Stoic and Peripatetic ideas, but a critical, and arguably intelligent, reinterpretation of Aristotle.

Why would anyone feel that he *needed* Stoic terms to explain Aristotle? In all the *Quellenforschung* insufficient attention has been paid to this question. We can come at the answer if we consider the structure of Cicero's *de Finibus*. Ethical theories are in the Hellenistic period in *competition*; students learn which the major theories are, and what the major arguments are against them. As in our own day, there is no intellectual consesus on a favoured ethical theory, though it is clear which the major contenders are, and what the major arguments for and against are.

In an atmosphere of contention and argument, theories are likely to develop in ways that respond to objections and alternatives. One form this may take is restating your own position in a way which can more adequately repel an objection. But another way is to take over part of the opponents' position, neutralizing opposition and strengthening your position by showing that you can take on board what was supposed to be an objection to you. In modern moral philosophy we have seen utilitarianism move from a rejection of rights and deontological principles to an acceptance of them, together with an explanation of them within a utilitarian system. We can read the Arius passage in something of the same way. The Peripatetics have given up defending their own moral psychology in terms of *orexis* and gone over to the Stoic model in which what is basic is *hormē*. They have given up talking as Aristotle does of the difference between a just act and a just act performed as a just person would do it, and started talking of *kathēkon* and *katorthōma*. In these and other cases we can see how Aristotle's school may have felt that, while Aristotle's works were fundamentally more correct than Stoic ethics, they could not be defended in their original form against Stoic attacks, and could be rendered more defensible by incorporating Stoic formulations and Stoic ideas. Insofar as they thought that the ideas were still basically Aristotelian, they thought that "the ideas were the same, and only the words different.'' But we should give them credit for thinking this in a *critical* spirit, trying to use Stoic formulations to rearm Aristotle against the Stoic alternative.

A utilitarian who can defend a utilitarian position on rights has thereby forced the rights theorist to look for a new argument against utilitarianism. And Arius, or his source, has, in basing Aristotelian ethics on a form of *oikeiōsis*, shown that accepting such an account can lead to Aristotelian rather than Stoic conclusions, and thereby forced a Stoic to concede that *oikeiōsis* does not necessarily lead to a Stoic position. In an intellectual atmosphere where debate tends to start from Stoic assumptions, this is an intelligent way to proceed, one step ahead of the opposition rather than one step behind.

If we are entitled to look at the Arius passage this way, a host of interesting questions arise. Do these Stoic ideas strengthen Aristotelian ethics, or do they undermine it? We need not, of course, expect the same answer in every case. Does *hormē* psychology in fact fit Aristotle's model of deliberation? If we see Aristotle in terms of *kathēkonta* and *katorthōmata*, are we covertly expanding the role of general rules in the Aristotelian agent's ethical thinking? Answering these and other questions will, I think, be illuminating about both Aristotle and the Stoics, and show what is at stake in the debate between them. In this paper I shall focus on only one change, though the largest: the way Aristotelian ethics are in Arius introduced and explained by the Stoic notion of *oikeiōsis*. The relation of this to some things that Aristotle says about self-love is, I shall argue, a highly interesting one. My account will inevitably be partial and sketchy, but I hope that it will encourage more work on the Arius passage in the thought that it is the product of debate about the form and content of ethics, and not of mechanical patching.[7]

Arius' account of Peripatetic ethics begins with a familiar Aristotelian theme: *ēthos*, character, derives from *ethos*, habit, and ethics is concerned with the habituation that leads to good moral character. But this is at once explained as our achieving the completion or perfection in our habits and ways of life of the things whose beginnings and seeds are given us by nature. We are to be given a genetic or developmental account of the establishment of virtuous dispositions.[8] The particular account we are to be given is a consciously altered version of the Stoic account of *oikeiōsis*.

What is the Stoic account? *Oikeiōsis* has no single natural English equivalent; I shall use 'familiarization' as the best available.[9] The verb *oikeioō* introduces a three-term relation: A familiarizes B with C. The Stoics are concerned with the case where the subject is nature, and their theory can be summed up by the two claims that nature familiarizes a human with himself and that nature familiarizes a human with other humans. Often it is said that humans "are familiarized" with themselves or with others, "by nature" being understood. Nature has thus equipped us with two instincts, two sources of unlearned behavior. Chrysippus irritated Plutarch "by writing in all his books . . . that we are familiarized with ourselves as soon as we are born, and with our parts and with our own offspring" (*de Stoic. repugn.* 1038B). As we grow and become more rational, our familiarization develops in two ways, corresponding to these two different instincts. What has been called "personal" *oikeiōsis*, familiarization with oneself, develops from an initial concern with what is harmful or beneficial to oneself to a more complex concern for acting so as to get what is beneficial for oneself. In a rational agent, claim the Stoics, this concern will develop into a concern with *how* one acts; one's actions will acquire a rationally based consistency and stability. Eventually, one will come to value one's exercise of rationality in the acquisition of various goods over the goods that it enables one to achieve; and it is at this point that one grasps the nature and the value of virtue. A rational being, then, will develop from a child's concern with things that hurt or harm to a concern with herself as a rational being, and hence with the ethical demands that her reason imposes.[10] This is not an argument from rationality to virtue; rather it is an account of how we develop from primitive self-concern to concern for ourselves as rational beings, and so to valuing virtue in the distinctive way that it demands.[11]

Familiarization with others, so-called "social" *oikeiōsis*, starts from our instinctive concern for others. As the Chrysippus quote indicates, we have unlearned, instinctive concern only as far as our own offspring, which are ours, as our parts are ours. Unnecessary difficulty has been found with the point that we have this concern at birth, since we obviously do not have offspring at birth. The point is surely that what we have at birth is instincts; this instinct does not come into play until we actually have offspring, but when we do, we do not have to learn to love them. But again a rational being will develop rationally to the point of having concern for others far beyond the scope given by instinct. From our offspring our concern spreads to other relatives and then further out beyond kin to concern with fellow-citizens and ultimately with all human beings; a fully developed rational being is capable of impartial concern for all humans, just as such.[12]

What we find in Arius is this Stoic story, but adapted so as to produce an Aristotelian, rather than a Stoic conclusion—for it is adjusted so that the agent's concern for reason and virtue retains a stronger connection to external and bodily goods than it does on the Stoic story; the definition of happiness emerging at the end of the passage includes them as well as virtue.

The passage begins by emphasizing that virtue develops as a result of three factors: nature, habit and reason. For virtue of character is not just knowledge, but involves choice (*proairesis*) of what is noble,[13] and so involves both the rational and irrational parts of the soul.[14] A human first of all "strives to exist, since he is familiarized with himself" (118.11–13). So he is pleased by things that accord with his nature, and shuns those that are contrary to it, and accordingly strives for health, pleasure and other natural advantages.[15] The beginnings of right action come from concern to obtain these things, and hence so do the beginnings of virtue, which is explained as being a correct and systematic understanding resulting in correct choice of natural advantages; it is emphasized that these are the sphere and the subject of virtuous and vicious actions.

But before reaching the end of the story about personal *oikeiōsis*, we find that social *oikeiōsis* breaks in, and from 119.22–122.7 we get an account of this which does not diverge from the standard Stoic story. We love our offspring for their own sake, and not for the sake of the advantages they bring. And this concern spreads out through the family to ever more outlying members to fellow-citizens and ultimately the whole human race. Much is said even about common-sense indications that we have concern for all humans. (The section ends with a caveat about this impartial extension of concern to all, to which I will return.)

We now return to complete the story about personal *oikeiōsis*, via a bridging passage which explains the odd procedure. It has been shown, the author says, that external goods are choiceworthy for their own sake (friends being conventionally the greatest of external goods); if so, this will apply with even more force to bodily goods and goods of the soul. We find the goods of the body choiceworthy for their own sake—goods such as health, strength and beauty; if so, *a fortiori* we find the goods of the soul choiceworthy for their own sake, without an eye to advantage. Then we resume (123.21ff) the lines of the account of personal *oikeiōsis*. Virtue begins from the external and bodily goods (for, as we have seen, it takes the form of a stable and well-reasoned attitude to getting these). But now virtue "turns towards itself and contemplates that it itself is much more something according with nature than the bodily virtues, and is familiarized with itself as with something choiceworthy for itself, even more so than with the bodily virtues." (123. 21–26) Virtue "turns towards itself" in the sense that it involves not just consistently right action but also an understanding of the proper value of virtue; the virtuous person must value her own virtuous state more than the results it produces. Since appreciating the value of virtue is the culminating point of rational development, virtue, which is a good of the soul, is more valuable than bodily goods.[16]

The conclusion (125.14–128.9) stresses that, although the process has culminated in the agent's concern for herself as a rational being, and hence as virtuous, virtue and the exercise of rationality are not the agent's only aims; the agent will regard both bodily virtues or excellences and external goods like friends as choiceworthy for their own sake. Virtue is greatly superior to these goods (126.12–14); happiness is not a combination of these goods, but rather an active life of virtue which in some way uses or acts on these goods (126.12–127.2). For happiness is not just good things, but a life of actions, so that the other kinds of good do not make for happiness on their own, but only as put to service by virtue. But despite the superiority of virtue the other goods are genuine goods, choiceworthy for their own sake and required for happiness.

We can now see why the straightforward Stoic story (rational development of familiarization to oneself, rational development of familiarization to others) has been interrupted and recast to accomodate the threefold distinction of external goods, goods of the body and goods of the soul. Although this produces the odd distortion that familiarization with others is no longer co-ordinate to familiarization with oneself, it has the advantage of enabling the author to give an account of familiarization with oneself that results in an Aristotelian, rather than a Stoic definition of happiness. Development of concern for oneself results in concern for oneself as a rational being, but this includes and transforms, rather than replacing, concern for one's friends and other external goods, and concern for health, beauty and other bodily excellences.

In Aristotle the definition and discussion of happiness emerges out of consideration of the "function" of humans, and from common beliefs about it. Why has this been replaced by an adaptation of the Stoic *oikeiōsis* account?

One answer is: intellectual fashion. The Stoics seem by the first century B.C. to have dominated the discussion of ethics, so that their terms became the current ones of debate. Arius in his introduction to ethics, before his accounts of the Stoics and Peripatetics, introduces the notion of a *hupotelis* or subordinate end, an idea which he says that older philosophers had, although they lacked the word; and he explains this allegedly universal ethical notion by an *oikeiōsis*-story (47.12–48.5). The anonymous Commentator on the *Theaetetus* calls *oikeiōsis* commonplace and regards Socrates and the Sophists as its originators. But this on its own will not do; intellectual fashion does not compel philosophers to take over terms and frameworks that are not satisfactory for what they want to say.

Another answer, which has played a dominant role in discussions of this passage, is that *oikeiōsis* was introduced by Theophrastus, and so was a part of the Peripatetic tradition anyway.[17] And scholars have also pointed to terminology in Aristotle which is strikingly similar to later Stoic terminology. (The verb *sunoikeiousthai*, for example, occurs five times in the *NE*.)[18] But verbal parallels prove nothing if the concepts in question are clearly distinct; the Theophrastus fragments do not amount to *oikeiōsis* as the Stoics understood it;[19] and in any case the Arius passage as a whole clearly draws predominantly on Aristotelian material. Further, hypothesizing a Peripatetic tradition of *oikeiōsis* does not really help. What we have in the Arius passage is something that educated readers would recognize as an adapted version of the Stoic story. Even if this happened to be identical to an earlier purely Peripatetic theory, this would not answer the contemporary question, how the theory in its version in Arius related to the Stoic version.

The question, "why in terms of *oikeiōsis*?" can best be answered by reference to the context of critical discussion I mentioned earlier. Aristotle's way of producing his definition of happiness from considerations of human functioning had been challenged by the Stoic developmental account of how a human develops from primitive self-concern to concern for himself as a rational being, and hence for the demands of virtue which reason works out. This was part of the Stoic claim that virtue actually suffices for happiness. Some Peripatetics clearly tired of repeating Aristotle's claims about happiness in Aristotle's form, and replaced them with what we find in Arius. The Stoic account has been taken over, but recast to accommodate the threefold division of goods. The result is that the definition of happiness that emerges is the Aristotelian one. In a context of debate, this move can be seen as an intelligent one. If the Stoic account can be adapted to produce an Aristotelian conclusion, then the burden of the debate shifts back to the Stoics. To show what, in their terms, has gone wrong with the conclusion, they have to pinpoint what in the account has gone wrong. They have to engage with the restated Aristotelian theory, rather than regard it as bypassed by their new approach.[20] So the recasting of *oikeiōsis* that we find in the Arius passage is a sign of critical engagement in contemporary debate, not of scribal muddle or imperfect patching of different layers of text.[21]

We are inevitably reminded of Antiochus' procedure in *de Finibus* V. But a question arises with the Arius passage which does not with Antiochus, who is avowedly constructing his own new system of ethics, and who can therefore take over other philosophers' material without staying faithful to their intentions. The Arius passage is supposed to be an account of *Aristotelian* ethics. Has this aim been undermined by incorporating so much by way of Stoic material and approach? If we judge that what we have does not answer to any Aristotelian concern, then the move will have been too costly. Aristotle's followers will have in effect conceded to the Stoics by meeting Stoic claims with a new theory, not a recognizably Aristotelian kind of theory.

This is a legitimate worry, but in the end unfounded. For we can find signs which are, I think, adequate to show that using *oikeiōsis* as the Arius passage does can be seen as an attempt to develop coherently and in an "up-to-date" way a theme of some importance which is genuinely Aristotelian.

In the books on friendship Aristotle raises the question of how self-love is related to concern for others. In *NE* IX 4 he argues that friendship for others is an extension of self-love, since friendship is marked by five crucial relations, such as wishing good things to the person for their own sake, and all of these are found paradigmatically in the good person's relation to himself. This is not a derivation of friendship from self-love, or a demonstration that self-love is more basic. However, in IX 8 Aristotle raises the question whether one should love oneself or others more, and gives a highly interesting answer. Briefly, he makes a distinction between kinds of self-love, and argues that in the popular sense one should not be self-loving, for in this sense one assigns oneself more of goods like money and honors. But there is a sense of self-love, already introduced in IX 4, in which the true self which is loved is the person's practical reasoning, which guides what he does, so that the person identifies with his reasoned judgement and commitment, and not with various temptations to go against this. In this sense, Aristotle says, we should be self-loving. For self-lovers in this sense will compete—but they will be competing to be virtuous, and this kind of competition turns out to be not selfish but just what virtuous action is: benefitting others and restraining one's own claims if need be. Further, self-love in this sense leads to what we recognize as altruistic behavior. The virtuous person is motivated to sacrifice her money, or honors, or even chances of virtuous action, to others; and this is really self-love of the good kind, since the person is gettng more of what matters to her, virtue and its own kind of reward. Aristotle should not be interpreted here as saying that the agent consciously aims at acting virtuously and also at getting more of the rewards of virtue for herself. Rather, the agent is motivated only to act virtuously, and this is just because she is someone who identifies herself with her practical reasoning and its virtuous conclusions. Virtuous and altruistic actions are expressions of the agent's self-love (if this is the right kind of self-love) not what directly motivates the agent.[22]

Aristotle thus puts forward in IX 8 the striking idea that the kind of aims a person has reveal and express the kind of conception they have of themselves. The greedy, competitive person shows that he conceives of himself as ambitious and ruthless; the just person shows that his conception of himself is as a rational and virtuous person. Their actions show what kind of self it is that they are showing love for in each case. This idea is a striking one because it posits that all action is formally a case of self-love or self-seeking. It is compatible with virtuous and altruistic action if the self in question is virtuous; and self-seeking is not even part of what the agent is aiming at, and hence not part of his thoughts. Still, it brings together selfish and altruistic action alike as both being formally cases of self-love. And this has wide implications; it suggests that all action is a case of self-love, and that the crucial difference between selfish and virtuous action lies in the conception of the self that the agent has.

Aristotle gives no indication that he means his point about self-love to be extended beyond its context, that of solving a problem arising in the books on friendship. However, whatever Aristotle's own intentions, it is certainly capable of such extension; self-love as Aristotle discusses it in IX 8 could be used in a much wider role in Aristotle's ethics, as a starting-point from which to build the accounts of virtue and happiness. This is, I suggest, what has happened in the Arius passage; self-love is made the starting-point for Aristotelian ethics, the point from which we develop the account of virtue and the definition of its role in happiness. Confronted by Stoic ethics, some of Aristotle's followers have proceeded to extend the role of self-love from its context in IX 8 to make it a starting-point for the ethics. But instead of merely contrasting common self-love with love of oneself identified with one's reasoning, they have done two things. They have, following the Stoic lead, given a developmental account: we start with a primitive self-love and from there, as we develop rationally, develop towards a love of ourselves as rational beings. And they have given this developmental account the form of an adapted Stoic *oikeiōsis* theory.

There are three striking external indications that this is what has happened. Firstly, when we find the summary of Aristotelian ideas on *philia* in the second half, we find (143.1–16) a small shrivelled remnant of the ideas in the books on friendship in the *Ethics*. Six types of friendship are listed, those appropriate to foreigners, kin, etc.; their bases are listed, together with the idea, familiar from the *Ethics*, that all friendship is for one of the three ends of the noble, the pleasant or the advantageous. But instead of any consideration of the basis of friendship in one's relationship to oneself, we find the following: "The first friendship, as we said, is that towards oneself, the second towards one's parents,[23] then in turn towards others, kin and strangers." This is clearly a reference to the initial *oikeiōsis* passage, and referring to it as an account of self-love indicates that the account of self-love has been transferred from the account of friendship to become, in expanded form, the introduction to the ethics in the form of an adapted account of *oikeiōsis*. It is especially noteworthy that the later passage refers to the earlier one as an account of self-love (which it was not there explicitly called). It even uses this to create a highly artificial application of the doctrine of the mean: we should avoid the extreme in friendship towards ourselves, for this carries the reproach of self-lovingness (*philautia*), and the deficiency in friendship towards others, for this carries the reproach of stinginess (*pheidōlia*).[24] This, the one clear reference back in the passage to the first part from the more doxographical second part, indicates clearly that self-love has been transplanted from its limited context in the account of friendship to bloom luxuriously in the updated introduction to Aristotelian ethics.[25]

Secondly, the initial passage itself, while otherwise parallel in terminology with Stoic accounts of *oikeiōsis*, contains many striking occurences of *philos* and related words.[26] While the terminology of friendship and self-love is not altogether absent from the Stoic accounts, it is not prominent in anything like this way.[27]

And thirdly, the conclusion of the passage seems to echo Aristotle's puzzle about self-love that gave rise to the conclusions of IX 8. "Virtue is on this theory not self-loving (*philautos*) but social and political; and since we said that virtue is most familiarized with itself, clearly it is naturally familiarized necessarily with knowledge of the truth" (125.21–126.2). Aristotle's special refined sense of self-love in which it is good to be self-loving is no longer necessary once the Stoic framework has been adopted. And it probably always sounded artificial anyway; the author of the *Magna Moralia*, in the passage corresponding to *NE* IX 8, refuses to extend "self-loving" to describe the virtuous peson, calling him "good-loving" (*philagathos*) and reserving, like Arius, the word *philautos* for common or garden self-love of the selfish variety (*MM* II 13–14). But the idea remains: the normal development of a rational being starts from a concern that is self-centered, but at the end of this development, although the person is still formally concerned with himself, what concerns him does not in fact amount to selfishness but is actually a concern for acting virtuously and considering the needs of others. It is formally self-centered but other-directed in content.

It might be objected that the Arius passage, which is so much more heavily influenced by the *Eudemian Ethics* and the *Magna Moralia* than by the *Nicomachean Ethics*, cannot be interpreted in a way that lays so much stress on a *Nicomachean* passage that has no echo in the *Eudemian* version. But, apart from the point that there is a passage corresponding to the crucial one in the *Magna Moralia*, the Arius passage does at some points stress a *Nicomachean* formulation, and does so on important issues like happiness and virtue. The author had read all three ethical works, and felt free to select from them all.[28]

Apart from particular indications, the Arius passage can reasonably be seen on general grounds as an attempt to introduce and explain Aristotelian ethics in terms of an expanding notion of self-love. And once Aristotle's followers had started to think of the *Ethics* in this way, with virtue as what the agent appreciates when she has reached the right stage of development and conceived of herself as a rational being, it is easy to see why Stoic *oikeiōsis* provided an accessible way of doing this. What was needed was a way of making self-love the starting-point of Aristotelian ethics in a way which would provide a coherent account of virtue and the place of virtue in happiness. Further, such an account would have to be developmental, as Stoic and Epicurean accounts were. Taking over the Stoic account could seem the natural thing to do to achieve all this; and it also had the advantage I have already stressed, that it met the Stoics on their own ground and thus forced them more on to the defensive.

But might the cost not still be too high? In the Arius passage virtue is dominant in the agent's happiness, but external and bodily goods are still required. Does this really answer to Aristotle's demand that the true self-lover identify herself with her reason? There is no real difficulty here. Aristotle in IX 4 and 8 does not mean that the true self-lover identifies herself only with her reason to the extent, say, of regarding the body and its needs as irrelevant to the true self. What identification with one's reason implies is that one identify oneself with the virtuous course, and this does not involve neglect or repudiation of bodily and external goods, merely the recognition that virtue overrides them, as we would say. In this respect the later Peripatetics were not unfaithful to Aristotle.

One might also worry about one result of displacing familiarization with others, as the passage does, and making it in effect part of familiarization with oneself. The result is that, as with Antiochus' version, the theory becomes, as the original Stoic theory does not, a theory in which self-love is always formally basic; the place in the theory of a properly developed concern for others is as part of a properly developed concern for oneself.

But this could be seen as an advantage, if one has a concern for the *Aristotelian* nature of the theory. For it now looks, as the Stoic theory does not, like a plausible extension of what Aristotle says about self-love in *NE* IX 8. All concern is formally self-directed; but the rightly developed self will identify with concern for others. A Stoic might complain, of course, that this makes the theory in effect too self-centered, since it gives us no source of concern for others which is independent of our concern for ourselves. An Aristotelian could respond, however, that their theory does account for our concern for others; it is not reduced to self-concern, since the good of others is what we aim at and direct our ethical training towards, while our conception of our own good is what is expressed in our doing this, but not what we aim at. An Aristotelian could even go on the offensive, and say that a theory of the kind in the Arius passage is simpler and more explanatorily effective than a theory like the Stoics', which posits two distinct sources of instinct to familiarization. We should note, however, that at this point the discussion has moved to the question of whether the Peripatetics have *improved* the Stoic theory in taking it over; if this is what they are aiming to do they may risk losing touch with the original advantages in taking over Stoic approaches for anti-Stoic ends.

So far I have been championing the view that the recasting of Aristotle's ethics that we find in the Arius passage represents a critical and intelligent attempt to develop a genuinely Aristotelian point and give it a larger role in the interpretation of the ethical theory; and that the way that this is done in adapted Stoic terms probably represents a way of doing this that was both natural and well-adapted to meet Stoic attacks. The view that there is a connection between *oikeiōsis* and what Aristotle says in *NE* IX 8 is hardly new; it was noted and discussed in antiquity as well as modern scholarship.[29] I have tried to find a philosophically intelligible connection between what we find in Aristotle and what we find in the Arius passage in particular, a connection that reveals to us an intelligent Hellenistic engagement with Aristotle's own works in a changed philosophical climate.

There is, however, one large fly in the ointment, deliberately neglected hitherto. I have concentrated on the passage's development of familiarization with oneself; but its treatment of familiarization with others, apart from having its status somewhat altered, harbours a major difficulty.

The Stoics hold that normal ethical development will result in the agent's having equal concern for all humans just as humans, a remarkable insistence on the need for ethics to include an impartial point of view not paralleled in Aristotle or Epicurus. Familiarization with others thus is not complete until one gives oneself no more ethical weight in one's deliberations than "the remotest Mysian," as the hostile ancient commentator on the *Theaetetus* puts it. And this idea is quite unAristotelian. It is true that in *NE* VIII there are a few comments on having fellow-feelings for all humans, and extending friendship even to slaves insofar as they are human,[30] but Aristotle's considered account is that one has friendship to a limited number of other people. True friendship is limited to a few; the kinds one can have to larger numbers are merely friendships based on advantage; and even these one can hardly have to everyone. Further, he does not base his account of justice on a point of view impartial as between everyone; rather, the just person is fair in the respect required by the case in hand—he is fair as between A and B, he is not merely applying a perspective impartial between A, B, C and all other humans. The Stoic account of familiarization with others is therefore extremely unsuitable in an account of Aristotelian ethics that retains his account of friendship and justice. Although little survives in the Arius passage of the friendship books, what does, implies unambiguously that friendship is an essentially limited relationship, not a provisional stage in the extension of one's sympathies to include everyone. And although there is nothing from the book on justice, the Arius passage ends with scrappy summaries from the *Politics* that repeat the Aristotelian assumption that the ethical life is to be best lived in the limited social context of the Greek city; being a citizen is essential to the ethical life, not a stage on one's way to becoming a citizen of the world.[31]

A passage at 121.22–24, at the end of the passage on familiarization to others, expresses this unease. "But although there exists in us a general love of humanity (*philanthrōpia*), still the fact of being chosen for its own sake is more manifest with regard to the friends that we are intimate with." The author has seen the problem, though he has hardly solved it. If impartial concern for all humans is ethically demanded of us, then however much clearer the basis of our concern is in limited contexts it is still something to be finally rejected. Yet there is no sign anywhere else in the Arius passage that this was taken to heart.

The verdict on the passage's use of Stoic *oikeiōsis* must therefore be a mixed one: while it is in many respects successful and interesting, it ought to have been carried out either less or more thoroughly. Either familiarization with others should have been limited to respect Aristotelian limits, or Aristotelian ethics should have revised the scope of its demands on concern for others. This is, however, exactly the sort of problem which we would expect given the kind of "critical eclecticism" I have ascribed to Aristotle's successors. The passage as we have it is open to some obvious Stoic objections, which were probably made; we do not possess the later stages of the debate. But the important point for Aristotle's school, at a low point for them historically,[32] was that Aristotle's ethics were still alive and well in Hellenistic debate.

Julia Annas

University of Arizona at Tucson

NOTES

1. The ascription to Arius is certain for this section, circumstantial for the Stoic section and introduction. See the article by Charles Kahn, "Arius as a Doxographer," 3–13 in W. Fortenbaugh (ed.), *On Stoic and Peripatetic Ethics: the Work of Arius Didymus*, Rutgers University Studies in Classical Humanities vol. 1, New Brunsick, NJ: 1983. I use Wachsmuth's text (Berlin 1884). There is unfortunately no translation available of the whole passage (though one is forthcoming in the Clarendon Library of Later Greek Philosophy). A translation of the long *oikeiōsis* introduction is on pp. 168–69 of H. Görgemanns, "*Oikeiōsis* in Arius Didymus," pp. 165–89 of Fortenbaugh.

2. We cannot determine whether the striking features of this passage are due to Arius himself or to a Peripatetic source, though the latter is much more likely. See P. Moraux, *Der Aristotelismus bei den Griechen* vol. I, Berlin & New York: 1973 (*Peripatoi* 5), pp. 273–74, 349–50. It is not plausible that Arius is on his own account producing an Antiochean eclectic synthesis, quite unlike his procedures in the rest of his history of physical and ethical philosophy. Still, Arius' own attitude is not irrelevant. As Moraux stresses, he was surely aware of Andronicus' new edition of Aristotle, and was a friend of Andronicus' pupil Xenarchus, whose approach to Aristotle's texts was quite different (see below, n29); yet his own view of Aristotle remained under the influence of Peripatetics who were pre-Andronicus but post-Critolaus (a definition rejected at 126.14–16 is that of Critolaus (cf. 46.10–13)).

3. See H. Diels, *Doxographi Graeci* (reprint, Berlin: 1958), pp. 71-72; and cf. the judgement of E. Zeller, *Die Philosophie der Griechen in ihrer geschichtlichen Entwicklung*, reprint Hildesheim: 1961, Teil III Abteilung 1, pp. 635-39.

4. H. von Arnim, *Arius Didymus' Abriss der peripatetischen Ethik*, Wien-Leipzig: 1926, (Akademie der Wissenschaften in Wien, philosophisch-historisch Klasse, Sitzungsbericht 204.3); F. Dirlmeier, *Die Oikeiōsis-Lehre Theophrasts* (Leipzig: 1937), *Philologus* Supplement XXX, 1.

5. M. Pohlenz, *Grundfragen der stoischen Philosophie*, Göttingen 1940, (Abhandlung des Gesellschaft der Wissenschaften zu Göttingen, philosophisch-historisch Klasse 3.26); C. O. Brink, "*Oikeiōsis* and *oikeiotēs*: Theophrastus and Zeno on Nature in Moral Theory," *Phronesis* I (1956), 123–45; M. Giusta, *I dossographi di etica*, 2 vols., Torino 1964–67, P. Moraux, op. cit., 316–444. Surveys of the scholarly discussion can be found in Giusta, 74–84, Moraux, 333–50, Görgemanns, 166–68.

6. Cf. the interesting collection *The Question of "Eclecticism"*: studies in later Greek philosophy, eds. J. M. Dillon and A. A. Long (Berkeley, CA: University of California Press, 1988). Moraux denies that the Arius passage is eclectic in the sense of using diverse materials to produce a new combination; he regards it as an attempt to "modernize" Aristotle in a context where Stoic terms are common property and answers conventionally have to be recorded to Stoic questions, whether or not these were important questions for Aristotle. I am in sympathy with this, but would like to link the *oikeiōsis* passage more closely than Moraux does with Aristotelian concerns.

7. For some interesting work on the way the Arius passage contributes to our understanding of Aristotle on the relation of virtue and the external goods in happiness, see J. Cooper, "Aristotle on the Goods of Fortune," *The Philosophical Review* XCIV (1985), 173-96. Cooper focusses on what are in Arius called "preferred" circumstances. Also relevant are the distinction between the happy life and the noble life (p. 145) and the way that Aristotle's "external" goods tend to be reinterpreted as "natural" goods. On this issue the Peripatetics seem to have not so much absorbed Stoic ideas as reformulated their own to meet a sharpened Stoic challenge. And on some issues the original Aristotelian approach seems to have been regarded as old-fashioned, and simply discarded, for example on responsibility and pleasure.

8. It has been claimed, for example by H. Görgemanns, that "of habituation there is no trace at all" despite its emphatic introduction. Surely, however, the developmental account we get is meant to replace an Aristotelian account of habituation.

9. This follows a suggestion by Jonathan Barnes. It does better than other English words in suggesting the idea of "family" in *oikeios* as well as the idea of coming to belong, the opposite of *allotriōsis*, for which we do have an English equivalent, "alienation."

10. Seneca, *Letter* 121, 7-8; Diogenes Laertius VII 85-86; Cicero *de Finibus* III, 16, 20-21. The late Stoic Hierocles emphasises the role of perception and consciousness of self in the early stages. See *Hierokles: Ethische Elementarlehre*, ed. H. von Arni and W. Schubart, Berliner Klassikertexte Heft 4, Berlin 1906. On this see Brad Inwood, "Hierocles: Theory and Argument in the Second Century A.D.," *Oxford Studies in Ancient Philosophy* II (1984), 151-83.

11. The fact that the process of *oikeiōsis* does not itself provide an argument for the rationality of valuing virtue is made clear in G. Striker, "*Oikeiōsis* in Stoic Ethics," *Oxford Studies in Ancient Philosophy* I (1983), 145-67.

12. Cicero, *de Finibus* III, 62-63; Hierocles ap. Stobaeus, *Florilegium* 84.23 (pp. 61-62 in Diels and Schubart). Ancient objections to social *oikeiōsis* can be found in *Anonymer Kommentar zu Platons Theaetet*, ed. H. Diels and W. Schubart, Berliner Klassikertexte II (Berlin: 1905), with Cicero *de Officiis* III 90; modern objections in B. Inwood, "Comments on Professor Görgemanns' Paper: The Two Forms of *oikeiōsis* in Arius and the Stoa," pp. 190-201 of Fortenbaugh.

13. There seems to be something lacking in the text, and Wachsmuth supplies *hexis*, which is suitably Aristotelian, but perhaps rather a bold conjecture.

14. Although at 118.6-11 there is a confusing passage which connects immortal and mortal, rational and irrational and soul and body. This is one of the places where the effects of interpreting *oikeiōsis* via the distinction of external goods, goods of the body and goods of the soul, seems not to have been fully thought through.

15. The Stoics did not consider pleasure a natural advantage, but a mere supervention, if that (cf. Diogenes Laertius VII 86); but Aristotle's theory gives it a more positive role, though the Arius passage does not contain anything corresponding to either *NE* account of pleasure.

16. The point is buttressed by analogies between goods of the soul and those of the body. This passage is made rather odd by the addition of highly peculiar and bizarre analogies between external goods, goods of the body and goods of the soul; for suspicions as to this being an interpolation see Moraux, pp. 325-27, Görgemanns 179-81.

17. Von Arnim 142ff, Dirlmeier. Giusta accepts that Aristotle's school may have held *oikeiōsis*-theories, but rightly frees this from a debate about priority over the Stoics (vol. I, 276-88).

18. Dirlmeier 79-80. Von Arnim points out many similarities throughout the Arius passage to wording in all three of the ethical works.

19. As Pohlenz definitively points out, pp. 12-14.

20. The Stoics would, of course, fault the idea that virtue is the same kind of good as the other two; in their terms bodily and external goods are not goods at all. But this would force them to defend this claim in turn, for the Aristotelian way of dividing goods is more intuitive. We can at any rate see how "updated" Aristotle would be brought right into the middle of the kind of debate we can find in *de Finibus*.

21. The interference with the expected progression of *oikeiōsis* has greatly exercised scholars, but in the main their expectation that this text is "eclectic" in a pejorative sense has led them to interpret it as signs of unintelligent patching. See Pohlenz 30-31, Görgemanns 173-81, Inwood.

22. I have argued this in more detail in "Self-love in Aristotle," for the Spindel Conference on Aristotle, October 1988.

23. Not one's children, as we would expect. Inwood, pp. 196-97 points out that this links the passage with Antiochus' way of explaining extension of sympathies, rather than the Stoic one, which begins from instinctual affection for one's offspring. But the two are not really in competition: to begin from one's offspring is to point to the instinctual basis of other-directed sympathies, to begin from one's parents is to point to the order in which we begin to extend them. The two are quite compatible.

24. Friendship is not in Aristotle a virtue to which the mean applies. The artificial application clearly postdates the recasting of Aristotle's ideas on self-love in a Stoic mould, so that self-love becomes the start of a continuum which ends with impartial regard for all; such a continuum seems amenable to the application of the mean.

25. This reference back has exercised scholars. Some, e.g., von Arnim 81ff, have used it as evidence for an original Peripatetic *oikeiōsis*-based theory; others, e.g., Pohlenz 36-40, have treated it as an artificial join between two dissimilar parts.

26. Very strikingly at 118.20-119.2. Cf. also 120.12, 15, 18; 121.17, 23-24; 127.4-9.

27. Cf. Cicero *de Finibus* III 16: "sensum haberent sui eoque se diligerent" and "a se diligendo," and III 59: "se omnes natura diligant." But in Greek accounts *philia* and *philos* are not prominent.

28. Cooper discusses the definitions of happiness, pointing out that they correspond more closely to the *Nicomachean* version; but it is hasty to infer from this that

the main text appealed to in Hellenistic discussion was the *NE*. Von Arnim's correspondences show clearly that the Arius passage is also heavily influenced by the *EE* and *MM*.

29. After Andronicus' new edition we find Xenarchus and Boethus appealing to *NE* IX 8 in explaining Aristotle's views in terms of *oikeiôsis* and the *prôton oikeion*. Alexander of Aphrodisias records and criticizes this (*de Anima* II 150–53, esp. 151.3–18). But this scholarly, text-based activity, not so very different from modern journal articles on Aristotle, is different from Arius' attempt to use contemporary notions to present Aristotelian ideas.

30. See 1155a 16–28, 1161b 5–8.

31. The *Politics* references mean that we cannot solve the problem by appealing to the Theophrastus passages, interesting though they are, which talk of extending our sympathies over a wider area. See von Arnim 142ff, Moraus p. 341 and n83 for references.

32. See J. Lynch, *Aristotle's School* (Berkeley, CA: University of California Press, 1972), chs. V and VI for the decline of the Lyceum as an institution in the Hellenistic period.

Acknowledgments

Cooper, John M. "The *Magna Moralia* and Aristotle's Moral Philosophy." *American Journal of Philology* 94 (1973): 327–49. Reprinted with the permission of John Hopkins University Press. Courtesy of Yale University Sterling Memorial Library.

Allan, D.J. "Quasi-Mathematical Method in the *Eudemian Ethics*." In S. Mansion, ed., *Aristote et les problèmes de méthode* (Louvain: Publications Universitaires, 1961): 303–18. Reprinted with the permission of Publications Universitaires. Courtesy of Yale University Sterling Memorial Library.

Barnes, Jonathan. "Aristotle and the Methods of Ethics." *Revue Internationale de Philosophie* 134 (1980): 490–511. Reprinted with the permission of Editions Universa. Courtesy of Yale University Sterling Memorial Library.

Roche, Timothy D. "On the Alleged Metaphysical Foundation of Aristotle's *Ethics*." *Ancient Philosophy* 8 (1988): 49–62. Reprinted with the permission of Mathesis Publications, Inc. Courtesy of *Ancient Philosophy*.

Kraut, Richard. "Two Conceptions of Happiness." *Philosophical Review* 88 (1979): 167–97. Reprinted with the permission of AMS Press, Inc. Courtesy of Yale University Sterling Memorial Library.

Dybikowski, J.C. "Is Aristotelian *Eudaimonia* Happiness?" *Dialogue* 20 (1981): 185–200. Reprinted with the permission of the Canadian Philosophical Association. Courtesy of Yale University Sterling Memorial Library.

Engberg-Pedersen, Troels. "For Goodness' Sake: More on *Nicomachean Ethics* I vii 5." *Archiv für Geschichte der Philosophie* 63 (1981): 17–40. Reprinted with the permission of Walter de Gruyter, Inc. Courtesy of Yale University Sterling Memorial Library.

Hardie, W.F.R. "Aristotle on the Best Life for a Man." *Philosophy* 54 (1979): 35–50. Copyright the Royal Institute of Philosophy. Reprinted with the permission of the Cambridge University Press. Courtesy of Yale University Sterling Memorial Library.

Keyt, David. "Intellectualism in Aristotle." *Paideia* (1979): 138–57. Reprinted with the permission of the State University of New York at Buffalo. Courtesy of Albert Grande, Esq.

Whiting, Jennifer. "Aristotle's Function Argument: A Defense." *Ancient Philosophy* 8 (1988): 33–48. Reprinted with the permission of Mathesis Publications, Inc. Courtesy of *Ancient Philosophy*.

Cooper, John M. "Aristotle on the Goods of Fortune." *Philosophical Review* 94 (1985): 173–96. Reprinted with the permission of AMS Press, Inc. Courtesy of Yale University Sterling Memorial Library.

Cooper, John M. "Some Remarks on Aristotle's Moral Psychology." *Southern Journal of Philosophy* 27 (1988): 25–42. Reprinted with the permission of Memphis State University. Courtesy of *Souuthern Journal of Philosophy*.

Leighton, Stephen R. "Aristotle and the Emotions." *Phronesis* 27 (1982): 144–74. Reprinted with the permission of Van Gorcum en Co. B.V. Courtesy of Yale University Sterling Memorial Library.

Hursthouse, Rosalind. "A False Doctrine of the Mean." *Proceedings of the Aristotelian Society* 81 (1980–1): 57–72. Reprinted with the permission of Basil Blackwell Ltd. Courtesy of the Aristotelian Society.

Charles, David. "Aristotle: Ontology and Moral Reasoning." *Oxford Studies in Ancient Philosophy* 4 (1986): 119–44. Reprinted with the permission of the author. Courtesy of Yale University Sterling Memorial Library.

Kraut, Richard. "Aristotle on Choosing Virtue for Itself." *Archiv für Geschichte der Philosophie* 58 (1976): 223–39. Reprinted with the permission of Walter de Gruyter, Inc. Courtesy of Yale University Sterling Memorial Library.

Young, Charles M. "Aristotle on Temperance." *Philosophical Review* 97 (1988): 521–42. Reprinted with the permission of AMS Press, Inc. Courtesy of Yale University Sterling Memorial Library.

Hardie, W.F.R. "'Magnanimity' in Aristotle's Ethics." *Phronesis* 23 (1978): 63–79. Reprinted with the permission of Van Gorcum en Co. B.V. Courtesy of Yale University Sterling Memorial Library.

Long, A.A. "Aristotle's Legacy to Stoic Ethics." *Institute of Classical Studies Bulletin* 15 (1968): 72–85. Reprinted with the permission of the Institute of Classical Studies. Courtesy of Yale University Sterling Memorial Library.

Annas, Julia. "The Hellenistic Version of Aristotle's Ethics." *Monist* 73 (1990): 80–96. Copyright (1990), the *Monist*, LaSalle, IL 61301. Reprinted by permission. Courtesy of Yale University Sterling Memorial Library.

BIBL. U. DE/OF SUDBURY LIBR.
Withdrawn / Retiré
3 0007 00676006 9